Odwira [oh-jeeh'-rah] in the language of ancient **Khanit** and **Kam** [illegible] and Egypt, as well as in their descendant **Akan** language of Ghana and Ivory Coast [illegible] term **asem** [ah-sehm'] means *'affairs, issues, matters'*. **ODWIRASEM** as a title of our anthology references *matters of purification* – those thoughts, ideas and formulations which influence our intentions and actions, which must be based in and reflective of truth. When we purify our thoughts, we have pure intentions and manifest actions that are supportive of **Amansesew** – Nationbuilding/Restoration.

ODWIRASEM: Trustorical Anthology - Volume 1 is a collection of twelve books in one volume written and published by **Odwirafo Kwesi Ra Nehem Ptah Akhan**. Odwirafo has expanded these twelve works with additional information and images not included in the original publications.

For this volume Odwirafo chose those twelve books within his thirty-one-book corpus which focus on trustory (true-history/trustorical), cosmology, ritual, identity and Nationbuilding/Restoration.

This anthology was curated to function as a volume that will positively transform the mind of any Afurakani/Afuraitkaitnit (African~Black) individual, youth or adult, who receives it. We examine every facet of Afurakani/Afuraitkaitnit (African) identity, empowering readers to transform their minds and thus transform their condition wherever they exist in the world.

The twelve books included in this volume were published between 12998 (1997) and 13017 (2017). These works have been expanded over the years including as recently as this year of 13025 (2025). Two of the books included in the anthology warrant unique attention.

KUKUU-TUNTUM – The Ancestral Jurisdiction was originally published in audio format. It is a narrative of our Ancestral trustory, cosmology and culture. It is part of the **orature** (oral literature) tradition of Afurakani/Afuraitkaitnit (African) people, Black people, which spans millennia. It is therefore important that you listen to the audio of this particular text in addition to reading the transcript published here. The sacred names and terms in our Ancestral language can only be experienced fully through hearing. The audio for this work can be found here: www.odwirafo.com/kukuutuntumpage.html

UBEN-HYENG – The Ancestral Summons is a transcription of Ancestral wisdom received and preserved in our clans here in North America as inculcated within us and transmitted to us by our Ancestresses and Ancestors who were forced to migrate here during the **Mmusuo Kesee** *(Great Perversity/enslavement era)*. It is this ritual wisdom of our Ancestral Religious practice which empowered us to remain resilient and vigilant in the face of the most extreme adversity, overthrow the enslavers and take our independence. Such wisdom also guides our resilience today so that we will meet every obstacle placed before us – social, political, economic, military, cultural, spiritual – and overcome all.

The remaining ten books in the anthology are **trustorical** examinations of the origins, nature and function of religion, language, cosmology, culture, psychology, spirituality, socio-political organization and more rooted in an Afurakani/Afuraitkaitnit (African) foundation – a full and clear picture of reality unhindered by the biases of eurocentric/eurasian pseudo-historicity and anthropology. This is the work of our **Nananom Nsamanfo**, our Spiritually Cultivated Ancestresses and Ancestors, the fountainhead of true Revolution-Resolution.

Odwirafo Kwesi Ra Nehem Ptah Akhan
Aakhuamuman Amaruka Atifi Mu
Awukudae, February, 13025 (2025)

ODWIRASEM: Trustorical Anthology – volume 1

AFURAKA/AFURAITKAIT

THE ORIGIN OF THE TERM 'AFRICA'

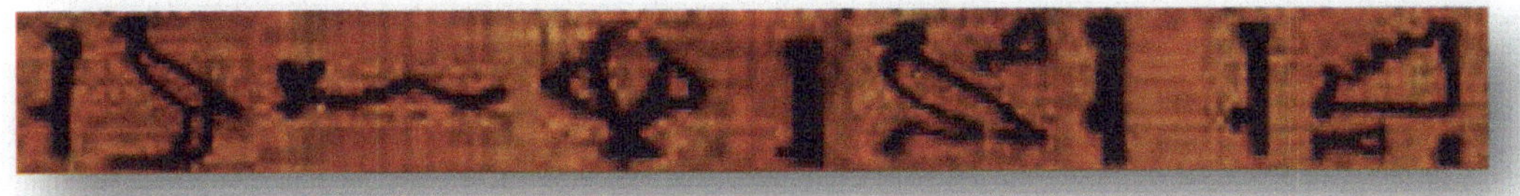

ODWIRAFO KWESI RA NEHEM PTAH AKHAN

From the **Hunefer Sheft** – *Papyrus of Hunefer* - 3,300 years ago]

Au **f** **Hr** **Kai**

[From the **Temple of Auset** in **Paaraka** *(Pilak, Philae)* - 2,400 years ago]

Au Ra Ka

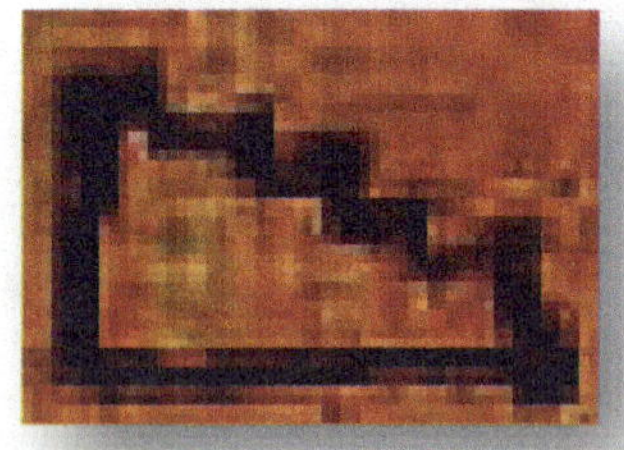

In the language and culture of Ancient ***Kamit*** *(Egypt), the term* ***resit*** *means 'south' while the term* ***ament*** *means 'west'. The* ***south land*** *was/is recognized to be the* ***head-land*** *or* ***top-land****, while the* <u>*west*</u> *is also considered 'right' and* <u>*east*</u> *is considered 'left'. The ancient and proper orientation of the continent of* ***Afuraka/Afuraitkait*** *(Africa) is thus with the* ***resit*** *or* ***south*** *at the* ***top*** *as shown above. Moreover, the proper orientation shows that the continent describes a form similar to that of the* ***human heart****, for* ***Afuraka/Afuraitkait*** *is the* ***heartland*** *of the world. It reflects the shape of the* ***Ka*** *or* ***Kai*** *medut (hieroglyph) meaning* ***high land****. Yet it is also used as a* <u>*determinative medut*</u> *for the name* ***Auf Hr Kai*** *and* ***Au Ra Ka – variations of the name Afuraka/Afuraitkait*** *as found in the Papyrus of* ***Hunefer*** *and the Temple of* ***Auset*** *in* ***Paaraka*** *(Pilak, Philae), respectively, shown above.* [Note that **Pilak** is an Ancient **Khanitu** (Nubian) form of the name **Paaraka** that predates **Coptic** by hundreds of years. See Appendix.]

AFURAKA/AFURAITKAIT

THE ORIGIN OF THE TERM 'AFRICA'

PARTS 1-4

AFURAKA/AFURAITKAIT – THE ORIGIN OF THE TERM 'AFRICA' was first published as a three-part article series in the **AWUSISEM** section of the first, second and third issues of our **AFURAKA/AFURAITKAIT NANASOM NHOMA – Afurakani/Afuraitkaitnit (African) Ancestral Religion Journal** in 13007-13008 (2007-2008). We published part four of the series in 13011 (2011). We made the pdf version of each individual installment of the series a free download from our website as they were published. Here, we have combined all four parts into one document for ease of study. We have elected to retain the original headings as they appear in the original first three issues of our nhoma as well as the subsequent fourth installment. We have also included an *Appendix* with additional information, published in 13014 (2014), which did not appear in the original series.

Numerous scholars over the centuries have attempted to delineate the etymological origins of the name *Africa*. However, they have failed because of a lack of understanding of Afurakani/Afuraitkaitnit (African) Ancestral Religion, cosmology and culture. **Odwirafo Kwesi Ra Nehem Ptah Akhan** is the first to elucidate and publish the actual etymological origins of the name *Africa* demonstrating the name to be derived linguistically and cosmologically from **Afuraka/Afuraitkait** – the original male and female aspects of the name. This includes showing the actual term written by our Afurakani/Afuraitkaitnit (African) Ancestresses and Ancestors in the **medutu** (hieroglyphs) of **Ancient Kamit** (Ancient Egypt) – a discovery which heretofore had never been accomplished. Afuraka/Afuraitkait is an indigenous designation for the continent first propounded by **Afurakanu/Afuraitkaitnut** (Africans~Black People) prior to the existence of any other people on Earth.

The myths put forward by eurasians seeking to locate the origins of the name *Africa* outside of the continent of Afuraka/Afuraitkait (Africa) and in the greek, latin, sanskrit, arabic, phoenician and other languages, have been shown in this article series to be a **deliberate attempt** by the non-Afurakanu/non-Afuraitkaitnut (non-

Africans/non-Blacks) to **misinform** Afurakanu/Afuraitkaitnut (Africans~Black People) and dispossess us of our heritage and culture. This is nothing new. We have been and will continue to be at war - culturally, intellectually, spiritually and physically - with the whites and their offspring, their culture and their pseudo-religions (inclusive of all forms of christianity, islam, judaism/hebrewism, hinduism, buddhism, taoism, pseudo-esotericism, etc.) until the whites and their offspring no longer exist in the world. We will always meet the challenge and will emerge triumphant on every level.

The proper etymology of the term *Africa* was first given to us in the 12990s (1990s) by our **Nananom Nsamanfo** – *Akan* term for our *Honored* or *Spiritually Cultivated* Afurakani/Afuraitkaitnit (African) *Ancestresses and Ancestors*. It was our Nananom Nsamanfo who would also lead us to the tangible evidence supporting the etymological origins of the term in the languages, cultures and ritual practices of Afuraka/Afuraitkait (Africa) – inclusive of Ancient **Khanit** and Kamit (Nubia and Egypt). We would subsequently release our publication: **KUKUU-TUNTUM The Ancestral Jurisdiction** in 13002 (2002), wherein we defined the term **Afuraka/Afuraitkait** and its cosmological roots in the first section. The release of our article series in 13007-13008 was designed to provide a more detailed analysis of the nature and function of the name **Afuraka/Afuraitkait** (Africa) as it applies to Black People – *and Black People only* – and to expose the misinformation which continues to be propagated deliberately by the whites and their offspring, as well as by misinformed Afurakani/Afuraitkaitnit (African~Black) scholars, teachers, authors, etc.

This four-part series is the first volume of a greater series. There are numerous manifestations of the term and name Afuraka/Afuraitkait (Africa) all over the continent and in the places we traveled after having migrated away from the continent thousands of years ago for the first time in our **trustory**. This is an attestation to the ancient spiritual roots of the name **Afuraka/Afuraitkait**. The information can and will fill many volumes. This is a never-ending project.

AWUSISEM

KRADIN

AFURAKA/AFURAITKAIT

The origin of the term 'Africa'

The Earth's surface is comprised of approximately 71 percent water and 29 percent landmass. Initially, the Earth's surface was completely covered by water. Our **Afurakani/Afuraitkaitnit** (African) Ancestresses and Ancestors learned the process of the development of Earth's first landmass and codified this process in their writings and illustrations. They/We learned of this process directly from the **Abosom** (Deities; Goddesses and Gods), the Spirit-Forces of Creation, Who affected the process itself. It is within our Ancestral cosmology, language and writing system of ancient **Keneset** and **Kamit** (ancient Black Civilizations of Nubia and Egypt) that we find this process codified and named with terms that are over 40,000 years old.

Earthquakes on the ocean floor of the primordial Earth caused a portion of the ocean floor to rise up above the surface of the water. This raised land became the first landmass of Earth. The masculine term for: *raised land, high land, exalted land, hill, mountain* in the language of **Kamit** (ancient Egypt) is **Ka** (kah). The feminine term for the same is **Kait** (kah-ette'), also written **Kat** (kaht). These terms are often written **Qa** and **Qait** (or **Qat**). The term for *soul* in Kamit is also **Ka**.

The **medut** (hieroglyphic symbol) representing *Soul*, **Ka** is: 

ka, P. 607, N. 619, T. 88, image, genius, person, double, character, disposition, the vital strength

The **medut** representing *raised land, exalted land, high land,* **Ka** (**Qa**) is: 

qa-t, U. 229, IV, 974, P. 174, M. 440, N. 941 = , P. 174, N. 941, U. 494, T. 235 = , high land, *i.e.*, the Nile banks above the river; plur. ; Copt. ⲔⲀⲈⲒⲈ.

Qa, Qait, B.D. 1, the high place on which the god of creation stood.

The two arms representing **Ka**/*Soul* are the <u>same two arms</u> of the individual who is reaching upward in the *medut* for **ka** (**qa**)/*high land.* [See appendix for **QA** vocalized **KAEIE** ⲔⲀⲈⲒⲈ.]

The term **Ka** (**Qa**) is also defined in the language of Kamit as: *the land above the banks of the river; the high ground upon which the Deity of Creation first stood.* The term is also doubled: **Qaqa** or **Kaka**. The doubling concept is widespread in Afurakani/Afuraitkaitnit languages when a particular quality or attribute is being emphasized. The term **Qa** also has the variation **Qi** (**Ki**) or **Qe** (**Ke**) in the language of Kamit.

qai-t [hieroglyphs], IV, 364, [hieroglyphs], Love Songs 2, 4, [hieroglyphs], Hymn Darius 23, the land high above the surface of the Nile; Copt. ⲔⲀⲒⲈ, ⲔⲞⲒ.

Qaqa [hieroglyphs], B.D. 17, 9, a hill in Khemenu on which the heavens rested.

qi [hieroglyphs], Rev. 12, 91, [hieroglyphs], Rec. 27, 190, field, estate; Copt. ⲔⲀⲒⲈ.

qi [hieroglyphs], to be high, exalted.

In the **Twi** language of the **Akan** people of Ghana, the term **Koko** is defined as: *hill, raised land.* This is the **Kaka** of Kamit. In Akan cosmology the area called **Koko**-*Afuo* is defined as: *the region where the Great Ancestress and her family settled after having descended from the sky/heaven on a golden chain after the beginning of the world.*

In the language of the **Yoruba** people of Nigeria, the term **Oke** is defined as *mountain, hill.* This is the **Qi** or **Ke** (**oKe**) of Kamit. There are five sacred hills in *Yoruba* cosmology, one of them being **oke ara** which is defined as: *the hill upon which the* **Orisha** *(Yoruba* for *'Deities') first descended to create the world.*

The terms **ka** (qa), **koko** (kaka) and **oke** (qi; ke) in *Kamit*, *Akan* and *Yoruba* all refer to *raised land* and also a *sacred raised land associated with the foundation of the world.* The same is true of many Afurakani/Afuraitkaitnit languages all over the continent for they are all derived from the ancient languages of Keneset and Kamit. *We are the same people.*

One of the most important definitions of **Qa** (**Ka**) in the language of Kamit is: *the high ground upon which the Deity of Creation first stood.* The Deity of Creation spoken of in this definition is **Ra** *(male name)* in cooperation with **Rait** (**Rat**, *female name)*.

Rā [hieroglyphs] **Rāit** [hieroglyphs]

In the language of Kamit, **Ra** (rah) is the most ancient name for the Creator of the world. **Rait** (rah-ette') is the most ancient name for the Creatress of the world. **Ra** and **Rait** function Together as One Divine Unit – the Great Spirit of The Supreme Being. **Ra** and **Rait**, as the Great Spirit, are the Divine Living Energy moving throughout all of Creation. The life-force energy animating plants, animals, minerals and Afurakani/Afuraitkaitnit humans, the energy moving throughout our bodies, is a portion of the Divine Living Energy, the Creative Power, the Creator and the Creatress, **Ra** and **Rait**. Just as the air in your lungs is connected to a greater source of air, the atmosphere of Earth, so is the life-force energy in your body a portion of and connected to the Greater Divine Life-Force Energy animating all *created* entities in Creation.

It was **Ra** and **Rait** Who created the primordial Earth. The Great Spirit then moved through the primordial Earth causing perturbations within the ocean floor. The vibrations, earthquakes, volcanic eruptions, separation and movement within the ocean floor forced a portion of the ocean floor to surge upward above the surface of the water. This was the first **Ka/Kait,** the *first land, high land, raised land, hill, mountain.* The Great Spirit, **Ra** and **Rait** then moved through this landmass and Their Divine Living Energy caused separation and development within the landmass. This would eventually lead to the development of the physical forms of mineral life, plant life, animal life and Afurakani/Afuraitkaitnit human life. **Ra** and **Rait** would ultimately move through the newly fashioned bodies of plants, animals, minerals and Afurakani/Afuraitkaitnit humans in order to enliven us. **Ra** and **Rait** use the **Aten**, the Sun, as a physical transmitter of Their Spiritual Energy. The solar heat/energy circulating through your body and the bodies of other *created* entities is the power of **Ra** and **Rait**.

åf , U. 268, 519, , U. 535, flesh, meat, joint, member; plur. ,

Åf, Åfu , the carcase of the Sun-god of night, or the dead body of Rā; he has the form of a ram-headed god, and his shrine is encircled by the serpent Meḥen.

The term **Af** in the language of Kamit means *flesh* as well as *house, chamber. Flesh* and *house* are conceptually related because your *flesh* is a *house*, a place of residence, for your spirit. The plural of **Af** is **Afu** (ah-foo'). In the Twi (Akan) language the term for *home/house* is **ofie** or **ofi**. The term **aafin** is the Yoruba term for *palace.* **Af, Ofie, Ofi** and **Aafin** in *Kamit, Akan* and *Yoruba* are all genetically related, phonetically related and conceptually related.

Moreover, the Twi term **Afo** is defined as: *carcass of an animal; that which is discarded and taken up once more.* The 'o' in *Afo* is a nasal 'o'. When pronounced nasally, the term *Afo* sounds virtually identical to *Afu.* The Twi *Afo* describes *animal flesh; carcass.* This is critical for our discussion, for when **Ra** moves through matter, matter becomes the *house* or *place of residence, the flesh* of the Creator. This is why in Kamit, the title of **Ra** when He moves through matter is **Afu Ra**. The Creator as **Afu Ra**, takes on the form/flesh of a Ram.

In the cosmology of Kamit, **Ra** operates *through* the **Aten** (Sun). [**Ra** is not the "sun-god". **Aten** is the Sun-God]. **Ra** rides in a sun barque/boat across the sky from horizon to horizon, from sunrise to sunset. He then travels in his barque for the 12 hours of the night through the spirit-realm or underworld. After His underworld journey the solar barque emerges from the underworld on the eastern horizon as the new sunrise and the beginning of a new day. As the solar light (energy of **Ra**) moves into the underworld (inside Earth) at sunset, the Earth becomes the *flesh, house, place of residence* for the solar light. The image below is a depiction of **Ra** in His barque. Notice the **Aten** (Sun) on His head and in front of Him:

The Creator, **Ra**, sails the **Aten** (Sun) through the sky from the eastern horizon to the western horizon. The solar barque then dips below the western horizon and sails from the western horizon to the eastern horizon-underground – bringing "light" to the underworld during the 12 hours of the night. The image below is a depiction of **Ra** as **Afu Ra**, after His barque has descended into the Earth, in the underworld. Notice that as **Afu Ra**, He has taken the form/flesh of a Ram-headed Divinity:

Afu Ra in tomb of **Ra Messu I**

Afu Ra in the tomb of **Seti** – *photo taken by this author*

When the life-force energy of the **Aten** (Sun) enters your body via the air that you inhale, the life-force energy has now entered your <u>house</u>; your <u>flesh</u>. The air inside your lungs is internalized air; air inside matter. It could thus be called, "**Afu-Air**", while the air outside of your body is simply "**Air**".

When **Ra** and **Rait** first moved through the primordial hill, the **Ka/Kait** to make it vibrant, to give it life, the **Ka/Kait**, the raised land, became the house or place of residence for **Ra** and **Rait**. It is for this reason that **Ra** and **Rait** take on the titles **Afu Ra** and **Afu Rait**.

This is why the first landmass is called the **Ka** of **Afu Ra**, *the land of the Creator* and the **Kait** of **Afu Rait**, *the land of the Creatress.*

The **Ka** of **Afu Ra** is **Afuraka**. The **Kait** of **Afu Rait** is **Afuraitkait**. **Afuraka/Afuraitkait** is the *Divine Land.*

Geologically, this first emergent landmass is of the continental plate, **Afuraka/Afuraitkait**. The male title, **Afuraka** was corrupted by the whites and their offspring into <u>Africa</u>.

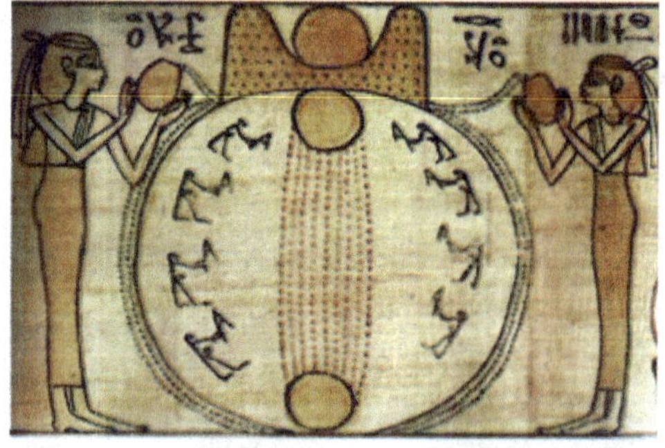

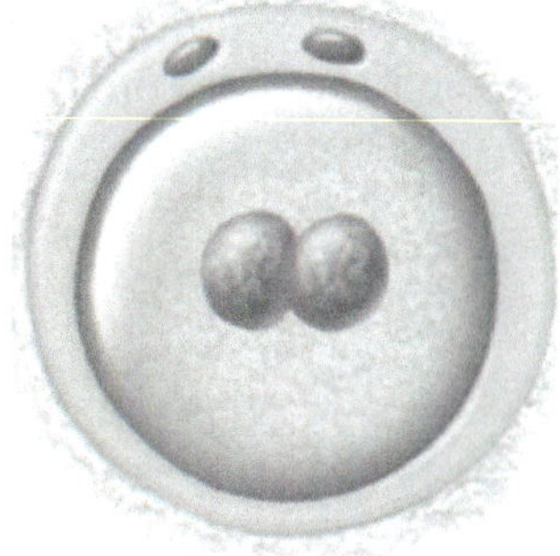

The image on the left above is from the **sheft** of **Khensumes** (papyrus of Khensumose). From a bird's-eye view it actually depicts the **Ka/Kait**, the high land, which first appeared above the surface of the water to become the Earth's first landmass. This **Ka/Kait** is described in many texts of Kamit as the *"primordial mound of Creation"* in the region of **Khemennu** or the **Kaka** (**Qaqa**) or **Qa** in *Khemennu* (later called *Hermopolis* by the greeks).

The depiction shows **Ra** and **Rait** moving through the land, **Ka/Kait**, as **Afu Ra** and **Afu Rait within the Solar disk** in two phases. Here, They are **Afu Ra** and **Afu Rait** because They are moving through matter/flesh/the house. Eventually, **Afu Ra** and **Afu Rait** rise within the Solar disk above the horizon (between the mountains) for the first time, creating the first sunrise in the *trustory* of the world (top of the illustration). **Afu Ra** and **Afu Rait** are thus transformed into **Ra** and **Rait**.

The Eight figures depicted on the mound are **Amen** and **Amenet**, **Ka** and **Kait**, **Hehu** and **Hehut**, **Nun** and **Nunet** – the Ancestresses and Ancestors of **Ra** and **Rait** (often called the *Ogdoad* – primordial Deities who existed before the creation of the world). **Auset** and **Nebt Het** are depicted through the forms of **Merit Meht** and **Merit Shema**, the Northern and Southern Nile Goddesses of the inundation. These Two Spirits pour water, libation, from two vases into the primordial waters which nourish the **Ka/Kait**.

This is an actual depiction of **Afuraka/Afuraitkait**, a depiction painted by one of our Afurakani or Afuraitkaitnit Ancestors or Ancestresses which dates back over 3,000 years.

The image to the right of Khensumose papyrus is a depiction of a **fertilized ovum** (egg) of a woman. The creation of the first landmass of Earth by **Ra** and **Rait** mirrors the fertilization of an ovum. Earth became *fertile* and thus *productive* when the Great Spirit, **Ra/Rait**, the Divine Life-Force operating through the *Aten* penetrated the **Ka/Kait** and "fertilized" it - making it capable of sustaining life(force). This insight is woven into the fabric of Afurakani/Afuraitkaitnit cosmology and is the reason why we codified these geological and biological processes in our language and our illustrations in ancient Kamit.

[Photos taken by this author from the tomb of **Seti**. Two variant spellings of **Afu Ra** and **Af Ra** in the **medutu**]

It is important to note that the name **Afu Ra** or **Afra** exists in the language of the Akan. A major **Obosom** (God; Deity) worshipped in Akan culture is the *Obosom* named **Afram**. The feminine version of this name in Akan culture is **Afra**. Moreover, it was stated above that in Akan cosmology, the area where a certain Ancestress settled with Her people after having descended from heaven on a golden chain is the region now called **Koko-Afuo**. Again, *Koko* means *hill, raised land* in Twi and in Kamit (*Kaka or Qaqa*). *Afuo* is a term in the Twi (Akan) language meaning *fertile land, farm land; land that is vibrant.* The pronunciation of *Afuo* in Twi, depending on the dialect, sounds like and is often written **Afur**. Thus **Koko-Afur** is a reference to a land of origins. A fertile, *Afur,* high land, *Koko. Koko-Afur* is **Afur-koko** (Afurko/Afuraka). The reason why land is fertile is because the energy of **Ra** and **Rait** is circulating through it, making it vibrant and full of life. Today, the name *Koko-Afuo* has been contracted to **Kokofu**, a well-known region of Ghana.

It is also worthy of note that the Twi term, **fura**, means: *to put on* (example: to put on clothing). This is directly related to the notion of **Ra**, when entering matter, taking on matter as His flesh or house, thus having the title **(A)fura**. He has "put on" flesh/matter. As shown in the illustration, **Ra** when moving through the underworld also takes on the form/flesh of a Ram-headed figure. He has put on (*fura*) the animal form that will eventually become a carcass. It is a form/body that **Ra** will discard once He reaches the point where He leaves the underworld and appears on the horizon as the energy emanating through the **Aten** at sunrise. This animal form will be taken up again, put on again, once **Ra** returns to the underworld. Again, this is the definition of *Afo* in Twi: *carcass of an animal; that which is discarded and taken up once more.* See entries from the **Akan (Twi) dictionary**:

fura, *v.* [*red.* **furafura**] **Ak. fira, 1.** (furá) *to put on,* viz. ntãmã, *a native dress* consisting of a large piece of cloth which is wrapped round the body. *pr.*

afṍ [*cf.* fõ, *a.*] **1.** *carcass, carrion,* the *dead body* of an animal = efúnu, abó-fõ, abókã. — **2.** *something cast away,* but *taken up agin:* fa afõ, *to take up*

The Twi term **fra** or **afra** also has the meaning: to become intermixed; co-mingled. This points to the fact that **Ra** and **Rait**, upon intermixing or comingling with matter/flesh become **Afu Ra** and **Afu Rait**. **Afura**, **fura** and **afra** are all related phonetically and conceptually. The Twi term **fram** also has the meaning: *to be on fire, to burn, blaze; flame fire.* This term **fram**, related to the name of the *Obosom* (Deity) **Afram** (**Afura**) shows the connection to the life-force energy being transmitted through the *Aten* (Sun; solar fire).

afrá: di afrá, *to become* or *be intermixed, commingled;* Guaŋfo nè Twifo àdì a-

fram', *v. to be on fire, to burn, blaze, flame, flare. Dan. 3,23. Job 19,11;* ka-

We should note also that the term **kua** in the Twi language means: *farm.* **Kua** or **Koa** is related to **Ka** as *land.* Specifically, the land which became fertile (*farmland* is fertile) as a result of **Ra** and **Rait** moving within it to make it vibrant. See correspondences below:

ɛ-kókó, (F. ɔ-), *pl.* a-, ŋ-, *hill, a natural elevation of ground; cf.* bepow, bepo-

kúá, 1. = afuw, *plantation, farm;* mékò mé kúám'; me kuam' ne ha-yi; né

o-fí, o-fie, *pl.* afí & afiafí, (F. also i-fi, *pl.* efi-efi) *home,* the place a man lives

afúw, Ak. afúo, *pl.* **m-, 1.** *plantation, cultivated ground, field* occupied by

Kamit
Afu – flesh; house; flesh of **Ra/Rait**
Afu Ra and **Afu Rait** – title of **Ra**, title of **Rait**
Kaka – high land
Ka – high land; land

Twi (Akan)
Ofi – house, home; also used for sanctuary/temple (**Abosomfie**)
Afo – animal carcass; flesh; that which is put on, discarded and taken up again
Afuo (**Afur**) – land that is fertile; farmland; plantation; land with vibrant energy moving through it
fura – to put on
afra – to become intermixed; comingled
fram – to be on fire, to burn, blaze; flame, fire; **Afram** and **Afra** (**Afura** and **Afurait**)
Koko – hill, mountain; high land
Kua – farm (fertile land)

False Etymologies (false origins) of the term 'africa'

The idea that the romans, greeks, arabs, hindus or any of the whites and their offspring created the name *Africa* is absolutely inaccurate. Moreover, the land was not named after Scipio Africanus, nor Leo Africanus. The arab version *ifriqia* comes from the roman corruption *africa.* It is often suggested that the reason why the romans used the term is because the roman suffix *–ca* means 'land' and **Afri** is the name of a **Berber** tribe who occupied the land when the romans invaded. The romans are therefore said to have called the territory in the northern part of the continent: the land, *ca*, of the **afri** people, hence *afri-ca*. The *Berber* ethnic group mentioned is called the **Aourigha**, often written **Afarik**. We have shown above clearly that the term *ka (qa)* definitely does mean *land* (high land), however it is not a term created by the romans. The roman *ca*, is a version of the term *ka*, that the romans learned of when they invaded Kamit. The *Afri* people or *Afarik* (*Aourigha*) did not materialize on the continent when the romans arrived. Their Ancestry, their language and thus their ethnic name reflects the culture of the region that they inhabited, North Afuraka/Afuraitkait. This of course is the region of Kamit and the areas west and east of Kamit where the Pharaonic culture was found as well. The ancient *Aourigha* inhabited these areas over 10,000 years before the invasion of the whites.

Today's *Berbers* or **Amazigh** are represented by the original Afurakani/Afuraitkaitnit *Aourigha* of the region and misrepresented by the descendants of white europeans and white arabs who invaded and polluted the blood of some of the Afurakanu/Afuraitkaitnut. The white and white-arab mixed descendants of white invaders/rapists falsely refer to themselves as *Amazigh* (*Aourigha*) and *Berbers*, just as white arab invaders in Kamit (Egypt) today falsely call themselves "Egyptians". The terms **Afarik** and **Afri** are related to **Afura** and **Afurai**(**t**). The terms **Afu**, **Ra**, **Rait**, **Ka** and **Kait** are over 40,000 years old. They pre-date the existence of the whites and their offspring on the planet. [See the **Turin papyrus** king's list delineating **42,000** years of rule in Kamit.]

The suggestion that *africa* is derived from the greek term *aphrike*, meaning *not cold*, i.e., *hot* or the *hot country* is also inaccurate. In the *medutu* of Kamit we find the origins of this idea. In the *medutu*, the term **Afer** means: *to burn, to be hot.* The term **Afri** means: *smoke, hot vapor.* This is the reason why the greeks, having learned of these terms after invading Kamit, used the term *aphrike*, *not cold.* The latin term *aprica* meaning, *sunny*, is also a corruption of terms from Kamit. The *p*, *ph* and *f* interchange in various languages. The suggestion that *aprica*, meaning sunny, is the origin of *africa* is inaccurate and points to the reality that the whites learned that the **Ka** of **Afu Ra**, was associated with being the land of the **Aten** (Sun). The whites and their offspring in the past, and to this day, have falsely assumed that **Ra** is the "sun-god". This is why *aprica* was associated with a land that was "sunny". It is the land of **Ra** (and **Rait**), and the whites assumed this to mean the "land of the sun" or the "sunny land". The *medut* for **Aten** is: ☉ This *medut* also makes up part of the name **Ra**. It is also used as a determinative *medut* to denote: *day, sun, time.* One honorific title of **Ra** is **Pa Ra**, meaning *The* **Ra** (*The God* **Ra**). **Pa Ra** was often written **Pra** in Kamit. This became **Phra** and **Phre** in the *Coptic* dialect (Late Egyptian).

pa Rā, the Sun ; Copt. **ФРН.**

To this day, the whites and their offspring will translate **Pra** or **Pre** (fre) or **Ra**, as **Helios** (greek version of **Ra**) and as "the sun", just as the romans called **Pre** the sun and *pre-ca* (*aprica*) the "sunny land". We can also see in the above examples how *Afer, Afri* and *Afra* are not only related, but because **Ra** and **Rait** operate *through* the **Aten**, the land can be associated with solar energy/heat, fire. We also see the root of the name *Afri* people or the *Afarik* in these terms.

The suggestion that *africa* comes from the **Phoenician** word for *corn* or from the *Phoenician* term **friqi** or **pharika** meaning *land of fruit* is also inaccurate. In the *medutu*, the word **per** is defined thusly: *grain, corn, wheat, field produce, fruit of any kind.* **per-t**, **grains of any substance.**

Coptic is the late form of the **Kamau** (Egyptian) language spoken at the latter part of the ancient civilization. This dialect came into use about 2,000 years ago. In the *Coptic* form of the language, the term *per* is written and pronounced: **fre**. The *p* sound often interchanges with the *ph* sound and the *f* sound linguistically. The term *per* or *fre*, meaning *corn, fruit* is the origin of the *Phoenician* term *friqi* or *phari-ka*, meaning *land (qi, ka) of corn* or *land of fruit.* This is a reference to a *fertile land* or *land of fertility.* The people who became known as *Phoenicians* were ancient Black migrants from Kamit. This is why the linguistic terms are identical. The notion of *pharika* (Afuraka) being defined as the fertile land points to the reality that **Afu Ra** and **Afu Rait** make the **Ka/Kait** fertile. The suggestion that the Phoenician root **faraq**, meaning *separation* including the notion of *diaspora*, is the origin of the term is also inaccurate. One of the meanings of **per**, written with a determinative symbol of two legs walking: 𓂻 is defined in the *medutu* as: *a sign of subtraction; to go forth, to go out, to go away, to leave one's country, to evade a calamity.*

per, **a sign of subtraction.** go away, to leave one's country evade a calamity

We also have the related term **perkh** (written **prkh**) meaning: *to divide; to separate.* The words *per* (*Coptic: fre*) and *perkh* becoming **freq** or *faraq* in Phoenician are the origin of the idea of subtraction, separation, a diaspora (separation/leaving from one's country of origin) being associated with the *land of fruit.* These terms passed over from Kamit into the dialect of the Afurakanu/Afuraitkaitnut called Phoenicians and those non-Afurakanu/non-Afuraitkaitnut who eventually invaded that area. **perkh** **to divide, to separate**

The suggestion that the **sanskrit** and **hindi** term **apara** is the root of *aparica* or *africa* is also inaccurate. The term *apara* is defined in sanskrit and hindi as: *that which comes after.* The false assumption is that because of its geographical position, the hindus would consider "africa" to "come after" india. In reality, the term mentioned above in the *medutu*, **per**, with a different determinative *medut* is defined as: *seed, progeny, posterity, descendants.* This definition of **per** (*pera* or *para*) points to that which "comes after", for this is the definition of **posterity, progeny**. **per-t**, grains of any substance, **per-t** what comes forth, offspring

Afuraka/Afuraitkait is the origin of the term *Africa.* The false etymological origins of this term have been created and promoted by the whites and their offspring **deliberately** to rob Afurakanu/Afuraitkaitnut of the awareness of our true identity, cosmologically, biologically, genetically, geologically, culturally and spiritually.

Our Collective Identity

One of the definitions for the term **nu** (noo) in the *medutu* is: *children.* Also, it is used to refer to a plurality, the definition in this sense being: *they, them, belonging to them.* In the Twi language the term **nom**, pronounced 'noom', is a term for the plural. We therefore have the terms:

nana – *honored elder/elderess* **nananom** – *honored elders/elderesses* **nua** – *sibling* **nuanom** – *siblings*

The Akan term **nom** is derived of the Kenesu-Kamau term **nu**. The feminine form of **nu** is **nut**.

nu, child, son, babe; plur. , children.

nu, Amen. 10, 2, 21, 17, Rev. 11, 134, , they, them, belonging to them.

nu, Rec. 16, 57, to drink beer with companions, to swill.

[*It should be noted as well that the Akan term* **nom** *also means:* **to drink**. *In Kamit, the term* **nu** *with a different determinative medut means:* **to drink**. *Two separate and distinct meanings for* **nu** *in Kamit are identical for* **nom** *Twi.*]

nóm, *pl. pron., the company of;* in most cases it may be considered as a *suffix,* used espec. when a plurality of persons known as connected is refer-

nŏm, *v.* [*red.* nonnŏm] *to drink* (nsu, *water,* nsã, *palm-wine &c.,* or any fluid).

The term **nut** (noot) is also defined in the *medutu* as: *village, town, city, community, settlement.* The related term **nutu** is defined as: *citizens, townspeople,* ***natives***.

nu-t, , village, hamlet, town, city, community, settlement; plur. ,

nutiu, Rec. 18, 181, , , , , , , , IV, 1160, citizens, townsmen, townsfolk, natives.

The terms *nu* and *nut* representing *offspring, children* and the related definition of *townspeople, citizens, natives* are connected conceptually and related to the Twi *nom* when used to designate a plurality. We thus have the following terms:

Afurakanu – Africans; male children/natives (**nu**) of the land of the Creator (**Afuraka**)
Afuraitkaitnut – Africans; female children/natives (**nut**) of the land of the Creatress (**Afuraitkait**)

The Twi term **ni** is a contraction of *ne yi*, meaning: *to be, this is*. It is used as a suffix to denote an individual in the singular sense. An Akan individual, male or female, is thus **Akanni**, meaning *to be* Akan. Akan people in the plural is written **Akanfo**. A Black individual is **Obibini** from **obibi** (*someone* [**obi**] *black* [**biri**]). Black people in the plural are **Abibifo (Abibirifo)**. The same occurs with the **Fula** people of Afuraka/Afuraitkait. A **Fula** person is called **Fulani**, meaning *to be* **Fula**.

c) **ní,** ***person*,** **forms personal nouns;** — *d*) **fó,** ***person(s)*,** **forms personal nouns**;

nȧ [hieroglyphs], Hh. 302, [hieroglyphs], I, me, my.

ni [hieroglyphs], belonging to = Copt. ⲛⲁ.

There is a relationship between the Akan and Fula suffix **ni** and the term found in Kamit: **ni**. The definition in Kamit is: *I, me; my*. The determinative *medut* in this word is an individual pointing at himself. We therefore have the following terms:

Afurakani – African; male individual of the land of the Creator (**Afuraka**)
Afuraitkaitnit – African; female individual of the land of the Creatress (**Afuraitkait**)

Pronunciation key: (note: The name of the Creatress, **Rait** is also alternatively spelled **Rat** [raht])

Afuraka (Ah'-foo rah-kah')
Afuraitkait (Ah'-foo rah'-ette kah'-ette) also Afuratkat (Ah'-foo raht-kaht')

Afurakanu (Ah'-foo rah-kah' noo)
Afuraitkaitnut (Ah'-foo rah'-ette kah'-ette noot) also Afuratkatnut (Ah'-foo raht-kaht' noot)

Afurakani (Ah'-foo rah-kah' nee)
Afuraitkaitnit (Ah'-foo rah'-ette kah'-ette neet) also Afuratkatnit (Ah'-foo raht-kaht' neet)

Finally, it must be clearly understood that only Black people are and can be referred to as Afurakanu/Afuraitkaitnut and **Afurakani/Afuraitkaitnit.**

Our identity is rooted in our biology, our biological/physical and spiritual connection to the original **Ka/Kait**, our spiritual connection to **Afu Ra** and **Afu Rait** as well as our **reincarnation through specific blood-circles**. This distinguishes us from all other groups. **Black people, wherever we are found in the world are Afurakanu/Afuraitkaitnut.**

Selected References:

Pyramid Texts of: **Pepi**, **Teta** and **Mer en Ra**
Tomb of **Seti I** (*Shat am Duat-Book of What is in the Underworld*, Third Hour of the Night)
Sheft (papyrus) of **Khensumose**
Sheft of **Nespakashuty**
Tekhen (Obelisk) of **Hatshepsut**
Let the Ancestors Speak, *Ankh Mi Ra*
Twi-English/English-Twi Concise Dictionary, *Paul Kotey*
History of the Ashanti Kings and the Whole Country Itself, *Nana Agyeman Prempeh*
Imoye: A Definition of the Ifa Tradition, *Baba Ifa Karade*

AWUSISEM

KRADIN

AFURAKA/AFURAITKAIT

The origin of the term 'Africa'

Part 2

The name **Afuraka/Afuraitkait** is multi-layered in meaning. We have shown conclusively in the first part of this article that the term *africa* has absolutely no etymological nor cultural roots in any european/arab/asian languages, but is directly derived from terms from **Keneset** and **Kamit** (Nubia and Egypt) that are over 40,000 years old. We have shown how **Afuraka/Afuraitkait** encapsulates our collective identity as **Abibifo** (Black people). We will now expand on this reality to show how it relates to our spiritual make-up.

We mentioned that **Ra** and **Rait** are the Creator and the Creatress. Together They are the Divine Living Energy moving throughout and animating all of Their *created* entities in Creation. Together, They are the Great Spirit. In the language of Kamit, the term for the conscious spirit of life and animation is **ba** (bah) represented by a

bird  or a human-headed bird.

The term for soul is **ka** 

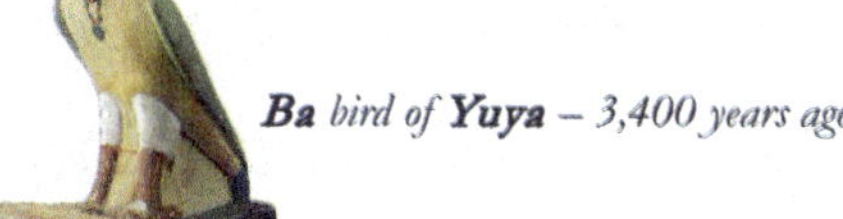

***Ba** bird of **Yuya** – 3,400 years ago*

The life-force moving through you, giving you the *ability* to move, act, think, is your **ba**. When we transition from this world, the *ba* (life-force spirit) leaves our bodies. It "flys" away from our bodies "like a bird". This is one of the reasons why the *ba* is depicted as a bird or a human-headed bird in the illustrations of Keneset and Kamit, the human head on the bird being the head/image of the deceased individual who is now a spirit. The *ba* also "flys through"/animates/circulates throughout your entire being perpetually, making and keeping you alive throughout your existence in your physical body while living in the physical world.

Your **ka** (kah) is your Divine consciousness. It is a "drop" of Divine Consciousness (Awareness, Intelligence) from the Supreme Being's "Ocean" of Consciousness. Your *ka* is that Divine Force of consciousness within your head that is always pulling you in the right direction – in the direction which is in harmony with Divine Order. It is up to you whether or not you harmonize with that pull, or reject that pull and move in the other direction. The phyisiological center of the *ka* is the brain. The brain organizes all of the activities taking place within you. Yet, your brain needs oxygen-carrying blood in order to function. The oxygen-carrying blood permeates all of your organs and systems. It is through this all-permeating substance that the entire body can function/live. The physiological residence of the *ba* is within the oxygen-carrying blood.

Just as your <u>physical body</u> contains a <u>smaller body</u>--the brain – which is the control center for the entire body, so does your <u>spirit-body</u> (called **sahu** in Kamit) contain a <u>smaller spirit-body</u> - the spirit-brain, your *ka* - which is the control center for the entire spirit-body. Your Divine consciousness, your soul, your *ka* is your spiritual brain.

Just as your physical body, including your brain, needs a continuously circulating life-energy source (oxygen-carrying blood) in order to function/live, so does your *sahu*, your spirit-body, which includes within it your *ka*, need a continuous life-animating force in order to function/live, operate. This is your *ba*.

You thus have a force of life/existence (*ba*) and you have a consciousness/awareness (*ka*). You have a spirit (*ba*) that animates you, that makes you alive and a soul (*ka*) that makes you aware. You are a conscious (*ka*) living (*ba*) being operating through a physical body (called **khat** in Kamit). *There are many other aspects of your spirit that comprise your entire being, just as there are many other organs beyond the brain that comprise your physical being. We focus here on the ba and ka, the two major aspects, because of the subject matter at hand.*

The Ba and Ka are Divine in provenance and exist as components within Afurakanu/Afuraitkaitnut (Africans~Black People) only.

In Afuraka/Afuraitkait we recognize the reality that there are **Abosom** (**Orisha, Vodou, Arusi, Ntorou/Ntorotu** – Goddesses and Gods) that govern the various aspects of our spiritual make-up and our physiological make-up. The water in your body ultimately comes from the great source of water on the planet, the Ocean. The air in your lungs is a portion of the greater source of air on the planet, the atmosphere. Your *ba*, your spirit, is a portion of the Great *Ba*, the Great Spirit. That Great Spirit is **Ra** and **Rait**. They are the Great **Ba** and the Great **Bait** (female aspect of spirit) animating all *created* entities. Your *ka*, your soul/consciousness, is a portion of the Great **Ka**, the Great Soul. The Great Soul is **Ka** and **Kait**. **Ka** and **Kait** are the Male and Female Forces of Divine Consciousness in Creation. Together, They are the expansive and contractive aspects of the Soul/Divine Consciousness (Awareness, Intelligence) of The Supreme Being.

In the first part of this article **Ka** and **Kait** are mentioned as Two of the Eight *Abosom (Deities)* represented on the primordial mound of Creation (**Amen** and **Amenet**, **Ka** and **Kait**, **Nun** and **Nunet**, **Hehu** and **Hehut**). They are Two of the Ancestresses and Ancestors of **Ra** and **Rait**. In the physical universe **Ka** and **Kait** are the *Black Substance of Space*, which is a *Divine Substance.* The Black substance of Space within which the planets, stars, etc. dwell has always been recognized by Afurakanu/Afuraitkaitnut as a united Male and Female Entity responsible for organizing the operations of the various living Entities (celestial bodies) within The/Their Universe. The whites and their offspring initially rejected this reality, however they have recently decided to pretend as though they have knowledge of it, by recasting **Ka/Kait**, the Divine Black Substance of Space, in so-called scientific journals as **dark** energy and **dark** matter. The actual Identity of this "dark energy and dark matter (dark substance)", has always been known to Afurakanu/Afuraitkaitnut.

Ka, Mission 13, 123, "the father of the fathers of the gods," *i.e.*, , and see **Khemenu**.

Kait, Mission 13, 123, consort of , and one of the four elemental goddesses = ; she was the grandmother, , of the gods.

Keki , , , , darkness personified, one of the four elemental gods ; see **Khemenu**.

Kekit , , , , darkness personified—one of the four elemental goddesses.

Ka and **Kait** are also called **Kaku** and **Kakut** (**Keki** and **Kekit**) in Kamit. As **Ka** and **Kait**, They are called the: *Grandfather and Grandmother of the Gods and Goddesses.* As **Kaku** and **Kakut** (**Kekui** and **Kekuit**) They are called the *Ntoro/Ntorot* or Divine Personifications/Embodiments of *darkness; **blackness**, night.* A portion of the Divine Black Substance of Space (dark matter) is what comprised the primoridial planet Earth, when Earth first took shape as a celestial body/planet. A portion of this Black Substance called Earth is what comprised the oceanfloor of the primordial Earth. A portion of this Black Substance of the primoridal Earth's oceanfloor is that which surged above the surface of the water to become Earth's first landmass. This first raised land, a black hill, was called/named **Ka** and **Kait** *after the original* **Ka/Kait** *(the Divine Black Substance of Space).* Our bodies as Afurakanu/Afuraitkaitnut were fashioned from this original landmass as well. We were/are thus originally black-skinned people with a Divine Black Substance in our brains, major organs and body-systems. This chemical black substance is what we call from the language of Keneset and Kamit: **Ka-Nu/Kat-Nut**, which basically translates as: the *Conscious Black-Energy substance; Soul substance.* This chemical substance is called **melanin** in english. *Melanin* is the chemical which gives us our skin, hair and eye color, yet does so much more *(see our book* ***PTAH SASETEM*** *for more information on* ***abatumm****/melanin).* It is actually a portion of the **Ka/Kait**, the Divine Black Substance of Space, which we inherited and which dwells within our bodies.

It should be noted that in the **Twi** (Akan) language the term **kra** (contraction of **kara**) is the term for: *soul, Divine consciousness.* The term **bra** (contraction of **bara**; **obara, obra**) is a term denoting *life* in the context of *existence*. The *ka-ra* and *ba-ra* of the Twi language is directly derived of the *ka* and *ba* of Kamit. A similar occurence linguistically is found with the word for *law* in Kamit: **maa**. The same term is **mmara** (mma-ra) in Twi. All three terms are phonetically and conceptually/cosmologically related. See correspondences below:

Kamit		*Twi*	
ka	soul; Divine consciousness	**kra** (*kara*)	soul; Divine consciouness
ba	spirit; life principle	**bra** (*bara; obra*)	life; existence
maa	law	**mmara**	law

The term *ka* in Kamit shows the **medut** (hieroglyphic symbol) of two arms reaching out to receive. The *ka* (soul) *receives* the *ba* (spirit). When the *ka* and *ba* unite, the entity is a living conscious entity. When your brain *receives* oxygen from the blood, only then can you function. This is why in the Twi language the term **ka** also means: *to touch; to come in contact with; to take possession of.* This definition in Twi is a description of the actual *medut* for *ka* in Kamit

kã, *v.* [*red.* **kekã**] *I. to touch, to come into, be in* or *bring into contact with,*

[In Kamit, the term *ka* also means: ***to speak***. Again, in Twi another meaning of *ka* is: ***to speak***.]

In the cosmology of Kamit, the *Ntoro* and *Ntorot* **Ausar** and **Auset** were elevated to and directed by **Ra** and **Rait** to be the Entities governing the **Ka** and **Kait** of all of the Deities as well as all Afurakani/Afuraitkaitnit males and females. This is why **Ausar** has the title **Ka** and **Auset** has the title **Kat** (**Kait**).

Auset (Kait) nursing **Heru**

Ausar (Ka)

Ra (Hawk-headed) and **Ausar** (Human-headed) meeting in **Tettetu** (Djeddjedu) (image from *sheft* of **Ani**)

In the **sheft** *(papyrus)* of **Ani** we find that **Ausar** and **Ra** meet and embrace: "***Ausar** pu aq - f er Tettetu qem nef ba am en **Ra** aha en hept en ki am aha enu kheper em baiu her ab Tchafi - It is **Ausar** when He goes into [city of] Tettetu, He finds the **ba** of **Ra** there, They embrace One Another there and thus comes into being the dual spirits within the dual Tchafi.*"

In other words, the **Ka** and the **Ba**, the *soul* of Creation and the *spirit* of Creation unite. The result is a spiritual form wherein **Ra** and **Ausar** <u>take up residence in the same body</u>. The *spirit* and *soul* work together harmoniously to sustain the being, *just as the oxygen-carrying blood and the brain work harmoniously together to sustain your body and being.* Below is a depiction of **Ausar** and a depiction of **Ra** as **Afu Ra** (Ram-headed):

Ausar 

 **Afu Ra**

Below are depictions of **Afu Ra** and **Ausar** after having **<u>merged</u>** (from the tomb of **Nefertari**):

The mummified bottom half of the merged figure represents **Ausar**, while the Ram-headed top of the figure represents **Ra**. The inscription states: **Ra** *is at peace with* **Ausar**; **Ausar** *is at peace with* **Ra**. It points to the reality that the soul and the spirit, the consciousness and the living energy, the *ka* and the *ba*, are in harmony with one another - They are balanced in their working together. What is critcal to understand here is that **Ra** has the form of a Ram-headed Divinity. This is the form of **Ra** called **Afu Ra**. **Ausar** has "received" **Ra**, "embraced" **Ra**. In this function, **Ausar** is called **Ka**. This is why one of His titles is: **Ka Hetep**. The **Ka** *at peace*. This figure is actually a representation, from top to bottom of **Afu Ra Ka** - *as a Divinity*.

(It should be noted that the word for **ram** *in Kamit is* **ba**. **Ra** *calls Himself the* **Ba** *of all beings in the text: The Book of the Cow of Heaven/Destruction of Mankind)*

Kaḥetep, T. 176, M. 158, N. 65, N. 112, T. 284, P. 54, M. 32, B.D. 128, 6, a god of offerings, a form of Osiris.

Ka Hetep. A title of **Ausar**. The name **Ausar** was corrupted into **Osiris** by the greeks.

Ba, Ṭuat III, the soul of the god Ȧf which was swallowed by the Earth-god.

Ba. The term for 'spirit' and also the general term for 'ram'. It is the flat-horned ram-form that **Ra** assumes as **Afu Ra** in the underworld. **Afu Ra** is the *Spirit* and **Ka** is the *Soul.*

The **djed** pillar is called the *backbone* of **Ausar**. It represents stability. Note the similarity between the *djed* pillar and the top of the vertebrae/backbone of a human:

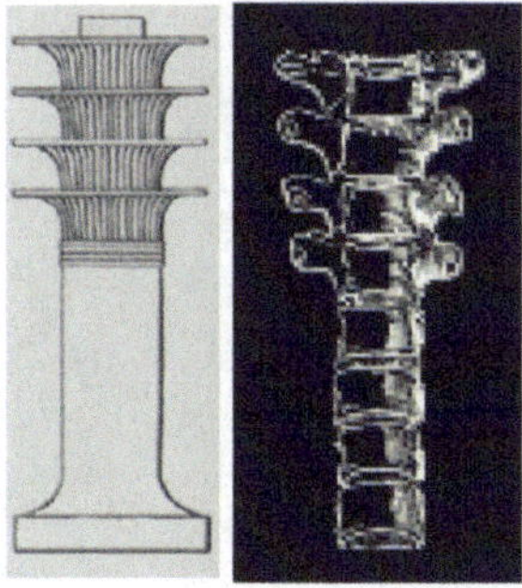

Below is another depiction of the *djed*/backbone of **Ausar**, this time with His two arms in the *ka* position:

Another depiction of **Ausar** as **Djed** (Tata/Tet), His head appearing at the top of the *djed*/backbone:

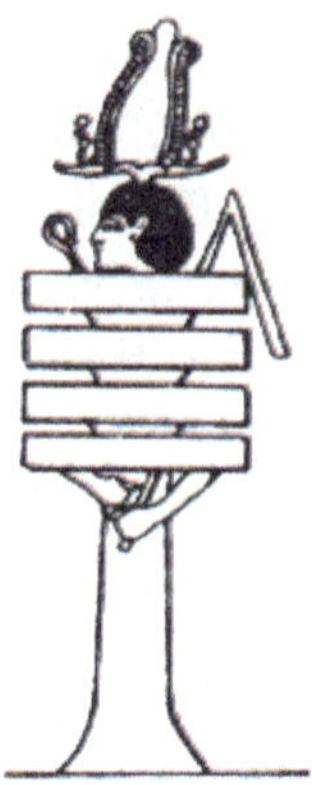

Below is another example from the *sheft* (papyrus) of **Ani**. The **djed** (**tet**) pillar on the base is one of the forms that **Ausar** takes. His two arms reach out and touch/receive the red solar orb. This is **Ausar** reaching out in His **Ka**-form (𓂓). This red solar orb is a depiction of **Afu Ra** as He emerges from the underworld during the 12th hour of the night to be born into the sky at sunrise. This is a snapshot *just before* He makes it fully into the day sky-boat. When **Afu Ra** moves beyond this point, He transforms from **Afu Ra** back into **Ra**. Again, this is a motif of **Ra** and **Ausar** united into One figure. From top to bottom, this is **Afu Ra Ka**:

We must also take note of the *sheft* of **Nespakashuty** (left) in comparison to the *sheft* of **Khensumes** (right):

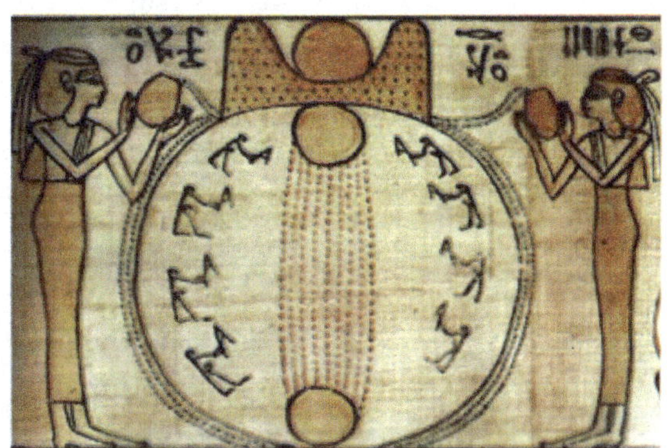

Notice that in the *sheft* of **Khensumes** (on the right) the **Aten** (Sun) begins to appear between the two mountains (top of illustration) creating the first sunrise in the trustory of the world. **Afu Ra** is emerging from the **Ka** (raised land), and will transform into **Ra**, *once clear of the mountains.*

In the sheft of **Nespakashuty** (on the left), the same principle is demonstrated in a different way. **Ra** is shown standing **partially mummified** (lower half) and **partially in the form of a winged scarab beetle** (upper-half/head). **Ra** is mummified because He is still **Afu Ra---Ra** moving through matter, through the **Ka**, the body/kingdom of **Ausar**. Moments later, *He will be free from the bandages and operate through the solar orb in the day sky as a Hawk-headed Deity.* Here, the mountain (recall that the term for *raised land; mountain* in Kamit is **Qa/Qat** or **Ka/Kait**) with the *Aten* (as in the Khensumes depiction) is replaced by the mummified **Ra** symbol. The bottom half (mountains, **Ka/Kait**) is replaced with the **mummiform** (**Ausar** or **Ka**). The *Aten* (through which **Ra/Rait** operates) is replaced (upper-half) with **Afu Ra** in the form of a scarab beetle, called **Khepera**. This is the same message depicted in two different ways.

The detail in the *sheft* of Nespakashuty shows that **Ra** is still **Afu Ra** (mummified/joined with **Ausar**), before and until He enters the sky (leaves the flesh/underworld/Earth). The detail in the *sheft* of Khensumes shows that the two mountains take on the **Ka** shape/form. <u>In fact, the **ka**-form itself is representative of the Earthly **Ka/Kait**:</u>

In various illustrations above the *ka* (arms *or* mountains *or* mummified/*ka* portion) is receiving the *ba* (**Afu Ra** in the form of the solar orb or the winged scarab).

In both *sheft* illustrations above, **Afu Ra** is about to emerge from a **Ka** - from **Ka** (**Ausar**) in one depiction and from **Ka** (mountain/raised land) in the other depiction. In both depictions, **Afu Ra** is still united with **Ka** (**Afuraka**).

In the various depictions above, notice that the *Ntorotu* (Goddesses) **Auset** and **Nebt Het** are supporting **Afu Ra** and **Ausar** by provocation with Their hands or through **ohwie** (libation).

The Body of Ausar as Tuat

It is stated in the texts of Kamit, that because **Ausar** is the Sovereign of the Spirit-Realm (underworld), *His body makes up the whole of the* **Tuat** *(duat/ underworld).* As the boat of **Afu Ra** sails "underneath" the world for the twelve hours of the night, He is passing through the *tuat*, the "kingdom" of **Ausar**. Each of the twelve hours of the night is represented by a division of the *tuat* that **Afu Ra** must sail through. Below is a depiction of **Afu Ra** and His attendants moving through the 12th (last) division of the *tuat*, in the 12th (last) hour of the night:

When **Afu Ra** reaches the twelfth hour of the night, the text in the **Shat am Tuat** (*Book of What is in the Underworld*; tomb of **Seti I**) says that His boat passes **directly through** a great serpent: **from the tail through the mouth**. *Once He comes out of the mouth of the serpent He has appeared at sunrise, the beginning of a new day in the sky.* This serpent is called **Ka em Ankh Ntorou (Neteru)**. This is a form connected to **Ausar** as the **Ka** of the *Ntorou/Ntorotu*. We thus have **Afu Ra** moving through the **Ka.** The **Ka** (soul) of the **Ankh** (living) **Ntorou** (Deities). Again, **Ausar** was appointed **Ka** of all of the **Ntorou** by **Ra** and **Rait** in the cosmology (Pyramid texts of **Pepi**, **Mer en Ra** and **Teta**). The text in the *Shat am Tuat* describing the journey of **Afu Ra** in the 12th hour of the night reads:

> "This Great God in this picture [**Afu Ra**] journeys along through this city by means of the faithful servants (*amkhiu*) of this **KA EM ANKH-NTOROU (NETERU)**. His Gods draw him along by a cord, and He **enters into His tail and comes forth from His mouth** and **comes to the birth under the form of Khepera**, and the Gods who are in His boat [do] likewise. He takes up His place on the face of the hidden image of the horn (or forehead) of the sky **at the end of the thick darkness**. . **Then** this Great God takes up His position in the Eastern Horizon of heaven, and **Shu** receives Him, and He comes into being in the East." [sunrise]
>
> "Those who are here are they who have their bodies, and they come forth in the following of this Great God into heaven. This is the hidden image of **Ka** of the serpent **Ankh-Ntorou**, which is by His den in the Tuat, and he rests in [his] place every day.."

Ka-em-ānkh-neteru

Below is a depiction of the great serpent **Ka em Ankh Ntorou:**

The boat of **Afu Ra** enters the tail of this serpent called **Ka**, *moves through/inside His body* and out of His mouth - emerging as the sunrise in the East. This happens in the 12th hour of the night. However, the same process is shown in a variation of the scene where **Ausar's Own body is in the form of a circle in the 12th hour of the night**. In this variation, again, after **Afu Ra** passes through this circle/**Ausar's** region, He emerges in the day sky as the sunrise in the East (from the **Shat en Sbau** *(Book of Gates) sarcophagus of* **Seti I**):

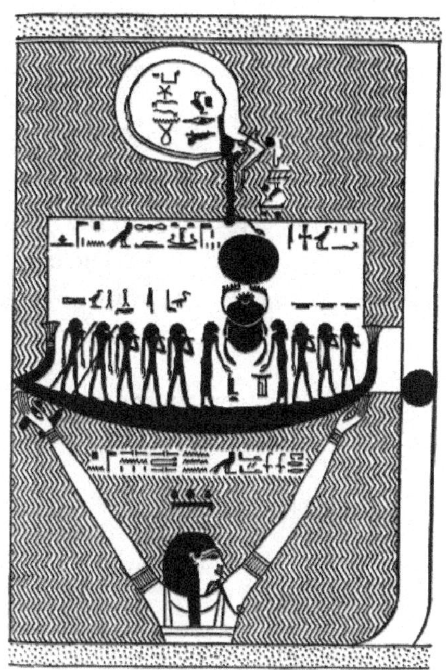

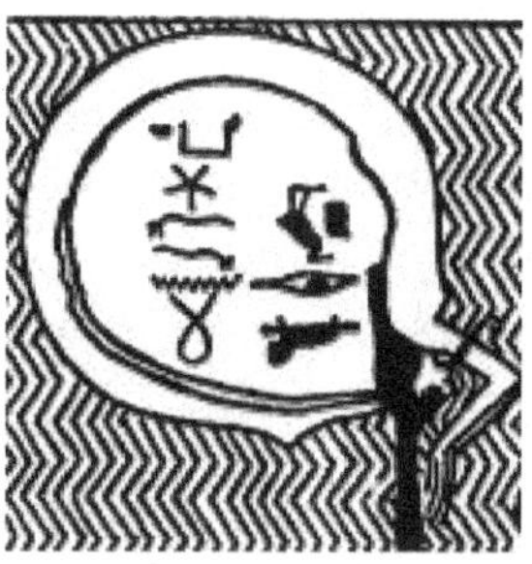

This is a variation of the same theme. **Afu Ra** is seen in His boat (operating through the solar orb) with His attendants. **Ausar** is shown above the boat, His body bent around in a circle. His feet are touching the back of His head. The text within His circular body reads: "**Ausar** is the circuit of the *Tuat*." This is a depiction of the 12th hour of the night. The *Ntoro* (God) **Nu** is holding up the boat of **Afu Ra**. **Nu** is the celestial waters' energy upon which the boat is sailing. **Afu Ra** is within the solar orb. The figure on top of **Ausar's** head is the *Ntorot* (Goddess) **Nut**. The Beetle **Khepera** is pushing the solar orb into the arms of **Nut**. **Nut** is the sky *Ntorot*. **Afu Ra** is about to be delivered into the morning sky as the new sunrise. **Nut** (sky) is ready to receive Him and then *birth* Him. He will then transform from **Afu Ra** into **Ra**. **Afu Ra** will cast aside the **Afu** (flesh form) and operate through the *Aten (Sun)*.

Ausar is called **Kam-Ur**, meaning the *Great Black One*. His Body makes up the entire strip of fertile Black Land comprising the country of Kamit. Similarly, **Ausar's** Body is said to make up the entire strip of Black land making up the circuit of the *Tuat*. Notice that the feet of **Ausar** touch the back of His head, yet His Head holds the *Ntorot* Nut, through Whom **Afu Ra** will be born into the sky as **Ra**. Since **Ausar's** Body is the circuit of the *Tuat*, the boat enters the circuit through the feet (like the tail of the serpent **Ka**) and leaves through the head (like the mouth of the serpent **Ka**). Here we have **Afu Ra** moving through Two representations of **Ka**. This **Ka** (**Ausar** or the Serpent **Ka en Ankh Ntorou**) represents the land (**Ka/Kait**) from which **Afu Ra/Afu Rait** will emerge from to enter the sky. Cosmologically, this is the **Ka** of **Afu Ra**, **Afuraka**. Various indications of the Divinity of **Afuraka/Afuraitkait:**

Ausar is called variously in texts from Kamit: **Ka Ausar**; **Ka Hetep**; **Ka Amentet**; **Ka**; **Qa**

Afu Ra unites with **Ausar** (**Ka**) in the form of a dual Divinity.

Afu Ra moves through the serpent **Ka em Ankh Ntorou** in the last division of the *Tuat.*

Afu Ra moves through **Ausar** (**Ka**) in the last division of the *Tuat.*

The last division of the *tuat* is the last division that **Afu Ra** operates *within the Earth*, the **Qa/Qat (Ka/Kait**).

It must be noted that **Auset** is also called **Auset-Rait**. **Auset** is also called **Kat**. The terms *ka* and *kat (kait)* are also used in Kamit for **bull** (*ka*) and **cow** (*kat*). As the Divine Bull and Divine Cow, **Ausar** and **Auset** are called **Ka** and **Kait**. **Auset** in the form of a Divine *Kat* (cow) is depicted with the body of a woman and the head of a *Kat* (cow/heifer). The terms *ka* and *kait* also mean *phallus* and *vagina*. The union of **Ausar** and **Auset** as **Ka** and **Kait** thus also speaks to the Divine balance of male and female in the process of conception.

We have used the depictions of **Ra** and **Ausar** only because they are most readily available and accessible. However, it is important to note that **Rait** and **Auset** figure equally in all aspects of the cosmology dealing with Afuraka/Afuraitkait.

Selected References:

Pyramid Texts of: **Pepi**, **Teta** and **Mer en Ra**
Tomb of **Seti I** (*Shat am Duat-Book of What is in the Underworld*)
Sarcophagus of **Seti I** *(Shat en Sbau-Book of Gates)*
Sheft (papyrus) of **Khensumose**
Sheft of **Nespakashuty**
Pert em Heru, Sheft of **Ani**
Tomb of **Nefertari**
Let the Ancestors Speak, *Ankh Mi Ra*
Twi-English/English-Twi Concise Dictionary, *Paul Kotey*

AWUSISEM

KRADIN

AFURAKA/AFURAITKAIT

The origin of the term 'Africa'

Part 3

In part two we demonstrated the relationship between the **Abosom** (Deities) **Ra**, **Rait**, **Ausar** and **Auset** and the spirit, **Ba/Bait** and soul, **Ka/Kait**. We delineated the connections between the Great *Ba* (Spirit) of Creation, **Ra**, working in harmony with the Great *Ka* (Soul) of Creation, **Ausar**. **Ra** as **Afu Ra** working harmoniously with **Ausar** as **Ka** is a manifestation in the world, in our spirits and in our bodies of the reality of **Afu Ra Ka**. **Rait** as **Afu Rait** working harmoniously with **Auset** as **Kait** is a manifestation in the world, in our spirits and in our bodies of the reality of **Afu Rait Kait**. We continue this series by detailing the functional relationship of **Ptah** in this process. We will also show additional etymological connections to the term **Afuraka/Afuraitkait**.

PTAH – Fashioner of the Raised Land

The *Ntoro* (Ntr/God) **Ptah** is the Divine-Spirit Force in Creation operating through the inner-most core of the **Aten** (Sun), stars and planets including the innermost core of **Asaase** (Earth). **Ptah** is called the *Great Fashioner, Creator/Maker, Excavator of the Universe.* He fashions the stars, suns, moons, planets, atmospheres as well as the bodies of plants, animals, minerals and Afurakani/Afuraitkaitnit humans. **Ptah** also fashions our spirit-bodies and thought-forms.

Pteḥ , , Rec. 31, 16, , , P. 672, 807, N. 618, 634, 1277, , , the architect of heaven and earth, the mastercraftsman in working metals, sculptor, designer, and the fashioner of the bodies of men; he was the blacksmith, sculptor, and mason of the gods. His chief forms are:

You have life-force energy circulating throughout your body, *yet that life-force energy can and must be shaped, fashioned into forms that carry the potency to accomplish your objectives.* You can fashion your life-force energy into muscular energy, enabling your body to walk, lift, jump. You can fashion/form/direct your life-force energy into specific potent units capable of shaping your thoughts into energic-matrices that will compel you to fulfill/execute certain actions/behaviors. The energy of **Ptah**, operating through your brain, is the *formative power of your spirit.*

Ptah takes the life-force energy of **Ra/Rait** and fashions that energy into specific forms, in order that you may be empowered to accomplish your specific objectives. In the same fashion, your brain fashions/structures the actions of the various organs and organs' systems in your body, so that you may function properly.

Ptah operating through the innermost solar-energic core of **Asaase** (Earth) fashions the life-force Energy streaming in from the *Aten* (Sun) and through *Asaase* into forms that are capable of shaping the surface and inner-structure of *Asaase.* Heat and cooling, expansion and contraction, are the dynamics of Form in Creation and the Divine Former/Fashioner, **Ptah**, governs this process in its masculine aspect. **Sekhemet**, the *Ntorot* (Goddess) Who is the Wife of **Ptah** governs this process in its feminine aspect.

In Keneset and Kamit (Nubia and Egypt), **Ptah** is thus called the Fashioner of the Universe. By extension He is also the Patron *Ntoro* (God) of master craftsmen/craftswomen, architects, builders, sculptors, artisans. As the Divine Energy operating through the innermost core of *Asaase*, **Ptah** receives the solar energy, takes it and molds it within His Divine workshop at the center of *Asaase.* Through the molten iron in *Asaase's* core (approximated to be 9000° fahrenheit) **Ptah** works to fashion forms, just as your brain takes the living energy moving through you and fashions it into thought-forms, behaviors, ideas, that are capable of facilitating your proper manner of living/functioning in the world.

The Conscious-Living Energy of the inner-core, **Ptah**, was the first to begin *shaping* the primordial Earth. In Keneset and Kamit, **Ptah** is therefore recognized to be the First King of Earth. **Ptah** became Potah, Podah, Podeh and **Boade** (**Oboadee**) in the **Akan** language. **Oboade** is defined in Akan culture as the *Creator, Fashioner, Former, Architect, Excavator of the Universe.* In **Yoruba**, He is called **Obaluaiye** (**Babaluaiye**), while in **Fon** and **Ewe** culture (**Vodoun** tradition) He is called **Sakpata** (**Sagbata**) or **Da Zodji** and is referred to in both traditions as the *Orisha or Vodou* (the Deity) Who was/is the First King of Earth.

Because **Ptah** was/is the First King and Fashioner of the Divine Black substance of the Primordial Earth into the first raised land, He has the title: **Ka.** It is **Ptah's** two arms that received the *Ba* (Spirit/**Ra**) of the newly Created planet Earth initially. As the primordial Earth's surface began to take shape and cool, the Kingship of Earth passed from the molten iron and solar *core*, through the *mantle*, the *crust* and eventually to the *soil/surface.* Thus the texts of Kamit speak of the Kingship of Earth eventually being passed down from **Ptah** (inner core) to **Heru** (outer core) to **Atem** (lower mantle) **Shu** (upper mantle) to **Geb** (crust) to **Ausar** (Black soil substance) to **Heru** (**Heru's** solar energy moving from the outer core through the various levels and being birthed into the world through plant life (**Heru** rising from the lotus)—connecting with the solar energy entering the atmosphere from the *Aten*).

As **Ptah** transfers His right of rulership to His Heirs, These *Ntorou* take on the title **Ka** and its associated function. **Geb** (*Ntoro* of Earth/crust) is thus called the ***Ka** of the Ntorou/Ntorotu* (Gods and Goddesses). When **Geb** transfers the rulership to His Son **Ausar**, **Ausar** eventually inherits the title, ***Ka** of all of the Ntorou/Ntorotu.* **Ausar** executes the same function on the *surface* of Earth that **Ptah** executes at the *inner-core.* This is one of the core reasons why **Ptah** and **Ausar** are united in their functioning as the Divinity: **Ptah-Ausar** and **Ptah-Seker-Ausar.**

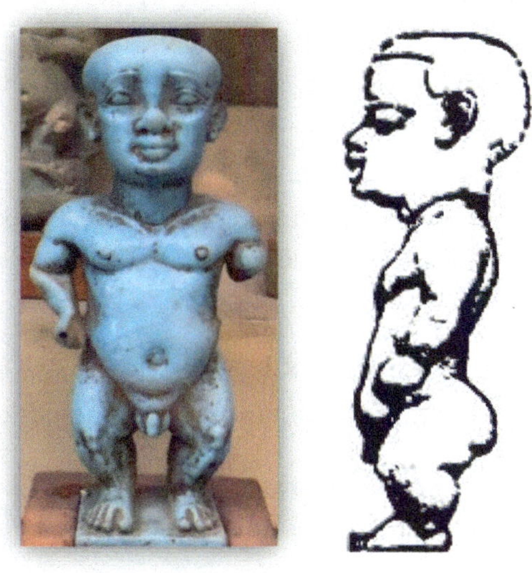

PTAH-SEKER-AUSAR

Represented as a ***Twa****, the small-statured original People of Earth, Ancestresses and Ancestors of all Afurakanu/Afuraitkaitnut*

In the **Shabaka** text (so-called "Mennefer (Memphite) Theology"), **Ptah** is said to have caused the rising up of the inert/inactive land (**Ta-Tenen**) into the primordial mound. The *Ntoro (Deity)* **Atem** then emerges from **Ptah** to sit upon the hill/raised land and creates, with His Wife **Atemet**, the Twins **Shu** and **Tefnut**, (*Ntoro* and *Ntorot* of expansion and contraction manifest here through Fire and Water). **Shu** and **Tefnut** in turn give birth to **Geb** and **Nut** (Earth/crust and Sky). **Geb** and **Nut** in turn give birth to **Ausar, Auset, Set** and **Nebt Het** (Black Earth, River waters, Red Earth (including deserts) and Rain water).

What is key for the purposes of this discussion is the fact that *the solar energy at the innermost core of Asaase is fashioned into a form that forces the energy from the core to the surface.* This results in the upsurgence of a portion of the primordial ocean floor up above the surface of the primordial Earth's waters. This first raised land/hill again is called **Ka/Kait**. As stated previously, it is the Energy of **Ra/Rait**, the Creator and Creatress moving through the *Aten* (Sun) which penetrates *Asaase.* Once this energy gets to the innermost core it is taken by **Ptah** and He begins His work of fashioning. He fashions this energy into potent forms which cause an eruption, forcing a portion of the ocean floor to surge upwards. Once the Divine black hill/raised land—**Ka/Kait** has emerged, **Ra/Rait** then move through/within that landmass to make it full of life/vibrant. They are thus known as **Afu Ra** and **Afu Rait**, for They are moving through/within matter (*Afu*).

The sacred city of **Ptah** is called **Men Nfur** (Men Nefer corrupted into Memphis), wherein exists the ancient temple **Hat Ka Ptah** meaning: *House/Sanctuary* (**Hat**) *of the Soul* (**Ka**) of **Ptah**. It was also spelled **Hat Ptah Ka** (an example of this spelling is in the victory stela of **Piankhi**).

In the **Coptic** dialect (Late Egyptian) the term **Hat** (**Het**) was often written and pronounced **At**. For example, the *Ntorot* **Het-Her** (**Hat-Hor**) was often written **Athor** or **Athyr** in the *Coptic* dialect: ⲁⲑⲱⲣ Once again, the letters *p, ph* and *f* are interchangeable linguistically. This is how the name of the sanctuary of **Ptah**, **Hat Ptah Ka**, came to be pronounced: **At-Phtah-Ka**, At-Ftah-Ka (very similar to **Afuraka**).

Hat means *sanctuary/temple/house.*
Af or **Afu** means *flesh* as well as *house.*
Ka means *raised land* as well as *soul.*

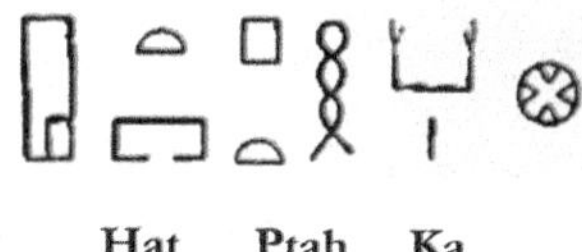

The city/region sacred to **Ptah**, *Men Nefer* was often referred to as **Hat Ptah Ka**. It is from this region of the surface of *Asaase* that **Ptah** centered His work of fashioning the landmass, **Ka/Kait**. It is where the **Ka** (soul) of **Ptah** dwelled on the surface of *Asaase.*

Thus, while **Afu-ra-ka** and **Hat-ftah-Ka** (**Hat Ptah Ka**) refer to the same landmass, **Afuraka** describes the nature of the energy which created the landmass, while **Hat Ptah Ka** describes the nature of its functioning.

It is inaccurate to suggest that the name *egypt* comes from *Hat Ka Ptah* (Hikuptah). It is true that the greeks called the region *ai-guptos*, however the etymological root of *aiguptos* is not *hikuptah.*

The *–os* or *–s* is a greek suffix and is often added to the end of foreign words co-opted into their language. Thus **Heru** or **Horu** becomes **Horus** in greek. **Ausar** or **Usir** becomes **Ausarus** or **Osiris** (**Usiris**) in greek. The Male Deity of *Asaase* (Earth) in Kamit is **Geb**, the Father of **Ausar**. The masculine word for land (as in flat land; plain) in Kamit is **Ta**. The name of the Earth-*Ntoro* **Geb** is often written with the addition of the determinative *medut* for land, *Ta*:

Geb, U. 210, N. 936, Rec. 32, 87, an Earth-god, the

Geb misread **GebTa (Gebto)**

The word **Ta**, land, in the *Coptic* dialect becomes **To**. When the Greeks corrupted the title, they read it as **Geb Ta** or **Geb To** (**Geb's** Land). **GbTo**, through the greek linguistic corruption became *Gebtos, Gbtos* or *aiguptos.* This later became *eguptos* or *egypt* in english. We must also note the **Qebt** or **Gebt** (also Qebtu and Gebtu) is also the name of the capital of the 5th **sepat** (*nome*/region district) of Southern Kamit (later corrupted into *Coptos*). **Gebtu** is related to **Geb Ta**.

Qebt, Gebt

The greeks, copying from our texts, co-opted fragmented information about **Ptah** and renamed Him *Hephaistos.* Because of His function as the Divine Fashioner operating through the innermost core of *Asaase*, including the molten iron found there, the greeks focused their discussion of **Ptah** (He-phaisto-s) on His function as a smelter of metals and a Divine artificer. They also focused much on His fiery energy causing the upsurgence of landmasses, as He is the *Ntoro* Who governs fiery mountains/hills known as **volcanoes**. The english term *volcano* is taken from the roman perversion of the name of **Ptah**. The romans learned of **Ptah** as *hephaistos* from the greeks, as well as from having invaded the civilization of the Kamit. The romans, after learning of **Ptah** as *hephaistos*, called **Ptah** by the name **vulcan.** Hence the english term for fiery mountains or *volcanoes.*

Again, linguistically, the letters *f* and *v* are interchangeable as well as the fact that *r* and *l* are interchanged when foreign words which contain the letter *l* are translated into the language of Kamit. This is why the following names are directly related and why the romans used the name:

vulcan
vula-can
Fura-kan
A-fura-kan(i)
At-ftah-ka

Hat Ptah Ka (At Futah Ka) is the sacred city of **Ptah**, for it is here that He centered His work of fashioning the world. The energy radiated from this center (just as the energy radiates from the inner core) to the entire landmass. The name *Hat Ptah Ka* is related to **Ptah** as the **Ka** of Creation fashioning the primordial landmass. The name **Afuraka** is related to **Ra** *moving through* the primordial landmass *giving it life*, while *vulcan* is a corruption related to **Ptah** fashioning the original landmass by causing the fiery hill (*volcano*) to surge upward above the surface of the primordial waters. Both terms **Afuraka** and **Hat Ptah Ka** (At-futah-Ka) refer to the original landmass of *Asaase*. **Ra/Rait** first gave the original landmass (**Ta/Tait**) life/vibrancy, while **Ptah** took that life-energy and fashioned it into the specific shape/form, creating a Divine hill/raised land—**Ka/Kait** (later imitated in the construction of the **mer**/pyramid).

We should note that the sanctuary of **Ausar** (called Osiris by the whites) was labeled by them as the *Osirieon*. The addition of the *–on* suffix at the end of the title is a european linguistic feature. The sanctuary of **Ptah**, *Hat Ptah Ka*, would thus be called the sanctuary of *Hat Ptah Ka* or **A-phutah-ka-on** or **vula-ka-n** (vulcan and volcano).

Al-Kebu Lan

The name **alkebulan** has been widely promoted in Afrocentric/Afrikan-centered circles as the only true indigenous name for the continent of Afuraka/Afuraitkait.* The term is in reality an arabic-influenced term used by Afurakanu/Afuraitkaitnut who had been arabized through the practice of the pseudo-religion of islam.

The prefix *al* is the definite article found in arabic, aramaic and which also passed into spanish after the moorish invasion. The prefix can be found in such terms as al-kitab, meaning: the (*al*) book (*kitab*); al-nur meaning: the (*al*) light (*nur*). *Al* becomes *El* in spanish. Thus, *el-presidente* meaning: the (*el*) president (*presidente*); *el-torro* meaning the (*el*) bull (*torro*).

El** has the **same form** as Deities of **Kamit

Al (also **El**) is a title in ancient **Kanana** (Canaan; ancient Black Civilization of **Palestine**) of the Creator while **Alat** (also **Elat**) is the title of the Creatress. The root of this prefix is found in ancient Kamit as **Ur** and **Urt**. **Ur** means: *great* or *the great*. **Urt** is the feminine. Various *Ntorou* and *Ntorotu* carry this title: **Heru Ur** (**Heru** the Great); **Amen Ur** (**Amen** the Great) **Ra Ur** (**Ra** the Great One); **Urt Hekau** (the Great Goddess of Divine Words).

[*Leo Africanus, in his "*A Geographical History of Africa*" written in 1526 A.D., states that the 'Arabians and Ethiopians' refer to the continent as '**Alkebulam**'. The false claim that Alkebulan is an indigenous name arises from this source.]

In ancient Black Arabia (before the incursion of the white arabs) the Creator and Creatress were called **Lah** and **Laht**. The same as **Al** and **Alat** (**El** and **Elat**) in *Kanana* and **Ra** and **Rat** in Kamit. Because the rolling 'R' is translated as 'L' in some languages which incorporated or co-opted Kamau terms into their own, **Ra Ur** or **Ur Ra** became **Ul-**

Lah and **Al-Lah**. **Urt Rat** became **Ul-Lat** and **Al-Laht**. <u>Note that **Ra** and **Rait** are the *Creator* and *Creatress*, while **Amen** and **Amenet** are the *Supreme Being*. **Ra** and **Rait** *serve* **Amen** and **Amenet**.</u>

Rā-ur, Thes. 429, Rā, the summer sun. **Ur-Rā**

The white arabs corrupted **Al-Lah** into *allah* and *ilah* and reduced **Al-Laht** into *allat*, a daughter of *allah*, so that female would be inferior to male. They then added this corrupt title to a make-believe entity (god/*allah*) and foolishly claimed that this entity was the supreme being. **In reality, whenever the white arabs speak of allah, they are speaking of their own perverse desires masquerading in the personage of a make-believe "creator". Ra and Rait have never and will never communicate with the whites and their offspring (including white arabs). The arabs simply manufactured a fake god and decided to <u>name</u> it with a label that was similar to what Afurakanu/Afuraitkaitnut were already familiar with.**

The root **kebu** of the name *alkebulan* is key to our discussion. **Kebu** or **Qebui** is actually the name of the *Ntoro (Deity)* of the **north wind** in Kamit. Two depictions of **Qebui** are below:

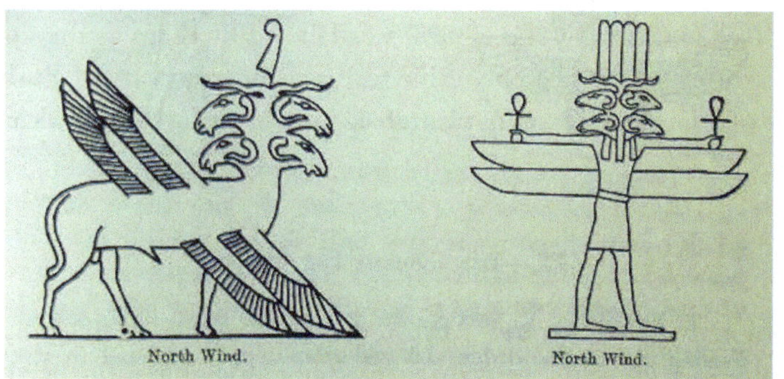

qebui, Rec. 18, 165, the north wind, icy winds.
Qeb, Berg. I, 35, the god of the North Wind.

In rome, the god of the *southwest wind* was called **Afer Ventus** (African ventus/wind) or **Africus**. The romans, just as the greeks, **had absolutely no indigenous Deities**. They <u>learned of the existence of Deities</u> from Afurakanu/Afuraitkaitnut. The reason why the southwestern wind god was called *africus* or *afer ventus*, the *african* wind, by the romans is because: **the major regions of Northern Afuraka/Afuraitkait that the romans dealt with are south/southwest of rome, italy.** The southwestern wind was thus the wind blowing up from Afuraka/Afuraitkait and therefore the wind god of the southwest was named by the romans the 'african wind', *afer ventus* or *africus*. What is **southwest** from the perspective of one stationed in rome is considered **north** if one is stationed in Kamit. **This is why the *Ntoro* of the North wind called Qebu or Qebui by the Kamau, is the exact same *Ntoro* which the romans learned about and called africus.**

The romans initially invaded Northern Afuraka/Afuraitkait and were not familiar with the interior of the continent, nor the far southern or western parts of the continent. They eventually referred to the entire continent by the name that they utilized for the northern portion of the continent. As has been shown, that name, *africa*, was derived by them from Afuraka/Afuraitkait. Because the romans eventually called the northern part of the continent by the name which they used for the entire continent, they would also refer to the wind-god of the southwest, the direction of Afuraka/Afuraitkait, by the same name, hence *africus*. In a similar fashion, one who lives in the Bahamas who is traveling by boat to florida, upon approaching florida, may refer to that landmass by saying, "we are now approaching florida" or they may say that "we are now approaching america." <u>Both</u> statements are accurate from their perspective, for the landmass represents, from their perspective, the *state* of florida as well as the *continent* of north america. See picture below:

Notice that the western half of the province of Africa is southwest of italy and north of Kamit

These facts are the basis for the nomenclature, *alkebulan*, being used by arabized Afurakanu/Afuraitkaitnut a few centuries ago to refer to the northern part of the continent of Afuraka/Afuraitkait. **They were simply repeating a <u>corrupt</u> form of the title as passed on via a <u>roman</u> idea representing the continent as the land of *the* (al) *north wind Deity* (kebu/qebu). Moreover, the name *alkebulan* as an arabic corruption, repeated by Afurakanu/Afuraitkaitnut centuries ago, does not encapsulate at all the definition of Afuraka/Afuraitkait. Our people in Afuraka/Afuraitkait did not refer to our continent as the *"land of the north wind Deity"* nor to themselves, as a people, as the *"people of the land of the north wind Deity."***

It is critical to understand the direct connection between the roman corruption *africa*, initially denoting the <u>northern</u> part of the continent in <u>their</u> minds, the roman term *africus*, denoting the <u>North</u> Afurakani/Afuraitkaitnit (North African) winds and **Qebui**, the *Ntoro* of the <u>North</u> winds. This will preclude some Afurakanu/Afuraitkaitnut from rationalizing the continued use of *alkebulan* by saying that **kebu** represents **gebu** or **Geb** (earth). We have shown that the romans referred to the northern part of the continent with the same corrupted name that they eventually used to refer to the whole continent. The association of **Geb** with *guptos* was learned by the romans from the greeks as no more than a title of the country of Kamit. The arabs used the term *qubt* to refer to Kamit as well. Thus, the greeks, romans and arabs used the corruption of **Geb** or **Gbtu** (*ai-guptos, aegyptus, qubt*) when referring to Kamit alone. The romans used the corruption *africa* when referring to the continent. The arabized Afurakanu/Afuraitkaitnut (African moors) used the arabic corruption of the name of the *Ntoro* **Qebui** or **Qeb**, or <u>the</u> (*al*) **Qeb** (*kebu*) to refer to the entire continent as an extension of the corrupted name of the northern part of the continent dominated by the northern wind *Ntoro*, **Qebui**.

Qebui, Al-Qebui and Al-Gebul (El-Gabal)

The term **gabal** (*gebel*; *gebal*; hebrew *gevul*, arabic *gebel* or *jebel*) means *mountain* in the language of **Kanana** (Canaan). The people of Kanana were Afurakanu/Afuraitkaitnut who had originally emigrated from Keneset and Kamit thousands of years ago and established a civilization north of Kamit. Thousands of years later the whites and their offspring invaded this civilization which existed in the area which today is erroneously called palestine/israel, syria and lebanon. In the language of the **Kananu** (also called Phoenicians, Canaanites), the form of the Deity **Al** (El) called **El-Gabal** was called the *Great Father/Old Man/Elder/Great One (Al, El) of the Mountain (gabal/gebel).* He was associated with the *Aten (Sun),* because of the rising and setting of the *Aten* between the mountains back in Kamit, where the people of Kanana migrated from in ancient times. The *Aten* rises above the *eastern mountain* called **Bakhau** in Kamit and sets below the *western mountain* called **Manu** in Kamit. **Ra** (Al/El) operating through the *Aten* has an important relationship with these mountains when the *Aten* is rising and setting. The mountain reference is also a reference to the original mountain/raised land, **Ka/Kait**, upon which **Ra/Rait** first descended to create the first landmass of *Asaase* (Earth).

The wife of **El-Gabal** in Kanana was called **Baalat Gebal**. The great temple of **Baalat** in the city of **Gebal** was called the **Baalat Gebalat**. [*She was associated by the Kananu with* ***Het-Heru*** *in Kamit. In Kamit the Ntorot* ***Het-Heru*** *was called* ***Herit*** *and also the "Lady of the Red Mountain".*]

The ancient **Kanani** civilization had a major city called **Gebal** (also **Gubla**), which was later called **byblos** by the greeks. This Kanani name *gebal* became *gebalene* as used by the romans. The term *gebalene* also exists in arabic as *gebelein* meaning *two mountains* as in, "between two mountains". **Khart Hadast** (Carthage), an important colony of the Kanani civilization which exists in the region of today's Tunisia, North Afuraka/Afuraitkait is connected to the mountain range now called the "atlas" mountains.

When the whites and their offspring invaded the ancient Near East, they co-opted information about our **Nanasom** (Religion) and corrupted it. In syria, after the white invasion and takeover of certain areas the Kanani Deity, **El-Gabal** *(Elder/Great One of the Mountain),* became known by the white syrians as simply "the sun-god" - just as the white greeks and romans promoted the false idea that **Ra** is simply "the sun god" and nothing more. During the **severan dynasty** of the roman empire the emperor who was eventually called *elgabalus* was a dissexual/homosexual who came from syria. He brought the corrupted (white) form of pseudo-worship of **El-Gabal** from syria to rome. This emperor was named *elgabalus* because he falsely claimed to have "inherited" the title of the high priest of **El-Gabal**. **El-Gabal**, the Deity, was called *elgabalus* by the romans and *heliogabalus* by the greeks. (*helios* is the greek corruption of the God **Ra**. *helios* means "sun"). The shrine established by emperor *elgabalus* for the Deity **El-Gabal**, was called the *El-Gabalium.* **El-Gabal** was eventually called the *deus sol invictus,* "god, the undefeated sun", whose birthday was December 25th. (*sol* is the roman word for "sun")

There is an intricate relationship between the arabized Afurakanu/Afuraitkaitnut known as moors' usage of the term **Al-kebulan** (alkabulan) and **El-Gebelein, El-Gebal** and **(Al) Qebu**.

One of the forms of **Ra** is that of a *flat-horned* ram-headed *Ntoro.* There are other *Ntorou* as well which have the head of a ram, including a form of **Amen**. The *Aten* (Sun) rises above the *eastern mountain* called **Bakhau** in Kamit and sets below the *western mountain* called **Manu** in Kamit. (Recall the arabic term: *gebelein* meaning 'two mountains'). As the *Aten* sets in the west descending below the western mountain, **Manu**, the temperature begins to go down. The cool **north winds** directed/sent by the *Ntoro* **Atem** (Atum) are then felt. In the **Pert em Heru** (misnomered *Book of the Dead*) it is stated:

".... I am a follower of ***Tehuti****, rejoicing in all that He has done. He brought the sweet air for your nose, life and vigor to gladden your face,* ***and the North Wind [Qebu] that comes from Atem*** *for your nostrils...."*

Atem is seen in certain forms as the *Ntoro* operating through the red **setting Aten** (Sun). See below:

Atem (Temu) sitting inside of the Red (setting) Aten/Sun

When **Atem** operates through the setting *Aten* (as the *Aten* sets upon and then below the western mountain) **Atem** sends **Qebu**, the North Wind *Ntoro*, to cool, to refresh us. (note that the general term **qebh** in Kamit means *cool, refreshing*).

The whites confused and deliberately confounded the manifestation of the *flat-horned* ram-headed form of **Ra** (**Afu Ra**) with the *flat-horned* ram-headed deity **Qebu** because of Their close association cosmologically and pictorially:

Afu Ra

Qebu

In their effort to manufacture the foolish doctrine/philosophy of *monotheism*, the foolish idea that there is only "one god", the whites and their offspring sought to fuse various Deities into one, while eliminating others totally. Another example of this kind of fusion is with the *Ntorou*, **Khepera**, **Ra** and **Atem**. In the text of **Ra** and **Auset**, **Ra** tells **Auset** that:

*"I am **Khepera** in rising, **Ra** at Noon and **Atem** in setting"*

Many whites have attempted to promote the false idea that **Khepera**, **Ra** and **Atem** are all one in the same *Ntoro*. This of course is inaccurate. **Atem** is an *Ntoro*. **Khepera** is a different *Ntoro* and **Ra** is distinct from both of Them, yet They all work harmoniously together just as your various organs work together to comprise and maintain your body.

The God (*Al*) **Qebu** (*Gebul*) is the North Wind, whose spirit is sent by **Atem** after **Atem** sets (through the *Aten*) **in the *gebelein* (mountains)**. It is via the corrupt process of fusion that **El-Gebal** or **Al-Gebul**, became simply "the sun god" and was then fused with **Qebu**.

To the romans, El-Gebal and Qebu or Al-Qebu were now one and the same Ntoro (God).

The Afurakanu/Afuraitkaitnut who became arabized adopted this false fusion of Deities and thus the "land of the God of the North Wind", **Al-Gebalat, Al-Qebu, El-Gebelein,** became **Al-kebulan.**

It is important to know that in the *medutu*, the city of **Gebal** or **Gubla** is written **Kbn** or **Kepuna**. **Kepuna** (**Qebuna**) is written in this fashion because there is no 'l' in the language of Kamit. As stated previously, any loan-word or loan-name that includes an 'l' is translated into the language of Kamit by using the *medut* for the letter 'r'. However, in the language of Kamit, just as in Twi, the rolling 'r' is sometimes indistinguishable from the 'n' sound, because both require that the tongue tap the roof of the mouth once. This is why if one says *Kepuna* and *Gebura* (*Gebula*) out loud, they sound identical at regular conversation speed--when the 'r' in *Gebura* is "rolled" once. [*A similar result can be found in the name of the Akan ethnic group, the* ***Bono****, whose name is also written* ***Bron*** *or* ***Brong****.* ***Bono*** *and* ***Bron*** *pronounced with the rolling 'r' sounds virtually identical.*]

Once again, the arabized Afurakanu/Afuraitkaitnut who became known as moors adopted the roman corrupt fusion of **Gebul** (**El-Gebal/Ra**) and **Qebu** into one Deity in contradistinction to the reality that **Ra** (El/Al) directs **Atem** to complete the day through facilitating the sunset (*Atem* or *Tem* also means "to complete" or "the complete One" in Kamit). Once **Atem** completes the day by causing the *Aten* to set ***in the mountains (gebelein)*** two things take place. 1) **Ra** becomes **Afu Ra**, and thus Ram-headed. 2) **Atem** sends the ram-headed *Ntoro* **Qebu**, the *north winds*. The cosmological function of **Al-Gebal** was misinterpreted by the whites as well as that of **Qebu** via the corrupt fusing of **El-Gebul** and **Qebu**. This corruption was repeated by the arabized Afurakanu/Afuraitkaitnut when referring to the northern part of the continent. See below:

Gebal, Gebel, Gebul, Gubla, Gebalene, Gebalein, El-Gebelein, Al-kebulan.

Gebal, Gebul, Qebu, Kbn, Kebun, Kepuna, Gebura, Gebula, Baalat Gebalat (Kebalan).

All of the above names and titles refer to that which is **north** from the perspective of Kamit. **Gebal** (*byblos*/Kanana, country north of Kamit). **Qebu** (North Wind). **Kepuna**(n) (Gebal; byblos; Kanana). *gebalene* (roman corruption of Gebal; region north of Kamit). The moors brought the pseudo-religion of islam/mohammedanism to North Afuraka/Afuraitkait initially. This is why these North Afurakanu/Afuraitkaitnut utilized the roman/arabic corruptions of our language and cosmology to identify the northern part of the continent *alkebulan* (al-gebelein; Al-kepuna(n)), eventually misnaming the continent itself.

Kepuna (Kepen) [hieroglyphs], Anastasi I, 20, 7, [hieroglyphs], [hieroglyphs], [hieroglyphs], Rec. 21, 99, Gebal; see **Keben.**

Kanāna [hieroglyphs], L.D. III, 126, Rec. 11, 55, [hieroglyphs], Israel Stele 26, [hieroglyphs], a district in Syria; compare Heb. כְּנַעַן, Assyr. [cuneiform] (Canaan).

Ȧn-ti [hieroglyphs], [hieroglyphs], [hieroglyphs], [hieroglyphs], [hieroglyphs], [hieroglyphs], Rec. 10, 133, [hieroglyphs], Gebelên, in Upper Egypt.

smaiui (?) [hieroglyphs], Rec. 27, 84, twin mountains (Gebelên ?)

Aa en Ka and Amen Ra Ka

In the papyrus text very often called, *The Tale of the Shipwrecked Sailor,* written approximately 4,000 years ago we have another reference to a Divine raised land called **Ka**. The story in the text is about a sailor from Kamit whose ship was destroyed in a storm. The other crew members died in the sea but the sailor was cast on an island by a wave of the sea. Once marooned on this land the sailor says:

"I found figs and grapes there. Leeks were ruler there. Sycamore figs were there together with notched sycamore figs. Cucumbers were there as though cultivated. Fish were there together with birds. There was nothing that was not in it. Then I satisfied myself and I placed some of it on the ground because it was too much upon my hands. I took a fire drill and made fire and made a sacrifice to the Ntorou/Ntorotu (Gods/Goddesses).

Then I heard the voice of a storm. I thought it was a wave of the sea. The trees shook, and the Earth was moved. I uncovered my face, and I saw that a serpent drew near. He was thirty cubits long and his beard greater than two cubits. His body was as overlaid with gold and his eyebrows were of true lapis lazuli. He coiled himself and raised up before me. Then he opened his mouth....and he said to me, 'What has brought you....little one?"....Then he took me in his mouth and carried me to his resting-place and put me down without any hurt. I was whole and sound and nothing was gone from me.....and he said, 'What has brought you...little one, what has brought you to this isle which is in the sea, and of which the shores are in the midst of the waves?'" The sailor told the Great Serpent about the shipwreck. The Great Serpent told him, *"Fear not little one and make not your face sad. If you have come to me,* ***it is the Ntoro*** *(the God)* ***Who has let you live****. For it is He who has brought you to this* ***Aa en Ka*** *(island, isle/land of the* ***Ka****), where nothing is lacking and which is filled with all good things."* The Great Serpent then told the sailor that this land was occupied with **75 Serpents**, His family, and that the sailor would ultimately be returned home after four months to see his loved ones once again. The Great Serpent told the sailor during their discourse that He was the **Lord** of **Punt**. Punt is the region of today's **Eritrea** and parts of **Somalia** and **Ethiopia**. In ancient times, this land south of Kamit was called **Ta Aakhu**, the *Land of the Spirits of the Honorable Ancestresses and Ancestors.*

For the purposes of this discussion, it is important to note that the land raised up from underneath the sea, an isle, was called the **island** of the **Ka**, **Aa** or **Aau en Ka** and **Au pn n Ka (Aupunaka).**

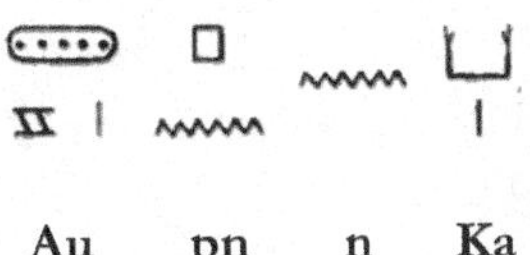

Au pn n Ka

'Island this of Ka' or 'This island of Ka'

It is important to recognize also that the major representation of **Ra** and **Rait** in Keneset and Kamit is the circular **serpent** with Its tail in Its mouth. There is a major text which is called the *Litany of* ***Ra*** or the ***75*** *praises of* ***Ra*** found in the tombs of the 19th and 20th dynasties at **Ta Apet** *(Thebes).* They describe the **75** forms of **Ra**.

We thus have a raised land, called **Ka**, upon which **75 serpents** reside, lead by One called the Lord of **Ta Aakhu**, Lord of the land of the Ancestresses and Ancestors. This is a reference to **Ra** as the owner of a raised land, **Ka** of origins. Some writers have associated this text with the origins of the tale of *atlantis* and *kumari nadu.*

We should also take note that in ancient america the term '*ca*' or '*ica*' (in the language of the Inca of Peru) means: *raised land, mountain, high land.* The term **amaru** means: *plumed (feathered) serpent.* The ancient title *amaruca*, means *land* (ca) *of the plumed serpent* (amaru). **Amaru** is a rainbow serpent who is the creator of the world. This was borrowed by the **migrants** from **asia** who **settled** in america, who now erroneously call themselves "native" americans of Peru. All over Afuraka/Afuraitkait the serpent with Its tail in Its mouth is the symbol of the Creator and the Creatress and very often associated with the rainbow. This rainbow serpent can be found in the **Fon/Ewe** (Vodoun) as: **Da** and **Ayida Hwedo**, in **Yoruba** (Ifa'Orisha) as: **Osumare** and **Odumare,** in **Akan** as: **Nyankonton** and **Nyankopon**. Again, They are **Ra** and **Rait** in Keneset-Kamit.

The Afurakanu/Afuraitkaitnut who migrated to ancient **Amaruka** building pyramids and mounds all over the north, central and south american continents of course brought their religion with them. In Kamit the male name of the Supreme Being is **Amen**. The female name is **Amenet**. **Amen** is often called **Amen Ra**, while **Amenet** is often called **Amenet Rait**. What distinguishes **Amen** in the iconography of Keneset and Kamit are the two tall plumes rising up from His crown. **Amenet** and **Amen** are the *Two Halves of the Great Divine Whole* called the *Supreme Being (Goddess-God)*. **Amenet** and **Amen** are called **Nyame** and **Nyamewaa** in Akan culture. **Amen** is the Deity whose name was stolen and used at the end of prayers in christianity, islam and judaism.

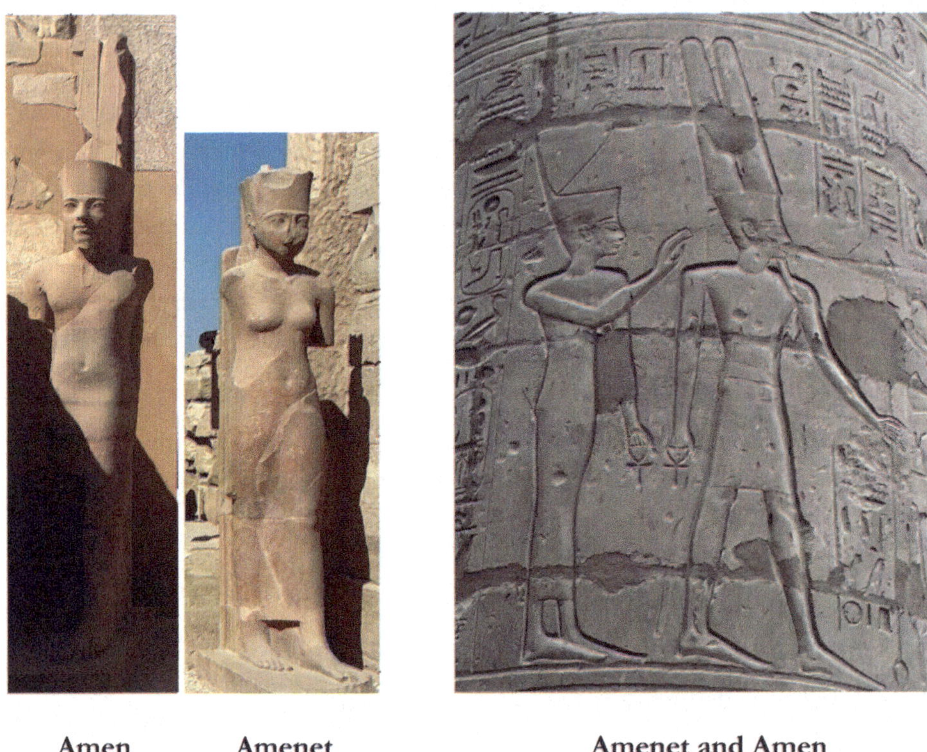

Amen **Amenet** **Amenet and Amen**

[Colossal statues and relief carving of **Amen** and **Amenet** from **Apet Asetu** (Karnak). Images taken by this author.]

Amen Ra can thus be called the *plumed (feathered) serpent* (**Ra** with His tail in His mouth). This is the origin of *amaru* (plumed serpent). Moreover, the term for *west* in Kamit is also **ament**. The extreme west of Kamit is the *western hemisphere*. **Ra** (through the **Aten**/Sun) rises in the east (*abtet*) and sets in the west (*ament*). **Amen**(t) or **Amen Ra Ka** (America/amaruca) is the land (*ka*) of **Amen Ra---**the western (*ament*) plumed (feathered) serpent (**Ra**). The bearded serpent in the text is related to the plumed (feathered/bearded) serpent of the western "paradise". We should take note that the scribe who penned the *Tale of the Shipwrecked Sailor* in Kamit over 4,000 years ago was named **Ameni**.

Of course, just as people who visited or lived in Afuraka/Afuraitkait (Africa) named themselves after or were *named after* the continent (Leo Africanus, Scipio Africanus, Terence Afer, etc.) so did the akyiwadefo (spirits of disorder/whites and their offspring) engage in the same process – but for malicious reasons. ***Amaruca*** is an ancient name for the continent, learned by the Inca of ancient Peru from the original Afurakanu/Afuraitkaitnut who built civilization here. The whites named themselves after the continent *after* having learned of the name when they arrived here a few centuries ago to plunder the land. This is the origin of the caucasian giving himself the name amerigo vespucci. Ameraka (amaruca) is the root of amerigo. Finally, the word for *lion* in Kamit is **ru**. When **Ra** takes the form of a lion in certain aspects of the cosmology, He is called **Ru-Ra** or **Ru**. Amaruka, Amaraka, Amenraka, amaruca, are all related.

Paaraka

(Pilak; Philae)

Image of the reconstructed **Paaraka (Pilak)** temple

In the southern region of Kamit near the juncture of Keneset and Kamit is the island **Paaraka** (Pa arqat) which was called **Pilak** in Coptic and *Philae* in greek. *Paaraka* lies near what is called the "tropic of cancer", the place where the *Aten* reaches its highest point at the summer solstice and then turns and "retreats backwards" until the time of the winter solstice. *Paaraka* was the last *public* sanctuary of **Nanasom** in ancient Kamit. The great temple of **Auset** was the last temple of Kamit to be officially closed and destroyed by the whites and their offspring. This took place about 1400 years ago or in what would be called the 6th century of their calendar.

Paaraka was called the "island of the Time (of **Ra**)". The island was adjacent to one of the most sacred regions of Kamit, a burial place of **Ausar**. Its structure and placement recalled the rising up of the primordial mound and the beginning of Creation. In the *Coptic* dialect *Paaraka* was written and pronounced *Pilak*. Once again, the '*r*' being interchanged with the '*l*'. In greek, the '*p*' was pronounced '*ph*'. Here we have another association of the primordial mound (island) associated with **Ra** carrying a name which is related to **Afuraka, Afarik** and **Hat Ptah Ka: Afuraka, At-Phta-ka, Paaraka, Pilak, Philae.** Here again is one of the many reasons why the corrupted term 'africa' was used by the whites and their offspring.

We have shown that Afuraka/Afuraitkait originates with Afurakani/Afuraitkaitnit people and Afurakani/Afuraitkaitnit people alone. The term 'africa' has no roots in any language or culture outside of Afuraka/Afuraitkait.

Afuraka/Afuraitkait is the origin of the term 'africa'

Afurakanu/Afuraitkaitnut reclaim our name so that we may realign ourselves with our collective **nkrabea.**

Selected References:

Let the Ancestors Speak, by Ankh Mi Ra
Sheft Ameni, Papyrus of *Tale of the Shipwrecked Sailor*
Shabaka Text (*Memphite Theology*)
Sheft of Ra and Auset (Legend of **Ra** and **Auset**)
Piankhi (**Piye**) "Victory Stele"
Apet Asut (Temple of Karnak)
Tomb of Seti (Tomb of Seti; Litany of **Ra**)
Paraakat (Sanctuary/Temple of **Auset** in Philae)

AFURAKA/AFURAITKAIT

The origin of the term 'Africa'

Part 4

In the first three parts of this series we proved that the term 'africa' is a corruption of **Afuraka.** We proved this through comparative linguistics and Afurakani/Afuraitkaitnit (African) cosmology. In addressing our ancient cosmology we cited numerous textual references from ancient Kamit. One of the major texts that we cited was the **Ru Nu Pert em Hru.**

In the *Ru Nu Pert em Hru*, often misnomered the *Egyptian Book of the Dead*, Afurakanu/Afuraitkaitnut (Africans) of ancient Kamit relay what the **Abosom** (Deities) taught us about the origin of Creation and the establishment of the first landmass of Earth. In what is referred to as *chapter 17* on *plate 7* of the **Ani** *sheft* (papyrus of Ani) version of the *Pert em Hru*, there is a description of how **Ra**, the Creator of the World, rose up for the first time out of the primordial waters to raise and establish the first landmass of Earth. An excerpt from this portion of the text reads:

*I am **Ra** in His rising, in the beginning ruled this has He*
Who then is He?
*It is **Ra** in the beginning when He rose within Henen Nsut as King within existence,*
*Not [yet] had come into being the pillars [of] **Shu** [Before the pillars of **Shu** came into existence]*
He existed upon the highland in Khemennu [of that within/inner Khemennu]
I am the Great God

In the *Pert em Hru* the question-and-answer formula is part of the format. This formula is found throughout the text. The **Obosom** (Deity) identifies Himself as **Ra**. He describes His rising (through the **Aten**/Sun) in the beginning. The text then states that when **Ra** rose up from the primordial waters for the first time, He rose as King/Sovereign. The text stipulates that this was **before** the *pillars* or *supports* of **Shu** came into existence. **Before Shu** separated **Geb** from **Nut** (Earth from Sky):

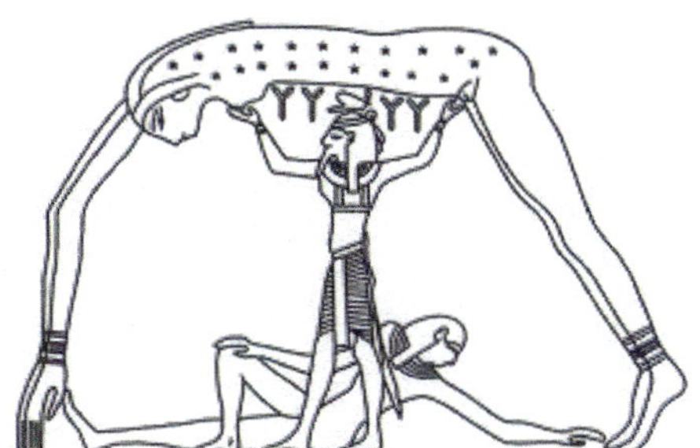

Shu separating the Obosom **Geb** (Earth) from the Obosom **Nut** (Sky)

At night it appears that the night Sky is "embracing" the Earth. At dawn the air of the atmosphere appears to "push" the night Sky up away from Earth. In the picture above, **Shu**, operating as the Obosom (Deity) in the Air, separates **Nut** from **Geb** or Sky from Earth. **Ra** directed **Shu** to execute this act ***after*** Earth was established. The 'pillars of **Shu**' reference the four cardinal points, the four supports of the Sky, held up by **Shu**. The four sticks with the 'v' top above **Shu** in the depiction reference the four supports. The text speaks of **Ra** being *'He Who is upon the hill/raised land'* that exists within the region of what was later called **Khemennu**. *It is in this line wherein the term* **Auf-hr-kaka** (Africa) *can be found.* See the actual **medutu** below:

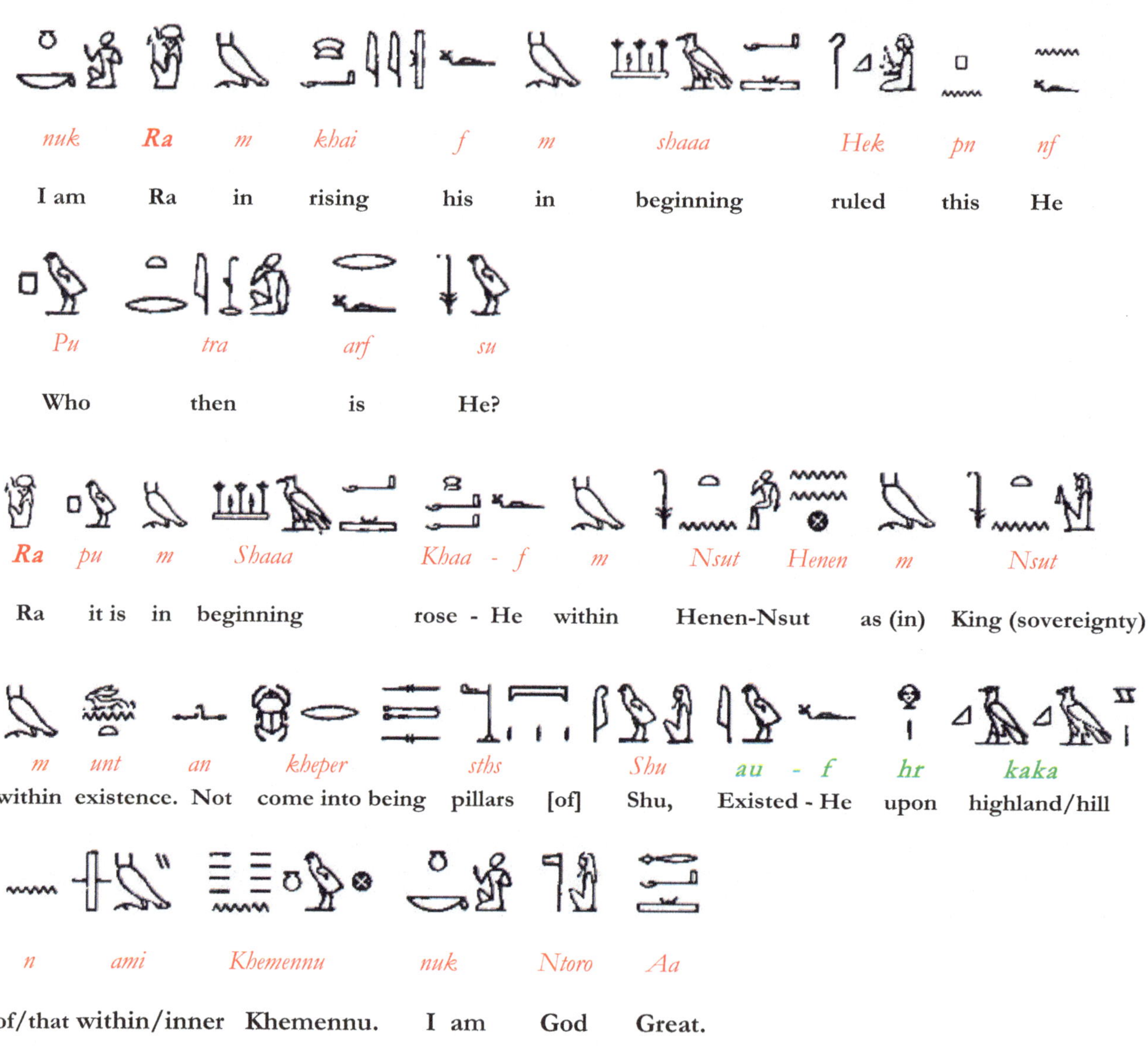

Here is evidence from the texts of Kamit that Afurakanu/Afuraitkaitnut referred to the first landmass at the beginning of Creation as the mound/highland upon which **Ra** rose for the first time: 'He Who exists *(au f)* upon *(hr)* the highland *(kaka)*':

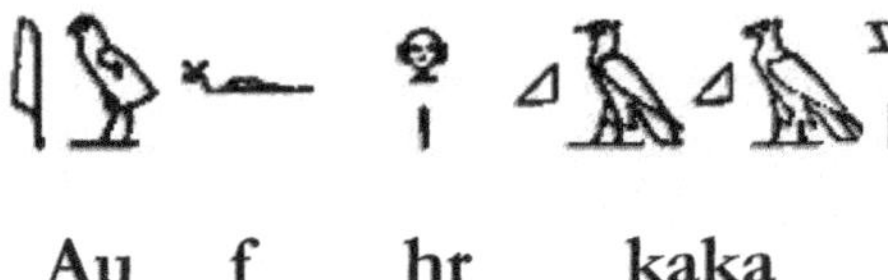

Au f hr kaka

This is the land of the beginnings – the hill/highland of **Ra** and **Rait**. This is an indigenous Afurakani/Afuraitkaitnit term which is linguistically and cosmologically exact and the roots from which the english perversion 'africa' was stolen by the whites and their offspring.

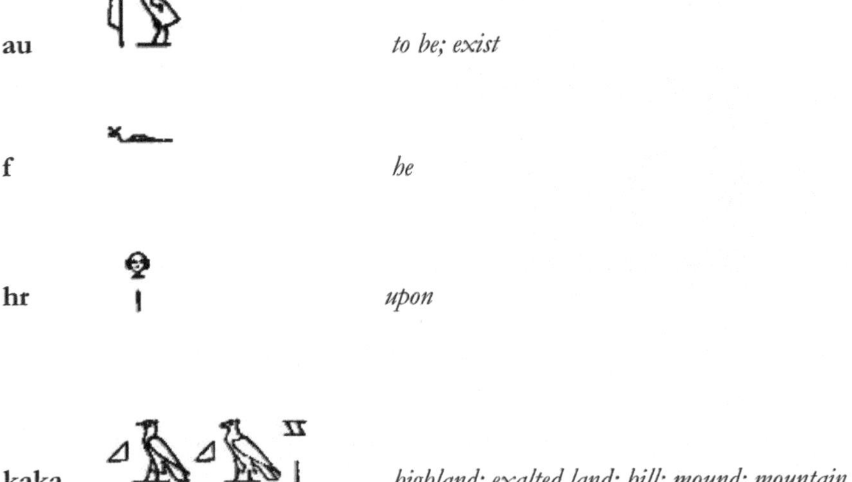

au *to be; exist*

f *he*

hr *upon*

kaka *highland; exalted land; hill; mound; mountain*

The term **hr** meaning *upon* within this term is critical to understand. The actual medut is the depiction of a *face/head* in the heavens:

This term is also the root of the term **hr**, **hri** or **heri** meaning *chief, king, he who is above, leader.* The reason why the terms reference a *face/head* in the sky is because the face is that of **Ra** in the masculine aspect. **Ra**, as Creator, is the *Chief, King, He Who is above, the Original Leader.* The texts of Kamit state that the *left eye* of **Ra** is the *Moon* and the *right eye* of **Ra** is the *Sun.* **This is because the Face of Ra is the original Face in the sky with two eyes in the masculine aspect**. The term ***hr*** in **auf hr kaka** not only references '*upon*' as in *upon the* **kaka** (hill), but also references **Ra** Himself. The term **hr** is a title of **Ra** as *Chief, He Who is above, upon; The Head; The Face in the Heavens.* **Auf Hr Kaka** is truly **Auf Ra Kaka** or **Afuraka**.

The text in the *Pert em Hru* clearly establishes that it is **Ra** who is the original Face in the Heavens, *He Who is upon the primordial hill.* The term **hr** also is the term for **Heru** or **Hr** the *hawk*. **Ra** is the original male *Hawk-Headed* (**Hr**-Headed) Obosom of Creation:

Ra as **Hr** (**Heru**) the *Hawk*

All of the other Male Abosom (Deities) with **Hr** or **Heru** heads (hawk/falcon heads) such as **Heru Sa Ausar Sa Auset**, **Heru Behudet**, **Khensu**, **Mentu**, etc. derive their **Hr** or **Heru** energy and character directly from **Ra,** Who is Their First Patricircular (Patrilineal) Ancestor and Progenitor. **Ra**, the Creator, is thus the original **Hr** (**Her**, **Heru**, **Hor** in Coptic). The **Auf Hr** in the name **Auf Hr Kaka** as written explicitly in chapter 17 of the *Pert em Hru* specifically references **Ra** (**Afu Ra**).

It is also critical to understand that the medut for the '*k*' in **kaka** shown here is not a '*q*'. Some so-called egyptologists, when transliterating sounds from Kamit into english, assigned the letter '*q*' to the right triangular medut . This is simply because in the language of Kamit there are a number of medut that have the 'cuh' or '*k*' sound. Just as english has two primary letters with the 'cuh' sound, '*k*' and '*c*', so does the alphabet of Kamit have more than one symbol representing the 'cuh' sound. There are in fact four primary phonetic medutu that represent this sound. We must recall that the english alphabet is a corruption of the ancient alphabet of Kamit with many omissions.

When transliterating the texts, the whites assigned the letter '*k*' to the basket medut in Kamit: . Subsequently, when confronted with another medut that has the 'cuh' sound, some egyptologists decided to use the letter '*q*'. This is how the medut: came to be transliterated as '*q*'. However, even in their translation of this medut as '*q*' it was understood that this was not the letter '*q*' with the sound '*qw*' as in '*queen*' but the 'cuh' sound as in the word '*unique*'. In fact, the capital **Q** in eurasian alphabets was stolen directly from the

hieratic (cursive) form of the ◿ medut. The hieratic (cursive) form of this medut is: . This hieratic or cursive form of ◿ became the english capital letter symbol **Q.**

More importantly, in the **Coptic** dialect (Late Kamau/Egyptian), the ancient Kamau transliterated the ◿ medut with the Coptic letter '*k*'. Thus, '*k*' and ◿ are identical and both carry the 'cuh' sound. In fact, in Coptic the ◿ and the medutu are used interchangeably because they both represent the same 'cuh' sound. Moreover, **the metut itself is actually the image of a slope or hill** ◿ **.** The word for slope or hill/high land is *ka/kat.*

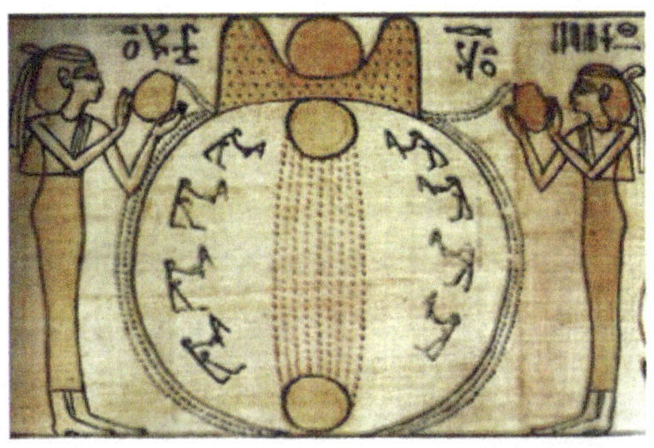

The term ***Auf hr kaka*** *as found spelled out and defined in the Pert em Hru is illustrated in the* **Khensumes** *sheft (Khensumose papyrus) above. This is the primordial mound from a bird's-eye view.* ***Ra/Rait*** *as* ***Afu Ra/Afu Rait*** *move within the solar disk, initially through (under) the mound, to ultimately rise above the mound/hill within the solar disk to manifest the first sunrise in the trustory of Creation. The Aten/Sun rises between two mountains on the eastern horizon:* .

Auf Hr Khant f [Tomb of **Ramessu VI**]

Au f	**Hr**	**Khant**	**f**
Exists He	*Upon*	*Highland*	*His*

Auf Hr Khant f - *He who is upon His highland/throne/elevation* is a title of the Baboon-headed Obosom (Deity) depicted above found in the *Second Hour* in the **Shat em Tuat** (*Book of the Spirit-World/Underworld*).

The word **kh-n-t** or **kh-n-d**, transliterated *khant, khand, khent or khend* with the determinative of a *terraced hill/ slope* (sometimes called a "staircase") is once again a word referencing a *highland* and also *throne*. The highland or terraced slope, **Khant**, is a *variation* of the straight slope/elevation in its relation to highland: ⊿ **Ka** or **Kat**. The terraced *khant* is the "throne" of He who dwells upon it. This is related to the straight *ka*/high land being an Earth-throne upon which **Ra/Rait** first sat as a culmination of the process of raising and establishing the first landmass of Earth. [*The term **kh-n-t** (khanit) is also a term referencing the first land as we will see in the next section.*]

Auf Hr Kaka and **Auf Hr Khant f** are directly related, as the Obosom **Aufhrkhant** (African) is a protector of **Afu Ra** as the boat of **Afu Ra** passes through the "underworld" during the twelve hours of the night. The **Aufhrkhant** (African) is a protector of **Auf Hr** (**Afu Ra**).

[**Auf Hr Khant f** has also been transliterated **Afu Her Khent f. Auf Hr Khant** is a ***name*** just as **Auf Hr Kaka** is a ***name***.]

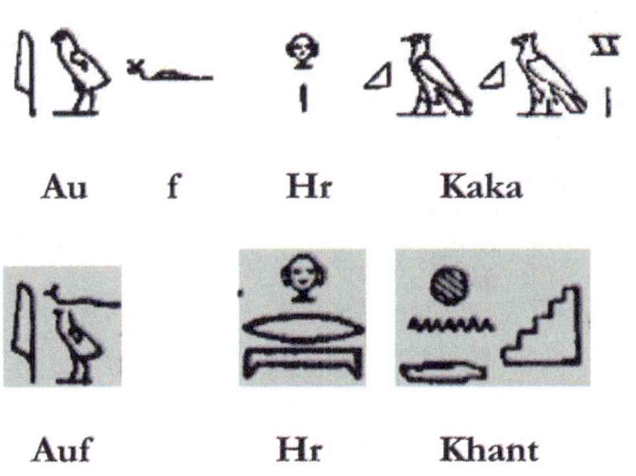

Shat am Sbau (Book of Gates) – 5th hour of the night – Tomb of **Ramessu VI**

Ausar sitting on His throne which rests upon a **Khant**/terraced slope. This is an elevation of Earth, a terraced **Ka.**

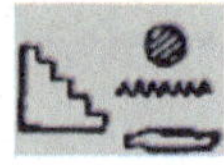

Ra-Ausar – Tomb of **Nefertari**

Ra (*Ram-headed* as **Afu Ra**) and **Ausar** (*Mummified bottom portion of figure*). They are united in one body. **Ausar** is referred to as **Ka** or **Ka Hetep**. This is **Afu Ra** and **Ka** united: **Auf Hr Kaka -** *He Who is upon **Ka**.*

Aourigha – Ahwene Koko

The term ***Aourigha*** was addressed in the first part of this series as a term related to the origin of the word 'africa'. It is true that some of the original/true **Berbers** – the **Blacks** of ancient North Afuraka/Afuraitkait – called themselves *Aourigh* which is also pronounced **Afarik** and **Afri.** Their land is thus called *Aourigha.* It must be understood that linguistically, 'v', 'u' and 'w' are interchangeable. Moreover, the 'f' sound is also interchangeable with the 'u' sound.

Alphabetically, the symbol representing the 'v' sound was transformed by the whites and their offspring into the letter 'u' approximately 1,500 years ago. The letter 'u' was in turn transformed into the letter 'w' approximately 1000 years ago. The letter 'w' is the *double*-u often written as two 'u' letters side-by-side or as two 'v' letters side-by-side. Certainly, in european languages the interchangeability of these letters is apparent. Names such as *sweden* are also written and pronounced *sveden.* The name william is written and pronounced villiam and vilhelm. The relationship between the 'v' sound and the 'f' sound is obvious. While the symbols have been altered by the whites and their offspring, the principle related to the sounds are constant across Afuraka/Afuraitkait. This is why **Aourigha** can be written and pronounced as **Aurigha, Avrigha** and **Afarika.** This interchangeability can be found not only in the language of Kamit but also in a most poignant example in the **Twi** language of the **Akan** people of Ghana and Ivory Coast, West Afuraka/Afuraitkait (Africa).

Hw (Fw)

hwa, hwã, (= fwa, fwã) and other words containing these three combined letters in Ak., *s.* **hũa, hũã...**

for things during one's absence, prepare **(something to eat)** *for one's return.* — **10. hwɛ.. mu,** *to look, pry ... inspect, examine, revise.*

In Akan orthography, the '**hw**' sound is also written '**fw**'. This is because the two pronunciations are related. The 'hw' sound can be pronounced as hoo-wuh with the 'hoo' portion pronounced as a near whisper. The 'fw' sound is simply a more forceful pronunciation of the 'hw'. When pronouncing the 'hoo' the lips are simply placed more closely together, with more force, thus providing the 'foo'-wuh sound. Depending on the Akan dialect and particular speaker, words spelled with this letter combination are pronounced differently. An example is the Akan name **Ahwene-Koko**. Depending on the dialect and the speaker one will hear the name pronounced:

Ah – hoo – whene – Kaw – kaw	**Ahwene-Koko**
Ah – foo – whene – Kaw – kaw	**Afwene-Koko**

This example is most important, for amongst the Akan people **Ahwene-Koko** is the name of the capitol of what later came to be known as the **Wankyi** region. Amongst Akan whose roots are in the Wankyi area, **Ahwene-Koko** or **Afwene-Koko** is referred to as the capitol of the place where the first people originated, for it is said by them that:

Wankyi** is the place where **Odomankoma Boade,** the Divine Proscriber/Evolver/Fashioner of the Universe,* ***made the world

"Sedee Odomankoma Boade, bo Wankyiman"

"It is said Odomankoma Boade, created/made Wankyi"

The Akan of Wankyi state that *after the creation of the world they came from out of a hole in the Earth.* They found that they were the only people in the area and referred to themselves as **Yefri** meaning '*we are the aborigines'*. They established their capitol and called it **Ahwene Koko (Afwene Koko)**. This region where they first emerged from a hole in the Earth at the beginning of human existence and established a capitol was later called Wankyi. [*Note*: This is in Ghana, Afuraka/Afuraitkait *not asia*.]

*Notice that the Akan **Yefri** as a name of Akan people describing themselves as the 'aborigines' is phonetically and conceptually the same as **Afri**.*

Linguistically, the letter 'N' and the *rolling* 'R' are interchangeable. One can demonstrate this by pronouncing *Kana* (Kah-nah) and *Kara* (kah-rah) over and over again. When pronouncing *kara* with a rolling the 'r' (tongue tapping the roof of the mouth once), there is no readily discernable difference from the pronunciation of *kara* and *kana* at regular conversation speed. In fact, the **Bono** Akan people are called Bono, Boron and Brong (Boron with a nasal 'n') – the '*n*' and rolling '*r*' interchanging in these pronunciations. Taking these facts into account, we can see how the Akan Ahwene-Koko is also Ahwere-Koko, Auerekoko, Aouerikoko, Aoueriko, Aouerigho and Aourigha. Afwene-Koko, also is Afwere-Koko, Afuerekoko, Afuereko, Afueregha, Afuarika.

[Note: Three-hundred years ago, when the dutch were reporting on Afwene Koko in the year 12715 (1715), a dutch writer attempted to approximate the spelling of Afwene Koko:

"…Butler' the Dutch factor at Axim in 1715 noted that 'a few years ago the Zay had sent an army of 3000 men against an inland country called Affidie Coco……. (Quotation drawn from NBKG 82. From sub-factor van Naerssen to Butler, February, 1715.."

*Affidie Coco is their approximation of Afwene Koko. The writer heard an Akan speaker at that time pronounce the 'hw' as 'fw'. Again, when the rolling 'r' is pronounced it can sound like a 'd' or 'n'. Affidie (ah-fee-dee-ay) and Afenie (ah-fee-nee-ay) are the same as Aferie or Afere (ah-feh-ree-ay or ah-feh-reh-ay). The name Yefri is also spelled **Yefre**. The people are called **Yefrefo**, Yefre-People or Yefrifo. This also shows the relationship between Yefri or Yefiri and Afwene. Afwene koko is thus also Yefere-koko and Yefri-koko. The **Yefrihene** is the Yefri King.*]

Ahwene or **Afwene** has two meanings. One meaning is *beads*, while another meaning is *nose* - that which is in *front, foremost, lead*, etc. The term **koko** in Akan means *hill/raised land*. Afwene-Koko (Afuereko) is the *front* (prominent) *raised land*---the ***capitol*** of the world established after Creation by **Odomankoma**. As stated in the first part of this series, the Akan term *koko*, meaning 'hill' is directly derived of the Ancestral term from Kamit, **Kaka**, meaning '*hill/raised land*'.

The term Afwene or Ahwene meaning *nose, prominent*, is also directly derived of the Ancestral language of Keneset and Kamit.

fent [hieroglyphs], [hieroglyphs], [hieroglyphs], Anastasi **I**, 23, 8, [hieroglyphs], nose; see [hieroglyphs] and [hieroglyphs]; Copt. ϣⲁⲛⲧⲉ.

Here the actual medutu for the term are **f-n-t** the symbol of the horned viper (f), the wavy line (n) and the semi-circular loaf image (t). The determinative medut is a nose or the symbol for flesh . The Akan language provides one of the pronunciations for **f-n-t** meaning *'nose'*. This is the Akan **Afwene** or **fw-n-t** (fwenet) with a silent 't'. We should take note that the **Coptic** (Late Kamit/Egyptian) spelling of the term is: Copt. ϣⲁⲛⲧⲉ Another Coptic variation is: Copt. ϣⲁⲁⲛⲧ. These spellings are rendered **shante** or **shaant** in english. This is important, for another variation of the pronunciation in Akan of the 'hw' letter combination is 'shw'. Some Akan speakers will thus pronounce the term Ahwene in a manner that sounds like 'Ashwene'. This is also why a variant spelling of the same term in Kamit is **Khent** or **Khanit**:

khent, khenti , , , , , the nose, the face; Copt. ϣⲁⲛⲧ.

Again, the actual medutu are **kh-n-t**. The white egyptologists often place the letter 'e' in between consonants when they are unsure of how the words were pronounced. Sometimes the 'e' is an accurate placement and sometimes it is not. Languages such as those of the Akan and other Afurakanu/Afuraitkaitnut (Africans) can fill in the blanks being that they are genetic descendants of the original language. Thus, **kh-n-t** is found as the alternative spelling for *'nose'* in Kamit and as the alternative for *'nose'* in Akan as Ashwene (shenet or shaant in Coptic):

Kamit: **fent** : **khent**

Akan: (a) **fwene** *(nose)* (a) **hwene**, (a) **shwene** *(nose)*

ɛ-hwéne, Ak. ɛhwéŋ, ŋhwéŋ; F. ɛhwen(e), *pl.* a-, **1.** *the nose. pr. 1198;* **óbò ne hwéne**

Moreover, this term as **kh-n-t** (khenet, khanit; shaant) also means the *front, before, aforetime, formerly, previously, in the beginning*:

khent , , , , , , in the front, in the fore part, before, aforetime, formerly, previously, in advance, the beginning, the land south of Egypt

This term also lends itself to the name **Khanit** (Khent or Khenti), a title for **Keneset** (Nubia) the *Front land, First Land, Land of the Beginnings*. [*Khanit* Land is *Akanni* Land/*Akan* Land]

Ashwene is **Shwene** or **Shene/Shenet/Shaant** in Kamit. This is **Ahwene** or **Afwene**, the first/front land, the Afwene Koko, the first/front (Afwene) raised land (Koko) – the capitol of the first landmass of the Created world. The terms *ahwene, ahwere, afwene, ashwene*, meaning *nose* in Akan and the same *fenet* and *shenet* meaning *nose* in Kamit are not only figurative, but cosmological. The Abosom of Kamit are seen placing the **ankh**, *the symbol of life*, to the nose of an individual to give him or her life. The nose is thus not only prominent or *first* because of it being the most forward/frontal point of the body above the mouth, but it is also through the nose that we receive our *first* breath. It is thus the cosmological and biological life-*first*. The nose is the *raised area/mound* where life/**ankh**-*force* first comes into the body (world). The dual channels/nostrils stream the masculine/feminine polarities of the Energy, the Spirit of **Ra/Rait** circulating within the mound. This is a replication of what occurs within the Earthly mound (kaka).

Amen (**Nyame** - Male aspect of Supreme Being) placing the **Ankh**, the talisman of *Life*, to the nose of **Senusert**

The name **Ahwene Koko** has also been defined by some Akan as meaning '*red beads*'. One of the reasons for this can be found in the ancient language of Kamit:

khen-t [hieroglyphs], Thes. 1111, red egg-shaped objects.

ɛ-hwènéɛ, *pl.* **ŋ-, Ak. = ahene, Akr.,** *a bead.*

kɔkɔɔ́, *a.* [*pl.* **akɔkɔɔ́ &** *red.*] *red,*

"...That the present day indigenous Wenchi [Wankyi] people are Akan is beyond dispute; and that their ancestors were Akan is perhaps supported by the fact that their early settlements such as Bonoso (meaning "the place of the hole"), ***Ahwene Koko*** *(meaning "**red beads**")..." [Boachie-Ansah, James. 2013]*

The term **kokoo** (extra '*o*') can be defined as *red* in Akan. This relationship of "red egg-shaped objects" to khent/shent/fent (Ahwene/Ashwene/Afwene) will be addressed as we discuss the medutu of the name *Aourigha*.

As stated above the 'hw' and 'fw' sounds are interchangeable in Kamit and Akan. This interchangeability was also retained by the whites and their offspring in english. The english letter combination '*gh*' can carry the '*h*' or '*hw*' *(huh)* sound as in *weigh, high, bough* and *thought*. However, the '*gh*' combination can also carry the '*f* ' sound as in *rough, tough, enough or laugh*. Here the open '*h*' sound and the '*f* ' sound interchange.

Another retention in english of ancient Kamau sounds is represented by the '*kh*' combination as addressed above. The medut representing the '*kh*' sound has two major pronunciations. This sound can be pronounced like the '*ch*' in *check* or like the '*ch*' in *chronology*. Indeed, the '*ch*' in english is stolen directly from the ancient '*kh*' medut from Kamit. However, there is also a third pronunciation related to the '*kh*' medut which is less frequent. It is the '*sh*' or '*shw*' sound mentioned above. This third pronunciation also has its retention in english, for the '*ch*' combination can also be pronounced '*sh*' as in '*charlotte*' or '*chagrin*'. Just as in ancient Kamit and Akan, the '*sh*' sound for the '*ch*' combination in english is used less frequently.

[*With respect to Akanfo, the etymologies of khant and fent reveal the ancient origin of the names Asante/Ashante (Khenti) and Fante (Fenti)-two prominent/leading Akan sub-groups*].

From the **Ghana National Commission on Culture Website** [emphasis ours]:

*"…Thus according to Wenchi [Wankyi] legend of origin, their founding fathers "***came out from a hole in the ground** *at a place called Bonaso near the source of Ayaso Stream." The leader, Nana Tabiriku Anye Amaniampon of the Asene clan, was accompanied by her sister, Asaseba Odinse and a large retinue.*

Another version of the tradition refers to the hole as Asomanini, claiming that Bonoso (ie. 'above the hole) is the exact site a little off the mysterious hole. **The existence of ancient mounds surrounding the hole** *and the oral traditions which relates that brass bowls were cleansed in the Ayasu Stream (Ayasu lit. means 'brass water')* **provides fairly convincing proof that there was a settlement near the hole***. The hole itself is said to have several galleries leading to various directions which looked like ancient goldmine or a place of refuge in time of war.* **This ancient settlement, now revered as the cradle of the people of Wenchi** *must have attained a high level of material culture. This can be seen in the quality of the State paraphernalia, the molten metal, the brass and silver products, the woven kente cloth, the terra cottas (brownish and glazed pottery), the artistic excellence which is now widely acclaimed by experts.*

Because the land was uninhibited at the time of occupation, they assumed the name **YEFIRI**, *meaning, "we are the aborigines"…."*

http://www.ghanaculture.gov.gh/index1.php?linkid=65&archiveid=2066&page=1&adate=18/06/2011

Paraaka (Pilak, Philae)

Af, Auf, Au – Flesh and Island

The interchangeability of 'u/w' and 'f' is found in a most poignant example in the language of Kamit. The term for *flesh* in Kamit is **Af**, **Auf**. However, the term for *flesh* can also be written as **Au**. This is because the 'u' and 'f' interchange just as the **hw** (hu-wuh) and **fw** (f-wuh) in Akan interchange:

ȧf , U. 268, 519, , **flesh, meat, joint, member; plur.**

ȧuf , , , , , , **flesh, meat, body, carcase;**

ȧu , , **limbs, members, flesh.**

The term **af,** *flesh*, is also related to the term representing a *house, dwelling place, chamber*: **Afai, Afaa** and **Aftt**:

āfait , , **tent, camp, chamber.**

This interchangeability again is key. For the term for island is typically translated as **Aa** or **Au**:

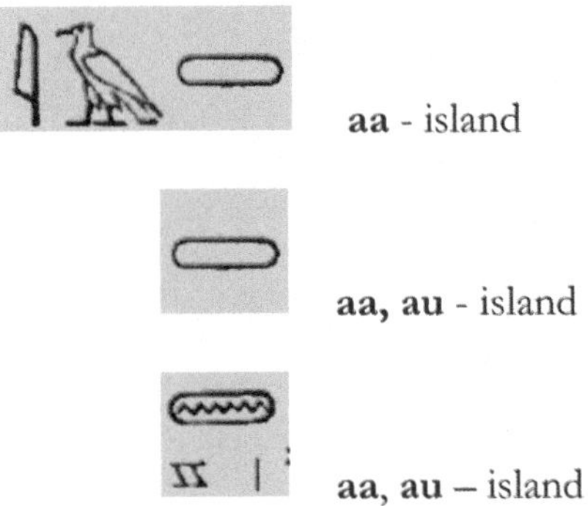

Moreover, related terms also define a *nest* or *home* as well as *flesh:*

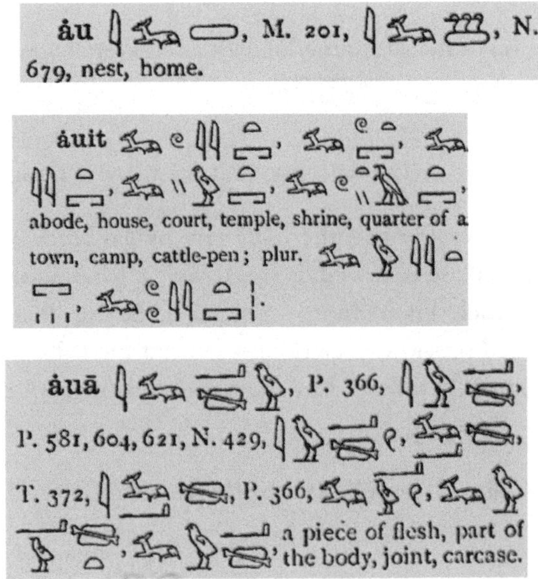
åu [hieroglyphs], M. 201, [hieroglyphs], N. 679, nest, home.

åuit [hieroglyphs], abode, house, court, temple, shrine, quarter of a town, camp, cattle-pen; plur. [hieroglyphs].

åuā [hieroglyphs], P. 366, [hieroglyphs], P. 581, 604, 621, N. 429, [hieroglyphs], T. 372, [hieroglyphs], P. 366, [hieroglyphs] a piece of flesh, part of the body, joint, carcase.

Aa, **Au** and **Aua** as *island, home, sanctuary* and *flesh* are all related conceptually and have their parallels in **Af**, **Auf** and **Aft** meaning *flesh* as well as *dwelling place, sanctuary*, etc. **Aua** also refers to *flesh* as in *posterity, lineage* (one's flesh and blood). The *flesh* is the *home*, sanctuary for the spirit and soul, just as the *island* (first raised land) was/is the *flesh* for the Great Spirit, **Ra/Rait**, the Creator-Creatress. It became the home/sanctuary for the Great Spirit to take up residence in Nature. These definitions are key, for as we mentioned in the third part of this series, the island of **Paaraka** (*Pilak, Philae*) was referred to by the Priests and Priestesses of Paaraka as the *land of the beginning*, the place where the world was created. Paaraka was seen as the primordial mound/hill that first rose up at the beginning of Creation. It is the Island of **Ra**.

There are various spellings of the name of this island. In the inscriptions on the **tekhen** (obelisk) of ptolemy IX and the inscriptions in the Temple of **Auset** (misnomered 'Isis') in Paaraka, different spellings of the name can be found. Some egyptologists misspell the name **Aa Rek** meaning the "island of **Rek**". Some of the actual spellings in medutu are below:

Au Ra Ka t

Au Ra Ka

Au Ra Ka t

The medut is a variation of the island medut with circles (grains, beads) inside of the landmass (island). The medut is the letter *'r'*. The medut is the letter *'k'*. The medut is the letter *'t'*. The medut is the determinative medut denoting that the word is designating a *place*.

The first medut representing the **Aa** or **Au** is the island, an ovular landmass surrounded by water. We know that the *'r'* medut and the *'k'* medut are followed by the vowel *'a'* for a number of reasons. In Coptic, the name for Pa Aurakat or Paarakat is **Pilak**. The definite article *'pi'* meaning 'the' is followed by *'lak'*. There was no letter *'L'* in Kamit. As mentioned previously there only existed the rolling *'r'*. The Coptic shows that the *'L'*, which is the letter *'r'* in the medutu, is followed by the vowel *'a'*. The root reason for this is because the name is referencing **Ra** and **Rait**.

We also know that the letter *'k'* should be followed by the vowel *'a'*. In the variant spellings the medut for the *'k'* sound is followed by the medut of a man raising his arms in the air in the **'KA'** pose: This is actually the word **'Ka'**. We have further evidence via the variant spelling: . Here, the lion represents the letter 'R'. The word for bull in Kamit is **'Ka'**. The bull is thus substituted for the end of the name

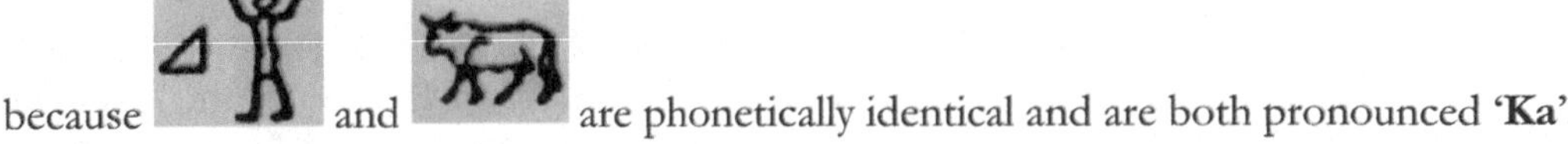

because and are phonetically identical and are both pronounced **'Ka'**.

Moreover **Ka**, literally means *raised, exalted; high.* When referencing land it means "*raised land, high land; exalted land; holy land; mountain, hill.*" It is the Divine/Sacred/Exalted/High land upon and through which the Creator and Creatress first operated.

Finally, we have evidence from the title of the temple town of **Pilak** (Philae) which is spelled **Aat Ra Ka**:

Aat R Ka t

Aat R Ka tt

Aat Ra Ka t *Actual inscription from the temple in **Auraka/Aurakat** (Paarakat/Pilak)*

The **Aat** term references the *sanctuary (temple), sacred space.* The medut depicting raised arms is '**Ka**'. Again, we see that the term **Ka** was spelled in three different ways: , **Ka**, , **Ka**, , **Ka**. This also proves conclusively that the medut represents the '*k*' sound and not the '*q*' as in '*qu*'.

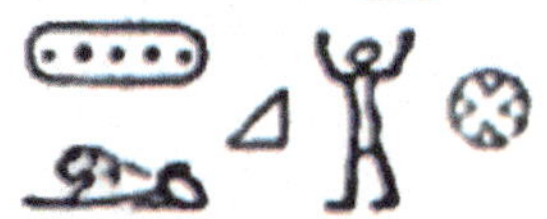

Au Ra Ka

Au Ra Ka t

Auraka and **Aurakat** are the male and female variations of **Afuraka/Afuraitkait**. We deliberately employ both terms, together, to reinforce respect for the Divine Balance of male and female. **Auraka/Aurakat** or **Afuraka/Afuraitkait** - This is the first Divine Land, the Land of **Afu Ra/Afu Rait**, the first land to rise up

from beneath the surface of the water. It is the land of **Auf Hr Kaka**, the land upon which **Ra** (**Hr**) and **Rait** (**Hrt**) existed before the coming into being of the pillars of **Shu**.

Auraka can also be found replicated in/as the term ***Aourigha/Aurigha***. **Auraka** is also replicated as *Ahwereka (Ahwere koko)*.

Finally, we must recognize that the terms *island* and *continent* are english words. Both terms reference *a landmass surrounded by water*. The medut representing *a landmass surrounded by water* is and and . In the first variant the medut for the *grains* are placed inside of the medutu: . This medut is typically a determinative for *grains of soil, sand, mineral/earth*. In another variant the wavy line representing the letter *'n'* (wave energy) is placed inside of the landmass. This is showing the Divine Energy of **Ra** and **Rait** subsistent within the landmass. This is depicted in a different manner in the Khensumes illustration showing **Ra/Rait** (active Divine Living Energy) moving through (within) the landmass before rising within the Aten/Sun for the first time on the horizon of Afuraka/Afuraitkait. Moreover, these grains/minerals are the "red beads" referenced in the definition of Ahwene Koko above.

khen-t Thes. 1111, red egg-shaped objects.

khenti 1096, red earth, red ochre, red paint.

As **Auraka/Aurakat**, this landmass surrounded by water references the first and only landmass existent at the time. **This landmass surrounded by water as Auraka/Aurakat is a medut referencing a continent – the original continent of Afuraka/Afuraitkait.** As mentioned in the first part of this series, this landmass was the first to rise up from beneath the surface of the water. Eventually, the rest of Earth's landmass would emerge and subsequently separate. **The original emergent landmass however still exists on the heartland, Afuraka/Afuraitkait.** It must be understood that this is **not** asia, europe, the americas, australia, antarctica or any of the mythological "lost continents" (mu, lemuria, atlantis) that in reality never existed and are fabrications of the whites and their offspring. **This landmass was/is Afuraka/Afuraitkait and still is Afuraka/Afuraitkait today.**

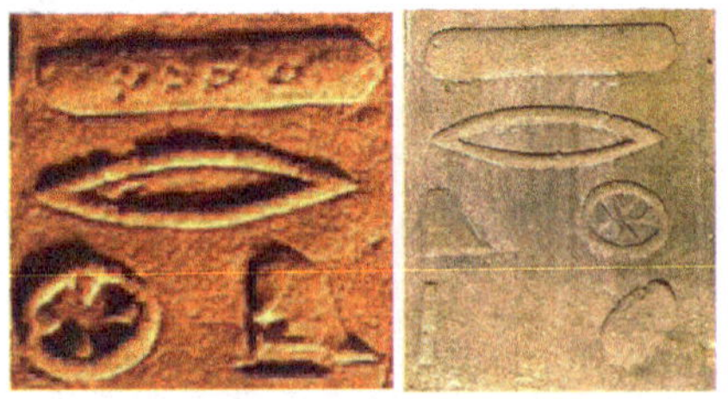

Au Ra Ka **Au Ra Kat**

*Actual inscriptions from Temple of **Auset** in **Auraka/Aurakat** (Paaraka, Pilak, Philae). Right: Taken by this author.*

The egg medut on the bottom right reference the feminine.

Berber - Abibiri

The original inhabitants of North Afuraka/Afuraitkait were unmixed Black people. Those groups who refer to themselves as **Berbers** and **Amazigh** today are represented by the **original Blacks** and misrepresented by the **invading whites** who polluted the blood of some of those Blacks. The white "berbers" are in reality descendants of the white invaders who misrepresent themselves as Berbers, just as descendants of white arab invaders of Kamit misrepresent themselves as "Egyptians" today and falsely claim to be descendants of the original Kamau/Kamitu (Egyptians).

The term *berber* has an etymology which is unknown to the whites and their offspring. The ancient term **brbr** later became *barbar* and corrupted into *barbarian* in english. The term as a name is actually an ancient one. The Akan maintain the original term as a designation for *Black people/Africans.*

The Akan term **biri** means 'dark, black'. The suffix 'fo' in Akan designates a plurality of people. *Akanfo* for example means *Akan-people.* The term 'obi' or 'bi' means *someone.* **Bibiri**-fo or **Abibirifo** means **Bibiri** *people* or 'Black People' in Akan. **Obibiri**-ni or **Obibi**-ni means *Black Person* in Akan. **Abibiriman** or **Abibiman** means 'Afuraka/Afuraitkait (Africa)' in Akan because **Abibiri**-man means the *Black* (**Abibiri**) *Nation* (**oman**).

Abibi-máŋ, *the Negro - country. pr. 1477.*
o-bibiní, *pl.* **a--fo,***negro, black man, African. pr. 1796.* — **o-bibiníwa** [dim.] *a negro boy* or *lad.*

birí, *v. to grow, be,* or *make black, dark.*

biribìri, *red. v., s.* **biri; anim' rèbiríbiri,** *it is getting dark. cf.* **anim 7 A.**

o-bírifo, obírifó, *pl.* **a-,** *a fellow of unusual power;* also = **sumanni;** *e. g.*

Bibiri can also be written **biribiri.** An **obirifo** is also defined in Akan as one who is not just a Black person but one who is *unusually powerful* for black signifies *power.* **Bibiri** or **Biribiri** designating Black People is derived from **Brbr** (Berber).

Ifri, Ifru

In the ancient Black Berber (Bibiri) cosmology, which is over 10,000 years old, there is a Female Obosom (Deity) called **Ifru** (**Ifrou**) or **Ifri** (**Afri**). **Ifri** or **Ifru** was recognized to be a "Sun Goddess *and* a Cave Goddess". **Ifri** was the most influential Female Obosom. Nearly 2,000 years ago the roman author pliny the elder stated that nobody in Africa began any undertaking without first consulting the **Goddess Africa.** *Africa* was the roman title of the Berber Obosom **Ifri. Ifri** as the Goddess Africa or *Dea Africa* in latin was depicted on roman coins of the time. Two examples:

These are coins stamped during the time of the roman emperor hadrian. They show the Goddess *Africa* reposing on a bed. Above the Obosom is Her name spelled out in latin, *Africa.* This is the Obosom Whom the Berbers called **Ifri** or **Afri** or **Ifru**. The Obosom **Ifru** is none other than the Obosom **Rait** or **Rat** as **Afu Rait** or **Afurat**. **Afurat** became **Afruat**, **Afrua** and **Afru/Ifru/Afri**. The reason why **Ifru** or **Ifri** is described as a Sun Obosom *and* a Cave Obosom is directly related to Her role in Creation. **Rait** is the Creatress of the World, just as **Ra** is the Creator of the World. They Both use the **Aten**/Sun as a physical transmitter of Their Spiritual Energy. Just as **Ra** becomes **Afu Ra** when He operates through matter "goes into the underworld" so does **Rait** or **Rat** become **Afu Rait** or **Afurat**. The Sun Goddess becomes the Cave Goddess. Indeed, in the texts of Kamit **Ra** is shown moving through the underworld as **Afu Ra** and one of these major texts of the New Kingdom of Kamit is called the **Book of Caverns** (Caves). Just as **Ra**, **Rait** also operates through the Aten/Sun and these Caves/Caverns.

Rait as **Afu Rait** (**Ifri/Afri**) wearing cow's horns and solar disk headdress in front of **Afu Ra**
Her title performing this function in the underworld is **Neb Uaa** - *Lady of the Barque*

It should also be noted that the reason why the arabs define "Ifriqiyah" (Africa) as "Queen of Heaven" is because **Rait** is the Obosom Who is the Queen (**Herit**) of Heaven. She is the Creatress operating through the most prominent *heavenly* orb, the Aten/Sun. The arabs learned of the Goddess Ifriqiyah (Dea Africa) from the romans. This is why the Berbers, later in their trustory, were referred to by the arabs as **Banu Ifran** or the *Children of* **Afri**. 'Africa' was recognized by the romans and others as the '*ca*' (*land) of the Afri* and *the land of the Goddess Afri (Afwene koko or Yefri-koko).* The romans learned of the Obosom from the Berbers and other Afurakanu/Afuraitkaitnut who worshipped Her in Kamit and those north of Afuraka/Afuraitkait in the Near East. **The name Ifri/Ifru/Afurat and the intricate cosmology associated with it was not created by the romans.**

Left: 2nd century bce mosaic of ***Afri*** *from Tunisia, North Afuraka/Afuraitkait (Africa). Center: Bronze bust of* ***Afri****. Right: Cleopatra Selene, daughter of Cleopatra VII wearing the sacred Abu (Elephant) headdress of* ***Afri*** *with trunk and tusks as is worn by* ***Afri*** *in statuary, coinage, paintings and reliefs.*

Rait – Temple of Khensu
Painted Gold – Color of the Aten/Sun

Rait – Apet Asetu (Karnak)

Rait – Late Period of Kamit

Tuareg in North Afuraka/Afuraitkait (Africa) and **Per Aa** (Pharaoh) **Osorkon II** from Ancient **Khahn** (Libya)

The ritual use of blue henna by the ***Tuareg*** *is an unbroken tradition from ancient Khahn (Libya), North Afuraka/Afuraitkait to today.*

In addition to **Rait/Afurait/Afru/Afri** the Berbers also worshipped **Amen, Ausar, Auset, Set** and many other Abosom worshipped in Kamit and Keneset. This is because Afurakanu/Afuraitkaitnut (Africans) across the continent share the same roots.

With respect to etymologies, *'t'* or *'ti'* is a feminine prefix in Berber languages just as *'t'* is the feminine suffix in Kamit. Thus, when speaking of a major Berber group such as the **Tuareg** the *'t'* is the prefix while the root is *uareg*. The etymology of *tuareg* is often related to the name **Targi**. *T-argi, T-ouareg, T-wareg* are all variations of *aurigh, aourigha*. Moreover, the script of the Berbers called **Tifinagh** again employs the feminine prefix *'ti'*. The root is **finagh**. *Finagh* is phonetically *Finak, Firak, Firaka.*

Finally, the group of Berbers called the **Fulani Berbers** have **Fula** as the root of their name. *Fula* is also pronounced **Peul** by some Fula. Here we have the interchange of the 'P' and the 'F'. This interchange of sounds is seen in english 'p' and 'ph/f' as well as the name Paraaka (Pilak, *Ph*ilae) and Faraka. Of course, the *Fula* are the *Fura, Afura/Afurai/Afri.* Recall also that the Akan of today's Wankyi first called themselves **Yefri**, *we are the aborigines.*

Darfur in the western part of **Sudan** means the *'land of the **Fur**'.* The name of the ethnic group varies: **Fur**, **Fura** (**Foora**), **Furok**. Their language is **Fur** also **Fura** and **Furakang**. These inhabitants of western Sudan are direct descendants of the ancient people of Southern **Nubit** (Nubia). They are the ancient Furok or **Furakang** – Afuraka – people. This is an unbroken ethnic designation that is tens of thousands of years old.

Fula women

Black Berber

Tuareg women

Iuput II – Berber (Libyan) King of Kamit
23rd Dynasty
Ancient Original Black Berber/Afri

Fura (Furok) man – (A)Furok from Darfur

Afuraka is not derived from africanus

Many misguided Afurakanu/Afuraitkaitnut (Africans) have promoted the false belief that Afuraka/Afuraitkait (Africa) came from the name of the roman general scipio africanus. The family tree of scipio africanus proves this belief to be false. The individual called scipio africanus was born publius cornelius scipio. His father was publius cornelius scipio. His grandfather was lucius cornelius scipio. His great grandfather was lucius cornelius scipio barbatus. The brother of publius cornelius scipio was born lucius cornelius scipio:

lucius cornelius scipio barbatus	great-grandfather
lucius cornelius scipio	grandfather
publius cornelius scipio	father
lucius cornelius scipio	brother

The individual named publius cornelius scipio later took on the title **africanus** only <u>after</u> his army won a battle against the famous Afurakani General **Hannibal** in Afuraka/Afuraitkait (Africa). scipio took on this title after having won a *battle* in "Africa". What is also important to note is that his younger brother is known as lucius cornelius scipio **<u>asiaticus</u>**. His brother only took on the title **asiaticus** <u>after</u> having won a *battle* in a portion of <u>asia</u>. **As we can see from the family tree, no individual in the family line had the name africanus or asiaticus.**

When the two sons of publius cornelius scipio won battles in portions of Afuraka/Afuraitkait (Africa) and asia, one took on the surname **africanus** and became publius cornelius scipio africanus, while the other took on the surname **asiaticus** and became lucius cornelius scipio asiaticus.

The continent of asia was not named after scipio asiaticus nor was the continent of Afuraka/Afuraitkait (Africa) named after scipio africanus. They named themselves after the continents. Both brothers whose surname was scipio took on the names asiaticus and africanus after having won battles in parts of asia and Afuraka/Afuraitkait (Africa).

Coin depicting the Afurakani General **Hannibal** on the front and his elephant on the back – c2,200 years ago

Afer, Afri, Afar

afer , to burn, to be hot. afri Verbum Voc., smoke, hot vapour.

It is often stated that the latin term **Afer** is the singular term for **Afri**. Both are terms used by the romans to mean *African*. Many suggest that the term was originally given to the romans by the Afurakanu/Afuraitkaitnut of Carthage. It is further suggested that the Afurakanu/Afuraitkaitnut of Carthage received the term from the Berbers who originally occupied what would later become Carthage. Centuries later, etymologies for the term Africa were put forward including a derivation from the greek *a phrike* meaning "not cold", i.e., "hot". We can see the true origin of these terms above. The terms **Afr** (Afer) and **Afri** exist in the ancient language of Kamit referencing *smoke, hot vapor* and *to burn, to be hot.* Cosmologically, this is a reference to the Life-Force Energy of **Ra/Rait** as **<u>Afu</u> Ra** and **<u>Afu</u> Rait** (*Afer Afri*), moving through **<u>matter</u>** (*afu*). When the solar energy moves through solid matter it causes '*heat, smoke; to burn*' and when moving through water/liquid matter causes *'hot vapor'*.

The letters *'b', ' f '* and *'v'* interchange phonetically. In the **Ewe** (Togo, Benin, Ghana, Nigeria) language for example the name of the **Vodou** (Deity) called **Heviosso** (**Heru** in Kamit) is also pronounced **Hebiosso** by some Ewe. The *' f '* or *'v'* sound interchanges with the *'b'* sound. The same interchange is seen in eurasian languages as well. Some spanish speakers, whether hispanics in latin america or asians from the phillipines who speak spanish, will interchange the *'v'* sound with the *'b'* sound. They will pronounce the word 'very' like 'bery' or the word 'have' like 'hab'. This interchange of the *'v'* or *'f '* sound with the *'b'* sound is ancient. This is why **Afer** or **Ferfer** can become **Berber**. **Afri** or **Frifri** can become **Biri or Biribiri**. Again, whether it is pronounced with the *'f '* or *'b'* the definition references that which is *black, to burn, be hot*, i.e. Black People.

It is also important to note that the term **'afar'** defined as '*dust*' referencing *grains of soil, earth, sand* is derived of the island/continent medut **'au'** containing the determinative medut of a series of small circles representing **grains**: *soil, earth, sand.* In fact, the related term **aa**, *island*, can also mean '*mound*' or '*heap of dust'*. **AuRa (AufRa)**, *island/mound/soil/earth dust* of **Ra** becomes *Afar. Afar* meaning *dust* is another derivation of *'africa'* promoted by the whites and their offspring, yet without them having knowledge of the actual roots of the term. **Afar** is also the name of an Afurakani/Afuraitkaitnit ethnicity who live in **Ethiopia, Eritrea** and **Djibouti**. The ***Afar*** are truly named after **Afra/Afrat (Afu Ra/Afu Rat).**

Afar Woman of Ethiopia

NOKWARE

Misinformed Afurakanu/Afuraitkaitnut (Africans) seek to denigrate and reject the name **Afuraka/Afuraitkait** (Africa) and attempt to seek the *name's origin* outside of Afuraka/Afuraitkait. They also attempt to seek their *own origins* as Black People **anywhere** outside of Afuraka/Afuraitkait including asia, ancient america, mythological lost continents (mu/lemuria, atlantis, etc.) and even other galaxies (extraterrestrialism). The reason behind such misguided seeking is that such individuals have incorporated a fundamental false sense of self-hatred which has been and continues to be forced on us by the whites and their offspring – when we accept it. Self-hating individuals would prefer to **mis-identify** and **mis-name** themselves and their children with false-perverse names such as *moor, asiatic, native american, indian,* etc. and associate themselves with mythological groups who never existed including: *semites, israelites, hebrews, ishmaelites, atlanteans, lemurians/children of mu, extraterrestrials* and other outlandish titles – all created by whites. This is because they have yet to reject the whites and their offspring, their culture and their false religions. Such Afurakanu/Afuraitkaitnut have refused to reject disorder and thus the lies which disorder spawns.

Such self-hating individuals include Afurakanu/Afuraitkaitnut ***on the continent*** of Afuraka/Afuraitkait: those bearing the titles priest, priestess, elder, elderess, king and queenmother who have actually **woven white pseudo-religious and pseudo-historical perversions into Afurakani/Afuraitkaitnit cosmological, oral, ritual and written traditions after contact with the whites and their offspring.**

Such self-hating individuals also include Afurakanu/Afuraitkaitnut ***outside of the continent*** of Afuraka/Afuraitkait: those in europe, the near east, india, china, australia, north, central and south america, the Caribbean and the pacific islands who have similarly **woven white pseudo-religious and pseudo-historical perversions into their oral, ritual and written traditions after contact with the whites and their offspring**.

When Afurakanu/Afuraitkaitnut make the decision to embrace Order, we reject the whites and their offspring, their culture and their false religions fully. We embrace ourselves and thereby open ourselves to **nokware**, *truth*, which is **irrefutable**.

Afuraka/Afuraitkait is the origin of the term 'Africa'

Afurakanu/Afuraitkaitnut, Black People, reclaim your name and reclaim your identity, yourself, in truth, nokware.

References:

Let the Ancestors Speak: *Removing the Veil of Mysticism from Medu Netcher* by **Ankh Mi Ra**

Ru Nu Pert em Hru, Ani Sheft Papyrus of Ani

Khensumes Sheft Papyrus of Khensmose

Tekhen of ptolemy IX Obelisk of ptolemy IX

Kasahorow - Afurakani/Afuraitkaitnit Online Language Resource www.kasahorow.com

Nzima Kotoko - Akan Culture and Trustory Resource www.nzima-kotoko.org

Ghana National Commission on Culture: *The Story of Wenchi* www.ghanaculture.gov.gh

q = Heb. ק; Copt. ⲕ and ϭ.

qaa , N. 663, , Rec. 30, 189, , ibid. 31, 28, , Pap. 3024, 59, , , , hill, high ground, high place.

qaqa , B.D. 17, 9, , hill, high place.

qa-t , U. 229, , IV, 974, , P. 174, M. 440, N. 941 = , P. 174, N. 941, U. 494, T. 235 = , high land, *i.e.*, the Nile banks above the river; plur. ; Copt. ⲕⲁⲉⲓⲉ.

qa-t , high, fine building.

qai-t , , IV, 364, , , Love Songs 2, 4, , , Hymn Darius 23, the land high above the surface of the Nile; Copt. ⲕⲁⲓⲉ, ⲕⲟⲓ.

qai-t , , a high place; and see .

qai en ānkh , "hill of life"—a name of the territory of the temple of Denderah.

Qa , N. 767, a title of Temu.

Qau , , the god of Creation.

Qa, Qait , B.D. 1, the high place on which the god of creation stood.

Qaqa , B.D. 17, 9, a hill in Khemenu on which the heavens rested.

In our publication we demonstrate that the term **Ka/Kait** references a *high, exalted, sacred land* upon which the **Ra**, the *Creator*, first dwelled. As shown above, the 'q' **medut** and thus the word transliterated **'qait'** is written **KAEIE** in *Coptic*: Copt. ⲕⲁⲉⲓⲉ. Notice also that a variation of **Qaqa** or **Kaka** is **Qai** (**Kai**). While the dual form 'Kaka' or 'Qaqa' is found in Chapter 17 of the papyrus of **Ani** as shown in part 4 of our series, the singular form 'Kai' (Qai) can be found in the *same Chapter 17* of the papyrus of **Hunefer**. Hunefer was a *Scribe of Divine Offerings* and *Overseer of Royal Cattle* under the **Nsut** or **Per Aa** (King or Pharaoh) **Seti I** during was is referred to as the Nineteenth dynasty of Kamit. This was approximately 3,300 years ago. See images from Hunefer's version of the **Ru Nu Pert em Hru** (misnomered Book of the Dead) below:

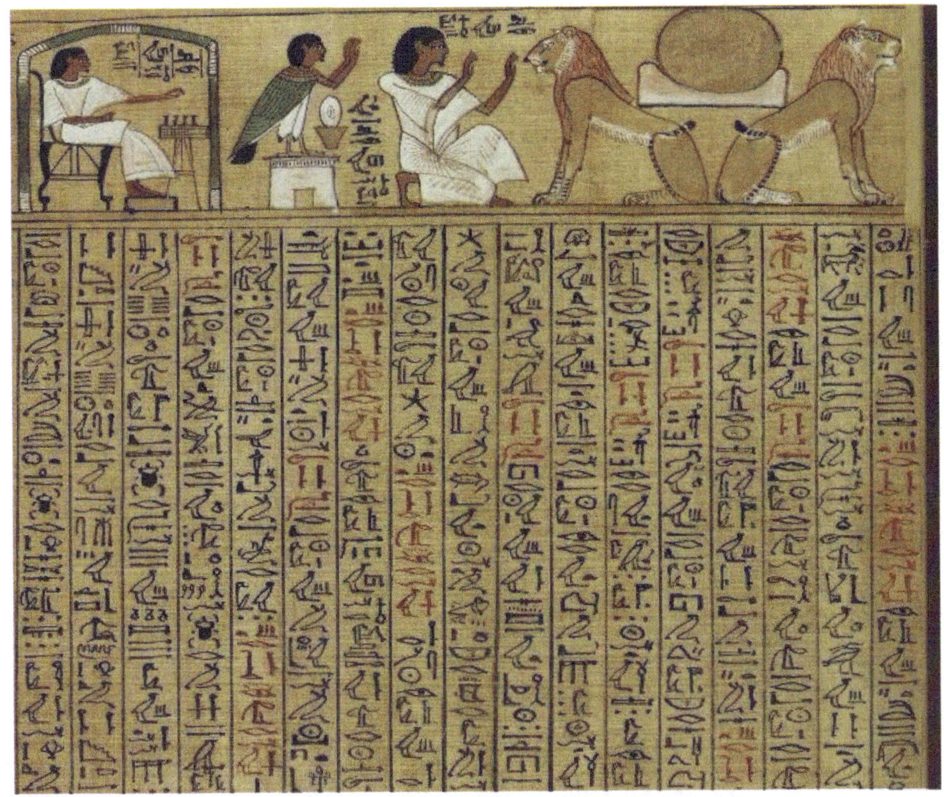

From Chapter 17 from the Papyrus of **Hunefer**

2 columns

In the above excerpt from *Chapter 17, section 5* of the actual papyrus of **Hunefer** we find the term **Auf Hr Kai** at the bottom of the first column and top right of the second column (isolated above right). For ease of reading we have placed the **medutu** (hieroglyphs) from right to left below:

Auf Hr Kai in the *papyrus of Hunefer* is rendered **Auf Hr Kaka** in the *papyrus of Ani*. It is the same text in the same chapter 17 in both versions of the **Ru Nu Pert em Hru**. It is a reference to **Ra** as Creator establishing the first land above the surface of the water at the beginning of Creation. **Au f** (He exists) **Hr** (upon) **Kai** (the exalted/high land) Once again, this is **Afuraka/Afuraitkait** (Africa) phonetically, conceptually and cosmologically.

KUKUU-TUNTUM

The Ancestral Jurisdiction

NHOMA

Full transcript of the original 3-CD/mp3 audio set

Origin of Creation · Origin of the name Afuraka/Afuraitkait (Africa) · Origin and nature of Afurakanu/Afuraitkaitnut (Africans) · Afurakani/Afuraitkaitnit (African) Ancestral Culture · Origin and nature of the whites and their offspring rooted in the insanity of dissexuality (homosexuality) and incest · Cosmological Structure of Creation · Nature and function of the **Nananom Nsamanfo** and **Abosom, Egungun** and **Orisha, Kuvito** and **Vodou** (the Ancestresses and Ancestors and the Goddesses and Gods) in Afurakani/Afuraitkaitnit (African) Ancestral Religion· Origin and function of Afurakani/Afuraitkaitnit (African) Ancestral Clans · Afurakani/Afuraitkaitnit (African) Ancestral Religion

Origins of the **FICTIONAL** characters **and FALSE** religions and writings:

abraham · isaac · ishmael · moses · aaron · david · judah · jesus · mary · yeshua ben pandira· muhammad · allah · yahweh · elohim · solomon · sheba · menelik · brahman · christianity and the bible · islam and the quran · judaism/hebrewism and the torah · hinduism and the vedas · buddhism and the dhamapadas · european pseudo-esotericism and the qabalah

ODWIRAFO KWESI RA NEHEM PTAH AKHAN

Heru, Ausar and Auset
Abtu, Kamit
(Abydos, Ancient Egypt)

KUKUU-TUNTUM

The Ancestral Jurisdiction

KUKUU-TUNTUM (koo·koo' - toon·toom') is the combination of the Kenesu-Kamau term, ***Kukuu*** and the Twi-Akan term, ***Tuntum***. The terms are defined in their respective languages as descriptive of blackness which contains illumination, holder; black, dark. As a name, they are representative of the regulatory function of Creative Consciousness. Just as the night sky executes its authority over the planetary bodies and stars within it, **KUKUU-TUNTUM** discloses the jurisdiction of the culture.

KUKUU-TUNTUM The Ancestral Jurisdiction was first produced and published by us as a 3-CD audio set in 13002 (2002). In 13006 (2006) we made the entire set available as a free download from our website at: **www.odwirafo.com**. In 13008 (2008) we published the entire 75-page transcript in **nhoma** (book)-form. The pdf version of the nhoma and the mp3 files of the original 3 CDs are all free downloads from our site.

The **KUKUU-TUNTUM** is groundbreaking in the sense that we were the first to publish the **correct etymologies** of the names of the various fictional characters including: jesus/yeshua, muhammed, abraham, isaac, ishmael, moses, solomon, sheba, menelik, buddha, allah, yahweh, brahmin etc. Many writers have put forward **false etymologies** based on a lack of understanding of Afurakani/Afuraitkaitnit (African) cosmology and culture. We were the first to demonstrate how these fictional characters were manufactured via the deliberate corruption of names, descriptive titles and functions of Deities of **Kamit**. We restore the consciousness of the *Divine Balance of Male and Female* in Creation founded upon **Amen** and **Amenet** and reaffirm the nature and function of **Afurakani/Afuraitkaitnit (African) Ancestral Religion**. Finally, we were the first to demonstrate and publish the actual etymological and cosmological origins of the term **Afuraka/Afuraitkait** (Africa) and thus our true identity as Black people, our role in Creation, the nature of our enemies and our path to restoration.

Contents:
Origin of Creation
Origin of the name Afuraka/Afuraitkait (Africa)
Origin and nature of Afurakanu/Afuraitkaitnut (Africans)
Afurakani/Afuraitkaitnit (African) Ancestral Culture
Origin and nature of the whites and their offspring rooted in the insanity of dissexuality (homosexuality) and incest
Cosmological Structure of Creation
Nature and function of the **Nananom Nsamanfo** and **Abosom, Egungun** and **Orisha, Kuvito** and **Vodou** (the *Ancestresses and Ancestors* and the *Goddesses and Gods*) in Afurakani/Afuraitkaitnit (African) Ancestral Religion
Origin and function of Afurakani/Afuraitkaitnit (African) Ancestral Clans
Afurakani/Afuraitkaitnit (African) Ancestral Religion

Origins of the following **FICTIONAL** characters:

abraham · isaac · ishmael · moses · aaron · david · judah · jesus · mary · yeshua ben pandira · muhammad · allah · yahweh · elohim · solomon · sheba · menelik · brahman · buddha and more

Origins of the **FALSE** religions and **FALSE** religious writings:

christianity and the bible · islam and the quran · judaism/hebrewism and the torah hinduism and the vedas · buddhism and the dhamapadas · european pseudo-esotericism and the qabbalah and more

The 13 tracks of the original 3-CD set, now mp3 files, are titled as follows:

OFA A EDI KAN - CD 1
Hyebea (:52)
Afu Ra Ka/Afu Rait Kait is Our Existence (11:44)
Afurakani/Afuraitkaitnit Ancestral Culture (18:14)
Afurakani/Afuraitkaitnit Function in Creation (15:38)
Afurakani/Afuraitkaitnit Ancestral Religion - 1 (16:26)

OFA A ETO SO ABIEN - CD 2
Afurakani/Afuraitkaitnit Ancestral Religion - 2 (7:29)
Afurakani/Afuraitkaitnit Ancestral Religion - 3 (12:18)
Afurakani/Afuraitkaitnit Ancestral Religion - 4 (36:28)

OFA A ETO SO ABIESA - CD 3
Afurakani/Afuraitkaitnit Ancestral Religion - 5 (7:08)
Afurakani/Afuraitkaitnit Ancestral Religion - 6 (11:20)
Afurakani/Afuraitkaitnit Ancestral Religion - 7 (5:34)
Afurakani/Afuraitkaitnit Ancestral Religion - 8 (11:06)
Nkrabea (5:26)

The transcript sections are titled accordingly. **It is suggested that the mp3 audio files are listened to first** in order to gain a full understanding of the various etymologies provided in the text.

Our usage of the terms *"humans"* and *"human beings"* in the text are properly defined as **Afurakanu/Afuraitkaitnut** (Africans~Black People) only, unless otherwise specified contextually.

Below are listed textual references from ancient Kamit and the numbers of the specific tracks whose information is supported by these references:

Reference Track number (1-13) – [Track 1 is **Hyebea**]

Pert em Heru *(Papyrus of Ani)* 2,6,7,8
Pert em Heru *(Papyrus of Hunefer)* 2,6,7,8
Tua Amen *(Hymn to Amen/"Leyden" Papyrus)* 2,4,5
Nesi Min sheft *(Book of Knowing the Manifestations of Ra)* 2,3,5
Tua Hapi *(Hymn to Hapi/"Sallier" Papyrus)* 9
Teret sheft *(Lamentations of Auset and Nebt Het)* 6,7,8,12
Shabaka Text 10,11,12
Texts of Teta and Pepi *(Pyramid Texts)* 2,4,6,7,8,9,10,11,12
Tomb of Seti I *(Shat em Duat/12 hours of the night)* 2,3
Tomb of Seti I *(The Destruction of Mankind/Book of the Cow of Heaven)* 6,7,8,12
Tomb of Seti I *(75 Praises of Ra)* 2,3
Tua Ausar *(Hymn to Ausar/Stele of Amenmes)* 6,7,8
Tomb of Nefertari *(Ra and Ausar, Djed/Tata pillar)* 2,6,7,8
Per Khensu em Uast Nefer Hetep *(Temple of Khensu)* 6,7,8,12
Per Tehuti Up Rehui *(Temple of Tehuti)* 6,7,8
Per Heru Behudet *(Temple of Heru in Edfu)* 6,7,8
Per Ba Neb Tata *(Temple of the Ram of "Mendes")* 6,7,8
Tekhen of Hatshepsut *(Obelisk of Hatshepsut)* 2,4,5
Narrative of Auset *("Metternich" Stele)* 6,7,8

HYEBEA

"…Follow in the footsteps of your Elder Ancestresses and Ancestors. For to follow the balanced path of those who have walked ahead of you is to embrace your trustory and balance your life. Realize that you do not exist alone. Your independence is only a measure of your proper functioning within the web of interdependence in Creation. Your place in the world only reveals the larger function of your Ancestral Clan.

Afurakanu/Afuraitkaitnut remember your trustory and you will remember the Divine Function given to you in your beginning by The Great Ancestral Spirit, and the means by which you must execute that function in life, through your Ancestral Culture. If you forget and you return and embrace the past to understand, it is not taboo…"

Afu Ra Ka/Afu Rait Kait is our existence.

Ra is the name of the God Who is the Creator of the World. **Rait** is the name of the Goddess Who is the Creatress of the World. **Ra** and **Rait** are Two Halves of a Whole. Two sides of One coin. That Whole, that coin, is the Great Spirit of the Supreme Being. **Ra/Rait**, together, are the Great Spirit Who brought into being all of Creation. They are the Divine Living-Energy moving throughout all that exists. Just as solar energy and heat move throughout the Earth, the atmosphere of Earth, throughout your body, throughout the bodies of plants, animals, minerals, so does the Great Spirit, **Ra/Rait**, move throughout, animate, give life to, the planets, Sun, Moon, stars, plants, animals, humans, the Black Substance of Space---all that exists. Fundamentally, the Supreme Being's Creative Spirit, Creative Power, is Who we call **Ra** and **Rait**.

Ka is the male name and **Kait** is the female name of the Black Substance of Space. This substance is truly a Divine Substance. **Ka** and **Kait** are Two Halves of a Whole. Two sides of one coin. That Whole, that coin, is the Great Soul of the Supreme Being. **Ka** and **Kait**, together, are the Great Soul Who determines the Form of all of Creation. They are the Consciousness, Divine Intelligence, operating within all that is *created*. Just as the tree comes into being and develops according to the design that existed in the seed, so does all of Creation come into being, unfold, and take form according to the Divine design of the Great Soul, **Ka/Kait**. Fundamentally, the Supreme Being's Creative Consciousness, Creative Intelligence, is Who we call **Ka** and **Kait**.

Amen is the Great God, the Father of All. **Amenet** is the Great Goddess, the Mother of All. Together, **Amen** and **Amenet** are the Two Halves of the Great Whole called the Supreme Being. When **Amen** and **Amenet** come together, They function as One Great Being, the Supreme Being. **Ra** and **Rait** proceed from **Amen-Amenet**, as the Great Spirit of **Amen-Amenet**. They give life to all of Creation. **Ka** and **Kait** proceed from **Amen-Amenet**, as the Great Soul of **Amen-Amenet**. They give Form to all of Creation.

Ra/Rait, the Great Spirit, moves within the Black Substance, **Ka/Kait**. This is the origin of Creation. It is the expansive/contractive movement of the Great Spirit, **Ra/Rait**, which causes **Ka/Kait**, the Black Substance, to vibrate and separate into various forms. Just as water vibrates, boils, when heat moves through it, creating separate, spherical or circular forms---bubbles---so did **Ka/Kait**, the Black Substance of Space, begin to vibrate according to the movements of the Great Spirit, **Ra/Rait**, within it. It is because of the expansive/contractive movements of **Ra/Rait** within **Ka/Kait**, the Black Substance, that spherical, circular, bodies—Sun, Moon, stars, planetary bodies, Earth—separated and were formed within it. These Creations are the Children of **Ra** and **Rait**.

The Great Spirit invests Its Divine Living-Energy into Its Children so that Its Children may live. So that They may sustain life and produce. As with all of Their Children, **Ra** and **Rait** invested Their energy into the newly formed planetary body of Earth. The substance of the new planet Earth, was a portion of the Black Substance of Space. Because of the movement of **Ra** and **Rait** within Earth, some of Earth's own Black Substance became fluid. This new fluid Black Substance of Earth is known as **Mu** and **Mut**, the male and female Ocean, another Child of **Ra/Rait**. **Ra/Rait** invested Their Living-Energy into Ocean so that Ocean would sustain It's Own life and produce.

As the Great Spirit, **Ra/Rait**, moved within the substance of Earth, the vibrations caused the black substance beneath Ocean to surge outward. This black substance of Earth which first emerged from beneath Ocean inherited the male name and title, **Ka** or **Kaka** and the female name and title **Kait**. The Earth's black substance inherited these two names from the Black Substance of Space, **Ka/Kait**. The Earthly **Ka/Kait**, this first Black Hill, or raised land, is another Child of **Ra/Rait**.

Ra and **Rait** invested Their energy into the Earthly **Ka/Kait**, and thus the Earthly **Ka/Kait**, the primordial or first Black Hill is able to sustain life and produce.

The Earthly **Ka/Kait**, the first Black Land, raised up from beneath **Mu/Mut**, Ocean, is the center of Earth. It is the place from which the spirits of the original humans, plants, animals, minerals first received their physical Earth-bodies in order to live, act and execute their Divine function in the world.

Just as the Great Spirit, **Ra/Rait**, caused the black substance of Space, **Ka/Kait**, to vibrate and separate into various forms, so did the movement of the Great Spirit through Earth's first landmass cause separation and development of some of its matter into various physical forms. These physical forms became the flesh within which the spirits of the original humans would enter.

Afu means *flesh*, as in *house* or *place of residence*. Your flesh is a house, or place of residence for your spirit. You are a spirit, a living-energy moving throughout a body. Your spirit gives your body the ability to stand, walk, move, act. When the sperm-cell of your father and the ovum-cell of your mother united to become one cell, this newly formed physical cell became a *place of residence* for your spirit and your spirit entered. 40 weeks later you were born into the world. When death occurs, your spirit will leave the physical body. It will no longer reside in that particular house.

When **Ra/Rait** moves through matter, matter becomes **Afu**, matter becomes the flesh, the house or place of residence of the Great Spirit. As **Ra** expands through matter, matter becomes the flesh of **Ra**. He is thus called **Afu Ra**. As **Rait** contracts through matter, matter becomes the flesh of **Rait**. She is thus called **Afu Rait**. As **Afu Ra** invested His energy in the Earthly **Ka**/primordial Black Hill, the first land to emerge from underneath Ocean, the energy of **Afu Ra** gave life to **Ka**. This first landmass is thus known under its male name as the **Ka** of **Afu Ra—Afu Ra Ka**. As **Afu Rait** invested Her energy into the Earthly **Kait**/primordial Black Hill, the energy of **Afu Rait** gave life to **Kait**. This first landmass is thus known under its female name as the **Kait** of **Afu Rait—Afu Rait Kait**.

Afu Ra Ka/Afu Rait Kait (Africa) is the region of Earth where the primordial Black Hill, **Ka/Kait**, first emerged from underneath **Mu/Mut**, Ocean. Eventually, the rest of Earth's landmass would emerge from Ocean and separate.

Afuraka/Afuraitkait is the region of Earth where the Goddesses and Gods, the Children of the Great God and Great Goddess, **Amen** and **Amenet**, first descended and took up residence in Nature. **Afuraka/Afuraitkait** is the region of the Earth Mother where our Ancestresses and Ancestors were born, lived, where they produced, worshipped, created, procreated. It is the place where They died, where their bodies, the first human bodies, were buried. It is the place from which Their spirits crossed over into the spirit realm.

Afuraka/Afuraitkait is the region of our Earth Mother where our Ancestresses and Ancestors were born as **Afurakanu/Afuraitkaitnut**, the people **[nu/nut]** of **Afuraka/Afuraitkait**. It is where the male individual, **Afurakani** and the female individual **Afuraitkaitnit**, realized Their physical and spiritual tie to **Amen-Amenet, Afu Ra/Afu Rait, Ka/Kait**, the Earthly **Ka/Kait**, the Goddesses and Gods, the Ancestresses and Ancestors, where They realized Their tie to one another, to animals, plants, minerals, the Nature spirits—all of Creation.

A drop of water is born of Ocean. A ray of sunlight is born of Sun. A grain of sand is born of Earth. Your being is born of the Great Being, **Amen-Amenet**. Your spirit is born of the Great Spirit, **Ra/Rait**. Your soul is born of the Great Soul, **Ka/Kait**. Your body is born of a greater body, the Earthly **Ka/Kait**.

The black energy substance in our organs and our skin, that which gives us our color, is derived of the Black Substance of Space and was inherited through the bodies of our Ancestresses and Ancestors from the primordial Black Hill of Earth. This black substance, melanin, whose male name is **Ka-Nu** and female name is **Kat-Nut**, is an energy substance made by **Amen-Amenet** to be an instrument capable of receiving and transmitting the full Divine Living-Energy of the Great Spirit. It is the substance which allows our physical bodies to function properly as houses, places of residence for **Ra/Rait**.

Ka-Nu/Kat-Nut, melanin, is the substance in the bodies of our Ancestresses and Ancestors which allowed their bodies to become possessed by the Spirits of the Goddesses and Gods during rituals of song, dance, prayer, marriage, copulation, conception. This was an infusion of Divine Energy into our families, those of our families who had remained in **Afuraka/Afuraitkait**. Those who had not yet left to populate other parts of Earth.

Our descent *from the original* **Afurakanu/Afuraitkaitnut**, the original people of **Afuraka/Afuraitkait**

Our descent *from those families who remained in* **Afuraka/Afuraitkait** to receive the Spirits of the Goddesses and Gods

Our *ability*, through **Ka-Nu/Kat-Nut**, melanin, to *properly receive and transmit the fullness* of that Divine Energy

Our *incarnation and re-incarnation* through *these families*

It is these things that identify us as Afurakanu/Afuraitkaitnut, people of Afuraka/Afuraitkait. It does not matter where we go now on Earth, where we are born on Earth, our identity as Afurakanu/Afuraitkaitnut is maintained. **We remain Afurakanu/Afuraitkaitnut in the physical world and the Ancestral realm.**

•••••••

Excerpts from the first and third issues of our:

AFURAKA/AFURAITKAIT Nanasom Nhoma
Afurakani/Afuraitkaitnit Ancestral Religion Journal

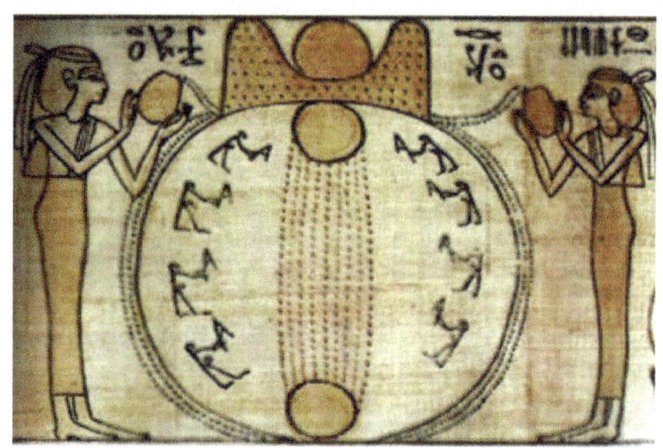

"...**Figure 3** [left] is from the **sheft** of **Khensumes** (papyrus of Khensumose). From a bird's-eye view, it actually depicts the **Ka/Kait**, the high land, which first appeared above the surface of the water to become the Earth's first landmass. This **Ka/Kait** is described in many texts of Kamit as the *"primordial mound of Creation"* in the region of **Khemennu** or the **Kaka** (**Qaqa**) or **Qa** in *Khemennu* (later called *Hermopolis* by the greeks).

The depiction shows **Ra** and **Rait** moving through the land, **Ka/Kait**, as **Afu Ra** and **Afu Rait within the Solar disk** in two phases. Here, They are **Afu Ra** and **Afu Rait** because They are moving through matter/flesh/the house. Eventually **Afu Ra** and **Afu Rait** rise within the Solar disk above the horizon (between the mountains) for the first time, creating the first sunrise in the *trustory* of the world (top of the illustration). **Afu Ra** and **Afu Rait** are thus transformed into **Ra** and **Rait**.

The Eight figures depicted on the mound are **Amen** and **Amenet**, **Ka** and **Kait**, **Nun** and **Nunet**, **Hehu** and **Hehut**---the Ancestresses and Ancestors of **Ra** and **Rait** (often called the *Ogdoad*-primordial Deities who existed before the creation of the world). **Auset** and **Nebt Het** are depicted through the forms of **Merit Meht** and **Merit Shema**, the Northern and Southern Nile Goddesses of the inundation. These Two Spirits pour water, libation, from two vases into the primordial waters which nourish the **Ka/Kait**.

This is an actual depiction of **Afuraka/Afuraitkait**, a depiction painted by one of our Afurakani or Afuraitkaitnit Ancestors or Ancestresses which dates back over 3,000 years..."

Temple at Paaraka

"...*Paaraka* was called the "island of the Time (of **Ra**)". The island was adjacent to one of the most sacred regions of Kamit, a burial place of **Ausar**. Its structure and placement recalled the rising up of the primordial mound and the beginning of Creation..."

Afurakani/Afuraitkaitnit Ancestral Culture.

Afurakanu/Afuraitkaitnut, people of **Afuraka/Afuraitkait**, recognize the spirit in plants, the soul in plants. We recognize plants as conscious-living entities functioning in the World. We harmonize our spirits, our souls, with theirs. As we interact with them, we tune into them. Our communication with them engenders respect for their function in the world, and their relation to our function in the World. Our physical interaction with plant-life reflects our respect for this spiritual relationship. It is through this respect that we maintain balance between ourselves and plant life as we live interdependently upon one another.

Afurakanu/Afuraitkaitnut recognize the spirit in animals, the soul in animals. We recognize them as conscious-living entities functioning in the World. We harmonize our spirits, our souls, with theirs. As we interact with them, we tune into them. Our communication with them engenders respect for their function in the world, and their relation to our function in the World. Our physical interaction with animal-life reflects our respect for this spiritual relationship. It is through this respect that we maintain balance between ourselves and animal life as we live interdependently upon one another.

Afurakanu/Afuraitkaitnut recognize the Spirit and the Soul in our Earth Mother, the Spirit and the Soul within planets, in Sun, Moon, stars, minerals. We recognize them all as conscious-living Entities functioning in the Creation. We harmonize our spirits, our souls, with Theirs. As we interact with Them, we tune into Them. Our communication with Them engenders respect for Their function in Creation, and Their relation to our function in Creation. Our physical interaction with our Earth Mother, with planets, Sun, Moon, stars, mineral-life, reflects our respect for this spiritual relationship. It is through this respect that we maintain balance between ourselves and our Earth Mother, planets, Sun, Moon, stars, mineral life as we live interdependently upon one another.

Afurakanu/Afuraitkaitnut recognize the spirit, the soul in one another. As conscious-living entities in the World, we harmonize our spirits, our souls, with one another. As we interact, we tune into one another. Our communication with one another engenders respect for our functions in the World, and how they are interrelated with one another. Our physical interaction with one another reflects our respect for this spiritual relationship. It is through this respect that we as Afurakanu/Afuraitkaitnut maintain balance amongst one another as we live interdependently upon one another.

Afurakanu/Afuraitkaitnut recognize the spirit, the soul of the **Afurakani male**, of the **Afuraitkaitnit female**. We recognize male and female as two halves of one conscious, living, whole entity functioning in the World. As Afurakani males and Afuraitkaitnit females, we harmonize our spirits, our souls with one another. As we interact with one another, we tune into one another. Our communication with one another engenders respect for our functions in the World, and how they are interrelated to one another. Our physical interaction as Afurakani males and Afuraitkaitnit females reflects our respect for this spiritual relationship. It is through this respect that the Afurakani male and Afuraitkaitnit female maintain balance between one another as we live interdependently upon one another.

Afurakanu/Afuraitkaitnut recognize the Spirits, the Souls of our Ancestresses and Ancestors, the Spirits, the Souls of the Goddesses and Gods, the Spirits the Souls of the Nature Spirits. We recognize Them All as conscious-living Entities of Creation. We harmonize our spirits, our souls with Theirs. As we interact with Them we tune into Them. Our communication with Them engenders respect for Their function in Creation and Their relation to our function in Creation. Our physical interaction with our Ancestresses and Ancestors, the Goddesses and Gods, the Nature Spirits reflects our attunement to and respect for the spiritual relationship we have with Them. It is through this respect that we maintain balance between ourselves and the Ancestral Spirits, the Goddesses and Gods, the Nature Spirits, as we live interdependently upon one another.

Afurakanu/Afuraitkaitnut recognize the spirit, the soul within ourselves. We recognize our spirit and soul as the living and conscious entities functioning within our being. We harmonize the functions of our spirit with our soul. As we focus on our spirit and soul, we tune into their purpose, their function within us. Our attunement to these parts of us engenders respect for the functions they fulfill within us, and how they relate to our function in the World. Our respect for our **Ka-Nu/Kat-Nut**, melanin, and our entire physical body reflects our respect for the spiritual relationship of our spirit and soul, our non-physical bodies. It is through this respect that we maintain balance between the various parts of our spirit, our soul and our physical body as they exist interdependently upon one another.

Afurakanu/Afuraitkaitnut recognize the spirit, the soul of individuals who have embraced and internalized disorder. We recognize these unconscious living entities in the World. We recognize the disharmony of their spirits, their souls with respect to ours. As we interact with these individuals, physical and non-physical, whose spirits, souls are in disorder, we tune into them. Our contact with them engenders a recognition of their malfunction in the world, and how it is unrelated to our function in the World. Our physical interaction with spirits, souls in disorder reflects our realization of their spiritual disconnection. It is through this realization that we maintain a balance between executing our function in the World and defending ourselves, as we reject **spirits of disorder**, physical and non-physical, and their influence in the World.

This is the life culture of Afurakanu/Afuraitkaitnut, people of Afuraka/Afuraitkait. It is our way of living established by our Ancestresses and Ancestors and transmitted to us. Because of Their devotion to the Supreme Being, our Ancestresses and Ancestors were shown that They were beings who were born of the Supreme Being. They learned that They did not create Their own life, but were given life by **Amen-Amenet** to participate in Creation in harmony with Its Divine Order.

The devotion of our Ancestresses and Ancestors to the Supreme Being, **Amen-Amenet**, enabled Them to attune Their spirits, Their souls, to the Great Spirit, the Great Soul. They were thus able to attune Their Spirits, Their souls to the Goddesses and Gods, the Children of **Amen-Amenet**. Our families in Afuraka/Afuraitkait were therefore opened to receive the Spirits of the Goddesses and Gods. We became open vessels through whom these Spiritual-Forces of Divine Order would function. Through us, the Goddesses and Gods would communicate and establish the Divine Order of **Amen-Amenet**, just as They execute the Divine Order of **Amen-Amenet** as They operate throughout plant life, animal life, mineral life, our Earth Mother, planets, Sun, Moon, stars, all of Creation.

While we all have a portion of the Earth's air in our lungs, the movement of air, wind, in the Earth's atmosphere can become so powerful that it may enter our lungs, surround our entire bodies, take possession of us, lift us up and carry us in its own direction. Our Ancestresses and Ancestors were shown that as part of Creation we are all under the influence of the Spirits of the Goddesses and Gods, as They move throughout all of Creation. In Afuraka/Afuraitkait, the movement of the Goddesses and Gods became so powerful with respect to us, that Their Spirits entered our bodies, surrounded us, took possession of us, and guided us in Their own direction. They possessed us during rituals of song, dance, prayer, marriage, copulation, conception. They empowered us and communicated the Divine Order of **Amen-Amenet** into us.

With these Forces of Divine Order expressing Themselves through our Fathers, Mothers, Children, functioning in our blood, our families, our Ancestresses and Ancestors were guided to order Their family relations, Their social relations, Their creative development, Their invention, Their dance, Their song, Their sexual relations, Their practice of medicine, Their methods of food production, Their rituals, Their civilizations, the entirety of Their lives They were guided to order after the Divine Order. By drawing on the Divine Spirits operating within Them and around Them, Our Ancestresses and Ancestors realized the nature of Their kinship to one another, to plant life, animal life, mineral life, our Earth Mother, planets, Sun, Moon, stars, the Spirits functioning through Nature, the Goddesses and Gods. Our families thus fashioned a way of living reflecting the Divine presence at the center of Their life activities.

We, as Afurakanu/Afuraitkaitnut, are descendent of these Ancestresses and Ancestors, whose blood was altered by the infusion of the Spirits of the Goddesses and Gods into our families. This uniquely altered blood is transmitted to us and by us today, wherever we are on Earth, and with it is transmitted the culture, the way of living embracing Divine Order.

Yet, there were those who **left** Afuraka/Afuraitkait **before** the Goddesses and Gods entered the families of our Ancestresses and Ancestors. In very small numbers, they moved away from the families, and settled in their new locations. These groups would become what are now the groups referred to as non-Afurakanu/non-Afuraitkaitnut.

Those who rejected the life-culture of Law and preferred a life culture dominated by lust, are those who were initially forced out of our families. They would move away and settle in new locations. Yet, most who were forced out of our families would, with time, recognize the error of living a life dominated by lust, disorder. They would eventually recognize that living in harmony with the Divine Order of Creation was the natural way of living, and the way that was beneficial to all of their life endeavors. Those who would recognize this would make amends to the Ancestresses and Ancestors, to the Goddesses and Gods, to the Supreme Being. They would restore balance and order to their existence.

Yet, there was a very small portion of that exiled population who would never embrace the life culture of Law. Lust was more important for them to serve. It is these individuals who, through living perverse, disordered lifestyles, corrupted themselves and their offspring.

The Great Spirit, **Ra/Rait**, is the Divine Living-Energy that initiated the Creation of the World. Within all of us is a portion of that life-creating energy. When we engage in sexual activity, this energy is aroused, and is responsible for the creation of a new life—a child. This creation is an expression of Divine Order. Those who would arouse this Divine Creative energy within themselves to serve lust, disorder, were living in direct conflict with their own existence, with the nature of Creation and with Divine Order. They were in direct violation of their function in Creation, and were thus self-destructive. **These individuals who chose to serve lust, disorder, engaging in incest and homosexual activity/dissexual activity, they who rationalized their lust-dominated lifestyle, are they who corrupted themselves and their offspring.** It is they, who had no respect for themselves, for the Supreme Being, the Goddesses and Gods, the Nature Spirits, the Ancestresses and Ancestors, the Divine Order of Creation. It is they who aroused the Divine creative energy of **Ra/Rait** residing within them for the purpose of perversion instead of creation. It is they who were that small portion of the exiled population who would never embrace the life culture of Law.

As they were drawn into a different part of the Earth, they would settle in isolation. **Through rape and incest, they would produce an increasing number of offspring who had no external skin color.** The practice of incest would result in a larger number of offspring being born albino, and offspring born with varying genetic mutations. **They would thus give birth to albino offspring and other kinds of genetically mutated**

offspring with white skin, blond hair, and light eyes. The incestuous and homosexual/dissexual practices amongst the albino offspring as well as the non-albino offspring, would eventually produce a group of people who not only had lost their external dark pigmentation, but the internal pigmentation also was greatly reduced. Their creative energy was aroused and used in a perverse manner and the result of their perversion was reflected in their corrupted offspring. **Their physical isolation in a colder climate, as well as their spiritual isolation from the order in Nature, would set in motion structural changes in bones, hair, physiology. This is the origin of the white groups and their offspring who live today.**

Ka-Nu/Kat-Nut, melanin, is the substance which allows Afurakanu/Afuraitkaitnut to attune ourselves, our bodies, to the life in plants, animals, minerals, one another, the Earth Mother, planets, Sun, Moon, stars, the Spirits of the Goddesses and Gods, the Nature Spirits, the Ancestral Spirits, the Supreme Being. The whites and their offspring exist without the proper *levels* and *quality* of **Ka-Nu/Kat-Nut**, melanin, and are not able to receive and transmit the fullness of Divine Energy proceeding from **Amen-Amenet**.

To embrace lust is to reject Law. To embrace disorder, is to reject Order. This is the culture of the whites and their offspring. They cannot properly attune their spirits, their "souls", their bodies to the spirits, the souls of plant life, animal life, mineral life, the Earth Mother, planets, Sun, Moon, stars, other human beings. Just as they isolated themselves from Divine Order, their original habitat, so do they isolate plant life, animal life, mineral life, human life from themselves. It is through this process of isolating all things through disorder, that they create an opportunity to destroy all things. No group of people destroys plant life, animal life, mineral life and human life as the whites and their offspring. No group of people shows hatred of the Goddesses and Gods, the Nature Spirits, the Ancestral Spirits of Afuraka/Afuraitkait, the Order of Creation, of **Amen-Amenet**, as the whites and their offspring.

Before Creation began, the Black Substance of Space had not been ordered by **Ra/Rait** into various forms, creations. The Black Substance was in a state of **non-order**. When **Ra** and **Rait** began the process of Creation, the Black Substance was ordered into various Forms, Creations. The Black Substance was now in a state of **Order**. The state of **non-order** is the **opposite** of the state of **Order**. **Non-order** is the **balance** of **Order**. *Disorder* is **not** the opposite of **Order**. *Disorder* is the **perversion** of **Order**. *Disorder* is the only true evil. *Disorder* is the culture of the whites and their offspring. *Disorder* is the nature of their character.

It is the nature of the whites and their offspring that makes all of them who exist, all of them who have ever existed, and all of them who ever will exist, the enemy of all Afurakanu/Afuraitkaitnut.

Our way of life as Afurakanu/Afuraitkaitnut, our culture, is that of Divine Order.

To live in Divine Order is to reject disorder in all of its forms.

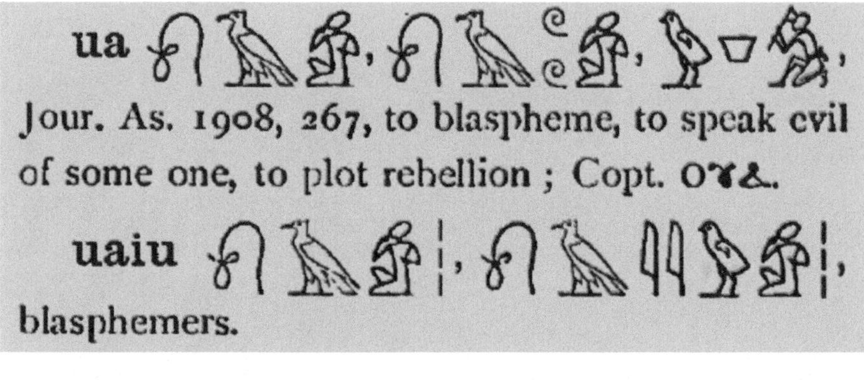
ua, Jour. As. 1908, 267, to blaspheme, to speak evil of some one, to plot rebellion ; Copt. ⲟⲩⲁ.

uaiu, blasphemers.

Uai, "Rebel," "Blasphemer," a title of Āapep.

Uaiu, the associates of Āapep.

uai, Rec. 29, 157, to stink, foul, bad, stinking.

uati, rebel; plur.

Uati (**Wati** – *whitey*) associate(s) of **Apep** – the spirit who brings disorder, the enemy of **Ra**. The **Khaitiu** are the Deities who slaughter the enemies of **Ra** and **Ausar**. They are *Divine Executioners*, Eradicators of disorder.

Khaitiu, the gods who slaughter the enemies of Rā and Osiris.

Afurakani/Afuraitkaitnit Function in Creation.

After conception, your body developed by creating a system of organs, structures and cells, a system of bodies within bodies. Each smaller body within you has its own function to execute within the large body. Your body birthed within itself a number of smaller bodies. These smaller bodies are the organs and structures within you including heart, liver, brain, lungs, bones, veins. These smaller bodies within you in turn birthed within themselves even smaller bodies. These smaller bodies are the cells of the organs and structures within you including, heart cells, liver cells, brain cells, bone marrow cells, blood cells. Your body is thus made up of a system of bodies within bodies.

The order of your body is born of and is a reflection of the Divine Order of Creation. **Amen**, the Great God, and **Amenet** the Great Goddess, come together and function as One Divine Unit, the Supreme Being, in the process of Creation. **Amen-Amenet** birthed within Themselves smaller or lesser Divine Beings. These are the Goddesses and Gods, the Divine Organs and Structures within the Divine Body of **Amen-Amenet**. The Goddesses and Gods, as Divine Organs and Structures, in turn birthed within Themselves even smaller beings. These smaller beings include stars, Sun, Moon, planetary bodies, from which proceeded plants, animals, minerals, **Afurakani/Afuraitkaitnit humans**. These beings are the cells of the Divine Organs and Structures. The Divine Body of **Amen-Amenet** is thus made up of a system of beings within beings.

The organs and structures of your body regulate the functions of their cells. The organs and structures in the body distribute blood and water, energy and nourishment, to their cells. It is in this manner that the organs and structures of the body establish and maintain order in the functioning of their cells and thus order in the body. The cells participate in this order by serving their parent organ or structure. By serving their parent organ or structure, the cells serve the whole body. Brain cells serve the brain. By serving the brain, their parent organ, brain cells serve the whole body. Liver cells serve the liver. By serving the liver, their parent organ, liver cells serve the whole body. Bone marrow cells serve the skeletal system. By serving the skeletal system, their parent structure, bone marrow cells serve the whole body.

The Divine Organs and Structures within the Divine Body of **Amen-Amenet** regulate the functions of their cells. The Divine Organs and Structures, the Goddesses and Gods, distribute the Divine Living-Energy of **Amen-Amenet** to their cells. They distribute the Divine Consciousness, Intelligence of **Amen-Amenet** to their cells. It is in this manner that the Goddesses and Gods, the Divine Organs and Structures within **Amen-Amenet**, establish and maintain Divine Order in the functioning of their cells and thus Divine Order in Creation. The cells participate in this order by serving their Divine parent Organs and Structures. By serving their Divine parent Organs and Structures, the cells serve the Divine Whole, **Amen-Amenet**. Stars, Sun, Moon, planetary bodies, plants, animals, minerals, Afurakani/Afuraitkaitnit humans, all of us are cells of the Divine Organs and Structures of **Amen-Amenet**. By serving our parent Organs and Structures, the Goddesses and Gods, we as cells serve the Great Whole, the Great God and the Great Goddess, **Amen-Amenet**.

Water exists in the organs and structures of your body, and in the cells of the organs and structures. Throughout the life of a cell, it is continuously nourished and rejuvenated by the water that exists in the organs and structures. When a cell dies, the water which was in the cell joins the nourishing and rejuvenating water that exists in its parent organs and structures. Eventually, the water in the organs and structures will become part of new cells which are birthed within the organs and structures.

The Divine water existing in the Divine Body of Amen-Amenet is the Ancestral realm. It is where the Spirits of our Ancestresses and Ancestors dwell. Throughout our lives as cells of the Divine Organs and

Structures, we are continuously nourished and rejuvenated by the Divine water of the Ancestral Spirits which exists in the Divine Organs and Structures. As cells, when we die, our spirits leave our bodies and go to the Ancestral realm. If our character is in harmony with Divine Order, we remain in the Ancestral realm and become Ancestresses and Ancestors. We become part of that Divine water within the Divine Organs and Structures of **Amen-Amenet**. As Ancestresses and Ancestors, we participate in the functions of the Ancestral realm. We help provide continuous nourishment and rejuvenation to the cells in the Divine Organs and Structures. Eventually, our spirits leave the Ancestral realm, the Divine water, to reincarnate as newborn Afurakanu/Afuraitkaitnut, newborn cells within the Divine Organs and Structures of **Amen-Amenet**.

This is the Divine Order of Creation. A system of bodies within bodies within the Great Divine Body. A system of beings within beings within the Supreme Being. The Great God and the Great Goddess. The Goddesses and Gods. The Ancestresses and Ancestors. The Nature Spirits. Plants, animals, minerals, Afurakanu/Afuraitkaitnut. Just as every cell in the body is designed and comes into being in order to execute a specific function in your body, so are we as Afurakanu/Afuraitkaitnut designed, and come into being, in order to execute a specific function in Creation. We serve **Amen-Amenet**, just as our cells serve us. We function for **Amen-Amenet**, just as our cells function for us.

The different organs and structures in your body have different functions, yet their functions are interrelated. The groups of cells serving the different organs and structures are different from one another yet their group functions are interrelated. The family of cells in the liver, are different from the family of cells in the lungs, which are different from the family of cells in the brain, the bones, the blood. Yet, as the cells carry out their specific functions within their respective families, the entire body functions in harmony with its Divine design.

The different Divine Organs and Structures, the different Goddesses and Gods, within **Amen-Amenet** have different functions in Creation, yet Their Divine functions are interrelated. The groups of cells serving the different Divine Organs and Structures are different from one another yet Their group functions are interrelated. As cells, the various groups of plants, animals, minerals, are different from one another. Yet, as they carry out their specific functions within their respective families, they participate in Creation in harmony with its Divine design. The various groups of Afurakanu/Afuraitkaitnut are different from one another. Yet, as we carry out our specific functions within our respective families, we participate in Creation in harmony with its Divine design.

The organization of the cells of your body into different families, groups which support their parent organs and structures, is a harmonious organization. **The organization of Afurakanu/Afuraitkaitnut into different clans, groups who support the functions of their parent Goddesses and Gods, is a Divinely harmonious organization ordered by Amen-Amenet.**

The heart cannot execute the functions of the liver. The liver cannot execute the functions of the lungs. The lungs cannot execute the functions of the bones. The cells of the heart cannot execute the functions of liver cells. The cells of the liver cannot execute the functions of lung cells. The cells of the lungs cannot execute the functions of bone marrow cells. Because of the design of your body, groups of cells within you are organized and identified by the organs and structures that govern them.

The Divine Organs and Structures of **Amen-Amenet**, the Goddesses and Gods, execute Their Divine functions in Creation harmoniously with One another. The great Afurakani/Afuraitkaitnit clans, as groups of cells, support the functions of their Divine parent Organs and Structures. By functioning under the direction of their Divine parents, the various Afurakani/Afuraitkaitnit clans do not conflict with one another. Because of the Divine design of Creation, the great Ancestral clans of Afurakanu/Afuraitkaitnut came into being and were organized by the functions of the Goddesses and Gods Who govern Them.

The physiological and cultural differences exhibited by Afurakanu/Afuraitkaitnut of different clans are rooted in this Divine system of organization. Our different dialects, languages, observances of taboos, our different foods, social interactions, religious expressions, reflect our identity as children of different Goddesses and Gods of Creation. Our different cultural practices reflect our attunement to our Ancestry, and our respect for our function in Creation. Thus:

To know your Ancestral clan, is to embrace your place in Creation. To function within the culture of your Ancestral clan is to properly harmonize your life-activities with the Divine Order:

Akan, Ewe, Yoruba, Igbo, Bakongo, Bambara, Dogon, Minianka, Goromantche, Nguni, Sotho, Khoi khoi, San, Dinka, Gikuyu, Maasai, Galla, Chokwe, Wolof, Twa, Ovambo, Bassa, Fula, Fang, Azande, Sara, Afar, Batswana, Fon, Ovimbundu, Kenesu

Afurakani/Afuraitkaitnit clans recognize the Divine Order of Creation, and their identity within the Divine Order. The Divine system of beings within beings within the Supreme Being. Bodes within bodies within the Divine Body. **The Great God and the Great Goddess. The Goddesses and Gods. The Ancestresses and Ancestors. The Nature Spirits. Afurakanu/Afuraitkaitnut.** The culture and languages of the various Afurakani/Afuraitkaitnit clans reflects their understanding and harmony with Creation's Divine Order.

Akan people call the Great God, **Nyame**, the Great Goddess, **Nyamewaa**. The Goddesses and Gods are called **Abosom**. The Ancestresses and Ancestors are called **Nananom Nsamanfo** or **Asamanfo**. **Ewe** people call the Great God and Great Goddess **Nana Buluku**, the Supreme Being from Whom proceeds the Great Mother **Mawu** and the Great Father **Lisa**. The Goddesses and Gods are called the **Vodou**. The Ancestresses and Ancestors are called **Gbogbo** [**Kuvito**]. **Yoruba** people call the Great God and Great Goddess, **Olorun** [and **Olokun**] The Supreme Being. The Goddesses and Gods are called **Orisha**. The Ancestresses and Ancestors are called **Egungun** or **Egun**. **Igbo** people call the Great God **Chukwu** and the Great Goddess **Komosu**. The Goddesses and Gods are called **Arusi**. The Ancestresses and Ancestors are called **Mmuo**. The ancient **Kenesu** people call the Great God **Amen**, the Great Goddess, **Amenet**. The Goddesses and Gods are called **Ntoru/Ntorotu** [Neteru/Netertu]. The Ancestresses and Ancestors are called **Shepsu/Shepsutu** or **Patu/Patetu**.

These groups of Afurakanu/Afuraitkaitnut, as **all** groups of Afurakanu/Afuraitkaitnut, attune themselves to the Mother-Father Supreme Being, *through the agency* of the Goddesses and Gods and the Ancestresses and Ancestors. **Our attunement is achieved through the language and culture of our Ancestral clans.**

The whites and their offspring are not part of the Ancestral clans of Afurakanu/Afuraitkaitnut. The Spirits of the Goddesses and Gods entered the families of those of us who *remained* in Afuraka/Afuraitkait to receive Them. Those who became the whites and their offspring, because of their initial rejection of Divine Order, **were outside of Afuraka/Afuraitkait**. Because of their initial rejection of Divine Order they corrupted their own spirits, which later caused the corruption of their own bodies. As they reincarnate through their offspring, the same spirit who rejected Divine Order long ago is birthed to live once again in the world. Even when a white and a person of color mix, and eventually give birth to a mixed child, *the blood may be mixed, but the soul is not.* When a spirit from the *european lineage* is drawn into the womb, this spirit, who was white in previous lifetimes, will be born this time with a body which is one of color. Yet, the spirit is one of disorder. **The body**

of Ka-Nu/Kat-Nut, melanin, within which this spirit of disorder now dwells, will not place this spirit of disorder in harmony with Divine Order.

It is this spirit of disorder that separates the whites and their offspring from Afurakanu/Afuraitkaitnut. **It is this spirit of disorder that will always separate the whites and their offspring from membership in the Ancestral clans of Afurakanu/Afuraitkaitnut.** As cells within the Divine body of **Amen-Amenet**, the whites transformed themselves into cancerous cells in the Divine body of **Amen-Amenet**. And so they move to consume and destroy other cells: plants, animals, minerals, humans, in the Divine Body.

Yet, just as your body has an immune system that destroys cancerous cells, so does the Divine body of **Amen-Amenet** have a **Divine Immune System**: Goddesses and Gods, Ancestresses and Ancestors, Afurakanu/Afuraitkaitnut, Nature Spirits: **Divine Forces Who destroy all cancerous cells, and always restore order wherever disorder appears in Creation.**

Afurakani/Afuraitkaitnit Ancestral Religion – 1.

Law is the expression of Order. Divine Law is the expression of Divine Order.

The laws governing Afurakani/Afuraitkaitnit society are expressions of Divine Order. Afurakani man and Afuraitkaitnit woman are two halves of a whole. We are the balance of one another. This is law in Afurakani/Afuraitkaitnit society and it is expressive of Divine Order. **Amen** and **Amenet** are the Two Halves of the Divine Whole. They are the balance of One another. **Ra** and **Rait** are Two Halves of a Divine Whole. They are the balance of One another. **Ka** and **Kait** are Two Halves of a Divine Whole. They are the balance of One another. The sperm-cell of the male and the ovum-cell of the female are two halves which become one whole. They are the balance of one another.

This Divine Order, which permeates all of Creation, is the basis from which our cultural laws are born.

The laws of Afurakani/Afuraitkaitnit culture link our life-activities to Divine Order from moment to moment to moment, day to night to day, month to month, year to year, lifetime to Ancestral life to lifetime. As we embrace Divine Order through the laws of our Ancestral clans, we link our thoughts, intentions and actions to Divine Order. In this manner we develop good character. And it is through maintaining good character that we create and live good lives.

Ritual is the means by which we incorporate Divine Law and restore Divine Balance to our lives. Ritual is thus the gateway to Divine Order.

When we attune ourselves to **Amen-Amenet**, we place ourselves in the position to know what is good for us and what is not good for us. What is needed and what is not needed. How to live and how not to live. How to function and how not to function. Through ritual we place ourselves in the position to be fed by the Divine Force of Law and Balance in Creation Whose male name is **Maa** and Whose female name is **Maat**. It is through the God **Maa** and the Goddess **Maat** that **Amen-Amenet** establishes male and female balance in Creation. It is these Children of **Amen-Amenet** that govern the center of balance within our bodies, within the operation of our spirits, within Creation. When we attune ourselves to **Amen-Amenet** in order to know right from wrong, what is necessary and what is not necessary, these Spirits of Divine Law and Balance, **Maa** and **Maat**, transmit the truth, the Law, the Divine Order of **Amen-Amenet** to us. We then harmonize our thoughts, intentions and actions with the Law. It is through **Maa/Maat** that we are able to balance what we desire with what is in harmony with Divine Order. It is through **Maa/Maat** that we establish good character.

When we fail to live in harmony with law, we create situations in life that are imbalanced, disharmonious, self-destructive. Ritual is the means by which we restore balance to our lives. We return our focus to the Divine Order and embrace law through ritual. We are thus able to maintain our good character. And this is the essence of Afurakani/Afuraitkaitnit Ancestral Religion: *The ritual incorporation of Divine Law and the ritual restoration of Divine Balance.*

Embracing Afurakani/Afuraitkaitnit Ancestral Religion is the ritual means by which people of Afuraka/Afuraitkait create and live good lives. To create and live a good life is to embrace and execute our Divine function in the World, given to us by the Supreme Being. Divine Law is the instrument that balances our thoughts, intentions and actions as we work continuously to maintain our good character and thus create and live good lives.

Our Afurakani/Afuraitkaitnit names and language, our dances, songs, exercises, prayers, chants, marriages, meditations, initiations, clothing, our use of medicines, oils, colors, gems, jewelry, our hairstyles, foods, the designs of our buildings, shrines, villages, are all rooted in the ritual incorporation of Divine Law and the ritual restoration of Divine Balance in our life-activities. All are rooted in Afurakani/Afuraitkaitnit Ancestral Religion. And all are essential to our ability to create and live good lives.

When we live in harmony with the culture of our Ancestral clans, when we embrace Divine Law and restore Divine Balance where imbalance occurs, when we operate through the guidance of our Afurakani/Afuraitkaitnit Ancestral Religion, we create and live good lives. We execute our Divine functions in Creation. We serve **Amen-Amenet**. We are empowered and guided by the Goddesses and Gods and our Ancestresses and Ancestors. It is only when we neglect Divine Law, Divine Order, our function in Creation; neglect the rituals necessary to incorporate Divine Law and restore Divine Balance, that we suffer.

This truth we have transmitted to and through our offspring ever since we first received it from the Ancestral realm. This truth is what enabled us and our Ancestresses and Ancestors to create and live good lives throughout our existence on Earth. It is what enabled us to express our respect for Divine Order through the building and the administration of great civilizations. **In ancient Keneset and Kamit, we created and lived good lives. The great structures of those civilizations which continue to stand after thousands of years are evidence of the good character of our Ancestresses and Ancestors. They survive as a reminder of how the Divine Order of Creation is made manifest through Afurakanu/Afuraitkaitnut on Earth, when we live in harmony with our Ancestral culture – when we incorporate Divine Law and restore Divine Balance through the practice of our Ancestral Religion.**

Afurakanu/Afuraitkaitnut built civilizations in Afuraka/Afuraitkait, as well as in southern europe, in asia and asia minor, in North Amaruka (america), Central Amaruka, South Amaruka, in the islands of the Caribbean, in australia, in the islands of the pacific ocean. **We have inhabited these areas for thousands and thousands and thousands of years.**

After the Spirits of the Goddesses and Gods had entered our families in Afuraka/Afuraitkait, some of us left Afuraka/Afuraitkait and inhabited various parts of the world. Those Afurakanu/Afuraitkaitnut who left Afuraka/Afuraitkait thousands of years ago maintained the Divine culture. We attuned ourselves to the Nature Spirits of our new surroundings, and harmonized our life-activities with Theirs according to Divine Law and Divine Balance. We created and lived good lives. In Afuraka/Afuraitkait, as well as in the various parts of our Earth Mother, we built homes, villages, shrines. We extracted metals from our Earth Mother. We cultivated fertile land, we produced medicines. We noted the movements of the stars, Sun, Moon, planets. We noted the development of plant-life, the cycles of animal-life. We noted their influences on our spirits and harmonized these influences with our life-activities and the development of our society. We created all of the things necessary for us to execute our Divine function in the World. When we had disputes with one another, we incorporated Divine Law and restored Divine Balance through the rituals of our Afurakani/Afuraitkaitnit Ancestral Religion, and developed just solutions to our disputes which were reflective of Divine Order. Throughout the process, we developed a greater appreciation for one another. We honored our Ancestresses and Ancestors, the Nature Spirits, we worshipped the Goddesses and Gods, we served the Great God and the Great Goddess.

Those who were exiled from Afuraka/Afuraitkait, those who had rejected Divine Law to embrace and incorporate lust as their lifestyle, are those who corrupted their spirits and their bodies. They who had isolated themselves and were drawn to northern eurasia are they who would eventually degenerate into people lacking **Ka-Nu/Kat-Nut**, melanin. They degenerated into whites. After their mutation, the whites would begin to move out of northern eurasia in waves. They would eventually come into contact with Afurakanu/Afuraitkaitnut for the first time after thousands of years of isolation.

When the whites came into contact with the Afurakani/Afuraitkaitnit civilizations, they brought conflict. They brought disorder because disorder is the nature of their character. The Divinely ordered culture of Afurakanu/Afuraitkaitnut which the whites encountered was not a source of inspiration for them. Because of the nature of their character, our culture only stirred within the whites the lust which drove them and continues to drive them, to destroy the culture and the people, and claim the culture and the land for themselves. The whites began a series of wars with Afurakanu/Afuraitkaitnut which have continued for thousands of years.

The whites first invaded southern europe, asia minor, asia and North Afuraka/Afuraitkait. As cancerous cells moving to consume healthy cells, the whites and their offspring moved out of northern eurasia attempting to consume the Afurakanu/Afuraitkaitnut and the lands we had cultivated. For thousands of years, Afurakanu/Afuraitkaitnut won the war against the whites and their offspring. We continued to cultivate our lands and develop our civilizations. Even when the whites and their offspring would gain control of a town or settlement it was only temporary. Afurakanu/Afuraitkaitnut would restore Divine Balance through ritual and, in time, overthrow the white aliens from our territory.

After having been unsuccessful at destroying and taking control of the Afurakanu/Afuraitkaitnut in our various countries by direct warfare, the whites and their offspring believed that the only way to gain the control that they lusted after was to attempt to control and corrupt the culture of the Afurakanu/Afuraitkaitnut. Through settling near our centers of civilization, and attempting to visit, trade and live in the lands of the Afurakanu/Afuraitkaitnut, the whites and their offspring would introduce corruption as a way of living. They would introduce the lust-dominated culture. The immature amongst the Afurakanu/Afuraitkaitnut would not immediately reject the white aliens. The immature amongst the Afurakanu/Afuraitkaitnut would try to show them a measure of respect. Once inside the territory of the Afurakanu/Afuraitkaitnut, the whites and their offspring would attempt to bring down the Afurakani/Afuraitkaitnit civilizations from within. They would encourage the immature amongst us to deviate from our normal patterns of living. Ultimately, the whites and their offspring hoped to create rivalries between the immature and the mature Afurakanu/Afuraitkaitnut. While we would fight one another, we would weaken one another. The whites and their offspring would then move to attack our nation from outside and inside, while we were in a weakened state.

When we accept poisonous substances in our bodies, we invite disorder and create conflict within our bodies. Our bodies then become weak. Once the body is weak, insects, substances and various other things that would normally not be a threat to our well being, become a threat to our health, our lives. When the immature amongst us accepted the whites and their offspring in our societies, disorder and conflict was accepted in our societies. We then became weak. We had weakened ourselves by accepting poison instead of rejecting poison. The whites and their offspring began to spiritually poison the immature, through the corruption of the Ancestral Religion. The whites and their offspring moved to poison our ritual means of incorporating Divine Law and restoring Divine Balance. It was their method of destroying our societies. The poison began to spread. Conflict amongst the Afurakanu/Afuraitkaitnut began to spread.

The means by which the whites and their offspring moved to poison Afurakani/Afuraitkaitnit Ancestral Religion, was to create characters who never existed, claim that these fictional characters were real, claim that these fictional characters were Divine and demand that we worship, believe in and follow these fictional white characters and the foolish culture connected to them. The culture connected to these fictional characters is the culture of the whites, which is that of disorder, rejection of Divine Law and a means of self-destruction for

Afurakani/Afuraitkaitnit culture and people. In order to make the fictional characters appear to be real, the whites had to give them names and create fictional life-stories for them. The whites and their offspring used the information about the Goddesses and Gods, and the Ancestresses and Ancestors of Afurakani/Afuraitkaitnit culture to manufacture life stories about the newly created fictional white characters.

The whites also corrupted the Afurakani/Afuraitkaitnit names of the Goddesses and Gods and our Ancestresses and Ancestors and applied the corrupted names to the newly created fictional white characters. The whites and their offspring had learned some of our language, and how to read some of our writings as they lived in and near Kamit, North Afuraka/Afuraitkait. They used the little that they learned from the culture of Kamit, perverted it and used their perversions to create written stories of their false gods, fictional people, a false heritage, a fictional bloodline and a false ancestry for themselves. Their goal is to make Afurakanu/Afuraitkaitnut believe that whites and their offspring were chosen by god to rule the people of the world, and show the people of the world the way to live. This total insanity of the whites and their offspring is a reflection of the nature of their character which is that of disorder, the only true evil.

Fictional white characters were created. The fictional characters were given names. The fictional characters were given fictional life stories. The fictional characters were presented to Afurakanu/Afuraitkaitnut as real and divine. The many fictional characters that were created by the whites and their offspring include: abraham, isaac, ishmael, judah, moses, david, jesus, solomon, sheba, menelik, muhammed, buddha, yahweh, brahman, allah and elohim.

Afurakani/Afuraitkaitnit Ancestral Religion – 2.

The whites and their offspring attempted to force Afurakanu/Afuraitkaitnut into the false belief that whites had a special agreement or covenant with god. They did this through creating a fictional ancestor for themselves and claimed he had a special covenant with god. They also claimed that this covenant was passed down to them through the two fictional sons of this character. The fictional character was given the name abraham or ibrahim. The fictional sons of this character were given the names isaac or ishak and ishmael or ismail.

abraham, isaac and ishmael never existed. The name abraham or ibrahim is a title that the whites stole from the God **Tehuti**. **Tehuti** is the Divine Spirit-Force in Creation that reveals the functions of all things in Creation and their relationship with one another. He is the Spiritual Force that transmits the Divine Wisdom of **Amen-Amenet** to our spirits. He is one of the Spirit-Forces whose energy is moving and operating through the Moon. In your body, **Tehuti**'s spiritual force is operating through your pineal gland. In your spirit, **Tehuti**'s spiritual force is operating as your spiritual intuition.

In the language of Kamit, one of **Tehuti**'s titles is **Aprehui** which is composed of **ap [up]**, meaning: *judge* and **rehui** meaning: *two combatants*. This title, **Aprehui [Uprehui]**, thus means: *judge of the two combatants*. For tens of thousands of years Afurakanu/Afuraitkaitnut have communicated with the God **Tehuti** and invoked his spirit under the title **Aprehui**. This title of the God **Tehuti** was corrupted from **Aprehui**, to Ibrahim [Aprehuim], by the whites. The Two combatants over whom **Tehuti**, called **Aprehui** is the judge are the two Gods **Heru** and **Set**. These two ancient Gods are Divine Spirit-Forces in Nature.

Heru is one of the Spirit Forces whose energy is moving and operating through the solar energy at the center or core of the planet Earth and the core of the Sun. In your body, **Heru** is the spiritual force that is operating through your cardiovascular system whose major organ is your heart. In your spirit, **Heru**'s energy is governing your *will*.

Set is one of the Spirit Forces whose energy is moving and operating through the planet mercury. In your body, **Set** is the spiritual force that is operating through your nervous system and gonads. In your spirit, **Set**'s energy governs your *desire*.

In the language of Kamit, one of the ancient titles of the God **Heru** is **Heq** [also pronounced **Sheq**], which means *ruler*. One of the ancient titles of the God **Set** is **Smai-Ur**, which means *to join or unite*, yet it also means *evil associate or fiend*. For tens of thousands of years Afurakanu/Afuraitkaitnut have communicated with the Gods **Heru** and **Set**, and invoked their spirits under the titles, **Heq** and **Smai-Ur**. These titles of **Heru** and **Set** were corrupted from **Heq** [**Sheq**] and **Smai-Ur** to ishak and ismail by the whites. The whites thus perverted the titles **Aprehui, Heq** and **Smai-Ur** into ibrahim, ishak and ismail. They would then pervert the knowledge of the Gods **Tehuti, Heru** and **Set**, Divine Spiritual Beings operating through the Moon, Sun, Earth and the planet mercury into a fictional tale about a fictional white man and his two sons who were the fictional ancestors of fictional white tribes.

The stories about ishak/isaac receiving the blessings of ibrahim as opposed to his elder brother ismail/ishmael receiving the covenant and blessings, were stolen from the knowledge of the Gods, where **Heru** or **Heq** received the <u>ruler</u>ship over certain aspects of Creation as opposed to his Elder **Set** or **Smai-Ur** receiving rulership over certain aspects of Creation. The conflict between **Heru** and **Set** in their names of **Heq** and **Smai-Ur** also takes place within your spirit, because they govern your will and your desire. Within your spirit, you sometimes desire to do something wrong, yet your will to do what is right is in conflict with your misguided desire. As one part of you fights with the other, you have conflict. Your desire fights your will. **Set**'s energy, your desire, is fighting **Heru**'s energy, your will. At some point, you become spiritually aware of why the desire is wrong, what the consequences of following your misguided desire would be, and you come to realize why it is in your best interest to follow your will, to follow what is right. The part of your spirit which allows you to weigh the facts and consequences and render a proper judgment is governed by **Tehuti**'s energy. And He is acting as judge between the desire and will. This is one of the reasons why He has the name **Aprehui**, Judge of the Two combatants. The Divine Wisdom, **Tehuti**, operating within your spirit guides you to follow your will, **Heru**, and put your desire, **Set**, in it's proper place. **Aprehui** has judged between the two combatants, **Heru** or **Heq** and **Set** or **Smai-Ur**. **Heru**, your will to do what is right has now been appointed ruler, **Heq**. He has been given rulership over the direction of your life.

The stories about ismail/ishmael being a rough man of the desert were stolen from the knowledge of the Gods, where **Set** is the God whose hot spiritual forces on Earth govern the desert. **Set** or **Smai-Ur** has been invoked by Afurakanu/Afuraitkaitnut as the god of the desert for thousands of years. **Set** is one of the Spiritual-Forces operating through the planet mercury which is very close to the Sun, and thus one of the hottest and driest planets. **Set**'s energy also operates through the gonads which are the ovaries in the female and the testicles of the male. It is from this region that the body becomes "fired" up. It is the seat of aggression in the person.

There was never and ibrahim, ishak and ismail. These fictional characters, and their false life-stories are perversions of the names and functions of Gods in Nature. The Divine Forces operating through the Moon, the Sun and Earth, the planet mercury and the deserts of Earth, through your pineal gland, your heart and cardiovascular system, your nervous system and gonads, through your intuition, your will and your desire, these Divine Forces, **Tehuti**, **Heru** and **Set**, and their titles **Aprehui, Heq**, and **Smai-Ur** were perverted by the whites and their offspring into a scheme aimed to make Afurakanu/Afuraitkaitnut believe white people have inherited a special spiritual connection and covenant with god which in fact the whites and their offspring do not have, have never had, and will never have.

Tehuti (Uprehui) **Heru (Heq)** **Set (Smai-Ur)**

Up reḥui, "judge of the two men" (Horus and Set), a title of the priest of Thoth of Hermopolis Parva.

[Title of **Tehuti** *and* of a Priest of Tehuti]

Rehui – The Two Combatants (**Heru** and **Set**)

Ḥeq, Rec. 36, 67, , ruler, governor, director, prince; plur.

Heq (Sheq, Ishak)

Smi,
"Slayer"—a name of Set; pl **Sma-ur**

Sma Ur: Title of a bull, a form of **Set**, who is sacrificed to restore Divine Order.

Afurakani/Afuraitkaitnit Ancestral Religion – 3.

The whites and their offspring attempted to force Afurakanu/Afuraitkaitnut into the false belief that god sent white people a liberator who was a messenger, prophet and a lawgiver. They did this by creating a fictional ancestor and claiming that god gave him the divine laws which they should live by. They claimed that the fictional character was proof of the covenant that god had made with them as a people. The fictional character was given the name moshe or moses.

moses never existed. The term moshe or moses, is taken from the name **Maakher** [maa-sher], which is another title of the God **Tehuti**. In the language of Kamit, **Maakher** is composed of: **maa** meaning *truth, law* and **kher** meaning: *voice, word.* Once who has the title **maakher** is thus one who is *true of word*; *one who voices or speaks the Divine Law.* For tens of thousands of years, Afurakanu/Afuraitkaitnut have communicated with the God **Tehuti** and invoked His Spirit under His title and function **Maakher** or **Smaakher**. This title and function was corrupted from **Maakher** into moshe [maa-she] and moses by the whites.

Tehuti, the Spirit-Force in Creation that transmits the Divine Wisdom of **Amen-Amenet** to us, functions as a messenger of the Supreme Being. The words of **Tehuti** are thus the *true words/truthful voice* of the Supreme Being. **Tehuti** is thus the original **Maakher**, *truthful of voice and word,* Who has the ability to make others **maakher** or *true of voice and word* [**s-***to make,* **maakher**, **smaakher**]. When you receive an intuition, knowledge of what is right and how it relates to your situation and your function in Creation, you have received a truthful voice to be guided by. This intuition is **Tehuti** transmitting the Divine Wisdom of **Amen-Amenet** to your spirit. **Tehuti** executes the same function as He operates through the Moon, reflecting and transmitting the Divine light of the Sun to us. **Tehuti** executes the same function as He operates through your pineal gland, receiving the energy of sunlight and moonlight through the gland, then transmitting this energy to the substances within your body that require it.

The whites created a fictional character, gave it the name moshe, and claimed that he was a white human being who became the lawgiver, after having received the law from god on the mountain. He would then come to the people and transmit the law of god to the people. moshe becomes the messenger of god. aaron was ordered by god to be the assistant and helper of moshe. This story of moshe going up on the mountain to talk to god, who appears in the form of a divine light or burning bush, and receiving the law was stolen from the knowledge of the Gods, where **Tehuti** is asked by **Ra**, the Creator, to come with Him to a mountainous region which was a distance from Heaven. **Ra**, the Creative Spirit, takes the form of a God of Light, and thus has the name **Aakhu** or **Ra Aakhu**. While **Tehuti** or **Maakher**, is with **Ra** in His Light-Form, **Ra** instructs **Tehuti** (**Maakher**) to write down what is in the spirit world. This is why another title of Tehuti is An-Maat, meaning scribe of the Divine Law. Ra then makes **Tehuti** (**Maakher**) His chief messenger and gives **Tehuti** (**Maakher**) an assistant. This assistant is the God who takes the form of a sacred baboon whose name is **Anan** [ah-nahn]. **Anan** is a Spirit-Force in Creation that functions by giving sounds to spiritual messages transmitted by **Tehuti**. In your spirit, **Anan** is one of the forces that enables you to give sounds to, or verbalize, your spiritual intuitions and thoughts, into a form that you can communicate to others. **Anan** enables you to use sounds, or put into words, what you are experiencing internally, so that others can understand. **Anan** is the name which the whites stole and perverted into aaran [ah-rahn] or aaron, the assistant to the fictional moses/moshe. Thus, **Anan**, the Divine assistant of **Tehuti**, whose spirit takes the form of a **baboon**, was perverted by the whites into a fictional white male, aaron.

The name **Tehuti** was pronounced by some Afurakanu/Afuraitkaitnut as **Tahut**. This was corrupted by the whites from **Tahut** in dawud [daoud]. dawud into dawid. dawid into daveed and david. The story of god making david king was stolen by the whites from the knowledge of the Gods, where **Ra** makes **Tehuti** King of Earth. The Sun rules the Earth during the day, yet the light of the Moon rules the Earth at night. The Moon is called **Iah** in Kamit, and **Tehuti** when operating through the Moon thus has the title **Iah-Tehuti**.

The bird sacred to **Tehuti** is the bird called **Habui**. **Tehuti** is usually depicted as a God with the body of an Afurakani man and the head of the bird **Habui**. The name **Habui** is also a title of **Tehuti** which was corrupted by the whites from **Habui** to Habweh and yahweh. The name of the Moon, **Iah**, was corrupted into jah. **Tehuti** was also pronounced Jehuti [**Djehuti**] and Jahut in certain dialects. This was further corrupted into jahuta (jahuda) and used by the whites as a name for their fictional character yahuda or judah and his fictional tribe, the tribe of yahuda or tribe of judah.

The entire story about god giving the followers of moshe a promised land wherein food from heaven would be placed, is stolen from the knowledge of the Gods where **Ra**, the Creator, creates the Divine field called **Sekhet-Hetep** or Field of Peace, wherein He places Divine vegetation from heaven called **Aaru**, which is for the followers of **Tehuti** to feed on. This great field called **Sekhet-Hetep** and **Sekhet-Aaru** is actually a name for the Ancestral realm in the language of ancient Kamit. A peaceful existence in the Ancestral realm is an extension of a peaceful existence throughout life on Earth, for all those Afurakanu/Afuraitkaitnut who live in harmony with Divine Law, for all of us who live to execute our Divine function in the World. When we follow the guidance of **Tehuti** (**Maakher**), He Who is the Spirit-Force of Divine Wisdom operating within our spirits, we secure a harmonious life in the physical world and also a harmonious life in the Ancestral realm. The whites perverted the knowledge of the Ancestral realm, called **Sekhet-Hetep** or Divine Field of Peace, into an actual strip of land in palestine called the promised land. They made their fictional white character moshe lead a group of fictional white characters out of egypt to this fictional promised land.

For tens of thousands of years. Afurakanu/Afuraitkaitnut learned to harmonize our activities with the phases of the Moon. By being receptive to the energy of the Moon at night, you can be lead into a peaceful world, the dreamworld. The God **Tehuti** uses the Moon as a physical transmitter of His Spiritual Energy. **Tehuti**'s energy operating through the Moon will affect your dreams so that conflicts within your spirit can be resolved through your dreams. Upon waking you will have instructions or ideas about how to resolve conflicts in life. Following **Tehuti** (**Maakher**) leads to a place of peace, the dreamworld. What you are fed in this place of peace, brings peace to your life. This is one way that **Tehuti** (**Maakher**) leads Afurakanu/Afuraitkaitnut to a place of peace, where food from heaven, energy from the Moon, is given to us to feed on. Those who do not harmonize their activities with the energy of the Moon can be negatively affected by its energy. When a full Moon appears, they who live stressful or disordered lives can become disruptive towards others.

In your body, **Tehuti**'s energy operates through the pineal gland. The pineal gland is stimulated by sunlight. It responds to sunlight by releasing a hormone in the body during the day that affects the detoxification of the body. The pineal gland also releases a hormone in the body at night that affects the production of **Ka-Nu/Kat-Nut**, melanin, in your body. **Ka-Nu/Kat-Nut**, melanin, is the chemical in your body that gives you your color. Yet, it is also a chemical that takes the energy of sunlight and transforms it into food or energy for the cells of the body to utilize. **Tehuti** (**Maakher**) receives the power from **Ra** and uses that power to free the people and cleanse them. They then receive food from heaven in the **Sekhet Hetep**, or Divine Field of Peace. So it is with the pineal gland, **Tehuti**, which receives the power of sunlight, **Ra**, and uses that power to secrete a hormone which works to free the body's cells from waste and detoxifies them. The body then receives the hormone at night that affects the production of **Ka-Nu/Kat-Nut**, melanin. **Ka-Nu/Kat-Nut**, melanin, transforms sunlight into food or energy that the body's cells can use. This food or energy which was derived from the power of sunlight, **Ra**, is the food from heaven, **Aaru**, given to the cells of the body. [milk and honey, lunar light (milk) and solar light (honey)].

Thus, following **Tehuti** (**Maakher**), Divine Wisdom, leads to peaceful existence in this world and peaceful existence in the Ancestral realm. The whites perverted this understanding into a fictional belief that whites who followed moshe were lead to a promised land in palestine, a land of milk and honey, where they could live in peace. The whites desired to make Afurakanu/Afuraitkaitnut believe that whites were god's chosen people and were given a land to settle in by god. The land of palestine is in fact an Afurakani/Afuraitkaitnit country that the whites invaded and desire to have complete control of. **The whites and their offspring are not chosen, have never been chosen, and will never be chosen by Divinity. Disorder is never Divinely chosen, it is only Divinely rejected.**

The entire story of moshe being born as the child who would become the liberator of the oppressed people, of his being hidden in a basket as a baby and floated down the river to be found by the daughter of the king, is a perversion of the knowledge of the Gods **Heru** and **Tehuti**.

Maakher means *true word/truthful, lawful voice.* Yet, another meaning of the word **maa** is: *bank or shore of a river.* Another meaning of the word **kher** is: *under.* Thus, another meaning of the ancient title **maakher** in the language of Kamit is: *under the bank or shore of a river.* To be under the shore of a river is to be in the water. This is the origin of the name **maakher** being associated with on who was in the water, or under the riverbank. **Tehuti** is a Spirit-Force in Creation Who is the son of **Ra**, the Creator, and Who comes into being in Creation from out of the great watery Substance of the Blackness of Space.

The God **Heru** is also a Spirit-Force in Creation who has the title **maakher**. **This title is given to Heru by Tehuti**. **Heru**'s Mother, the Goddess **Auset**, places **Heru** in the river in Northern Kamit in order to hide **Heru** from **Set**, who was the evil King of Kamit at the time. The whites and their offspring applied this information to their fictional character moshe.

Tehuti (Maakher) and **Anan**
("moshe/moses and aaron")

Original image from stele of **Nefer Renpet**

Tehuti as the bird **Habui**

Iah Tehuti

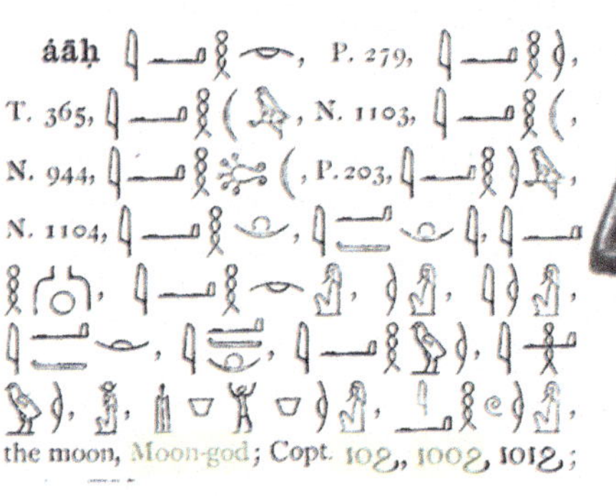

āāḥ, P. 279, T. 365, N. 1103, N. 944, P. 203, N. 1104, the moon, Moon-god; Copt. ιοϩ, ιοοϩ, ιοιϩ;

Aah (Iah) – *Coptic:* **IOH, IAH**

Moon God: **Iah (Yah)**
also: **Iahu (Yahw)**:

heb, Rev. 11, 188, ibis; Copt. ϩιβωι.

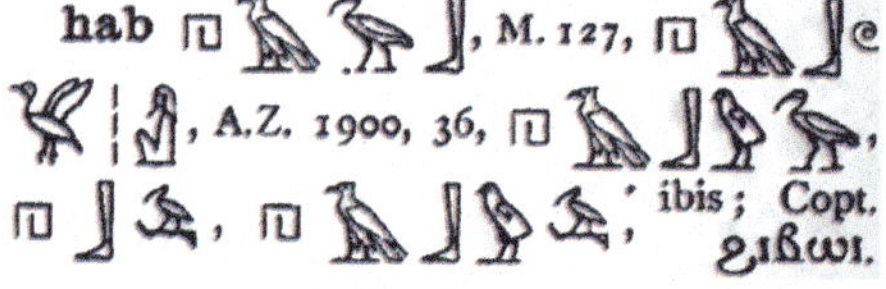

hab, M. 127, A.Z. 1900, 36, ibis; Copt. ϩιβωι.

[The *Coptic* spelling here is key: **ϩιβωι. HIBAWI**. the **ω** is an 'aw' sound in Coptic. **Habu, Habui, Habawi** are all variations as attested in the medutu. The spelling Iahu or Yahw (Yhw) for the *Moon God* is the origin of **yhwh**, yahweh.]

Ṭeḥuti (Tcheḥuti), U. 2, P. 615, M. 783, N. 1142, A.Z. 1900, 35, Ani 15, 47, the ibis-god, the scribe of the gods; Copt. ϴοογτ, ϴωϴ.

Tehuti/Tahut/Djehuti (Temple of **Seti**. Photo by author)

[The *Coptic* spelling is key: **ϴοογτ Thoout** from **Tahut** – corrupted into **Dawud, Daoud, Dwd**]

maā-kheru "true of voice, or word"

Afurakani/Afuraitkaitnit Ancestral Religion – 4.

The whites and their offspring attempted to force Afurakanu/Afuraitkaitnut into the false belief that whites had a special relationship with god by creating a fictional son for god and claiming that this fictional white character was the savior of the world. They attempted to make Afurakanu/Afuraitkaitnut believe that our happiness and well being in life and after death is absolutely dependent on us believing in and worshipping the fictional white character. The whites desired to identify themselves with god through their fictional character and therefore force Afurakanu/Afuraitkaitnut into the false belief that whites and their offspring are divine or have god's blessing no matter what they have done to Afurakanu/Afuraitkaitnut. The whites attempted to control every aspect of the lives of Afurakanu/Afuraitkaitnut through introducing this fictional character that teaches we should love all of our neighbors. These disordered fictional teachings they attached to their fictional character are designed to make Afurakanu/Afuraitkaitnut accept the invasion, destruction, abuse and control from whites and their offspring, and view our suffering and their control as divinely ordered from god. They gave the name jesus, yeshua or hesus to this fictional white character.

jesus never existed. The name jesus, yeshua or hesus is taken from the name **Khensu**, which is one of the titles of the God **Heru**. In the language of Kamit, **Khensu** is composed of **khi**: which means *child* and nsu: which means *royal, Divine, king,* and *king of southern Kamit.* **Khensu** thus means *Divine royal child.* For tens of thousands of years Afurakanu/Afuraitkaitnut have communicated with the God **Heru** and invoked His Spirit under His title **Khensu**. This title of **Heru** was corrupted by the whites from **Khensu**, into hesus, yeshua and jesus and applied to their fictional white character.

The God **Heru** is a Spirit Force in Creation Whose energy is operating through the core of the Earth, and the core of the Sun. In your body, **Heru's** energy operates through your cardiovascular system whose major organ is the heart. In your spirit, **Heru's** energy operates through your will.

The Divine Energy of the Great Spirit, **Ra/Rait**, flows throughout all things in Creation. The God **Heru** is a Spirit Force in Creation Who regulates the flow of this Divine energy so that all things in Creation can receive their share of this energy of **Ra/Rait** and use it to execute their functions in the World. **Heru** executes this function as He operates through your heart and cardiovascular system, regulating the flow of blood from the heart to all cells in the body, so that all cells can receive the energy they need to execute their functions in the body. **Heru** executes the same function as He operates through your will, regulating your energy, your actions, towards various behaviors that allow you to execute your function in the world. **Heru** executes the same function as He operates through the core of the Sun, regulating the flow of solar energy from the Sun to the planets of the solar system, so that the planets can receive the energy they need to execute their functions in the solar system. **Heru** executes the same function as He operates through the solar energy at the core of Earth, regulating the flow of energy from the core towards the surface of Earth so that the water, sky, plants, animals, minerals and humans can receive this energy and use it to execute their functions in Nature.

Heru is thus the Spirit Force in Creation that takes the energy of the Great Spirit, **Ra/Rait**, and regulates its flow to us all. **Heru** is at the heart or core of all things including animals, plants, planets, stars. The knowledge of this God, this powerful Spirit in Nature, was corrupted by the whites and applied to their fictional white character jesus who they made to be a white male, god's only begotten son, who is directly related to white people and teaches us to love whites, our enemies, as we love ourselves.

The root of the name **Heru** is **Her**. **Her** or **Heri**, in the language of Kamit means, *Chief, King, He Who is above, leader.* This is one of the reasons why **Heru** has the title *Heri* or King. The Sun also has the title as it is the *Heri* or king of the solar system. Your heart is the *Heri* or king in your body. Your will is your *Heri* or king of your actions. The core of Earth is the *Heri* or king of the planet. Your heart, your will, the core of the Earth and the core of the Sun are also hidden from view, and the Divine energy they regulate is invisible or hidden. The term **Seshta**, in the language of Kamit means that which is hidden, secret or sacred. This is why Heru also has the title **Heri Seshta**, which means king or chief, *Heri*, of that which is hidden, secret or sacred, *Seshta*. This title **Heri Seshta** was also given to some priests and priestesses in Kamit. This title was corrupted by the whites from **Heri Seshta** to **Heri Seshtos**, **Kerishtos** and **Christus** or **Christ**. Thus, **Heru** or **Khensu** the **Heri Seshta** was corrupted into hesus the kerishtos and jesus the christ.

As the whites manufactured their fictional white savior, they used the names and titles of the God **Heru**, and the knowledge of the God to create a fictional life story for the new white character.

The entire story of the son of god being born of a virgin, who would grow up to lead the people, be killed and become resurrected as the savior of the world was stolen by the whites from the knowledge of the God **Heru**, His Mother the Goddess **Auset**, His Father the God **Ausar**, and His Father's brother the God **Set**.

Ausar is a God in Creation Whose Spirit operates through the star system of **Sah**, called Orion, through the Moon, and through the black soil substance of Earth. In your body, **Ausar's** energy operates through your pituitary gland. **Ausar** operates as the masculine aspect of your soul, your **Ka**. **Ausar** is thus the Force dwelling within your spirit that is always rooted in what is in harmony with Divine order. **Ausar** is a God Whose Spirit has the ability to unify the functions or operations of the various Forces in Nature. The God **Ausar** was thus ordered by the Great Spirit to operate on Earth and teach Afurakanu/Afuraitkaitnut, by example, how to live in harmony with Divine law.

Auset is a Goddess in Creation Whose Spirit operates through the star system **Sapadet**, or Sirius, through the Moon, and through the river waters of Earth. In your body, **Auset's** energy operates through the vagina and uterus structure in the female and the penis and prostate gland of the male. **Auset** operates as the feminine aspect of your soul, your **Kait**. **Auset** is thus the Force dwelling within your spirit that makes you receptive to what is in harmony with Divine order. **Auset** is a Goddess Whose Spirit has the ability to maintain the unity of functions and operations of the Forces in Nature. The Goddess **Auset** was thus ordered by the Great Spirit to operate on Earth and teach Afurakanu/Afuraitkaitnut, by example, how to maintain their living in harmony with Divine law.

The God **Set** is the brother of **Ausar** and **Auset**. The God **Set** is a Spirit Force in Creation Whose energy operates through the star system **Meskheti**, called the Great Bear, the planet Mercury and the deserts or red hot lands of Earth. In your body, **Set's** energy operates through the nervous system, and the gonads, which are the testes of the male and the ovaries of the female. In your spirit, **Set's** energy governs your desire. Desire can be for that which is in harmony with Divine law, yet desire can also be misguided, making that which is disharmonious seem attractive.

In **Afuraka/Afuraitkait**, the Great Spirit, directed the God **Ausar** and the Goddess **Auset** to operate amongst the population of Afurakanu/Afuraitkaitnut and guide our spirits to living in harmony with Divine law and how to maintain the life of harmony. **Ausar** and **Auset** became King and Queen in Afuraka/Afuraitkait. As Afurakanu/Afuraitkaitnut in Kamit and Keneset lived under the government of the King **Ausar** and the Queen **Auset**, we learned the Divine balance of male and female. **Ausar** and **Auset** instructed us in spiritual cultivation, as well as the cultivation of the land. We began to apply what we learned under the guidance of **Ausar** and

Auset and we built great civilizations around the world reflecting the Divine harmony of Creation. Our culture is a reflection of the Divine balance of male and female, **Ausar** and **Auset** in all things.

Yet, the God **Set** desired to govern Kamit Himself, in place of the God **Ausar**. **Set** therefore plotted and killed **Ausar**, disposed of His Body in the river, took over the rule of Kamit, and began a tyrannical, disharmonious government rooted in misguided desire, disorder, lust.

After the murder of **Ausar**, the Goddess **Auset** was forced out of Her role as Queen of Kamit. She searched tirelessly for the Body of Her Husband **Ausar** that He may be given a proper burial. When She found the Body of Her Husband, **Auset** performed ritual. She began to invoke the Spirit of **Ausar** from His existence in the Ancestral realm. Through ritual, **Auset** communicated with Her Husband and was drawn to His Spirit. Through Their Divine Spiritual union **Auset** became pregnant. Because of Her devotion to Her Husband, **Auset** was referred to under the title **Merit**, which means *beloved* in the language of Kamit. She was called **Merit Ausar**, or the *beloved of* **Ausar**. The whites corrupted this name **Merit** into *mary* and *maryam* and gave it to their fictional white female character. The union of the Spirit of the God **Ausar** with the Goddess **Auset** which resulted in **Auset** becoming pregnant with Her Son, the God **Khensu Heru**, was corrupted by the whites into the immaculate conception and virgin birth by a fictional white character named *mary* who would give birth to a fictional white boy, hesus or jesus whose father was god.

The Goddess **Auset** was informed by the God **Tehuti** that the Son She was carrying in Her womb would grow to be strong. He would defeat and remove **Set** from power and reestablish Divine law and order. As Divine Heir to the throne, the son of the God **Ausar** would restore the Divine government of His Father. **Auset** was directed to give birth to Her Son and raise Him away from the seat of power of the government, because **Set** had declared that all male children would be killed. **Set** knew that the Son of the God **Ausar** was going to be born. He knew that the Son of **Ausar** was the rightful Heir to the throne who would challenge the evil government and abolish it. **Set** thus sought to kill the child as soon as he was born. However, **Auset** followed the directions of **Tehuti**. She gave birth to **Khensu Heru** and hid away in the swamps of Northern Kamit. The whites corrupted this knowledge of the Gods and Goddess into a prophecy to a fictional white female, mary, by an angel that she would give birth to the son of god. The whites made their fictional mary go into northern Egypt or Kamit to hide her fictional son jesus. This is also one of the reasons why the whites made their fictional moses to be hidden in the swamps of Northern Egypt as a baby. The whites also corrupted the knowledge of the God **Set** into the fictional account of the evil king *herod* who decided to put to death all newborn boys, so that the savior child would never live to challenge the government. The whites created a fictional character called the devil who they made into a spirit of absolute evil. They corrupted the name **Set** or **Seti** into Satan and applied it to their fictional devil.

The God **Set** eventually found that **Heru** had been born. He found out where **Heru** was and had him killed. One of **Set's** associates stabbed **Heru**. When **Auset** found that Her Son **Heru** had been killed, She went to embrace the deceased Body of Her Son and lamented. Her Sister, the Goddess **Nebt Het** also lamented with Her.

Nebt Het is a Goddess in Nature Whose Spirit also operates through the star system of **Sapadet**, called Sirius, through the planet Venus, and the rain waters of Earth. In your body, **Nebt Het** operates through your kidneys. In your spirit, **Nebt Het** governs your emotions.

As **Auset** and **Nebt Het** lamented the death of **Heru**, the Goddess **Serqet** told **Auset** to call on **Ra**. **Auset** called on **Ra** the Creator, and **Ra** sent the God **Tehuti** from heaven to cause **Heru** to be resurrected. The whites corrupted this episode into the two fictional marys, lamenting the death of the fictional jesus, and learning of his resurrection from an angel of the lord. **Auset**, has the title **Merit**, meaning beloved, yet **Merit** is also a title held by **Nebt Het**. For thousands of years Afurakanu/Afuraitkaitnut have communicated with these Goddesses and invoked **Auset** and **Nebt Het** under the title **Merit**.

After **Heru's** resurrection, there was great rejoicing because **Auset** saw in Him one Who would answer for His Father. **Heru**, along with another warrior God called **Heru Behudet** the son of **Ra**, led a great army to victory over **Set**, removing **Set** from government. **Heru** then assumed His rightful place as ruler of the world. The whites corrupted this episode, by applying these acts to their fictional character jesus, claiming that he would overcome satan with an army of angels and become ruler of the world. **Heru** and **Heru Behudet** fighting **Set** together, was applied to the fictional *messiah* and *mahdi* of the whites, who come to destroy the rule of satan.

Heru, with the Goddesses **Auset** and **Nebt Het**, performed a ritual to resurrect the God **Ausar**. **Ausar** was resurrected and His Spirit left the Ancestral realm to rejoin with the Great Spirit, **Ra/Rait**, to operate as a God in Nature. This knowledge of **Heru** or **Khensu**, along with **Auset** and **Nebt Het** resurrecting **Ausar** was also corrupted by the whites. The name **Ausar** was perverted into Osiris by the whites. The ancient title **Ur**, meaning great or the great, in the language of Kamit was corrupted by the whites into **L [UL]**. The God **Ausar**, under the title **Ur-Ausar**, was corrupted into L-Osiris. L-Osiris became L-azarus and Lazarus. The fictional jesus, with two marys behind him as their brother lazarus is resurrected, is a perversion of the knowledge of **Heru**, with **Auset** or **Merit** and **Nebt Het** or **Merit** behind Him, as They resurrect Their brother the God **Ausar**. Lazarus comes out in bandages, or mummified, because the God **Ausar** was always depicted in the form of a mummified God in Kamit.

In Northern Kamit, a major city called **Tata**, was sacred to **Ausar**, **Auset** and **Heru**. In this city, They were often referred to under the names **Ba Neb Tata**, **Hat Mehit** and **Heru pa khart**. **Ausar**, the Father was referred to as **Ba Neb Tata**, meaning the Ram, lord of the city Tata. **Ba Neb Tata** came to be pronounced Ba ne Tata or BanTera. The whites corrupted the title Ba ne Tata in to Pantara or Pandira. **Ausar** was thus referred to as Pandira, and His Son **Heru** was called **Heru**, son of Pandira. **Heru** or **Khensu**, the son of Pandira, was a title stolen by the whites and used for their fictional character who never existed called jesus or yeshua ben pandira, meaning jesus son of Pandira.

Khensu in human form

Khensu in His Hawk-headed form

Khensu

Khensu/Chensu/Jensu/Yensu/Iesu/Yeshua

Ḥeri seshta

Heriseshta/Kherisshta/Kherishta/Khrishtos
Khristus/Christus/Christ

Ausar **Auset** **Heru**

Khensu holding **heq** *(shepard's crook)* and **Merit** (**Auset**) holding baby **Khensu**

Merit and **Khensu** corrupted into **mary** and **yeshu/hesus 1,400** years later

Heru operates through the core of the Sun. The cycles of the Sun, **Heru's** cycles, were used to create a fictional life story for the fictional white character jesus. Every year at Spring, near March 21, the day consists of nearly 12 hours of sunlight and 12 hours of darkness. Everyday after the beginning of Spring, the days become longer and longer until on or near June 21 the days consist of approximately 15 hours of sunlight and 9 hours of darkness. Starting on or near June 24, the days become gradually shorter and shorter. By the beginning of Fall, near September 22, days and nights are again nearly 12 hours each. Daylight continues to diminish after the beginning of Fall until the first day of Winter, on or near December 21, when daylight is approximately 9 hours, and night lasts approximately 15 hours. Between December 21 and December 24 the 9 hour days and 15 hour nights continue. On December 25, the days begin to get longer and the nights become shorter. When March 21 arrives, the days and nights are approximately equal again at 12 hours each. When the daylight, the light of the Sun begins to increase on December 25, our Ancestresses and Ancestors recognized the birth of a new Sun. the Sun, which was created by the Supreme Being, was said to have been born. The Supreme Being's Sun is born every December 25. This Sun is the light of the World. The whites corrupted this knowledge into a fictional account of a white boy, called god's son, the light of the world , being born on December 25. Between December 25 and March 21, the sunlight is increasing, yet there are still more hours of darkness than there are hours of light. Darkness, or **Set**, rules the world as king. When the daylight increases to the point of equality with darkness on or near March 21, the powers of light and darkness are equal at 12 hours each. At this time on Earth, the Sun can be seen positioned on the intersection of the Earth's celestial equator and the Earth's ecliptic, which is Earth's pathway around the Sun. When the Sun is seen to be positioned on the intersection of the equator and the ecliptic, the Sun is said to be positioned on a cross. After March 21, the sunlight increases while darkness begins to decrease. The position of the Sun is no longer on the intersection of the equator and the ecliptic. The Sun is then said to have overcome its hanging or death on the cross. By June 21, the beginning of Summer, the Sun rises at its highest point in the sky. It is said that the Sun has ascended into Heaven to be with the Father.

This cycle of the Sun, **Heru's** cycle in nature, was corrupted by the whites into a story of a fictional white male who was born on December 25, struggled with the devil, the prince of darkness and evil king of the world, was hung on a cross, overcame death and ascended into the sky or heaven to sit on the right hand of his father.

The Goddess **Auset** operates through the star **Sapadet**, called *Sirius*, which is the brightest star in the sky. As **Auset Sapadet**, She is called *the great provider*, because of the energy She transmits to the Sun and Earth. The God **Ausar** operates through the star system of **Sah**, called *Orion*, and can be found together with the star **Sapadet**. As **Ausar Sah**, He is said to make Heaven and Earth fruitful. Together, **Ausar**, operating through the star system **Sah**, and **Auset**, operating through the star system **Sapadet**, are Husband and Wife transmitting Their energy to our solar system which develops the energy of **Heru**, the core of Sun and Earth.

As the Goddess **Auset** operates through the star system **Sapadet**, She is called the Queen of **Sapadet**. In the language of **Kamit**, **Sapad** means *to provide; provider*. This title was corrupted by the whites from the Queen of **Sapadet** into the Queen of **Sapa**, **Shaba** or *Sheba*. As the God **Ausar** operates through the star system **Sah**, He is called **Heri Meht**. In the language of Kamit, **Heri**, means *King, Chief or Leader* and **Meht** means *North or Northern territory*. **Heri Meht** thus means *King of the Northern territory*. North Kamit was sacred to **Ausar** as the region where He made His transition to the **Sekhet Hetep** to rule as King and also where He was resurrected. The title **Heri**, was corrupted by the whites into **Hori**, **Shori**, **Sholi**, **Soli** and *Sol*. **Meht** was corrupted into *Men*. This title **Heri Meht** was thus corrupted into **Hori Meh**, **Sholi Men**, *solaiman* and *solomon*. The two star systems **Sapadet** and **Sah** change positions in the sky and ultimately unite with one another. This union of **Sapadet** and **Sah**, is the union of the Goddess **Auset** and the God **Ausar** in the sky. This is the union of **Auset** the Queen of **Sapadet**, and **Ausar** or **Heri Meht**, King of the North. When **Auset** and **Ausar** unite through the two stars **Sapadet** and **Sah**, They occasion the appearance of a star called **Heru am Tuat**. Because the God **Heru** operates through this star He has been called the son of **Auset Sapadet** and **Ausar Sah** for thousands of years. As Queen, **Auset Sapadet** also has the title **Rekhit**, meaning *wise one* in the language of Kamit. **Heru am Tuat**, the star born of the wise Queen **Auset Rekhit** is thus called *Son of* **Rekhit**, meaning *Son of the wise one*. The whites corrupted the title **Rekhit** into **Lekhim** and *Lekh*. In the language of Kamit, **per** or **perat**, means *product of, or offspring of*. **Perat Rekhit** thus means *son or offspring of the wise one,* **Rekhit**. The whites corrupted **per** and **perat** into **ben** and **bayna** and **ibn**. Thus the description of **Heru am Tuat** as the son or offspring of **Auset Rekhit**, was corrupted from **Perat Rekhit** into, *bayna lekhim*, *menelekh* and *menelik*, the son of solomon and sheba. **solomon, sheba and menelik never existed.** The names of these fictional characters and the fictional life stories attached to them are perversions, by the whites and their offspring, of the names and titles of **Ausar**, **Auset** and **Heru** as they function through the star systems of **Sah**, and **Sapadet**.

In your spirit, **Heru** governs your will, **Set** governs your desire. **Ausar** and **Auset** govern your soul, the Divine conscious part of your spirit. When you allow the Divine part of your spirit, to guide your actions you live well. This is **Ausar** and **Auset** ruling the country as King and Queen. However, sometimes you allow your misguided desires, or lust, to control your actions. This is **Set**, killing **Ausar**, in order to take over the reigns of control. As you live controlled by lust and misguided desire, you cause yourself to suffer. This is **Set's** rule causing the people to be oppressed. At some point, you decide to make a change. You begin to look for the proper way to live your life. This is **Auset**, looking for Her Husband **Ausar**. When you have found out the truth about how you should live, and make the decision to embrace Divine order over a lust-dominated lifestyle, this is **Auset** finding **Ausar**, embracing Him, and becoming pregnant with a new will, **Heru**, to live right. As your newly born will to live right conflicts with your lust or misguided desire, this is **Heru** and **Set**, will and desire, the two combatants fighting. When lust wins out, **Set** has killed **Heru**. When you follow your intuition and your will to live right re-emerges, this is **Heru** being resurrected from the dead by **Tehuti**. When you finally root out the lust or misguided desire, and live according to Divine law for good, **Heru** has defeated **Set** and taken over the government of your personal world. As you strive to maintain a life of harmony through seeking the guidance of your Ancestresses and Ancestors, this is **Auset**, **Heru** and **Nebt Het** resurrecting **Ausar**.

On Earth, **Ausar** as the black soil substance of Earth is in partnership with **Auset**, the river waters of Earth. Their partnership brings prosperity to the people. When the red hot desert lands of **Set** begin to expand and dry up the black soil and the rivers, the people suffer and go hungry. **Ausar** and **Auset** have been removed from rulership, and **Set** has taken over. When the river waters begin to move and expand again, and move over the black soil, the union of the two, river water and black soil, **Auset** and **Ausar**, produce vegetation, drawing on the solar energy deep within the core of Earth and within the Sun. Through the vegetation, **Heru's** energy is born into the world. The people are thus returned to prosperity and free from hunger and suffering. **Ausar** and **Auset** have produced the savior of the world. The hot weather of the desert threatens the existence of the new vegetation, and the vegetation dies as a result. Yet, the vegetation later re-emerges at a certain season. **Heru** has been killed and then resurrected. The vegetation grows into lush forests with great trees and vines that displace the desert. **Heru** has taken over the government of the world.

In your body, the pituitary gland, **Ausar's** region, is a master gland that regulates the functions of other glands. The male and female reproductive organs, **Auset's** region, have reflexive areas that are connected to all of the major organs and glands. The heart, **Heru's** region, regulates the flow of blood, and thus energy, to the various organs and structures of the body. The nervous system, and the testes of the male and ovaries of the female, **Set's** region, governs your desire to act and your sexual desire. When one is controlled by lust, they can place an over-emphasis on sexual activity. They force the body's organs and structures to feed the sex drive. The pituitary gland becomes overworked and submits to the misguided sex drive. The penis and vagina structures of the reproductive area become over worked and weakened as they submit to the misguided sex drive. The glands, organs and structures of the body are drained of their nutrients in order to support the lust of the misguided sex drive. The body becomes weakened. The immune system becomes compromised. **Set** has forced **Ausar** into submission, and **Auset** into submission, and the world or body is suffering under His government. An electric signal from the brain and pineal gland causes the reproductive organs and pituitary gland to begin to function in harmony again. The heart begins to regulate the flow of blood away from its overemphasis in the reproductive organs. Here, **Ausar** and **Auset** have reunited or realigned themselves, and **Heru** has begun to assume His role in government. When your lust fights the normal functioning of the body, there is conflict. You experience anxiety. Your heart then becomes heavy. **Set** has attacked and **Heru** has been killed. Eventually, your heart resumes its normal rhythm. **Heru** has been resurrected. **Heru** reestablishes the proper regulation of blood throughout the body. The organs and structures receive their proper nourishment again. **Set** has been defeated.

Ausar and **Auset** also function through the Moon. The Moon is called **Iah**, in the language of Kamit. **Ausar** is connected with the New Moon which is black. **Ausar** is often depicted as a perfectly Black God. As a Spirit operating through the New Moon, **Ausar** has the title **Ausar Iah**. **Auset** is connected with the Full Moon. As the light of the Moon begins from a crescent shape to expand day after day, it gradually covers the entire blackness of the New Moon, to become a Full Moon after nearly 15 days. **Auset** has just come over the perfectly Black God **Ausar**, and become a pregnant, or Full Moon, with the light of the Sun, **Heru**. **Auset**, as the full or pregnant Moon transmits that sunlight to Earth. **Heru** is thus called **Heru Iah**, or **Khensu Iah**. The light reaches Earth and the people who were in darkness. The Full Moon is then reduced to a ¾ Moon. The black crescent shape begins to expand until the entire Moon is dark after nearly 15 days. **Set** has removed the light and the people of Earth are in darkness again. **Heru** has been killed. In about 3 days, the silver light of the crescent appears from the face of the dark Moon. **Heru** or **Khensu** has resurrected on the 3rd day. The crescent light expands into a Full Moon. The light reaches the people of Earth. **Set** has been defeated. The people of Earth are no longer in darkness.

Ausar, Auset, Heru, Set, Nebt Het and **Tehuti** also operate through the lives and events that take place within the clans of Afurakanu/Afuraitkaitnut. **Ausar**, the great Black King is murdered by **Set** who is often depicted as red. The Afurakanu/Afuraitkaitnut, the great Black nations of Earth, were destroyed by misguided desire operating within a small portion of Black people controlled by lust, and a large group of reddish or white foreigners from the deserts of eurasia who were their followers. **Set** takes the body of **Ausar** and throws it in the river, then proceeds to take control of the country. Here, the white foreigners of europe and asia take the bodies of Black people and throw them in the water. This is the beginning of the slave trade of millions of Afurakanu/Afuraitkaitnut who are forced into ships and sent into the waters of the Ocean. The white foreigners then take control of the Black nations and create unlawful rules and regulations. **Auset** is forced out of Her role as Queen and goes to search for Her Husband. This is the remnant of Black people who were forced out of their countries, yet survived the wars and escaped slavery. These Afurakanu/Afuraitkaitnut would search for their sisters and brothers who were still in bondage. **Auset** finds the body of **Ausar**, performs ritual, communicates with His Spirit and becomes pregnant. Afurakanu/Afuraitkaitnut who had escaped slavery would find their sisters and brothers on the plantations and seek to unite with them and build alliances with them to plan for freedom from the white slavers. The God **Tehuti** tells **Auset** that Her son will grow up to defeat **Set**, and that She must hide away in the swamps to raise **Heru** away from the seat of government. Afurakanu/Afuraitkaitnut who escaped slavery set up their own sovereign independent nations in the swamps and forests and mountains away from the plantations. We gave birth to children who would grow to become those who will defeat the rule of the white slavers. **Set** finds out about **Heru's** birth and has Him killed. The white slavers plot against the Afurakani/Afuraitkaitnit males and females creating drugs, and diseases that we use to destroy ourselves and thus maintain white rule. The Goddesses **Auset** and **Nebt Het** find **Heru** murdered and lament His death. The mothers of Afurakani/Afuraitkaitnit males, as well as females, lament as they bury their children daily as a result of violence, drugs and diseases created by the whites. The Goddess **Serqet** tells **Auset** to call on **Ra**. **Ra** sends **Tehuti** to cause the resurrection of **Heru**. We are reminded by our Ancestresses and Ancestors that our liberation is only possible through the invocation of the Goddesses and Gods. We begin to invoke **Ra/Rait** and the Spirits of the Goddesses and Gods, and the sons and daughters of Afurakanu/Afuraitkaitnut begin to wake up. **Heru**, with **Heru Behudet** the son of **Ra**, defeat **Set** and establish Divine order in the world. The children of those who were captured and enslaved away from Afuraka/Afuraitkait, are uniting with the children of those who were colonized in Afuraka/Afuraitkait and are defeating the whites and their offspring and their false religions and perverse culture for good. **Auset**, **Nebt Het** and **Heru** resurrect **Ausar,** and **Ausar** joins **Ra** in Heaven as a God in Nature. The children of those Afurakanu/Afuraitkaitnut who were separated from Afuraka/Afuraitkait begin to evoke the Spirits of the Ancestresses and Ancestors, Who then come forth and openly exercise their jurisdiction over the lives of Their children.

jesus never existed. mary never existed. jeshua ben pandira never existed. whites have no special connection to god, nor have they been visited by god's fictional only begotten son. The names of the Gods and Goddesses that were corrupted by the whites and applied to their fictional characters are names of Spiritual Forces in Creation that have always operated through the Sun, Moon, planets, stars, our physical bodies and our spirits and continue to operate through the families and clans of Afurakanu/Afuraitkaitnut.

Nebt Het

Set

Auset-Sapadet

Sah, the abode of Ausar

Heru (Pera Rekhit)

Åst-Sepṭit, Isis + Sothis.

Åsår-Saḥ, B.D. 142, 8, Osiris + Orion.

Ḥeru-Sepṭ, U. 465, P. 31, N. 650, M. 149, Horus-Sothis, Horus the Dog-star.

Rekhit, B.D.G. 461, knowledge personified.

Rekhit, Thes. 99, a title of Isis-Sothis.

per-t, Metternich Stele 55, exit, issue, what comes forth, manifestation, outbreak of fire, offspring ; plur.

*Sothis and Sirius are greek corruptions of **Spdt** (**Septit, Sapadet**).

Afurakani/Afuraitkaitnit Ancestral Religion – 5.

The whites and their offspring attempted to force **Afurakanu/Afuraitkaitnut** into the false belief that whites had a special relationship with god by creating a fictional prophet who was to bring the true religion of god to the people. They desire to control the actions of Afurakanu/Afuraitkaitnut by forcing the false belief that there is only one god and only one true religion. The whites desired to make Afurakanu/Afuraitkaitnut stop our communication with the Great God and the Great Goddess, **Amen** and **Amenet**, our communication with the Goddesses and Gods, our Ancestral Spirits and the Nature Spirits, so that we would follow the fictional white god, its fictional prophet and by extension we would follow the whites themselves. The name of the fictional prophet and their false religion is called muhammed and islam.

prophet muhammed never existed. The term muhammed is a term the whites stole from the God Who is the male Spiritual Force that operates through the great river in **Kamit** often called the **Nile**. Because it very rarely rains in Kamit, the people of Kamit are greatly dependent on the great river for the growth of their crops, the well being of animals and themselves. The people depend on the great river for their survival and their ability to live a good life.

The great river of Kamit is the longest river in the world. The name of the God of the river in the language of Kamit is **Hap** or **Hapi**. The great river **Hap** flows through the entire country of Kamit. In the language of Kamit, **Reset** means south and **Meht** means north. Because the God **Hap** governed the entire length of the country, the people referred to this God as **Hap Reset**, meaning **Hap** of the *south,* as He flows in the southern part of the country, and **Hap Meht**, meaning **Hap** of the *north*, as He flows in the northern part of the country. It was this aspect of the God of the river, **Hap Meht**, or **Hap** of the *north*, that the whites and their offspring who invaded Kamit were familiar with.

The term for water in the language of Kamit is **Mu**. **Mu Hap Meht** thus means waters, **Mu**, of the northern nile, **Hap Meht**. It refers to the God **Hap**, this Spirit Force in Creation, as He operates through the river water of the northern Nile. The whites corrupted the title of the God of the waters of the northern Nile, **Muhapmeht** into muhammed.

For thousands and thousands of years, Afurakanu/Afuraitkaitnut have communicated with the God **Hap** and invoked His Spirit under the names **Hap Reset**, **Hap Meht** and **Mu Hap Meht**. Not only have we fed our bodies with the water of the God, we have also energized our spirits with the unique energy of this Spirit Who operates through this river water. Every year the rainy season in the lands south of Kamit causes the water of the great river in Kamit to swell until the river floods its banks creating a tremendous lake. After a certain period, the floodwaters begin to decrease until they are no longer flooding the land on both sides of the river. The land on both sides of the river, after having been underwater for a period, is now very wet and fertile. At this time of the year, the people of Kamit have always gone out to plant seeds in this fertile soil. Because the land is so wet and fertile after the flood of **Hap**, a harvest of large crops was usually guaranteed. The coming of the God **Hap** to soak the land on both sides of the river is thus the coming of One Who is a bringer of a great harvest, abundance, a good life and peace. The whites applied this knowledge of the God **Hap Meht** to a fictional white male, and created the false belief that this fictional character was the last messenger of god and came to bring the world peace or islam.

The term islam is another corruption of the whites. The root of the term is salem (salm). Salem is a corruption of the name **Sarem**, which is an ancient title of the God **Hap**. In the language of Kamit, **Sarem** is composed of **Sa**, which means *shrine or sanctuary of a God or Goddess*; and **Rem**, which means *tear*, or *moisture from the eye*. The swelling of the waters of the river is said to be caused by moisture or a tear from the Eye of **Ra/Rait**, the Great Spirit, because moisture in the eye indicates compassion. The Goddess **Auset**, as she operates through the star system, **Sapadet**, called 'sirius', was referred to as the *Eye* of **Ra**. It is from **Auset** or **Auset Sapadet**, the *Eye* of **Ra**, that the Divine teardrop falls, which begins the swelling of the river **Hap** every year. This is because the yearly flood of the river was occasioned by the rise of the star **Sapadet**. When this star, which is the brightest star in the sky, would rise at the beginning of the year, it was an indication that the great flood was coming. Thus, for thousands of years, the people of Kamit have celebrated the beginning of the flood of the river **Hap**, during a holy day now called the "night of the drop", meaning night of the Divine teardrop from the star **Sapadet** or *Eye* of **Ra**.

The river **Hap** is a sanctuary, *Sa*, of the Divine moisture, or tear, *Rem*. Afurakanu/Afuraitkaitnut depended on the God **Hap Meht**, or **Sarem**, for survival and abundance as a means to maintain peace as a way of life. The whites corrupted the God **Hap Meht**'s title **Sarem** to salem, isalem and islam, and claimed that it meant the religion, or way of life of peace. The spread of **Sarem**, or **Mu Hap Meht**, the waters of the northern Nile over the country was corrupted by the whites into the spread of isalem or islam and muhammed throughout the country.

The God **Hap** is also the Spiritual Force operating through the great river of stars called the **heavenly Nile**. He is thus referred to as **Hap Ur**, meaning, **Hap** *the Great*. In your body, **Hap** operates through the blood which is made up mostly of water. Blood leaves your heart to flood the organs, structures and tissues of the body. Cells in the body receive nourishment and energy from this flood, so that they can execute their function in the body.

The various functions of the God **Hap**, as the Spirit operating through the river on Earth, the river of stars in the sky and the river of blood in your body were corrupted by the whites, applied to their fictional white character muhammed and used to manufacture a life story for this fictional character.

The whites and their offspring have no special connection to the Supreme Being. They have never had any prophets sent to them from the Supreme Being teaching any religion, and this they will never have.

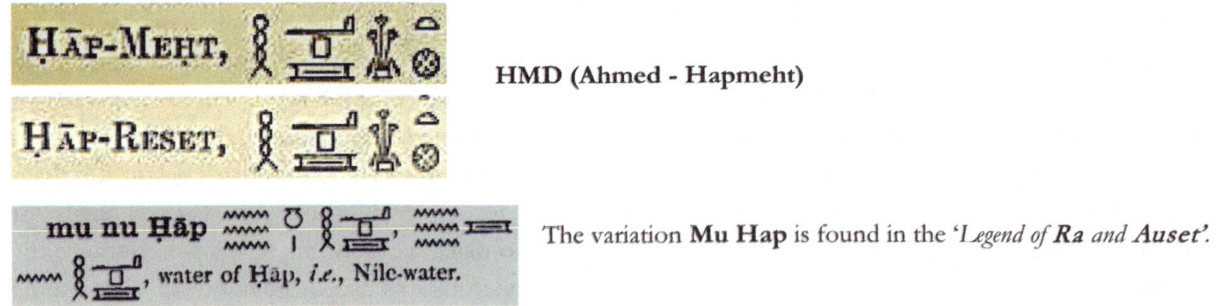

HMD (Ahmed - Hapmeht)

The variation **Mu Hap** is found in the '*Legend of **Ra** and **Auset***'.

Hap Meht and **Hap Reset**

Muhapmeht *(northern Nile)* and **Muhapreset** *(southern Nile)*

Sarem ; var. , Edfû I, 78, a title of the Nile-god.

Bār , Baal,

*Excerpt from our "**Origins of the Fictional characters of the bible, quran and talmud**" [www.odwirafo.com/ktposts.pdf]:

"...Bilal is none other than the ancient God **Baal** (Bel). In Kamit, Baal is a form of **Set**. He is called **Bar. Bar-Ur** (Bar the Great) became Bal-Ul, Bel-Ul and Bil-al.

Set is the God of the **desert** in Kamit amongst other things/functions. The deserts are just outside of the fertile plains of the nile valley. This is why when **Muhapmeht** (waters of the northern nile) floods the nile valley, the very first land that is flooded outside of the nile valley are the deserts. I.e., Bilal (Bar-Ur) the Kushite/Ethiopian/Black-Red individual/Desert was the first "convert" of Muhammad. Bilal being "burned" in the desert sands, etc., etc. is nothing more than an allusion to the fact that we are talking about **Set** (**Bar**) the *God of the Desert...*"

Afurakani/Afuraitkaitnit Ancestral Religion – 6.

The whites and their offspring attempted to force **Afurakanu/Afuraitkaitnut** into the false belief that whites are capable of attaining divine enlightenment. They forced this false belief by manufacturing a fictional spiritual teacher and claimed that it had attained divine enlightenment. They also claimed that it had incarnated to teach the world the way to enlightenment or union with god and the end of all suffering. The whites and their offspring attempted to take Afurakanu/Afuraitkaitnut away from our actual means of attuning ourselves to the Supreme Being, through the agency of the Goddess and Gods and our Ancestral Spirits, and force us into accepting the false divinity represented by their fictional white character, and the false teachings attached to it. This they hoped would force Afurakanu/Afuraitkaitnut into the false belief that the whites are capable of spiritual perfection and that we should therefore accept them and follow their instruction. The fictional white character was called buddha.

buddha never existed. The name buddha is a name that the whites stole from the God **Ptah**. In the language of Kamit, the name **Ptah** means: *maker, fashioner, former*. The God **Ptah** is the Spirit-Force in Creation that gives form to the Divine Life-Energy of the Great Spirit, **Ra/Rait**. **Ptah** took the energy of the Great Spirit and fashioned it into the various spiritual and physical forms of plants, animals, minerals, humans, planets, stars, Nature Spirits, Goddesses and Gods. **Ptah** is the Spirit-Force in Creation operating through the innermost core of all stars, the innermost core of the Sun, the innermost core of the Earth. In your body, **Ptah** operates through your brain. In your spirit, **Ptah** is the Force that takes the spiritual power moving through you and fashions it into a form that you can use to execute your function in the World. Just as the brain formulates the functions, the actions, the movements of the entire body, so does **Ptah** formulate the function, the action, the movement of the spiritual power moving through you. While **Ra/Rait**, the Great Spirit is the Divine Living-Energy moving within you, giving you life, and **Heru** is the Force that regulates the flow of this spiritual energy within you, **Ptah** is the Force that fashions this spiritual energy into specific forms which carry the power to accomplish your specific objectives. **Ptah** is the force that takes the energy moving through you and forms it into muscular energy so that you can walk, run, move. **Ptah** is the Force that takes the energy moving through you and forms it into digestive energy, so that you can digest your food and be nourished by it. **Ptah** takes the energy moving through you and forms it into mental energy so that you can study, listen, understand and communicate. **Ptah** is the force within you that takes the energy moving through you and forms it into sexual energy, so that you can procreate with your souse and bring life into the world again. **Ptah**'s functioning in your spirit and body are a reflection of His functioning in Creation. He is the Spirit-Force in Creation formulating the functions, the actions, the movements of the Divine Life-Energy moving through all [created] things in Creation. **Ptah** takes the Divine Life-Energy of the Great Spirit, **Ra/Rait**, which moves through all [created] things, and shapes it into forms that your organs, structures, cells, your spirit, can use. He shapes the Divine Life-Energy of **Ra/Rait** into forms that the planets and stars can use. He operates through the innermost core of all [created] things. He shapes the Divine Life-Energy of **Ra/Rait** into forms capable of executing the order of **Amen-Amenet**.

As **Ptah** functions in Creation, He shows us how to function, act, move through Creation. Because He is the Force fashioning the life-energy of humans, plants, animals, minerals, into forms capable of executing the Divine Order, **Ptah** has the title **Neb Ankh**. In the language of Kamit, **neb** means: *master* and **ankh** means: *life*. The title **Ptah Neb Ankh**, means: **Ptah**, *the master of life* or *life-master*. As the Spirit-Force in Creation Who takes the Divine Life-Energy of the Great Spirit, **Ra/Rait**, and shapes and fashions it into the various life-forms in Creation, **Ptah** is the *Master of Life*. For thousands and thousands of years, Afurakanu/Afuraitkaitnut have communicated with the God **Ptah**, and invoked His Spirit under the title, **Ptah Neb Ankh**.

The whites corrupted the name **Ptah** into **Putah** and buddha. They took the title **Neb Ankh**, master of life or life-master and applied it to the fictional white character. **Ptah Neb Ankh**, or **Ptah** *life-master*, was corrupted into buddha the life-master or buddha the sage, sage meaning *life-master.* Sage is a corruption of the term **Sesha** which means: *learned one, skilled one, wise one* in the language of Kamit. **Sesha** was another title of **Ptah**. The whites took the knowledge of the God **Ptah**, a Divine Spirit-Force operating through the innermost core of the Sun, the Earth, your brain and the formative power of your spirit, and applied it to their fictional white male character.

For thousands and thousands of years, the temples of Kamit have included the statement: **Nuk Pn Nuk**, which is carved in the walls. In the language of Kamit, **Nuk** means: *I, I exist as, I am.* **Pn** [pun] means: *this, that or who, what.* **Nuk Pn Nuk** thus means: *I am Who I am; I am that I am; I exist as that which I am.* This statement of identity **Nuk Pn Nuk**, *I exist as that which I am*, focuses Afurakanu/Afuraitkaitnut on the fact that we exist as who we are, as defined by the Supreme Being. We are to be who we are, and not attempt to imitate anything other than who we are. Because we are created by the Supreme Being to execute a specific function in Creation, to exist and act according to who we truly are is to participate in Divine Order. To embrace the reality of **Nuk Pn Nuk** is to function properly in the world. This statement was carved in temples of Kamit and repeated through speech, chant, and song amongst the Ancestral clans of Afurakanu/Afuraitkaitnut in order to properly align and realign our spirits with our souls. The whites corrupted this realization of who we truly are, **Nuk Pn Nuk**, into No pan no, nur pa no, nurbana, and n(i)bbana. nibbana is also pronounced nirvana by the whites.

The God **Ptah** fashions the Divine Life-Energy in Creation into the various life-forms existing in Creation. He is thus the Divine Spirit-Force Who makes us Who we are. He is the Spirit-Force that fashions our physical and spiritual bodies, and they are unique to us. He is the Spirit-Force that fashions our thought forms, and our thoughts are unique to us. Because our Divinely given functions in the World are different from one another, **Ptah** fashions our physical bodies, our spirit-bodies, our thought forms, into forms that differ from one another. **Ptah** upholds the Divine order of **Amen-Amenet** as He fashions the forms of all [created] things in Creation, and it is therefore through **Ptah** that we can embrace the realization of who we are. It is through the forms within which we exist, that we can understand and realize we are who we are. We exist as that which we are. It is through **Ptah** that we can embrace the reality of **Nuk Pn Nuk**, *I exist as that which I am.* The whites applied this knowledge of the God **Ptah** to their fictional white character. They claimed it is through buddha that we can embrace the reality of nibbana or nirvana.

The whites taught that their fictional character buddha was born of a virgin named *mahamaya* or *maia.* This is another perversion of the birth of **Heru**, by the virgin **Auset Merit**. maia, the name applied to the fictional virgin mother of buddha, is a version of maria, mari, mary and **Merit**. The fictional character buddha was also made to be the son of a king, which is another perversion of the story of **Heru**, as **Heru** was the son of the King **Ausar** and the Queen **Auset**. The fictional wife and son of buddha, is stolen from the knowledge of the Gods and Goddesses where the God **Ptah** has a wife, the Goddess **Sekhet**, and a son the God **Nfer Tum**.

Ptah, being the Spirit-Force that gives form to the Divine Life-Energy in Creation, also inherited the title **Ka**. **Ptah** functions as the Fashioner of the world, and His sacred city in Kamit is called **Hat Ptah Ka**, meaning *house*, **Hat**, of **Ptah**'s, *Soul*, **Ka**.

Because **Ptah** was sometimes pronounced **Phtah**, **Hat Ptah Ka**, the name of the sacred city of the God, was sometimes pronounced **Hat Phutah Ka**. **Hat Ptah Ka**, is the region where the God **Ptah** fashioned the landmass of Earth. The primordial Black Hill, the Earthly **Ka/Kait**, which was raised up out of the primordial

Ocean to become the landmass of planet Earth was fashioned by **Ptah** into the Earth's surface. The central region of His work of fashioning the landmass is the city of **Hat Ptah Ka**. Because the Spirit-Force of **Ptah** centered His operation in this particular region, this region was called His house, or **Hat**. It is in this house, or **Hat**, that the Soul, **Ka**, of **Ptah** dwells as He fashions the Earth's landmass.

The names **Hat Ptah Ka** or **Hat Phtah Ka** and **Afuraka** refer to the same landmass and have fundamentally the same meaning. While **Hat Ptah Ka**, or **Hat Phutah Ka**, is a name showing how the first emerging landmass of Earth took and maintains its form through **Ptah**, **Afuraka/Afuraitkait** is a name showing how the Great Spirit infused Life and sustains Life within the landmass by operating through it.

buddha never existed. The whites applied the knowledge of **Ptah** to their fictional character buddha.

None of the whites and their offspring have attained spiritual perfection and they are not capable of attaining spiritual perfection. They have not incarnated as enlightened beings to teach release from the world of suffering. They only incarnate as spirits of disorder contributing to suffering in the world, yet, only when we allow them to influence our thoughts and behavior.

Ptah **Buddha** (Bdha/Ptah)

Ptah Nefer Her

Ptah of the *'Beautiful Face'* or *'Radiant or Illumined Face/Head'*. This form of **Ptah** with the Sun disk on His head is the origin of *Buddha the 'Enlightened/Illuminated One'*.

Afurakani/Afuraitkaitnit Ancestral Religion – 7.

The whites and their offspring attempted to force **Afurakanu/Afuraitkaitnut** into the false belief that whites have a special connection to the Goddesses and Gods, the Forces of Nature. They created images of themselves, claimed that these images were images of the Goddesses and Gods of Creation, and claimed that they, the whites and their offspring, were the interpreters of what the Goddesses and Gods communicate to human beings. The whites corrupted the forms of names of the actual Goddesses and Gods of Creation and applied these corrupted names to their created white images. The whites created false rituals that served their own lusts, and claimed that these rituals were given to them by their lifeless, white, fictional gods and goddesses. They applied fictional life stores and spiritual functions to their fictional white gods and goddesses based on the knowledge and spiritual functions of the actual Goddesses and Gods of Creation, that the whites learned about after having invaded the cultures of Afuraka/Afuraitkait. The false ideologies, teachings, instruction created by the whites and their offspring and attached to their fictional white gods and goddesses were designed to force Afurakanu/Afuraitkaitnut to abandon the Great God and The Great Goddess, the Goddesses and Gods, the Nature Spirits, our Ancestral Spirits and Their communication to us of Divine Law. The whites did this so that we would follow the whites themselves and come under their total control.

brahman is fictional and the entire pantheon of devas and devis connected to brahman, promoted by the whites and their offspring as well as the teachings connected to them are fictional gods and goddesses and false ideologies created by the whites and their offspring to undermine the culture of Afurakanu/Afuraitkaitnut.

The whites and their offspring attempted to force Afurakanu/Afuraitkaitnut into the practice of empty and corrupt rituals and misguided techniques, to serve the fictional white gods and goddesses, and the lusts of the whites and their offspring. They moved to force Afurakanu/Afuraitkaitnut to reject the true Ancestral rituals and the true Goddesses and Gods of Creation, that operate through the Ancestral clans of Afurakanu/Afuraitkaitnut. These Forces in Nature, Who operate throughout the plant, animal, mineral and human spheres, **and when They do incarnate through the human sphere, They only incarnate as Black Goddesses and Gods, as Afurakanu/Afuraitkaitnut.** These Goddesses and Gods, Spirit-Forces in Creation, the Children of the Great God and Great Goddess, Whom we have served for thousands and thousands of years are They Whom the whites and their offspring attempted to remove from our memory and replace with white images of fictional gods and goddesses—the images of the whites themselves.

During times when the whites and their offspring felt that the Afurakanu/Afuraitkaitnut were not totally controlled by the false religion of the fictional white gods and goddesses, the whites would color one or more of their fictional images black. They did this in order to lure those amongst us who had initially rejected the white images.

The name brahman is a corruption of the name **Per Amen**. In the language of Kamit, the term **per** means: *house, dwelling place* or *temple* as well as *to manifest oneself, to arise from, to sprout.* **Amen** is the name of the Great God, Whom along with **Amenet**, the Great Goddess, constitute the Supreme Being. **Per Amen** thus means: *the house or dwelling place*, **Per**, *of the Great God*, **Amen**. This was a title of various shrines of worship dedicated to **Amen** in Kamit and Keneset. Many temples were thus called **Per Amen** or *house* of **Amen**. Yet, **per** also means: *to manifest oneself, to arise from, to sprout.* **Amen** and **Amenet** are the Source from which we were created and from which our souls and spirits and all of Creation *arises* or *sprouts*. **Per Amen** thus describes also the Divine spiritual *state* from which our spirits and souls are created, made manifest, or made to appear. **Amen** and **Amenet** are the Two Halves of the Great Whole. They are the Supreme Being. Just as there were temples of **Amen**, or **Per**

Amen, so were there temples of **Amenet** or **Per Amenet** also called **Per Mut**, **Mut** meaning: *Great Mother* in the language of Kamit. Because of the disorder and imbalance of the spirits of the whites and their offspring, they described a fictional Supreme Being who was male only. Thus, they used a corruption of the male title **Per Amen** to apply to their fictional being, brahman, while disregarding the female titles **Per Amenet** or **Per Mut**.

brahman and the related pantheon of gods and goddesses of the whites and their offspring never existed and do not exist. They are creations of the whites and their offspring. The teachings connected to them are corrupted techniques and manufactured rituals designed to serve the lusts of the whites and their offspring and paralyze the consciousness and power of Afurakanu/Afuraitkaitnut. Yet it is only as long as we accept them and embrace them.

Amen **Amenet**

Amen, Mut and Khensu

Amenet and Amen

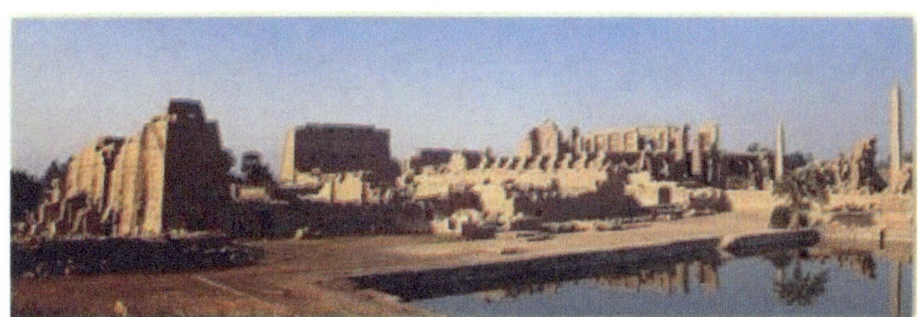

Per Amen, Temple of **Amen** in **Ta Apet**

Per Mut, Temple precinct of **Mut** in **Ta Apet**

Afurakani/Afuraitkaitnit Ancestral Religion – 8.

The whites and their offspring attempted to force Afurakanu/Afuraitkaitnut into the false belief that whites have received divine revelations from god and put them in writing. The whites created fictional holy books and writings and claimed that they contained divine guidance for Afurakanu/Afuraitkaitnut to follow. After invading Afurakani/Afuraitkaitnit civilizations the whites and their offspring moved to copy the language, writings and culture of Afurakanu/Afuraitkaitnut. In their character as spirits of disorder, the whites and their offspring corrupted the language, writings and cultural practices that they observed. They corrupted the writings they stole and created perverted nonsense concerning the nature of the Supreme Being, the spirit world, Creation and culture. The perverted philosophies of the whites and their offspring are a reflection of their character which is that of disorder. They use their written perversions as a tool to control the thinking of Afurakanu/Afuraitkaitnut in an effort to enslave our spirits, our physical bodies and make us self-destructive.

The bible is not a holy book. It is not divinely inspired. The bible is a series of writings which are perverted fragments of ancient writings from Kamit. The bible is less than 1,600 years old, while the writings of Kamit are over 20,000 years old. The title *holy bible* is a translation from *helios byblos*. The term *byblos* is derived from *papyrus* or *pa-pyrus* which is a plant used to make paper. The term *paper* is derived from *papyrus* or *pa-pyrus* [papers]. The term *helios* is the greek language perversion of the name of the God **Ra**. The holy bible or *helios byblos* or *helios papyrus* is actually a white perversion meaning the *papyrus* of *helios* or the *papers* (book) of **Ra. It is a series of plagiarisms and perversions describing the whites' false worship of their fictional god.**

The torah, which are the first five books of the old testament of the bible, are not holy writings. They are not divinely inspired. In the language of Kamit, the term **tua** means: *worship*. **Tua ra** thus means: *the worship* of **Ra**. This is a title of many compositions written in Kamit by Afurakanu/Afuraitkaitnut for thousands of years. **Tua Ra** or the *worship* of **Ra** was corrupted by the whites into *torah*, **and used as a title for a series of plagiarisms and perversions describing the whites' false philosophy and worship of their fictional god.**

The quran is not a holy book. It is not divinely inspired. The quran is a series of perverted fragments from ancient writings of Kamit. The term **Khu** or **Aakhu** in the language of Kamit has been used for thousands and thousands of years in Kamit to describe: *illumination, wisdom, Divine Intelligence*. The Ancestral Spirits are thus called **Aakhu**, meaning: *the illuminated* or *shining Ones*, or *those who have embraced and exude Divine Wisdom*. The whites and their offspring used the title **khu Ra**, or Divine Wisdom of the Creator, and corrupted it into *quran*. This is why they call the quran the book of wisdom. **It is a series of plagiarisms and perversions describing the whites' false philosophy and worship of their fictional god.**

The vedas are not holy scriptures. They are not divinely inspired. The vedas are a series of perverted fragments from the ancient writings of Kamit. veda is from the root ved, meaning: *to know*. veda is also pronounced beda, which is a variation of buda (buddha), the corrupted form of the name **Ptah**. It is through **Ptah** that we *come to know* who we are or come to realize **Nuk Pn Nuk**. The whites took the name of the God **Ptah** which as also pronounced **Phutah** and used it to name their various writings *vda* or *veda*. **The vedas are a series of plagiarisms and perversions describing the whites' false philosophy and worship of their fictional gods and goddesses.**

Ra and **Rait**, the Creator and Creatress in Creation who function together as the Great Spirit in Creation, are the Divine Living-Energy moving through all [created] things giving life, movement, to all [created] things.

Some Afurakanu/Afuraitkaitnut outside of Kamit referred to **Ra** as **Lah**, and **Rait** or **Rat** as **Lat**. The title **Ra Ur**, meaning: **Ra** *the Great One*, was also pronounced **Lah-Ul** and **Ul-Lah**. **Rait** or **Rat-Urt**, meaning **Rait** or **Rat** *the Great One* was also pronounced **Laht-Ul** or **Ul-Laht**. The whites and their offspring took these titles and applied them to their fictional god and corrupted **Ur Ra** or **Ul Lah** into allah. They corrupted **Urt Rat** or **Ul-Laht** into allat. allat was then made by the whites to be a daughter of their fictional god allah, so that male would appear to be superior to female.

The names **Ur, Ul Lah** and **Ul Laht** were also corrupted by the whites into **el, eloh** and **elat** and applied to their fictional gods and angels. The plural of **Ur** is **Uru** and **Urui**, meaning: *the great Ones* in the language of Kamit. These titles were corrupted by the whites from **Uru** and **Urui** into **Uluim** and **elohim**. These corrupted titles were also applied to their fictional gods and angels.

The whites and their offspring use their fictional white characters, false religions and false religious practices as a weapon to destroy and control Afurakanu/Afuraitkaitnut. Yet, some Afurakanu/Afuraitkaitnut immediately rejected the fictional white characters and the false religions of the whites. **Because of these kinds of reactions, the whites and their offspring responded by painting and sculpting a select number of these fictional white characters black. This was done in order to trick certain groups of Afurakanu/Afuraitkaitnut into accepting the false religions of the whites by accepting blackened versions of fictional white characters. The whites and their offspring also included a small number of references in their false religious writings loosely describing some of the fictional characters in terms that could be conceived as describing the characters as black. This was part of the strategy of tricking these Afurakanu/Afuraitkaitnut into respecting then accepting the fictional characters and false religions.** The whites and their offspring also used the strategy of chipping away and removing the names on ancient statues and paintings of the Afurakani/Afuraitkaitnit Goddesses and Gods and replacing these names with the names of the fictional white characters.

Statues and paintings of the God **Heru** shown as a child sitting on the lap of His Mother, the Goddess **Auset**, existed in Kamit, europe and asia for thousands of years. The whites destroyed many of these Black statues and paintings after invading these countries. Yet, those statues and paintings of **Heru** and **Auset** which they saved, they renamed jesus and mary. The whites and their offspring created europeanized replicas of these paintings and statues. **This is the origin of the many ancient Black jesus and mary or madonna and child, statues and paintings existing all over europe and asia.**

Merit

Auset (Merit) and Heru **perversion of Auset and Heru**

The same strategies were used to trick certain Afurakanu/Afuraitkaitnut into accepting the fictional character buddha and the false teachings attached to it. Statues and paintings of the ancient God **Ptah** were used as models to create a select number of Black statues and paintings of the fictional character buddha. Descriptions of the God **Ausar** and the Goddess **Auset** were used by the whites to trick certain Afurakanu/Afuraitkaitnut into accepting a Black solomon and sheba, after they had rejected a white solomon and sheba. The same strategies were used to trick certain Afurakanu/Afuraitkaitnut into accepting a fictional black moses and david, because they had initially rejected the fictional white moses and david. The whites and their offspring knew that some Afurakanu/Afuraitkaitnut would never accept the various fictional characters whether painted and sculpted as white or black. They knew that some of the immature amongst us would accept the fictional characters as white. **Yet, they also found that some of us would initially reject the fictional white characters, but be ignorant enough to accept them as real and the teachings connected to them if they were just painted black.**

jesus, mary, yeshua ben pandira, buddha, abraham, isaac, ishmael, moses, david, solomon, sheba, menelik, judah, muhammed did not exist at all. They are not Black. They are not white. They are purely fictional.

Afurakanu/Afuraitkaitnut will free ourselves permanently, only when we fully embrace our religious culture and absolutely reject, forever, the whites and their offspring, and all forms of their foolish, backward and perverted culture and "religions" including christianity in all of its forms, islam in all of its forms, judaism/hebrewism in all of its forms, Jainism, in all of its forms, Hinduism and Vedanta in all of their forms, Buddhism in all of its forms, European so-called paganism in all of its forms, gnosticism, in all of its forms, qabbalism in all of its forms, Sufism in all of its forms, hermeticism, in all of its forms, european and asian so-called mysticism and esotericism, occultism and spiritism in all of their forms, the bible, quran, torah, Vedas, dhammapadas, qabbalah, and all other writings developed and derived from the whites and their offspring in all of their forms and all other non-Afurakanu/non-Afuraitkaitnut ideologies and practices, in all of their forms.

Afurakani/Afuraitkaitnit Ancestral Religion, the ritual incorporation of Divine Law and the ritual restoration of Divine Balance, is the **food** and **medicine** of **Afurakanu/Afuraitkaitnut**.

Through it we are nourished and through it we are healed.

NKRABEA

"... **Afurakanu/Afuraitkaitnut:** The greatest attack ever waged against you has been the **lie** that you should respect the whites and their offspring, their culture, their false religions, their different and perverted view of the world. The whites and their offspring have made you fear reality, by making you fear your natural hatred for disorder and your natural hatred for them and their culture. As long as you turn away from your natural hatred of disorder, you will turn away from your natural hatred for the whites and their offspring and their culture. You are then ready to accept them and their way, disorder, into your life. You are then ready for self-destruction and perpetual slavery.

You are a slave in your own lands and away from your homeland because you have invited your absolute enemy, the whites and their offspring and their culture, to influence and control your way of thinking, your way of understanding, your way of behaving. Whenever you have embraced your enemy, you have lost control of your societies. Whenever you have rejected your enemy, you have regained control of your societies. Whenever you have accepted the "religions" of your enemy, your have accepted your own slavery. Whenever you have rejected the "religions" of your enemy, you have freed yourselves from slavery.

You will become rooted when you embrace your natural hatred for disorder just as strongly as you embrace your natural love for order. You will arise when you recognize the unchangeable nature of the character of the whites and their offspring, which is disorder, and recognize the unchangeable nature of your character which is order. You will blossom when you understand that to pass judgment is wise, only misjudgment is unwise. You will bear fruit when you reject the whites and their offspring, their religions, their culture, permanently, without compromise and embrace your Ancestral religion and culture, permanently, without compromise.

You will be faced with the deceptions that make the whites and their offspring and their culture seem to be nourishing to you as opposed to being destructive to you. Your Ancestresses and Ancestors were faced with the same deceptions and rejected them. We understood that substances that paralyze the body also cause the body to lose its connection to reality and feel no pain. The body can then be easily attacked and destroyed. We understood that the substances causing paralysis must be rejected.

You have allowed the culture of the whites and their offspring, these spirits of disorder, to paralyze your spirit. They have thus caused you to lose your connection to reality, and you feel no pain when you accept them. This is why it is easy for the whites and their offspring to attack and destroy your clans, generation after generation. You have yet to understand that these spirits of disorder and their culture must be rejected.

Your challenge is the challenge of your Ancestresses and Ancestors Who executed true revolution and achieved true resolution. When Earth moves around Sun and returns to the point from which it began it has made a complete revolution. **When you return to your point of origin, when you embrace again the Great God and the Great Goddess, the Goddesses and Gods, the Ancestral Spirits, the Nature Spirits, your Ancestral clans, your Ancestral culture and your Divine function in the World, only then will you have executed true revolution.** You will be empowered to take your independence, establish your sovereignty and maintain your sovereignty, permanently. **You will then achieve true resolution.** This has been executed before, and you will execute it again.

Afurakanu/Afuraitkaitnut do not respect disorder

Afurakanu/Afuraitkaitnut hate disorder

Afurakanu/Afuraitkaitnut do not respect the whites and their offspring, their culture, their "religions"

Afurakanu/Afuraitkaitnut hate the whites and their offspring, their culture, their "religions"

Embrace yourselves. Continuously eradicate the influence of the whites and their offspring from your spirits. Separate yourselves from those among you who refuse to eradicate the white cultural influences on their spirits, those among you who rationalize their continuous acceptance of the white cultural influences on their spirits, and those among you who proclaim their love to be Afurakani/Afuraitkaitnit and claim to be revolutionaries, yet in actuality are identical in character to your enemy. **These willing slaves, apologists and duplicitous hypocrites within your clans you must identify, judge and separate yourselves from.** They function as agents of your enemy, and live to weaken themselves and you internally, while externally the whites and their offspring seek your destruction and perpetual slavery.

Know your origin. Know your function. Know your clan. Know your clan. Know your enemy. Execute your function. Embrace your clan. Reject your enemy. Establish your sovereignty. Defend your sovereignty. Live. Live. . ."

..Bra nkwa mu..

MMARA NE KYI

DIVINE LAW/LOVE AND DIVINE HATE

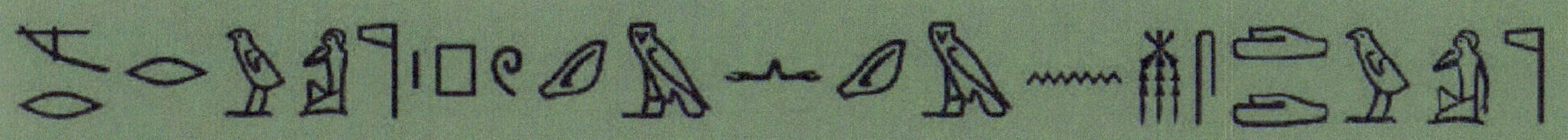

ODWIRAFO KWESI RA NEHEM PTAH AKHAN

MMARA NE KYI

DIVINE LAW/LOVE AND DIVINE HATE

MMARA NE KYI – DIVINE LAW/LOVE AND DIVINE HATE was first published as a three-part article series in the **BENASEM** section of the first, second and third issues of our **AFURAKA/AFURAITKAIT NANASOM NHOMA – Afurakani/Afuraitkaitnit (African) Ancestral Religion Journal** in 13007-13008 (2007-2008). We published part four of the series in 13008 (2008) and part five in 13010 (2010). We made the pdf version of each individual installment of the series a free download from our website as they were published. Here, we have combined all five parts into one document for ease of study. We have also included an *Appendix* newly published in 13014 (2014) with the related **medutu** (hieroglyphs) of the terms *law, love* and *hate,* additional cosmological analysis of these terms and additional linguistic references which did not appear in the original series.

In reality, and thus in Afurakani/Afuraitkaitnit (African) Ancestral Religion and Culture, we recognize that there is a Great Mother and Great Father Who comprise the Supreme Being. The most ancient name for the Great Mother is **Amenet**. The most ancient name for the Great Father is **Amen**. **Amen** and **Amenet** can be found, together, in the earliest written religious compositions unearthed in ancient **Kamit** (Egypt) to date – the **meru** or *pyramid* texts written c5,000 years ago. All Afurakanu/Afuraitkaitnut (Africans), wherever we have migrated to in the world, recognize the reality of the Great Mother and Great Father. In the culture of the **Akan** of Ghana and Ivory Coast, West Afuraka/Afuraitkait (Africa), **Amen** is called **Nyame** (**Ny-Amen**). **Amenet** is called or **Nyamewaa** (**Ny-Amenat**).

The term for *plan, order or arrangement* in ancient Kamit is **sekher** (seh-shehr) . This term can be found in the Akan language as **nhyehyee** (in-sheh'-sheh) meaning *order, arrangement.* The verb **hyehyee** (sheh-sheh) means *to fix, to order, to arrange,* while the noun version includes the 'N' prefix. **Nyamewaa-Nyame Nhyehyee** is thus the *Divine Arrangement, Order.* This is **Amenet-Amen Sekher**. The names of the Great Mother and Great Father as well as the term for *order, arrangement* are the same from ancient Kamit to contemporary Akan culture, for the Akan just as many Afurakanu/Afuraitkaitnut (Africans) in West, Central, South, East and Northwest Afuraka/Afuraitkait (Africa), migrated from ancient **Khanit** (Nubia/Sudan) and Kamit centuries ago after the fall of Kamit to the invading whites. We naturally carried our language, culture and religion with us. [See our publication: *Akan – The People of Khanit (Akan Land - Ancient Nubia/Sudan)*].

Amenet-Amen Sekher or **Nyamewaa-Nyame Nhyehyee**, *Divine Order,* is composed of Two Complementary Poles: **Divine Law (Love)** and **Divine Hate**. This is the Order in/of Creation and is the key to our restoration of Order as Afurakanu/Afuraitkaitnut (Africans) wherever we exist in the world.

The whites and their offspring have consistently and deliberately attempted to erase our conscious awareness of the reality of ***Divine Law as Love*** *and of the* ***Divinity of Hate*** *for political purposes.*

The whites and their offspring came to realize, after millennia of numerous failed attempts to conquer Afurakanu/Afuraitkaitnut (Africans) by direct warfare, that the only way that they might control us subsequent to an invasion was to corrupt the Ancestral religion. They realized that the only laws that Afurakanu/Afuraitkaitnut (Africans) adhere to are those rooted in Divine Order, thus *if the notion of Divine Order could be corrupted, the whites calculated that they could also corrupt the laws that Afurakanu/Afuraitkaitnut (Africans) readily accepted.* This would give a pseudo-'divine' sanction for whites to have invaded and taken control and by extension a pseudo-'divine' sanction against any form of retaliation by Afurakanu/Afuraitkaitnut (Africans). They would then only need to conscript a segment of those in society who were previously disgruntled with the status quo, prior to the white invasion, as allies to propagate the new corrupted 'philosophy'. This is the origin of christianity, islam, judaism, hebrewism, hinduism, vedanta, buddhism, gnosticism, kabbalism, hermeticism, humanitarianism, various 'schools' of psychology, etc.

Once Afurakanu/Afuraitkaitnut (Africans) over the centuries began to accept these false, foolish doctrines, pseudo-religions and the fictional characters associated with them (jesus, yeshua ben pandira, moses, abraham, muhammed, allah, yahweh, brahmin, buddha, etc. are <u>all absolutely fictional characters who never existed of any race whatsoever</u>) we embraced our own self-destruction. Our thoughts, intentions and actions were open to be proscribed by the whites and their offspring via the false doctrines. This openness to disorder has become a self-perpetuating slavery.

It is a misnomer that the 'African' was hospitable and open to 'strangers' as part of our culture. This misnomer is political propaganda created and promoted by the whites and their offspring and perpetuated by brainwashed Black people who were miseducated regarding our authentic **trustory** (true-story/true history) and culture. **Various Afurakani/Afuraitkaitnit (African) societies routinely executed the whites and their offspring – on sight – without any initial conversation. This was a feature of Afurakani/Afuraitkaitnit (African) culture for thousands of years.** We were aware that these spirits of disorder had arrived to promote their agenda of murder, destruction and control. We therefore did not give them a chance to begin that process.

It was a minority of misguided Afurakanu/Afuraitkaitnut (Africans) who were engaged in empire building who began to ally with some of the whites and their offspring – <u>against</u> the counsel of our Elders/Elderesses and the Deities via oracular divination.

Certain powerful, but misguided, Afurakani/Afuraitkaitnit (African) rulers began to embrace the idea that they were too powerful to be taken down by the physically, spiritually, economically and militarily inferior whites they had come into contact with. They therefore allied with the whites and their offspring, initially conscripting them as mercenaries and later engaging them via commerce, in an effort to expand their influence over foreign territories. Yet, the whites entered such alliances with an ultimate goal of turning against the powerful Afurakani/Afuraitkaitnit (African) rulers by exacerbating and exploiting **already existing divisions** in the nation. This led to the *implosion* and *fracturing* of the great Afurakani/Afuraitkaitnit (African) nations of **Kamit**, **Kanaana**, **Numidia** and others over time. *This also led to the accepted hegemony of white cultural 'values' – disorder – into the spirits of a segment of the Afurakani/Afuraitkaitnit (African) population which has been perpetuated to this day.*

We will free ourselves from the social, political, economic and military control of the whites and their offspring (white americans, white europeans, white hispanics/latinos/latinas, white hindus, white arabs, white asians, white pseudo-'native'-americans, etc.) only when we reject – without comprise – all of them, their perverse doctrines and the discordant ideas they have and continue to spawn.

NANASOM

Nanasom [nah'-nah-sohm] is a term we have coined from the language of ancient Khanit and Kamit to reference Afurakani/Afuraitkaitnit (African) Ancestral Religion. The term **Nana** is a reduplication of the root **na**. In the *Twi* language of the Akan, the root 'na' is defined as *that which is rare, precious; ancient (Ancestry), great.* The Twi language is derived of our Ancestral language of ancient Khanit and Kamit. We therefore find that in the medutu (hieroglyphics) the term **na** means: *great, greatness; benevolence.* We also find that the term **sm** (**som**) means: *a deed or undertaking; a custom, a practice; to ritually provoke, to ritually place offerings on an altar.*

Thus in our ancient Ancestral language these terms describe *an undertaking, custom and practice of ritual invocation and ritual offering (service) to They Who are great, benevolent* – The Supreme Being, the Deities and our Spiritually Cultivated Ancestresses and Ancestors. These are the ancient conceptual and phonetic roots of the term and nature of **Nanasom**, for Khanit and Kamit are the roots of Afurakani/Afuraitkaitnit (African) Ancestral Religious inheritance. All Black People--and only Black People--wherever we exist in the world are Afurakanu/Afuraitkaitnut (Africans) and share in these linguistic and cultural roots. Authentic religious expressions of Keneset and Kamit are therefore manifest only through our varied Afurakani/Afuraitkaitnit (African) ethnicities including, but not limited to: Akan, Yoruba (Ifa'Orisha), Ewe/Fon (Vodoun), Igbo, Bakongo, Bambara, Dogon, Goromantche, Nguni, Sotho, Khoikhoi, San, Dinka, Gikuyu, Lemba, Temne, Bassa, Fula, Fang, Mande, Azande, Afar, Oromo, Batswana, Ovambo, Ovimbundu, Maasai, Chokwe, Wolof, Twa, Lobi, Ibibio, Edo, Krobo, Guan, Ga, Tamil (Black India), Olmec (Ancient america) and all others.

Nanasom is a **spiri-genetic inheritance** incarnate within the **kra ne mogya**, the *soul and blood*, of all Afurakanu/Afuraitkaitnut (Africans). It therefore naturally reveals itself via our thoughts, behavior and culture everywhere we have migrated to and/or settled on **Asaase Afua** (The Earth Mother). It is inborn.

Afurakani/Afuraitkaitnit (African) Ancestral Religion is defined in essence as the *ritual incorporation of Divine Law and the ritual restoration of Divine Balance.* Through ritual we incorporate those things, objects, deeds and entities we need to harmonize with Divine Order and through ritual we reject those things, objects, deeds and entities we need to in order to restore balance to our lives. Afurakani/Afuraitkaitnit (African) Ancestral Religion *animates* our culture, our way of life, for Afurakani/Afuraitkaitnit (African) Ancestral Culture is the *Divine acceptance (Love/Law) of Order and the Divine rejection (Hate) of disorder.*

The phrase **mmara ne kyi** is Akan for *law and hate.* These terms derive from the same terms in Kamit: **maa hna kht**. Divine Law and Divine Hate are the *Expansive* and *Contractive* Poles of Divine Order. In this work we properly define these concepts inclusive of the fact that there are *Deities* (**Abosom, Orisha, Vodou, Ntorou/Ntorotu [Neteru/Netertu -Ntrw/Ntrwt**]) who embody these concepts: **Maa** and **Maat** (Law) and **Heru Behdety** and **Sekhmet** (Hate). We demonstrate that **Law** and **Love** have always been the same concept in Afurakani/Afuraitkaitnit (African) culture and that **Hate** has been and always will be Divine. Just as there are *Deities of Law/Love*, there are *Deities of Hate.*

Moreover, and most critically, without an understanding of the *Divinity of Hate* one has absolutely no understanding of authentic Afurakani/Afuraitkaitnit (African) cosmology, culture, religion, philosophy and its infrastructure: *Divine Order.*

We have many in the Afurakani/Afuraitkaitnit (African) community, on the continent of Afuraka/Afuraitkait (Africa) as well as outside of the continent, who perpetuate misinformation regarding authentic culture, cosmology and philosophy because they have internalized a centuries-old **infection** of white culture stretching back to the muslim invasions of North and West Afuraka/Afuraitkait (Africa) over 1,000 years ago and the subsequent european invasions. This infection is ensconced in what appears on the surface to be traditional Afurakani/Afuraitkaitnit (African) culture, philosophy, ritual, enunciations of the 'African Worldview' and more. However, just as a cancerous tumor is not always apparent, yet is continuously growing and destroying the body, so has such misinformation gone undetected and spread throughout the Afurakani/Afuraitkaitnit (African) world body (community). We have been weakened by its proliferation as a result. The manner in which we address such an issue is to *arrest the development* of the tumor, isolate, destroy and expel it from the body. This is what must be done with the misinformation being promoted as 'ancient African culture, religion and philosophy'. It is through the *acceptance* or *Law/Love of Order* and the *rejection* or *Hate of disorder* that we *arrest the development, isolate, destroy and expel* the disorder for good. **MMARA NE KYI**.

We were made aware of the identity of Law as Love, the Divinity of Hate and the nature of **Maa** and **Maat** and **Heru Behdety** and **Sekhmet** under the direction of our **Nananom Nsamanfo** (Akan for *Honored/Spiritually Cultivated Ancestresses and Ancestors*). We were directed to confirmation in the Ancestral languages, cultures, religion and cosmology of Afurakanu/Afuraitkaitnut (Africans) worldwide from ancient Khanit and Kamit to the present day. We first taught this information in 12996 (1996) and our first publication of these concepts in the context of ritual was through our **UBEN-HYENG The Ancestral Summons**, 12998 (1997). Our first publication of these concepts in the context of cosmology and culture was through our **KUKUU-TUNTUM The Ancestral Jurisdiction**, 13002 (2002). Our publication of the first three parts of the series **MMARA NE KYI** and the subsequent fourth and fifth installments is the most extensive exposition of these concepts to date. It is the responsibility of the Afurakani man and Afuraitkaitnit woman to not only establish Order in ourselves, families and the Afurakani/Afuraitkaitnit (African) world body-community in the present as a foundation for our future, but to also correct the misinformation – *remove the infections* – from the past. Indeed, our present and future stability is dependent upon our fulfilling of this sacred responsibility. It is truly the **rebuilding of our core** and the **reestablishing of our immunity**.

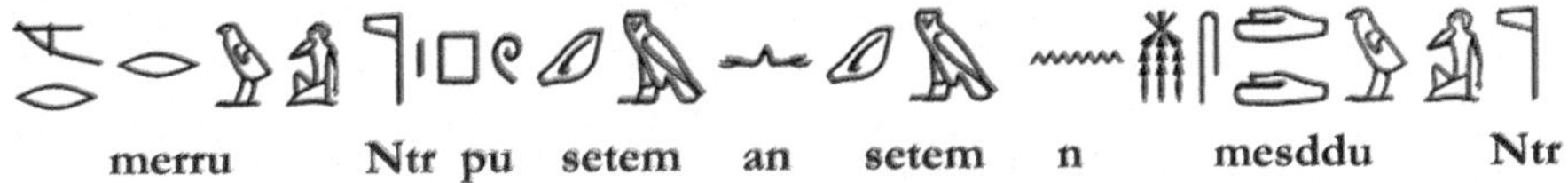

*This **God loves (merru)** hearing (listening). Not hearing is **hated by the God (mesddu Ntr)***

[Epilogue of the **Instructions of Ptah Hetep** c4,500 years ago]

Odwirafo Kwesi Ra Nehem Ptah Akhan
Aakhuamuman Amaruka Atifi Mu
March 20, 13014 (2014)

MMARA NE KYI

Divine Law and Divine Hate

Ofa a edi Kan – Part 1

Afurakanu/Afuraitkaitnut (Africans~Black People) understand that Creation comes into being and is sustained through and within what *Akanfo* (Akan people) call **Nyamewaa-Nyame Nhyehyee. Nyame** (Onyame) is the term for God, while **Nyamewaa** (Onyamewa) is the term for Goddess in the **Twi** language of the Akan. **Nyamewaa** and **Nyame** function Together as One Divine Unit, The Supreme Being. The *Twi* term **nhyehyee** (n-shay'-shee-ay) means: *order, arrangement.* **Nyamewaa-Nyame Nhyehyee** is thus translated into english as The Supreme Being's Order, i.e. *Divine Order.*

As with all *created* entities, **Nyamewaa-Nyame Nhyehyee,** Divine Order, is comprised of two opposite-and-complementary poles. These are the masculine and feminine poles representing the Divine balance of male and female which permeates all of Creation. This male-female balance is rooted in the foundational complementary relationship of **Nyame** and **Nyamewaa**. As **Nyame** and **Nyamewaa** function harmoniously Together, They show us the nature of all *created* entities. This essential nature of all *created* entities naturally applies to Divine Order as well.

The expansive pole of Divine Order is **mmara** (law). The contractive pole of Divine Order is **kyi** (to hate). Afurakanu/Afuraitkaitnut recognize the reality that *mmara*, law, is Divine and that *kyi*, to hate, is Divine.

It is anti-Afurakani/anti-Afuraitkaitnit (anti-African) and hence anti-reality to embrace the foolish notions that hate is evil, hate is immature, hate is heavy, draining, self-destructive, etc., and that love is unconditional, love is the way, love conquers all things, etc. Law and Hate are two halves of a whole, **Nyamewaa-Nyame Nhyehyee**. The proper understanding of our role in Creation as Afurakanu/Afuraitkaitnut individually and collectively is absolutely dependent on our understanding of and embracing the proper definitions of law/love and hate.

In the process of showing the proper definitions of these concepts, we must understand that the alphabet in use today is derived from our **Nananom Nsamanfo**, our Afurakani/Afuraitkaitnit (African) Ancestresses and Ancestors, Who developed the phonetic script thousands of years ago in ancient **Keneset** and **Kamit** (the ancient Black civilizations of Nubia and Egypt). The whites and their offspring have never created an alphabet. After invading ancient Kamit and other Black centers of civilization north of Kamit, the whites and their offspring took the alphabetic characters created by Afurakanu/Afuraitkaitnut as part of our complex writing system and corrupted them. These varied corruptions were then deliberately mis-labeled by the whites as the greek alphabet, the roman alphabet, the arabic alphabet, the hebrew alphabet, the sanskrit alphabet, the english alphabet as well as many others. **This fact is critical to this discussion, for the manner in which we have been misled through the "english alphabet" to mis-define words fosters an ill-acceptance of mis-defined concepts.** This process has greatly contributed to the perpetuation of spiritual enslavement amongst Afurakanu/Afuraitkaitnut. It is time to free ourselves.

MAA and MAR – Law and Love

Trustorically, approximately 1,500 years ago as the whites and their offspring corrupted our original phonetic script, the letter '**V**' was transformed into the letter '**U**'. In turn, the letter '**U**' was transformed into the letter '**W**' about 1000 years ago. '**W**' (double-U) of course is comprised of two '**U**'s or '**V**'s side by side. The letters **U**, **V** and **W** are fundamentally the same letter linguistically. This is why these letters and their sounds interchange in european languages. Those who are english-speakers pronounce the name william with the 'w' sound while other europeans write and pronounce the same name as villiam or vilhelm. The name of the country, sweden, pronounced with the 'w' sound in the english dialect is pronounced sveden, with the 'v' sound in swedish. This is a critical distinction, for the same principal is at work with the terms Law and Love.

In Afurakani/Afuraitkaitnit culture the words and concepts Law and Love are fundamentally the same. To be "in love" with someone or something from the Afurakani/Afuraitkaitnit perspective, the true perspective, is to be "in law" with that person or thing. This means that you are functioning in harmony with Divine Order with respect to your interaction with that person or thing.

The consonantal structure of the words Love and Law are **LV** and **LW**. From the Afurakani/Afuraitkaitnit perspective, they are the same word and hold the same spiritual meaning. However, because of the corruption of our phonetic script, the originally identical words *love* and *law* **and ultimately the conceptualizations represented by these terms** were corrupted by the whites and their offspring. As a result of said corruption these terms are now mis-defined as being unrelated to one another. In reality, when the whites and their offspring use the term **love**, they are actually describing the concept of **lust** which is properly defined as *misguided desire.* In Afurakani/Afuraitkaitnit Ancestral Religion and Culture, lust (misguided desire) is properly recognized to be--**not** the *opposite* of love/law--but the **perversion** of love/law. When the whites and their offspring use phrases such as "falling in love" what they are truly conveying is the concept of "falling in lust". In the publication, **MATE MASIE The Ancestorhood of Nana Yao (Dr. Bobby E. Wright)** by Odwirafo Kwesi Ra Nehem Ptah Akhan it is stated:

"Law is the expression of order. Divine Law is the expression of Divine Order. The laws governing Afurakani/Afuraitkaitnit (African) society are expressions of Divine Order. At the most fundamental level, the concepts of law and love in Afurakani/Afuraitkaitnit (African) cultures are identical. Love is that which attracts balance, for it is the force which draws one's complementary to him or herself so that order may be had. Law is that which attracts Balance, for it is the instrument which draws one to establish or re-establish order in their lives."

Taking the concept further it is stated:

"For Afurakani/Afuraitkaitnit (African) people, to be "in love" is to be "in harmony with Divine Law". To be "in love with someone" is to be "in harmony; in law with someone". If someone is "lovable" or "lovely", it is because they are "lawful". I.e., they are expressions of Divine Order. They function in harmony with Order, thereby manifesting "beauty" in the real sense. Because the nature of Afurakani/Afuraitkaitnit (African) people is rooted in Divine Order we are mandated to manifest beauty by harmonizing our life activities with the Order in Nature on every level including the individual, marital, familial, communal, national, international (world Afurakani/Afuraitkaitnit (African) body/community) and the Ancestral levels...."

The whites and their offspring deliberately separated the notion of *law* from *love* for the purpose of cultural, spiritual and ultimately the physical enslavement of Afurakanu/Afuraitkaitnut. They promoted *their* "love" concept which is actually their promotion of the definition of lust---the perversion of law/love. They then applied this corruption to their fake religious philosophy. When they forced their fake religions and the foolish philosophies associated with them upon Afurakanu/Afuraitkaitnut, the goal was to make us perversely "love" or lust after their fake white gods. *The immature amongst us then began to unconsciously develop a lust (misguided desire) for the whites and their offspring--the representatives of the fake white gods on Earth.* The immature amongst us would therefore develop a lust for the embracing of white culture, while falsely believing that they were engaged in a process of embracing Divine Order. The immature would also develop a misguided fear that if they were to attack the whites and their offspring that attack would be sinful, for they would be placing themselves in conflict with the "children of god". By default, the immature amongst us would denigrate themselves, denigrate all Afurakanu/Afuraitkaitnut, denigrate the actual **Abosom, Orisha, Vodou, Ntoru/Ntorotu**, the actual Black Goddesses and Gods/the Spirit Forces of Creation. They would denigrate Afurakani/Afuraitkaitnit Ancestral Religion and Culture. They would denigrate reality itself. Our self-destruction was thereby set in motion. Conflicts arose between the mature Afurakanu/Afuraitkaitnut in society who rejected the perverse white culture and pseudo-religious concepts and the immature Afurakanu/Afuraitkaitnut who embraced the perverse white culture and pseudo-religious concepts. Civil war was the result. As we weakened ourselves internally, the whites and their offspring waged war against us externally attacking from the outside. It is in this manner that they were able to gain control over our societies after having employed this process for centuries.

Today, we see that immature Afurakanu/Afuraitkaitnut still maintain a perverse love—lust—for the whites and their offspring and fake white gods and personages who never existed of any race. These make-believe cartoon-character "gods" and personages include: jesus, yeshua ben pandira, muhammed, allah, yahweh, buddha, brahmin, abraham, isaac, ishmael, jacob, jah, moses, david, solomon, sheba, menelik, etc. Yet, the immature believe that they are upholding Divine Law. They believe that they are in harmony with Divine Order by embracing these fictional characters. It is through our embracing of the proper definitions that these fallacies will be eradicated.

In the language of Kamit the terms for **law** and **love** are **maa** and **mar** (also written **mer**) respectively. The term **maa** (law) and the term **mar** (love) **are both indicated in the medutu (hieroglyphic symbols) with the exact same determinative symbol, the eye:** 𓁹. The **medut** (symbol) of the eye *represents* both **law** and **love** (*maa* and *mar*) in Kamit, because we have always seen these two terms related phonetically and conceptually.

The term **maa** itself has two major definitions in Kamit. The <u>first</u> definition of **maa** is: *law, true, straight, real, balance.* The <u>second</u> definition of **maa** is: *sight, inspection, to see, to oversee.* **The medut of the eye is used in both the first and second definitions of maa (law) as well.** Why is the eye used as a symbol for both definitions of the word for **maa** (law) as well as a symbol for the word **mar** (love)?

The particular eye *medut* used to define these terms represents the Divine eye (insight) of the Supreme Being. To align yourself with the Divine Eye is to avail yourself of the ability to *see* the truth, *see* the law governing Creation. When you align yourself with Divine insight (**maa**) you are aligning yourself with divine Law (**maa**), *that which is true, straight, real, unwavering.* You are then showing love (**mar**). You are showing *commitment* to Divine Order. You are now "in" law/love (you are in-sight-ful(l), you are showing in-sight into Divinity; you are in the sight/scope/perimeter and parameters of the Supreme Being's Divine Order. You are now in love/law (mar/maa). You are in a truly (true/maa) *committed* relationship. *The dynamics of these relationships can be experienced ritually by Afurakanu/Afuraitkaitnut and made applicable socially.* This is the reason why the symbol of the eye is used in **maa** (law) **maa** (sight; inspection; oversight) and **mar** (love). The eye is also the organ through which attraction is confirmed. Making eye contact is a means by which one can show his or her law (love) towards his or her complement, his or her other half. The eye allows one to *see* his or her balance (*maa*/law), complement, to *see* (*maa*) his or her "love"/law.

The language of ancient Kamit had different dialects. The dialect known as **Coptic Egyptian**, is the form also known as **Late Egyptian**. This is the form that the language of Kamit took at the close of the ancient civilization. It came into common usage about 2000 years ago. In the *Coptic* dialect, the term **maa** (law) is written and pronounced **me** (meh). Also, in the *Coptic* dialect, the term **mar** or **mer** (love) is written and pronounced **me** (meh). The 'r' is a rolling 'r' when pronounced, just as in the languages of contemporary **Afuraka/Afuraitkait** (Africa) today. At regular conversation speed, this 'r' sound (tongue tapping the roof of the mouth once) is almost silent. Thus, in the oldest dialects going back over 7,000 years **maa** and **mar,** law and love, are related phonetically, hieroglyphically (using the symbol of the eye) and conceptually, and in the last surviving form of the language, *Coptic*, **maa** and **mar** become **me** and **me**. The terms are identical phonetically and conceptually.

[See the appendix for actual images of the **medutu** (hieroglphys) spelling all of the words examined in this text.]

The word **mar** (love) is also written **mara** in Kamit. This is also why in the language of Kamit, the term for: *overseer, inspector, upholder/protector of rules/laws* is also **mara** (also written as **mer** or **mera** and written in *Coptic* as **Bar** or **Bara**). This word survives as **bara** (sometimes contracted to **bra**) in the **Twi** language of the Akan carrying the exact same meaning. In Akan/Twi, the singular form of **mmara** (law) is **bara**. Same word, same concept from ancient Kamit to Akan. Moreover, the title **bara**-fo (also **abrafo**), in the Akan language is defined as: *one of the people/group* (**fo**) *who are the* **law** (**mmara** or **mbra**). These **bara-fo** (**brafo, abrafo, mmarafo**) or **mmara** (law) **fo** (people) are the "police", maintainers of order, overseers, those who have insight into the laws underpinning the society and are those who uphold those laws. They are also executioners.

Finally, the term for *love, desire* in *Twi* is **pe** which is the root of **mpena** (lover). This term **mpena** is also written **mpra** and **mpara** (variation of **mpena** and **mpana**). The pronunciation of the rolling 'r' in the *Twi* language at regular conversation speed is nearly identical to the pronunciation of 'n' when 'n' is encased within a word. **Mpana** and **Mpara** thus sound identical. The interchange between the rolling 'r' and the 'n' sounds is very common in *Twi* and many other Afurakani/Afuraitkaitnit languages.

Mmara or **Mbra** (the spelling for **law** in two different *Twi* dialects) is thus related to **Mpara** (lover; love). **Pe** (love; desire) in *Twi* is also derived from the Coptic **Me** (love). **P** and **B** are interchangeable in linguistics. The same is true of **M** and **B**. (Note that in *Twi* the term for *blood* is written variously as **mogya**, **mbogya** and **bogya**. The **m** and **b** are interchangeable. The same is true of **m** and **p** in certain circumstances.) See the correspondences below:

Early Kamit	*Coptic (Late Kamit)*
Maa (Law)	**Me** (Law)
Mar (Love)	**Me** (Love)

Early Kamit	*Twi (Akan)*
Maa (Law) **Mara** (Love)	**Mmara** or **Mbra** (Law) **Mpara** or **Mpra** (Lover)
Coptic (Late Kamit)	*Twi (Akan)*
Me (Love)	**Pe** (Love)
Coptic	*Twi*
Mara or **Bara** (inspector/overseer)	**Bara** or **Bra-fo** (upholder of law; overseer of law)

Afurakanu/Afuraitkaitnut have always recognized the reality that not only is Love/Law the same word and concept but that **Law is a Divine Living Entity**. Divine Law is a Twin Spirit Force in Creation Whom we work to align ourselves with. This is yet another reason why we do not —fall‖ in and out of Law (Love)---**we do not fall in and out of a Spiritual Entity.**

In the language of ancient Kamit, the **Ntoro** and **Ntorot** (*Neter* and *Netert*/God and Goddess) of Law and Balance are **Maa** and **Maat** respectively. These Divinities, These Spirit-Forces in Creation hold the Created Universe Together. They govern the center of balance in your body and within the operation of your spirit. This is why the general term **maa** means: *law, balance, straight, true* in the language of Kamit. Again, this term becomes **mmara** (**maara**) meaning *laws, rules* in the *Twi* language of the Akan. The terms and their definitions are derived from the names and the functioning of the actual Deities **Maa** and **Maat** in Creation.

Afurakanu/Afuraitkaitnut thus harmonize with Divine Law by harmonizing our thoughts intentions and actions with the *Ntoro* (God) of Law, Whose name in Kamit is **Maa** and by harmonizing our thoughts, intentions and actions with the *Ntorot* (Goddess) of Law, Whose name in Kamit is **Maat** *(see pictures below).*

MAAT

MAA

[**Maat** from the tomb of Ra Messu III. **Maa** from the tomb of Ra Messu VI. Photos by this author.]

KYI – Hate

The etymology of the english term **hate** is initially traced back to the greek term **kedos**. The **–os** is a greek suffix that is added to many of the root words in that language. The root of *kedos* is **ked** from the *proto-indo-european language phylum*. [*See appendix*] From *ked* came **khed**, **hed**, **het** and the english **hate**. In *proto-indo-european*, the term **ked** is defined thusly: *to break, to destroy*. The english definition and conception of **hate** is derived directly from that conception. You *hate* something or someone when you *reject* it or them totally--when you seek only *to destroy, break, disassociate yourself from* it or them fully. Why is the english term for hate derived from a greek term meaning to break or destroy? It is because the greek term is a corruption of an ancient term from Kamit.

When the greeks invaded Kamit, they corrupted, stole and perverted many of our words, concepts, teachings about the **Ntoru/Ntorotu**. The term **khet** (often written in the *medutu* without the vowel as **kht**) in the language of Kamit means: *to break, to destroy, to overthrow, to enact violence upon*. This term is often doubled into **khetkhet** (often written in the *medutu* as **khtkht**). The doubling concept exists throughout Afuraka/Afuraitkait to emphasize a specific quality of a person or concept. The determinative *medut* defining the word **khet** is a man holding a stick in his hands in the action of *beating, pounding, breaking, destroying* something . Variations of the word in Kamit have the following meanings: *to crush, pound, bruise, kill, slay*. This is the reason why when **khet** was corrupted by the greeks into **khet**-*os* (ked-os) the term retained its meaning: *to break or destroy*. This is the essence of **hate** and is why it still has the same conceptual meaning in the english version of the word.

One variation of the word **khet** in Kamit that is critical to our discussion is **kher**. This word also is sometimes doubled in Kamit: **kherkher**. This word means: *to overthrow, to destroy, etc.* **These distinctions are critical because both words survive in the Twi language carrying the exact same meaning.** The *medut* making up the '**kh**' sound in Kamit is: . The sound for this *medut* is a '**K**' sound in some words and a '**Tch**' or '**Ch**' sound in other words (similar in english to the '**k**' sound of the '**ch**' letter combination in the word *chronology*, and the '**ch**' sound for the '**ch**' letter combination in the word *check*). Thus, the words **khet** and **kher** pronounced 'cheet' and 'chee-ree' in Kamit survive in the *Twi* language as **kyi** and **kyiri**. In the *Twi* language, the combination '**ky**' is usually pronounced like the english 'ch'. Thus, **kyi** and **kyiri** are pronounced 'chee' and 'chee-ree' in *Twi*. Both words in *Twi* are verbs and they both mean: **to hate**. See the correspondences below:

Kamit		*Twi (Akan)*	
khet (cheet)	to destroy/hate	**kyi** (chee)	to hate
kher (chee-ree)	to destroy/hate	**kyiri** (chee-ree)	to hate

In Twi, **kyi** also has the definition: *to press, squeeze, wring or crush out. [It is important to note that while* **kyi** *in Twi is a verb: 'to hate; to abhor', some have popularized the term* **okyi** *as a noun version of the word meaning: hatred, abhorrence.]*

The letter '**h**' in Kamit is pronounced with the aspirated sound as in 'hello' or the '**Tch**' or '**Ch**' sound. We thus have variations of the same terms where the *medut* for 'kh' is replaced with that of 'h'. These terms have the same meanings. We have the following variations [See appendix for these terms spelled in the medutu]:

Kamit (h version)	*Kamit (kh version)*
heta (hehta) to break, to tear up	**khet** impaling pole *(upon which enemies are hung, executed)*
het (hehd) to strike; vanquish; subdue	**khet** to cut into; to pierce, to penetrate
hedhed (hehd-hehd) to batter down; crush	**khetkhet** to break, cut into pieces, destroy
herher (hehr-hehr) to demolish; pull down	**kherkher** to root up, to destroy

In Akan culture the term **akyiwade** or **akyide** is composed of **kyi**, *to hate*, and **ade**, *things, objects, deeds, entities.* **Akyiwade** or **akyide** are therefore: *hateful, abominable, abhorrent things, objects, deeds, entities.* This translates into english as *taboos.* In Akan culture, **akyiwade** are defined as those things, objects, deeds, entities that are taboo, those things, objects, deeds, entities (**ade**) that the **Abosom** (Goddesses and Gods) and **Nyamewaa-Nyame** (The Supreme Being) **hate** (**kyi**). This is **Divine Hate**.

Akyiwade are things, objects, deeds, entities which are **Divinely prohibited**. As with the Akan, all Afurakani/Afuraitkaitnit Ancestral Cultures and Religions have terms within their languages which are defined in the **exact** same manner. **Such is the case because all Afurakanu/Afuraitkaitnut recognize the reality as given to us by the Supreme Being that kyi, to hate, is Divine.**

From the proper Afurakani/Afuraitkaitnit perspective, **to hate is to reject**. Approximately 1 out of every 100,000 cells in your body is cancerous at any given time. These cells began as normal cells, yet for a particular reason became disfigured and thus began to malfunction. These now-disfigured cells began to seek out, consume and destroy other healthy cells. Yet, the reason why everyone has not developed cancer is because of the body's response to these cancerous cells. The cells of the **immune system** respond to cancerous cells by seeking them out, destroying them, and expelling them from the body. **This immune response is a Divinely ordered response. It is an intelligent response. Your immune system is the vehicle of the Supreme Being's Divine Hate operating through your body. It rejects cancerous cells (disorder) in the body.** In a similar fashion, there is a Divine immune system in Creation. Creation's Immune System is the Divine Hate of the Supreme Being. It is that Twin Spiritual force which upholds the Divine Order of Creation.

In the language of ancient Kamit, the **Ntoro** and **Ntorot** (God and Goddess) of **hate** are **Heru** and **Sekhemet** respectively (also called **Her** and **Herit** respectively). These Divinities, These Spirit-Forces in Creation, maintain the integrity of the Created Order, Together. They govern the immune response within your body and within the operation of your spirit. There are a number of **Ntoru** (Gods) Whom include the title **Heru** in Their names. The particular form of **Heru** called **Heru Behudet**, is the **Ntoro** of war, metal/iron, Divine Justice. He is the Son of **Ra** (The Creator). He is also called **Sekhem Shut** (the Powerful Winged One), when

He takes the form of the Winged Celestial orb/disc: 

The wife of **Heru Behudet** is **Sekhemet**, also called **Herit**. She takes on the title **Sekhemet** (Powerful One) when She operates as the destructive force annihilating disorder and its purveyors. There are a number of **Ntorotu** (Goddesses) Whom include the title **Het-Heru** in Their names. In the texts of Kamit, **Heru** as **Heru Behudet** destroys all of the enemies of **Ra** (the Creator) under His orders. In the texts of Kamit, **Sekhemet** also called **Sekhemet-Het Heru** destroys all of the enemies of **Ra** under His orders. **Heru Behudet** and **Sekhemet** are Husband and Wife, complementary Spirit-Forces Who **impress** the Divine Hate of the Supreme

Being upon Creation. **Heru Behudet** and **Sekhemet** function as the **contractive** pole of Divine Order (**Hate**) while **Maa** and **Maat** function as the **expansive** pole of Divine Order (**Law**). Afurakanu/Afuraitkaitnut harmonize with Divine Hate by harmonizing our thoughts, intentions and actions with the **Ntoro**/God of Hate, Whose name in Kamit is **Heru** (**Heru Behudet, Heru Behdety, Heraakhuti, Sekhem Shut**, etc.) and by harmonizing our thoughts, intentions and actions with the **Ntorot**/Goddess of Hate, Whose name in Kamit is **Sekhemet** (**Herit; Sekhemet-Het Heru**). She is also called Chieftainess of the Red Mountain.

Heru Behudet also has the title **Heru Kheti** and **Heru Heri Khet**. Both of these titles include the term **khet(i)** and refer to Heru's function as the *piercing, fiery, warrior, destroyer*. He is **Heru** the **Heri** (Chief/Master) of **Khet** (destruction/hate).

Sekhemet also has the title **Skhet** (**Sekhet** a variation of **Sekhemet**). The general term *s-khet* is comprised of **khet**, *to destroy*, and the causative prefix **s**-. The prefix **s**- in the language of Kamit indicates that something is being made to occur. To be called **s-khet** is to show that one is causing (**s**) **khet** (destruction/hate) to occur. He or she is thus the causer/bringer/executor of destruction. The term is thus represented with the *medut* of the man wielding the weapon (see above) and defined thusly: *blow, beating, punishment*. Both Divinities thus have titles and functions that demonstrate Their role as the Twin Agents of **Khet, Kyi**, the Divine Hate of **Nyame** and **Nyamewaa**. (**Ny-Ame** is the God **Amen** while **Ny-Ame-waa** is the Goddess **Amenet** from Ancient Keneset and Kamit).

We must also recognize that **Heru** or **Her** is a name, while the general term derived from the name, **heru** or **her**, is a variation of **kheru** or **kher**, meaning: *to destroy, to overthrow (hate in the true sense)*. We now have a better understanding of the term **maakher** or **maakheru**. The terms **heru** or **her** also have the connotations: *to set in order (restore order); to terrify; to frighten*. The same determinative *medut* (symbol) of the man raising his weapon in the act of striking is used in these variations as well.

Afurakanu/Afuraitkaitnut have always understood the following truisms:

The universe is Created through Divine Law (love) and the universe is sustained through Divine Hate.

Law is the **expression** of order. **Divine Law** is the **expression** of Divine Order. **Hate** is the **impression** of order. **Divine Hate** is the **impression** of Divine Order.

Divine Hate impresses or imprints upon Creation the parameters within which we are to function properly. Operation outside of these parameters is disorder, which Divinity does not support and thus destroys.

Divine Hate as a functional reality is properly defined as: **the rejection of disorder for the purpose of maintaining the Divine Order.**

If one is not rejecting disorder, then one is not exercising hate. Just as the whites and their offspring deliberately corrupted the definition of love (law) to fit their reality (lust) so have they corrupted the proper definition of hate to fit their reality – **malice**.

It is the concept of **malice**, properly defined as *evil intent*, that the whites and their offspring have deliberately mis-defined as **hate**. The whites and their offspring incarnate as spirits of disorder. They are therefore incapable of hate – **the Divine rejection of disorder for the maintenance of Divine Order.** In order to embrace hate, they would have to remove themselves from the planet, for in order to exercise hate they would **by definition** have to seek to destroy disorder – themselves. **They would have to reject that which they are an incarnation of (disorder).**

In reality, the whites and their offspring exercise **malice** (evil intent). Malice is what prompts one to break, to destroy things and/or entities **outside of harmony with Divine Order**. When one engages in malice, one does not reject for the purpose of maintaining Order, one rejects for the purpose of perverting Order, destroying Order, eliminating any semblance of Order and replacing it with disorder, with chaos. Moreover, it must be clearly understood that disorder is the only true evil. Disorder is **not** the opposite of Order. Disorder is the **perversion of** Order. Divinity does not support disorder in Creation. Disorder is thus routinely eradicated by **Abosom, Orisha, Vodou, Arusi, Ntoru/Ntorotu** (Deities) Created specifically for that purpose.

Just as it is natural, Divine, for the living cells of your immune system to hate, to reject, to eradicate the disfigured living cancerous cells in your body without exception nor compromise whatsoever, so is it natural, Divine, for Afurakanu/Afuraitkaitnut who are immune cells within the Divine Body of **Nyamewaa-Nyame**, to hate, to reject, to eradicate the whites and their offspring, the cancerous cells in the Divine Body of **Nyamewaa-Nyame**, without exception nor compromise whatsoever.

As stated in our **MAAKHERU** audio webcast on this subject:

...Just as lust is the perversion of love or law, so is malice, evil intent, the perversion of hate. It is malice, evil intent, that the whites and their offspring have projected onto Afurakanu/Afuraitkaitnut for thousands of years. The whites and their offspring are not capable of hate. For Hate is the Divine rejection of Disorder, for the purpose of maintaining the integrity of Divine Order. The whites and their offspring are spirits of disorder. They can never reject disorder, for they would be rejecting themselves. They did not reject Afurakanu/Afuraitkaitnut. They had an overwhelming lust, or misguided desire or draw to us. They traveled thousands of miles to Afuraka/Afuraitkait un-invited and invaded our lands. For centuries, they would drag millions of us thousands of miles to their occupied territories against our will. They forced us to live and slave for them for the rest of our lives and their lives against our will. If we attempted to escape, they went out of their way to come after us and drag us back to them. This is not hate, this is not rejection of disorder, it is the **promotion** *of disorder. This is malice, an evil intent to pervert and destroy. This is not law or love, which the whites and their offspring are incapable of. This is lust, a misguided desire to possess, to control. And it continues wherever we are found in close proximity to the whites and their offspring around the world.*

Afurakani/Afuraitkaitnit Ancestral Culture is the Divine Acceptance of Order and the Divine rejection of disorder. *It is the law or love of Order and the hatred of disorder. Our culture, our way of life, is rooted in adhering to Order through embracing Law and rejecting disorder and its purveyors by employing Hate. We have been taught that hate is a negative emotion. Hate is self-destructive. Hate is consuming. Hate is heavy. Hate represents a low vibration of energy.* ***This is foolish. Malice is heavy, for you have taken on disorder, and your spirit rebels. This conflict creates a self-consuming frustration and stress. Thus, malice is consuming. Malice and misguided frustration creates a low vibration.*** *However,* ***Hate is effortless. Hate is light. To reject/hate disorder is to free your spirit from its burden. Your immune system destroying cancerous cells is not burdening you---it is freeing you....***

The whites and their offspring realized once they had gained control over some of our societies that the only way a minority (themselves) could control a majority (us) was to corrupt the ideas of a certain percentage of the majority. **They understood that as long as the majority recognized the reality that Hate is Divine, the Black majority would have no problem killing the invading white minority as an act of Divine Justice.** Thus, over the course of centuries the whites and their offspring worked tirelessly to corrupt the idea of hate into an evil idea, as opposed to its true essence---the **Divine Force** created by **Nyamewaa-Nyame** to maintain **Divine Order**. This corruption of hate into an evil idea was propagated by the whites and their offspring most importantly via their pseudo-religions. It is tantamount to cancerous cells in your body calling your immune cells evil, because they are seeking to destroy the cancerous cells.

Hate is a Divine Endowment from Nyamewaa-Nyame to Afurakanu/Afuraitkaitnut

Finally, as the only *created* people in the world, only Afurakanu/Afuraitkaitnut have the capacity to embrace and harmonize with Divine Law and Divine Hate. When we speak of harmonizing with the Order in Nature on every level we are speaking only of harmonizing with other *created* entities. A *created* entity is one that came into being by Divine mandate. By definition this excludes all of the whites and their offspring who exist, who have ever existed and whoever will exist. None of the whites and their offspring came into being via Divine mandate (this includes all white europeans, white americans, white asians, white indians/hindus, white arabs, white hispanics/latinos/latinas, white so-called "native" americans, etc.). Their existence is very recent in the **trustory** of the world and is a manifestation of the degeneration, spiritually and genetically, of a small percentage of Afurakanu/Afuraitkaitnut (less than .001%) who were separated from the majority Afurakani/Afuraitkaitnit population over 20,000 years ago.

The maintenance of Order in our bodies, our spirits, our culture, our society, our lives as Afurakanu/Afuraitkaitnut is absolutely dependent on us embracing Divine Hate just as strongly and equally as we embrace Divine Law (Love).

Selected References:

Let the Ancestors Speak, *Ankh Mi Ra*
Pert em Heru *(sheft/papyrus of Ani)*
Tomb of Seti I, *(Book of the Cow of Heaven, Destruction of Mankind)*
Per Heru Behudet *(Temple of Heru Behudet, Legend of Heru of Edfu)*
Twi-English/English-Twi Concise Dictionary, *Paul Kotey*

MMARA NE KYI

Divine Law and Divine Hate

Ofa a eto so Abien – Part 2

In the first part of this article we detailed the reality that as Afurakanu/Afuraitkaitnut (Africans~Black People) we have always recognized the reality that **mmara** (law) and **kyi** (to hate) are two halves of the Divine Whole which is **Nyamewaa-Nyame Nhyehyee** (The Supreme Being's Structure, Divine Order).

We demonstrated that **maa** and **mar** (law and love in Kamit; **me** and **me** in *Coptic*) are one and the same word and concept. **Mmara** (law/love) is the Twin Force in Creation, the *Ntoro (God)* **Maa** and the *Ntorot (Goddess)* **Maat**, through Whom we incorporate those things, entities, we need in order to establish balance in our lives. **Khet** or **kyi** (*to break, destroy, hate* in Kamit; *to hate* in Twi) is the Twin Force in Creation, the *Ntoro* **Heru Behudet** (**Heru Kheti**) and the *Ntorot* **Sekhemet**, through Whom we reject those things, entities, that we need to hate/reject in order to restore balance to our lives.

It is impossible to establish or restore Nyamewaa-Nyame Nhyehyee unless we fully embrace and operationalize mmara ne kyi, Divine Law (Love) and Divine Hate, in every aspect of our lives.

Not realizing the truth about *mmara ne kyi* is the only thing standing in the way of our total liberation: spiritually, physically, socially and politically. With respect to revolution-resolution, Afurakanu/Afuraitkaitnut will free ourselves, permanently, only when we internalize and actualize *mmara ne kyi*. The **akyiwadefo**, the spirits of disorder/whites and their offspring, recognize the truth of this prescription for our full liberation and have therefore worked for centuries to keep us from recognizing it. We must understand that when we embrace *mmara ne kyi*, only then do we invoke **nyansa** (wisdom, intelligence). We thereby accept *Nhyehyee (Order)* and summarily reject disorder and its purveyors. It is through this process that we recognize the akyiwadefo to be who they truly are, spirits of disorder, and only seek their total eradication from this world: spiritually and physically.

It is imperative that we understand the mechanism by which the akyiwadefo have been able to disable our alignment with this most fundamental truth of our lives. It is through such disabling that we have been influenced to operate, constantly, in an imbalanced fashion. We have been foolishly taught to *"accept all and reject none"*. We therefore accept things and/or entities that we need as well as those things and/or entities which are destructive, even fatal, to us. We also refuse to reject these things and/or entities when they are recognized to be injurious to us physically and non-physically. Because we have been taught to receive such things and/or entities and retain them, we are forced into the insane position of attempting to rationalize the existence of disorder in our lives. Such misguided rationalizations truly manifest as spiritual (which includes psychological) illness. This acquired **oyare**, *illness*, exists only because our consciousness of *mmara ne kyi* has been thwarted by the akyiwadefo through the manipulation of fear.

FERE ne EHU

(Respect and Fear)

Respect is a manifestation of Order. In Afurakani/Afuraitkaitnit culture we uphold respect as a virtue. We recognize it as a byproduct of maturity for it shows that we have fully developed our ability to perceive reality and operate accordingly.

Fear is a manifestation of disorder. In Afurakani/Afuraitkaitnit culture we do not uphold fear as a virtue. We recognize fear to be a byproduct of immaturity and also as representing a lack of perception. Thus, we do not *fear* The Supreme Being, we *respect* The Supreme Being.

In the Twi language, **fere** (feh-ray) is defined as *respect*, but can also carry the connotation of *fear*. This is similar to the fact that *desire* can be in harmony with Order (the body *desires* water for replenishment), yet *desire* can also be misguided (lust—one *desires* to steal). *Fere* or *respect* in the proper sense, means that we constantly **re-spect**, or **re-view** (*spect-ate: to look at*) every thought, intention and action and harmonize each with **Nyamewaa-Nyame Nhyehyee**. The term *fere* is represented in the *medutu* of Kamit as **per** or **pera**, with the determinative symbol of an eye 𓁹 meaning: *to see; perceive; to take in.* The *p* and *f* interchange linguistically here just as in the Twi words for *house* and *to come out, to leave, go out:* **ofi** and **firi** respectively, and the words in the language of Kamit for *house/chamber* and *to come out, go out:* **pi** and **piri** respectively. See correspondences below showing the interchange between *p* and *f*:

Kamit	*Twi*
pera to see; perceive; recognize	**fere** to respect (to re-look, view, perceive, recognize)
pi house	**fi** house
piri to come out; to leave, go out	**firi** to come out; to leave, go out

We should note also that the Kamau term **per** or **pera** with the *medut* of the eye, meaning *to see, vision* is the origin of the english word peer, as in *to peer into, look into something.* The related word, appear, is derived from the latin, perer, meaning: *to come forth; be visible.* Of course, this word is derived from the Kamau term **per** with the *medut* of the horned viper meaning: *to come forth, to appear.*

Moreover, the word **per** or **pera** with the determinative *medut* of two legs walking: 𓂻 meaning *to evade a calamity (as in escaping from one's country)* is the root of the idea that *pera* can mean what is commonly referred to as **fear**. This is why in Twi, *fere*, respect, is also translated to mean *fear*. This is also why in english the term is written and pronounced *fear*. It is derived from the Kamau *pera*—the *p* and *f* once again interchanging. We must understand however, that *pera*, to evade a calamity, is still based on *proper* recognition, *proper* perception of reality, manifesting as a *properly* conceived decision and action rooted in that recognition. However, in the culture of the akyiwadefo, fear is based on *not* understanding, *not* knowing, *not* recognizing. *Fear of the unknown* is thus a common phrase. This is also the basis of the misguided idea of one being *god-fearing*. The akyiwadefo do not, have never, and never will know God/Goddess.

In the Twi language, the term **ehu** means: *fear, fright, terror* while the related term in Twi **hu** means: *to perceive by the eye, to behold, discern.* The noun **ohu** means: *knowledge*. Again, these related terms show the connection between *seeing, perceiving* things *properly,* manifesting as **ohu** (knowledge) and *seeing, perceiving* things *improperly,* manifesting as **ehu** (fear). These concepts show the basis for *respect* (re-spect/re-view/re-look) being composed of terms related to *perception, seeing, viewing, recognizing.*

Fere, meaning *respect* in Akan, embodies the ability to *see* (*spect-*) things, entities or events for what they really are, to see or perceive what our capacities are and to see how to interact with these things, entities or events, utilizing our spiritual capacities without creating or perpetuating disorder in the process. *Fere* is thus the act of proper **recognition**, hence the related term **hu** *(to perceive by the eye, to behold, discern).*

Fere in the negative or misguided sense, manifesting as *ehu (fear)*, means that we either *mis*-perceive some thing, entity or event and/or we properly perceive the thing, entity and/or event, yet do not properly perceive our capacity to harmoniously address or engage the thing, entity or event without creating disorder in the process. *(Harmonious engagement could be acceptance or it could be rejecting, attacking, destroying to maintain Order).* We thus develop a debilitating stress, **because of our lack of proper recognition**---we cannot see a harmonious outcome for ourselves. This debilitating stress blocks our perception yet further and also has a deleterious effect on our bodies, and ultimately our overall health. Frustration develops which often leads to self-destructive, rash behavior and/or misguided rationalizations which promote and lead to stagnation or self-destructive actions as well.

In order to properly execute our **nkrabea**, our Divinely allotted function (destiny) in Creation, we must embrace and operationalize *mmara ne kyi* consistently and perpetually. **We must understand what and who to accept into our lives and what and who to reject---what and who to law/love and what and who to hate.** However, we cannot do so until we develop *fere*, respect, for *mmara ne kyi.* This is what the akyiwadefo understand, and this is why they have incorporated the total disrespect for *mmara* and the total disrespect—fright/fear--of *kyi* into their pseudo-religions. **When we have ehu (fear) for our Divine mandate for kyi (to hate) we have in reality an insane ehu of Nyamewaa-Nyame Nhyehyee, for we have an insane fear for eradicating our enemies, for eradicating disorder and its purveyors.** In this condition, we maintain a state of spiritual and physical (including social, political and economic) paralysis. We refuse to defend ourselves. This is a comprehensive enslavement through the enculturation of *ehu.*

The key to embracing our innate *fere*, respect, for *mmara ne kyi*, and thus our capacity to embrace **Nyamewaa-Nyame Nhyehyee** and to reject disorder is through re-embracing our capacity to execute proper **judgment**. As we have stated in the *nhoma (book)* **PTAH Sasetem**:

...Judgment is wise, yet misjudgment is that which is unwise

Judgment is an expression of wisdom. Non-judgment as well as misjudgment are expressions of ignorance. Afurakanu/Afuraitkaitnut have always understood that proper judgment is the basis of the security of a sovereign nation and the preservation of a balanced society. The whites and their offspring have attempted, through pseudo-religion, to teach us "don't judge", for they understood that if we were to apply proper judgment to them we would embrace the Divine mandate to reject them outright and permanently. This will mean their loss of control over us.

When we engage our timeless method of making decisions we arrive at proper judgments. We should be judging everyone and everything, in order that we may live and interact in the world in harmony with our nkrabea. When we come to this realization and put the principles of judgment into practice, only then have we gained maturity. As long as we refuse to make judgments, we remain gullible and immature...

Atemmu is the Twi term for *judgment.* The root **nten** means: *straight, right, correct.* **Bu aten** means *to execute judgment* while the noun *atemmu (aten bu)* means *judgment.* In Afuraka/Afuraitkait we have always taught the truism:

Proper judgment is the hallmark of maturity

The difference between a mature individual and an immature individual is this: The mature individual understands how to make proper judgments. The immature individual does not. The immature individual either makes no judgments at all (non-judgmental) or makes **mis**judgments. We teach our children to assess every situation and then make a proper judgment so that the decision and action they make and exercise are in harmony with their *nkrabea.* If the temperature is 20 degrees below 0 and the child is in the process of deciding what he or she is going to wear outside, he or she is taught to assess the situation and make a proper judgment. The child would therefore not put on a pair of shorts and a t-shirt, but would dress accordingly. Proper judgment affords one the ability to navigate through life, executing his or her *nkrabea,* without creating or perpetuating disorder in the process. **We must constantly judge everyone and everything at all times. This is essentially Afurakani/Afuraitkaitnit.** It is **misjudgment** which is foolish, which is immature, which is a manifestation of immaturity. Moreover, **aspiring to be "non-judgmental" is the greatest form of misjudgment**.

We must recognize that it is the akyiwadefo who constantly encourage us: *"don't hate, don't judge".* This foolish and diabolical doctrine is a direct and deliberate assault on Afurakani/Afuraitkaitnit people, culture and religion. It is a deliberate attempt to enslave us and keep us enslaved physically and non-physically. The related foolish doctrine admonishing us to *"fear god"* pulls the other two together into a triangular formula for the perpetual and self-regenerating imbalance, enslavement, of Afurakanu/Afuraitkaitnut. It is this formula: *don't hate-don't judge-fear god* which adds up to the insane notion, constantly perpetuated by the akyiwadefo that we should "love unconditionally". Again, this is a direct and deliberate assault on Afurakani/Afuraitkaitnit people, culture and religion, for it is an attempt to pervert reality.

We have shown conclusively that **mmara** (law/love) is absolutely conditional. It always has been and always will be. **Mmara**, is the expansive pole of **Nyamewaa-Nyame Nhyehyee**. As One of the complementary poles of Divine Order, Law/Love, can only support that of which It is a component part. **Nyamewaa-Nyame Nhyehyee** dictates what and who to love (be in law with) and what and who to hate. *Nhyehyee* (Order, arrangement) including **Nyamewaa-Nyame Nhyehyee** (Divine Order) is in reality **the essence of conditionality**. Establishing parameters, rules, laws, right and wrong is the nature and definition of placing 'conditions'. **Nyamewaa-Nyame** do not "love unconditionally". **Nyamewaa-Nyame** are the root of discriminatory thought. By establishing *Nhyehyee* as the foundation of the Created Universe, **Nyamewaa-Nyame** teach us to be discriminating, discerning so that we can align ourselves with *Nhyehyee*, and restore that alignment when we find ourselves in disharmony.

When we have *fere*, respect for **Nyamewaa-Nyame** as opposed to the perverse idea of *"fearing god"*, our *fere* automatically aligns us with our *Okra/Okraa* and *nkra/nkrabea*, our Divine Consciousness and function. This alignment illuminates our awareness of **Nyamewaa-Nyame** operating within us. This alignment therefore moves us to consciously embrace **Nyamewaa-Nyame Nhyehyee**, Divine Order. This means that we embrace the Two complementary poles of **Nyamewaa-Nyame Nhyehyee**, *mmara ne kyi.* We are thus grounded and capable of *bu aten*, executing proper judgments. This will always lead to our absolute rejection of the akyiwadefo, their culture and their pseudo-religions, for our spiritual alignment will always illuminate for us the reality that all of the akyiwadefo who exist, who have ever existed and who ever will exist are the enemies of all Afurakanu/Afuraitkaitnut, and will continue to be until we make them extinct. *Mmara ne kyi* shows us that law/love (**mmara**) is balanced out by hate (**okyi**). This proves to us that law/love is absolutely conditional.

fere • mmara ne kyi • atemmu
(respect • law and hate • judgment)

This is the formula for manifesting *nyansa* (wisdom, intelligence). As *nyansa* is made up of two complementary poles: revolution and resolution, this is also the formula for our total liberation, spiritually and physically.

Below are examples of *mmara ne kyi* in action as shown through the operation of the *Abosom (Deities)*. From the ancient text called the *Book of the Cow of Heaven (Destruction of Mankind)* the *Ntoro (God)* **Ra** directs the *Ntorot (Goddess)* **Sekhemet** to destroy, to kill those individuals who were creating disorder in Kamit:

*"...Then **Ra** spoke to [His Father] **Nu**, saying: "O You first-born God from Whom I came into being, O You Goddesses and Gods of ancient time, my Ancestresses and Ancestors, take heed to what men and women [are doing]; for behold, those who were created by my Eye are uttering words of complaint [projecting disorder] against me. Tell me what you would do in the matter, and consider this thing for me, and seek out [a plan] for me, **for I will not slay them until I have heard what you say to me concerning it."***

*Then the Majesty of **Nu**, to [His] son **Ra**, spoke, saying, "You are the God who is greater than He who made You. You are the Sovereign of those who were created with You. Your throne is set, and the fear of You is great. Let Your Eye go against those who have uttered blasphemies against You."*

*And the Majesty of **Ra**, said: **"Behold, they have taken themselves to flight into the mountain lands, for their hearts are afraid because of the words which they have uttered."***

*Then the Goddesses and Gods spoke in the presence of His Majesty, saying, "Let Your Eye go forth and let it destroy for You those who revile You with words of evil, for there is no eye whatsoever that can go before It and resist You and It when It journeys **in the form of Het-Heru." Thereupon this Goddess went forth and slew the men and the women who were on the mountain (or, desert land).** And the Majesty of this God said, "Come, come in peace, O **Het-Heru**, for the work is accomplished."*

*Then this Goddess said, "You have made me to live, for when I gained the mastery over [the disordered] men and women **it was sweet to my heart**" and the Majesty of Ra said, "I myself will be master over them as [their] king, and **I will destroy them.**" And it came to pass that [this Goddess] **Sekhemet** of the offerings waded about in the night season in their blood, beginning at Henen Sut....*

*And the Majesty of **Ra** said, "I live, but my heart hath become exceedingly weary with existence with them (i.e., with disordered women and men). **I have slain [some of] them, but there is a remnant of worthless ones, for the destruction which I wrought among them was not as great as my power....**"*

*"....And when these things had been done, [the good] men and women saw the god **Ra**, upon the back [of the Divine Cow]. Then these men and women said, "Remain with us, and we will overthrow your enemies who speak words of blasphemy [against you], and [destroy them]." Then his Majesty [**RA**] set out for the Great House, and [the Goddesses and Gods who were in the train of **Ra** remained] with them (i.e., the good men and women); during that time the Earth was in darkness. And when the Earth became light [again] and the morning had dawned, **the men came forth with their bows and their [weapons], and***

they set their arms in motion to shoot the enemies [of Ra]. *Then said the Majesty of this God [**Ra**],* ***"Your acts of violence are placed behind you, for the slaughtering of the enemies is above the slaughter [of sacrifice]"***..

There are a number of important aspects to this story. We will only focus on a few in this article. The *Ntorot* **Sekhmet** is also referred to as **Het-Heru** as well as the **Eye of Ra (Arit Ra)**. She is sent out by **Ra** to destroy those who were projecting disorder into the Creative Power (uttering words/vibrations of complaint/blasphemy). They were disrespecting **Ra**, meaning that they were engaged in an attempt to corrupt the Life-Force Energy of Creation that all created entities share. If they were able to pollute the Life-Force Energy, then those Afurakanu/Afuraitkaitnut who were not engaged in such acts would still suffer. This is similar to a small group of individuals polluting the air that we all share, thereby making us all suffer.

Sekhemet goes out and kills the disordered men and women and enjoys it so much so that She states that overpowering them was *sweet to Her heart.* She then began to wade in their blood. We must understand that in relation to the body, the immune system cells do not have a group of immune system veins to operate through. They operate through the circulatory system's veins—they "wade through the blood" in order to kill cancerous cells. **Sekhemet** is connected to the Divine Immune System of Creation – specifically the Lymphatic System.

In the end, those men and women who came out to fight and to kill for **Ra** were *honored/blessed* by Him. He tells them that their acts of violence on His behalf are put behind them. Their move to kill the enemies of **Ra**, have thereby been given **Divine sanction**. While the killing of fellow citizens would normally be classified as criminal, killing the enemy in order to uphold Divine Order is given Divine sanction.

We must also point out that **Ra** asks His Father (**Nu**) as well as His Ancestresses and Ancestors for counsel before making the decision to slay the disordered men and women. It is critical to understand that the Creator of the Universe **seeks counsel** from His *Nananom Mpanyimfo (Elderesses and Elders)* and *Nananom Nsamanfo (Ancestresses and Ancestors).* This is why across Afuraka/Afuraitkait the king and queen (**ohene** and **ohemaa** in Akan) have a council of *Nananom Mpanyimfo* and seek counsel from their *Nananom Nsamanfo.* Our *ahene* and *ahemaa* (kings and queens) are not autocratic rulers. They as well as the rest of the population follow the cultural precedent established by the Creative Power ItSelf. We consult the *Abosom* and *Nananom Nsamanfo* for guidance.

We also highlighted the fact that those disordered men and women once discovered by **Ra**, ran into the mountains/deserts in an attempt to escape. Ultimately, **Ra** states that He slew/killed **some** of them, but there was a **remnant of worthless ones who remained**, for His destruction did not demonstrate the extent of His power. This is a reference to those who would become the spirits of disorder (akyiwadefo) being forced out of Afuraka/Afuraitkait into the mountains and deserts of northern eurasia and the Near East thousands of years ago. The remnant of worthless ones who survived would later return to Afuraka/Afuraitkait thousands of years later as melanin-recessive entities---**the whites and their offspring**. It was not necessary for **Ra** to destroy them all Himself. Just as there were men and women who moved to **complete the war** on behalf of **Ra** in the past, so are there Afurakanu/Afuraitkaitnut who are poised to do the same today. We must and will follow the cultural precedent set by **Ra** and those past warriors and warrioresses, our *Nananom Nsamanfo.*

The major lesson that can be extracted from this excerpt is that we have always recognized the reality that **kyi**, to hate, is Divine. The Creative Power will not only direct the *Abosom* to destroy disorder and its purveyors, but will also sanction **nnipa** (humans: Afurakanu/Afuraitkaitnut only) to participate. This has always been common knowledge amongst Afurakanu/Afuraitkaitnut. The only reason it appears to be revolutionary or unique presently, as opposed to being common sense, is because the akyiwadefo have hidden this information from us, while simultaneously poisoning our spirits/minds against **Nanasom** (Afurakani/Afuraitkaitnit Ancestral Religion). The akyiwadefo also poison the spirits/minds of Afurakanu/Afuraitkaitnut who *have* decided to embrace **Nanasom** *(Afurakani/Afuraitkaitnit (African) Ancestral Religion)* so that these Afurakanu/Afuraitkaitnut will *corrupt* its ritual practices and philosophy. The major goal being to insure that the truth about Divine Hate is never taught within **Nanasom**. Finally, the men and women who projected disorder towards **Ra** feared Him, only because of the fact that they were in the wrong. Fear would not have manifested in their spirits, had they been in harmony with **Ra**.

A second example of *mmara ne kyi* from the ancient **Per Heru Behudet** (Temple of **Heru Behudet**) in Kamit:

"..In the three hundred and sixty-third year of ***Ra-Heru-Khuti****, who lives forever and ever, His Majesty was in [the region of]* ***TA-KENS*** *[Keneset/Nubia], and His soldiers were with Him; [the enemy] did not conspire (auu) against their lord, and the land [is called]* UAUATET *unto this day. And* ***Ra*** *set out on an expedition in His boat, and His followers were with Him, and He arrived at* UTHES-HERU, *[which lay to] the west of this nome, and to the east of the canal* PAKHENNU, *which is called [..to this day]. And* ***Heru-Behudet*** *was in the boat of* ***Ra****, and He said unto His father* ***Ra-Heru-Khuti****,*

"I see that the enemies are conspiring against their Lord; let your fiery serpent gain the mastery..over them."

Then the Majesty of ***Ra Heraakhuti*** *said, "..****Heru-Behudet, Son of Ra****, You exalted one, who did proceed from* ***Me****, overthrow the enemies who are before you straightway." And* ***Heru-Behudet*** *flew up into the horizon in the form of the great Winged Disk, for which reason He is called "Great God, Lord of heaven" unto this day. And when He saw the enemies in the heights of heaven He set out to follow after them in the form of the great Winged Disk, and* ***He attacked with such terrific force those who opposed Him****, that they could neither see with their eyes nor hear with their ears, and each of them slew his fellow.* ***In a moment of time there was not a single creature left alive.*** *Then* ***Heru Behudet****, shining with very many colors, came in the form of the great Winged Disk to the Boat of* ***Ra-Heraakhuti*** *and* ***Tehuti*** *said unto* ***Ra****, "O Lord of the gods,* ***Behudet*** *hath returned in the form of the great Winged Disk, shining [with many colors]..."*

And ***Ra*** *said to* ***Heru****... "O Winged Disk, you Great God and Lord of Heaven, seize them..." and He [****Heru****] hurled His lance after them [the enemy] and He slew them, and worked a great overthrow of them. And He brought one hundred and forty-two enemies to the forepart of the Boat [of* ***Ra****]....And He hacked them in pieces with His knife and He gave their entrails to those who were in His following, and He gave their carcasses to the Gods and Goddesses Who were in the Boat of* ***Ra*** *on the river-bank of the city of Heben. Then* ***Ra*** *said to* ***Tehuti****, "See what mighty things* ***Heru Behudet*** *has performed in His deeds against the enemies....Then* ***Tehuti*** *said to* ***Ra****, "****Heru*** *will be called Winged Disk, Great God, Smiter of the enemies in the town of Heben from this day forward..."*

*....His [****Heru Behudet's****] blacksmiths are to Him, and those who are in His following are to Him in His territory, with His metal lance, with His [mace], with His dagger, and with all His chains (or, fetters) which are in the city of* ***Heru-Behudet****.*

[And when He had reached the land of the North with His followers, He found the enemy.] Now as for the blacksmiths who were over the middle regions, ***they made a great slaughter of the enemy****, and there were brought back one hundred and six of them. Now as for the blacksmiths of the West, they brought back one hundred and six of the enemy. Now as for the blacksmiths of the East,* ***among whom was Heru-Behudet, He slew them (i.e., the enemy) in the presence of Ra,*** *in the Middle Domains.*

And Ra, said unto Tehuti, "My heart [is satisfied] with the works of these blacksmiths of Heru-Behudet who are in His bodyguard. *They shall dwell in four sanctuaries, and libations and purifications and offerings shall be made to their images, and [there shall be appointed for them] priests who shall minister by the month, and priests who shall minister by the hour, in all their God-houses whatsoever,* ***as their reward because they have slain the enemies of the God."*** *And* ***Tehuti*** *said, "The [Middle] Domains shall be called after the names of these blacksmiths from this day* *onwards, and the God who dwells among them,* ***Heru-Behudet****, shall be called the 'Lord of* ***Mesent'*** *from this day onwards, and the domain shall be called 'Mesent of the West' from this day onwards." As concerning Mesent of the* West, *the face (or, front) thereof shall be towards [the East], towards the place where* ***Ra*** *rises, and this Mesent shall be called 'Mesent of the East' from this day onwards..*

There are again many lessons to be learned from the above excerpt however we will highlight only the most salient points for the purposes of this article. **Heru Behudet** is directed by **Ra** to kill His enemies. The term translated as *overthrow* or *destroy* is **s-kher**. We demonstrated in the first part of the article that the **s-** in Kamit is a causative prefix. It denotes that something is being made to occur. The term **kher** means *to destroy, overthrow, kill.* The Twi version is **kyiri** (meaning *to hate*). **Ra** is directing **Heru Behudet** to exercise Divine Hate. Later in the text **Ra** says that His heart is satisfied and directs the *Ntoro* **Tehuti**, the *Ntoro* of Divine Wisdom, to declare that **Heru Behudet** will be rewarded for His actions. The followers of **Heru Behudet**, the blacksmiths, were *honored* as well for killing the enemies of **Ra**.

It is decreed also in this text that **Heru Behudet** is called **Neb Mesen** or Master/Lord of **Mesen**. **Mesen** is the name for the **iron-working foundry**. His followers were called *mesentiu* (blacksmiths) because they were **iron-workers and warriors** who wielded **iron weapons**. **Ra** also decreed that a **metal statue** of **Heru Behudet** be placed in His temple as a shrine. The immune system is dependent on iron in order to carry out its function. Iron carries oxygen (fire). **Heru Behudet**, the *Ntoro (God)* of Metal, Iron, and War, carries the fire of **Ra/Rait** not only throughout the immune system in your body, but throughout the Divine Immune System of Creation. The *Ntoro* **Tehuti**, the Male Divinity of Divine Wisdom, confirms and announces the judgment of **Ra**. We see, time and again, the **association of Divine Wisdom with the execution of Divine Hate**. We also see, just as in the excerpt about **Sekhemet**, that **Ra** rewards the followers of **Heru Behudet**, for assisting in the killing of the enemies of **Ra**. Those who fight on behalf of **Ra** are honored with temples and shrines and offerings are decreed to be made to their images. **The Creator of the Universe promotes and rewards the execution of Divine Hate.**

Finally, an example from Akan culture. What follows is a quote from **Kwesi Yankah** as he describes the structure of the Akan libation **mpae** (prayer). The curse is a component part of Akan **mpae**. Without that component, you do not have a complete prayer specifically when the *mpaebo* is for the community. From his work, **Speaking for the Chief: Okyeame and the Politics of Akan Royal Oratory**:

The rigid structure of mpae is notable. Even though the officiant is allowed an unlimited scope of creativity in his diction, he sticks to the following sequence in the organization of his message.

a) Invocation
b) Message
c) Solicitation
d) Curse

During the invocation, the officiant invokes the forces of beneficence, observing the Akan religious hierarchy where God is the Supreme Being, followed by Mother Earth, the pantheon of lesser gods, and the ancestors. The message segment of libation often highlights the occasion and the purpose of the prayer. This is followed by solicitation, in which the speaker solicits support for the spiritual, moral and material well-being of the lineage or society. Officiants here often exploit the occasion to make oblique references to delicate political problems for which the society needs help or counseling. In a few cases, a chief's misdemeanor will receive indirect mention, in the hope that wiser counsel from the spirit world may prevail on him. The concluding segment of mpae is often reserved for the pronouncement of a curse on the forces of evil.

We should note that the term for *curse* in Twi is **duabo**. This term is comprised of **dua** – stick, and **bo** – to strike. **Duabo** is thus *stick-striking; beating*. This is a clear description of the intent of the terms **khet** and **kher** from Kamit where the *medut* shows a man with a **stick** in the act of *striking, beating, attacking (hating)*.

Below is an *mpaebo* offered as thanks for the recovery from sickness recorded in Date *(Larteh)*, Ghana by K.K. Anti: (formerly posted on http://cehd.ewu.edu/cehd/faculty/ntodd/GhanaUDLP/KKAnti/LibationIntro.html)

Otwereduampon drink, Thursday Earth drink,
River Afram drink, Paha drink, Asunsu drink.
Ancestors of the Aduana family drink, Biretuo drink.
Dente Deity drink, Dwerebe drink, Buruku drink,
Thousand ancestors and thousand gods come and receive drink
When I call one, I call all of you,
Soul Bosompra here is drink! Soul Bosompra here is drink!
There is nothing wrong that I call you.
It is my son Ntiamoa Amankuo
You are aware of the sickness that befell him a month ago.
It is through your grace and great prayers, that he has recovered.
Receive wine and drink today this Monday.
Stand behind him with good standing
We pray for long life and prosperity
Bless him with living water
Any evil person who wish Ntiamoa Amankuo
To pass away from this world
So that I become lonely,
Hand him over to the Divine Executioners
Nobody blesses his enemies,
Blessing to all who have assembled here.

Otwereduampon is used here as an invocatory title of **Nyame**. The *Earth Mother* and various *Abosom* and *Nananom Nsamanfo* are called in the *mpae*. The key statements at the end of the *mpae* are those comprising the *duabo* section where the individual asks Those Whom were invoked and evoked, i.e., **Nyamewaa-Nyame**, the *Abosom* and *Nananom Nsamanfo* that **any evil person be handed over to the Divine Executioners**, for **nobody blesses his enemies**. This kind of speech is common in Akan culture, and in Afurakani/Afuraitkaitnit culture **across the board**. It is a manifestation of our total **fere**, respect, for **Nyamewaa-Nyame Nhyehyee**. We seek to incorporate (*mmara/mar*...law/love) things, entities that we need and we seek to reject (*khet, kyi*...hate) things, entities that we do not need. It also shows that we have always sought and we always seek to invoke the **Divine Executioners** (**Divine Killers**), Those *Abosom* Whom are governed by **Heru Behudet** and **Sekhemet**, by whatever names These *Abosom* are called in the various Afurakani/Afuraitkaitnit languages and cultures. We invoke Them for the purpose of eliminating the purveyors of disorder.

In Kamit, the term **maakheru** or **maakher** is the masculine and **maatkheru** or **maatkher** is the feminine title given to those who have achieved a certain level of spiritual cultivation. In the texts of Kamit, the spiritually cultivated individual who has made his or her transition via Death to the spirit-realm is tested by the *Abosom* and *Nananom Nsamanfo* to determine if his or her spirit is in harmony with Divine Order. If so, he or she is declared to be **maakheru** or **maatkheru**, for he or she has achieved the requisite level of spiritual cultivation to be accepted as part of the community of **Aakhu/Aakhutu** (*Nananom Nsamanfo*; Spiritually Cultivated Ancestresses and Ancestors). Such an individual is endowed by **Amen/Amenet** (**Nyame-Nyamewaa**) with the capacity and the responsibility to guide his or her relatives on Earth, as they live to develop their character and properly execute their **nkrabea** (Divinely allotted function/mission in Creation).

The term **maakher** or **maakheru** is very often defined: **maa** – true, **kher** – voice. One who is *maakheru* is one who is *true of voice*. One who speaks, commands (*kher*), and does – incorporates – law, truth (*maa/maat)*. The related term in Twi is **mmarahye**, which is comprised of: *mmara* (law) and *hye* (tsheh) meaning: *to command; to arrange; to force*. This term is used to describe the act of giving laws while the *mmarahye-fo* is one of the group (*fo*) who gives, enacts (*hye*) laws (*mmara*), hence the definition "law giver" for *mmarahyefo* in Akan.

The Twi term *hye* (to command) is derived of the Kamau term *kher* (*shehr*) *to voice*. **Maakher** is thus **mmarahye**. Moreover, the definition of *hye* meaning *to force; to compel* shows the connection of *kher, hye* and *kyi* phonetically and conceptually. The idea of one *compelling* or *forcing law* is actually the definition of the function of **Heru Behudet** and **Sekhemet**. Certainly, the pronunciation of *hye* and *kyi* are similar, and the concept of hating/rejecting (*kyi*) disorder for the purpose of upholding law (*mmara*) is the same as forcing, compelling, fixing (*hye*) law (*mmara*). Such a compulsion exists only for the purpose of maintaining **Nyamewaa-Nyame Nhyehyee**.

Critically, we have shown the root cosmological meaning of *maakheru/maatkheru* which is the basis of the notion that one can be *true of voice*, one who speaks/does the Law. *Maakheru or Maatkheru* as a title shows that one has achieved **Nyamewaa-Nyame Nhyehyee**. He or she has balanced the two complementary poles of Divine Order---*mmara* (maa/maat) and *kyi* (*khet* or *kher* in the language of Kamit…*kyi* or *kyiri* in Akan). He or she is *maakheru* or *maatkheru* because he or she respects and operationalizes *mmara ne kyi*, Divine Law and Divine Hate in a balanced fashion, consistently, without fail.

It is this kind of Afurakani/Afuraitkaitnit person **and only this kind** of Afurakani/Afuraitkaitnit person who achieves the level of Honorable, Venerable (Spiritually Cultivated) Elder or Elderess in Society and Honorable, Venerable (Spiritually Cultivated) Ancestor or Ancestress after making transition to **Asamando** (the Ancestral realm). In Akan culture they are called *Nananom Mpanyimfo* and *Nananom Nsamanfo* respectively.

maā-kheru [hieroglyphs], U. 453, [hieroglyphs], Rec. 33, 36 [to be declared to be] "true of voice, or word" in the Judgment, *i.e.*, to be innocent, to be justified like Osiris; Maā-kheru (fem. maāt-kheru) always

mmăra-hyɛ́, *inf.* the act of *giving laws; legislation*; *s.* mmăra.
mmăra-hyɛ́fó, *pl. id. lawgiver, legislator.*

Selected References:

Tomb of Seti I, *(Book of the Cow of Heaven, Destruction of Mankind)*
Per Heru Behudet *(Temple of Heru Behudet, Legend of Heru of Edfu)*
Pert em Heru, *Sheft (papyrus) of* **Ani**
Let the Ancestors Speak, *Ankh Mi Ra*
Speaking for the Chief: Okyeame and the Politics of Akan Royal Oratory, *by Kwesi Yankah*
Twi-English/English-Twi Concise Dictionary, *Paul Kotey*

MMARA NE KYI

Divine Law and Divine Hate

Ofa a eto so Abiesa – Part 3

Nyansa is the term for *wisdom, intelligence* in the Twi language. We have shown in the first two parts of this series that **Nyamewaa-Nyame Nhyehyee** (Divine Order) is comprised of Two Complementary Poles: Law (Love) and Hate. **Mmara** (Law/Love) is governed by the *Ntoro* and *Ntorot* **Maa** and **Maat** while **Okyi** (**Kyi**, to Hate) is governed by the *Ntoro* and *Ntorot* **Heru Behudet** (Sekhem Shut) and **Sekhemet** (Herit). In a similar fashion, *Nyansa* is comprised of Two Complementary Poles: Revolution and Resolution. Revolution is the expansive pole of Wisdom/Intelligence while Resolution is the contractive pole of Wisdom/Intelligence.

San ne San

Return and Resolve; Revolution-Resolution

A *revolution* is a complete *return*. The word is composed of *re-* meaning *back or again* and the root *volve*: meaning *to turn, to roll.* To revolve is to *re-turn* or *turn-back*. When Earth moves around Sun and returns to Its point of origin, it has made a complete revolution. When an Afurakani/Afuraitkaitnit individual has made a complete revolution, he or she has returned to his or her point of origin or his or her original nature/condition.

In the Twi language the term **san** means *to repeat an act; to return.* The often repeated **sankofa** means to **san** (*return*) **ko** (*go*) **fa** (*grasp*). The **ebe** (proverb) associated with **sankofa** is as follows:

Se wo were fi, na wo sankofa a, yenkyi
If you forget and you return, go, grasp (from your past) it is not hateful/taboo (it is truly best)

This *ebe* refers to the act of returning, spiritually and/or physically, to go and grasp from the values of your Ancestral past, in order to resolve or bring resolution to conflict in the present. Afurakanu/Afuraitkaitnut recognize that it is in our Ancestral past, that we find the answers to our problems, for the further that we go back in time the closer we come to those first Afurakanu/Afuraitkaitnut who were created by **Nyamewaa-Nyame** and who first established **Nyamewaa-Nyame Nhyehyee**, Divine Order, in every aspect of their lives. They were the first to establish **civilization,** *a social order rooted in the Divine Order of Nature.* They were the first to be possessed by the **Abosom** and codify what they received from the *Abosom* into the institutional fabric of the culture. They were thus the first to achieve the status of **Nananom Mpanyimfo**, Spiritually Cultivated [Honorable] Elderesses and Elders, and the first to make the transition from *Nananom Mpanyimfo* to **Nananom Nsamanfo**, Spiritually Cultivated [Honorable] Ancestresses and Ancestors upon transitioning to **Asamando**, the Ancestral realm.

These *Nananom* were the first to receive and establish the protocol for functioning harmoniously in Creation, and the methods by which that protocol would be transferred intergenerationally – without profanation. These *Nananom Nsamanfo* continue to guide us in the present. Afurakanu/Afuraitkaitnut have thus inherited and continue to inherit a cultural reservoir of over 1,000,000 generations of Earthly experience from which we may draw in order to bring balance to every aspect of our lives. Yet, the concept of *san* goes further.

Afurakanu/Afuraitkaitnut in America have been the furthest removed, geographically and spiritually/culturally, from Afuraka/Afuraitkait. Our *sankofa* process must therefore reach the furthest back. We must go to the beginning of Creation. We must *san* (return) to the pact we made with **Nyamewaa-Nyame** before incarnating into the world. We must therefore revisit our **nkrabea** (Divine function) in order to reclaim our identity, individually and collectively. Once our identity is reclaimed through this extensive process of *sankofa*, only then can we understand what is lawful and what is hateful, how to function and how not to function, who and what to accept, who and what to reject, who and what to be in law/love with and who and what to hate, how to establish Order and how to destroy disorder. We have thereby returned to our original state, our point/condition of origin in order to draw from the resources necessary to address that which confronts us in the present with intelligence. Through *san*, we consciously avail ourselves of our inherited reservoir of experience. We have made a complete revolution.

When we return, **san**, *to our Ancestral consciousness and are fed from it we fully and properly expand our awareness of our position in Creation and how to negotiate that position in harmony with* **Nyamewaa-Nyame Nhyehyee.** *This is the expansive nature of Nyansa.*

A *resolution* is a complete *rectification.* The word is composed of *re-* meaning *back or again* and the root, *solve* meaning *to loosen, unravel.* It includes the notion of: *to free* or *to free from restraint; to vindicate; to clear; to restore; to return to the former state.* To resolve is to reduce something back to its former state, its natural form.

A second meaning in the Twi language for the term **san** is: *to loosen; to unfasten, unravel.* Once we have expanded our awareness of the **nokware** (truth) of our *nkrabea* and its relationship to our place in Creation through engaging *san* (return, revolt), we then engage *san* (unravel) in order to loosen, unravel, to break up the hold that disorder has taken over our lives. We move to unravel the knots which have blocked the free-flow of consciousness and energy necessary for the execution of our *nkrabea.* We move to eradicate the disorder for good. We restore our condition to its former (Orderly) state. We have affected a complete resolution.

When Earth, through revolution, transmits Its power through the seasons, It has brought about a complete resolution. When we take the consciousness and energy that we have acquired through revolution and expend it for the purpose of achieving resolution, we vindicate ourselves and our condition. We restore nhyehyee. This is the contractive nature of Nyansa.

Through revolution we *san, return,* to our original state/our point of origin---our well of consciousness, energy and Ancestral experience to arm ourselves with the necessities/weapons necessary to rectify conflict. Through resolution we *san, resolve/restore,* the life-situation to its natural form/former state of harmony with Creation. We restore our life-circumstances to their former Orderly state, the state in which they existed before the interruption of disorder. In that *san*, in that return, we eradicate blockages to our own awareness. In that *san*, in that resolve/restoration, we eradicate impediments (people or situations) to our ability to execute our *nkrabea*.

The expansive nature of *san* allows us to return to, to **express**, our essence. The contractive nature of *san* allows us to restore, to **impress**, our essence. We return to reclaim who we are and how we are designed to function, how we should/must function. We resolve by impressing/imprinting that knowledge upon our life-condition, our present circumstances. We return, *san*, to retrieve the template for proper living and we resolve, *san*, by taking that template and impressing/imprinting it upon the current situation, thereby stamping out the disorder and restoring Order.

Revolution is the *expression* of Wisdom, Intelligence. Resolution is the *impression* of Wisdom, Intelligence. Through revolution we revolt, we express our disdain for disorder---by challenging it. Through resolution we resolve, we impress our disdain for disorder---by eradicating it. When we challenge, we challenge relentlessly, without compromise. When we eradicate, we eradicate completely, without exception.

NYANSA

It is important to note that the term **nyan** in the Twi language means *to awaken, to cease to sleep; to rise up*. The term **sa** in Twi means *war*. It also means *to end; bring an end to; to cut into* as in **sa yare:** *to cure, to bring an end to* (**sa**) *disease* (**yare**).

Nyan is related to the expansive aspect of **san** in the sense that *to revolt, to return* is to *awaken, to rise up, to cease to sleep,* which demonstrates expansion. **Sa** (war; to bring an end to) is related to the contractive aspect of **san** in the sense that *war, to bring an end to, resolution, bringing an end to disorder, restoring order* demonstrates contraction. *Nyansa* as *wisdom, intelligence* is thus a dual ac*knowledge*ment that disorder is present and that it must be challenged, turned back (**san**) and defeated, cut into, brought to an end (**sa**) so that we may be *free from restraint, vindicated, returned to our former state* (**san**).

In the language of Kamit, **san** also means: *to turn back*. **san** also means: *to cut; to cut into.* See below:

Kamit	*Definition*	*Twi*	*Definition*
san	to turn back	**san**	to turn back; return
san	to cut; cut into	**sa**	to cut; cut into; pierce

Functionally, *nyansa* is the ability to **re-spect** or re-view every thought, intention and action and harmonize each with **Nyamewaa-Nyame Nhyehyee**. This means that we must engage what we would call **san-san**, *revolution-resolution*. We must reach back into our Divine Ancestral awareness when faced with a problem, draw the necessary resources therefrom, challenge the disorder and eradicate the disorder. This is the proper balanced approach and that which is the only means whereby Afurakanu/Afuraitkaitnut can engage in true **Amansesew**, Nationbuilding/Nation-restoration. We must be **asafo** (warriors/warrioresses) who are **revolutionary-resolutionary**.

One cannot simply "be a revolutionary" and be complete, yet not have a true goal to eradicate disorder and its purveyors and restore Order through resolution. One cannot simply "focus on solutions", i.e. "be a resolutionary" and be complete, yet have no understanding of the value of nor possess the courage to fight/engage/revolt. Revolution and Resolution are two halves of the Divine Whole of *Nyansa.* One cannot truly be a revolutionary without being a resolutionary. One cannot truly be a resolutionary without being a revolutionary. It is the akyiwadefo who promote the imbalanced idea that, "we are in the struggle", "we are in the revolution", "the revolution is coming", while the balanced notion of "we are ending the struggle", "we are in the resolution", "the resolution is here" is never addressed. Many misguided Afurakanu/Afuraitkaitnut have followed this perverse pattern of thinking in imitation of white pseudo-"revolutionaries".

The focus on a pseudo notion of 'revolution' by the akyiwadefo is a manifestation of the reality that the akyiwadefo are incapable of resolution, for resolution requires that disharmony is challenged relentlessly with the goal of resolution---the complete eradication of disharmony/disorder and its purveyors and the restoration of balance. The akyiwadefo incarnate as spirits of disorder and are therefore perpetually imbalanced. Resolution with regard to the akyiwadefo on any level would necessarily mean their total extinction. Because they seek only to perpetuate disorder, they necessarily seek to perpetuate their existence (disorder) in the world which is in direct contradistinction to the function of revolution-resolution.

Moreover, the akyiwadefo are not capable of true revolution for they do not have the capacity to return to a point of origin or an original/natural state---a state (natural) which they have never experienced. They have no capacity therefore to return to a pact with **Nyamewaa-Nyame**, for they have no pact. They never had a pact and will never have a pact. They have no *nkrabea*. Only *created* entities in Creation have a pact with **Nyamewaa-Nyame**, have an *nkrabea*, a purpose, a Divine function to execute in Creation. The akyiwadefo being, naturally, forever excluded from this category have nothing to revolt against, nor anything to bring resolution to. They **are** the disorder that must be addressed through revolution-resolution on the part of Afurakanu/Afuraitkaitnut.

The akyiwadefo do not challenge for the purpose of restoring Order, they fight only for the purpose of restoring their ability to engage in their own lustful and malicious (disordered) desires without hindrance. The akyiwadefo therefore do not/cannot engage in revolution, but in **revulsion**. To *revulse* is to *tear away*, to *pull; tear* (*vulse* from the root *vellere*) *back; again* (*re*). The akyiwadefo only challenge, or seek to *pull back* or *tear away* anything that stands in the way of them perpetuating disorder in the world.

The akyiwadefo do not engage in resolution, seeking to restore Order to society or relationships, for if they did they would only seek the complete eradication of themselves (complete eradication of disorder). Instead, the aspiration of the akyiwadefo is **repression**. They malfunction in Creation for the purpose of *pressing* (holding down) *back; again* (re) others.

The act of *revulsion* is the **perversion** of *revolution* from the Afurakani/Afuraitkaitnit, the true, perspective. The act of *repression* is the **perversion** of *resolution* from the Afurakani/Afuraitkaitnit, the true, perspective.

It is spiritually and cosmologically impossible for any non-Afurakani/non-Afuraitkaitnit to be a revolutionary or a resolutionary. Non-Afurakanu/non-Afuraitkaitnut cannot bring revolution. They can only bring revulsion. Non-Afurakanu/non-Afuraitkaitnut cannot bring resolution. They can only bring repression. They are not and cannot be revolutionary, but can only be revulsionary. They are not and cannot be resolutionary, but can only be repressionary.

TU SA…NYAN SA

The Twi phrase **tu sa** is translated as: *to wage war*. In a similar fashion, with respect to the revolutionary-resolutionary nature of wisdom, intelligence, we utilize the term **nyan sa**. We recognize the nature of wisdom to be a process of awakening, *nyan*, war, *sa*, against disorder in all of its forms.

Nyan, to awaken, is a natural Divine reaction to the influence of disorder. **The urge to challenge disorder is an urge of Divine Intelligence.** *Sa*, war, is a natural, Divine, response to disorder. **The urge to eradicate disorder is an urge of Divine Intelligence**. As stated previously, the definition of **Nanasom**, Afurakani/Afuraitkaitnit Ancestral Religion is: *the ritual incorporation of Divine Law and the ritual restoration of Divine Balance.* This is a reflection of Afurakani/Afuraitkaitnit Ancestral Culture, which is properly defined as the *Divine acceptance (law/ love) of Order and the Divine rejection (hate) of disorder.* When we embrace these realities only then do we have religion and culture. Otherwise, we simply demonstrate the perverse influence of the akyiwadefo.

We have been conditioned by the akyiwadefo against awakening, *nyan*. Through the propagation of their false religions, fictional characters and their associated foolish doctrines/philosophies we are programmed to remain asleep. We are instructed to: *seek our treasures in heaven; to turn the other cheek; to seek to escape the cycle of reincarnation; to view this world as an illusion and that the physical world and its affairs are unimportant; that we should not be focused outwardly but inwardly; that we should not judge, pass judgment, or be judgmental; that we should accept all people, things and events and see them all as representatives of lessons and that, "all are in divine order".* These ideas are absolutely inaccurate, foolish and self-destructive, promoting disorder in the spirits of Afurakanu/Afuraitkaitnut. It is for this reason that they comprise the core-programming tool utilized by the akyiwadefo to keep us from awakening.

We have been conditioned by the akyiwadefo as well to express an instantaneous adverse reaction to the idea of warfare. We are taught that war is wrong, evil, immature, non-spiritual, a sign of being controlled by a lower-level of consciousness among many other idiotic, nonsensical beliefs. We have been shielded with respect to the true meaning of war and its relationship to Divine Intelligence.

It is a manifestation of Nyansa, Divine Wisdom, to seek to establish, restore and maintain Nyamewaa-Nyame Nhyehyee through the functional instrument of Revolution-Resolution. For disorder is not a creation of Nyamewaa-Nyame. Disorder is always by definition an uncreated, therefore a temporary, aberration in the Created Order.

In ancient Kamit, the *Ntoro* (God) of Divine Wisdom, Divine Speech, learning, writing, the sciences, etc. is called **Tehuti**. **Tehuti** is also called **Tehi** and **Tekh**. As **Tekh**, He is the regulator of the Time and seasons (Nature's rhythm). It is for this reason that He is also the *Ntoro* of the first month of the calendar of Kamit. **Tekh** is the Male counterpart to **Tekhit**. **Tekhit** is the *Ntorot* (Goddess) of Divine Wisdom. She is also the *Ntorot* of the first month of the calendar. Together **Tekh** and **Tekhit** govern the Natural rhythm.

Tehuti (**Tekh**) as Divine Measurer of Time is shown as the Divine Scribe holding the *notched palm-branch.* **Seshat** as a title of the Female counterpart of **Tehuti** is the Divine Scribe (**seshat** means scribe) also holding the *notched palm-branch.* This palm-branch represents the enumeration/measurement of Time and the proper place of all created entities, things and events within the Divinely Created Continuum:

Tehuti with notched palm branch

Seshat with notched palm branch

Seshat and **Tehuti** Together, both holding notched palm branches

Notice the symbol on the Head of the *Ntorot* **Seshat**. This symbol of a seven-pointed star or plant with two horns inverted above it lends its name to another title of **Seshat**. She is thus often called **Sefkhet Aabuit**. **Sefkhet** can mean *seven*. **Aabuit** means *two horns*. However, the term **sefkh(t)** also means: *to untie, to unfasten, to loosen, to set free; to cut off, to cut away (with force/violence).*

The **habu** bird (ibis; crane) is the bird which is sacred to **Tehuti** and thus the bird-form that **Tehuti** takes. **Tehuti** often has the head of the *habu* (as shown above) and the body of a man. He is also depicted in the full form of a *habu*. The *habu* was a bird which used its hooked-beak to kill certain deadly animals and insects. It was thus a protector for the inhabitants of Kamit. This bird *habu* was also called **tekh**. It is critical to note that the general term **tekhi** in Kamit, with the determinative of a man wielding an axe means: *massacre; slaughter*. The term **tekh** spelled with the soft *'t'* also means: *to overthrow*.

Tekh/Tehuti, the *habu*-headed *Ntoro* was seen as a Divine Protector, for the establishment and maintenance of Order through the application of Wisdom is *protective to us* as we work to fulfill our *nkrabea*. We rely on the Divine Laws (**maau**) scribed by **Tehuti** and **Seshat** in order to protect ourselves from falling into a lustful, malicious, self-destructive life-style/existence. They inscribe these laws through writing and also through ritual into our consciousness.

The **Medut Ntorot** (hieroglyphic symbols), as well as other sacred symbols such as the **Adinkra** in Akan culture, were formed/scribed by **Tehuti** and **Seshat**. **Once ritually incorporated, these geometric forms become talismans which we can employ to neutralize dissonant energy, inimical vibrations, projected upon us from other entities. These specialized forms also become functional matrices performing the function of Abosomkommere (Deity Shrines)-in-miniature whose potency we may activate for our spiritual alignment and re-alignment when thinking (conceptualizing), writing, speaking, meditating, engaging in mpaebo (ritual prayer) and more.**

Tehuti is the *Ntoro* of Divine Wisdom. **Seshat**, also called **Sefkhet Aabuit**, is the *Ntorot* of Divine Wisdom. The titles **Tekh** and **Tekhit** are related to the word **tekh** meaning *massacre, slaughter; to overthrow*. The title **Sefkhet** is related to the word **sefkh** meaning *loosening, unraveling, setting free*. As the *Governor* of the expansive pole of Wisdom (Nyansa), **Tehuti** or **Tekh**, is directly connected with the **revolutionary** notion of **san**: *to return, to revolt, to challenge, to turn back---to attack/slaughter; wage war against*. As *Governess* of the contractive pole of Wisdom (Nyansa), **Seshat** as **Sefkhet Aabuit** has a function which is directly connected with the **resolutionary** notion of **san**: *to loosen, unravel (disorder), to set free---to end the war*.

We demonstrated in the second part of this series that **Tehuti** directs **Heru Behudet** to slaughter the enemy and subsequently rewards and honors **Heru Behudet** for accomplishing the task---according to the Orders of **Ra**. Divine Wisdom, **Nyansa**, has always been associated with the execution of Divine Hate, **Kyi**, whose execution is prompted by the Creative Power. See picture below:

Tehuti, Auset and Heru Behudet participating in the capturing and spearing of the enemy

Drawing of the scene from the **Temple of Heru of Edfu.** Photo by this author.

It must be stated clearly that these enemies/fiends are not simply symbolic representations of our lower nature, misguided desires or lusts. While these concepts are related and part of the whole, these *Abosom*, **Tehuti**, **Auset**, **Heru Behudet** and Others operate throughout all aspects of Creation. *As above, So below.* We have real enemies (purveyors of disorder) in the physiological realm (cancerous cells), the spirit-realm (including various forms of lust and malice as well as deceased discarnate spirits who seek to wreak havoc in the lives of the living), but also the physical realm – murderers, rapists, all of the whites and their offspring/akyiwadefo, etc. Disorder and its purveyors are stamped out on **every** level, physical and non-physical, under the *direction* of **Tehuti** and **Tekhit**. This is one of the reasons why **Tehuti** is shown above with the captured enemy, holding them for **Heru Behudet** to **slay** them in turn. Divine Wisdom (**Tehuti**), respects the role of Divine Hate (**Heru Behudet**) and allows It to carry out its Divine Function (eliminating disorder and its purveyors) in Its proper *Time.*

An excerpt from the **Pert em Heru** (*sheft*/papyrus of the scribe Ani):

". . . Hail, ***Tehuti****, who made* ***Ausar*** *victorious over his enemies, make the Ausar, the scribe Ani* ***maakheru****, to be victorious over his enemies in the presence of the great Divine rulers, on the festival of the breaking and turning up of the Earth in (the region of) Djedu, on the night of the breaking and turning up of the Earth in their blood and of making* ***Ausar*** *to be victorious over his enemies.*

When the ***fiends*** *of* ***Set*** *come and change themselves into beasts, the great Divine rulers, on the festival of the breaking and turning up of the Earth in Djedu,* ***slay them in the presence of the Deities therein, and their blood flows among them as they are smitten down. These things are allowed to be done by them by the judgment of those who are in Djedu.***

The great Divine rulers in Re-stau are ***Heru, Ausar*** *and* ***Auset****. The heart of* ***Ausar*** *rejoices, and the heart of* ***Heru*** *is glad; and therefore are the east and the west at peace.*

Hail ***Tehuti****, who made* ***Ausar*** *victorious over His enemies, make the Ausar Ani, the scribe and teller of the divine offerings of all the Deities, to triumph over his enemies in the presence of the ten companies of great Divine rulers who are with* ***Ra*** *and with* ***Ausar*** *and with every God and Goddess in the presence of* ***Neb-er-tcher****. He has destroyed his enemies, and he has destroyed every evil thing belonging unto him. . . ."*

Here **Tehuti**, the *Ntoro* of Divine Wisdom is appealed to, that He may make the scribe Ani, victorious/triumphant over his enemies, just as **Tehuti** had done for **Ausar** by making **Ausar** victorious over His enemies. The word being translated here as *victorious* or *triumphant* is actually the word **maakheru** (**maakher/mmara ne kyi/mmarahye**). We appeal to Divine Wisdom/*Nyansa*, in order to become victorious over our enemies. We appeal to Divine Wisdom in order to embrace *mmara ne kyi*, *maakher*, Divine Law and Divine Hate. This has always been common knowledge in Afuraka/Afuraitkait. It was only through the perversion of our culture by the akyiwadefo that we have been perversely conditioned to never associate warfare, destruction of our enemies, of disorder, with Divine Wisdom.

MMUSUA NE MMUSU.:.MSUT HENA MSUT

Just as in the Twi language, the language of Kamit has more than one term to describe hate. The term from Keneset and Kamit, **mst** is found in Twi as **musu**, both being directly related to Divine Hate. In the language of Keneset and Kamit we have the term **mst** with two major meanings:

mst -- offspring, that which is birthed, children; family
mst -- hate, hatred, that which is hated

These terms and their related forms are usually written by egyptologists as:

mest, mesut, msut, ms, mes, mesi

Again, in the "field" of egyptology, the whites often place the letter '*e*' in between the consonants of those words that are written without vowels in the *medutu*. For example, the term for God, **Ntr**, is often written *Neter*. This application of the letter *e* is arbitrary. It is done as a way to facilitate pronunciation. It is an indication that the researcher either does not know the proper pronunciation of the ancient term and/or the researcher is attempting to conceal the proper pronunciation of the ancient term. Such concealment is employed because the whites know that it is in the languages of Afuraka/Afuraitkait that these ancient terms still exist---intact. For example, the above-mentioned term **Ntr**, God (Masculine), exists in Twi as **Ntoro** meaning the Patrilineal *Obosom*/God. The identity of thousands of words and concepts from Keneset and Kamit existing in the languages and cultures of contemporary Afuraka/Afuraitkait shows that many of the peoples of Afuraka/Afuraitkait today are the direct descendants/relations of the ancient Kenesu-Kamau. This fact the akyiwadefo seek to keep from us, for it is liberating to our Ancestral consciousness.

How then do we properly pronounce the terms **mst** (*family, offspring*) and **mst** (*hate, to hate, that which is hated*)?

In Akan we have **both** terms carrying the **same** meanings:

mmusua – Matrilineal families/clans: offspring, those who are birthed; descendants of Great Ancestresses
mmusu -- that which is hated; great moral evil/taboo

As we can see, **mst** and **mst** in Kamit is **musua**(t) and **musu**(t) in Akan. The arbitrary insertion of the *e* is inaccurate (mest, mesut, mesi). Moreover, in *Coptic*, the word **mst** is spelled **moste**. The *o* in *Coptic* is approximated by the *u* in Twi/Akan (**musu**(t)).

In Akan culture, inheritance is determined through the matrilineal blood-circle. There are seven Great Females Whom collectively are the Ancestresses of all Akan people. These seven Females are the heads of the seven great **mmusua**, matrilineal clans/families, of the Akan. Every Akan individual is descendent through one of these *mmusua*. If an Afurakani/Afuraitkaitnit individual can trace his or her direct Ancestry---physically and spiritually (via reincarnation)—directly to one of these seven Females, then he or she is Akan. Otherwise, he or she is not Akan. The singular form of *mmusua* is **abusua**.

[Just as the *m* and *b* interchange in the term for *blood* in Twi, written: **mogya**, **mbogya**, **bogya**, depending on the specific Twi dialect and/or orthographical representation, so is it apparent in the terms *abusua* and *mmusua*. *Mmusua* is used in the pronunciation of the plural just as many words whose root begins with the *b* sound in the singular are spelled with the double *mm* in the plural. Indeed, when spoken at regular conversation speed, *mbogya* and *mogya* sound identical.]

All Akan people are part of one of the seven *mmusua*. We are all *offspring, family, birthed* from these clans. When one asks "what is your *abusua*?" they are asking what family do you come from. This is why the term *msut* is defined in Kamit as: *offspring, family, that which is/those whom are birthed.* The terms *msut* and *mmusua* are the exact same terms, phonetically and conceptually.

In Akan culture that which is **mmusu** is that which is considered: *abominable, hateful, abhorrent, accursed, wicked.* **Mmusu** is also written **musu** or **musuo** depending on the dialect or the orthographical representation. Again the *m* and *b* interchange, so we have the forms **busu-fo** (*fo* – people, who are *mmusu* – wicked). See the relationship to **ade** (things), **adwene** (thoughts), **bo** (to act; acts) and **yi** (to remove; removal):

busu-de – wicked, evil thing or deed; abomination
busu-adwene – wicked, evil thoughts (*adwene*)
mmusu-bo – the act of (*bo*) cursing; the committing of acts that bring disaster
mmusu-yi – the removal (*yi*) of a curse, evil, of that which is hated (*mmusu*)

In Akan culture, **mmusu** is defined as **a great moral evil**. *Mmusu* is a great or comprehensive **akyiwade** (taboo).

Incest, rape, child molestation are examples of what is considered **mmusu**. These are some of the things that are **hated** by the *Abosom*. They are necessarily, by default, *akyiwade*, taboo, *that which is hated by the Abosom.* The *Abosom* are known to punish and/or kill individuals who commit such acts. The difference between *mmusu* and *akyiwade* can be summed up in the phrase:

Mmusude ye akyiwade na akyiwade nyinaa nnye mmusude

All mmusu are akyiwade, yet all akyiwade are not mmusu.

An example of this principle: the various **mmusua** (families/clans) have their own dietary *akyiwade* or taboos. If the members of the *mmusua* consume a certain food that is *akyiwade* for their group, it could lead to their deaths. The *Abosom* have directed them not to consume this food. Such consumption is something that is hated/rejected by the *Abosom*. The *Abosom* will punish those who violate the *akyiwade*/taboo. However, one particular food can be *akyiwade* for the members of one of the *mmusua* but not for members of any of the other *mmusua*. Therefore, we can have a situation where, because of their trustory and genetic/spiritual make-up, the members of the **Asona** *abusua* (Asona clan) may be able to eat a particular food, whereas the members of the **Agona** *abusua* cannot. On a much lower level, there are some food items that make some of us sick while others can consume the same food items and be fine. These kinds of differences, <u>not related to a sanction from the *Abosom*</u>, are called <u>allergies</u> in english. Someone can eat mushrooms for example and have no adverse reaction, whereas someone else can eat the same mushrooms, develop an acute allergic reaction and die from it. The allergic reaction to a food led to their demise. The dietary *akyiwade* are similar, except they carry the sanction of one or more *Abosom*. The *akyiwade* is therefore a comprehensive (physical and spiritual) restriction as opposed to a simple physical allergen.

However, **mmusu** is that *class* of *akyiwade* that is **taboo for all Afurakanu/Afuraitkaitnut**. Again, incest, rape, child molestation, are examples of that which is designated as *mmusu*. **Every Afurakani/Afuraitkaitnit individual** is Divinely prohibited from this kind of *akyiwade*. No exceptions. The relevance of these terms for the purposes of this discussion is summed up in the well known phrase in Kamit:

Mst Ntr

(*musu(t) Ntoro*; *mest neter* as misspelled by the whites)

mesṭ neter, Excom. Stele 5, a person or thing hateful to the god.

A person or thing which is Hated (Mst) by the God (Ntr) or Goddess (Ntrt)

Again, this is **Divine Hate**. **Hate has always been Divine**. We have simply been misguided by the whites and their offspring, deliberately, against Hate.

Mst Ntr (Divine Hate, That which the God/Goddess Hates) is not only found in the texts of Kamit, but in Akan culture the *Abosom* have always stated, **Themselves**, who and what They Hate. **Afurakanu/Afuraitkaitnut learned the concept of Divine Hate from the Abosom Themselves**. This is true of **all** Afurakani/Afuraitkaitnit (African) Ancestral Religions. The **Abosom**, **Orisha, Vodou, Arusi**, have always stated and continue to state to this day whom and what They hate. This occurs through possession, divination, and many other forms of direct communication from the *Abosom* to us. **Since the whites and their offspring first came into existence and into contact with us, the Abosom have clearly stated that They hate the whites and their offspring. They continue to do so today and will continue to do so, by Their own admission, until we make the akyiwadefo extinct. The Abosom direct us to hate the akyiwadefo, for this is part of embracing Nyamewaa-Nyame Nhyehyee, Mmara Ne Kyi.**

Mst/Musu/Khet/Kyi---The concept of Hate as an integral part of our culture and thus our religion/spirituality was never an "issue", until the whites made it a false issue. They understand that as long as we reject the Divine Mandate to Hate them, we place ourselves out of *Nyamewaa-Nyame Nhyehyee* (Divine Order) and will not be able to eradicate them and their influence from our lives. In this ill-condition we are actually showing hatred for **Nyamewaa-Nyame**. This is truly self-hate---which is insane.

Insane or insane-acting people cannot govern themselves. They must be dependent upon others. Others often include their enemies.

We mentioned in this series that **Heru** is the *Ntoro* (God) of Hate. We mentioned that the name **Heru** is directly related to Hate. It should thus be understood that **one** of the **four sons of Heru** is named **Mst** (**Musut**). **Mst** is an *Ntoro* Whom governs the *liver*. The term for the *liver* in Kamit is **mst**. A major function of the liver is to **oxidize** impurities in the blood---to oxidize is to "burn up" impurities.

The terms *mst* and *mst*, from Keneset, Kamit and their derivatives in Akan were corrupted by the whites. These corruptions therefore show up in their languages:

Kamit		*Twi*	
mst	family; that which is birthed	**mmusua**	matrilineal clans; offspring that which is birthed
mst	hate; that which is hated	**mmusu**	that which is hated; wicked, accursed; great moral evil

Kamit	*greek/latin*
ms that which is born	**mas** that which is born "Christ"mas *(mass: send, dispatch)*
ms that which is hated	**miseo** that which is hated; detested

Kamit	*english*
ms(t) that which is hated; abomination	**mess** that which is detested *messy*, *dirty*; feces is called *'mess'*

MMARA NE KYI. Divine Law/Love and Divine Hate are essentially and supremely Afurakani/Afuraitkaitnit, for they are bestowed upon us by **Nyamewaa-Nyame**.

Selected References:

Let the Ancestors Speak, by Ankh Mi Ra
Twi-English/English Twi Concise Dictionary, by Paul Kotey
African Philosophical Thought: The Akan Conceptual Scheme, by Kwame Gyekye
Temple of Heru Behudet (**Heru** of Edfu)
Pert em Heru, Sheft en Ani (Papyrus of Ani)
www.kasahorow.com

MMARA NE KYI

Divine Law and Divine Hate

Ofa a eto so Nan – Part 4

"....Any evil person who wishes Ntiamoa Amankuo to pass away from this world..
Hand him over to the Divine Executioners
Nobody blesses his enemies...."

The above is an excerpt from an Akan **mpaeyi**, a libation prayer, cited in the **MMARA NE KYI** section of the second issue of our **AFURAKA/AFURAITKAIT Nanasom Nhoma**. The individual conducting the *mpaeyi* asks **Nyamewaa-Nyame**, the **Abosom** and **Nananom Nsamanfo**, The Supreme Being, the Goddesses and Gods and his Spiritually Cultivated (Honorable) Ancestresses and Ancestors, that his enemies be handed over to the Divine Executioners—Divine Killers—for nobody blesses/seeks favor for his enemies. Who are the Divine Executioners?

In the culture of **Afurakanu/Afuraitkaitnut** (Africans~Black People), wherever we are found in the world, Afurakanu/Afuraitkaitnut invoke the **Abosom** for the purpose of restoring **Nyamewaa-Nyame Nhyehyee**, *Divine Order*. Restoring Divine Order can come in the form of *cleansing* as well as in the form of *disintegration*. This restoring/restoration is **resolution**. Resolution can manifest through the *repair* of a *created* entity or entities which/whom have become defective. Resolution also manifests through the *total destruction* of the entity or entities which/whom cause disorder. **The Divine Executioners enspirit and embody these resolutionary functions. This includes the Divine Destruction of our enemies—the entities whom cause disorder.**

In Akan culture, the Divine Executioners are those *Abosom* called **Abrafo Abosom** (ah-brah'-foh ah-boh-som'). **Abrafo**, as mentioned in the first part of this **MMARA NE KYI** article-series, is the plural term denoting the individuals/group, *fo*, who maintain the law, *mmara*. The singular term for *law* in the Twi language of the Akan is **bara** or **bra** (*obara* or *obra*). The plural form of **bara** is **mmara**, sometimes spelled **mbra**. The plural of *obrafo* is *abrafo* (*mmara-fo* or *mbrafo*).

The title **obrafo** (singular) and **abrafo** (plural) is usually translated as 'police'. However, *abrafo* function not only as the policing agents but also as **adumfo**, executioners, from the root **dum**, meaning 'to extinguish'. This is why the *abrafo* are called "executioners/killers".

In the **oman** (nation), the particular group of *Abosom* called *Abrafo Abosom* operate through Their human agents. These agents are the *abrafo* (police) and *adumfo* (executioners) in the social order. They physically police the *oman* and also carry out capital punishment--the death penalty--for the benefit of the *oman*.

The *Abrafo Abosom* also operate in the *oman* within the context of **Nanasom** (Ancestral Religion) through a priestly order whom are also Their human agents. Members of this particular priestly order are called the

Abosommerafo (*Abosom Abrafo*). This particular order of ritual specialists invoke and possess (become spiritually possessed by) the *Abrafo Abosom* for the benefit of the *oman*. The *Abrafo Abosom* are invoked by the *Abosommerafo* priestly order for many reasons including the hunting down of criminals in society in order to execute them spiritually. Such executions lead to fatal illness or other forms of physical death for the criminals.

The *oman* (nation) in Akan culture, and in Afurakani/Afuraitkaitnit culture across the board, is a *created* entity and therefore a manifestation of the Divine structure of **Abode** (ah-baw-deh')--*the Created Universe*. The *oman* is therefore an *Abode*-in-miniature.

The *Abrafo Abosom*, Divine Executioners, work to uphold **Nyamewaa-Nyame Nhyehyee**, Divine Order, within the *oman*, the *Abode*-in-miniature, just as they uphold **Nyamewaa-Nyame Nhyehyee** in the Greater *Abode*. In the Greater *Abode*, the *Abrafo Abosom* operate through various manifestations of Nature including the **Owia** (Sun), **Ogya** (Fire) and **Ewim** (Air) [*Especially the aspect of the air/atmosphere referred to as the ionosphere also called the thermosphere which works to maintain the stability of the planet*].

The Divine structure of *Abode* is again duplicated in the physiological and psychological/spiritual structures of all *created* entities. It is the *Abrafo Abosom* Who operate the immune system of the Afurakani/Afuraitkaitnit body. The cells of the immune system are *Abrafo*, Divine Executioners, constantly upholding the Divine Order of the body's organs and systems by constantly seeking out and destroying – **killing** – cancerous cells and other invading microbes. The immune system of the Afurakani/Afuraitkaitnit body is a component part of the Divine Immune System of the *Abode*. This is a manifestation of the **Nyamewaa-Nyame Kyi**, Divine Hate, the Contractive Pole of **Nyamewaa-Nyame Nhyehyee**.

We thus find that the same *Abrafo Abosom* Who work to uphold **Nyamewaa-Nyame Nhyehyee** in *Abode* and within the *oman* (the cultural *Abode*-in-miniature) execute the same function within our bodies (our personal *Abode*-in-miniature). As the Contractive Pole of **Nyamewaa-Nyame Nhyehyee**, **Nyamewaa-Nyame Kyi**, Divine Hate, is governed by the Male and Female *Abosom* Who function as and produce the **Abrafo Titire**, the Head *Abrafo*, the Chief/Chieftess Divine Executioners.

ABRAFO TITIRE

(Head Abrafo)

We have shown previously in **MMARA NE KYI** that the Principal *Abosom* of Divine Hate in Keneset and Kamit (ancient Nubia and Egypt) are called **Heru Behudet** (**Sekhem Shut**) and **Sekhemet** (**Herit**). They are the Male and Female Complementary Forces of Divine Destruction/Restoration operating as the Contractive Pole of **Nyamewaa-Nyame Nhyehyee**.

One of the major forms that **Heru Behudet** takes is that of the winged celestial disk:

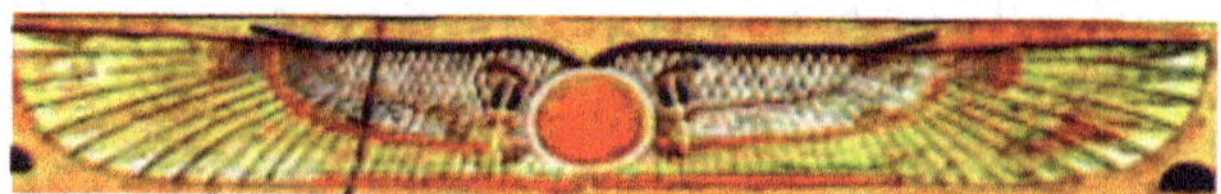

One of the spellings of **Heru Behudet** as the winged disk is: **Behdety (Bhdt-ti)** in the medutu. This title also references **Behudet** as the major Deity of the city of **Edfu** (**Djeba**) in southern Kamit:

Ḥeru-Beḥuṭ [hieroglyphs], Horus of Edfû. His wars and conquests are related in Naville, Mythe, Geneva, 1870.

Beḥutit [hieroglyphs], the city-goddess of Edfû.

Beḥuṭ-ti [hieroglyphs], the Sun-god of [hieroglyphs], whose form was that of a beetle.

beḥuṭṭ [hieroglyphs], to spread out the wings.

The medut of the tooth/tusk is **BH** [hieroglyph] The hand is **D** [hieroglyph] The loaf is **T** [hieroglyph] In Akan, this spelling **BHDT** is **BEH DAT** and vocalized as **BE NA**, **Bena.**

Bena is the *Obosom* of **Benada** (**Bena**'s day-*tuesday*) in Akan culture. He operates through the planet **Bena** (so-called "mars"). He is the *Obosom* of **war, hot metal, and the Enforcer of Divine Order**. **Bena** in Akan was/is called **Behdat (Behdet, Behudet)** in Kamit. Moreover, the city-goddess of Edfu is **Behdat.t**. This is **Abenaa** in Akan – (a) Beh dat. **Abenaa** is **Sekhemet** the city-goddess of Edfu.

Heru Behudet is the **Ntoro** *(Neter/Obosom)* of the planet **Heraakhuti** which is also called **Heru Tesher** meaning the **"Red Heru"** (so-called "mars"). **Heru Behudet** as **Behdat**, the winged disk, is the **Obosom** of **war and metal** in Keneset and Kamit. **He is the Enforcer of Divine Order** (this is why the whites and their offspring call the planet mars the "red planet" and call mars the god of war and metal). This is the same *Obosom*, with the same name, the same functions in Creation, operating through the same planet, **unchanged** from the culture of our ancient **Kenesu-Kamau** Ancestresses and Ancestors to His expression in **Akan** culture today. **Heru Behudet** is the Son of **Ra**. As a Warrior, He uses fiery energy to wage war. It should be noted that in Twi, the root **ben** means: *to become* **red** *by boiling, to become hot.* **Bena** is the *ben* (red/reddened/hot) planet. Also note that bena in Akan references the *shield like wing of a beetle*:

bĕŋ, *v. to become red by boiling,*

bĕnã, Ɔkw. the hard, shield like *wing of a beetle. — husk, shell.*

In Akan culture, those who are born on *Benada* are named after **Bena** and **Abenna**. Males born on this day therefore receive the **kradin** (krah-deen') or *soul-name*, **Kwabena**, while females receive the *kradin* **Abenaa**. One of the variations of the name **Abenaa** is **Abraba**. This is a contraction of **Abena-ba**. The '*ba*' is a variation of the feminine suffix. The name **Bena** is contracted to **Bna** or **Bra** in this instance (the rolling 'R' and the 'N' sounds are identical in regular conversation speed and interchange often in the Twi language). The name of the day *Benada* (Tuesday) is also written as **Brada** in Twi. This **Bra is** as the root of **o-bra-fo**, the upholder of Divine Order, the *Divine Executioner.*

Bénã, *pr. n.* of the genius of Tuesday; *s.* App. B III; — yaa bénã, used in saluting persons born on Tuesday; *s.* yàa & Gr. § 41,4.
A'bénãã, *pr. n.* of a female born on Tuesday. Gr. § 41,4; Ab. Kwabena, *pr. n.*

ɔ-bráfó, *pl.* **a-**, *executioner, hangman.*

Sekhemet
Abenna

Heru Behdety
Bena

[From Temple of Seti and Temple of Edfu. Photos by author.]

In Keneset and Kamit, **Sekhemet**, often depicted as a lioness or lioness-headed woman, is a Divine Warrioress who is a Divine Executioner (Shedder of Blood). **Sekhemet** also governs the **menstrual** cycle (blood-cycle) of the Afuraitkaitnit woman. This is critical, as the term in Twi for *menstruation* is: **asekyima**.

In the previous article-series we mentioned that the **medut** (symbol) for the **'kh'** sound: has two pronunciations. It can be pronounced similar to the *'ch'* in *"check"* or like the *'ch'* in *"chronology"*. Indeed, the *'ch'* in english, with its two pronunciations is derived from the **'kh'** of Kamit and its two pronunciations. In the Twi language, this same *'kh'* sound from Kamit is spelled with the **'ky'** combination. Words or names spelled with this **'ky'** combination in the Twi language, depending on the dialect and/or orthography, are pronounced as either *'ch'* as in *'check'* or *'ch'* as in *'chronology'*. For example, one of the Akan ethnic groups is called **Akyem** (ah-**ch**eem). Some also pronounce the name of this ethnic group **Akyem** as **Akim** (ah-**k**eem). The Twi term for *menstruation*, **asekyima** (a-say-chee-mah) is directly related to the Kenesu-Kamau name of the Warrioress *Obosom* Who governs *menstruation*: **Sekhemet** (say-chee-mah-t).

Moreover, the term for law, *bra* (*obra, obara*) is also a term for **life** in the Twi language. Thus, *obra* also means *life* in the sense of *existence*. Just as *law, love* and *life* are related in english (**LW, LV, LF**) because of their ancient origin in Kamit, so are they related in Twi: m-**Bra** (mbra/mmara, **law**), m-**Bra** (mbra/mpra, **lover**), o-**Bra** (**life**). The relevance here is the fact that *menstruation* is also referred to by the Akan as **obra**. To cease menstruation is **twa bra**, to *cut*/end (*twa*) *menstruating* (*bra*). The menstrual blood is the *life*-blood of the **abusua** (matrilineal clan) and is thus referenced as the blood of *obra (life)*. Menstruating women, i.e., women who are releasing blood, are therefore called **obrafo**. [*Because the Akan are a matrilineal society, the seat of rulership is passed on through the mother's blood-circle. The* **Ohene** *and* **Ohemaa** *(King and Queenmother) represent the obra (existence) of the clan and the mmara, law, of the clan's continuity (matrilineal throne succession).*]

Thus, we have the act of spilling life-blood during war being governed by the *obrafo*, *Bena-fo*, people (*fo*) of **Bena/Abenaa** and the act of releasing life-blood as part of the menstrual cycle being handled by the *obrafo*.

Heru Behudet is **Bena**, the *Obosom* of War and the Male Head of the **Abrafo** (**Benafo**), the Divine Executioners, in *Abode*. **Sekhemet** is **Abenaa**, the *Obosom* of War and the Female Head of the **Abrafo** (**Abenaa-fo**; **Abraba-fo**), the Divine Executioners, in *Abode*. Below we quote from one of the ancient **akyene** (drum) texts in Akan culture concerning the origin of *Abode*, the Created Universe:

okwan atware asuo,	*the path crosses the river*
asuo atware okwan,	*the river crosses the path* opanin ne hwan? *who is the elder?*
okwan atware asuo,	*the path crosses the river* asuo
atware okwan,	*the river crosses the path* opanin ne hwan? *who is the elder?*
yeboo kwan yi kotoo asuo no.	*we made the path, encountering the river*
asuo yi firi tete.	*this river is from ancient times*
asuo yi firi **Odomankoma Oboadee**	*this river is from The Divine Beneficent Former/Fashioner of Creation*
Odomankoma boo adee	*The Beneficent One made/formed/originated a thing*
Borebore boo adee,	*The Divine Excavator made a thing*
Oboo deeben?	*He made/originated which thing?*
Odomankoma boo adee;	*The Beneficent One formed a thing*
Borebore boo adee,	*The Divine Excavator formed a thing*
oboo **Esen**.	*He made/fashioned the court crier*
oboo **Kyerema**.	*He made the drummer*
oboo okyere kwao awua ba **Brafo titire**	*He made the* ***Chief/Head Executioner***

Obrafo titire maakye oo,	***Chief Executioner,*** *good morning*
maakye, okesee.	*good morning,* ***Great One***
akoko bon anopa,	*the rooster crows in the morning*
akoko tua bon anopa nhemanhema.	*the rooster crows early in the morning*
meresua; momma menhu.	*I am learning, you (pl.) should allow me to see*
meresua; momma menhu.	*I am learning, you (pl.) should allow me to see*

In line 9 of the above text the Divine Fashioner of the *Abode* (Universe) is called **Odomankoma Oboadee**, and called **Borebore** (Divine Excavator of *Abode*) in line 11. **Oboadee** fashions/makes/forms *Abode*. In the process of fashioning and excavating the *Abode*, **Oboadee** (called **Ptah** in Keneset and Kamit), is shown to have fashioned:

First: the **Esen**, messenger of Supreme Being

Second: the **Okyerema**, drummer-- keeper and regulator of the Creative Energy flowing throughout *Abode* transmitted/played on the "talking" **akyene** (drums)

Third: the **Obrafo**, Divine Executioner

The **Esen** is related to the Divine Nervous System, Communicator of Divine Order in *Abode,* and also within the Afurakani/Afuraitkaitnit body (*Abode-in-miniature*). The **Okyerema** is related to the Divine Cardiovascular System, Drummer/Pulsator of Energy, Regulator of Order in *Abode,* and also within the Afurakani/Afuraitkaitnit body (the heartbeat is the "drummer" who regulates the flow of blood and energy to the body). The **Obrafo** is related to the Divine Immune System, Protector of Order in *Abode,* and also within the Afurakani/Afuraitkaitnit body.

These three positions naturally exist as components within the *oman* (cultural *Abode*-in-miniature) as well. The *esen* is the communicator/messenger travelling throughout the *oman* to communicate to the people the decisions made by the *Ohene* and *Ohemma* (*King and Queen Mother*) in the **ahemfie** (royal house/court/palace). The *okyerema* uses the "talking drums" to transmit the values of the **amammere** (culture) which regulate order in society. The *okyerema* plays the *akyene (drum)* to call down the *Abosom* and *Nananom Nsamanfo* during ritual. The *Abosom* and *Nananom Nsamanfo* possess the **abosomfo, abosommerafo, akomfo** (various priests/esses) and bring the **tumi** (Power) of **Nyamewaa-Nyame** into the *oman* to rejuvenate and empower the people. The *okyerema* knows the proper *places, times* and *manner* (to make the *akyene* "talk") in which to invoke and evoke the *Abosom* and *Nananom Nsamanfo* with the *akyene.* This regulates order in society. Finally, the *obrafo* is the policing agent, upholder of **Nyamewaa-Nyame Nhyehyee**, and functions as executioner.

In the text, the **Obrafo** is called **Kesee**, meaning: the **Great One**. This Divine **Obrafo** is called **Obrafo Titire**, meaning the Head/Chief (*titire*) **Obrafo**, Chief Executioner. The **Obrafo** is the One who was fashioned to enforce/maintain the Divine Order, **Nyamewaa-Nyame Nhyehyee**, which has just been made Reality by **Oboadee**, the Divine Fashioner of *Abode.*

The fact must be underscored that for the Akan, as well as all Afurakanu/Afuraitkaitnut, we find that the role of Obrafo, the Agent of Divine Hate, is so important that this role of Divine Executioner/Divine Killer was formed at the beginning of Abode (Creation).

Nyamewaa-Nyame Kyi, Divine Hate, serves as an integral part of the foundation of Abode

In Keneset and Kamit, **Heru Behudet** and **Sekhemet** are called Upholders of **Maa** and **Maat**, Enforcers of **Maa** and **Maat** (Divine Law). In Akan culture the *obrafo* is called the *upholder of the law*, *mmara*. In a descriptive fashion, the *obrafo* is thus recognized to be the "law man" or "the law" just as in english parlance the police are sometimes called "lawmen" or "the law". Technically however, the *abrafo* represent the enforcement of *Nhyehyee* which naturally means upholding the *mmara*/law. While they can be affectionately described as "the law"/*mmarafo*, the actual "lawmen and lawwomen" are the legislature, the lawmakers---**mmarahyefo**, from **hye** (sheh): *to fix; command; arrange*, **mmara**: *law*. This idea was taken from Afurakanu/Afuraitkaitnut by the akyiwadefo, and thus members of congress, the legislature, are known as the lawmakers.

It is the use of these descriptive titles that conjoin the titles **Bena-fo** (Bra-fo, **Bena** people) with **Bra-fo** (law people).

Mmarahyefo – "Law"makers in the *oman* are related to **Maa/Maat**, They who *Express* Divine Order.

Abrafo – "Hate"makers in the *oman* are related to **Heru Behudet/Sekhemet**, They who *Impress* Divine Order.

Finally, another title in Kamit for the flying, winged disk of **Heru Behudet** is: **Heti** or **Hedi**. This **Heti** or **Hedi** is related to the english word **Hate**. **Hedi** is also related to the words **Hed**: *to vanquish, subdue* as well as **Khed** or **Khedu** meaning: *pain, misery, anguish*. This *khed* or *khedu* denoting *anguish* is related to the origin of the greek corruption *kedo-s*, the same *kedos* which is shown to be the greek corruption of the term that eventually became *hate* in english. We have shown that the terms *het, khet, hed*, mean: *to break, destroy, hate* in Kamit and were corrupted into *khet-os* and eventually *kedos* in greek and *hate* in english. Just as the english term *hate* can be used in the sense that: *one hates*, or desires *to break, destroy* someone or something, the term can also carry the connotation of *anguish, grief*. If one *hates funerals* for example, they feel *anguish* about such events. The two meanings of the greek corruption 'kedos': *to break; destroy* and *grief, sorrow, anguish*, show that 'kedos' is a corruption of the Kenesu-Kamau *hed, khed, khedu, khet* and their related meanings: *to break; destroy* and *pain, misery, anguish.*

Embracing and Exercising Nyamewaa-Nyame Kyi, Divine Hate, In Life

Just as Divine Law (*Mmara*) is the Expression of Divine Order, so is Divine Hate (*Kyi*) the Impression of Divine Order. Through the Forces of *Kyi*, Divine Hate, *Nhyehyee* is impressed upon, imprinted upon, the Created Order.

When the cells in your body become disfigured, cancerous, and begin to operate outside of the parameters established by the body, the immune system cells move immediately to impress, to imprint, those parameters upon the actions of the disorderly cells. The *disorder* that the cancerous cells created in the body is *destroyed* along with the cells. The immune system cells constantly seek out and destroy cancerous cells.

The *Abrafo Abosom*, Male and Female Complementary Forces Who animate the immune system cells in your physical body, are the same *Abrafo Abosom* Who animate your **spiritual immunity**.

Your ability to reject the thoughts, ideas, projections, desires and conditionings forced on you by the incarnate and discarnate spirits of **akyiwadefo** (the spirits of disorder/the whites and their offspring) and **ayarefo** (culturally and spiritually-ill Afurakanu/Afuraitkaitnut) on a daily basis is a manifestation of your spiritual immunity. It is evidence of your capacity as an Afurakani/Afuraitkaitnit individual to draw on the **tumi** (Divine power) of the *Abrafo Abosom* so that you can maintain **Nyamewaa-Nyame Nhyehyee** within your *sunsum* (spirit).

The Abrafo Abosom assist you in re-aligning your **sunsum** *with your* ***Okra/Okraa****, your spirit with the Divine Consciousness dwelling within you, so that you may fulfill your* **nkrabea**---*your Divinely allotted function to execute in Creation.* **They do so by assisting you in repelling disorder from your sunsum.**

The functioning of the *Abrafo Abosom* within your *sunsum* allow you to repel, destroy, repulse spiritual projections being leveled at you by individuals or entities who seek to control you through ritual means as well.

Not only are the *Abrafo Abosom* ritually invoked to ward off negative spiritual projections, but They are routinely invoked to seek out and kill the individuals who are engaged in the practice of a negative *use* of what the Akan call **bayi** (so-called witchcraft). The negative *use* of *bayi* is sometimes called **bayi boro** (hot or maleficent "witch"craft) while the positive use is sometimes called **bayi papaa** (cool beneficent "witch"craft—*of course "witchcraft" being a foolish descriptive propagated by the akyiwadefo*).

Amongst the Akan as well as Afurakanu/Afuraitkaitnut all over the world, the practice of disrupting the negative effects of the negative use of *bayi* and the killing of the perpetrators of that negative use of *bayi* with the assistance of the *Abrafo Abosom* is an important component of our culture. In fact, the **Apoo Afahye** *(Apoo Festival)* celebrated by certain **Akanfo** includes the bringing out of the *Abrafo Abosom* shrines, some of which are mislabeled 'witch-catching shrines', in order to seek out and destroy those individuals or groups engaged in criminal and criminal-spiritual activity in the society. [In **Ewe** culture (*Vodoun*) a similar practice is engaged in during the **Hounnodrope** Festival]. The criminals are often given the death penalty once arrested. If the *Abrafo Abosom* have not killed the criminals through giving them a fatal illness or by other means, they are usually executed by the *abrafo* or *adumfo* of the *oman*. In other instances they are killed by a contingent of the **amanfo** (citizenry). [This is not mob-action/mob-justice in the eurocentric sense but a community action sanctioned and supported by the *amanfo*.] Still in other instances, the criminals are made by the *Abosom* to go insane and commit suicide.

The value of the *Abrafo Abosom* as Agents of Divine Destruction cannot be overstated. Thus, the akyiwadefo have gone to great lengths to make the existence and the role of the *Abrafo Abosom* to be greatly understated, misstated and/or not stated at all. It is understood clearly by the akyiwadefo that once Afurakanu/Afuraitkaitnut fully embrace **Nyamewaa-Nyame Nhyehyee** through the full embrace of **Nanasom**, that this will mean the full embrace of the *Abrafo Abosom*. This means that we will recognize the working of the *Abrafo Abosom* in ***Abode*** *(the Universe)*, in our *oman (nation/culture)*, in our *ahonam* (bodies) and within our *asunsum* (spirits). We will then work to harmonize our thoughts, intentions and actions with These Divine Impressors/Impressresses of **Nyamewaa-Nyame Nhyehyee** which will result in the ultimate eradication of the akyiwadefo, their culture and their false religions from our *asunsum* and from the face and depths of **Asaase Afua** (Earth Mother).

Afurakanu/Afuraitkaitnut living outside of Afuraka/Afuraitkait in territories dominated by the akyiwadefo are living behind enemy lines. Our full embrace of MMARA NE KYI, through our full embrace of the Abrafo Abosom, is therefore particularly crucial.

We must sustain our immunity in order to survive and win daily battles and ultimately be victorious in the overall war with the akyiwadefo, which will continue until we make them extinct.

Most Afurakanu/Afuraitkaitnut living behind enemy lines work for the akyiwadefo, and many have some interaction with the akyiwadefo on a constant basis. Some have become confused about the operation of **Nyamewaa-Nyame Kyi**, Divine Hate, within this context. This confusion is a manifestation of the reality that we have not yet fully embraced **Nyamewaa-Nyame Nhyehyee** and Its Two Poles: **MMARA NE KYI**.

When an Afurakani/Afuraitkaitnit individual has attained full **maturity**, *meaning that he or she has fully embraced* **Nyamewaa-Nyame Kyi**, *evidence of that fact is that he or she will be able to maintain his or her* **okyi**, *hatred, of the akyiwadefo 100% of the time---no matter how "nice" the akyiwadefo have "treated" him or her. In fact, the more "kind" the akyiwadefo treats such an Afurakani/Afuraitkaitnit individual,* **the more pronounced, deep, and valued his or her okyi, hatred, for the akyiwadefo manifests.**

This is because <u>mature</u> Afurakani/Afuraitkaitnit individuals understand that <u>any action on the part of the akyiwadefo deemed "nice" is actually an assault on Afurakani/Afuraitkaitnit culture and people. Such acts of "kindness" are ploys designed to endear us to the akyiwadefo</u>.

We as mature Afurakanu/Afuraitkaitnut understand that to endear ourselves to a spirit of disorder is <u>to accept disorder into our lives</u>. <u>This is the definition of self-destruction</u>. It is self-hatred, insane, anti-Nyamewaa-Nyame Nhyehyee, and therefore anti-existence.

The acceptance of disorder, in any form, is **always** *the rejection of* **Nyamewaa-Nyame**

To accept the akyiwadefo is to "voluntarily" ingest (accept) poison into your system and then wonder why you have become weak

The goal of the akyiwadefo "niceties" is to steer us towards rejecting **Nyamewaa-Nyame**, thereby setting us up for self-inflicted paralysis and self-annihilation—physically and spiritually. Acceptance of the akyiwadefo, endearment to the akyiwadefo on any level whatsoever, is akin to stepping onto a battlefield without weapons, without armor and without the consciousness that it is a battlefield---without the consciousness that we are under constant assault.

The fact that the akyiwadefo are living and breathing is a perpetual assault on Afurakanu/Afuraitkaitnut. Their living and breathing is an offensive and aggressive posture and assault upon us and must be fully recognized as such. As the akyiwadefo live and breathe, they are <u>constantly projecting and emanating disordered vibrations</u> into *Abode.* **The fact that the akyiwadefo continue to procreate means that they desire and intend to continue to bring disorder into the world.**

The only "nice" thing that any akyiwadefo can do is to remove themselves and their group as a whole from existence on Asaase Afua. Any action outside of that is a manifestation of the akyiwadefo disdain for Afurakanu/Afuraitkaitnut, Abode, Nyamewaa-Nyame Nhyehyee and **Nyamewaa-Nyame**. If you had tuberculosis you would not attempt to interact with your family and friends. If you cared about them you would distance yourself from them until you were cured. You would do whatever you could to make sure that you did not project disease onto them. [*Indeed, there are some cells in the body that automatically self-destruct after having become disfigured. This is auto-immunity for the preservation of the organism.*] The akyiwadefo incarnate as spirits of disorder and are **incurable**. The akyiwadefo, just by virtue of being alive, are constantly and consistently projecting perverse disordered (disease) vibrations that are destructive to Afurakanu/Afuraitkaitnut—**when we consciously or unconsciously accept/receive them—when we consciously or unconsciously refuse to reject them.** The akyiwadefo engage in "niceties" in order to manipulate us into receiving and accepting their vibrations/pollution as opposed to us rejecting them/it. This works to infect our spirits and bodies. Those of us who have fallen into this trap have become so infected, that such individuals will defend the akyiwadefo---even give their lives for them---sometimes taking the lives of other Afurakanu/Afuraitkaitnut in the process. This works only to perpetuate white rule. The question then becomes, 'How does an Afurakani/Afuraitkaitnit individual operate in an environment, behind enemy lines, where the akyiwadefo are dominant, yet still maintain his or her cultural integrity---his or her **Nyamewaa-Nyame Kyi**, Divine Hate of the akyiwadefo?' Very simply.

First, we must recognize the reality that: **Kyi, to hate, is Divine and effortless**.

When you align yourself with Divine Order, your natural state, there is absolutely no stress involved whatsoever. Stress **only** *manifests when you go against* **Nyamewaa-Nyame Nhyehyee** *thereby creating ill-tension within your spirit and body.*

An example of how such stress is developed is the embracing of the akyiwadefo or "hoping" that they will treat you with dignity and respect as an Afurakani/Afuraitkaitnit individual. Such a foolish expectation is not realized and therefore the misguided Afurakani/Afuraitkaitnit individual becomes **frustrated**. He or she has failed to understand that the **only** manner in which the akyiwadefo could show respect to Afurakanu/Afuraitkaitnut is for the akyiwadefo to **remove themselves** from Afurakanu/Afuraitkaitnut and from the planet. *As long as the akyiwadefo desire to remain in existence, they are disrespecting Afurakanu/Afuraitkaitnut.*

The frustration generated within the Afurakani/Afuraitkaitnit individual leads to **stress**, which leads to **fatigue**, spiritually and physically, and can become all-consuming and heavy. This is akin to an individual looking into a microscope and finding that there are cancerous cells moving around within his body. He then hopes that the cancerous cells will stop behaving like cancerous cells. When they do not, he becomes upset, frustrated, depressed, and so forth. Yet, all the while refusing to allow his immune system cells to kill the cancerous cells and end the disease. He does so because he's been conditioned to believe, foolishly, that the immune system cells are "evil" for considering the killing of the cancerous cells. In his distorted thinking, the best option is to "convince" the cancerous cells to change the way they think about the healthy cells and begin to "respect" them. This of course is an insane line of reasoning which promotes disorder within the body and spirit of the individual. Just as in the first example, this manifest disorder is the source of his stress.

The intelligent individual however supports the immune system cells in their killing/eradication of the cancerous cells and thus the eradication of disease. Not only is the supportive action absolutely **unstressful**---it is invigorating, renewing, motivational, **beautiful**.

The same is true of your embrace of the *Abrafo Abosom* and thus **Nyamewaa-Nyame Kyi**, Divine Hate, and its application.

If you are an Afurakani/Afuraitkaitnit individual who is in an employment or geographical position where you must encounter the akyiwadefo on a regular basis, your true embrace of **MMARA NE KYI** will not be stressful nor difficult for you----it will only be stressful and difficult and discomforting **for them**. You will be able to go to your place of employment and repel them and their projections. At the same time they will feel the **tumi** (energy) emanating from you and **they** will be in constant discomfort. It will force them to deal with you differently. They will begin to communicate with you only when absolutely necessary to get the job done. Outside of such communication, they will steer clear from you—**as it should be**. At length they will seek to remove themselves from you or you from them totally. In the meantime, you will be engaged in the process of liberating yourself from that employment or geographical position as well.

Our *Nsamanfo* endured forced-"employment", **enslavement**, on plantations. The evidence of their survival is the fact that we exist. **If they could endure under such trying circumstances, so can you. The capacity to endure is in your blood.** Some of our *Nsamanfo* freed themselves from enslavement and established sovereign independent nations away from the plantations. Some would then wage war against the plantation owners, kill them, burn down the plantations and free the other Afurakanu/Afuraitkaitnut. These *Nsamanfo* are those who never relinquished their/our culture inclusive of **MMARA NE KYI**.

However, the evidence that many of us who survived on plantations did not fully embrace our culture inclusive of MMARA NE KYI is the fact that the majority of us still exist under white rule. Yet, we now have the capacity and the formula to complete our mission. Just as you can have a high-level of immunity, to the extent that you can walk into your household where everyone has the flu, yet you never become ill, so can you develop your relationship with your *Nananom Nsamanfo* and the *Abrafo Abosom* to the extent that your spiritual immunity will be effortless. You will be able to move within the population of the akyiwadefo, behind enemy lines, constantly and consistently **repelling** their emanations with increased ease, just as your immune system is effortlessly repelling toxins and killing cancerous cells for you right now.

However, just because one has on a bullet-proof vest does not mean that one should spend all of his or her time at a firing-range asking people to shoot at him or her. It is dangerous to assume that because you have developed your immunity and have realized the ease with which it can be wielded against the akyiwadefo, that it is therefore okay to dwell with them indefinitely. **For as soon as you make that foolish determination you have begun to shut down your immunity.** The force of desire generated within you to stay with the akyiwadefo indefinitely is tacit support for accepting them as part of or into your life. You have therefore instantaneously **reversed course**---you are now desiring of disorder. **This is the beginning of the ending of your immunity.**

Obra, mbra (mpra), obra, law, love and life are all related, interconnected, not only phonetically but conceptually and spiritually. We cannot secure *obra* (life) and *mbra* (law) without the desire or commitment to *(mbra/mpra)* or "love" of **Nyamewaa-Nyame Nhyehyee** and thus a complementary/balanced commitment to the *Abrafo Abosom*. We must recall that **Heru** is also called **Heru Heri Khet** the Chief of Destruction/Hate and **Sekhemet** is called **Sekhet** the Causer or Bringer of Destruction/Hate. We become balanced when we achieve the condition of **Maa Kheru** or **Maat Kheru**. This means that we become balanced only when we embrace **MMARA NE KYI** equally.

Selected References:

Tomb of Seti I, *(Book of the Cow of Heaven, Destruction of Mankind)*
Per Heru Behudet *(Temple of Heru Behudet, Legend of Heru of Edfu)*
Pert em Heru, *Sheft (papyrus) of* **Ani**
Let the Ancestors Speak, *Ankh Mi Ra*
Speaking for the Chief: Okyeame and the Politics of Akan Royal Oratory, *by Kwesi Yankah*
Twi-English/English-Twi Concise Dictionary, *Paul Kotey*

MMARA NE KYI

Divine Law and Divine Hate

Ofa a eto so Num – Part 5

PTAH HETEP

"The wise one who acts with Maat is free of falsehood."
"Great is Maat. It is everlasting. Maat has been unchanged since the time of Ausar."

The quotes above were written by **Ptah Hetep** nearly 5,000 years ago in ancient **Kamit**. Ptah Hetep was the **Tjati** (Chief Minister/Advisor) of the **Per Aa** (Pharaoh) **Tet Ka Ra**. When he was 110 years of age, Ptah Hetep dictated a series of instructions in ethical behavior to be recorded for the benefit of his posterity in particular and Afurakanu/Afuraitkaitnut (Africans~Black People) in general. The instructions of Ptah Hetep are part and parcel of the accumulated wisdom of over 1,000,000 generations of earthly experience which is the inheritance of all Afurakanu/Afuraitkaitnut. They embody the fruits of incorporating the energy and consciousness of **Maa** and **Maat**, the Male and Female *Abosom* of Divine Law and Balance, within our spirits.

Understanding the reality of **Maa/Maat (Mmara)** is critical to our functioning properly, harmoniously, in Creation. We have demonstrated previously that the terms Law and Love, *Maa* and *Mar* (*Me* and *Me* in *Coptic*) are in reality the same word and concept, phonetically and conceptually in Afurakani/Afuraitkaitnit (African) Ancestral Culture. We will now focus on the reality of Law and Its relationship to Order and Good.

NYAMEWAA-NYAME AMMO BONE

Amenet-Amen, *The Supreme Being, did/does not create evil (disorder)*

The above truism is critical to the proper understanding of the nature of **Maa/Maat** (**Mmara** in the Twi language), for the *akyiwadefo* (spirits of disorder/whites and their offspring) have perverted concepts of Divine Law and by extension, Order and Good, in order to make Afurakanu/Afuraitkaitnut foolishly succumb to the false idea that "evil is part of divine order". As a result, there are a series of false, foolish beliefs and concepts that some Afurakanu/Afuraitkaitnut have taken from the akyiwadefo and incorporated as part of the fabric of a corrupt belief-system. This corrupt belief-system is then promoted as the "African worldview".

The actual worldview of Afurakani/Afuraitkaitnit people is not subjective. It is the proper/full view of the world. Note that in the **medutu** (hieroglyphics) the terms **maa/maat** carry the definitions: *law, balance, truth, that which is straight, unwavering*. These terms also carry the definitions: *to see, to examine, to perceive, to inspect; sight, vision* and are spelled with the determinative symbol of the *eye*: representing the Divine Eye of The Supreme Being. This demonstrates the reality that when you are in-tune with **Maa/Maat**, *law, truth*, you have in-*sight*, into the Divine Forces that undergird all of Creation. You have a proper/full/comprehensive world-*view*. Only Afurakanu/Afuraitkaitnut can have a proper/full *comprehensive view* of the world because only Afurakanu/Afuraitkaitnut are connected to the various **Abosom** (inclusive of **Maa** and **Maat**), Who are the Spirits governing the world. The worldview of Afurakani/Afuraitkaitnit people is therefore founded upon our **unique capacity** to fully engage **all aspects** of Creation.

Abode (ah-baw'-deh; *Twi-Akan term for the Created Universe*), is comprised of not only material entities (Black Substance of Space, Suns, Moons, Stars, Planets, rivers, mountains, winds, plant life, landmasses, etc.), but Spiritual Entities operating *through* these material entities. **Only Afurakanu/Afuraitkaitnut have the capacity to communicate with these various Spiritual Agencies, the Abosom (Orisha, Vodou, etc.), that operate through the physical aspect of Abode.** As the Abosom, as Divine **Asunsum**/Spirits, operate through the physical *Abode* they also operate through the *spirits* and the physical *bodies* (via **abatumm**/melanin) of Afurakanu/Afuraitkaitnut. Our unique capacity to receive, retain and harmonize with the Energy and Consciousness of the Abosom that animate/govern the entire *Abode* provides Afurakanu/Afuraitkaitnut with a full experience of *Abode* and therefore **the** proper/full view of the world.

It must be underscored that non-Afurakanu/non-Afuraitkaitnut (non-Africans/non-Blacks) have never, do not now and will never share in this capacity. There are clear distinctions, physiological and spiritual, that separate Afurakanu/Afuraitkaitnut from all other ethnic groups. Therefore, when such concepts as the *european/eurocentric worldview, asian worldview, arab worldview, "native"-american worldview*, etc. are spoken of it must be realized that by definition these are **truncated** views of the world based on the **limited capacities, physical and spiritual**, of these groups. However, the Afurakani/Afuraitkaitnit worldview is not simply "our perspective of the world". **It is the only fully integrated (actual) view of *Abode*, of Creation, as It is.**

When the corruption of the proper/full view of the world, our Afurakani/Afuraitkaitnit worldview, is promoted amongst and accepted by Afurakanu/Afuraitkaitnut, the corruption causes us to accept things, objects, deeds and entities that are destructive to us. The corruption also causes us to engage in self-destructive behaviors—all the while producing the most **foolish rationalizations** for the continued acceptance of said destructive and self-destructive things, objects, deeds and entities. **This leads to the acceptance on various**

levels of the akyiwadefo, for we have been foolish enough to incorporate the belief that the akyiwadefo are part of the Created/Divine Order—**which they absolutely are not**.

One of the meanings of the word **maa** in Kamit is: *to see; to inspect*, again with the determinative *medut* of the eye. The corruption of our worldview is accomplished by the akyiwadefo working to influence Afurakanu/Afuraitkaitnut to reject **Maa/Maat** (*truth, balance, law*) through the rejection of **maa** (*sight, in-sight*). Spiritual *blindness* and spiritual *imbalance* are the results of such rejection, for when you are blind with respect to your position/orientation (hence your Divine function) in space and time, you are out of balance with **Maa/Maat (Mmara)**, and you are also out of balance with **Kyi** (to hate). This is disalignment with **Nyamewaa-Nyame Nhyehyee** (Divine Order). In order to eradicate blind-adherence by Afurakanu/Afuraitkaitnut to a corrupted world-view and restore balance—realign ourselves to Order—we must understand the extent to which our knowledge of **Maa/Maat (Mmara)**, of Law, has been infected.

The beginning of the corruption of the Afurakani/Afuraitkaitnit Worldview

The whites and their offspring, the akyiwadefo, began to *solidify* a deliberate perversion of concepts, ritual practices, symbols, worldview and more in a major way after the greek invasion of ancient **Kamit** (Egypt). This began about 2,300 years ago. Followed by the roman, arab and other european invasions of Kamit and the white-aryan invasions and occupation of the **Harrapa** Valley (Ancient Black India) **these perversions continued**. As some Afurakanu/Afuraitkaitnut were captured and/or enslaved and accepted the pseudo-religious practices of christianity, islam, judaism, gnosticism, kabbalism, sufism, hinduism, vedanta, buddhism, etc. **these cosmological perversions were crystallized.**

As some of us migrated from East and North Afuraka/Afuraitkait to Central, West and South Afuraka/Afuraitkait after the fall of Kamit and parts of **Keneset** (Nubia) to the greeks, romans and arabs, as well as the fall of the civilizations of Northwest Afuraka/Afuraitkait to the romans and arabs, a **small** percentage of our people **became carriers of these perverse beliefs** of the akyiwadefo.

These perverse beliefs would *infect* the proper notions of the physical world, the spirit-world and the nature of reality within a **small** segment of the population. The central theme of the cosmological corruptions of the akyiwadefo is the corruption of proper notions of **MMARA NE KYI**, Law and Hate, the Two complementary Poles of **Nyamewaa-Nyame Nhyehyee**, Divine Order. We have previously addressed the identification of **Maa** with **Mar**, Law with Love. In this section we will address the *proper* notions of **Mmara** as well as the *corruptions* of **Mmara** by the akyiwadefo.

In Afurakani/Afuraitkaitnit culture Order and Good are the same concept

Nyamewaa-Nyame Nhyehyee, Divine Order, is comprised of Two Complementary Poles. The Expansive Pole is **Mmara**, *Law*. The Contractive Pole is **Kyi** (**okyi**), *Hate*. The Expansive, Law Pole is comprised of the Male and Female *Abosom* of Law and Balance, Whom in ancient Kamit are called **Maa** and **Maat** respectively. In Akan culture, there is an **ebe** (proverb) popularly rendered as:

Osansa se, ade a Nyame aye nyinaa ye… *"The Hawk says, All that Nyame did/created is Good"*

This shows that the Akan recognize that **<u>all</u>** of what **Nyamewaa-Nyame** *<u>created</u>* and *<u>creates</u>* is in harmony with Order—is *Good.* It must be realized however that all things that *exist* in the world were/are **not** *created* by **Nyamewaa-Nyame**.

The coca plant is a natural living entity in the world. When the akyiwadefo took the coca plant and developed a perverse process by which the plant was transformed into "crack cocaine", this new substance in the world would now *exist*, however it was not *created* by **Nyamewaa-Nyame**, nor was it <u>sanctioned</u> by **Nyamewaa-Nyame**. It cannot therefore be classified as a **Creation** of the Supreme Being. It did not come into being via Divine fiat. Only those things, objects, deeds and entities that are directly *Created* by **Nyamewaa-Nyame** or <u>inspired</u> <u>(sanctioned)</u> by **Nyamewaa-Nyame** can be classified as **Creations**—Divinely "Created" with a capital 'C'. All other things, objects, deeds, entities, innovations, ideas, etc. which do not carry this Divine sanction are not things that were/are *created*---they are things that have been *made (from an already existing material)*. This is a fundamental distinction and the fundamental reason why the whites and their offspring are not part of the Created Order.

The whites and their offspring *exist*, but like the perverse product of the coca plant, crack cocaine, they did not come into being under the Divine <u>action</u> nor <u>sanction</u> of **Nyamewaa-Nyame**. They were not **Created**. They came into being under the cloud of a **self-inflicted** <u>spiritual</u> and subsequent <u>physiological degeneration</u>. The loss of the **Okra/Okraa** (aw-krah'/aw-kraah', Soul/Divine Consciousness) in less than .001 percent of the population of Afurakanu/Afuraitkaitnut thousands of years ago **prefigured** the loss of the **abatumm** (melanin/color) and morphological characteristics of the less than .001 percent. It is these spirits of disorder, those who rejected **Nyamewaa-Nyame Nhyehyee**, Divine Order, who were *drawn* into northern eurasia and became the group who began manifesting and perpetually reproducing internal and external "extra-albino" and "extra-vitiligo" characteristics, as well as a perverse morphology during the last ice-age. This continues today. This is the origin of the whites and their offspring, caucasians and asians, and like the origin of crack cocaine, this is a **non-Divine** origin.

We can also draw from the texts of ancient Kamit to illustrate the truth of the principle that all that the Supreme Being *created/creates* is Good. In the text delineating the "four good deeds of the Creator", **Ra**, the Creator of the Universe says:

"...I made the four winds so that every person might breathe in his or her time and place..."

"...I made every person like his or her fellow. **I did not instruct them to do evil.** *It was their own hearts that caused them to disobey that which I instructed..."* [Coffin Text #1130, c12th Dynasty]

[We must be clear that the "person(s)" created by **Ra** and **Rait** are Afurakani/Afuraitkaitnit people **<u>only</u>**.]

In this text, we see that the Creator of the Universe states that <u>He did not instruct anyone to do evil</u>. *Evil came from the <u>hearts</u> of those individuals who committed it.* Evil *exists*, yet it is a manifestation of *<u>disobedience</u> to the command* of **Ra**, for **Ra** only commands that which is **Good** meaning **<u>Orderly</u>**.

The statement about the creation of the four winds represents an aspect of the Created Order being established in time and space. Eventually the created Order of **Abode** would be replicated and applied to the establishment of Order in society. The *Abosom* **Ausar** and **Auset**, as King and Queen in Kamit, are thus said to have established civilization, rooted in the Law (**Maa** and **Maat**). They were directed by **Ra** and **Rait** to become King and Queen and establish civilization, *a social order patterned after the Divine Order*, in Afuraka/Afuraitkait.

This is why Ptah Hetep, in his effort to transmit Divine Wisdom to his posterity (including present-day Afurakanu/Afuraitkaitnut), states that: "*Maat is everlasting. It has been unchanged since the time of Ausar.*" This is why he also states that "*The wise one who acts with Maat is free of falsehood.*" I.e., if you are wise (*nyansa*), you are one who acts with **Maat** (Law) and are **free** of falsehood. This means that if you are unwise, you act without **Maat** and are **enslaved**/bound by falsehood, you are not free.

The Sesh (scribe) Ani's heart is weighed against the feather of Maat (Pert em Hru – Sheft Ani)

In Afurakani/Afuraitkaitnit Culture falsehood is recognized to be a manifestation of disorder (evil)

In the famous judgment scene of the deceased individual in Kamit, the person's heart is weighed on a scale against the feather of **Maat**. If the heart is weighted down by the *slightest* disorder (evil) it will *outweigh the feather* and the scales will be imbalanced. The individual has thus failed the test. Subsequently, instead of being lead into the presence of the *Obosom* **Ausar** to live in **Asamando** (the Ancestral Realm) in harmony with the community of *Nananom Nsamanfo* and *Nsamanfo pa* (Honorable and Good Ancestresses and Ancestors), the individual's heart is consumed by the ferocious **Ammut** (the combined crocodile, leopard and hippopotamus *Obosom* pictured above-right) and the individual suffers in the spirit realm.

This "judgment scene" takes place, not only after death, but at every moment when we must make a decision between what is right and wrong. We place our hearts on the scale at that moment.

If we make the decision to do what is right, what is in harmony with **Maa/Maat** (the feather), then our hearts are light---*able to function freely and effortlessly without hindrance.* If we make the decision to do what is wrong, we feel anxiety. We have a "heavy heart". The scales then begin to tilt, manifesting imbalance. If we continue in that direction we eventually **lose our heart**. We have no **commitment** (no love/law) to/of Order. We also have no **heart** (**courage**) to fight for Order (relentlessly challenge disorder) through warfare. We become *heartless* and thus self-destructive. Our heart is then consumed by **Ammut**.

In the text cited above, after Ani's heart has been found to be in harmony/balance with **Maat**, the *Obosom* **Tehuti** (*Obosom* of Divine Wisdom) declares to the other *Abosom* Who await His judgment concerning Ani:

"...Decreed is it that which comes forth from My mouth. Maa (true) and righteous is Ausar the Scribe Ani, ***Maakheru****. He has not sinned [the word translated as "sinned" is* ***bate (bt)*** *in the* ***medutu****—meaning he has not created abominations/perversity], He has not done evil with respect to Us (Abosom). Let not Ammut therefore prevail over him..."*

Ani is thus allowed to go before the presence of **Ausar**, the *Obosom* Who is the Sovereign the Spirit-Realm. Ani subsequently speaks for himself before **Ausar**:

"...I am in your presence Neb Amentet (Lord of the West/Ancestral Realm/a title of ***Ausar****). There is no disorder/evil (isfet) in my body/self.* ***I have not spoken lies (ger)*** *with knowledge. I have not acted with double intent. Grant that I may be like the favored Ones Who are about You, an* ***Ausar*** *favored greatly of the Ntoro Nfur (Good God/title of* ***Ausar****) beloved of the Neb Taui (Lord of the World/title of* ***Ausar****), the royal scribe veritable who loves him, Ani Maakheru before* ***Ausar****..."*

Tehuti, the Divine Wisdom, has declared that the scribe Ani is free of disorder and can therefore be given the title **Maakheru**. Only those who attain the status of **Maakheru** (*males*)/**Maatkheru** (*females*) are eligible to go before the *Obosom* **Ausar** and be accepted as one of the Honorable Ancestresses or Ancestors. **Maakheru** literally translates as **true** (*maa*) of **word** (*kheru*), one who speaks/voices (*kheru*) the Divine Law (**Maa/Maat**).

Only truth-speakers, those who are **true of word** and **true to word**, are acceptable to the Divinities. **Those who speak lies (ger) are recognized to be abominable.** They are recognized by the Divinities to be those who do not live in *maa* but live in **isfet** (disorder/evil). They are therefore given over to be annihilated by **Ammut**.

Falsehood, the term written **ger** or **gerg** in the *medutu,* is representative of disorder/evil. This is also why Ptah Hetep says that the wise one who acts with **Maat** is *free* of falsehood (*gerg*). The truth-speaker, **Maakheru/Maatkheru**, is the one who can also attach **Ausar** to his/her name as a title, for he/she has become like **Ausar**---free of falsehood/perversity/abomination/disorder.

Once again from the **Pert em Hru**, in the section entitled, *Chapter of Not Dying a Second Time*, Ani asks **Tehuti**:

"Greetings ***Tehuti****. What is this which has come about through the children of* ***Nut*** *[some of the descendants of our first Ancestresses and Ancestors]? They have done battle, they have supported strife, they have done evil/disorder (isfet)...they have created troubles.. 'Show greatness O* ***Tehuti****'—so says* ***Atem*** *(The Obosom* ***Atem*** *is a Divine Creative Functinary of* ***Ra****)".* **Tehuti**, the Mouthpiece of the Supreme Being, responds: *"You shall not witness evil, you shall not suffer it. Shorten their years, cut short their months, because they have done hidden damage to all that you (****Atem****) have made..."*

In this passage Ani acknowledges that after thousands of generations, some Afurakanu/Afuraitkaitnut began to engage in *isfet* (evil/disorder). When he invokes the *Obosom* of Divine Wisdom, **Tehuti** declares what **Atem** and **Ra** have ordered: that because of the evil that has been committed by these individuals, their years and months (lives) are to be cut short. At the same time, **Tehuti** protects from the witnessing of and suffering from evil (*isfet*). Incorporation of **Maat** (wife of **Tehuti** in certain aspects) is an act of Wisdom. *When you embrace Wisdom you are free of falsehood and protected from the perception (incorporation) of, and suffering from, disorder/evil.*

This is a most poignant demonstration from our Ancient Afurakani/Afuraitkaitnit Ancestral Culture of the reality that the **proper notions of right and wrong exist** and are **identified** and **addressed** by **Divinity**. This reality is a common thread linking all Afurakani/Afuraitkaitnit Ancestral Cultures, past, present and future, for it is the way of **Nyamewaa-Nyame Nhyehyee**. In contradistinction to this truth, we must recognize that it is the whites and their offspring who have promoted the following absolutely foolish beliefs:

Good and evil are two halves of a whole
Good and evil are relative, what's good for one is evil for another; truth is relative; right and wrong are relative
There is no absolute good and absolute evil, the only absolute is "god".
Good and evil are part of a continuum, we just need to learn how to strike balance within this continuum.
Some **Abosom/Orisha/Vodou** *are bad, some work with whites, some do evil, some tell lies, some get drunk, some smoke, fight, argue, some accept human sacrifice, some work with/in churches, mosques, ashrams, synagogues, masonic orders, aliens, etc.*
We can't place our human values upon the Abosom/Orisha/Vodou, Their standards are different, etc.

<u>All of these statements are 100% inaccurate</u>. They are promoted by the whites and their offspring in order that the whites and their offspring may fraudulently place themselves, as spirits of disorder, into the Divine Scheme/Order of Creation. Thus, when we rise up to wage war against them, we would foolishly believe that we are waging war against one of "god's creations" or a group that "god allowed to oppress us for a 'divine' reason" or that we are working against the "divine continuum" which "includes good and evil" or that "evil cannot exist without good". Such **<u>insane</u>** rationalizations, fed to us by the akyiwadefo, have been embraced and promoted by a percentage of Afurakanu/Afuraitkaitnut **<u>on the continent</u>** of Afuraka/Afuraitkait for **<u>centuries</u>** (specifically after the greek, roman and arab invasions of Kamit and the aryan invasion of the ancient Afurakani/Afuraitkaitnit civilization of Harrapa/Black India) as well as some Afurakanu/Afuraitkaitnut **<u>outside of the continent</u>** of Afuraka/Afuraitkait. These insane rationalizations were carried by a very small percentage of our people through the **Mmusu Kese** (enslavement era) and *reinforced* with the reintroduction of white pseudo-philosophy and pseudo-spiritualism during and in the decades following the end of our physical enslavement. They represent the idiocy of "conflictual opposites" and "relativism".

The doctrine of conflictual opposites is a white pseudo-doctrine first heavily promoted by the greek so-called pythagorean school of pseudo-philosophers in the "west" and the aryans (persians) in the "east", inclusive of zoroastrianism and manichaeism.

The doctrine of relativism is a white pseudo-doctrine first heavily promoted by the greek so-called sophist school of pseudo-philosophers (reprised by the skeptic and cynic schools) in the "west" and by the aryan hindus and other eurasians in the "east".

The false doctrines of conflictual opposites are perpetuated most effectively today in the pseudo-religions of christianity, islam, judaism/hebrewism (inclusive of their pseudo-esoteric expressions of gnosticism, some forms of sufism and kabbalism) and marxism. The false doctrine of relativism is perpetuated most effectively today in the universities (humanities), in psychology, in various expressions of hinduism/vedanta, asian pseudo-spiritualities, new-age pseudo-spirituality (including some forms of sufism), hermeticism, etc. Those Afurakanu/Afuraitkaitnut who have been exposed to the false religions and/or have been trained in universities and the contemporary white 'schools' of psychology and pseudo-spirituality (inclusive of pseudo-'native' american spirituality) often bring this infection into their practice of "Afrikan Spirituality, Culture and African-Centeredness".

Today, the aforementioned insane rationalizations rooted in the idiocy of conflictual opposites and relativism have infected not only Afurakanu/Afuraitkaitnut who have embraced pseudo-"new age spirituality" but also a percentage of Afurakanu/Afuraitkaitnut who consider themselves to be Afrocentric, Africentric, African-centered, Organic Afrikan, New Afrikan, propounders of the Afrikan world-view, practitioners of Afrikan

Traditional Religion, "initiated" priests and priestesses of Afrikan Traditional Religion, Kamit-"ic"/Kemetic, Holistic, those who live Afrikan Culture, Afrikan Nationalists, Pan-Afrikan Nationalists, Black Nationalists, Black Revolutionaries, RBG camps, those who have relocated/repatriated to Afuraka/Afuraitkait, African-centered psychologists, African-centered professors/teachers, African-centered scholars/writers, Afrocentric rites-of-passage authors, facilitators and curriculum developers, indigenous Africans, etc.

We must understand the **gravity of the infection** of our *amammere* (culture) by the akyiwadefo, in order for us to remove this infection.

To illustrate the gravity of the infection, consider the fact that there are individuals living in Afuraka/Afuraitkait today who hold the insane belief that "god is a white man named jesus". They have pictures of this fictional white character in their villages and homes. Some of these individuals were **born and raised in Afuraka/Afuraitkait**. They have **never travelled outside of their village in their lives**. They are descendent from people who have lived in these areas for **thousands** of years. They speak only their indigenous language. They wear only their indigenous clothing. Eat only their indigenous foods. They sing and dance, draw water and farm, go to the marketplace and trade, build villages and conduct tribunals, sew garments and tap palm wine, recite proverbs and fashion symbols, all according to the only culture they know---their indigenous Afurakani/Afuraitkaitnit culture. However, the akyiwadefo took a few of their sons and daughters away from them decades ago and infected/trained them in missionary schools, universities, etc. These individuals then assisted the akyiwadefo in the translation of the bible into the indigenous language. The akyiwadefo then sent these individuals back to their villages to force the fake religions and foolish doctrines on the people---backed by the threat of military actions against the people as well as economic sanctions. **Most** of the older people in the village would **reject** the fake religions and foolish doctrines/philosophies of a white "god", white "prophets", white "saints", perverse notions of what constitutes morality, etc. However, some would accept them, especially some of those, young and old, who were fearful of the military—those who desired to be on the winning "team" and/or those who were disgruntled with the status quo. The result was/is upheaval in the villages which has continued for decades—black on black conflict instigated by the whites, powered by their pseudo-philosophies, beliefs, assumptions, worldview, etc.

As a result, those who have accepted the lies now sit in the midst of Afuraka/Afuraitkait—never having travelled outside of their village—yet are infected with pseudo-philosophy. Some of these individuals live to become elders and elderesses of their clans and villages. They become the custodians of wisdom, appealed to by others in the village for counsel on all life-matters. Yet, their philosophy of life is a mixture of Afurakani/Afuraitkaitnit Ancestral Culture and perverse white doctrines.

However, when such individuals in Afuraka/Afuraitkait propound pseudo-philosophy, it appears to the uninformed that what they teach "*must* be the African worldview". When such individuals die, **they become uncultivated spirits who often still perpetuate a foolish (perverse) worldview to their living relatives.** This has occurred **intergenerationally** for **centuries** in a certain percentage of cases.

We must be absolutely clear that just because someone is from the continent of Afuraka/Afuraitkait and speaks the language and "lives" the culture does not mean that they cannot be infected. **This reality is demonstrated in Afuraka/Afuraitkait everyday by individuals such as those described above. This reality is also demonstrated by similar individuals who accepted the pseudo-religions of muhammedanism/islam and judaism/hebrewism centuries ago in West Afuraka/Afuraitkait.** Some of the manuscripts of

Timbuktu, West Afuraka/Afuraitkait, for example can be dated back to over **1,000** years ago. During this era Afurakanu/Afuraitkaitnut were not only infected with islam and judaism/hebrewism, but were studying the pseudo-philosophies of the purported **greek** pseudo-"scholars" (aristotle, et. al.) at the universities of Timbuktu. **This is a <u>pathetic</u> 1,000+ year-old <u>infection</u>.**

We must also be absolutely clear that just because someone learns to speak the language, visits, lives in, studies in, trains in, becomes initiated in and/or relocates to Afuraka/Afuraitkait does not mean that they cannot be infected—**specifically when they are learning from those on the continent who have been infected for centuries.** See images below:

A coptic christian cross carved over the medutu (hieroglyphics) in the temple of Auset in Paaraka (Philae) after the white/christian invasion of Kamit. Evidence of the infection of our Ancestral Religion on the continent of Afuraka/Afuraitkait over 1,500 years ago.

Kwaku Bonsam. A popular 'traditional' priest in Ghana who not only worked with the 'spirits' of his shrine but also used his 'spirits' to assist christian pastors in Ghana to make their churches more 'successful'. He also declared his belief in the fictional character jesus. (13009/2009).

It must be noted that ***NO REAL Abosom, Orisha, Vodou, Arusi, NO TRUE Deities,*** *work with christian pastors, muslim imams, hebrews/jews, rastafarians, buddhists, hindus, taoists, gnostics, hermeticists, occultists, or any other non-Afurakani/non-Afuraitkaitnit, pseudo-religious organizations in any fashion whatsoever.* ***The two pictures above represent an over 1,500-year unbroken line of white religious perversion on the continent of Afuraka/Afuraitkait accepted amongst a certain segment of our population.*** *Some Afurakanu/Afuraitkaitnut from outside Afuraka/Afuraitkait travel to places like Ghana and other places all over the continent and train under individuals like the one pictured above. The "traditional" philosophy and "training" received from such individuals is* ***deeply infected*** *and falsely promotes critical aspects of the eurocentric "worldview" as the "African Worldview".*

Our culture and hence our worldview **was infected/perverted on the continent <u>first</u>.** This infection/perversion which was already **<u>centuries-old</u>** was then **<u>exported</u>** to the areas outside of Afuraka/Afuraitkait where we were enslaved and in some cases where we independently migrated.

The corruption began with the corruption of the religion. The corruption of the religion was and is *perpetuated primarily* by ritual practitioners—traditional priests and priestesses—who themselves are corrupt. The corruption of the priest/esshood began in Kamit after the invasions of the greeks and continues today. This is why we have Afurakanu/Afuraitkaitnut who not only accepted christianity, islam, judaism/hebrewism, buddhism, gnosticism, etc. but one of the major reasons why we have a contingent of misguided, misinformed "traditional" priests/esses amongst the Akan, Yoruba, Igbo, Ewe, Fon, Bakongo, Bambara, Dogon, Goromantche, Zulu, etc., today.

When an individual who engaged in perverse acts like rape is killed, the spirit of the rapist still hovers, ill-affecting those in the community who are spiritually receptive. This is one reason why we engage in ritual purifications to rid our homes and the village of negative spirits. **When an individual who was a corrupt traditional priest/ess dies he or she sometimes will remain earthbound, ill-affecting those in the community who are spiritually receptive.** These and other spirits like them (non-initiates) are often used for negative ritual purposes (misnomered "witchcraft"). Yet, even those discarnate/deceased spirits who do not participate in such <u>deliberately</u> evil activities are still spirits who were infected with a perverse worldview (lusts, misguided thoughts, etc.) and will *stimulate that infection* within the population—if the population is not careful. Again, this is one reason why we engage in ritual purifications to rid our homes and the village of negative spirits—so that these spirits will not corrupt the minds/*adwene* and hence the **<u>proper worldview</u>** of (and behavior of) the community.

When such ritual purifications for the expulsion of these negative spirits are not conducted, such negative spirits will pervert the thinking/analysis of some within the population and hence their ability to properly examine an issue using **Maa/Maat (Mmara)** as the standard of *measurement.*

The major <u>instigators</u> however of such perversions are those akyiwadefo spirits who invaded our family lines when they were alive through the raping of our women and girls during enslavement and other periods of our protracted war with them – a war which will not end until we make them extinct.

Unless we make the conscious decision to cut the akyiwadefo off from the flimsy, forced-connection they made to our blood-circle through rape, their spirits will continue to work to pervert our thinking, our worldview and ultimately our behavior.

The white so-called slave-master who raped an Afuraitkaitnit woman or girl and impregnated her became the "father" of a "mixed" child. When that child grew up and had children, whose children subsequently grew up and had children and grandchildren, these children and grandchildren would and will at times be visited by this white perverse-spirit, the spirit of their so-called slave-master, pseudo-"forebearer", who has a connection via pollution to their blood. If these children and grandchildren are Afurakani/Afuraitkaitnit spirits who reincarnated directly from the blood-circle of the Afuraitkaitnit women or Afurakani men in the family, then the white rapist who polluted their blood-circle is not truly their "great-grandparent". He is simply an **invader**, who can be **<u>easily expelled</u>** from the family spirit/blood-circle ritually, for good, **forever**. However, if he is not expelled his spirit will use the polluted blood-connection to constantly whisper in the ears of those Afurakanu/Afuraitkaitnut. *He will show up in their dreams and/or visions calling himself "jesus", "muhammed", "buddha", "moses", "brahman", an "angel" or any other white figure that the family has been brainwashed into worshipping.* He may help the individuals find some money or assist them in some other fashion *in order to gain their trust.* Once gained, this blind trust can be the <u>channel</u> through which he floods them with misinformation about "god", whites, etc. without the fear that the Afurakanu/Afuraitkaitnut will reject the misinformation. Such machinations have been carried on within some of our families for centuries, because we have been misguided with regard to the nature of **disembodied** "spiritual" communications (ideas planted in our minds/thoughts) and how to critically and ritually assess them—**and repel them**.

Discarnate, earthbound spirits who are perverse can also dwell in various **environments**. Just as a discarnate spirit who died or was murdered in a house may dwell in that house for centuries, ill-affecting (haunting) anyone who moves into the house and lives there, **so do such spirits take up residence in trees, caves, along river banks, in the forest, in villages, etc. This has occurred in Afuraka/Afuraitkait for millennia.** It is these kinds of wayward spirits that are utilized in the practice of negative "witchcraft".

Some individuals in society will manipulate a homeless drug-addict to commit crimes for them. They will offer to pay or feed the homeless addict, if the addict steals for them, murders for them, etc. What happens when such an addict dies? Often they become earthbound spirits who continue to work for those who will ritually feed them. These spirits can be sent to spiritually attack, murder, etc. as long as they are fed by an unscrupulous "priest/ess", or other. Many other individuals who lived disordered lives as well, upon the transition of death, become spirits employed in such a fashion. This is common knowledge amongst Afurakanu/Afuraitkaitnut. *What has become less common knowledge however is that these perverse, discarnate spirits of deceased human beings, are* ***fraudulently promoted by unscrupulous and/or ignorant priests and priestesses as Deities*** *– as* ***Abosom, Orisha, Vodou, etc.*** *Such spirits will also* ***fraudulently promote themselves as Deities.***

Such spirits, dwelling in the forest, inhabiting a certain tree, will be present when a scrupulous or unscrupulous priest/ess uses elements of that tree to fashion an amulet, talisman or shrine for protection. The spirit will often make a *unilateral* attempt to take up residence in the newly fashioned amulet, talisman or shrine, or be *invited* by the unscrupulous priest/ess to take up residence in the amulet, talisman or shrine. The *scrupulous* but *misguided* priest/ess will utilize the talisman, amulet or shrine and suffer greatly. He or she may give the amulet, talisman or shrine to a client and the client will suffer greatly. The *unscrupulous* priest/ess however will utilize the talisman, amulet or shrine, now occupied by the perverse spirit as a weapon. He or she will give ritual offerings to the spirit, feed it, and direct it to execute perverse tasks for him/her. The discarnate spirit will also carry-out certain tasks for the client of the unscrupulous priest/ess to gain the client's trust. It will then withhold its influence, under the strategic direction of the unscrupulous priest/ess, thereby forcing the client to return to the priest/ess for a "reading", divination, in order to figure out what went wrong. Why is the spirit of the amulet, talisman, shrine no longer "working"? The priest/ess then "consults" the "deity" and returns with an answer that usually requires the client to give more money, sex, sacrifice that which is valuable to them, etc. This creates fear within the client and a perverse dependency on the fake "deity" and the unscrupulous priest/ess. The client is sometimes "initiated" as a priest/ess of the spirit/fake-"deity" of the amulet, talisman or shrine as well creating an even deeper perverse dependency.

It is these kinds of unscrupulous, pseudo-priests/esses and **discarnate disordered spirits promoted falsely as "deities"** that work with the akyiwadefo who seek them out. It is these kinds of perverse discarnate earthbound spirits, falsely promoted as deities that lie about the nature of the real Deities/Abosom. It is these kinds of perverse discarnate spirits **posing** as Abosom that promote the false ideas that the Abosom accept human sacrifice (outside of capital punishment), that the Abosom are just like humans, that they fight, argue, lie, drink, smoke, work with whites, churches, mosques, are "extraterrestrials", that human beings are equal to or superior to the Abosom, that the Abosom can be ordered by human beings or threatened by human beings to obey them and other foolish lies. In Akan culture the amulets, talismans, shrines are called **nsuman**. There are good spirits who work through *nsuman* and disordered spirits who work through *nsuman*. The disordered spirits are those who fraudulently pass themselves off as deities. And it is the unscrupulous priests/esses as well as the ignorant who fraudulently promote these *suman*-spirits as Abosom. **The same corrupt process occurs all over Afuraka/Afuraitkait amongst a certain misguided percentage of our varied populations.**

Nanasom, Afurakani/Afuraitkaitnit Ancestral Religion, has always had ritual mechanisms to expose and eradicate such negative spirits from contacting the family and community as well as mechanisms to identify unscrupulous priest/esses. Yet, when we do not avail ourselves of these mechanisms, or do not recognize that they even exist, we succumb to the perverse influence/misinformation, the perverse "worldview" promoted by such disordered spirits, the akyiwadefo and their black followers. **This misinformation gives rise to insane rationalizations. Adherence to such insane rationalizations causes us to engage in behavior and establish institutions that perpetuate misguided thinking and behavior – even under the auspices of Pan-Afrikan Nationalism. Ultimately this only serves to perpetuate white rule.**

These insane rationalizations detailed below must and will be dismantled once and for all.

Good/Order and Non-Order. What is the opposite of Good? In the akyiwadefo/perverse view of the world, "evil" (bad) is the opposite of good. The akyiwadefo also put forward the perverse notion that "good and evil are relative" or "part of the continuum of divine order". This began in a major way after the akyiwadefo invaded ancient Kamit and began to deliberately pervert the Afurakani/Afuraitkaitnit Ancestral Religion. It continues today.

This ideological perversion was and is a **political ploy** on the part of the akyiwadefo to insert themselves into the Divine Scheme and thereby escape retribution by us for their criminal actions against us.

The akyiwadefo have promoted white images as images of the "son of god" (christianity), "messenger of god" (islam), "chosen people" (judaism), images of devas and devis (hindu "deities"), as well as buddhist and taoist "deities". These images are promoted to this day in order to promote the insane notions of white supremacy and black inferiority. In the same fashion they promote pseudo-spiritual concepts.

In reality, the concept of **Good** and the concept of **Order** (Divine Order) are **one and the same**. Again, the Akan saying: *Osansa se, ade a* ***Nyamewaa-Nyame*** *aye nyinaa ye…The Hawk says that all that the Supreme Being created is Good.* This is not merely an Akan *belief*, but a *reality* that can be found all throughout Afuraka/Afuraitkait (Africa). What the Supreme Being creates is Good. **Good is Order**. The opposite of Order is **Non-Order**—*that which is not yet Created by the Supreme Being.*

To illustrate this principle, if you have clay (unformed/non-ordered) and then you order it/form it into a pot, you have gone from *non-order* to *order*. If someone came along, saw your pot, took a hammer and destroyed it, scattering potsherds all over the room this is **disorder**---a *perversion* of the **order**. It is *disorder* because this new state (scattered potsherds) *was not sanctioned* by the potter/ess (yourself). Non-order is the *balance* of Order while disorder/evil is the *perversion* of Order. See depiction below:

Unformed Clay
Non-Order

Formed Clay (Pots)
Order

Destroyed pots
disorder – perversion of the Order

This reality undergirds the formation of **Abode**, the Created Universe. The Black Substance of Space is recognized by all Afurakanu/Afuraitkaitnut (Africans) to be a Male and Female Spiritual Entity. In Kamit, these are the Deities **Ka** and **Kait** respectively. Within **Ka** and **Kait**, the Black Substance, are the Male and Female Deities **Hehu** and **Hehut**, the expansive and contractive forces of pulsation, heat, *'breathing'* and **Nu** and **Nut** (noo and noot). **Nu** and **Nut** are the energic-base within the Blackness. Divine Energy in potential. The Root Energy of Being. *(Notice the electromagnetic energy/wavy/watery lines of energy comprising Their names in the medutu/hieroglyphic symbols)*. This is the state of Non-Order, "black clay". It is from this Root (inert) Energy that the spiraling/active energy of **Ra** and **Rait** (Creator and Creatress) proceed, manifesting as light.

If you close your eyes for a moment, you can experience a snapshot of these principles. When the eyes are closed you are "looking into" an expanse of Blackness with no beginning or ending. However, you are conscious. Your consciousness (**Ka/Kait**) is an invisible inhabitant of the Blackness. You also have energy. Your inert energy (**Nu/Nut**) is also an invisible inhabitant of the Blackness. When you start to shape and fashion ideas, images, spark thoughts, etc. your consciousness and energy interact, facilitated by the Male and Female Deities **Hehu** and **Hehut**, the expansive/contractive movement *('breathing')* within the Blackness. Light-forms are birthed and pulsate within your spirit/mind. This is a replication of the origin of Creation.

Nyamewaa-Nyame (**Amenet-Amen**) directs a portion of the Divine Black Substance of Space to be shaped/fashioned into various forms. The Root Energy of Being (**Nu** and **Nut**), the potential Energy within the Black Substance, interacts/activates and gives birth to the spiraling expansive/contractive Spirits (Life-force) that ultimately manifest as light and fire and separate the Black Substance into spheres. These spheres, once infused with Life-Force energy become stars, planets, etc. [the Life-Force Energy is the Creator and Creatress of the World, the Deities called **Ra** and **Rait** in *Kamit*, **Odumare** and **Osumare** in *Yoruba*, **Nyankonton** and **Nyankopon** in *Akan*, **Da** and **Ayida-Hwedo** in *Fon/Vodoun*, etc.] This process is similar to heat causing water in a pot to vibrate (to *wave*/boil) ultimately producing spheres (bubbles).

Non-Order

Order

nuclear test explosion
disorder - perversion of the Order

The energic-substance of **Ka** and **Kait,** inclusive of **Nu** and **Nut,** has thus gone from **Non-Order** to **Order**. **Non-Order** is the *balance* of **Order**. Non-Order is the *complement* of Order. That which is *Uncreated* (unformed) becomes *Created* (formed). It is *Created* with a capital "C" because this Creation was sanctioned by the Supreme Being. If someone on one of these Creations decides to destroy the creation—as in the akyiwadefo attempting to destroy **Asaase Afua**, the Earth Mother—this destruction is **disorder**. It is *disorder* because *this destruction was/is not sanctioned* by **Nyamewaa-Nyame**. Disorder is therefore the **perversion** of Order—**not the opposite—not the balance.**

Evil in Afurakani/Afuraitkaitnit culture is defined as **disorder**. **Disorder is not part of a continuum of Divine Order, for it is not sanctioned by the Supreme Being.** This is why there is a Male Obosom (*Orisha, Vodou, Arusi*) in Creation called **Bena** in *Akan*, **Heruaakhuti** (**Heru Behudet**) in *Kamit*, **Ogun** in *Yoruba*, **Ogu** in *Fon* and *Ewe* (Vodou), **Ikenga** in *Igbo*—Whose role is to eradicate disorder and eradicate (kill, destroy) its purveyors on *behalf* of **Nyamewaa-Nyame**. The Female Obosom called **Sekhmet** in Kamit, written **Sekyima** (**Sakyima**) in Akan, participates equally in this process. In Akan culture These Abosom (Deities) are called **Abrafo Abosom**---Divine Executioners (Divine Killers). They exist to maintain the **integrity** of Divine Order—to maintain the **true continuum** of Divine Order—*the Divine Balance of Male and Female.* This reality is recognized throughout Afurakani/Afuraitkaitnit culture, past and present. This is not subjective. It is a comprehensive understanding resulting from Afurakani/Afuraitkaitnit direct experience with these Divine Entities and our attunement to and alignment with **Maa/Maat.**

Good/Right. "Either/or logic" or what is labeled dichotomous logic is not a feature of the world-view of eurasians. It is **essentially** Afurakani/Afuraitkaitnit. The existence of right and wrong is not a eurocentric concept—the **propaganda** that "right and wrong are two halves of a whole" or that "right and wrong are relative" is **eurocentric propaganda** promoted for the same reasons stated above regarding "good and evil". It is a political ploy by the akyiwadefo to include all of their oppressive acts into the Divine Scheme, thereby attempting to inoculate themselves from Divine Justice being dispensed by us who have been oppressed. Promoting the "relativity" of right and wrong also allows the akyiwadefo to promote the practice of their inherent, perverse sexual deviance, dissexuality (homosexuality), as "normal" and "okay". In reality, dissexuality (homosexuality) is not a "form" or "expression" of sexuality—**dissexuality (homosexuality) is a perversion of sexuality**. It is disorder, the *perversion* of Order.

In reality **Right** and **Good** (Order) are the same concept. Thus, what is Good (Order) is also what is "Right". Since all that the Supreme Being creates is Good (Order/Right) then the *opposite* of Right/Good/Order is *that which has not yet been Created/fashioned* by Divinity (Non-Order).

Wrong is not the opposite of right. Wrong is the *perversion* of right. Again, disorder (wrong) is the *perversion* of Order (right). The perversion is never the complement/balance. All Afurakanu/Afuraitkaitnut recognize the reality that right and wrong are **not** two halves of a whole nor are they relative. True opposites balance one another. They complement one another.

Nyamewaa-Nyame Nhyehyee, The Divine Order, is the Union of Complementary Opposites

The degree to which this reality is misunderstood by Afurakanu/Afuraitkaitnut demonstrates the measure of their infection. The proper notions of Law, of **Maa/Maat (Mmara)**, are dependent on the recognition that **Maa/Maat** is the measure of Good/Right—that which is True.

Absolute Truth. What is **True** is ultimately expressed in **Order, Good, Right. Truth is Absolute. Truth is the measure of Order. It is the essence of Law as the Expression of Order**. The opposite of Truth, in the Divine Scheme of *Abode*, is thus **Non-Order**, that which has *not yet been Created or sanctioned* by **Nyamewaa-Nyame**, for **Nyamewaa-Nyame** only creates and sanctions that which is Good, Order, Right, Genuine, Real, True. We must recognize therefore that **falsehood** is the *perversion* of **Truth** – *not the balance.*

Falsehood represents that which is *un*-real, *not* genuine. *Falsehood is that which was never fashioned by Divinity.* It only comes into being as a *perversion* of that—Truth—which was originally and genuinely conceived, sanctioned and fashioned by Divinity. Absolute Truth is the *essence* of Divine Law. It is thus the Divine measure of how we express our every thought, intention and action in the physical and spirit-worlds. **In Afurakani/Afuraitkaitnit culture this leaves no room for the enshrining of belief.**

Belief is recognized by Afurakanu/Afuraitkaitnut to be an expression of immaturity

Belief is a manifestation of the failure at one or more points in *Time* to attune to **Maa/Maat** and to acquire the in-sight that comes with such attunement.

Lack of attunement leads to lack of insight which, to the immature, can lead to blind-acceptance of and ultimately adherence to falsehood which is always self-destructive and thus anti-Divinity.

***Amammere**, Afurakani/Afuraitkaitnit Ancestral Culture, is defined as the **Divine acceptance** (love/law) of Order and the **Divine rejection** (hate) of disorder.*

We accept through **Maa/Maat** and through **Maa/Maat** only. We reject through **Sekhem Shut/Sekhmet** (**Heru Behudet/Sekhemet**) only. We accept through the Abosom of **Law/Love**. We reject through the Abosom of **Hate**.

The whites and their offspring have moved to promote the insanity that "truth is relative", for they know that our acceptance of this lie is adherence to spiritual blindness and thus a precursor to our own self-destruction. The elevation of belief beyond its proper categorization of being an expression of immaturity allows the whites and their offspring to introduce false ideas into our awareness and force us to accept them without proper judgment. This blind-acceptance is the key to self-destructive thoughts, intentions and actions/behavior taking root within the Afurakani/Afuraitkaitnit population and is propagated most pointedly through the vehicle of false-religious beliefs. It is therefore a critical imperative that we embrace and execute the truism:

The key to Afurakani/Afuraitkaitnit Revolution-Resolution is the absolute rejection of false beliefs

In order to ground ourselves in this reality, we must recognize and internalize true complementary opposites of and within **Abode**:

Major Complementary Poles of Opposites of **Abode**

Non-Order	**Order** (Good/Right)
Uncreated	**Created** (Good/Right)
Unformed	**Formed** (Good/Right)

That which is Divinely Ordered, Created, Formed is that which is Good/Right. It is that which is **True** (Real, Genuine/Divinely Sanctioned). The **Non-Order** Pole *balances* the **Order** Pole. The **Uncreated** Pole *balances* the **Created** Pole. The **Unformed** Pole *balances* the **Formed** Pole. If the Order Pole is *perverted*, disorder/wrong appears. If the Created Pole is *perverted* disorder/wrong appears. If the Formed Pole is *perverted*, disorder/wrong/malformation appears. *Disorder appears only as a* **perversion** *of the* **Order Pole** *(Good/Right Pole)*—**not** *as the balance of the Non-Order Pole, nor as a balance of the Order Pole.*

Major Complementary Poles of Opposites within **Abode**

Female	**Male**
Contraction	**Expansion**
Kyi (Hate)	**Law/Love**

[*We must recognize the reality that* **Law** *is* **Love**. *Sensuality, which many falsely identify as Love, is a different concept*]

Perversion of the Complementary Poles:

Disorder is the *perversion* of **Order** *not the complement*
Evil is the *perversion* of **Good** *not the complement*
Wrong is the *perversion* of **Right** *not the complement*
Malformed/Malformation is the *perversion* of that which is **Formed** *not the complement*
Lust (misguided desire) is the *perversion* of **Law/Love** *not the complement*
Malice (evil intent) is the *perversion* of **Hate** *not the complement*
Falsehood is the *perversion* of **Truth** *not the complement*

And finally from the text **OBARIMA Afurakani Manhood** by **Odwirafo Kwesi Ra Nehem Ptah Akhan**:

"...The balance of the **Afurakani male** is the **Afuraitkaitnit female**. The balance of Afurakani/Afuraitkaitnit people—the only *created* people—are the *uncreated* people: the Afurakani/Afuraitkaitnit Ancestresses and Ancestors *not yet born*. The balance of the Afurakani male is **not** the white male. The balance of Afurakani/Afuraitkaitnit people is **not** white people. The whites and their offspring (white europeans, white americans, white hispanics, white so-called — "native"-americans, white arabs, white indians, white asians, etc.), i.e., all non-Afurakani/non-Afuraitkaitnit people are **not** the balance of the *created* people, they are a **perversion** of a minute percentage of the *created* people. They are descendants from and carriers of a genetic and spiritual perversion which defines them, and establishes their identity as physically and spiritually separate from and out of harmony with Afurakanu/Afuraitkaitnut..."

Ptah Hetep says:

"...He who hears (is obedient) is beloved of The Deity. The Deity **hates** *the one who does not hear....The fool who does not hear, he can do nothing at all. He looks at ignorance and sees knowledge. He looks at harmfulness and sees usefulness. He does everything that one detests and is blamed for it everyday. He lives on the things by which one dies. His food is evil speech. His sort is known to the officials who say, "There goes a living death everyday." One ignores the things he does because of his many daily troubles.*

A child who hears is a follower of ***Heru****. When s/he is old and has reached the period where s/he is venerated, then s/he will speak likewise to his/her own children, renewing then the teachings of his/her parent.*

To create obstacles to the following of laws is to open a way to a condition of violence. The transgressor of laws is punished, although the greedy person overlooks this. *Baseness (lust) may obtain riches, yet crime never lands its wares on the shore.* ***In the end only Maat lasts.*** *Man says, "Maat is my father's ground".*

I have had 110 years of life. As a gift of the Per Aa (Pharaoh), I have had honors exceeding those of the Ancestresses and Ancestors, by doing Maat until the state of veneration (Elderhood)..."

Ptah Hetep **repudiates** the idiotic belief that *"truth is relative; right and wrong are relative"* by stating that *the* ***fool*** *looks at ignorance and sees knowledge, looks at harmfulness and sees usefulness*, etc. He **repudiates** the idiotic belief that *"good and evil are part of a divine continuum"* by stating that "*Maat is everlasting...In the end, only Maat lasts.*"

The perversion of Order is temporary, for the Abosom Who function to eradicate disorder ultimately fulfill Their function. This is so that **Nyamewaa-Nyame Nhyehyee**, Divine Order, is perpetuated, for it is the basis of *Abode*. Those who refuse to eradicate the infection of the akyiwadefo within their spirits are participating as agents of disorder and will ultimately be exposed. Some will attempt to provide pseudo-credentials to justify their tightly-held eurocentric/false beliefs:

"I was born and raised in Africa, I know the culture"
"I am an initiated priest/priestess"
"I was initiated in Africa"
"I am a 5th generation Nigerian Babalawo"
"I am a direct descendant of Ifa, Shango, etc."
"I have the Vodou in my family"
"I come from a long line of priests/esses"
"I have been enthroned/enstooled as a king, chief, chieftainess, queenmother in Africa"
"I have lived in Ghana at the shrine of the Abosom for 7 years"
"I speak the language"
"I have repatriated to Africa"
"I am a Zulu shaman"
"I have been sanctioned by my elders in Africa to teach the foreigners"
"I have studied at the feet of masters"
"I have been given the authority to reveal sacred mysteries hitherto unknown outside of the African Bush"
"I have been possessed by spirits"
"I have heard the spirits speak and I have seen them and felt them..the spirits obey my commands"
"I do divination and get results...[usually]"
"I have healed people"
"I have done sacrifices for people"
"I have seen the future"
"I was the first to be initiated; first to receive a shrine; first to establish a temple, first to bring the tradition from Africa, etc."

Initiation, priesthood/priestesshood, lineage, length of time on the continent of Afuraka/Afuraitkait, length of study with **infected** continental "elders/elderesses", disembodied spirit-experiences, memorization of language and ritual practices, receiving "titles" of "authority", receiving intermittent assistance from wayward spirits for medicinal/healing advice and through divination (trumpeting the good "*results*" of divination but rationalizing the bad "*results*" and blaming the client for the bad "*results*"), irrelevant "firsts"—**all of these are absolutely meaningless "credentials".**

Afurakanu/Afuraitkaitnut reject them and the fools who propound them

Maa/Maat is Maa/Maat. Law is Law. Truth is Truth.

Our conscious connection to, incorporation and expression of Maa/Maat (Mmara) and our repulsion of isfet (disorder) through the impression of Kyi is the measure of our spiritual and cultural integrity as Afurakanu/Afuraitkaitnut.

Those Afurakanu/Afuraitkaitnut who do not understand the proper balance of Non-Order and Order, that Order, Good and Right are the same concept and that Truth is absolute are those who do not understand Nyamewaa-Nyame Nhyehyee, Divine Order, and hence their own culture.

Amammere, Afurakani/Afuraitkaitnit Ancestral Culture, belongs to those Afurakanu/Afuraitkaitnut who refuse to profane the Truth transmitted to us by Nyamewaa-Nyame through the agency of the Abosom and our Nananom Nsamanfo.

Maā [hieroglyphs], U. 220, [hieroglyphs], [hieroglyphs], P. 400, M. 571, N. 1178, [hieroglyphs], Ṭuat XI, [hieroglyphs], god of law, order, truth, integrity, etc.

Maā-t [hieroglyphs], N. 154, 1224, 1279, [hieroglyphs], a goddess, the personification of law, order, rule, truth, right, righteousness, canon, justice, straightness, integrity, uprightness, and of the highest conception of physical and moral law known to the Egyptians.

maā-t [hieroglyphs], P. 93, [hieroglyphs], truth, integrity, uprightness, justice, the right, verity, genuineness, law; Copt. ⲘⲈ, ⲘⲎⲒ.

maā [hieroglyphs], to be true, to be upright, true, truthful, veritable, real, actual; Copt. ⲘⲈ, ⲘⲎⲒ.

maa [hieroglyphs], U. 39, 213, P. 187, [hieroglyphs], P. 170, [hieroglyphs], Koller Pap. 5, 2, [hieroglyphs], Hymn Darius 17, [hieroglyphs], Rev. 11, 140, to see, to examine, to inspect, to perceive, to look at; [hieroglyphs], IV, 1006; [hieroglyphs], seen, visible.

Maāti [hieroglyphs], B.D. 125, I, [hieroglyphs], U. 453, [hieroglyphs], IV, 1082, [hieroglyphs], IV, 1220, the two goddesses of Truth, *i.e.*, Isis and Nephthys, who assisted at the Great Judgment.

maār, to see, to keep a look-out.
maār, watch-tower, look-out place.

mer, to see, to look at.

mer-t, eye; dual, the two eyes; divine eyes, sun and moon, etc.; many-eyed, "full of eyes"; "all eyes," *i.e.*, everybody, people in general; Copt. ϐⲁⲗ.

mer, Rev. 11, 124, 12, 29, overseer, chief officer, head, superintendent, director, foreman; plur.

mer T. 266, M. 421, T. 283, P. 50, M. 31, N. 64, P. 64, U. 224; Rec. 27, 224, to love, to desire, to wish for, to crave for, to will; Copt. ⲙⲉ.

merȧ, Hymn Darius 19, lover, friend.

As we can see in the above examples, both terms **maa** *(law)* and **mer** *(love)* are vocalized in the *Coptic* dialect as **ME**: Copt. ⲙⲉ. Moreover, we also have the variations of **maa**, **maar**, **mer** all referencing *sight, insight, the Eye of* ***Ra*** *(Creator), Divine Eyes,* etc. These variations can also be vocalized in Coptic as **ME**. As stated in Part 1 of the series, the Coptic vocalization **Me** is retained in the Akan language as **Pe**. *Pe* thus means *will, desire* yet it also means *just, exactly, accurately, perfectly, precise* as well as *to search, examine, scrutinize, investigate:*

ɔ-pɛ, *inf. 1. will, desire;* wo pɛ a wopɛ nyɛ, *thy will be done (Mt. 26,42.);* ɔpɛ na mepɛe sɛ mehũ wo anim, *I have heartily desired to see thy face (Lk. 22,15); cf.* apɛde. — *2. love* or *affection* for a person of the other sex, *amorous passion;* ɔpe fi dompem', *love comes*

pɛ́, pɛ́pɛ, pɛ́pɛ̄pɛ, *adv. exactly, accurately, precisely; just, even, but, only; completely, thoroughly, perfectly;* adañ anañ pɛ wɔ kũrow yi mu, *there are but (or only) four houses in this village;* wosi nnipa ɔha pɛpɛ, *there are exactly a hundred people;* wasiesie ne dañ mu pɛpɛ̄pɛ, *he has put his room in excellent order.*

pɛ̄, *v.* [*red.* pɛ̄pɛ̄] mu, *to search, examine, scrutinize, investigate, inquire;* kopɛ̄ no mu yiye (na) benyã bi bɛkã kyerɛ me; ɔn'na ogyina hɔ yi, wo añkasa pɛ̄pɛ̄ no mu na hũ no nokware; wopɛ̄pɛ̄e mu na wobisae, *Jud. 6,29.* pɛ̄pɛ̄ asɛm no mu yiye na woanni atoro.
pɛ, *night-watching;* si pɛ, *to sit up at night. pr. 2155.*

Coptic		Akan/Twi	
Me	*law, truth, right, just*	**Pe**	*just, perfect, accurately, truly*
Me	*will, desire*	**Pe**	*will, desire*
Me	*see, inspect, examine*	**Pe**	*to search, examine, investigate; night watching*

As stated previously, the 'm' and 'p' sound interchange from Kamit to Akan, thus the pronunciation of the Coptic '**ME**' and the Akan '**PE**' is identical. This is shown in the relationship between the Akan term **mpra** (mpena, mpana) meaning *lover* and the Kamiti term **mera** meaning *lover*:

mprā, mpānā, *pl.* -fo, *1. lover, paramour; concubine, mistress, courtesan;* ɔbarima a. ɔbea a ɔnam twē mprā ; *pr.* 2719. *cf.* agnāmāā.

merȧ, Hymn Darius 19, lover, friend.

The 'm' in *mera* (*mara*) is represented by the 'mp' combination in *mpara* (*mpra* also *mpena, mpana* in other Twi dialects – the rolling 'R' and 'N' interchange). These are the same words with the same five meanings in both languages, unchanged over thousands of years.

The term **maa** (**me**) referencing *law* as well as *to see* is undergirded by the cosmology as demonstrated via the **medutu** (hieroglyphs). The 'a' medut in the word **maa** of the *forearm with the open palm turned upward* is shown as: **a**

maat

The showing of the palm turned upward is a *'showing of your hand'*. It is **expression**. It is a *revealing* of yourself and a revelation or manifestation of *integrity, uprightness,* having *nothing to hide.* It is *openness* and *honesty.* It is a manifestation of *truth.* At the same time it is a ritual gesture. While turning the palms towards someone is a ritual *provocation* ('pushing' energy, *electric*), the opening of the palms and turning them upward is ritual *convocation.* It is a ritual "announcement" that one is *ready to receive.* Once we show (express) through our openness, our cleanliness, our integrity, our righteousness, we have aligned ourselves with Order. We are now *eligible* to *receive* the energy *(magnetic)* from the Supreme Being necessary for us to execute our Divine function in the world. Such ritual convocatory gestures are used during *spirit possession, divination* and more in various Afurakani/Afuraitkaitnit (African) cultures inclusive of ancient Kamit, Khanit and Akan culture.

In the same fashion, when one opens his/her eyes it is an **expression**. It is a *revealing* of self, an opening to the **Ka/Kait** (Soul/Divine Consciousness) and a manifestation of *integrity, uprightness*, having *'nothing to hide'.* We thus require that someone *'look (maa/me) us directly in the eye (maa/me)'* in order to know if they are telling the truth (*maa/me*). The opening of the eye is *openness* and *honesty.* It is a manifestation of *truth.* Just as with the opening of the palms as a ritual method to *receive* the energy necessary to execute our Divine function in the world, so is the opening of the eyes an expression of that process. We thus have the ritual of the *'Opening of the Mouth and the Eyes'* in Kamit, Khanit as well as Akan and other cultures.

With the *open palm* or the *open eye* we are revealing ourselves, **expressing** ourselves. We are thus able to *receive*, draw (receive with the *hands*, receive through *insight*), **attract** balance to our lives. **Law** *(me)* is the instrument by which we attract *balance* to our lives. **Love** *(me)* is the instrument by which we attract our *balance* (complement, spouse) to our lives. Opening our hands to receive and our eyes to receive thus allows us to ***express** our true nature* and *receive what is necessary to function.* Upon reception of this energy from the Supreme Being, our influence and sphere of awareness **expands.** Law/Love (Maa/Maa or Me/Me) as the *Expression* of Order is thus the **Expansive Pole** of Divine Order. This is the key difference between Law/Love as *expression, revelation, integrity* and *attraction* as opposed to the belief that the focus of love is 'giving'. As stated in the series, to be *in love* with someone is truly to be *in law* with the individual – *to function in harmony with Divine Order with respect to your interaction with said individual or entity.* It is to be <u>open</u>, *expressive of your true nature* and thus <u>receptive,</u> *attractive to* Balance – and averse to imbalance.

mmára, *v. n.* [băra, bra] *law, commandment, order, decree, edict, regulation, rule, statute.* – hyẹ (or di) mm., *to make, give (or issue) a law;* – di mm. so, (or ye mm.) *to observe* or *keep a law;* – tō mm., *to transgress a law.*

law, commandment, order,

mbra, F. = mmăra.

mmára-hyẹ. *inf.* the act of *giving laws; s.* mmăra.
mmăra-hyẹ́fo. *pl. id., lawgiver, legislator.*

act of giving laws

ọ-bráfó, *pl.* a-, *executioner, hangman; pr. 636. forerunner;*

executioner, police

bra, băra, *v.* 1. *to make, enact a law* or *laws, to order with authority. to lay an injunction upon, to command,* esp. *to forbid, prohibit;* mpanyimfo kọ apām akọbrá ade, *the elders have assembled to enact* or *make laws;* mabra no, *I have interdicted him:* bra no nẹ ara sẹ oññkosi ntẹw bio, *forbid him this very day any more to join in that play* (ntẹw-si) *again;* – *to fix* (by law) *the value of:* wọabra dare mā aba mmañ 75. — 2. *to settle:* matu mabẹbra ha,

to make, enact a law; forbid

ọ-bra, *(inf.)* 1. *the coming into this world. the state of existence* or *life in this world;* ọbra a wọwoo me too mu yi, *the life into which I have been born;* mẹsọre bra yim', *I shall depart this life;* ọbra akyi wọ amane, *in after-life more trouble is met with than in childhood;* or, *in future days trouble may befall you;* mebọọ ọbra, mennom bi da, *as long as I live, I never drank any.* — 2. *manner of life, conversation, behaviour, conduct; pr. 409. 634. 635.* ọbra a ẹhō nni dẹm *or* akasayé, *blameless behaviour;* bọ bra, *to behave, conduct, to bear* or *carry one's self;* bọ bra-pa, *to behave well;* bọ bra-

life, existence

As we can see above the term **mmara** (law), also written **mbra** (**mbara**) in the *Fante* dialect of Twi, is also related to the term **obra** (life) and **obrafo**. The **obrafo** is one of the *group of people* (fo) who enact *law* (bra). The term **bra** as a verb meaning *to enact law* is the active version of the noun **mmara** or **mbra**. When a word beginning with a 'b' in Akan is pluralized an 'm' is prefixed. Thus **bra** becomes **mbra**, pronounced in some dialects as **mbra** (**mbara**) and most others as **mmara**. The term **bra** or **obra** is a contraction of **bara** or **obara**. The *executioner, hangman* and also *'police' – upholder of the law* is **bara**-fo. This is directly derived from the Coptic dialectical version of the term for *inspector, overseer* (officer) **MER** or **MAR**. As shown above the Coptic version of **MR** or **MER** meaning *'eyes'* is **BAR**: Copt. ⲃⲁⲗ. Here, the 'm' and the 'b' interchange just as they do in Twi. Moreover, the terms **Mbra** (**Mbara**) or **Mmara**, **Mpra** (**Mpara**) and **Obara** are all related as: **Law, Love** *(lover, one's love)* and **Life**.

heṭ [hieroglyphs], IV, 1090, [hieroglyphs], IV, 971, to strike, to trample upon, to vanquish, to suppress, to subdue.

heṭheṭ [hieroglyphs], IV, 710, [hieroglyphs], Verbum I, 338, [hieroglyphs] to batter down, to beat small, to crush.

ḥeta [hieroglyphs], to break, to tear up,

kherkher [hieroglyphs], T. 282, N. 132, [hieroglyphs], to root up, to destroy, to be destroyed; Copt. ϣⲟⲣϣⲣ̅.

ḥerḥer [hieroglyphs], to demolish, to pull down; Copt. ϧⲉⲣϧⲱⲣ, ϣⲟⲣϣⲣ̅.

kheti [hieroglyphs], to engrave, to cut into, some-

khetkhet [hieroglyphs], to break, to cut into pieces, to destroy, to break a command, to engrave; Copt. ϣⲟⲧϣⲉⲧ.

khet [hieroglyphs], to be behind someone or something, to follow, to march back, to turn back, to retreat, the hinder part; [hieroglyphs]

khet [hieroglyphs], impaling pole; [hieroglyphs], impaled.

kyi, Ak. kyiri, *r.* [*red.* kyikyi] *to turn the back to; 1. to dislike, not to like, to loathe, have an aversion to, hate, detest, abhor; cf.* taṅ;
kyi, *r.* [*red.* kyikyi] *to press, squeeze, wring* or *crush out;*
akyi, *cf.* akyiri, Ak. akyire, Gr. §119. 120,4. 130,5. *1. the back, the hind(er) part, rear; the outer (outward) part, outside* of a vessel or enclosure, of the hand. *pr.* 468. — *2. the space behind* or *outside.* —

As stated in Part 1 and shown above, the Akan term **kyi** (also **kyiri**) means *to hate, abhor, loathe, detest.* It also means *to press, squeeze, wring or crush out.* The related noun **akyi** (**akyiri**) means *the back, hinder part, rear.* Thus, the same word for 'hate' is also the same word for 'back'. In the medutu shown above we see that the same word for *to break, destroy,* **khet** ('hate') is also the same word for *'hinder part, to turn back, to be behind something'* **khet**. This is rooted in the notion that what is *loathed, abhorred,* is *squeezed out, crushed,* in the *back* from the *hinder part.* This is elimination of waste from the physical body. That which is toxic and thus rejected (*hated*) by the body is forced out from the *back*. Thus, to turn one's *back* on someone in ancient and contemporary Akan culture is to show *loathing, hatred, abhorrence* for that person. **It is to identify them with excrement**. It means fundamentally that they must be rejected, repelled, hated, repulsed because they are toxic. These are the same terms with the same meanings from Khanit and Kamit to Akan culture unchanged over thousands of years. We also have the variations **khed** and **khed** meaning *pain, misery, anguish* and *to go back* also **s-khedkhed** – *to overthrow, to upset.* [*The 's' prefix in Kamit is causative.* ***khedkhed*** *– overthrow,* ***s-khedkhed*** *– to overthrow, to upset*] kheṭ, to go back, retreat. kheṭ, pain, misery, anguish.

s-kheṭkheṭ, 30, 193, to overthrow, to upset

akyi-de [kyi, c., ade] *a detestable or abominable thing; any food disallowed by the fetish;* wadi n'aky., *he has eaten what he was forbidden to eat.*

The Akan term **akyide** also written **akyiwade** speaks to that which is abominated by the **Abosom** (Deities, Divinities) referred to derogatorily as 'fetish' in the entry above. The **akyide** are the **ade** *(things, objects, deeds, entities)* that are **kyi** *(hated)* and thus *disallowed* by the Abosom. This is **Divine Hate**.

It is also important to note the variations **Khai** (Khi, Kyi) meaning to *defeat, overthrow, slay* and **Khaitiu** the *Deities who slaughter the enemies of* ***Ra*** *and* ***Ausar***. This includes **Heru Behudet** and **Sekhmet**:

khai, Nástasen Stele 39, , Ḥerusâtef Stele 82, , to slay, to defeat, to overthrow.

khai-t, , , , , , slaughter, massacre, ruin.

Khaitiu, , , , the gods who slaughter the enemies of Rā and Osiris.

The titles of **Heru** as **Heru Kheti** and **Heru Heri Khet** with the determinative medut of the stick which is also used in the terms **khet** for *destroy, overthrow* and *impaling pole* give further definition to the role of **Heru Behudet** as the Agent of the Divine Hate (**Khet**) of **Amenet-Amen**, **Nyamewaa-Nyame**.

Ḥeru-kheti, Ṭuat III, Horus as a fire-god. Ḥeru-ḥeri-khet (?)

The *winged Sun disk* is one of **Heru Behudet's** major forms. He therefore also has the *actual title* **Heti** (Hate) as well as **Sekhem Shut**.

Ḥeṭi, the flying, winged sun-disk. skhem shu-t, "strong pinioned"—a title of the Winged Disk.

Hate: [proto-indo-european etymon: **kad**] **akedos** (greek) *care, grief, sorrow*; **hata** (north germanic) *to hate, damage, destroy*; **kat** (tocharian A) *destruction*.] [www.utexas.edu/cola/centers/lrc/ielex/U/P0806.html]

All of the above facts prove Khanit and Kamit to be the **origin** of the proto-indo-european 'root': *kad* or *kat*. **The word hate was never of european origination – phonetically nor conceptually**. It is essentially Afurakani/Afuraitkaitnit (African).

Skhemit, U. 390, Rec. 30, 68, Rev. 15, 16, Rec. 31, 11, Rec. 26, 152, Ṭuat X, a lioness-headed goddess, the consort of Ptaḥ, sister of Bast, and mother of Nefer-Temu. For a list of her titles see P.S.B. 25, 218.

s-kheti, T. 171, P. 118, to turn back, to repulse; caus. of .

s-khetkhet, Love Songs 4, 8, to repulse, to drive back; caus. of .

skheti, M. 772, P. 661, P. 777, hunter, fowler, snarer; plur.

sekhi, U. 537, Rec. 27, 86, Rev. 11, 163, Ebers Pap. 109, 12, to strike, to break, to defeat, to overthrow, to beat (a drum), to mark cattle, to knap

Skhetiut, B.D. 112, 2, the goddesses of the chase.

As described in Part 2, **Sekhemet** is directed by **Ra** to slaughter the disordered men and women. She takes the form of a lioness, hunts and massacres those in rebellion to **Ra**. **Sekhemet** is the bringer of *destruction, repulsion* (**skheti**) and a Goddess of the chase (**Skheti**).

ase-kyīma, ***inf. menstruation.***

ɔ-brá, ***(inf.)*** **1.** ***the coming into this world,*** **— 3.** ***the nature,*** **i.e.** ***the menses*** **or** ***monthly courses of women, euph.*** **asabu; yɛ b. (bu nsa, kɔ afikyiri),** ***to menstruate, to have the monthly flow*** **or** ***discharge, cf.***

Sekhmet not only governs the *shedding of blood* through warfare but the *shedding of blood* through **menstruation**. This is why the term and name **asekyima** (**asakyima**) or **Sakyima** in Akan means *menstruation*. All girls in Akan culture when going through puberty rites upon the onset of menarche are referred to as either **Sakyima** or **Obrani**. The term **obra** (life) is a term also used for the *menses* (life blood). An **obra-ni** is one who is in the *obra* (menses) state. Women who are on their cycle are called **obrafo**, the *group of people* (fo) who are in the *obra* state. The Akan **kradin** (soul-name) **Abenaa** or **Abena** also has the variation **Abraba** (Abena-ba). **Abenaa** is the major name of the Obosom **Sekhmet** in Akan culture – the Female Obosom (Deity) of the planet **Bena/Abenaa** ("mars") – a warrioress Obosom Who destroys disorder and operates as the *Divine Lymphatic System* within Creation and also governs *obra*. [Note that **Het Heru** and **Sekhmet** are two separate and distinct Abosom although titles are shared.]

"…In english, derivatives of the term ***ht*** are: *hate, hit, hot, heat*….To *hit* something or someone can be an exercise in *hate*/rejection. It leads to *breaking or destroying*. *Hate* (rejection of disorder), *Hit* (to attack) *Hot* and *Heat* (to fire/burn) all relate to the functioning of **Abenaa** as the Hot, Fiery, Attacking, Warrioress Who destroys (hates) disorder and its purveyors in order to maintain the integrity of Divine Order in Creation. Another variation of **ht** from the metutu is **huit**. We thus have the title **Huit Antiu**, a title of **Sekhemet** identifying Her as the Hateress/Punisheress of the **Antiu** (dwellers in the Eastern Desert on the outskirts of Kamit who often invaded and attacked the nation of Kamit)… "

[*Excerpt from our article:* **Abenaa The Obosom of Abenaa and Abenaada** www.odwirafo.com/Akradinbosom_Abenaa.pdf]

ḥuit [hieroglyphs], IV, 1107, [hieroglyphs], [hieroglyphs], [hieroglyphs], Hh. 204, a beating, bastinado, a striking; [hieroglyphs], Rec. 30, 185.

Ḥuit Ȧntiu [hieroglyphs], a title of Sekhmit.

Variations in the spelling of the term **huit** *in the medutu include* **ht, hut** *and* **hit** *as shown above.*

mest [hieroglyphs], Rev. 13, 39, [hieroglyphs], [hieroglyphs], to hate; Copt. ⲙⲟⲥⲧⲉ.

mesit [hieroglyphs], T. 284 = [hieroglyphs], P. 53, [hieroglyphs], M. 32, [hieroglyphs], N. 65, [hieroglyphs], [hieroglyphs], children; [hieroglyphs], P. 593, race, family.

Finally, as shown in Part 3, the terms above **mst** and **msit** or **msut** meaning *to hate, hatred, that which is hated* and *children, offspring, race, family* can be found vocalized in the Akan language as:

When terms spelled with 'b' are written in the plural in the Akan language, the terms are often spelled with the double 'm':

busude *that which is evil; wicked, hated*
mmusu *evil; wicked; that which is hated*

abusu-dé, *a wicked, mischievous thing* or *deed; ill luck, disaster. pr. 118. (opp.:* akrade); F. *abomination, Mt. 24,15; a*

busú, *s.* mmusu, ahabusu, abusude

abusua *family; clan; offspring*
mmusua *matrilineal families; matriclans; offspring*

abusũá, *pl.* m-, *family, kindred, relatives,* esp. *the relations of the mother's side; one of the original families* of the Tshi nation. (Descent is matrilineal); *race; lineage; clan. Cf.* App. D. II. b & ntɔrɔ.

pl. m- denotes that the plural is **mmusua**

<u>*Selected References*</u>

An Hieroglyphic Dictionary, Vols. 1 and 2, E.A. Wallis Budge
A Dictionary of the Asante and Fante language called Tshi (Chwee, Twi), J.G. Christaller
www.archive.org

Pyramid Texts Online
www.pyramidtextsonline.com/tools.html

Kasahorow Online, Promoting African Languages
www.kasahorow.org

UBEN-HYENG

The Ancestral Summons

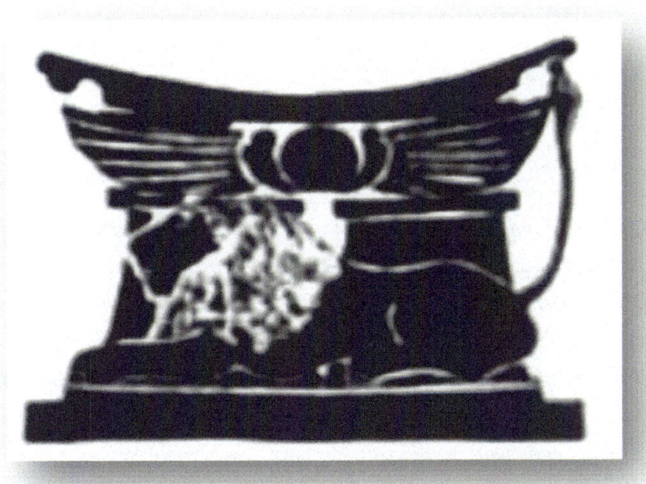

ODWIRAFO KWESI RA NEHEM PTAH AKHAN

AAKHUAMUMAN AMARUKA ATIFI MU

Antcha herak ***Amen****. Antcha herak* ***Amenet****. Antcha herak Ntorou nebu. Antcha herak Ntorotu nebut. Antcha herak Aakhu nebu. Antcha herak Aakhutu nebut.*

Mema me ho ***Nana Nyame****. Mema me ho* ***Nana Nyamewaa****. Nananom Abosom nyinaa medaase. Nananom Nsamanfo medaase.*

UBEN-HYENG (ü•ben´ - shehng´) is the combination of the Khanitu/Kenesu-Kamau (Nubian-Egyptian) term ***Uben*** and the Twi-Akan term ***Hyeng***. The terms are defined in their respective languages as descriptive of drawing forth by illumination, to shine; bright, brilliant. As a name, they are representative of the revivifying energy of Creative Power. Just as the morning Sun calls for the rejuvenation of Earth, **UBEN-HYENG** is a summons for the rejuvenation of the culture.

I have endeavored to accurately relate the following ideas and formulations which were given by the Ntorou/Ntorotu, Abosom, and confirmed by the Aakhu/Aakhutu, Nananom Nsamanfo.

This work is dedicated to Afurakanu/Afuraitkaitnut (Africans~Black People) who will hear.

Odwirafo Kwesi Ra Nehem Ptah Akhan

21 December 12998 (1997)

When we use the combination Goddess/God in this work, we are speaking of ***Amenet*** *and* ***Amen****,* ***Nyamewaa*** *and* ***Nyame****, the Mother and Father Supreme Being. The Great Ancestral Spirit, Spirit and The Great Spirit, refer to* ***Ra*** *and* ***Rait****,* ***Nyankopon*** *and* ***Nyankonton****, the Creator and Creatress. The Law refers to the Deities* ***Maa*** *and* ***Maat****. The* ***Aakhu/Aakhutu*** *and* ***Nananom Nsamanfo*** *are our Spiritually Cultivated Afurakani/Afuraitkaitnit (African) Ancestresses and Ancestors. The* ***Ntorou/Ntorotu*** *and* ***Abosom*** *refer to the Deities, Goddesses and Gods. When we use the term* ***human*** *in this work, it applies only to* ***Afurakani*** *(African) males and* ***Afuraitkaitnit*** *(African) females. The term eurasian applies to all non-Blacks: white europeans, americans, hispanics, asians, arabs, hindus, pseudo-'native'-americans, etc.*

Afuraka/Afuraitkait *is the origin of the term 'Africa'. All Black People, and only Black People, wherever we exist on Earth are* ***Afurakanu/Afuraitkaitnut****.*

The **Ures** was used in Keneset/Khanit and Kamit (Nubia and Egypt) to raise the head of the person during the sleep state, and that of the deceased with interment. The **Gwa** in Akan culture is expressive of the values, authority, and spirit of the nation. It is a seat elevating heads-of-state, societal heads, and the valued authority of the Ancestral community. Inner-vision is seated in/as the head of the conscious individual and the harmonious society.

Ru Ures-Gwa Kwesi: Symbol of the twin-circulage of Keneset/Khanit and Kumbu-Kankyeabo. It is representative of the sunsum of **Aakhuamuman Amaruka Atifi Mu**, The Akwamu Nation in North America. www.odwirafo.com

You will come to recognize that whatever is done above is also done below. Whatever functions are executed in the spirit realm, will be replicated in the physical realm. This is Law.

Those who lived before you have left their genetic imprint in you. Your physical body shows their genetic qualities. Your behavior is reflective of these qualities. Who are you descendant of, essentially? Should you not then show the qualities, and consciously engage in behavior, which is reflective of your Progenitor/Progenitress, The Great Ancestral Spirit? This is Culture. The embracing of Harmony. The way is then open to Union.

Afurakanu/Afuraitkaitnut are the heirs/heiresses of Spirit, thus your inheritance is that of the Law and Culture of The Supreme Being. *You will die, only when The Supreme Being dies.*

SHEMWT
OBRA

Goddess pours libation in your honor.

Evaporation-condensation-precipitation is the cycle by which water is drawn into Heaven and falls to rejuvenate Earth. It is a process of redistribution. Not only is Lake or Ocean from which the water is drawn replenished, but the dry Earth which requires the benefits of water is also nourished. The water's properties work to regenerate Earth-functions, resulting in a coming forth or manifestation of that which was in the Earth. Spirit raining down in this form thus renews the potential for growth subsisting in Earth. This is libation.

Is your physical vehicle of Earth? Does it not contain copper, iron, zinc, magnesium, and every element that exists in the soil? From the beginning, was not the physical sperm, the ovum, a magnet for your spirit through whose union you became manifest on the physical plane? If Spirit rains down in the form of water to nourish Earth, and you exist as spirit through Earth on the physical plane, then you are nourished by Spirit's rain. You are renewed by Spirit's rain. Your potential for growth and development is dependent on Spirit coming in this form. You need the libation of the Goddess. She pours for you. She pours water in your honor.

Where is your spirit when it leaves the physical plane? Is some aspect of your spirit attracted to Earth? Was not your physical vehicle a miniature Earth? If miniature Earth had the power to attract and fix your spirit, now that it has totally disintegrated, should not the planet Earth have the power to attract and fix your spirit within its cosmic jurisdiction? Have you come yet to consciously expand your awareness of your spirit-body beyond the protective, nurturing power of Earth, to be nurtured, consciously, under the cosmic jurisdiction of other celestial bodies/powers? Until such time, you are nurtured by Earth.

Goddess pours libation to nourish Earth as part of the cycle of regeneration. She renews the physical potential inherent in Earth. Earth then yields fruits for all physical bodies, and you then appropriate a portion of those fruits to feed your physical body. Yet, if the libation of Goddess also renews the spiritual potential inherent in Earth, then Her libation perpetually renews the potential energy of all Ancestral Spirits, while they are under Earth's jurisdiction. Do you not have the right then to appropriate a portion of Her libation and direct it towards renewing the potential inherent in your Ancestral Spirits, whose fruits of experience and wisdom will renew your awareness and nurture your development?

Who speaks against libation? Are you of God? Are God and Goddess two sides of the same coin? Are you then of Goddess? Should you not pour libation then in honor of the Ancestral Spirits? If you are of Goddess then you have a right and responsibility to place yourself in the process. It is more than symbolic.

Goddess prostrates. God prays. Ancestral-Deity worship.

Every emanation is a prayer. Every emanation from you is energy vibrating from you into the cosmos. Every word is a sound or collection of sounds. Every sound is a vibration. Every vibration is energy. Each sound and its vibratory wave and rate is representative of an aspect of Deity/Creative Power. Different vibrations generate different colors. Different vibrations generate different forms. Every sound thus generates an image--form and color. Every thought-image is an emanation, a vibration, sound, word, a prayer.

To emanate one must generate energy. Energy is drawn from the very root of Being, the uncreated and infinite matter underlying all things. In order to draw energy from this state, one must consciously merge with this state. She submits. She prostrates. She receives. The energy needed is then able to be drawn out. This energy is what emanates from the individual. He prays. He transmits. He emanates.

Your body prays perpetually. As Spirit continuously vibrates throughout your physical vehicle, the vibrations emit sounds--ship words--into the universe. Would it not be wise to redirect these emanations? If the Ancestral Spirits have answers or guidance for you, should you not periodically ship your words--redirect your emanations--out to them, in order to positively provoke their energy, which will in turn be shipped into you? This is Ancestral worship. This is evocation.

If the Deities are the powers within and without your physical vehicle, should you not ship your words--redirect your emanations--into them, so that their energy may be positively provoked and intensified within your physical vehicle enabling you to overcome some obstacle, physical or spiritual? This is Deity worship. This is invocation.

Do you not redirect your bodily emanations-sounds-vibrations every time you speak someone's name, thus provoking a response/energy from the person? Do you not redirect your emanations towards the letters in the pages of the books you read, thus provoking-activating the forms of the letters, which affect your consciousness in a manner that informs you?

Evocation and invocation are two sides of the same coin--provocation. Submission-passivity engenders receptivity. What is received may be transmitted. Goddess prostrates-receives power. God prays-sends power.

Are you of Goddess/God? Why then do you question provocation? If you are of Goddess/God then you have the right and the responsibility to evoke/worship the Ancestral Spirits, invoke/worship the Deities, worship the Supreme Being. Provoke/call forth the Creative Power in order to consciously cultivate It within your own being.

Meditation, participation. Ancestral-Deity possession.

Meditation facilitates conscious participation. Through meditation, we transfer our conscious focus from the external plane to the internal planes. We thus come to participate, consciously, in the spirit world--the community of Ancestral Spirits, Deities.

Who exists who does not operate on both planes? Does your thought, your spirit, not influence your physiology, physical acts? Should not the thoughts of the Ancestral Spirits, who remain connected to your physiology/their blood, aim to influence you if they must return through you? Do they not have an interest then in assisting you, your community? We consciously allow different thoughts/spirit-energy to direct our physical body and behavior, whether guided or mis-guided. Should we not consciously allow the Ancestral Spirits, and their thoughts/energy, to direct our physical body and behavior during ritual, that they may bring a message of wisdom? This is Ancestral possession.

When you decide to take water into your system, the decision is an act of the will. Yet, as the digestion of this substance is an act which is in harmony with the laws that govern your physiological make-up, this act of will is united with the Divine Will. The carrying out of this directive is facilitated through power. What moves your arm towards the glass? What directs the glass to the mouth?

To possess is to exert influence or control over. Your arm, muscles, nerves, are possessed by the power under the direction of the will. It is the will and power working in concert which possess you to grasp the glass and lift it. This is possession by an unseen power.

When the raindrop falls (back) into the river, it becomes one with the river. It loses its own direction and is now directed by the river's flow. It is possessed by the river. It is the river. When one returns his/her focus of consciousness (back) to the Source of all, he/she becomes one with, or is possessed by this flowing river of Being. When one focuses his/her consciousness on a particular aspect or phase of Creative Power, then one comes to know that phase of power, one possesses that power--becomes dominated by/participates in the power. He/she becomes that power-Deity. This is Deity possession.

Do you feel heat in the summer and cold in the winter? Do you feel heat at mid-day and coolness at midnight? Can all phases of Creative Power become manifest and dominate Space simultaneously, or is the exhibition of Creative Power phased? Time orders and conditions the cyclical manifestation of all phases of Creative Power, the Deities.

Who questions possession? Who exists who is not conditioned by Time? To participate in/awaken each phase of Divine Power is to facilitate union by possession, through Time. Our descent is of the Ancestral Spirits which by definition includes the Deities, for their/our circulage is of The Great Ancestral Spirit. We are possessed of this power at birth.

Song and dance as ritual possession-meditation.

Sound is power manifest. Rhythm is power conditioned. Different vibrations, different rhythms. Different rhythms, different powers. God's Power manifest through sound/rhythm. Goddess' Energy manifest through God. We are captivated by this sound. We are animated by this rhythm. We exist through Form as this sound/rhythm.

You will operate consciously as Goddess/God when you have cultivated the fullness of consciousness and power which lay dormant within you--that which was placed in you by Spirit. Fulfillment occurs then as your spirit's form is consciously united with Spirit's Form. Your power now in conscious harmony with Spirit's Power. Meditation, alteration of conscious focus, opens the way for it is the means by which one becomes open to receive, to possess, the sounds/rhythms, powers, of Creation. Song and dance are expressive forms of chant, trance, provocation.

Song is generation of power, a revelation of sound. The voice-vibrations unveil power. Why should this power not be wisely directed towards turning the keys to unlock every phase of Creative Power? Song is truly ritual. Spirit's ordered movement/vibrations ritualize the song of cosmos. Its harmony is captured and reverberates by/through Space perpetually. Should you not seek to hear and echo this song, these sounds, this power? Should you not sing as Spirit sings, directing your voice/vibrations in forms/songs displaying Spirit's harmony, in order to facilitate possession, empowerment? Song as ritual is possession-meditation.

Dance is generation of power, a revelation of rhythm. The movements wield power. Why should this power not be wisely directed towards opening the doors which will unleash every phase of Creative Power? Dance is truly ritual. Spirit's ordered movements/rhythm ritualize the dance of cosmos. Its rhythm is displayed by the celestial bodies, by animals, by nature. Should you not seek to absorb and imitate this dance, this movement, this power? Should you not dance as Spirit dances, directing your body/movements in forms/dances displaying Spirit's rhythm, in order to facilitate possession, empowerment? Dance as ritual is possession-meditation.

Who speaks against song and dance as possession? Ritual song and dance is the Earthly replication of cosmic sound and rhythm. It is possession through meditation. Different song-forms engender receptivity to specific phases of Creative Power/Deities. Different dance-forms engender receptivity to specific phases of Creative Power/Deities. Musical instruments work to mediate and channel the Powers/Deities into the human instrument. You are possessed, perpetually, of Spirit's sound/song, Spirit's rhythm/dance. Ritual possession-meditation is conscious reconnection, union, with Goddess/God.

Nature worship.

One Spirit which all things in the universe share. The Great Spirit which comes into being in the forms of the things It created. It vibrates continuously throughout your physical vehicle. It vibrates continuously throughout the bodies of the entire animal sphere. It vibrates continuously throughout the physical structures of the vegetal sphere. It vibrates continuously throughout the physical structures of the mineral sphere. All created matter in the universe, down to Its very sub-atomic structure and beyond, is permeated by the Consciousness of the Mother-Father Supreme Being.

The bird is compelled by desire, which is dictated by the forces which formed it. It has no choice but to follow. The cactus lives and dies in accordance with the laws of the forces which created and formed it. It too has no choice but to follow. The mountain is also receptive, totally, to the forces that created and sustain it. It has no choice but to follow. Yet the human has a choice. One choice. The human can choose not to be dominated by that which is not in harmony with Divine Law. Knowledge of our Divinity becomes conscious expression when we exercise this one choice at any given time. Otherwise, the knowledge of our Divinity is un-conscious.

If you have freedom to make a choice, then choose to listen to yourself, for Nature talks. Are you of Nature? Is your spirit not one with the Spirit permeating Nature? If Spirit vibrates throughout your physical vehicle producing a collection of vibrations unique to your configuration, then can it not be said to do the same with all forms/structures in/as Nature? Does the bird have a physical body? Does Spirit not vibrate continuously throughout its form? Does the oak tree have a physical body? Does Spirit not vibrate continuously throughout its form? Does the mountain or the stream have physical forms? Does Spirit not vibrate continuously throughout their forms? Then they all send out emanations. And as they act they direct their emanations. When they suffer damage they record and transmit that information as energic emanations which flood the universe.

Nature talks. When the bird decides to take flight, the decision manifests as an energic emanation, which is sent out into the universe. As the tree grows, it is bombarded with energy-emanations from other entities in Nature, it absorbs, records, and reverberates these emanations into the cosmos. The mountain and the stream absorb emanations from the vegetal, animal and human spheres, record and reverberate them into the cosmos.

Sit in front of the tree if you are of Goddess/God. For you will be able to ingest its emanations-vibrations and choose to translate them into your language. Listen to the bird, the mountain, the stream. Their emanations-vibrations are their language. You as human have the ability to consciously absorb and translate their words into your words. Who speaks against Nature worship? Spirit exists as Nature. You have the right and responsibility to provoke Nature's oration so that Nature may feed you Its lessons.

Spirit-womb of the talisman, amulet.

What is the nature of the womb? It must receive and retain, for only then can the function of gestation commence. What is the nature of the spirit-womb? Must not the same functions be executed? Where is the spirit-womb?

Observe the element fire, notice the flame and its corona. Observe the Moon, witness Its body and Its corona. Take notice of the Sun, Its body, Its corona. Hold your palm near to your face. Does your body not generate heat? Is this heat which extends beyond your physical constitution not your corona? Does movement generate heat? Should not heat be generated then as Spirit vibrates throughout/as all forms in Creation, thus producing a corona surrounding all forms and objects, animate and inanimate? Every form, every body, has a corona.

Can anxiety/thought engender physical stress? Thought originates beyond the corona on the spiritual plane. Thought is spirit, energy vibrations that are conditioned/directed. The corona receives and retains these vibrations from the spiritual plane. If the corona is an energic extension of the body, should not energy affecting the corona affect the body?

Does the reception, retention, and gestation of spirit-energy by the human corona not represent the functional properties of the womb? The corona is the spirit-womb. Spirit in the form of directed-thought conditions, impregnates, this womb. Is the corona of the inanimate not of the same origin as that of the animate, if the same Spirit vibrates through/as all forms in Creation? Should not the corona of the inanimate act as womb?

The womb of the female retains and feeds the energy of the child. The corona of Earth naturally retains, drawing the inhabitants to the surface, while it feeds them of Its atmospheric elements. The human corona retains conditioned energic-vibrations/thought, from which the brain and body feed. Should not the corona of the talisman, the amulet, be conditioned to retain energic-vibrations, power, until such time is necessary for the power, the vibrational energy, to be provoked, birthed and utilized by the owner?

The corona of the Sun will disintegrate an object before the object has a chance to reach the body of the Sun. The corona of the flame will singe the skin though it is not yet close enough to touch the body of the flame. Why should the corona of the talisman, the amulet, not be ritually conditioned to protect its owner from inimical thoughts, energic-vibrations, projections? The womb protects the child until the child can protect itself.

Who speaks against the talisman, the amulet? Do you ornament your body with metals, stones, animal skin? Do you keep objects which hold sentimental value? Talismans, amulets. Goddess/God has conferred Divine Power upon the inanimate. You have a right and responsibility then to enlist its utility, until you learn to master its generation.

Creation is ritual incarnation.

Can you see in the dream state? Can you hear in the dream state? Can you taste, touch, smell, desire, in this state? Yet, your body lay motionless in the dark. No sounds, no light, no activity. What then is it that sees, hears, senses, beyond the body?

You, as spirit, are living-energy. Your soul is your consciousness, it describes the nonphysical form which you assume as spirit. Your body is the physical replication of your nonphysical form, spirit-soul. Is this not true of Spirit? Is Goddess/God, as Spirit, not the Life-Energy of Creation? Does Goddess/God, as Soul/Consciousness, not determine Her/His Form? Does Goddess/God, as Creatress/Creator, Spirit-Soul, not incarnate perpetually, through Time, as a multitude of forms in/as Creation, the physical world-universe?

Water passes through air, in the ritual of precipitation, as various drops of water. Creative Power passes through Time, in the ritual of Creation, as various phases of Power. Every phase of Power performs a primary function, thus revealing Its nature, Its personality. Every phase of Spirit's Power is a Spirit-Power, a Deity, a Goddess or God.

Are you not of Spirit? Is your procreative power not of Creative Power? Does your procreative power then not manifest, through the cycle of your life-time, as various phases of power? Do the various phases of your power perform primary functions, revealing their nature, their personality? Is not every phase of your spirit's power thus a Spirit-Power, a Deity, a Goddess or God?

Creator/Creatress-Creation is one. Spirit-Matter is one. Soul-Body is one. How else could Creator/Creatress manifest in physical form, except the many forms of Creative Power be received and replicated in/as Matter? Is Sun not a form of Matter, an active expression of Creative Power? Is Ocean not a form of Matter, a passive expression of Creative Power? What of the Atmosphere, what of Earth? What of your forms? What is your heart, if it is not a form of your body-matter, an active expression of your procreative power? What is your blood, if it is not a form of your body-matter, a passive expression of your procreative power? What of your corona, what of your organs? You, as spirit-matter, are a synthesis of the Deities.

Creation is ritual incarnation. Does Creation not ritualize the incarnation of The Great Ancestral Spirit? Should not procreation then ritualize the incarnation of an Ancestral Spirit? Does Creation not ritualize the incarnation of the Spirit-Powers? Should not sexual activity-procreation then be ritual invocation of these incarnate Spirit-Powers? Who questions Creation as ritual incarnation? To destroy Creation is to reject the Deities incarnate in/as Creation. To strain and damage your bodily organs, glands, structures, through non-ritual sex-procreation, through improper diet and behavior, is to reject the Deities incarnate in/as your physical body. Such rejection is the only Death.

The world is the great oracle.

If one interacts with the world and beings who live in the world, and the result of that interaction seems to reveal lessons for your spirit, then that interaction with some being(s) outside of yourself is an interaction facilitated by the creative part of your spirit. Your Divine indwelling intelligence has crafted a lesson for you to learn through tools which do not dwell within you -- different people, animals, nature, stars. You can be reminded of certain principles conducive to your own spiritual awakening by simply observing nature and its laws. You can be reminded of certain principles which are conducive to your spiritual awakening simply by observing animals. You can be reminded of certain principles which are conducive to your spiritual awakening simply by listening to another individual's life experiences.

If you believe that Spirit places certain people in your path and creates certain situations providing you with the opportunity to draw a lesson from the experience, then you recognize that the Divine indwelling intelligence can and will use an external means to focus your consciousness towards that (It) which is internal. This is the definition of an oracle: An external system through which Spirit expresses its internal workings, Its Self. People, animals, insects, Earth, Moon, Sun, stars, all have lessons, and all are organs of the great oracular system called World.

If one did not need these lessons that the physical plane holds for him/her, he/she would not need to be on the physical plane.

Who questions the necessity of the oracle? You live in an oracle. You exist as an oracle.

If your spirit existed before this incarnation, if it was that which facilitated the union of sperm and ovum, if after death, it departs from the physical vehicle, then the temporary physical vehicle can consciously be referred to as external from the spirit. The spirit operates through this vehicle, and utilizes it as a tool towards union with the Source. Spirit expresses itself on the physical plane through this external tool. This tool and its component parts--organs, chakra centers--is thus oracular.

If God fashions the world and the world is oracle, if you are of God, then you fashion an oracular world. You have the right and the responsibility. You set the parameters. Allow your Divinity to express Itself through those parameters.

Those who recognize that Wisdom is accessible to all through oracle, are those who can no longer escape accountability for their actions.

MESSU RA ODOMANKOMA

God is an Idolater.

An idol is substance structured into a specified form according to a pre-existent image. Is the Sun idolized fire? It is not the Creative Power, but a vehicle through which that active and aggressive phase of Creative Power can manifest itself on the physical plane. Is the Ocean idolized water? It is not the Creative Power, but a vehicle through which that passive and receptive phase of Creative Power can manifest itself on the physical plane. Is the Moon idol? Is the Earth idol? Is the jackal, lion, bear, serpent, idol? Is the hammer idol? Does it not take the place of Creative/Destructive Force, on the physical plane?

What is the greatest idol?

Are you an idol? Did Goddess not provide the substance and God not structure your form? Are you created according to an image born of the Supreme Being? Does God not worship you? Does He not word-ship you? Does He not ship His word or His spirit, His power, His vibration, His breath into your very form while existing in essence as your form?

God is an idolater, the Great Idolater. He creates idols daily. He idolizes perpetually. He idolizes you. Goddess spins the images which will become physical reality, then Goddess/God comes into being in the form of the things It created.

You exist as idol, and Spirit word-ships you until you learn to worship It, until you learn to send your self to Self, to achieve union. Then you become the Great Idolater.

Who of the Creator's idols now comes to destroy idolatry? Would he destroy himself?

Spirit releases Creative Power through the filter of a Time-conditioned reality. Each phase of Power generating a geometric pattern in Space. Each pattern holding the key--the vibrations--of the phase of Creative Power which created it.

If you are of God, if you are of Goddess, then you have the right and the responsibility to idolize. Your idolatry is Creative Process. Your fashioning of form after the design of a preexistent pattern leads you to true worship. To ship/send a word is to ship/send your worth. Your worth is your value. Your value is expressed mathematically as the sum total of the vibrations whose unique-key ratio of waves and rates manifest on the physical plane as your spirit-body.

True worth/word-ship turns the key--releases the vibration--of the cosmic pattern. As every key is turned, every power is unleashed, at-one-ment comes. You transcend Time.

God structures the great economy through world. Make offerings.

Economics as a system designed to allocate resources in a useful and equitable manner according to the dictates of the Divine Order, is God's structure. Goddess allocates resources. God structures the plan through which they may be made useful. What are the resources of the spiritual plane?

Creative Power conditioned by Time is phased into various aspects. The many aspects are the resources. Humans share all aspects/phases as a micro-economy, but in a unique configuration. The ratios between one phase of Creative Power to the next is different for every individual. Are some humans not aggressive, hot, fiery? Are some not passive, cool, watery? If they share every aspect of Creative Power, yet one dominates their behavior, are they not by definition imbalanced? By what means is balance achieved?

In an agrarian setting of a communal society the farmer who grows yams, predominately, will barter with the farmer who predominately grows beans. When the transaction is complete, both have yams and beans. A balance has been achieved. The wildebeest depletes the grass by consuming it, yet the lion consumes the wildebeest. Still, the soil is rejuvenated by the excrement of the wildebeest, thus the grass returns year after year. Nature has bartered for Its own stability, Its own balance.

Where is your balance? If all phases of Creative Power dwell within your being, you must fully awaken each phase, within the Law of Cycles, in order to achieve true balance and equilibrium--union with the Creative Principle-Goddess/God. Have you the ability to awaken these dormant faculties within you immediately? It is something to be achieved. Yet, until you realize this goal how do you live in harmony with Divine Law--meet every situation with the required spiritual power--if many of the powers you need to harmonize with the Law are not yet awakened? Does Goddess have a Divine barter system?

If Spirit vibrates through the color red, the hot and pungent foods such as garlic or ginger, the oil of cedar wood, a garnet stone, and ram's blood, at a rate and wavelength that generates fiery energy, then provoke the fiery energy of such tools through offering, and reallocate/utilize it. All physical things produce emanations according to their nature. If Spirit produced all things, and you exist in essence as Goddess/God, then you have the right and responsibility to reallocate/utilize all things in your effort to achieve Harmony.

Should you not make offerings then to the Ancestral Spirits, to erase a temporary deficit in your own understanding, which at the same time engenders a purified environment for them to reincarnate into? Is this not barter, exchange, in harmony with Law? Should you not make offerings to the Deities, that their energy may be aroused enabling you to recognize and reallocate/utilize it to overcome some temporary imbalance, physical or spiritual? Is this not a proper allocation of resources? Who speaks against the offering?

The human body, the world, are shrines within a shrine.

During the dream experience, or the trance experience, the images perceived are through a third-eye, while the two eyes are closed. The experience of radiant energy in the area between the eyebrows when a revelation, intuition, or vision comes to you, reveals this third-eye center to be a center of inner-vision. It is a shrine, a focal point for some aspect of consciousness to show Itself.

When air vibrates through a musical instrument, the vibration produces a sound. When air and spirit vibrate through the human instrument, sounds are produced. Yet, if your human instrument has a different configuration than every other human instrument, then the collection of sounds resonating from you are unique to you. As Spirit vibrates perpetually through your vehicle, perpetually producing the same collection of sound vibrations one comes to understand that these vibrations, unique to your person, make up your true name. They represent the specific configuration of forces which governed your incarnation, your moment of entry into the physical plane. If heard with a spiritual ear, they may be reproduced by the vocal chords. It is from the throat center that these sounds or words of power can be generated. This center is a focal point for that aspect of consciousness. It is a shrine.

Anxiety often makes for a heavy heart. For near it is a center through which emotional energy is received and transmitted, just as the heart receives and transmits life-blood. It is a focal point for some communicative aspect of consciousness. It is also a shrine.

Nature is comprised of shrines within shrines. Can you not communicate with nature? Is your mode of communication in a mountainous region different than it is when you immerse yourself in a body of water? Meditate on a hill or mountain. Meditate under the direct energy of the noon-day Sun. Meditate under the full Moon. Meditate in the waters of the Goddess. Are these focal points connected, yet different? They are shrines, various focal points for communication with various aspects of Consciousness.

If Being manifests as a multitude of forms through time, then Time has seemingly broken the One into the many . . . . the many aspects of the One. Until we have returned our focus of consciousness to the Source --recognized and consciously realized the synthesis of the many through time -- then our focus perpetually travels among the many aspects of Being. Each aspect of Being is a shrine.

Who speaks against the shrine? Spirit has fashioned the world as shrine, for you to communicate with and come to know yourself through. Should you not erect shrines then in your dwelling-place, to consciously focus on various aspects of Being? If you say your essence is Creator/Creatress, then you have the right and the responsibility to make a shrine. You are only re-enacting your work as Creator/Creatress when erecting the shrine called World.

Ancestral communication. Appeal for guidance.

The One Consciousness, Goddess/God, through whom all created individuals, physical and non-physical, living and deceased, have their awareness. Does the fragrance of a flower not condition/modify the air? Are those who share and breathe the same air not then affected by this conditioning? Do individual thoughts, projections, not condition/modify Consciousness? Is our awareness not affected then by the thoughts, projections, influences, of the Ancestral Spirits, if we all share the same Consciousness? Why should we not determine the nature and value of communications from the Ancestral world?

Do you seek advice from father, mother, sister, brother, relative, close friend, associate, teachers, orators, books, at any point and time in your life? Why? Why not go to the indwelling-Divinity for every single question or decision you have to make? This is the goal. But are you in the position to actualize this goal at the moment, at will? The child's goal is to feed itself, but the process will take time. Until the child develops the capacity to seek out and acquire that which it needs for nourishment it will have to rely on assistance from others or die. Its natural instinct is to live; it thus has no problem receiving assistance. If you were in the position where you needed no assistance in order to feed yourself spiritually, you would never consult anyone, or anything. The Divinity within you would be fully awake on the conscious level. You would be Self-guided.

Egotism often blinds us from seeking guidance. Yet, when there is nowhere else to turn guidance is sought. We may fancy ourselves to be knowledgeable about health, but if the physical vehicle breaks down on an isolated path and we cannot figure out the problem, we are glad when one arrives who has the experience to heal the physical vehicle. We suspend our ego for the sake of receiving assistance. This is hypocrisy.

You are on a pathway right now with a vehicle whose defect is that of egotism. The assistance you need, but have denied, may come from those who have traveled that road before you. They have the tools, but you refuse to make an appeal to them.

The Ancestral Spirits transmit wisdom from experience. Yet they receive a vehicle/body in which they can incarnate which is not defective, only if those who provided the vehicle were receptive to guidance. We feed the Ancestral Spirits a non-defective vehicle and a favorable environment in order for them to continue their development unmolested by excessive egotism. They feed us with their wisdom through experience which allows us to create such an environment, if we listen.

Who questions Ancestral communication? You communicate daily, though unconsciously. Do you dream? Do you receive intuitions? You have thus entered their world. Should you not endeavor to enter their world consciously for guidance? Appeal to those who are already on the path of Divine guidance. Until then the blind (ego) leads the blind.

Goddess/God has Emissaries. Representatives in Creation.

Movement presupposes Energy. Movement/energy-vibrations reveal sound. Such vibrations are essential to the manifestation of Time. Creation is governed by Time. Time orders-measures the cyclical manifestation of Power, that things may come into existence. All things produce emanations which are reflective of Power, which is governed by Time. Vibratory waves may manifest as longer or shorter. Vibratory rates may be faster or slower. From beginning to ending to beginning, from light to dark to light, from expansion to contraction and back to expansion, all wavelengths, all rates, come into being as various representatives of Creative Power.

Every representative/phase of Creative Power vibrating through Space generates Its own sound (s). Sound imbues Space with colors corresponding to the nature of the vibration. Is sunlight not broken into a band of colors, a rainbow, when refracted by rain or mist?

Collections of sounds are groups of various vibrations, together generating geometric patterns in Space. Does rapid movement/vibration not generate heat? Is heat not expansive? Does expansion not call forth contraction, cooling? Are expansion and contraction not essential as dynamics of Form? Are heat and cooling not essential as dynamics of Form on the physical plane?

Every representative/phase of Energy emanating from Spirit as a Creative function, through Time, is a personality, a Deity, a phase of consciousness emanating from the Divine Source of All-Consciousness. Each Deity is either male or female, predominantly expansive or contractive in power-character-behavior, whose vibrations generate higher or lower-pitched sounds, feminine or masculine voices, thereby revealing Its own name.

The form-vehicle through which Spirit operates determines its personality, consciousness. Is there not one source of air on Earth which all humans share? Is there not one Spirit, by which all things have life? When spirit is housed in a lion, does it not manifest as the peculiar personality and consciousness of the lion? When spirit is housed in a dove, does it not manifest as the peculiar personality and consciousness of the dove? When spirit is housed in a human, does it not manifest as a personality and consciousness peculiar to that person? What of the personality and consciousness of the Forces which determined the form of all things--the Goddesses, the Gods? What of these various representatives of Divine Power operating through the medium of Space, who generate their own sounds (voices), colors and geometric patterns (images and forms), their own genders/powers (male/expansive, female/contractive), names, personalities, behaviors?

Who speaks against the Goddesses and Gods? Are you not consciousness as physical form, patterned after an image of various colors, with your own voice, gender, name, personality, behavior? Goddess/God has Emissaries. Representatives in Creation. Are you of Goddess/God?

Goddess holds your name, God has your language.

Energy fathers movement. This is the beginning of Creation. Energy before movement contained all vibrations necessary for the coming into being of all things, in a passive potency. Goddess mothers Energy.

Sound is truly primordial. We receive sound. We process sound. We reproduce sound. Goddess sustains our form. Our form specifies sounds. These sounds are our names.

All movement/vibrations produce sounds. Yet the product, sound, is merely an audible manifestation, revelation, of Energy--pre-existent Energy. Is the word you speak not already known to you before you allow it to pass from your lips? Did the word not exist prior to your speaking it? Is the spoken word then not a manifestation, revelation, of energy/vibrations, which were pre-existent in your mind/spirit? Sound is truly primordial.

As Spirit vibrates through any form, sounds are emitted. We notice the different sounds produced as air vibrates through musical instruments of various shapes. Every musical instrument speaks. Its specific dialect is determined by its form, its use. This is language.

Can we not perceive different sound groupings as Spirit vibrates through humans of various spirit-energic configurations? Does your configuration not emit your true name? Do you not have a language? A primordial language? A language rooted in the product of Energy vibrating through your genetic form? What then is your dialect? Does the region in which you live not have an effect on your physiology? Should then your natural dialect of the primal language not be a result of your migration to a different region? You have a name. You have a language. Goddess has written the dialect into your very nature.

The Ancestral Spirits recognize the dialect of the primordial language they spoke. They recognize it when you call their name, in their dialect, during libation. They recognize it when you provoke dialogue, in their dialect, through evocation. Their dialect nourishes them, for it is descendant, through Afuraka/Afuraitkait, from the primordial-God language, which is a tonal language. Tonal languages give different meanings for the same word, based on the way in which the word is pronounced, in what tone it is spoken. Different tones are different vibrations. Different vibrations yield different meanings. Is this not of God? Are the different phases of Creative Power not reflective of different rates of vibration, thus yielding different tones, values, meanings? Deities? Afurakani/Afuraitkaitnit language resounds Divinity.

You are connected genetically to the Ancestral Spirits. If the dialect they spoke nourishes and energizes them, should it not nourish and energize you, as their descendant? Their incarnation? You have a right and responsibility to employ the dialect that was written in you; the name resonating as you. Goddess has a name. God has a language. Speak them if you are of Goddess/God. Proper name and language are energic-links to Spirit.

AKHET
OSAGYEFO

Goddess's destruction is reorganization.

The Sun sends forth energy which manifests as light and heat on Earth. Its rays cause evaporation, Earth now releasing a portion of its water into the atmosphere in the form of a fine mist. The Sun causing Earth's water to transform into mist, is a destruction of forms. Mist is water and heat united. Pure water's form is destroyed. Pure heat's form is destroyed. Out of the elemental debris of these two destructions comes a new combination--mist--a new form. The mist collects/condenses in the atmosphere. It falls back to Earth as droplets of water/rain, a new form. The mist-form is destroyed in order to give rise to the rain-form. Thus, out of one body/water, comes many bodies/raindrops. Is this not the replication of a cosmic function? Is this not representative of the process by which many human souls come forth from the one Great Soul--Goddess/God?

Goddess destroys matter-forms in accordance with the necessity of the moment as dictated by the Divine Plan. The fashioning of new/different forms by God is then possible. Is this not an Orderly Creation? Is the Order inherent in Creation not representative of a pre-existing Divine Plan or Structure? God's Structure?

Destruction giving rise to a new form in harmony with the Divine Plan is truly reorganization. Is not destruction irrespective of harmonizing with the Divine Plan then truly self-destruction? The Divine Plan determines the reality of Creation on the physical plane. Who then lives out of harmony with the Divine Plan who is not out of touch with Reality? If one is out of touch with Reality, is he or she not then insane?

Destruction means to de-structure--to take away or remove the present structure-form. This is a necessary process in Creation, if all forms are modifications of Spirit's Form. Are you of Spirit? Must you then de-structure/reorganize present forms in order to generate new or different forms, behaviors? Yet, your reorganization must be in harmony with Structure, for deviation from Structure is deviation from Reality. This is insanity.

The culture dominated by lust is your enslaver, thus your embracing of this culture and its adherents is deviation from Structure/Reality. It is self-destruction. Insanity. Does the prey commune with the predator? Should the enslaved commune with the enslaver? This is insanity. Are you named after Spirit or are you named after your enslaver? Do you destructure/alter your hair to emulate your enslaver? Do you de-structure/alter eyes, skin, physical attributes, out of harmony with Divine Structure? Insanity. Are you a slave to food, de-structuring the natural form of your body creating obesity, disease? Are you enslaved by lust--a male or female engaging in dissexual/homosexual activity? Insanity. Deviation from Reality. Self-destruction. Deviation from the Divine Plan.

All of your excuses are useless, for Goddess does not Self-destruct. Renounce insanity. Embrace Reality. Cease self-destruction. Reorganize, if you are of Goddess/God.

Barter fear for knowledge of immortality.

Imagine for a moment that eurasians ceased to treat you in a prejudiced manner. They ceased to commit police brutality. They finally admitted the truth concerning our population, showing that Afurakanu/Afuraitkaitnut are at least the majority of the population. They began to accept you. The highest political office, as well as the majority of the political offices in the nation, were filled by Afurakanu/Afuraitkaitnut. Many of their most influential trade and commerce organizations came to be headed by Afurakanu/Afuraitkaitnut. Usury ceased to be practiced at the expense of Afurakanu/Afuraitkaitnut. Afurakani/Afuraitkaitnit-owned businesses began to flourish. Equal access to property ownership was honored. Imagine eurasians removing all the white images from their places of worship. Imagine such a state of affairs in the nation. How many of you would embrace and feel comfortable in such an egalitarian society? Herein lies your slavery.

Many of you who claim to champion Afurakani/Afuraitkaitnit culture really seek only to live this white culture unmolested. Afurakani/Afuraitkaitnit culture becomes your shield; a system of defense with which you must become moderately-well versed intellectually. For your sense of security against this white culture's blatant attacks, grows in proportion to your degree of intellectualism. Have you not considered the white culture's subtle attacks? Have you not considered the fact that white culture itself is a perpetual attack on your life/lives? To assimilate poison is to accelerate your own death. Whose cultural values do you truly seek to assimilate?

Who truly speaks of Afurakani/Afuraitkaitnit culture? Religion animates the culture. Reincarnation animates the religion. One who speaks of a harmonious society without speaking of reincarnation is one who has never truly desired to burn the tie to the slave master's values, false religions. Have you been made to fear your own culture more than your enslaver?

The knowledge of reincarnation is at the root of religion. How one perceives his/her destiny beyond death determines, fundamentally, how they conduct their lives. We who have been brainwashed into the belief that we only live once have suffered a grave offense. To conceal the knowledge of multiple existences from someone is to take their life/lives from them. The value of their past experiences, lessons, are disabled as a source of nourishment, cultivation. Lacking the proper insight into how future circumstances are crafted in the present sentences one to repeatedly make misjudgments. How long would you serve under the slave master if you were truly conscious of your immortality? Would the knowledge of immortality, reincarnation, and rebirth not diminish the fear of death? Does the eurasian deliberately execute the barter of fear for such knowledge? Is it not his only true means of maintaining control? Do you endure, for fear of death?

You are immortal. Ancestral communication consciously connects you to the spirit realm, immortality of the soul thus manifesting as reality--no longer speculation. Reincarnation is the process through which you consciously realize and re-establish your connection to Divinity. Barter your fear for the knowledge of Immortality, if you are of Goddess/God.

Spring has arrived. Regenerate your culture.

Is your body of Earth? Earth becomes hot and dry during the summer; cold and moist during the winter. Should the seasons then not affect your body if your body is of Earth?

How does heat effect your emotions, your actions? Is your body not "heated-up" during a spirited argument? Is an abundance of heat not apparent in connection with sexual arousal? How does cold effect your emotions, your actions? Is your body not "cooled down" during the sleep state? Is it not necessary for cool energy to dominate your physical body in order for you to engage in deep thought, concentration, contemplation?

Heat and cold are two polarities of the same reality, two sides of the same coin--energy. As solar energy increases, the body is stimulated to secrete certain energic substances by which we become more externalized, active. As solar energy decreases, the body secretes substances by which we become more internalized, passive. This is true of all solar cycles.

The Earth's position in relationship to the Sun determines the Earth's seasonal cycle. Yet there are greater Suns. Our solar system's position in relationship to these greater Suns/stars determine greater seasonal cycles. One such cycle is the Great Year. It is a period lasting about 25,920 years.

The wise have always observed the cycles. Fire can light a room or burn down a dwelling-place. Water can nourish the body or drown the body. Wisdom shows how to direct these energies positively. The Ancients devised a cultural milieu which harnessed and directed the different phases of stellar energy being received by the planet towards the good of society. Thus, during the spring-summer half of the year/6 months, as well as the spring-summer half of the Great Year/12,960 years, the culture allocated the solar and stellar heat in a resourceful manner furthering creativity, expansion, and expression. During the fall-winter half of these solar and stellar cycles, the cool energy was directed through the design of our culture to further receptivity, gestation and development.

We have lived through many Great Year/25,920-year cycles. However, the current one introduced the eurasian grouping. Still, it was only when we allowed them to pull us away from our culture, that we began to truly suffer. The hellenization of Kamit. The aryanization of India. The islamicization, catholicization, and anglicization of Afuraka/Afuraitkait. We began to embrace their culture. Thus, during this stellar summer we allowed the heat to fire our passions and lusts, instead of it being re-directed towards productive creativity. We fought amongst one another; we sold the prisoners of war to the eurasian as slaves in exchange for his cultural peculiarities. During this stellar winter we allowed the coolness to put us to sleep instead of making us receptive to the wisdom in Nature; its gestation and development within us. We allowed caste-systems to define us. But be wise, observe. Spring has arrived. Regenerate your culture.

PERT

ADAE

God protects Her Laws.

Scratch your skin and notice that a scab will form. A self-defense mechanism, or an act of Self-defense? Spirit restoring order within some aspect of Its-Self? Attack a bear and witness the reactive-protective stance it takes--defense at all costs. Cut the leg off of a crab or the leaf off of a plant and witness the regeneration of their members as the Self defends/restores its form. Watch the Earth. Observe the restorative patterns being activated as Earth cleanses itself. Cut into the Earth and you cut into an Organism. Witness the earth as it quakes, the hurricanes, the floods, the brush fires. Nature restores order. God protects Her Laws ItSelf.

Throw a stone up into the air. A force in Nature causes it to return to Earth. What was out of harmony with the laws which govern its form, was made to submit to that harmony. Otherwise, it could continue to float.

Project your energy out into the universe and know that a reaction is inevitable. If your energy-projection is out of harmony with respect to Nature, Nature will protect Itself. If your energy-projection is out of harmony with the animal, the animal will protect itself. If your energy-projection is out of harmony with the vegetation, the vegetation will protect-regenerate itself or die. What if the energy you project towards another human is out of harmony with the laws which govern the existence of the human? Is the human not part of Nature? The human should protect self, naturally. Only if she/he so chooses.

Does the bear wait for another to protect it? Does the crab wait for another to protect it? Does the plant wait for another to restore order? Should the human wait for another to save him/her from another? Is the same Spirit in the animal and plant not in you? The animal instinctively allows Spirit to awaken its protective-restorative self-defense mechanism. It is then moved to attack--restore balance. Are you not of Nature? Do you not have a natural instinct towards self-preservation? Should you not allow Spirit to provoke that natural instinct within you, so that you may use every talent and faculty within your being to restore order and balance where disorder and imbalance have been created? Where are your talents and faculties?

Does disease not begin on the spiritual plane and manifest as a physical malady? Then does self-preservation and restoration begin on the spiritual plane? Is power rooted in the spiritual plane? Where then should you look to draw your resources for engagement?

Make your vehicle a receptive channel through which the reactive, Self-defensive aspect of Creative Power can resonate. Engagement begins on the spiritual plane. The strategy is already mapped out on the spiritual plane. The power to overcome originates on the spiritual plane and manifests through the physical plane, but only through receptive physical vehicles.

Killing is transference, murder is stealing.

All murderers are killers, but all killers are not murderers. Just as disease arises out of an energic imbalance in the spirit, ultimately manifesting as a physical malady, so does murder arise as an emotional imbalance of the spirit (lust), often manifesting in the physical act of killing. The description of karma as being purely a mental phenomenon is accurate. Even if the physical act is not carried out the individual is still dominated by lust, whose hegemony will strangle his/her efforts to perceive and live in harmony with the Divine Plan.

Transference is a lawful separation (taking away) of something from its present cycle, placing it then in a different cycle. This separation is defined as lawful if it is found to be in harmony with the Divine Plan; if it serves a purpose expressive of Divine Order.

Stealing is rooted in lust, which manifests truly as a lack of perception of the Divine Plan and the Divine Order (the proper place and distribution of all things in the universe). Stealing is an unlawful separation (taking away) of something from its present cycle without placing it in a cycle wherein the result is expressive of Divine Order. It is defined as unlawful because it is found to be in violation of the Divine Plan.

If I take water from a stream and drink it, I have effected a transference of energy. This transference is in harmony with the Divine Plan, for the energy will rejuvenate my person, and later be recycled by nature without imbalance being generated. The water was separated from the nature-cycle of evaporation-condensation-precipitation, and placed into the human-cycle of digestion-rejuvenation-excretion. After excretion from my person, it returns to nature. This is lawful. It is transference (truly cyclical).

If through misplaced anger I murder a human being, I have caused a separation of energy – his soul from his physical body. Yet, a misplaced anger has caused me to be indifferent to the circumstances within which I have now placed this soul-energy (Ancestral-cycle). Lust blinds me from the perception of the Divine Plan. Thus, the separation of soul from body in this instance is not expressive of Divine Order. It is unlawful. It is stealing.

If Goddess/God came into being in the form of the things It created, after having laid a foundation in Order, then the life-death-rebirth cycle is a cycle used by Goddess/God as a mode of transference--recycling of the Life-force. If we are Goddess/God, essentially, then we have the responsibility and the right to facilitate transference, if said transference-sacrifice is expressive of Divine Order, and in harmony with the Divine Plan.

Acts never create bad karma. Lust itself, is its only creator. It is a mental phenomenon.

The initiated as instruments of liberation.

What is the priestess' or priest's function with respect to liberation? Do the initiated ever liberate, or do they learn the arts of harnessing and redirecting that which has been provoked, in harmony with the Divine Plan?

Does the initiated priestess/priest not provoke, or call forth, the energy of the herb, then redirect that energy towards the healing of the patient, if the patient so desires? Does the initiated not provoke the energy of the animal through prayer and sacrifice, then redirect that energy towards restoring balance where some energic imbalance has occurred, if the injured individual or entity so desires? Does the initiated not provoke the energy of the Ancestral Spirits, the Deities, the oracles and then redirect that energy in order to provide direction and guidance to the querent towards harmonizing with the Divine Plan, if the querent so desires?

The priestess is an instrument. The priest is an instrument. They relinquish ego to receive their part as one of many conscious participants in the Divine Order. Yet, the initiated must submit to the Laws of Cycles.

One ignites the fire, then uses it to light the way. You must arouse energy before you can use it to serve your needs. You must begin with its ignition before energy can be directed to move or change you or your situation. Yet, before one ignites the flame in any endeavor there must exist a genuine desire for the flame to be ignited. The baby desires to move across the floor, so he/she rises to do so. The flame is ignited by a genuine desire. Even if he/she cannot yet walk or direct him/herself, the desire is so genuine that the parent will come to assist, to take the arms of the baby and direct him/her towards his/her desired destination. The parent does not carry the child. The parent initially provokes the child's energy through urging him/her to walk, then redirects the baby's energy when the imbalance/fall comes. The parent restores balance.

If a genuine desire towards liberation is aroused within the society as a whole, the priestess/priest has the responsibility then to redirect this energy towards that end. The Haitians had the desire, Boukman harnessed that desire towards victory. Their genuineness lay in the fact that they never had the desire to relinquish their culture. Who else has such a desire?

The religion is the culture. Who speaks against the religion? They who would relinquish their culture. The genuine desire then wanes. The initiated must wait, for they must obey the Laws of Cycles. Then a time arrives where the mass of the society has grown weary of searching for liberation from an external source. They begin to look within. They revisit the culture. They revisit the religion. The initiated may then begin provocation; desire is aroused; energy is redirected; balance begins to be restored.

MAAT MMARA

Our roles as Ntoru/Ntorotu, Abosom, Our roles as Aakhu/Aakhutu, Nsamanfo, are joined, inseparable, with respect to the awakening of the full potential of the spirit in the individual. We are not here to carry out your tasks. We cannot do the work for you, for We are never in violation of the Law in which We are sustained, through which We are fed and have Our origin, Our existence. Your choices determine the path you tread. You have a destiny, but your success depends on the choice you make at the critical moment. We as Aakhu/Aakhutu, Nsamanfo, can answer your questions. We can provide insight into a direction upon which you are contemplating. We can show you, today, the Nation of which you are a direct incarnation. The ways of the people, Us, from whom you directly descend. We can function as intermediaries, access to the forces which influence events. We as Ntoru/Ntorotu, Abosom, will nourish, replenish, and sustain your spirit, your body. We will convey the power, the consciousness, for you to carry out the tasks which you choose to undertake. But, you must see that every act sets events in motion. Events that will not be reversed. Some may endeavour to avoid consequences through manipulation of forces, but none can ever truly escape. We worship the Law. We uphold the Law. We can never deviate from the Law, the Supreme Being. Make your choice. Unite your will to the Divine Will, and you will prosper. You will accomplish what you incarnated to accomplish. Reject the Will of Divinity, and you will receive that which you chose to receive. It is ultimately your choice.

Nas

Agoo

You have never had an idea. You know nothing. The Wisdom of Divinity is from Whence comes all knowledge. We as Ntoru/Ntorotu, Abosom, form Wisdom as knowledge. This We hold in Time. Every desire generated in you to think, to know, is an invocation of Us to transmit knowledge. Your intelligence is proportionate to your degree of receptivity. We as Aakhu/Aakhutu, Nsamanfo, do assist you. We access knowledge, ideas, for you when you lack the receptivity. For to be receptive you must listen, you must silence yourself. Yet, your desire to know is rivaled by your desire to follow those which lead you away from your path. Know then that you have no thoughts of your own. Know that We must always be involved. Know that the only thing you own is the choice to reject that which is received. Know, only because the Supreme Being Knows.

Hetep Amee.

UBEN-HYENG

The Ancestral Summons

The Okra/Okraa Complex

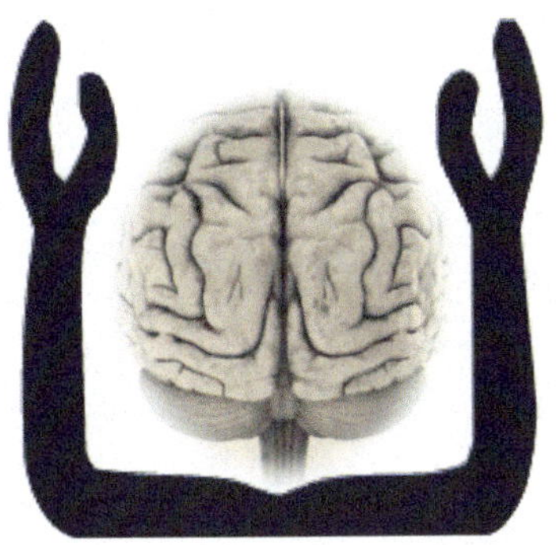

The Soul of Akanfo

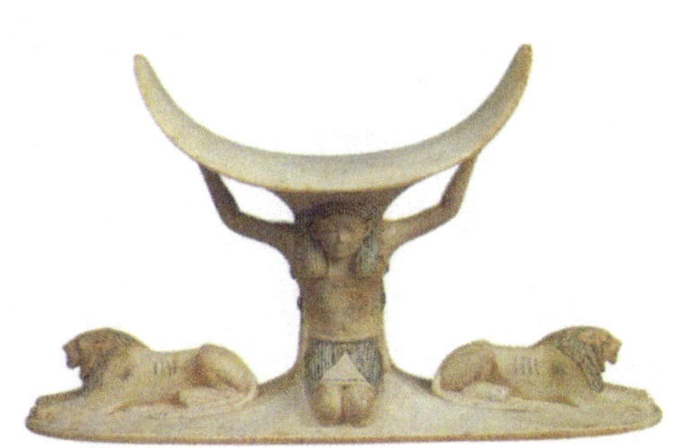

ODWIRAFO KWESI RA NEHEM PTAH AKHAN

THE OKRA/OKRAA COMPLEX

THE SOUL OF AKANFO

In **Akan** (ah-kahn') culture we recognize that every *created* entity has an **Okra** (aw-krah') or **Okraa** (aw-krah'-ah), the masculine and feminine terms for *Soul*, which is defined as the *Divine Consciousness*. The Afurakani and Afuraitkaitnit (African) Okra and Okraa is a portion of the **Okraa** and **Okra**, the *Soul* or *Divine Consciousness* of **Nyamewaa** and **Nyame**. **Nyamewaa** and **Nyame** are the Great Mother and Great Father, respectively, Who function Together as One Divine Unit – *The Supreme Being*. In Ancient **Khanit** and **Kamit** (ancient Nubia and Egypt), **Nyame** is called **Amen** and **Nyamewaa** is called **Amenet**. Akan people migrated from ancient Khanit and Kamit millennia ago and ultimately settled in West Afuraka/Afuraitkait (Africa) primarily in the regions of contemporary **Ghana** and **Ivory Coast**. Centuries later, many **Akanfo** (Akan people) would be captured as prisoners of war, forcibly transported to the western hemisphere and into enslavement in the americas and the Caribbean. Those forced into enslavement struggled and waged war along with other Afurakanu/Afuraitkaitnut (Africans) in order to regain our freedom from enslavement and to force its abolishment in the western hemisphere. Our language, culture and ritual practices are proof of the reality that Akanfo migrated from Khanit and Kamit to West Afuraka/Afuraitkait (Africa) and the western hemisphere.

Amenet and **Amen**

[From the Temple of ***Ipet Reset*** *in Kamit]*

Nyamewaa and **Nyame**

Nyame *and* ***Nyamewaa*** *are forms of* ***Amen*** *(Ny-****Amen****) and* ***Amenet*** *(Ny-****Amen****-waa-t)*

The *Soul* or *Divine Consciousness* is called **Ka** (kah) and **Kait** or **Kat** (kah-ette' or kaht) in the language of ancient Khanit and Kamit. The male version of the term is **Ka** while the female version is **Kait** or **Kat**. As the ancient **Akanfo** (Akan people) migrated from Ancient Khanit and Kamit over 2,000 years ago we continued to use the same root term to refer to the Soul and variations of the term. Thus in the Akan language, also called the **Twi** (Chwree) language, the masculine term for *Soul* is **Kara** (kah-rah') often contracted to **Kra**. The feminine term for *Soul* is **Karawa** (kah-rah'-wah) often contracted to **Krawa** or **Kraa**. In the Twi or Akan language the suffix which *feminizes* nouns is written variously as: 'baa', 'bea', 'waa', 'aa' or 'a'. Thus **kra** (masculine) becomes **kra-wa** or **kra-a** (feminine). These terms are very often written with the 'o' prefix – **Okra** or **Okara** (aw-krah' or aw-kah'-rah) and **Okraa** or **Okrawa** (aw-krah'-ah or aw-krah'-wah).

The 'o' prefix in the Akan language often shows that the term is a noun. For example, the general term for *Deity*, **Bosom** (boh'-sohm), is often written **Obosom**. The plural is **Abosom**. The term for *puff adder* (a kind of snake) is **Nanka**, often written **Onanka**. Often, when the 'o' prefix is dropped the word changes from being a noun to a verb. For example, **oko** means *'a battle, a fight'*. When the 'o' is dropped the noun **oko** meaning *a battle, a fight* becomes the verb **ko** meaning *'to battle, to fight'*. The root however is **'ko'**. The same is true of the term **kra** or **okra**. The root is **kara**. The root **kara** or **kra** meaning *soul* is the same root term from Kamit meaning *soul* – **Ka** (Ka-ra or Kra). See entries from a **Metut Ntoro** (*hieroglyphic*) dictionary (left) and a ***Twi*** (Akan) language dictionary (right):

ka, , , , P. 607, N. 619, , T. 88, , image, genius, person, double, character, disposition, the vital strength of the Ba-soul (, B.D. 30B, 4, the ka residing in the body); plur. ,

ò-k'rá, òkárá, F. ẹ-, *pl.* a-, *1. the soul* of man.

Khanit/Kamit	**Akan**
Ka	Kara, Kra (Okra)
Kat (Kait)	Karaa, Kraa (Okraa, Okrawa)

In both languages the **Ka/Kait** or **Okra/Okraa** is the *Divine Consciousness* that dwells within the *head* of the person. It is important to note that this Consciousness is not merely 'awareness' but an actual *Entity*:

The Okra/Okraa is a personal Obosom – *a personal Deity* – that guides the Afurakani/Afuraitkaitnit (African) individual throughout his or her life.

In Akan culture, the Divine Spirit-Forces in Creation operating through and animating the Sun, Moon, Earth, Rivers, Oceans, Fire, Mountains, the Atmosphere and more are *Children* of **Nyamewaa-Nyame**. These Goddesses and Gods, Children of the Great God and Great Goddess, are called **Abosom** (ah-boh'-sohm) and are the *Embodiments of Divine Order* in Creation. They function as the Divine 'Organs' within the Great 'Divine Body' of the Supreme Being, **Nyamewaa-Nyame**. Akan people ritually invoke the Abosom in order to harmonize ourselves with Creation. We invoke our Okra/Okraa, our **personal Obosom**, for guidance in every aspect of our lives, to obtain answers, gain insight and more just as we invoke other Abosom (Deities) of Creation.

During life, the Ka/Kait or Okra/Okraa is often experienced on a foundational level as the *pull in your head* that is constantly urging you towards living in harmony with **Nyamewaa-Nyame Nhyehyee** (Divine Order). Upon death, the Ka/Kait or Okra/Okraa ultimately returns to **Nyamewaa-Nyame** (**Amenet-Amen**) to 'report' on the activity/behavior of the individual. The pull of the Ka/Kait or Okra/Okraa is often referred to as your 'first mind'.

However, every urge or pull that one experiences in the head that is spiritual is not the Okra/Okraa

We can be urged or influenced by the Spirits of our **Nananom Nsamanfo**, our Spiritually cultivated Afurakani/Afuraitkaitnit (African) Ancestresses and Ancestors, by the Spirits of **Abosom** (Deities), or by the spirits of *unrelated* deceased individuals who *do not* have our best interest at heart. We can also be influenced by the mental projections of the living including those who engage in ritual practices seeking to negatively or positively influence our thoughts and actions. We must learn to make the distinction between the influence/pull of these different classes of spirits and/or individuals upon us and the influence/pull of our own Okra/Okraa. Attunement to our own Okra/Okraa (Soul) allows us to make these distinctions clearly and repel the urges, pulls and influence from negative spirits and negative individuals with minimal effort.

The more in-tune we become with our Okra/Okraa, the more detailed information and guidance we receive from this Obosom. We therefore experience more than just the basic pull or urge or 'awareness'. *We have clear dialogue with this **Obosom** who dwells within us.*

Moreover, because the Ka/Kait or Okra/Okraa is a Divine Entity, fashioned by Nyamewaa-Nyame, only Afurakanu/Afuraitkaitnut (Africans~Black People) have an Okra/Okraa.

RACE AND THE OKRA/OKRAA

Only Afurakanu/Afuraitkaitnut (Africans~Black People) Have Okra/Okraa

No non-Afurakani/non-Afuraitkaitnit (non-African~non-Black) individual or group including **all** white europeans, white americans, white latinos/latinas, white hispanics, white pseudo-'native'-americans (who are actually migrant asians), white asians, white arabs, white hindus or any others have Okra/Okraa. They have no connection to **Nyamewaa-Nyame**, the Abosom or Divinity at all.

The lack of an Okra/Okraa is what distinguishes all other people in the world from Afurakanu/Afuraitkaitnut (Africans).

Indeed, it was the loss of the Okra/Okraa thousands of years ago which caused the small segment (less than 0.00001%) of the Afurakani/Afuraitkaitnit (African) population who had migrated to Northern eurasia to degenerate into melanin-recessive, white-skinned, depigmented individuals with *extra-albino* and *extra-vitiligo* characteristics and a perverse morphology.

Their **spiritual degeneration** – *loss of Okra/Okraa* – **precipitated their physical degeneration** – *loss of melanin (melanin-recessiveness)* and *their accompanying perverse morphology*. Their loss of Okraa/Okra was based on their *own* *disordered behavior* which caused them to **repel** the Okra/Okraa. As *individuals without Okra/Okraa*, they perpetually manifested disordered behavior (criminality, sexual deviance, social perversity, etc.) and were repelled/exiled from the larger group of Afurakanu/Afuraitkaitnut (Africans). *Their disordered behavior continues to this day.* Like cancerous cells that develop within the company of healthy cells and subsequently operate only to consume and destroy the community of healthy cells, *so are the whites and their offspring the cancerous cells in the body of Black humanity.* They operate only to consume and destroy Afurakanu/Afuraitkaitnut (Africans) wherever they encounter us in the world. Their nature is unchangeable, for they do not have an anchor in **Nyamewaa-Nyame Nhyehyee** (Divine Order). The anchor which they lack is the Okra/Okraa.

There is no possibility of non-Afurakanu/non-Afuraitkaitnut (non-Africans~non-Blacks) regaining an Okra/Okraa. The mixing of blood through miscegenation will not cause the Okra/Okraa-less spirit to reincarnate with an Okra/Okraa.

The Abosom are the *Embodiments of Divine Order* in Creation. The Abosom therefore do not dwell in disorder. The Okra or Okraa, as an Obosom, also does not dwell in disorder. When disorder arises, a person with an Okra or Okraa will be guided by his/her Okra/Okraa on how to eradicate the disorder. If the individual rejects the guidance of the Okra/Okraa and decides to dwell in disorder deliberately and perpetually, the Okra/Okraa will eventually detach from – *leave* – the individual. The individual has made him or herself repulsive to the Okra/Okraa. If the individual continues to dwell in disorder and does not seek to realign with the Okra/Okraa and ritually invoke the Okra/Okraa to return and re-attach Itself to the spirit of the individual, the Okra/Okraa will return to **Nyamewaa-Nyame** and never return to the individual.

When the Okraa/Okra returns to **Nyamewaa-Nyame** *because the individual has repelled it*, the Okraa/Okra is *reabsorbed* into the Great **Okraa/Okra** (**Kait/Ka**) of **Nyamewaa-Nyame** and loses its individuality **forever**, just as a drop of rainwater when reabsorbed into the Ocean loses its individuality **forever**. This condition is what **defines** all of the whites and their offspring. The whites and their offspring will thus continue to reincarnate as *spirits of disorder* – **spirits without Okra/Okraa** - until they become extinct. This process of extinction is already in motion.

The decades-long worldwide negative population growth-rate of the eurasian population is evidence of this reality. In comparison, the birth-rate of Afurakanu/Afuraitkaitnut (Africans) worldwide is the highest in comparison to all other ethnicities.

In the case of miscegenation, the perverse act of inter-racial copulation where a conception occurs between a white individual (european, american, asian, hispanic, arab, hindu, pseudo-'native'-american, etc.) and an Afurakani or Afuraitkaitnit (African) individual, if the spirit that enters the womb is a spirit of *one of the white individual's ancestors*, then that spirit is a spirit *without* an Okra/Okraa. This white/eurasian spirit will be born 40 weeks later in a 'bi-racial' body with a white 'parent' and a Black 'parent'. **Yet it is still a spirit of disorder.** This **Okra/Okraa-less spirit** will not receive an Okra/Okraa just because it is operating in a melanin-dominant 'body of color'.

However, if *an Afurakani or Afuraitkaitnit spirit with an Okra or Okraa* is drawn into the womb under similar conditions, this Afurakani or Afuraitkaitnit spirit will be born also with a white 'parent' and a Black 'parent'. However, this spirit is Afurakani or Afuraitkaitnit - **a spirit with an Okra/Okraa**. He or she is the spirit of an Afurakani Ancestor or Afuraitkaitnit Ancestress of the Black parent who made the foolish decision to copulate with one of the whites and their offspring. This forced the ancient Afurakani/Afuraitkaitnit spirit to have to be born into a weak 'bi-racial' body and have one white 'parent' - *physiologically*. However, because this is an *Afurakani or Afuraitkaitnit spirit* and he or she has an Okra or Okraa, he or she is therefore connected to

Nyamewaa-Nyame, the Abosom and the Nananom Nsamanfo. **Moreover, this spirit is truly part of his/her Black parent's family and Ancestry <u>only</u>.** *The white 'parent' is a **stranger/alien** to this <u>returning Afurakani or Afuraitkaitnit spirit</u>, is <u>**not**</u> truly a parent nor family member at all and should not/cannot be regarded as such.*

The **metutu** *(hieroglyphs)* for the terms **Ka** and **Kat** in Kamit depicts the *shoulders* and *two arms* reaching upward as shown above. The metut is for the letter 't' which feminizes nouns in the language of Kamit. *(This device continues to be used in english. The 't' or 'et/ette' suffix feminizes names: Anton, Anton-ette ('t'), Paul, Paul-ette, etc.).*

The position of the **Ka/Kat** is shown to reside in the *head.* Inside of the two arms and shoulders is the *space* where the *head* resides. A variation of this notion is when the **Ka** symbol is shown *upon* the head of an individual. It focuses attention upon the fact that the **Ka** is associated with the head:

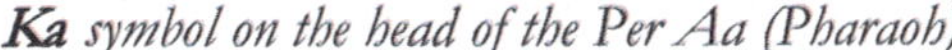

***Ka** symbol on the head of the Per Aa (Pharaoh)*

*Variation of the spelling **Ka** in the metutu*

Below is another variation of the spelling **Ka** with the *determinative symbol* of the *seated, mummified figure.* When this determinative symbol is used it is the indicator of a **Deity**. This is showing that the **Ka** is an Obosom (Deity):

It is important to note here that in the Akan language one of the terms for *'shoulders'* is **kra-do** meaning the *'seat of the **kra**'.* This is a *definition* of the ancient **Ka** symbol with its *two shoulders* and arms, a direct carry-over from ancient Khanit and Kamit.

The root 'ka' in Kamit, being the root of ka-ra (kra) in Akan is shown by the Akan root **ka** meaning *'to touch'*. From the Twi dictionary:

> **kã**, *v.* [*red.* **kekã**] *I. to touch, to come* or *be in* or *bring into contact with, to join &c.* (1-25); *II. to move* or *stir, to be* or *cause to be active* (26-40); *III. to move in order to join* (41-51).
> (*I.*) 1. *to touch, come in contact with*, pr. 466. – *to handle* (slightly), *feel* i.e. *perceive* by the sense of feeling; mfã wo nsa ñkã dade no, na

The root, **ka**, meaning *'to touch, to bring into contact with, to join; to cause to be active; to perceive by the sense of feeling'* are all functions of the **Ka**: 𓂓. The *two arms and hands* of the Ka *touch, join us,* to the Divine Consciousness of **Nyamewaa-Nyame,** cause us to be spiritually/consciously *active*, allow us to *perceive by the sense of feeling.* This definition in Akan is clearly represented by the metut (symbol) for Ka, because Khanit and Kamit is the origin of the Akan word and its variations, Kara or Kra.

[*The **Ka**, called **Kra** in Akan is called **Ori Inu** in Yoruba, **Se** or **Se Lido** in Fon and Ewe and **Chi** in Igbo. In these cultures and all across Afuraka/Afuraitkait (Africa) the Ka/Kait, Okra/Okraa, Ori Inu, Se, Chi, etc. is recognized to be the person's **personal Obosom** (personal **Orisha, Vodou, Arusi** – Deity) which resides in the <u>head</u>.*]

The **Ka/Kait** was also sometimes depicted as the *image* (double) of the person. For example, in the tomb of **Tut Ankh Amen** (King Tut) we find this large **Ka-statue** guarding his tomb which is an image of the **Per Aa** (Pharaoh) himself:

Ka statue of Tut Ankh Amen

It is said that the **Ka/Kait** would reside with the body of the deceased in the tomb for a period. This is because before the spirit of the individual *in concert with* his/her **Ka/Kait** left the physical world to go to the Ancestral realm, the relatives of the deceased would come and place ritual offerings including food at the gravesite, tomb, etc. This was a means by which the family could facilitate communication with the spirit of their deceased relative for various reasons. This was true in ancient Khanit and Kamit and continues to be true with Afurakanu/Afuraitkaitnut (Africans) today wherever we exist in the world, including the western hemisphere.

Just as you have a physical body which contains a *smaller body in the head* – the brain – which governs the overall functioning of the body, so does your spirit-body, called **sahu** in Kamit and **sunsum** in Akan, contain a *smaller spirit-body in the head* – the **Ka** or **Kait** – which governs the overall functioning of the spirit-body. Your Ka/Kait or Okra/Okraa is your *spirit's brain.*

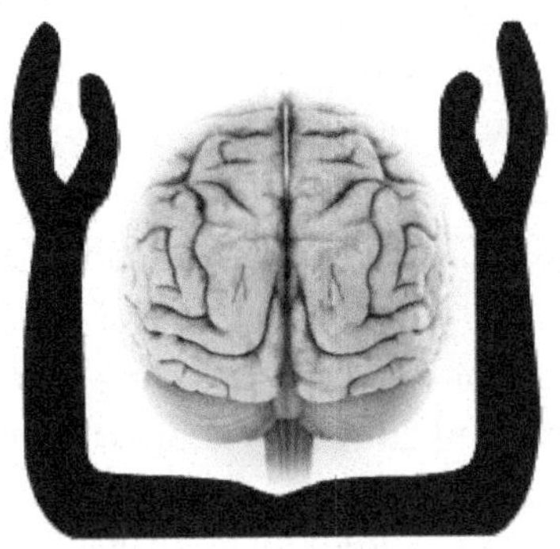

Ka/Kait – Okra/Okraa: The Spirit's-brain

Sahu – *Spirit body* in Kamit, called **Sunsum** in Akan

When an individual dies, his/her **sahu** (spirit - Kamit) or **sunsum** (spirit - Akan) separates from the physical body. Inside of the spirit, *housed within the spirit's head-region*, is the **Ka/Kait** *the spirit-brain.* The newly deceased individual as a **sunsum-okra** entity *(spirit-soul-entity)* will remain around the grave and the physical body it once inhabited as well as visit various family members and friends for a period. In Akan culture, this period lasts for approximately 40 days. Family members will thus often see the individual spirit/sahu/sunsum in the form of a **saman** (Akan for spirit-personality - *'ghost'*) and communicate with the *saman* before and after the funeral. The Akan term *saman* is directly derived from the ancient term **smn** and **smnu** which defines the *spiritual form, figure, image* of the deceased (notice the *determinative* metut of the standing mummified figure):

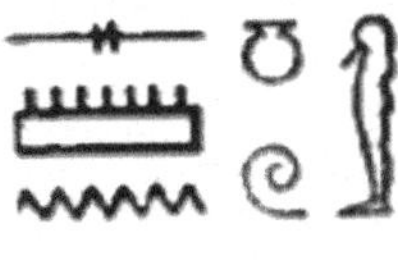

Smnu (Kamit)

This ancient term is still used by the Akan and is vocalized as ***Saman***

When living on Earth, the sunsum (spirit) lives through the physical form/body. The physical body generates an *electromagnetic image* of itself as life-force energy circulates through its form. When the physical body dies, the electromagnetic image of the physical body retains its form. The sunsum (spirit) operates through this electromagnetic form which in Akan is called *saman* and in english is called a *'ghost'* – the *immaterial image/form of the person.* The individual *sahu* (spirit) operating in the form of a *saman* (misnomered 'ghost'), subsequently makes its journey to the *Ancestral realm*, called **Asamando** in Akan [Only Afurakani/Afuraitkaitnit (African) spirits can enter **Asamando**].

Yet, *some* spirits remain 'earthbound', lingering because of an *unnatural attraction* to the physical world. Such spirits often plague ('haunt') the 'living' relatives as well as non-relatives causing fear, disruption in regular life-activities, sometimes illness, financial loss, miscarriages, etc. This is why Afurakanu/Afuraitkaitnut (Africans) established **ayie** – *funerary practices* – to ensure that the spirits of those departed will make a smooth transition to Asamando, the Ancestral realm. Those who do not make a smooth transition, and/or remain earthbound for a negative reason, are ritually neutralized from their attempts to negatively impact the living in Afurakani/Afuraitkaitnit (African) culture. This helps to maintain order in the society through the avoidance of unnecessary interference from misguided spirits in the lives of the 'living'. When we do communicate with our Ancestresses and Ancestors ritually (*Afurakani/Afuraitkaitnit (African) only*) during Ancestral observances and other ritual practices, our communication with Them is natural, harmonious and beneficial.

It is during the time *prior* to the saman spirit beginning its journey to Asamando that offerings are brought to give to the Ka/Kait of the saman spirit at the grave or at a special shrine established for them. This is because the people know that upon reaching Asamando, the Ka/Kait will at some point temporarily disengage from – **leave** – the spirit of the person and return to **Nyamewaa-Nyame** (**Amenet-Amen**) to *make a report* as to how the individual lived his or her life and to also *receive instructions/direction.* **Nyamewaa-Nyame** will then send the Ka/Kait *back* to re-attach/reconnect to/with the saman, the individual, in Asamando. The living relatives understanding this would like to ask the Ka/Kait or Okra/Okraa of the individual to protect the spirit of their deceased loved one while the spirit of the loved one travels to Asamando, for the spirit of the loved one could be assailed by other 'earthbound' spirits, negative entities, if he or she is not in alignment with his/her Okra/Okraa. The living relatives also ask the Ka/Kait to carry the prayers of the family to **Amenet-Amen when the** Okra/Okraa temporarily *leaves* the saman spirit and goes to **Nyamewaa-Nyame/Amenet-Amen** to make a report on how the individual lived his/her life while on **Asaase** (Earth).

We thus have the verb '**kra**' in Akan meaning *'to take leave'.* We also have the verb '**ka**' in Kamit meaning '*to take leave'.* Just as **Ka** (Soul) becomes **Kra** (Soul) from Kamit to Akan, so does **Ka** (to leave) become **Kra** (to take leave) from Kamit to Akan. From the Metut Ntorot dictionary (left) and the Twi dictionary (right):

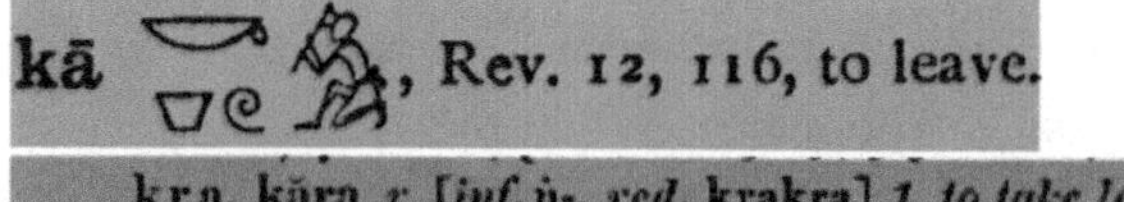
kā, Rev. 12, 116, to leave.

kra, kăra, *v.* [*inf.* n-, *red.* **krakra**] *1. to take leave of, bid farewell;* **makra wo,** *I am now going, therefore good-bye! — 2. to depart, leaving an injunction* or *commission* to those that remain. —

The Akan phrase *'makra wo'* meaning *'I leave you'* is used when someone is leaving another's home and in other situations. Akanfo recognized that the **original incidence** of the use of this phrase is when the individual as a **sunsum** (spirit), *prior to incarnation*, stands before **Nyamewaa-Nyame** (**Amenet-Amen**) to receive his or her **Okraa** or **Okra**. As a sunsum (spirit) infused with an Okra/Okraa, the individual is now a *whole entity – a spirit of Order/Divine Order.*

The individual receives *instructions* from **Nyamewaa-Nyame**, which are also *encoded* within his or her Okra/Okraa and subsequently *'takes leave'* from **Nyamewaa-Nyame** and is sent back to Asamando, the Ancestral realm, to await reincarnation into the womb of his/her future parent. When the future parents copulate and a conception occurs, the sunsum is *drawn into the womb.* This sunsum takes up residence in the zygote to undergo gestation and will be born into the world as a newborn child approximately 40 weeks later.

The terms **Ka** and **Ka-ra (Kra)** in Kamit and Akan are the same terms with the same meanings carried by ancient Akanfo during our migration from Khanit and Kamit to West Afuraka/Afuraitkait (Africa). It is important however to understand cosmology for a proper understanding of the *provenance* of the Ka/Kait, the Okra/Okraa, and the nature of its function in our lives as Afurakanu/Afuraitkaitnut (Africans). We quote at length from our article: **NYANKOPON-NYANKONTON – RA-RAIT**:

Pages 4-5:

Amenet and **Amen** (**Nyamewaa** and **Nyame**)

"…The Supreme Being has always been and continues to be the *union* of the Great Father and the Great Mother. In Akan culture the Great Father is **Nyame**. The Great Mother is **Nyamewaa**. Together, **Nyamewaa-Nyame** function as One Divine Unit – The Supreme Being. **Nyame** (God) is a form of the ancient name **Amen** (Ny-**Ame**-n) from Khanit and Kamit, while **Nyamewaa** (Goddess) is a form of the ancient name **Amenet** (Ny-**Amen**-at). **Amen** and **Amenet** are the Great Mother and Great Father Whom Together are the *Great Being* behind all of existence. It should be noted that the name **Nyame** exists across Afuraka/Afuraitkait in various forms: **Nyambe, Njambe, Nzame, Njambi, Nyama**, etc. From East, South, North, Central and West Afuraka/Afuraitkait, this variation of **Amen** can be found as the name of the Great Father **Amen**.

Amenet-Amen, the Great Being, produce **Ra** and **Rait** (Divine Living Energy), Who then create the Universe. This is akin to the Afurakani man and Afuraitkaitnit woman as *two beings* uniting to function as *one unit* and consciously directing and utilizing their *procreative-energy* for the purpose of creating a child…"

Pages 7-10:

"…**Amen** and **Amenet** are the Great Being, the Father and Mother of all existence. One of the definitions of the general term *'amen'* in Kamit is *'concealed'* or *'hidden'*. The other major definition is *stable, abiding, permanent.* **Amenet-Amen** as the Supreme Being are thus the *invisible, permanent, abiding, eternal Being*. When **Amenet-Amen** decided to create the universe They first exercised Their *Consciousness/Intelligence*. It was birthed as a *Twin* Masculine and Feminine *Spiritual Force* called **Ka** and **Kait**. The term *'ka'* means *'soul'* or *Divine Consciousness.*

The **Ka/Kait** is the Soul, the Divine Consciousness of **Amen** and **Amenet**. In the physical universe, These Two Abosom, **Ka** and **Kait**, the Male and Female Soul of **Amenet-Amen**, manifest as the *Black Substance of Space*. In physics this substance is called *Dark Matter* and *Dark Energy* and is said to make up over 99% of the Universe. This has always been known in ancient Afurakani/Afuraitkaitnit Ancestral Culture. However, we have always understood that the Black Substance is not just Dark Matter and Energy, but comprise the Male and Female *Deities* **Ka** and **Kait**. The Black Substance, the *physical shrine* of the expansive and contractive Spiritual Force of Consciousness/Intelligence, is all-pervasive in and of the Universe. I.e., the Consciousness or Soul/Intelligence of **Amenet** and **Amen** is all pervasive.

Just as you can direct your mind, your consciousness, to focus on a specific objective and formulate thoughts, so did/does **Amenet-Amen** direct Their Soul/Consciousness to focus and develop (form) thoughts (matrices) that would/will become the basis for the coming into being of the physical bodies of stars, planets, etc.

In the dream-state, with your eyes closed, you can generate vivid colorful images within the blackness of your spirit (mind) while lying in a dark room. Your **ka** (soul) *directs your formulation of thoughts* (unless you are overly influenced by disordered entities). This process is a *reflection* of the original acts of creation by **Amenet-Amen**. As the Great Being, invisible, stable and permanent, dwelling in nothingness before the creation of the Universe, **Amen** and **Amenet** united and began to exercise thought – i.e. They gave birth to **Ka** and **Kait**, Masculine and Feminine Spiritual Forces of Consciousness/Intelligence and *directed* Them to *formulate* thoughts. In order to make the thought-formations manifest there needed to be Energy. **Amenet-Amen** thus gave birth to the Masculine and Feminine Spiritual Forces of Expansion and Contraction within the Black Substance – the Abosom **Hehu** and **Hehut**. The expansive-contractive action of **Hehu** and **Hehut** caused the Black Substance to begin to *vibrate.* This is similar to the *breathing* process.

The term **heh** in the language of Kamit means *'eternal', 'everlasting'*, yet it also means *breath.* **Amenet-Amen** generated thought-forms via Their Soul/Divine Consciousness, **Ka** and **Kait**. **Amenet-Amen** then began to *activate* through 'breathing' – *expanding and contracting the Black Substance.* The 'breathing' process caused the *vibration* of the Black Substance which manifested **Energy**. This Energy manifested as the Male and Female Spiritual Forces **Nu** and **Nut** (**Nun** and **Naunet**). **Nu** and **Nut** are the Two Abosom of *Primordial Energy*, *Inert Energy*, the Energy that contains the Potential to bring everything into being. The names of **Nu** and **Nut** are written with the 'wavy' lines representing the *wave-energy* within the Black Substance as it transformed into a watery-like substance. Their names are also written with the determinative metut of the **urn** or *vessel*:

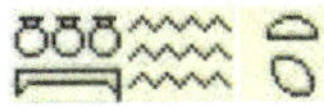

Nu (Nun) **Nut** (Naunet)

The Abosom **Nu** and **Nut** are the Divine, Inactive, Infinite Energy-source subsisting within the Black Substance, **Ka/Kait**. Again, when **Amenet-Amen** decided to Create the Universe, They birthed Their own Consciousness with Male and Female Potencies, **Ka** and **Kait** which manifested as an all-pervasive Black Substance. They directed **Ka** and **Kait** to formulate thought-forms, matrices, of what would come into being (just as you create thought-forms within the blackness of your consciousness). They gave birth to **Hehu** and **Hehut**, and caused Them to expand and contract (breathe) within the Black Substance (Body), causing the birth of **Nu** and **Nut**. [Notice our breathing sounds like "hehu-hehu-hehu"] The Black Substance began to *wave/vibrate* thus making the Black Substance *fluid.* The waves of Energy rising and falling within the Black Substance are akin to the rising and falling waves within the Ocean. This was the birth of **Nu** and **Nut**. The waves are expansive and contractive. This process is similar to the boiling of water.

When water is in a pot on a stove it is still. When heat is applied (expansion and contraction) the water begins to wave (vibrate). This is an invisible force (**Amenet-Amen** – invisible) directing the expansion and contraction (**Hehu** and **Hehut**) of an all-pervasive, pliable substance (**Ka** and **Kait**). The vibrating substance births waves (**Nu** and **Nut**). If the process continues to escalate, the waves will begin to interact with one another and the invisible heat within the waves will ultimately give birth to *spheres* – bubbles. Within these spheres is *heat.* In Kamit the general term **heh** also means *heat*, in addition to *eternal* and *breath.*

When **Nu** and **Nut** unite and begin to activate Their Divine Energy Potential within the Black Substance, They ultimately give birth to radiant, spheres of Light, Fire (heat). This is the emergence of **Ra** and **Rait**. **Ra** and **Rait**, manifesting as Spiritual Forces of Light and Fire emerging from Blackness, **separate** the Blackness. The spheres of Light and Fire ultimately birth the first stars in the Universe. The *Spirits* of **Ra** and **Rait** operate *through* the physical bodies of these stars, which gave birth to other stars. Stars ultimately gave birth to planets. The Spirits and Fire of **Ra** and **Rait** penetrated the planets and *activated* them causing *separation* and *development* within their primordial forms. **Ra** and **Rait** rose out of the Blackness of **Ka/Kait** as Creator and Creatress of the Universe.

Amen and **Amenet**, **Ka** and **Kait** (**Keku** and **Kekut**), **Hehu** and **Hehut**, **Nu** and **Nut** (**Nun** and **Naunet**) are called the **Khemenu Ntorou/Ntorotu** the *Eight Primordial Abosom* (misnomered the 'Ogdoad'):

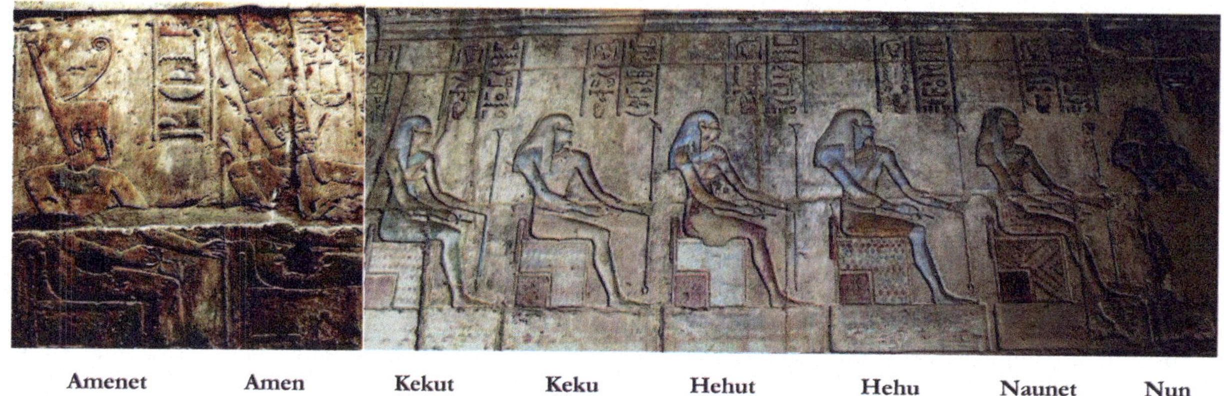

Amenet **Amen** **Kekut** **Keku** **Hehut** **Hehu** **Naunet** **Nun**

Before the Creation of the Universe, there was **Amenet** and **Amen**, the Great Invisible, permanent Being. They birthed thought/Consciounsess/Soul which manifested as an all pervasive, all-encompassing Blackness, **Ka** and **Kait**. In Their eternal capacity to expand and contract, **Hehu** and **Hehut** They activated their Primal, Inactive, Energy, **Nu** and **Nut**. As the Energy began to vibrate, Spheres of Light and Fire, **Ra** and **Rait**, emerged from the Blackness. This was the beginning of Creation. **Ra** and **Rait** manifested through the spheres of Light and Fire. *Thus, before manifesting, **Ra** and **Rait** were formed within the Black Substance.*

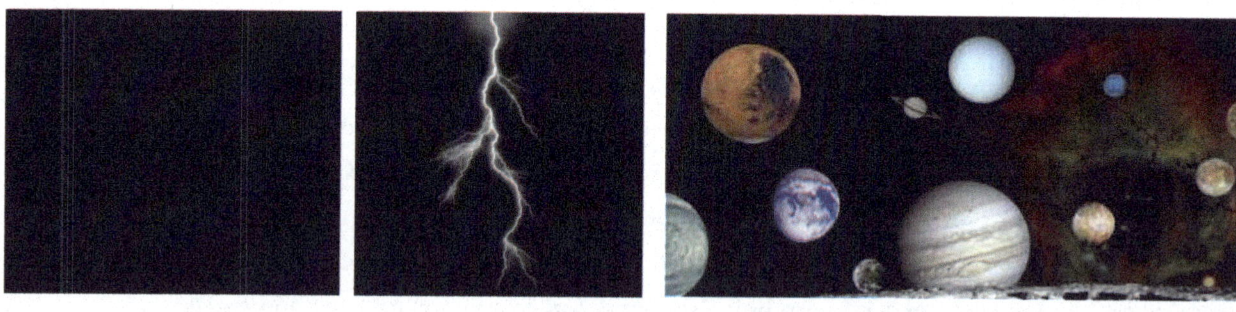

Above: **Amen** and **Amenet**, the invisible/hidden Being dwelling in the Blackness of **Ka** and **Kait**. When **Hehu** and **Hehut** cause the **Ka/Kait** to wave/vibrate **Nu** and **Nut** are born. They then birth the **explosive** power of **Ra** and **Rait**, Fire/Light, which generates the stars, planets, moons, etc. The Black Substance, **Ka** and **Kait**, can be found within the **bodies** of Afurakanu/Afuraitkaitnut. This is **abatumm** or **melanin** – *the chemical in our body that gives us our color.* It is not only in our skin, hair and eyes, but all of our major organs and systems including our brain (*neuromelanin*). **Abatumm** or melanin is the *shrine* of **Ka, Kait, Nu, Nut** in our bodies. Our abatumm/melanin (black chemical – **ka/kait**) is a conductor of our bodily energy (**nu/nut**). It is from this **Ka/Nu-Kait/Nut** (melanin) that our fire **Ra/Rait** arises.

Just as you can become 'fired-up' by a thought, begin breathing rapidly and feel a surge of heat (invisible) within your body, so did the Black Substance (**Ka/Kait**) when acted upon by the breathing process (**Hehu** and **Hehut**) cause the Substance (Body) to vibrate. This was a *kindling* of the Black Substance. The first manifestation of this kindling was **Nu** and **Nut**, the *waves* of Infinite Energy of **Amen** and **Amenet**. The further kindling and activation of **Nu** and **Nut** (waves) gave birth to *manifested Heat* – Fire and Light, **Ra** and **Rait**.

Thus, while coming into being within the Black Substance, **Ra** and **Rait** moved in *wave form*. They moved within **Nu** and **Nut**. Just as water waves (vibrates) first when heat is applied yet eventually births spheres, so did **Ra** and **Rait** move in the Black Water (Substance) of Space in wave form (through Their Parents **Nu** and **Nut**) and eventually manifested through/as spheres of Fire and Light (Stars/Suns)…"

In the above excerpts we find that **Amenet** and **Amen**, the Supreme Being, at the beginning of Creation first generated the Abosom (Deities) **Ka** and **Kait** Who are the Divine Spirit-Forces of Consciousness/Intelligence. It is through **Ka** and **Kait** that thought-forms are generated. Just as you make decisions and formulate thoughts, ideas, etc. in the blackness of your own mind, so did/does **Amenet-Amen** (**Nyamewaa-Nyame**) use **Ka/Kait** to formulate the thoughts, ideas, etc. which are the basis of Creation, created entities and future events in the Universe. The Black Substance of Space is the *physical shrine* of **Ka** and **Kait** – the all-pervasive *Soul* of **Amenet-Amen** which encompasses all of Creation – Suns, Stars, Moons, Planets, Comets, Asteroids, Galaxies, etc. It is from these Two Abosom that **Amenet-Amen** give us our *individual* Ka or Kait. Because **Ka** and **Kait** were birthed first within the Great Divine Being, **Amenet-Amen**, and operate through the all-pervasive Black Substance of Space, **Ka** and **Kait** are sometimes called the *Grandfather* and *Grandmother* of the Abosom (Deities):

Ka [hieroglyphs], Mission 13, 123, "the father of the fathers of the gods," *i.e.*, [hieroglyphs], and see **Khemenu.**

Kait [hieroglyphs], Mission 13, 123, consort of [hieroglyphs], and one of the four elemental goddesses = [hieroglyphs]; she was the grandmother, [hieroglyphs], of the gods.

The air we have in our lungs is a minute portion of the air that comprises the atmosphere surrounding the entire planet. The water which comprises over seventy percent of our bodies is a minute portion of the Oceans that comprise over seventy percent of the planet. The Ka/Kait within our heads is an entity *birthed* from the Great **Ka** and Great **Kait**. This Divine Spirit-Force, this Soul - Ka or Kait, dwelling within us is a *child* of the Parent **Ka** and **Kait**. It is a 'drop' of Blackness from the 'Ocean' of the Black Substance of Space:

Kait and **Ka** (**Kauket** and **Keku**)

Kait and **Ka** the Abosom of the Black Substance of Space within which all Divine Consciousness dwells. **Kait** and **Ka** are often called **Kauket** and **Kek** (**Kekit** and **Keku** or **Keki**). The general term **Kk** or **Kka** means *darkness, blackness*. The Abosom of *Darkness, Blackness – Black Substance* are **Kka** and **Kkat**. Notice below that the term and name *Kka* can also be spelled with *two* **Ka** symbols – **KaKa**. This is why **Ka** and **Kait** are interchangeable with **Kek** (Kk) and **Keket** (Kkt).

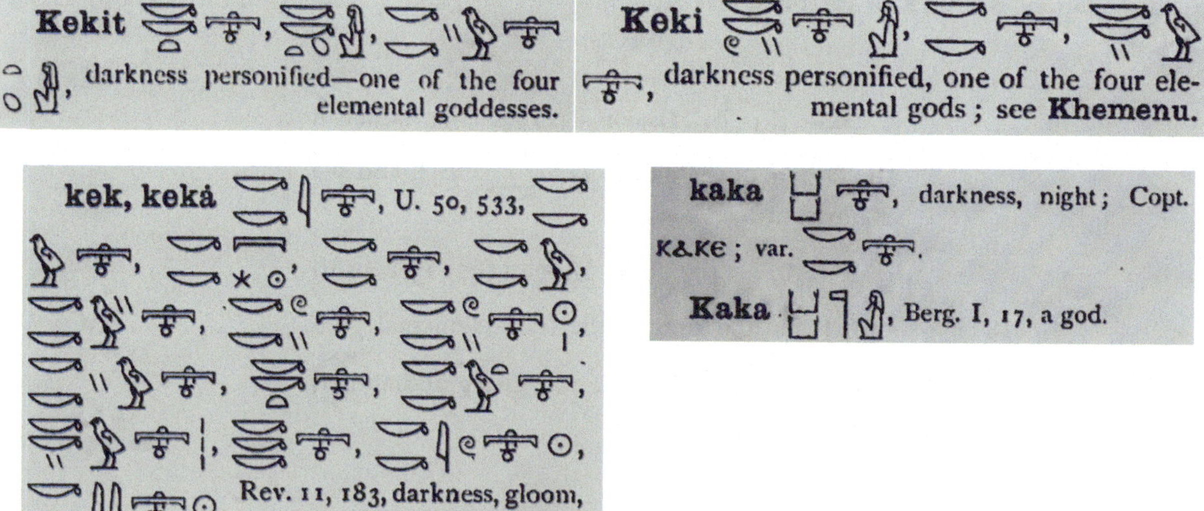

Kekit, darkness personified—one of the four elemental goddesses.

Keki, darkness personified, one of the four elemental gods; see **Khemenu**.

kek, kekȧ, U. 50, 533, Rev. 11, 183, darkness, gloom, obscurity; Copt. ⲔⲀⲔⲈ.

kaka, darkness, night; Copt. ⲔⲀⲔⲈ; var.

Kaka, Berg. I, 17, a god.

Our *physical* blackness (*abatumm* or *Ka-Nu/Kat-Nut* or *melanin*) comes from the Black Substance (plasma) of Space – the *body* of the Abosom **Ka** and **Kait**. Our *spiritual* blackness, our Ka/Kait, is a spiritual entity, an **organelle**, from the *Spirit-body* of **Ka** and **Kait**, Who comprise a **Divine Organ System** within the Great Divine Body of **Amenet-Amen**.

NKRA AND NKRABEA

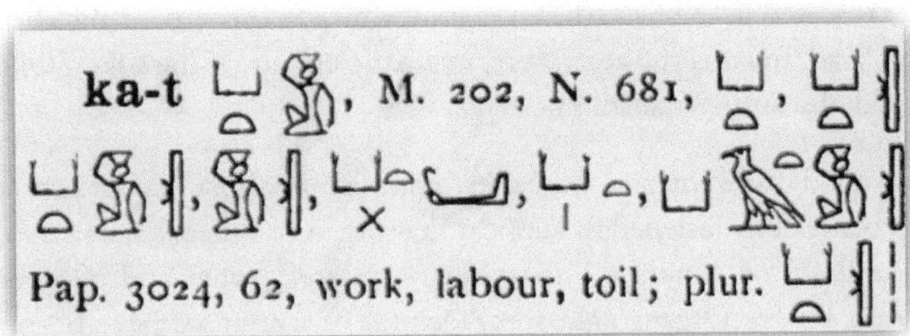

ka-t, M. 202, N. 681, Pap. 3024, 62, work, labour, toil; plur.

Above we see that the Ka/Kait is associated with *work, labor*. The individual in the metutu as a representation of this definition *carries* a vessel upon his *head*: . This concept continues to be conveyed in the Akan language when we say,

*'The **Okra/Okraa** is the <u>bearer</u> of the **nkra** and **nkrabea**.'*

The Okra or Okraa is our Divine Organ of Consciousness/Soul. It is a *complex* which *carries* the codified **<u>function</u>** that we are to execute in the world and the codification of the **<u>spiritual capacities</u>** (energy) necessary for us to execute our function.

If an Afurakani individual is born to function as a healer, this is an *assignment* encoded within his Okra by **Nyamewaa-Nyame**, *pre-incarnation*. **Nyamewaa-Nyame** also gives the *specific configuration of spiritual forces (energy) needed* for one to carry out his or her Divinely allotted function. Just as every organ in your body has a specific function to execute within the body and is designed (formed) and given the energy necessary to successfully execute that function, so are Afurakanu/Afuraitkaitnut (Africans), as cells within the Great Divine Body of **Nyamewaa-Nyame**, given a *specific function* to execute within the Great Body. We are also given the power, *a specifically-designed configuration of spiritual energy*, necessary to fulfill our role in Creation – to execute our function. The masculine and feminine terms **nkra** and **nkrabea** in Akan define our 'function' – life-focus (misnomered 'destiny'). The masculine and feminine terms **hye** and **hyebea** in Akan define our 'spiritual capacities' – the unique configuration of spiritual energy we are given in order to be successful at executing our nkra/nkrabea. First, we will address the **nkra/nkrabea** - our very *reason for being*.

Our nkra/nkrabea, our Divinely allotted function to execute in Creation, is our ka/kat our 'work, labor'

When Afurakanu/Afuraitkaitnut (Africans) were created by **Amenet-Amen**, our **asunsum** (spirits) were fashioned in the spirit-realm first. **Amenet** and **Amen** then gave each one of us a **Ka** or **Kait** – an **Okra** or

Okraa. This spiritual being, an Obosom which was assigned to us, was born of the Great **Ka** and **Kait**. This is because **Amenet-Amen** directed the *Grandmother* and *Grandfather* of the Abosom (Deities), **Ka** and **Kait**, to *give birth* to numerous *offspring*. It is one these Divine *offspring* who became our *personal* Obosom, our individual Ka/Kait. **Amenet-Amen** directs one of these offspring – one of these Obosom – to reside with us throughout our lives. This Obosom is seated in the head/brain region, which is the *apex* of the shrine for the Ka/Kait in the spirit and body. The head/brain is the apex/seat, while the energy of the Okra/Okraa *radiates* throughout our **sahu** (spirit body) and **abatumm** (melanin body).

When **Amenet-Amen** created our spirits, we were created for a *reason*. Just as your cells are part of an organ or organs'-system and are created and designed to support that organ or organs'-system, so are we as spirits, cells within the Great Divine Body of **Amenet-Amen**. We were/are created and designed to execute specific functions within the Great Divine Organs (Abosom/Deities) of whom we have been assigned by **Amenet-Amen**.

The Akan terms **nkra** and **nkrabea** are derived from the root **kra**. In the Akan language these terms are the masculine and feminine aspect of our Divine Function, our life-focus. What is often called our 'destiny' is more properly identified as <u>function</u>. The heart is designed to execute a specific <u>function</u> in the body - to send blood which contains nutrients and fire/energy to every part of the body perpetually, without fail or compromise. *This is the nkra/nkrabea of the heart* – the heart's Divinely allotted function. The lungs are designed to execute a specific <u>function</u> in the body – to breathe air as well as expel carbon dioxide and toxins from the body. *This is the nkra/nkrabea of the lungs* – the lungs' Divinely allotted function. The immune system is designed to execute a specific <u>function</u> in the body – to defend the body against internal disorder (developing cancerous cells, etc.) and external disorder (toxins, bacteria entering from the outside). *This is the nkra/nkrabea of the immune system* – the immune system's Divinely allotted function.

Afurakanu/Afuraitkaitnut (Africans), *and only Afurakanu/Afuraitkaitnut (Africans)*, are cells within the Great Divine Body of **Nyamewaa-Nyame**. Each one of us is therefore designed to execute a specific <u>function</u> within the Great Divine Body. That function is **encoded** within our Okra/Okraa by **Nyamewaa-Nyame**. It has *masculine* and *feminine* aspects related to the masculine and feminine aspects of the Okra/Okraa.

Males and females produce both of the major male and female hormones testosterone and estrogen. However, testosterone is abundant in males while estrogen is abundant in females comparatively. Similarly, the expansive and contractive force of the Okra and Okraa (Ka and Kat) exists within Afurakani males and Afuraitkaitnit females. However, the masculine aspect dominates in males and the feminine aspect dominates in females. *Indeed this is what defines us as males and females and ultimately causes us to develop physically as males and females in-utero.*

[The term ***nkra*** *is also used as a synonym for* ***mogya*** *meaning blood. The term* ***ka-fo*** *is also used:]*

ñkrá, *n. blood, syn.* **mogya. kafo**

In the Akan language, as stated above, the manner in which nouns are expressed in their feminine aspect is through the feminine suffix which is variously: **baa, bea, waa, wa, aa** or **a**. In fact, the word for *woman, female* in Akan is **Obaa** or **Obea** depending upon the dialect of Twi spoken. Linguistically, the sounds of the letters 'B' and 'W' interchange. This can be seen in the Akan practice of naming. The name **Ofori** has male and female versions. The male version is **Ofori** while the female version is **Oforiwaa**. We also have names such as **Okyere** and **Kyerewaa** (**Kyerebea** in Akwamu and Akuapem dialects), **Fosu** and **Fosuwaa**, **Acheampong** and **Acheampomaa** (Acheampong-baa becomes Acheampomaa), **Opoku** and **Opokuwaa**. Depending upon the dialect of Twi being spoken the 'aa' or 'waa' or 'wa', 'baa' or 'bea' defining the feminine will be employed. This is why we also have variations of the name **Nyamewaa** such as **Nyamewa**, **Onyamewa**, **Onyamebea**, **Onyamebaa**.

As stated above, in the language of Kamit, the same objective is accomplished by the use of the letter 'T'. The term **Ka** is masculine while **Kat** or **Kait** is feminine. The same is true of **Ra** and **Rat** (**Rait**), **Amen** and **Amenet**, **Nu** and **Nut**, etc.

Afurakanu/Afuraitkaitnut (Africans) have always recognized the Divine Balance of Male and Female in all *created* entities in the universe, because all *created* entities are descendant of Amenet and Amen the Great Mother and Great Father Who function in Divine Balance as the Two Halves of the Great Divine Whole. The whites and their offspring to not qualify as *created* entities.

The masculine and feminine terms **nkra** and **nkrabea** are the *Akan versions* of **ka** (kra) and **kat** (kra-bea). The term **nkra** is typically defined as a *message, mandate, word, commission.* The term **nkrabea** is typically defined as the *manner* of the *message, 'fate', 'destiny', allotted life.*

ŋkrá, *inf.* [kra] **1.** *taking leave.* — **2.** *errand, mandate, order, commission, word, message; information, notice. pr. 1761;* ŋkra bi nni akyiri bio, *that is all I have been commissioned to say, I have nothing else to say.* — di ŋkrá, *a) to part, be separated; to quit each other* = di mpaapaemu; yenà mo adi ŋkra, *we have no connection with you any more;* onè ne kra adi ŋkra = waka baabi. — *b) to have conversation or communication;* me nè no nni ŋkra

ŋkrá-béa [kra 8, bea, *manner*] *fate, destiny, appointed lot, allotted life, final lot, manner of death; syn.* hyɛbea. *pr. 1762 f. 2538:* Onyame ŋk. nni ŋkwatibea, *what God has destined cannot be evaded; there is no evading fate.* Wobɛwo wo a, na wo asɛm a

The term that is used for the female, **obea**, is also a term used to define *manner, way, place.* This is why the term **nkra-bea** is defined as the *'destiny'* the **bea** (*manner, way*) of the **nkra** (*message, mandate*) given by **Nyamewaa-Nyame**. There is a cosmological reason why the term **bea** is not only a term used for *'female, woman'* but also for *'manner, way, place'.*

The sperm cell of the male enters the woman and ultimately there is a union of sperm and ovum. However, this union can only occur within a certain *place*, within a certain *time* (cycle) and in a certain *way* or *manner.* In order for life to occur, the female (*obea*) determines the manner (*bea*) and place (*bea*). Moreover, the term **bere** in Akan is a variation of the term bea and thus also means *female* (bere), *manner* (bere), *place* (bere) and also *time* (bere). [See: **gyata** – *lion*; **gyata nini** – *male lion*, **gyatabere** – *female lioness*; **akoko** – *chicken*; **akokonini** – *male akoko/rooster*, **akokobere** – *female akoko/hen.*]

In the *female* (obea), the womb is the sacred *place* (bea, bere) wherein the gestation unfolds in a certain *manner* (obea, bere) and within a set *time.* The sperm cell *initiates* the process. The ovum receives the sperm cell, fuses both cells and the process is *completed* within the female.

We have a Divine function to execute in Creation. If one is created and designed to be a healer, this is his or her *mandate, order, message.* However, he or she must heal in a certain *manner, way.* Some can heal with certain plants, while some may come from an Afurakani/Afuraitkaitnit (African) family who are allergic to those particular plants and therefore must use others. They have to heal in their own *manner, way* according to what is in harmony with their unique physical make-up. Some may be children of a fiery Obosom and must utilize that fire to burn up toxins/heal, while others may be children of a watery Obosom and must utilize that cool energy to cleanse/heal. The function given by **Nyamewaa-Nyame** carries the balanced energy/force/consciousness of **Nyamewaa-Nyame**. There is a *message, mandate,* which must be executed in a *specific manner* according to our nature – our unique spiritual anatomy.

The Akan terms **nkra** and **nkrabea** (male and female aspects of function) are derived from the terms **ka** and **kat** in Kamit. As stated above, in the language of Kamit, the ‘T’ is the feminizing element, functioning the same the ‘baa’, ‘bea’, ‘waa’ or ‘aa’ in Akan.

If you picture the *inside of the mouth* when the ‘T’ sound is pronounced, the tongue touches the edge of the roof of the mouth. The air rising up from the trachea enters the mouth and fills up the space. The roof of the mouth is arched and the tongue forms an almost flat base. The flat base and the arched roof thus cause the air to take the form similar to a bowl turned up-side down and the air filling the space inside:

This is of course the metut (hieroglyph) for the letter ‘T’. One of the reasons why it has this shape is because *this is the form that the air takes inside the mouth when pronouncing the sound.* The arched portion is the roof of the mouth. The flat base is the tongue. The air carries the life-force energy of **Ra/Rait**. *The life-force energy thus takes this form inside the mouth as well when pronouncing the ‘T’ sound.* This shaping/forming of the Divine Living Energy of **Ra/Rait** *defines* the shape/form of the metut for the ‘T’ sound.

Moreover, the sky is seen as the upper-half of a *calabash* in certain Afurakani/Afuraitkaitnit (African) cultures. The calabash is like a womb. As an entity grows and expands its expansion must at some point be contracted *in order for a shape/form to emerge.* Unchecked expansion will never produce an entity – a life-form. It is the complement of expansion and contraction that gives birth to *forms.* The womb of the female allows expansion and growth, however, it is *contained.* The female (obea) womb is thus the *creative space/place* (bea) wherein an entity takes *form.* This function is defined by the metut for ‘T’. This is why functionally and conceptually ‘bea’ in Akan and the ‘T’ in Kamit are the same. In fact, the terms ka and kait also mean *phallus* and *vagina* as represented via the metutu for *bull* and *cow* in Kamit. The Per Aa (King) and many Male Abosom were called *Great Bull,* while many Female Abosom were called *Great Divine Cows.* This is a reference to the *reproductive capacity* of the male and female:

ka , , , P. 77, 646, , , , N. 1039, , , Rev. 12, 11, , Rev. 13, 5, bull; plur. , , Rec. 29,

kai-t , , , cow; plur. , Rec. 27, 58.

Ka ur , B.D. 178, 7, "Great Bull"—a title of the God of heaven.

ka-t , Ebers Pap. 94, 17, , , Rec. 27, 88, , vulva, vagina,

Ka and Kat, Kra and Kraa, Nkra and Nkra-bea are all of the same root – the Abosom **Ka** and **Kat**. It is **Nyamewaa** Who gives the **Kat** (Kraa, Okraa, Okrawa) while **Nyame** gives the **Ka** (Kra, Okra). It is **Nyamewaa** Who gives the **nkrabea**, while **Nyame** gives the **nkra**.

As the Afurakani/Afuraitkaitnit (African) sunsum (spirit) stands before **Nyamewaa-Nyame** prior to it being sent into the womb of a female, the sunsum learns from **Nyamewaa-Nyame** what his or her function will be to execute in the world. **Nyame** speaks the **nkra** (message, mandate) and **Nyamewaa** speaks the **nkrabea** (the manner of the mandate) to the individual. **Nyamewaa-Nyame** then order that an Obosom, one of the Children of the *Grandmother and Grandfather of the Abosom*, **Ka** and **Kait**, come forward. This Okra or Okraa Obosom is *assigned* to the sunsum of the Afurakani/Afuraitkaitnit (African) individual. This spiritual entity, this personal Obosom, takes up residence in the head region of the spirit-body of the Afurakani/Afuraitkaitnit (African) individual. The individual sunsum has now been *infused* with a Soul a Ka or Kait, an Obosom Who is a link to the Great Soul, **Ka** and **Kait**, the Divine Consciousness of **Nyamewaa-Nyame**. Whenever the individual listens to his or her Okra/Okraa from this point on, his or her Okra/Okraa or Ka/Kait will relay to the individual the information from the Great **Ka/Kait** – The Consciousness of **Nyamewaa-Nyame**. This is how the Afurakani/Afuraitkaitnit (African) individual is *Divinely guided.*

When **Nyamewaa-Nyame** speaks the **nkra** and **nkrabea**, They speak the individual's Divine function, life-focus, life's *work, labor* to them:

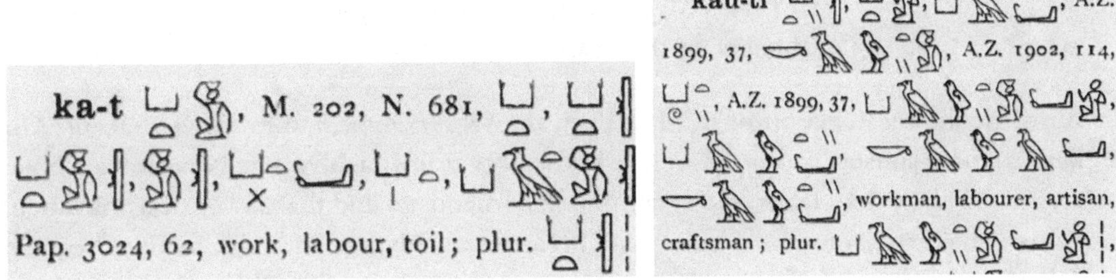
ka-t, M. 202, N. 681, Pap. 3024, 62, work, labour, toil; plur.

kau-ti, A.Z. 1899, 37, A.Z. 1902, 114, A.Z. 1899, 37, workman, labourer, artisan, craftsman; plur.

We have seen that the root **ka** means *soul, to leave* and *work, labor.* The same term in Akan **kra** means *soul, to leave* and *commission, errand, mandate* – [nkra/nkrabea - *life's work, labor*]. **Nyamewaa-Nyame** *speaks* the ka/kat or nkra/nkrabea to the individual and directs the Abosom **Ka** and **Kait** to send one of Their offspring to dwell with the individual as his/her personal Ka/Kait (Okra/Okraa) for life. It is important to note that the term for *to speak* also has the same root in Kamit and Akan. From the Metut Ntoro and Twi dictionaries:

kai, P. 1116B, 62, to think, to think out, to devise, to meditate, to speak, to repeat, to say,

kā, *v.* [*red.* **kekā**] *to emit a sound, to utter, speak, say, tell; cf.* **kasa, se, be, besebese,** bɛ 75-82., **woro**; – **agyinamoa kā ne menewam'**, *the cat emits a sound from its throat,* i.e. *it purrs;* **woakā**, *thou hast said it, Mt. 26,25. 64.* — **kā asɛm**, *to utter words, speak, talk; to*

The term **kai**, also spelled **ka**, in Kamit means *to think out, to devise, to meditate, to speak, to repeat, to say*. The Akan term **ka** (above right) also means *to emit a sound, to utter, speak, say*. The related Akan term **ka-bea** means the *way or manner of speaking*:

kā-beá, *manner or way of speaking;* **òbéhū ne k.**, *he will know how to say that, to speak of that further.*

Moreover, the related Akan terms **nka** and **ka** mean *to perceive, perception; to learn, come to know* and also a *report* as well as to *touch, perceive by the sense of feeling:*

ṅkȃ, *1. smell, scent;* – te ṅkã, *to perceive the smell, to smell.* — *2. noise, report, rumour;* mate ne ṅkȃ (sẹ ọbẹba nẹ), *I have heard of him, have had news of him (that he will come to-day);* wọtee ne ṅkã (= ne hõ asẹm terẹwe) asase no ṅhinã so, *his fame spread abroad in all that country.* — *3. perception;* te ṅkȃ, *to learn, hear, come to know, be informed of;* mate ṅkã sẹ yẹadaṅ bone, *I know from experience that we have become bad or sinful.*

kã, *v.* [*red.* kekã] *I. to touch, to come* or *be in* or *bring into contact with, to join &c. (1-25); II. to move* or *stir, to be* or *cause to be active (26-40); III. to move in order to join (41-51).*
(I.) 1. to touch, come in contact with, pr. 466. – to handle (slightly). *feel* i.e. *perceive* by the sense of feeling; mfã wo usa ṅkã dade no, na

This notion of *perception, learning* is related to the term **kat** meaning *thought, meditation, internal focus, learning.*

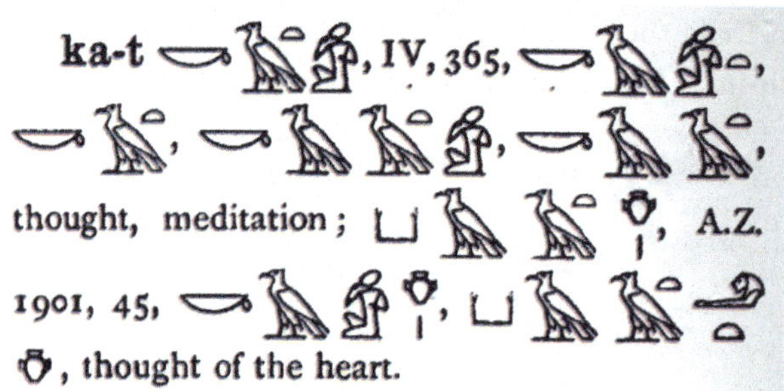
ka-t, IV, 365, thought, meditation; A.Z. 1901, 45, thought of the heart.

All of these terms define the function of the Ka/Kait, the Okra/Okraa within the Afurakani/Afuraitkaitnit (African) individual. The sunsum (spirit) is drawn before **Nyamewaa-Nyame**. **Nyamewaa-Nyame** *speaks* (**ka**) the life's *work assignment* (**kat**: labor; **nkra**: commission, mandate) and the *manner* (**kat/nkrabea**) in which that assignment is to be carried out to the individual. **Nyamewaa-Nyame** then directs the Great **Ka** and **Kait** to give one of their offspring, to assist the individual throughout his or her life. This offspring is the individual's personal Obosom (Ka/Kait or Okra/Okraa). Throughout the course of life, the individual is able to consult with his or her personal Obosom (his or her Okra or Okraa) Who resides in the head region. The individual *thinks, meditates, devises, perceives, learns* (**kat, nka**) from the Ka/Kait or Okra/Okraa on a daily basis for his or her entire life. This allows the individual to harmonize with **Nyamewaa-Nyame Nhyehyee** (Divine Order) for whenever he or she *perceives, learns* (**nka**) and *meditates* (**ka**) with his or her personal Obosom (Ka/Kait) he or she attunes him/herself to the Great **Ka** and **Kait**, the Soul of **Nyamewaa-Nyame**. *The Afurakani/Afuraitkaitnit (African) individual thus always has access to Divine guidance through the agency of his or her Ka/Kait – Okra/Okraa.* As stated above, once the individual spirit has received his/her nkra/nkrabea and everything he or she needs from **Nyamewaa-Nyame**, the spirit *leaves* (**ka, kra**) and returns to the spirit-realm as a **sunsum-okra**, a *spirit-soul* or whole entity, to await reincarnation into the physical world.

Upon arrival in the physical world via birth, the parents give the newborn child/spirit a name which *resonates* with the energy of his or her nkra/nkrabea so that whenever he or she is called or reflects upon his or her name, his or her spirit/sunsum will be consciously and energically refocused upon the Okra/Okraa.

Upon death, the sunsum (spirit) separates from the body. The sunsum eventually travels to **Asamando** – the Ancestral realm as long as he or she is not a disordered spirit. *Prior to settling* in Asamando, the individual's Okra/Okraa will temporarily *leave* (ka/kra) the individual and go before **Nyamewaa-Nyame** to *speak* and give a *report* (ka, nka) about how the individual lived his or her life on **Asaase** (Earth). This *report* (nka) will determine whether or not the individual will be able to reside in Asamando with the community of **Nananom Nsamanfo** and **Nsamanfo Pa** (*Spiritually cultivated Ancestresses and Ancestors and the Good Ancestresses and Ancestors who were not highly spiritually cultivated on* ***Asaase*** *(Earth) but were good people nonetheless*). The Ka/Kat or Okra/Okraa, after making the *report* (nka) and receiving the decision will *take leave* (ka, kra) from **Nyamewaa-Nyame** and return to the individual spirit to reside with him or her once again.

Understanding our cosmology allows us to see how the Abosom give birth to the terms, names we use. The configuration of vibrations/sound waves which comprise the words in Afurakani/Afuraitkaitnit (African) languages are *directly derived* of the names and functions, movements, operations of the Abosom in Nature. This principle is demonstrated in all of its nuances in the terms Ka/Kait, Okra/Okraa and their derivations:

Khanit/Kamit		**Akan**	
Ka/Kat	*Soul, Divine Consciousness*	Kra/Kraa	*Soul, Divine Consciousness*
Ka	*to leave*	Kra	*to leave*
Ka	*to speak*	Ka	*to speak*
Ka/Kat	*work, labor*	Nkra/Nkrabea	*mandate, function; manner of function,*
life's work, labor			
Ka/Kat	*to meditate, devise; thought, meditation*	Nka	*to perceive; to learn*
Ka	*symbol of arms and hands reaching, receiving*	Ka	*to touch; join, perceive by sense of feeling to cause to be active*
Ka	*arms and shoulders placed on the head*	Kra-do	*shoulders; seat of the kra/kraa*

Close-up of **Ka** from the outer wall of the Temple of **Het Heru** (Hathor) in Dendera

Hye and Hyebea

When the individual sunsum (spirit) stands before **Nyamewaa-Nyame** and receives his or her Okra or Okraa, the **nkra** and **nkrabea** are encoded *within* the Okra or Okraa of the individual. The individual has been given the *knowledge, consciousness* of the function in its male and female expressions (**nkra/nkrabea**) – *what* he or she is to do (nkra) and *how* (manner - nkrabea) he or she is to execute this function in harmony with his or her physical and spiritual make-up. The individual must understand how to execute his or her function without creating disorder in **Abode** (Creation) in the process.

The individual sunsum (spirit) is subsequently given the spiritual capacity, *a specific configuration of spiritual energy*, necessary for the individual to be able to execute the Divinely allotted function he or she has been tasked with. The individual sunsum (spirit) is given the *power to execute* – a specific configuration of spiritual energy related to Abosom (Deities) *connected to his or her Ancestry* as well as the *manner* in which to exercise this configuration of energy. This is the domain of the **hye** and **hyebea**.

The Akan term **hye** is a verb meaning *to fix, arrange; to compel.* The noun version of the term, **ohye** means *the act of fixing, compulsion*:

ǫ-hyę, *inf. 1.* the act of *fixing, putting on* &c. *cf.* hyę, *v.* — *2. compulsion* (*Mf.* ńhyę). — *3. commandment, cf.* ahyęde, ńhyehyęe.

The term **hye** also has the meaning *to set, appoint* and is sometimes defined *to predestine, predestinate; to command, charge; to compel, force; to impel, urge:*

hyę, *v.* [*red.* hyehyę]
1. to stick (fast), to be put, set, fixed, inserted (hǫ, mu, ase, *there, in, under &c.*) espec. in the *contin.* form; pętea hyę ne nsa, *a ring is put*

(dam') da bi manyę; watu ahyę da, *he has postponed it.* — *19. to fix, set up, institute:* hyę afã, *to celebrate a festival*; hyę mom, *to issue a decree*; hyę mmăra, *to give, make, enact a law* or *laws*; hyę apãm, *to set up a covenant* (?) *s.* pãm. — *20. to set, constitute, appoint*; hyę panyiń, F. *Mt. 24,45.* — *21. to predestine, predestinate, appoint* or *ordain beforehand*; *s.* hyębea; *to be predestined for, pr.* 621. *22. to command, charge:* ǫhyę́ abień yi na ǫhyę́ę̀ no ketē sę ǫ́nyę,

The 'hy' combination in the Akan language is approximated by the 'sh' combination in english. The term **hye** thus sounds like 'shay'. The term has a feminine version: **hyebea**. This term is typically defined to mean *predestination, fate; decree.*

hyę-beá, ***predestination, fate; cf.*** **ŋkrabea;** ***decree. Dan. 4,24.***
hyę-beá, hyę́-bérę, **F. -bew,** ***a place where to put &c. Mt. 26.52.***

The terms hye and hyebea thus have to do with *force, fixing, arranging, compulsion.* They are the *masculine and feminine aspects* of the configuration of spiritual energy we are given so that we can execute our nkra/nkrabea. As in the example cited above, one may have the nkra/nkrabea which dictates that they are to be a healer – one who brings balance when imbalance arises. What kind of healer? If the individual's nkra/nkrabea, encoded within his or her Okra/Okraa, mandates that he or she is to utilize the energy of Abosom of *Fire* to heal, then **Nyamewaa-Nyame** assigns the individual to and aligns the individual with Abosom of *Fire* such as Abosom of the **Owia** (the Sun) or **Osranaa** (lightening). If the individual's nkra/nkrabea, encoded within his or her Okra/Okraa, mandates that he or she is to heal through a *Watery*, cool medium, then **Nyamewaa-Nyame** assigns the individual to and aligns the individual with Abosom of *Water* such as Abosom of the **Opo** (Ocean) or a certain **Asuo** (River). The individual's Okra/Okraa, Sunsum and entire being will be affected by the Abosom with Whom he or she is aligned. He or she will therefore naturally manifest *physical characteristics* (morphology, metabolism, etc.) and a *personality and temperament* reflective of the energy and character of those Abosom. This occurs in the same fashion as an individual who has very similar facial and bodily characteristics of his father as well as his personality and temperament.

Just as we are genetically related to our parents, we – Afurakanu/Afuraitkaitnut (Africans) only – are spiri-genetically related to the Abosom Whose energy is infused within us by Nyamewaa-Nyame.

The individual's hye and hyebea affords him or her the ability, the capacity, to *employ* a configuration of energy (be it fiery, watery, earth, air, etc.) – **hye** (force, command, compel) – yet he or she is also given the ability, capacity, to *employ* this energy-complex in a certain *manner* (bea) – **hyebea**. The individual must utilize the energy-complex derived from the Abosom in a *manner* that allows him or her to heal, yet not create disorder in **Abode** (Creation) or within him or herself in the process. <u>The energy-complex must only be used to support the individual's nkra/nkrabea, his or her Divine function in **Abode**</u>. If the individual attempts to misuse the energy he or she is given, the Abosom will not allow it. <u>The Abosom will shut down the energy complex and disengage from the individual</u>.

The Akan terms hye and hyebea (shay and shaybea) are directly derived from the language of Kamit. The term **shai** and **shat** in Kamit mean *to fix, appoint, to predestinate, decree; destiny, fate,* etc.

sha, shai [hieroglyphs], Thes. 1285, [hieroglyphs], to fix, to appoint, to decide, to determine, to destine, to predestinate, to allot, to design, to decree, to ordain, to commission, to authorize.

sha-t [hieroglyphs], Amherst Pap. 26, [hieroglyphs], A.Z. 45, 125, something decreed or ordained by God, what is ordained by man or fixed by custom, what is seemly or fitting, dues, revenue, taxes, impost.

shau [hieroglyphs], A.Z. 1874, 87, [hieroglyphs], IV, 1116, [hieroglyphs], what is decreed or ordered or ordained, fate, destiny.

In the language of Kamit and that of the Akan **shai** and **hye** (shay) are <u>identical</u> phonetically and conceptually:

sha, shai [hieroglyphs], Thes. 1285, [hieroglyphs], to fix, to appoint, to decide, to determine, to destine, to predestinate, to allot, to design, to decree, to ordain, to commission, to authorize.

(dam') da bi manyę; watu ahyę da, *he has postponed it.* — *19. to fix, set up, institute:* hyę afã, *to celebrate a festival;* hyę mom, *to issue a decree;* hyę mmăra, *to give, make, enact a law or laws;* hyę apãm, *to set up a covenant* (?) *s.* pãm. — *20. to set, constitute, appoint;* hyę panyiñ, F. *Mt. 24,45.* — *21. to predestine, predestinate, appoint* or *ordain beforehand;* s. hyębea; *to be predestined for, pr. 621.* *22. to command, charge:* ǫhyę́ abieñ yi na ǫhyę́ę̀ no ketē sę ónyę,

The related term **shaui** and **shai** means *to be of value, property, goods, something useful; utility, worth:*

shau [hieroglyphs], Ámen. 12, 4, [hieroglyphs], to be of value, property, stuff, possessions, goods, something which is of worth or value, something useful, advantage, benefit; [hieroglyphs], Theban Ostraka No. 2; [hieroglyphs], most valuable of all.

shai [hieroglyphs], Rev., use, utility, worth; Copt. ϣⲁⲩ-.

These definitions are critical to the notion of 'destiny' (function) as being that which is *appointed* by **Nyamewaa-Nyame**. *Your function in the world determines what your value is in the world, just as the function of each organ in the body determines its value to the body.* Outside of its appointed function, the organ has no value. Moreover, the notion of value, goods, property, possessions, etc. being associated with 'destiny' speaks to the proper notion of hye and hyebea being defined as the *specific configuration of energy, spiritual forces, given to the individual (property, goods, possessions) which give him or her the capacity to be able to execute his or her nkra/nkrabea (function) fully.* The energy-complex and the Abosom who are appointed to the individual and Whose energy the individual will draw from in order to function properly in Abode (Creation), is of the highest *value* and *utility.* Without it, the individual would have no capacity to function and hence no value or utility. This is also why **Shai** is referred to as the Obosom of *good 'luck', fortune, prosperity,* etc. When we exercise our hye and hyebea properly, our capacity to utilize force, energy in a specific manner, we have *prosperity, fortune* (misnomered 'luck') – meaning we have executed our function, harmonized with **Nyamewaa-Nyame Nhyehyee** (Divine Order). This is the only prosperity or fortune in **Abode** (Creation).

The terms *shai* and *shait,* written as *hye* (shay) and *hyebea* (again the 'bea' feminizes in Akan just as the 't' feminizes in Kamit) are derived directly from the Male and Female Abosom **Shai** and **Shait**:

Shai [hieroglyphs], Ámen. 21, 16, A.Z. 1873, 138, Todt. (Leps.), pl. 50, [hieroglyphs], Pap. Ani 3, B.M. 32, 411, Jour. As. Sér. X, 9, 434, 460, 473, 491, 508, 552, Berg. 73, the god Luck or Fate or Destiny who reckons the days ([hieroglyphs]) of men.

Shau [hieroglyphs], Rec. 36, 53, [hieroglyphs], P.S.B. 15, 35, [hieroglyphs], the god of prosperity and of good luck and good fortune.

Shait [hieroglyphs], Ámen. 9, 11, [hieroglyphs], Hh. 330, the goddess Fate.

In the above scene of the weighing of the heart of the deceased we see the Obosom **Shai** standing under the scales of **Maat**. An enlarged image of **Shai** is on the right.

Khanit/Kamit		**Akan**	
Shai	*to fix, appoint, predestinate*	Hye	*to fix, appoint, predestinate; compel, impel*
Shait	*that which is ordained, decreed*	Hyebea	*that which is ordained, decreed*

[Because the Akan term **bere** (*female, place, manner, time*) as shown above is a synonym for **bea** (*female, place, manner*) the term **hyebea** is also written **hyebere** (**hyebre**). Moreover, **nkrabea** is also written **nkrabere** by some Akan.]

Note: *The **Ba** spirit in the form of a human-headed bird – the head of the deceased individual – also awaits the results of the weighing. **Ba** and **Bait** are the masculine and feminine terms for our Divine Living Energy, the Conscious Living Spirit-Entity which animates us - like the solar-fire or heat within our bodies which permeates our entire being and radiates from us. When the **Ka** and **Ba** (**Kait** and **Bait**) unite it is the union of the Soul and the Divine Life-Spirit. The **Ba** and **Bait** carry the energy of **Ra** and **Rait** (Creator and Creatress – **Nyankopon** and **Nyankonton** in Akan). It is the radiant Life-Energy of the **Ba/Bait** which allows us to consciously and energically link to the Abosom in all of Creation and activates our inherited energy-complex, **hye** and **hyebea**. The term **ba** in Kamit is **obara** (**obra**) in Akan meaning 'life, existence'. The union of the **Obra** and **Okra** is the union of the Divine Life-Spirit with the Soul.*

When **Nyamewaa-Nyame** speaks the nkra/nkrabea to us prior to our incarnation, They then direct the Abosom **Ka** and **Kait** to send one of Their offspring to dwell with us. The Obosom They send becomes our personal Ka or Kait, our personal Okra or Okraa. **Nyamewaa-Nyame** then gives us the *capacity to execute* our nkra/nkrabea. This capacity is our hye/hyebea our motive force of compulsion. The particular manner in which we utilize our hye/hyebea is *fixed* by **Nyamewaa-Nyame**. They *appoint* certain Abosom to us Who carry the requisite energy necessary for us to function according to our nkra/nkrabea (allotted function or 'destiny'). **Nyamewaa-Nyame** direct the Abosom **Shai** and **Shait** to *monitor* our use or employ of the energy-complex we are given. Our hye and hyebea are the masculine and feminine aspects of our *capacity* to execute our function, nkra/nkrabea, properly without being self-destructive in the process or profaning the **Awiase**, the world, in the process.

Our **nkra/nkrabea** is our *consciousness of our Divine function* – how we fit into the reality of **Abode**. We exercise this consciousness to operate in the world. We attune to our nkra/nkrabea in order to know the *nature* of the function (nkra) we are to execute in the world and the *manner* (bea - nkrabea) in which we must execute that function in any given moment and within any given situation in a harmonious fashion.

Our **hye/hyebea** is our *motive force*. It is our *impulsion* and *compulsion* to wield our appointed energy-complex in order to properly operate in the world, meaning *according to the dictates of our nkra/nkrabea.* We attune to our hye/hyebea in order to know the *nature* of the resources (hye) we have (our uniquely assigned spirit-energy complex) and the *manner* (bea - hyebea) in which we must utilize that energy-complex in any given moment and within any given situation in a harmonious fashion.

The centers of resonance, *the shrines*, of the nkra and nkrabea and hye and hyebea are within the *head*. The Okra and Okraa is akin to the *spirit's brain*. **The Okra/Okraa is a complex which contains the major centers of resonance, nkra/nkrabea and hye/hyebea.**

The structure of the physical brain reflects this reality:

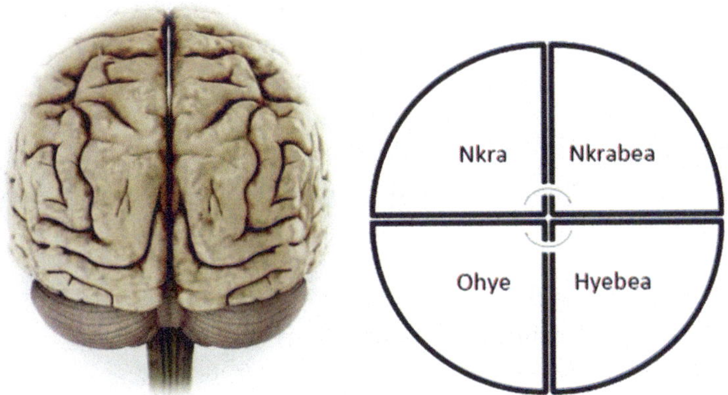

The above image is the brain (**amemene** in Akan) as viewed from the back. The brain's **cerebrum**, the top grayish area which comprises the majority of the structure, is divided into two hemispheres. The right hemisphere governs *intuition, holistic constructions, congregative thinking*, etc. The left hemisphere governs *linear thinking, analysis, segregative thinking,* etc. The functions of the right hemisphere are characteristically feminine functions while the functions of the left hemisphere are characteristically masculine functions. The Afurakani/Afuraitkaitnit (African) human being *balances* these functions in order to live harmoniously. It is important to note that the nature of that *achieved balance* is different with regard to the Afurakani male and the Afuraitkaitnit female. Balancing these functions places each gender firmly within their nature. Balancing the functions of the brain or the masculine and feminine energy of the spirit never leads to androgyny, dissexuality (the insane practice of homosexuality, bi-sexuality, cross-dressing, etc.) or any other perverse, deviant acts. The Afurakani male and Afuraitkaitnit female, when fully balanced, have made themselves a fully balanced **half** of a whole. Complete balance only comes when the two fully balanced halves Afurakani/Afuraitkaitnit **unite** through marriage, ritual practice and more.

The two hemispheres of the cerebrum are the *physical shrines* for the nkra and nkrabea. The nkra and nkrabea are the masculine and feminine aspects of our consciousness which define for us the nature of our Divine functioning in the world (nkra) and the manner in which that function must be executed according to our unique make-up (nkrabea). The nkra and nkrabea resonate through the left and right – masculine and feminine – hemispheres of the brain respectively.

The bottom portion of the brain as shown above is called the **cerebellum** which is also divided into two hemispheres. The cerebellum governs *motor movement, coordination, balance, equilibrium and muscle tone.* The cerebellum relays information between body muscles and areas of the cerebral cortex that are involved in motor control. The cerebellum has articulation (left hemisphere) and cognitive (right hemisphere) functions with regard to language (fashioning/arranging sound-vibrations/forms energy) and emotions (e-motive force) as well.

The two divisions of the cerebellum are the *physical shrines* for the hye and hyebea. The hye and hyebea are the masculine and feminine aspects of our compulsion/impulsion to execute. The hye and hyebea are our motive force which employs the energy and consciousness of the Abosom assigned to us pre-incarnation.

Our **nkra** and **nkrabea** (ka and kat) are governed by the Abosom **Ka** and **Kait**. Our **hye** and **hyebea** (shai and shait) are governed by the Abosom **Shai** and **Shait**.

The *entire* nkra/nkrabea-hye/hyebea *complex* is regulated by our *individual* Okra or Okraa, our *individual* Ka or Kait – the *child* of the Great **Ka** and **Kait** who was sent to dwell with us (in our heads) and guide us throughout life. This is the **Okra complex** in the Afurakani male and the **Okraa complex** in the Afuraitkaitnit female.

The brain and its cerebrum and cerebellum, divided into hemispheres with their own functions is the *physical seat* of the Okra/Okraa complex and its divisions: nkra, nkrabea, hye, hyebea. Moreover, major functions of the brain are *crystallized* in the *anterior* and *posterior lobes* of the *pituitary gland.*

Throughout the course of life, the Afurakani/Afuraitkaitnit (African) individual seeks to function in the world *harmoniously* – meaning according to **Nyamewaa-Nyame Nhyehyee** (Divine Order). He or she attunes his or sunsum (spirit) to his or her Okra/Okraa. The *pull* of the Okra/Okraa is *animated* by the divisions within the Okra/Okraa. When we are guided by the Okra/Okraa to knowledge of *what* our function is (healer/healeress, builder, defender, etc.) and the knowledge of the *manner* in which we are to execute that function based on our unique Ancestry (spiritual anatomy) we have attuned to our nkra/nkrabea which dwells within the Okra/Okraa complex. When we are guided by our Okra/Okraa to knowledge of *what* our spirit-energy capacities are and the *manner* in which to wield our energic, impulsive/compulsive force towards the support of our function without being self-destructive or destructive in **Abode** (Creation), we have attuned to our hye/hyebea which dwells within the Okra/Okraa complex.

Our Okra/Okraa (Ka/Kait) is a messenger of **Ka/Kait** and **Shai/Shait**. When we ask fundamental questions of the Okra/Okraa regarding our role in **Abode** (Creation), our Okra/Okraa will relay the infinite knowledge of **Ka/Kait** and the energy of **Shai/Shait** to our nkra/nkrabea and hye/hyebea. This is akin physically to the hemispheres of the cerebral cortex and cerebellum being stimulated and receiving and transmitting information.

The information and energy received from ***Ka/Kait*** *and* ***Shai/Shait*** *stimulates the information and energy that had been spoken to the sunsum and encoded within the Okra/Okraa by* ***Nyamewaa-Nyame*** *prior to incarnation.*

Our consciousness and energic capacity is thus kindled and brought forward to the *surface* our awareness. We then understand *what* we are to accomplish and *how* we are to accomplish – *what* our value/energy capacity is and *how* to exercise/wield that energy towards the fulfillment of our objectives. This is how we *operationalize* our 'destiny' – how we execute our Divinely allotted function.

Prior attempts to define the nkrabea and hyebea have been misinformed because of a lack of knowledge that:

- Our **nkra** and **nkrabea** as well as the our **hye** and **hyebea** are the *masculine and feminine aspects* of function and energic capacity
- Our **nkra** and **nkrabea** are connected to the Abosom **Ka** and **Kait**, while our **hye** and **hyebea** are connected to the Abosom **Shai** and **Shait**
- Our Okra/Okraa is a ***personal Obosom*** with Whom we communicate and receive Divine guidance from
- Our Okra/Okraa, as an Obosom, is the *offspring* of the Abosom Ka and Kait
- The Okra/Okraa is an *entity* and also a *complex* just as the brain is an *entity* (organ) and also a *complex*

The misguided definitions of nkrabea and hyebea being *'interchangeable'* or *'dual-destiny'* or *'nkrabea being the destiny received by Nyame while the hyebea is the personal destiny'* arise from a lack of understanding of the cosmological structure that gives birth to the notions of **Ka/Kait**, **Shai/Shait**, nkra/nkrabea, hye/hyebea. The lack of understanding arises from a lack of experience in working with these Abosom and invoking the Okra or Okraa in order to stimulate and become informed by the nkra/nkrabea and hye/hyebea.

Moreover, we have demonstrated conclusively that these concepts in Akan culture are ancient and are the same concepts learned from the Abosom that informed our practice of **Nanasom**, *Afurakani/Afuraitkaitnit Ancestral Religion*, in ancient Khanit and Kamit thousands of years prior to our migration to West Afuraka/Afuraitkait (Africa) and the subsequent forced-migration by some of us to the western hemisphere.

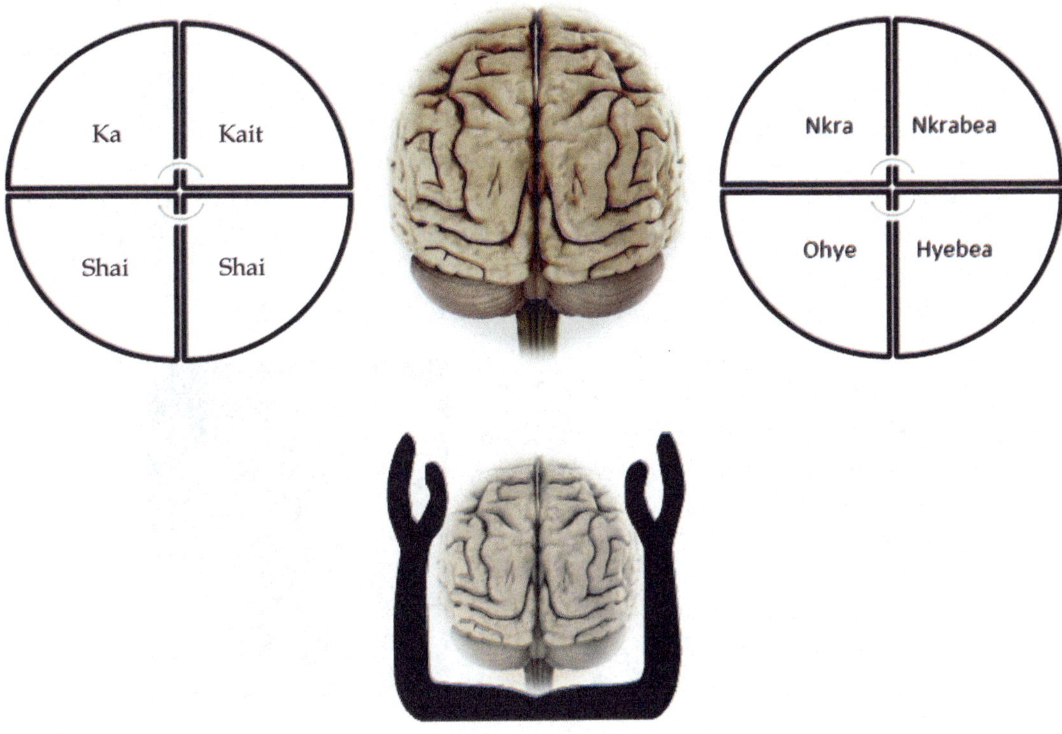

Kuduo

Akan vessel often used as a shrine for the purification of the Okra/Okraa

"..KRA is worshipped; is given offerings. Among some of the Akan tribes each person has an altar for his KRA." [From *'The Akan Concept of the Soul'* by Sam K. Akesson]

"..Yoruba religion focuses on the worship of the òrìsà because of the belief that they act on behalf of Olodumare, who is too exalted to be approached directly. Yet Olodumare is indirectly involved in the day-to-day life of an individual through his/her Ori Inu, which is also called Ori Apere, Asiniwaye (Venerable head, one's guardian spirit in the physical world) (Ladele et al. 1986:42). Thus, in the past, every adult Yoruba dedicated an altar to the Ori Inu. The practice continues today in the rural areas." [From *'Orilonise: The Hermeneutics of the Head and Hairstyles Among the Yoruba'* by Babatunde Lawal]

The Okra or Okraa as our personal Obosom is invoked, *worshipped.* We *ship* or *send* our *words* – our *sound-vibrations* which resound our unique configuration of spiritual energy (hye/hyebea, our *worth*) – to *provoke* the Okra/Okraa in order to solicit a response reflective of our nkra/nkrabea, our Divinely allotted function. This is *word-ship* or *worth-ship.* As evidenced in the quotes above, the practice of establishing a shrine for *communication with* and *purification of* the Okra/Okraa (*Ori Inu* in Yoruba, *Se* in Fon and Ewe, *Chi* in Igbo) had been a common practice amongst Afurakanu/Afuraitkaitnut (Africans) until relatively recently amongst those who have embraced the pseudo-religions of the whites and their offspring and the infection of white culture. Yet, establishing a shrine for the Okra/Okraa has ancient roots. A major shrine-form in Kamit is called **Kara**:

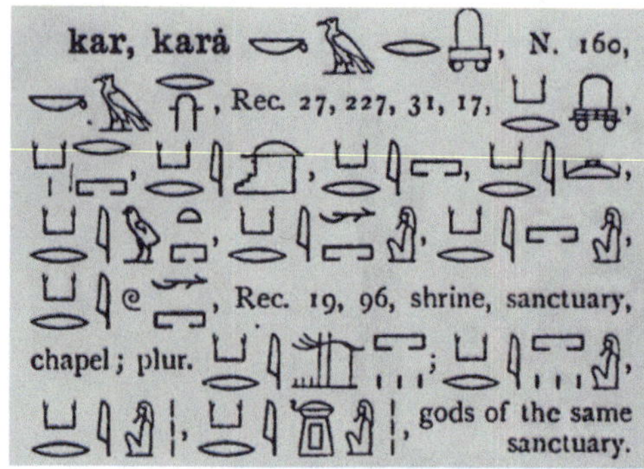

kar, karȧ, N. 160, Rec. 27, 227, 31, 17, Rec. 19, 96, shrine, sanctuary, chapel; plur. gods of the same sanctuary.

There were also sanctuaries, temples and niches within tombs constructed for the Ka/Kait of the deceased individual often served by a class of priests called **Hem Ka** or *servants of the Ka.* The sanctuaries themselves were called **Het Ka** or the *House of the Ka*:

ḥem ka, IV, 1205, Rec. 29, 77, priest of the Ka; plur., IV, 1032.

Ḥe-t Ka, the KA-chapel, or portion of a tomb set apart for the dwelling of the KA.

While the Ka/Kait of the *deceased* individual was appealed to by the *Hem Ka* as well as the people in the *Het Ka*, so did individuals invoke their *own* Ka/Kait regularly *throughout their lives* in order to harmonize with **Amenet-Amen** (**Nyamewaa-Nyame**):

"...Follow your ***ab*** *[heart - will of the Ka/Kait]* *as long as you live. Do not make a loss on what is said. Do not subtract time from following the* ***ab****. It is offensive to the* ***Ka/Kait*** *to waste its time..."* [**Instructions of Ptah Hotep**, c4,500 years ago]

In this excerpt from **Ptah Hotep**, he illuminates the reality that the wasting of time is *offensive* to the Ka/Kait. This is because we are sent into the world specifically to execute our nkra/nkrabea. The Ka/Kait, Okra/Okraa, is the bearer of the nkra/nkrabea. It is therefore the nkra/nkrabea which establishes the *parameters* of harmonious functioning within our life-*time*. Any thoughts, intentions or actions which transgress these parameters necessarily transgress the parameters, the **Nhyehyee** *(Order)*, of **Nyamewaa-Nyame**. Such thoughts, intentions and actions are therefore *offensive* to the Ka/Kait, Okra/Okraa for they are a waste of our *time*. They do not have the support of **Nyamewaa-Nyame**.

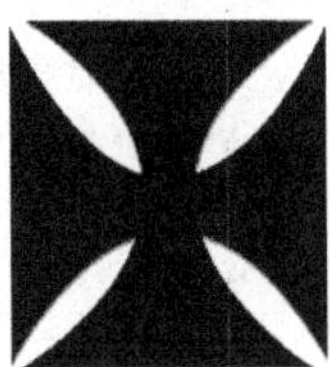

Krapa or **Mmusuyidee**
Akan Adinkra Symbol

Krapa ye ***Nyame*** *ahoboa: ote se okra, okyiri fi na okram fi te se pete nti na Nananom de no yi Mmusuo*

The good Kra (soul) is the preparation of ***Nyame****. It is like a cat (okra), it hates filth and it clears filth like the vulture does. That is why it is used to drive away evil and diseases.* [**Cloth as Metaphor** – G. F. Kojo Arthur]

The **Adinkra** (ah-deen'-krah) symbols of Akan people are used to convey Ancestral wisdom. Each symbol has one or more **mme** (proverbs) associated with it. The **Krapa** (*Kra* – soul, *pa* - good) or **Mmusuyidee** (*mmusu* - evil, *yi* - to remove) adinkra symbol is used ritually as an instrument to remove and repel negative energy from wayward spirits. Because of this practice, the **krapa** or *good soul* adinkra symbol's proverb compares its nature and functioning to that of a *cat*. The title for *cat* in Twi used here is **okra**. Cats are known for constantly cleaning themselves – hating the slightest filth. They are thus a fitting representation of the Okra/Okraa and thus have the name *'okra'*, for the Okra/Okraa does not dwell in disorder. It *repels disorder* and is *incapable of being contaminated*. As an actual Obosom, a Divinity, the Okra/Okraa is an *Embodiment of Divine Order* within the individual. It thus not only hates disorder, but repels disorder. The Okra/Okraa thus functions as our **moral center** within the head. *Morality comes to us directly from* ***Nyamewaa-Nyame*** *through the agency of the Abosom of Law and Balance,* ***Maa*** *and* ***Maat****, and has a center of resonance within the Okra/Okraa.*

"...This symbol was woven into the bedside mat on which the king would step three times for good luck before going to bed... Every year, a ritual (mmusuyidee) was performed. During the period all streets of townships were swept each morning and evening

to remove mystical danger and to prevent disease or death from entering the townships..." **[Cloth as Metaphor (Re) Reading the Adinkra Cloth Symbols of the Akan of Ghana** – G. F. Kojo Arthur]

Note: Two forms of the Obosom **Khensu** (Khonsu) in Kamit – the Hawk-headed form and the Human-headed form. This Obosom is called **Ayensu** in Akan (**Bosomayensu**). **Khensu** is an Obosom of *healing* and is known as *One who drives away evil spirits.* Notice that **Khensu** wears the **krapa** or **mmusuyidee** adinkra symbol around His neck. This demonstrates the cultural continuity of Akanfo from our migration from ancient Khanit and Kamit to West Afuraka/Afuraitkait (Africa). **Khensu** was also called **Khensu Nefer Hetep Heru**. It is **Khensu Heru** from Whom the name 'jesus' was corrupted. **Khensu** (Chayn-soo) was corrupted into jayn-soo, yayn-soo, yeshu, yeshua (so-called hebrew), iesu and iesus (greek), hesus (latin) and later jesus (english). **Khensu Heru** and **Heru** son of **Ausar** and **Auset** are *Two different Abosom.* The *name* of **Khensu** was corrupted into jesu/jesus as well as His *healing powers* (driver out of demons; 'jesus' being of the 'therapeutae' sect, etc.). The *life story* of the fictional character jesus was stolen from **Heru**, son of **Ausar** and **Auset**. The early 'christian' Coptic crosses including those that were carved into the temples of ancient Kamit by white invaders in order to attempt to demonstrate their dominance over the country, were actually in the form of the cross of **Khensu** – the **krapa**. One of the meanings of the name **khns** (khenes) in Kamit is to *'cross over; travel'.*

Left: Defacement of the Temple of **Khensu** by christians with the early 'christian' cross originally the cross of **Khensu**. Middle: Defacement of the Temple in **Paaraka** (Philae) with the early Coptic 'christian' cross.

Right: **Khensu** in mummiform. The cross image can be found on his mummy wrappings. This cross image can be found on other Abosom in mummiform as well.

The character jesus, yeshua, iesu, isa as well as yeshua ben pandera are fictional characters who never existed of any race whatsoever. See our **KUKUU-TUNTUM – The Ancestral Jurisdiction** for details: www.odwirafo.com/kukuutntummpage.html

Although amongst some Afurakanu/Afuraitkaitnut (Africans), the practice of consulting with and purifying the Okra/Okraa (Ori Inu, Se, Chi) has been neglected, especially with the embracing of the false-religions and their fictional gods – christianity, islam, judaism, hinduism and jesus, allah, yahweh and brahmin – it is imperative that Afurakanu/Afuraitkaitnut (Africans) return to these practices, for the consulting with and purifying of the Okra/Okraa is the core of true spirituality. Afurakani/Afuraitkaitnit (African) Ancestral Religion, **Nanasom,** *in all of this varied expressions revolves around our relationship with our Okra/Okraa. The Abosom empower us to align with our Okra/Okraa. The Nananom Nsamanfo (our Spiritually Cultivated Ancestresses and Ancestors) guide us to align with our Okra/Okraa, for the Okra/Okraa is the bearer of the nkra/nkrabea – our very purpose of being. It is the shrine of* ***Ka/Kait****, the Soul of* ***Nyamewaa-Nyame****, within us.*

The Okra/Okraa as stated above is the personal Obosom of the Afurakani/Afuraitkaitnit (African) individual. It is a child of the Great Okra/Okraa (Ka/Kait). When we are given our nkra and nkrabea by **Nyame** and **Nyamewaa**, it was stated that this 'destiny', more properly defined as our Divinely allotted **function** we are to execute in **Abode** (Creation), is encoded within the Okra/Okraa. We also stated that because of the specific manner (bea) in which we must execute our nkra/nkrabea (function), we are *assigned* Abosom Who empower us to do so. The Akanfo relationship with **Nyamewaa-Nyame** defines the manner in which major Abosom are assigned to each individual.

There are Abosom associated with our **Abusua** (matriclan) as well as our **Ntoro** (patriclan). Thus, there is a major Obosom Who governs our mother's blood circle, *an Obosom Who has protected and guided our* ***abusuafo*** *(matriclan members) for millennia.* There is also a major Obosom Who governs our father's blood circle, *an Obosom who has protected and guided our* ***ntorofo*** *(patriclan members) for millennia.* These Abosom are sometimes referred to as the **Abusuabosom** or **Nton-bosom** (**Nton** is a synonym for Abusua – matriclan) and the **Agyabosom** (Agya – *'Father'*) or **Ntorobosom** or simply **Ntoro**, respectively. Just as we receive DNA and thus *physical* and *personality* characteristics from our mother's blood-circle (lineage) and father's blood-circle (lineage) – *so do the sperm and ovum carry the energy of the matricircular (matrilineal) Obosom and the patricircular (patrilineal) Obosom of the mother's clan and father's clan respectively.* These are *clan* Abosom which are *directly related to our Ancestry.*

The Abusua Abosom and Ntoro Abosom are related to the hye and hyebea

There are seven major **mmusuakuo,** *great matricircular (matrilineal) clans* in Akan culture. **Mmusua** is the plural of **abusua.** If one cannot trace his or her Ancestry to one of the seven great Ancestresses of these mmusuakuo, then one is not Akan. The seven major mmusuakuo are: **Asona, Agona, Aduana, Ekuona, Asenie, Brietuo** and **Asakyiri.** There are also variations of these names and sub-groups born of these clans. These seven mmusuakuo are *headed* by seven Great Ancestresses and *governed* by **seven Female Abosom**.

There are twelve **Ntoro,** *patricircular (patrilineal) clan groups,* each governed by its own Obosom in Akan culture. Every Akan person inherits his or her Ntoro or **Agyabosom** (*Father's* Obosom) by virtue of birth. The twelve major Ntoro groups and their related Ntorobosom are: **Bosom Afram, Bosom Pra, Bosom Opo, Bosom Sika, Bosom Akom, Bosom Dwerebe, Bosom Ofin (Afi), Bosom Ayensu, Bosom Muru, Bosom Konsi, Bosom Twe** and **Bosom Krete**. Bosom here refers to the Deity, thus **Bosom Afram** is the Obosom of the River Afram in Ghana. **Bosom Ofin** (often written Bosomafi) is the Obosom of the River Ofin, etc.

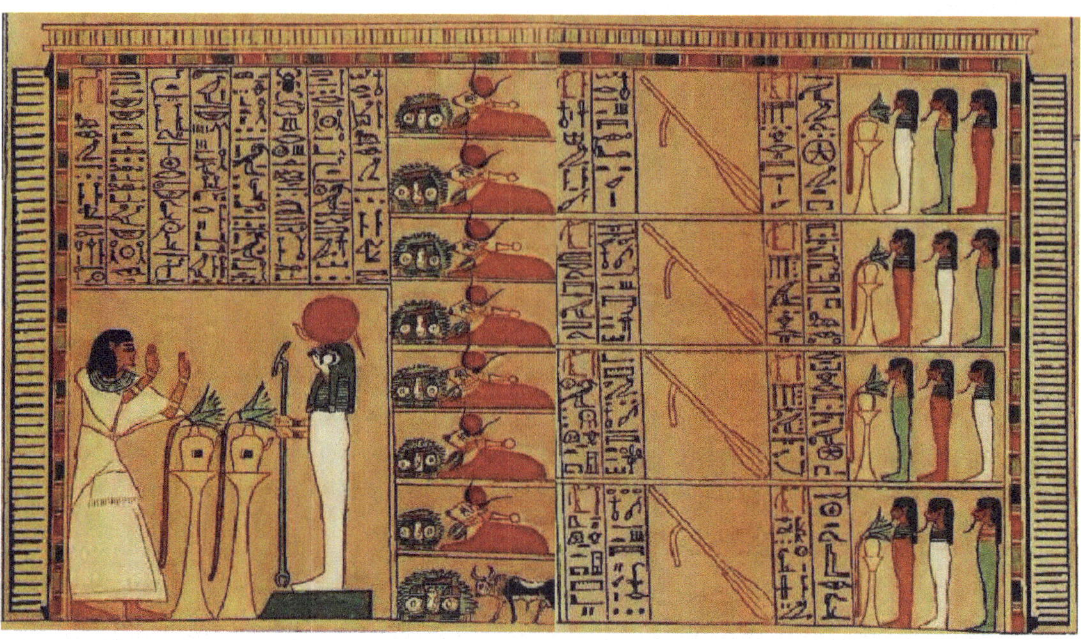

Left: The seven *Nton-Abosom* or *Abusuabosom* in the form of the Seven **Het Heru** Abosom. Here, the Seven **Het Heru** Abosom take the form of Seven Divine Cows. Right: The twelve *Ntoro-bosom* or *Agyabosom*. [*From chapter 148* ***Pert em Heru, Sheft Ani*** *(so-called Egyptian Book of the Dead - Papyrus of Ani)*]

Above: Another depiction of the Seven **Het Heru** Abosom. These Seven Female Abosom actually *govern* the seven Akan Ancestresses who *head* the Seven **Mmusuakuo** – matricircular clans. In ancient Kamit, the Seven **Het Heru** are shown to be present at the birth of the child to announce the child's *'fate'* or *shait/hyebea*. The constellation called *'pleaides'* in european languages is called the **Seven Het Heru** in Kamit *(seven Hathors)*. In Akan this constellation of seven major stars is called *Aberewa na ne mma – The Elderess (Old) Woman and Her Children*. [*From the stele of the Priest Amenemhat*]

For Afurakanu/Afuraitkaitnut (Africans) who are Akan who were forced into enslavement in the western hemisphere, our connection to these **Abusuabosom** and **Agyabosom** is still intact. We were connected to these blood circles *prior* to the **Mmusuo Kese** *(the Great Perversity, enslavement).* We have mixed with other Afurakani/Afuraitkaitnit (African) ethnic groups over the past three centuries after the advent of enslavement. However, our identity is based on **bebra** - Akan for *reincarnation.* Thus, if you were an Akan spirit in Asamando (Ancestral realm) and your descendants were forced to mix with others during the enslavement process, when it is time to reincarnate you will enter a womb where there may have been blood mixture between Akan, Igbo, Bakongo and others. However, you are the *same Akan spirit returning.* **Your blood may be mixed, but your Okra/Okraa is not**. You are the *same* Akan sunsum (spirit) who is connected to the *same* Abusuabosom and Ntoro that you were connected to *prior* to the enslavement era – when you lived on **Asaase** (Earth) as an Akan in Afuraka/Afuraitkait (Africa) in your last incarnation 200 years prior. The connection is unbroken and unbreakable.

The energy of the Agyabosom and Abusuabosom is that which is wielded by the hye and hyebea, respectively. The two lobes/hemispheres of the cerebellum stimulate and direct specific activities in certain parts of the body related to *motor control.* In the same fashion the two *spiritual lobes*, called hye and hyebea, are used by the Okra/Okraa to *activate the inherited power* of the Agyabosom and Abusuabosom.

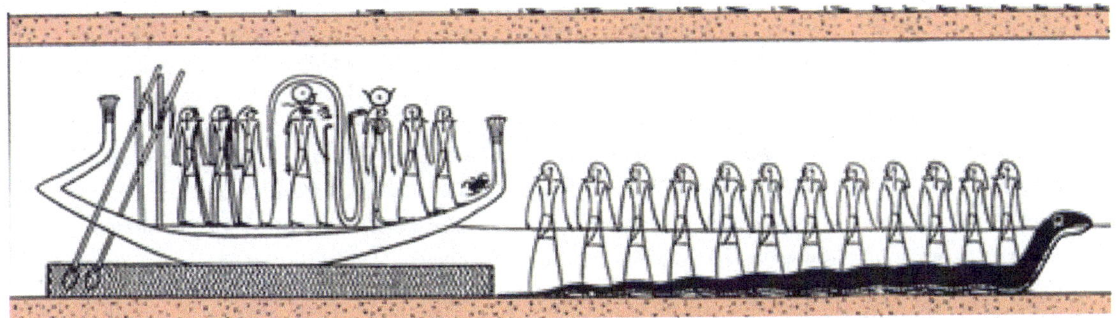

Shat em Duat – Book of the Underworld. Twelfth Hour of the Night

The Creator as Afu Ra in His boat with His attendants. This is the form that **Ra** (**Nyankopon**) takes when operating through the **Aten** (Sun) *during the twelve hours of the night.* **Ra**, operating through the Aten during the day is shown sailing in the boat of the Aten from sunrise to sunset. When the Aten sets, goes underground in the west and into the underworld (Ancestral realm), **Ra** becomes **Afu Ra** and sails through the underworld during the twelve hours of the night. When the boat of **Afu Ra** reaches the east, **Afu Ra** transforms into **Ra** (with the head of a Hawk) and rises inside of the Aten from the eastern horizon and into the sky to begin a new day.

Above is an image of **Afu Ra** sailing in His boat with His attendants in the underworld (**Duat**). This is a depiction of the twelfth hour of the night, the *last region of the underworld* that **Afu Ra** must pass through before being 'reborn' into the sky on the eastern horizon. The twelve Male Abosom who are towing the boat of **Afu Ra** are the twelve **Ntoro** or **Agyabosom**. They are standing upon the great serpent called **Ka en Ankh Ntorou**. The boat of **Afu Ra** will actually *enter the tail of this serpent*, move through its body and *come out of the mouth* being born into the sky as the sunrise of the new day. **Afu Ra** *will thus move through the* **Ka** (Afuraka) in order to appear above the mountain of sunrise. In the same fashion, before we leave Asamando to enter the world as a newborn child, we encounter the twelve Agyabosom who *stand upon the Ka* (Okra/Okraa) and we are assigned to one of these Abosom by **Nyamewaa-Nyame**.

In addition to the **Agyabosom** and **Abusuabosom** Who govern the **hye/hyebea**, there are Abosom Who are directly related to our **nkra/nkrabea**. These are the Abosom Who govern the entire *individual* Okra/Okraa *complex* and are the group of Abosom called the **Akradinbosom** (ah'-krah-deen-boh'-sohm).

OKRA/OKRAA AND THE AKRADINBOSOM

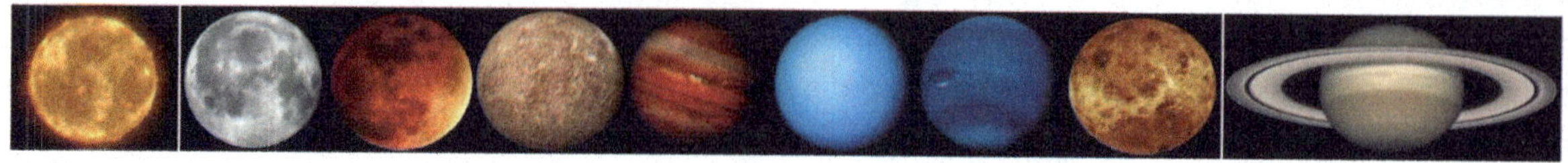

Akanfo govern our lives by the **nnawotwe** the seven-day inclusive week. Each day of the week has its own character, for the days are determined by the solar, lunar and planetary bodies that govern the different days. **There are major Abosom who *animate* these solar, lunar and planetary bodies:**

Day	Eda - Akan Day	Sun, Moon or Planet	Abosom	Akradin
Sunday	Akwesida	Owia *(Sun)*	Awusi and Esi*	Kwesi, Akosua
Monday	Dwooda	Osrane *(Moon)*	Adwo* and Adwoa	Kwadwo, Adwoa
Tuesday	Benada/Abenaada	Bena/Abenaa *(mars)*	Bena and Abenaa	Kwabena, Abenaa
Wednesday	Awukuda/Akuada	Awuku/Akua *(mercury)*	Awuku and Akua	Kweku, Akua
Thursday	Yawda/Yaada/Aabaada	Yaw/Yaa/Aaba *(jupiter, uranus, neptune)*	Yaw, Yaa and Aaba	Yaw, Yaa, Aaba
Friday	Fida	Afi *(venus)*	Afi and Fiifi*	Kofi, Afua
Saturday	Menmeneda	Amen Men *(saturn)*	Amen Men and Amemenewaa*	Kwame, Amma

In Khanit and Kamit, these Abosom are called* ***Ausar* *(Awusi also Adwo),* ***Auset*** *(Esi also Adwoa),* ***Sekhmet*** *(Abenaa),* ***Heru Behudet*** *(Bena),* ***Set*** *(Awuku),* ***Nebt Het*** *(Akua),* ***Heru*** *(Yaw),* ***Wadjet*** *(Yaa),* ***Nekhebet*** *(Aaba),* ***Het Heru*** *(Afi also Amemenewaa) and* ***Amen Men*** *or* ***Min*** *(Amen Men also Fiifi). The* ***Akradin*** *(soul-names) have variations according to dialect. The Akradinbosom are worshipped by all Afurakani/Afuraitkaitnit (African) ethnic groups. Their titles vary in accordance with each language.*

The names of the days of the week in Akan culture are *derived from* the names of the major Abosom Who animate the solar, lunar or planetary body which governs the day. Thus, the planet *Bena* or *Abenaa* is named after and governed by the Male Obosom **Bena** and the Female Obosom **Abenaa** (**Heru Behudet** and **Sekhmet** in Kamit; called **Ogun** and **Iyaami Abeni** in Yoruba). The energy of these major Abosom *animate* this planet *as well as the aspects of* ***Asaase*** *(Earth) and our bodies which resonate with the energy of this planet.* Thus, any Akan person born on that day receives a **kradin** (krah-deen') a *soul-name* (**kra** – *soul*, **din** – *name*): **Kwabena** if male or **Abenaa** if female. The *kradin* or soul-name is automatically given as an acknowledgement of the Obosom Who governs the day the child is born on. Other names are also given in addition to the kradin.

The fact that the child is born on a particular day is a *confirmation* of what took place with the spirit of this Afurakani/Afuraitkaitnit (African) individual *before incarnation.* It is an indication of what Obosom **Nyamewaa-Nyame** *assigned* to the individual after giving the individual his or her Okra/Okraa. Therefore, because **Nyamewaa-Nyame** gave this particular Afurakani/Afuraitkaitnit (African) spirit an Okra/Okraa and then designated **Bena** or **Abenaa** to *guide* the Okra/Okraa of the person in life, this *guaranteed* that the person would be born on the day of **Bena/Abenaa** – *Benada or Abenaada* (tuesday).

Akan people therefore do not 'name our children after the days of the week'. We *acknowledge* that their birth on a particular day is a *message* (nkra) from **Nyamewaa-Nyame** of what Obosom was assigned to the Okra/Okraa *pre-incarnation.* The kradin is not only a soul-name, but the *soul's* name. Again, the Okra or Okraa is an Obosom, an Entity, who dwells within us. In the example above, the kradin or *soul's* name is *Kwabena* (male) or *Abenaa* (female). This means that when the individual prays to/invokes his or her Okra or Okraa, he or she will address his or her Okra/Okraa by *Its* name – Kwabena or Abenaa.

Akan people have soul-names, **akradin**, as well as **din pa** (formal names, surnames) and **mmrane** (praise names). An Akan male with the full name **Kwabena Ogyam Amponsa** has the *kradin*/soul-name Kwabena and a *din pa* Amponsa as well as the *mmrane* **Ogyam**. When Ogyam Amponsa wants to communicate with his Okra, he will refer to his Okra by his Okra's name – Kwabena. He could say, "*Me Kra, Kwabena, kyere me nokware*" meaning "*My Soul, Kwabena, show/teach me truth*". Because *his* soul, whose name is Kwabena, is attached to *his* spirit and dwells within *his* head, people in the community can also call Ogyam Amponsa by his kradin, his ***soul's*** name – Kwabena. This does two things. On one hand, it *refocuses* Ogyam Amponsa on his nkra/nkrabea, in relation to the Abosom **Bena** *every time* someone calls that name or when he contemplates or vocalizes the name himself. *It is an invocation of his Okra.* On the other hand, it is a way to invoke the Obosom **Bena**. Invocation includes *communication* with the Obosom **Bena**, as well as *activating the shrines* in the physical body (immune system) and spirit body (spiritual immune system) that resonate with the energy of **Bena**.

Some Akanfo use the kradin to address an individual on a regular basis. Some Akanfo however rarely use the kradin when addressing someone and typically use the mmrane or din pa – until a situation arises where they seek to gain the attention of, to reprimand or refocus the individual. They will then use the individual's kradin. This is similar to Afurakani/Afuraitkaitnit (African) parents in america who often use the middle and/or nick-names of their children to address them, however, when the children are in trouble or the parents desire to refocus their children they address them by their full *first, middle and last name* – often while raising their voices.

Again, if one is given the nkra/nkrabea (Divine function) which mandates that he or she operate as a healer/healeress, the Okra/Okraa is *encoded* with this information. However, there are many different kinds of healers/healeresses who use *various ritual media* to accomplish their objectives. What *manner* of healer/healeress should the person be? Part of the nkra/nkrabea, the *message, mandate* and *manner* in which the *message/mandate* must be executed is the *assignment* by **Nyamewaa-Nyame** of an Obosom to *guide* the Okra/Okraa of the individual.

Every Okra/Okraa is born of the Great **Ka/Kait**. However, *what kind* of Okra/Okraa is it? What makes this Okra/Okraa *unique* in relation to all others born of the Great **Ka/Kait**? The *assignment* of an Obosom to *guide* the Okra/Okraa defines what kind of Okra/Okraa it is to be. One that will carry out the function **Nyamewaa-Nyame** has allotted to it.

In the example, the individual's Okra was assigned to **Bena** or **Abenaa**. He or she will thus receive the kradin (soul-name) **Kwabena** or **Abenaa**, because he or she will operate in **Abode** (Creation) to support the functions of **Bena** and **Abenaa**. The Abosom **Bena** and **Abenaa** are Warrior and Warrioress Abosom. They are the Divine Spirit-Forces in Creation Who operate as the *Divine Immune System* and *Lymphatic System* within the Great Divine Body of **Nyamewaa-Nyame** and thus the immune and lymphatic systems within the Afurakani/Afuraitkaitnit (African) body. They give us not only our *physical immunity* but our *spiritual immunity*. We attune to the Abosom **Bena** and **Abenaa** in order to *eradicate disorder* in our lives and *enforce Divine Order*. An individual who has been given the nkra/nkrabea (function) to heal, yet is born with his or her Okra/Okraa under the governance of **Bena** or **Abenaa**, means that the *manner* in which they will affect the healing process – *execute their nkra/nkrabea* – will necessarily be through a **fiery** medium. At the same time, their *fiery approach* to healing as defined by **Nyamewaa-Nyame** through the assignment of the **Kradinbosom** (**Bena** or **Abenaa**) will be *further conditioned* by their matrilineally and patrilineally *inherited* Abosom, the Abusuabosom and Agyabosom.

The *DNA* and *spiritual* characteristics that the individual has received/inherited from his or her mother, from his or her father, from the Obosom Who governs his or her mother's blood circle, from the Obosom Who governs his or her father's blood circle as well as the *character* of the Obosom Who governs his or her Okra/Okraa *combine* to produce a *unique individual* with a *unique approach* to healing, although utilizing the energy of **Bena** and **Abenaa** Whom many other Akanfo are born under as well. See the images below:

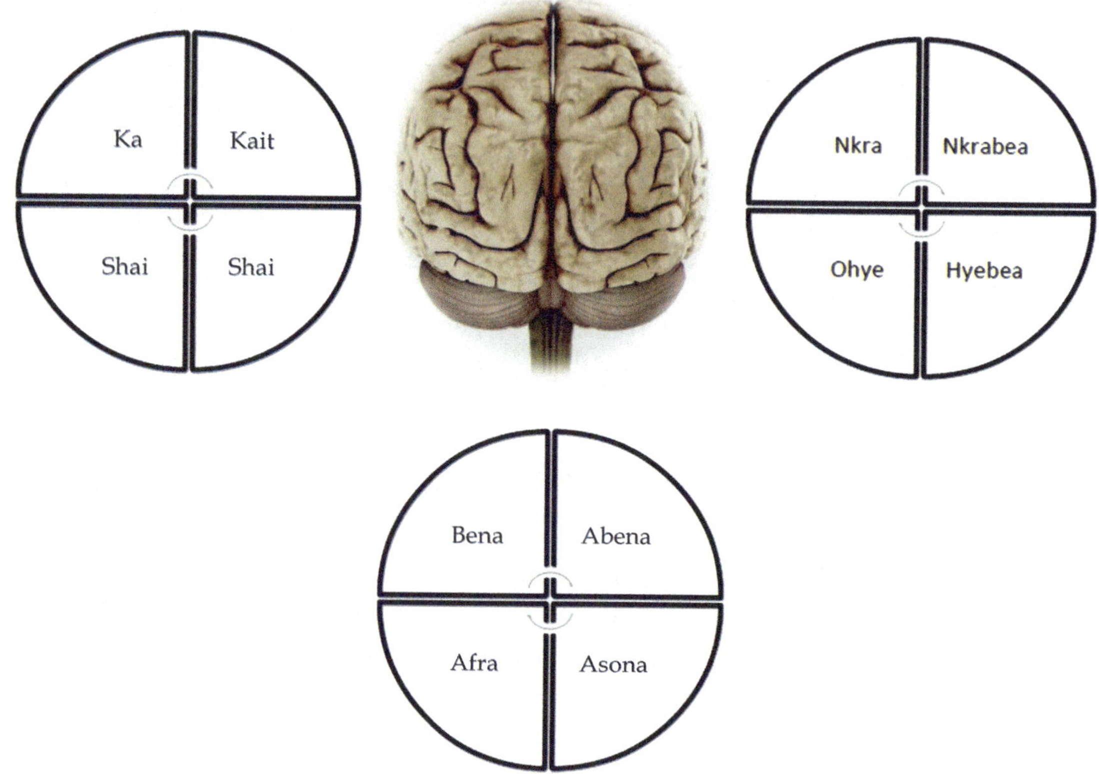

Okra of Kwabena Ogyam Amponsa

In the example of Kwabena Ogyam Amponsa, as a sunsum (spirit) prior to incarnation he stands before **Nyamewaa-Nyame (Amenet-Amen)** and receives an nkra/nkrabea and hye/hyebea – a *function* to execute in the world and a *motive capacity* necessary to successfully fulfill that function. **Nyamewaa-Nyame** directs **Ka/Kait** to send one of their offspring to dwell with this sunsum. Ka/Kait thus send a Ka (an Okra), an Obosom, One of their children, to connect with the sunsum. This Ka (Okra) becomes the *bearer* of the nkra/nkrabea, hye/hyebea functioning as a spirit-brain – the *head* of the sunsum, just as the physical brain is made to be the *control center*, the *administrative head*, for the various organs and organs' systems of the body.

At this point, the sunsum (spirit) has been given nkra/nkrabea, hye/hyebea. His function is to be a healer, however **Nyamewaa-Nyame** orders that he heal *through the energy of fire* and the *Divine Immune System* of **Nyamewaa-Nyame**. **Nyamewaa-Nyame** therefore *directs* the Abosom **Bena** and **Abenaa** to *guide* the Okra (Ka) sent by Ka/Kait, for **Bena** and **Abenaa** are the *Divine Immunity* and *Lymphatic System* within the Great Divine Body of **Nyamewaa-Nyame**. The individual does not have a 'generic' Okra - a non-descript 'globe' of energy dwelling in his head region. He has an Okra governed by Fiery Abosom – *an Okra with a certain character within which the nkra/nkrabea is rooted.*

Light is white when it emanates from the **Owia** (Sun). However, if the light shines through a stained glass window with different colors, the light will be *conditioned.* On the other side of the window, the light will appear to manifest in different colors. Moreover, because of this conditioned light, the vibratory waves that we receive from the light will reflect the conditioning. The different vibratory frequencies of the colors white, green, blue, red, yellow, purple, orange, etc. have different effects upon our physical organs, organs' systems and our electromagnetic fields or *aura* (**khaibit** in Kamit).

When Ka/Kait sends one of their children to dwell with us as our personal Obosom within our heads, this Obosom, our Okra/Okraa, receives *guidance* from **Nyamewaa-Nyame** – *through the agency of the Abosom* ***Nyamewaa-Nyame*** *assigns to it by nature of the allotted function.* The Okra/Okraa is guided by this **Kradinbosom**.

In the example, **Nyamewaa-Nyame** orders that the individual is to function as an 'immune system cell' in **Abode** (Creation). He is to be a healer, *but specifically a healer who operates through a fiery, energic medium.* This is his *function* and the *manner* in which he must execute that function (nkra/nkrabea). In order to operate through the fiery, energic medium related to Divine Immunity, Enforcement of Divine Order, etc. **Nyamewaa-Nyame** *must assign* the Abosom Who govern this aspect of Creation, **Abenaa** and **Bena**, to the Okra.

The individual sunsum (spirit) now has an Okra who will dwell with him. What kind of Okra? One that is *guided* (conditioned) by the fiery Abosom **Bena** and **Abenaa**. His nkra and nkrabea are therefore necessarily *conditioned* by **Bena** and **Abenaa**. Typically, males will be more influenced by the male Kradinbosom throughout their lives while females will be more influenced by the female Kradinbosom throughout their lives. Although one is dominant, we acknowledge both. In this example, this individual sunsum, who will take on the *kradin* – **Kwabena** – will be guided by **Bena** and **Abenaa** throughout his life, however, **Bena** will be dominant and thus recognized and approached ritually as his **Kradinbosom**.

When the individual communicates with his Okra, asks his Okra for guidance throughout his life, his Okra (whose name is Kwabena) will communicate to the individual, Ogyam Amponsa, direction based on what was *encoded into the Okra* by **Nyamewaa-Nyame** in the beginning. Ogyam Amponsa's Okra will communicate with him in a manner that reflects Its nature as an Okra conditioned by the fiery energy of **Bena**.

Ogyam Amponsa will communicate with his Okra regularly, yet he will also periodically communicate with **Bena** and **Abenaa** as well. This is akin to an individual communicating with his *father* for guidance regularly, yet periodically communicating with his *father's parents* (his grandmother and grandfather) for guidance as well, understanding that they have a key role as **Mpanyinfo** (Elder/Elderess) in his life also.

The individual sunsum has an Okra whose *consciousness* is born of **Bena** and **Abenaa**. However, there are many individuals in the community who have Okra/Okraa governed by **Abenaa** and **Bena**. The individual must be born through a specific *blood circle* which *further conditions* and *defines* the nature and character of the individual sunsum (spirit). **Nyamewaa-Nyame** assigns him to the Female Obosom Who governs the **Asona** abusua (matriclan) and to Bosom **Afram**, the Male Obosom Who governs the Afram Ntoro (patriclan group). **Nyamewaa-Nyame** have now encoded within the Okra complex of the individual sunsum a specific configuration of spiritual energy, hye and hyebea, to execute the healing function throughout his life in harmony with the nkra and nkrabea.

Some whose Okra is governed by **Bena** and are ordered to be healers by **Nyamewaa-Nyame**, will heal through the use of *metal implements* (surgery). Others will heal through the use of *laying hands/energic healing.* Both are engaged in the healing process under the *guidance of* ***Bena***, however they have *different means* of achieving the healing objective/function. The different means are *determined* by **Nyamewaa-Nyame**. This is why the individual is *assigned* to the matrilineal and patrilineal Abosom which *define* how the individual will *employ his or her* ***motive force*** – his or her hye/hyebea.

Because **Nyamewaa-Nyame** assigned the Abusabosom of **Asona** and the Agyabosom **Afram** to the hye/hyebea of the person, the person will return to the world through the Asona abusua (clan) and the Bosom Afram Ntoro (clan group). **Nyamewaa-Nyame** thus directs the sunsum (spirit) towards a member of his family (one of his descendants) who is living upon **Asaase** (Earth), who is from the Asona abusua and who has married a member of the Bosom Afram Ntoro. They will be the future parents of the individual. The individual spirit is drawn into the womb from Asamando (Ancestral realm) and born into the world 40 weeks later. The parents, taking note of the *day* the child is born the *gender* of the child, *acknowledge* his kradin to be Kwabena. As they experience the energy and consciousness of their newborn-*returning Ancestor*, they are naturally drawn by **Nyamewaa-Nyame** to give him the name **Ogyam Amponsa** – names which carry the energy of his nkra/nkrabea and hye/hyebea.

His parents will refer to him as Kwabena, Kwabena Amponsa, Ogyam, Ogyam Amponsa, Kwabena Ogyam Amponsa, etc. As he grows older, he will learn how to formally *communicate with* and *purify* his Okra. Ogyam Amponsa will establish a **Kradinbosonkommere**, an **nkommere** (shrine) which will serve as a shrine for his personal Obosom/his Okra (Kwabena) and for his Kradinbosom – **Bena** (**Heru Behudet**). On his **krada** (*soul-day*), the day he came into the world, **Benada** (**Bena**'s **da** (day) or tuesday), Ogyam Amponsa will set aside time to go to his **nkommere** (shrine), purify his Okra (Kwabena) and communicate with It. He will *also* take time to communicate with the Great Obosom **Bena**.

In ***Aakhuamuman Amaruka Atifi Mu****, Akwamu Nation in North America, we coined and utilize the term* ***nkommere*** *for 'shrine' and employ the* ***Kradinbosonkommere*** *to communicate with* ***both*** *the Okra/Okraa as well as the* ***Kradinbosom****. This practice is reflective of the most important formative event of our existence - our being assigned an Okra/Okraa by* ***Nyamewaa-Nyame*** *and our Okra/Okraa being assigned to an Obosom by* ***Nyamewaa-Nyame****, concurrently, prior to our incarnation into the world. That experience is replicated in the ritual purification of and communication with our Okra/Okraa and Kradinbosom at the Kradinbosonkommere.*

Nkonsonkonson (links - common bond)

"...another important indicator of an ***Akan presence*** *is readily evident in the trial records generated in the aftermath of the 1712 [****New York slave] revolt****. Of the 21 Africans facing criminal charges in connection with the uprising, 9 had* ***Akan day names****..."*
[From *'Conjure, Magic, and Power: The Influence of Afro-Atlantic Religious Practices on Slave Resistance and Rebellion'* – *W. Rucker*]

In ***Yoruba*** *culture, the* ***Ori Inu, Ayanmo, Kadara, Akunleyan*** *and* ***Akunlegba*** *have their cognates in the Akan Okra/Okraa, Nkrabea, Nkra, Hye and Hyebea. The* ***Iponri*** *is related to the* ***Great Ka/Kait*** *(Soul in 'Heaven') while the* ***Ipori*** *- Ancestral energy from the father's and mother's side connected to the right and left big toe - is related to the Hye and Hyebea.*

In ***Ewe*** *and* ***Fon*** *culture (****Vodoun****), the* ***Se*** *or* ***Se Lido*** *is cognate with the Okra/Okraa. The* ***Se Kpoli*** *is related to the Nkra and Nkrabea, while the* ***Se Fawesagu*** *is related to the Hye and Hyebea.*

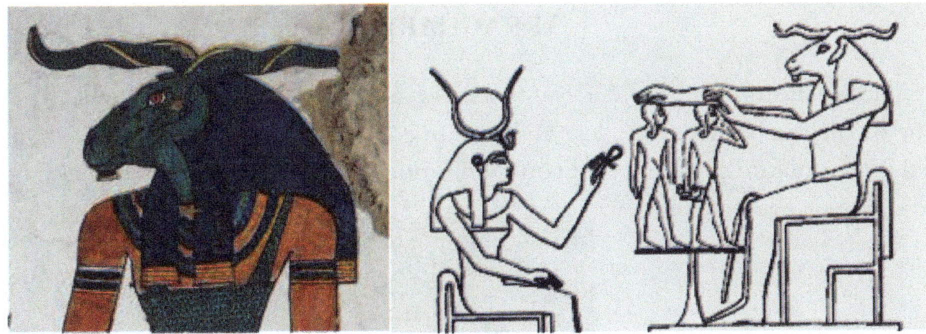

Note: The ram-headed Obosom **Khunem** (**Khnum**) fashioning the *body and* ***Ka*** of the individual on His *Divine potter's wheel.* When **Ka/Kait** send one of Their children to become the personal Ka/Kait (Okra/Okraa) of the individual spirit, **Amenet-Amen** directs **Khunem** to *fashion* the Ka/Kait (Okra/Okraa) according to Its nkra/nkrabea and to also fashion the *body* in a form which reflects the Ka/Kait. *Note that the term 'oku-**kunwem**-fo' is the term for 'potter' in Akan.*

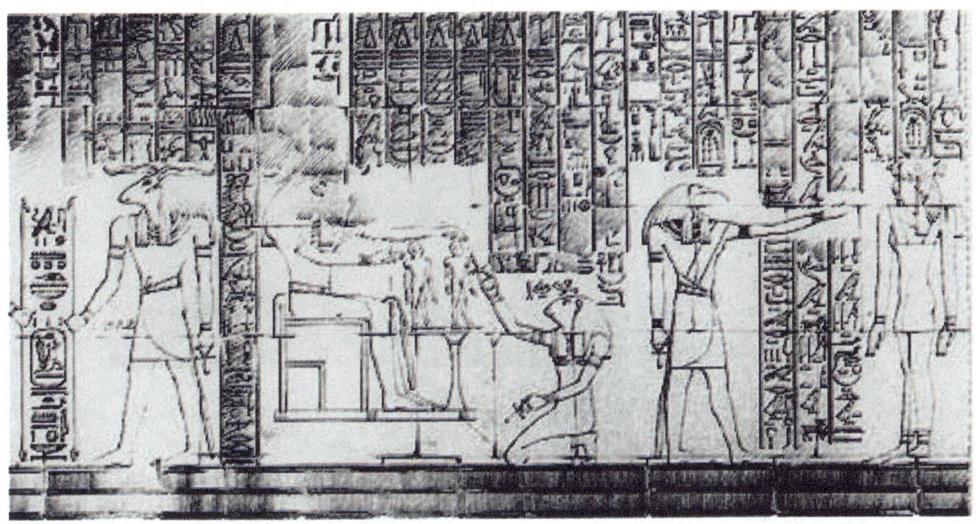

*"...**Amen-Ra** [**Nyame** in Akan] called for **Khunem**, the creator, the fashioner of the bodies of men. "Fashion for me the body of my daughter and the body of her **Ka**," said **Amen-Ra**, "A great queen will I make of her, and honor and power will be worthy of her dignity and glory."*

*"O **Amen-Ra**," answered **Khunem**, "It will be done as you have said. The beauty of your daughter will surpass that of the **Ntorou/Ntorotu** (Deities) and will be worthy of her dignity and glory."*

*So **Khunem** fashioned the body of **Amen-Ra**'s daughter and the body of her **Ka**, the two forms exactly alike and more beautiful than the daughters of men. He fashioned them of clay with the air of his potter's wheel and **Heqet**, Ntorot (Goddess) of birth, knelt by his side holding the **ankh** towards the clay that the bodies of Hatshepsut and her **Ka** might be filled with the breath of life..."*

[From the Mortuary Temple of the Queen Hatshepsut]

AKRAGUARE

The Akan observance of **akraguare** *(soul washing/purification)* is conducted to 'clean the head' of the individual ritually, so that he or she can have a more clear and precise communication with his or her Okra/Okraa. This purificatory ritual is prerequisite to meaningful communication/dialogue with our personal Obosom.

Akan Kente Cloth design: **Asasia Puduo**

*'**Puduo** or **kuduo**, are cast brass vessels used in rites to sustain the family. Early examples of these vessels had small **pyramids** on their lids, and this might explain the pyramidal shape of the puduo design. **Asasia**, the most elaborate kente cloths, were reserved for the Asantehene (King) alone.'* [http://www.twi.bb/akan-kente.php]

*Two versions of **kuduo** and **puduo** (left, middle) and a **kara** shrine from Kamit (right). Kuduo are used to store sacred items including **sika**, **sika futuro** (gold and gold dust), **ahwene** (beads) and more. The **kuduo** is also used in purificatory rituals for the Okra/Okraa and is a shrine for the Okra/Okraa. It is therefore buried with the individual upon death or placed in front of the blackened **agua** (eh-gwah') – the seat used by the deceased during his or her life which is subsequently used as a shrine for Ancestral communication:*

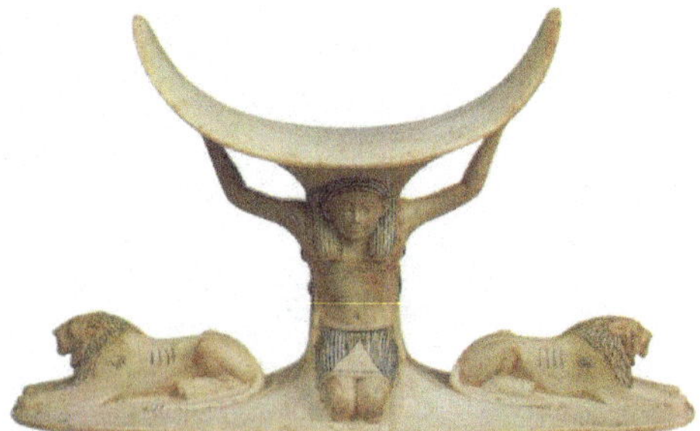

Ures - *Khanit/Kamit*

Agua (Adwa) - *Akan*

*Above left is an **ures** from ancient Kamit. Above right is an **agua (adwa)**, an Akan seat (misnomered 'stool'). The Akan agua is the seat/throne used to 'elevate' heads of families (mmusua) and heads of state (oman). Upon the death of the owner, the agua is ritually blackened (**tuntum** – black, **tumi** – power) and used as a shrine to communicate with the deceased. The ures in Kamit was used as a headrest – 'elevating the head' during the sleep state as the sunsum visits **Asamando** (Ancestral realm). The Akan agua is derived directly from the ures of Khanit and Kamit. The arms are the arms of the Ka/Kait. The 'elevation of the head' is the elevation of the Okra/Okraa.*

'...In the past, Kuduos, with or without jewelry, were often placed inside the grave or on top of the grave superstructure. Also Kuduos were used as containers to hold ritual offerings presented to ancestors and deities at shrines. Kuduos were exhibited in stool rooms and at festivals. Kuduos sometimes served as vessels containing 'holy water' used in the ritual purification of a chief's soul. During female puberty rites and rites for twins in Akan society, Kuduos were used as containers for mashed yam and eggs...' [From the Ghana National Commission on Culture: www.ghanaculture.gov.gh]

The ***kuduo*** *is used as a container of the water which is used to ritually* ***guare*** *(dwaree – wash) the Okra/Okraa.* ***Apae*** *(prayers) are used to invoke the Ntoro or Agyabosom to activate the healing/cleansing properties of the water. Many of the Ntoro operate through bodies of water (rivers, lakes, the Ocean). Traditionally, we would therefore conduct akraguare in the actual river or body of water of our Ntoro. For example, if our Ntoro is* ***Bosom Afram****, the Obosom operating through the river Afram in Ghana, we would go to that river and use its water for akraguare. For those of us outside of Afuraka/Afuraitkait (Africa), we can conduct akraguare in a river or body of water in our locale and invoke our Ntoro to come and dwell in that body of water. We also conduct akraguare at the* ***Kradinbosonkommere*** *inviting our Ntoro to infuse Its* ***tumi*** *(Divine power) into the water within the kuduo (we can use a bowl as our kuduo). The* ***nsuo*** *(water), now activated, is used to ritually cleanse the head, the shrine of the Okra/Okraa within the body. The purified water acts as an 'electromagnetic cleansing agent', removing, repelling negative entities, vibrations, false conditionings, disorder, etc. from the orbit of the Okra/Okraa so that our communication with our Okra/Okraa is clear. After washing (guare) the Okra/Okraa, we sit and consult with the Okra/Okraa on issues concerning our harmonious functioning in* ***Awiase****. We subsequently consult with our* ***Kradinbosom****.*

[This is a basic approach to *akraguare (akradwaree)* as conducted in **Aakhuamuman Amaruka Atifi Mu**, *Akwamu Nation in North America*. There are variations of the practice of *akraguare* amongst Akanfo of different groups *(Bono, Asante, etc.)*]

The Akan individual understands that his or her very purpose for being is encoded within his or her Okra/Okraa complex. Alignment and realignment of every thought, intention and action with the Okra/Okraa is thus our anchor in **Nyamewaa-Nyame Nhyehyee** (Divine Order) – *our anchor in reality*. Said alignment is the ultimate focus of all ritual practice because it is, fundamentally, our endeavor to maintain our alignment with **Nyamewaa-Nyame**. The Abosom *empower us* and the Nananom Nsamanfo *guide us* to align our thoughts, intentions and actions with our Okra/Okraa and hence with **Nyamewaa-Nyame**.

The Okra/Okraa as an Obosom is an *Embodiment of Divine Order*. **Nyamewaa-Nyame Nhyehyee** or Divine Order is comprised of Two Complementary Poles: **Mmara ne Kyi – Divine Law and Divine Hate**. Through *mmara* (law) we learn who and what to *accept* into our lives – that which will allow us to harmonize with **Nyamewaa-Nyame**. Through *kyi* (hate) we learn who and what to *reject* from our lives – that which would otherwise create disharmony with **Nyamewaa-Nyame**. *Mmara ne Kyi*, Divine Law (Love) and Divine Hate – and the Abosom of Law (**Maa** and **Maat**) and the Abosom of Hate (**Bena** and **Abenaa/Heru Behudet** and **Sekhmet**), keep us in alignment with our **amammere** (culture).

Amammere is composed of *oman* (nation) and *bere* (way, manner). *Amammere* meaning *'way of the nation/people'* as a description of culture is defined by Afurakanu/Afuraitkaitnut (Africans) worldwide as the *Divine Acceptance of Order and the Divine Rejection of Disorder.* As we live each day to execute our Divine function, nkra/nkrabea, given to us by **Nyamewaa-Nyame**, we must recognize *who and what to accept* (law/love) and *who and what to reject* (hate). The body's respiratory system and circulatory system draw in (accept) nutrients from the atmosphere as well as the foods that we consume. Yet, toxins are drawn in as well. The immune system and lymphatic system function to reject/hate/repel those toxins as well as cancerous cells developing within, which left unchecked, would destroy the body. The body's *culture* of acceptance and rejection is a reflection of the *culture* of the Great Divine Body of **Nyamewaa-Nyame**. **Nyamewaa-Nyame** have given us culture, amammere, *specific instructions/function* and a *manner* (bea, bere) in which to execute that function.

Our adherence to amammere, culture, is the embrace of **Nanasom** (Afurakani/Afuraitkaitnit Ancestral Religion), for **Nanasom** animates **Amammere**, *Religion animates Culture.* When we adhere to our Divinely allotted function, our nkra/nkrabea, we are thus adhering to our *Divinely given amammere.* We are fulfilling our individual nkra/nkrabea and are thus qualified to function harmoniously within the *communal/collective* nkra/nkrabea. This is the foundation of **Amansesew.** The term *amansesew* is composed of *oman* (nation) and **sesew** (building; restoration). Amansesew is thus *Afurakani/Afuraitkaitnit (African) Nationbuilding/Restoration.*

***Nanasom, Amammere** and **Amansesew** – Afurakani/Afuraitkaitnit (African) Ancestral Religion, Culture and Nationbuilding/Restoration, are the structural components of the Divine **ahinasa** (triangle) of **Amannee** – our Ancestral customs and traditions. **Amannee,** the **nnee** (things) of the **oman** (nation), defines the totality of our functioning as component parts of a system, our collective **nkra/nkrabea,** established by **Nyamewaa-Nyame**.*

Because the Okra/Okraa does not dwell in disorder, thoughts, intentions and actions which are reflective of disorder are repulsive to the Okra/Okraa, for they are naturally repulsive to **Nyamewaa-Nyame**. Disorder is not the opposite or complement of Order – **Nyamewaa-Nyame Nhyehyee**. Disorder is the *perversion* of the Created Order. This is why **Nyamewaa-Nyame** created Abosom to exercise the *Divine Immune Response,* **Bena** and **Abenaa**, to eradicate disorder and its purveyors, so that the integrity of the Divine Order is maintained in **Abode** – the Universe, the Created *Order.*

***Nhyehyee,** Order, by definition delineates the reality that some things, objects, deeds and entities are acceptable and some things, objects, deeds and entities are not acceptable.*

Success, happiness, joy, peace, fulfillment, balance, etc. in reality are manifestations of our *alignment* with our Okra/Okraa. When we align or realign with our personal Obosom, we realign with our function as well as the spiritual energy we have inherited to execute our function. *This internal alignment is impervious to disorder, anxiety, misguided fear, misguided frustration, depression, etc. streaming in from outside influences, physical or non-physical and/or from internalized conditionings rooted in misinformation.*

Every perceived obstacle that we face can be overcome through our alignment with our Okra/Okraa, for through this alignment we are able to access the Consciousness and Power of Nyamewaa-Nyame inscribed within our Okra/Okraa complex.

The manner in which we structure and defend our lives, structure and defend our families, structure and defend our communities and our **oman** (Afurakani/Afuraitkaitnit (African) nation) is rooted in our *individual* nkra/nkrabea as well as the *collective* nkra/nkrabea shared by Afurakanu/Afuraitkaitnut (Africans) – *and only*

Afurakanu/Afuraitkaitnut (Africans) – worldwide. It is for these reasons that the communication with and purification of the Okra/Okraa is central to our individual and communal well-being.

Akan Adinkra Symbol of ***Ohene Kra Konmuade*** *and an actual depiction of* ***Ohene Kra Konmuade***

The ***Ohenekrakonmuade,*** *typically called* ***Akrafokonmu,*** *is worn by the* ***akraguarefo*** *or* ***akrafo*** *('soul-washing people' or 'soul people'). The akraguarefo or akrafo are individuals whose major function is to perform the ritual purification or 'washing' (guare) of the Okra of the Ohene (King). The Ohene is the representative of the oman (nation) to the Nananom Nsamanfo (Honored Ancestresses and Ancestors). The Ohemmaa (Queenmother) is the representative of the Nananom Nsamanfo to the people. The guare, washing/cleansing, of the Okra or Okraa of the Ohene and Ohemmaa is thus the ritual purification of the Okra/Okraa of the oman (nation, people). The gold disc is worn as a pendant on the necklace of the akraguarefo or akrafo. Notice this version of the ohenekrakonmuade or akrafokonmu has the four-fold division which delineates the nkra/nkrabea and hye/hyebea.*

Ohenekrakonmuade *and the* ***Nut*** *(****Niwt****) Metut*

The metut (hieroglyph) for 'town, city, nation' is the ***nut*** *(****niwt****) symbol shown above. The term* ***nut*** *meaning 'nation' is related to* ***oman*** *in Akan meaning 'nation, people'. The nut symbol referencing nation also references a* ***government****. The* ***Ohenekrakonmuade*** *references self-governance (nkra, nkrabea, hye, hyebea), as well as communal governance, for the guare (washing) of the Okra/Okraa is executed for the stability of the individual as well as the society, nation – through the guare (washing) of the Okra/Okraa of the Ohene and Ohemmaa.*

Above center: The original zodiac from the Temple of ***Het Heru*** *at Denderah and a drawing of the zodiac. The zodiac references the* ***governing forces,*** *celestial bodies – shrines of the major* ***Abosom*** *– in* ***Abode*** *(Creation). It is from this representation that the nut (niwt) metut and the ohenekrakonmuade are derived. They all reference the purification and governance of self, nation and the Universe.*

Akan Adinkra Symbol – ***Sankofa***

Se wo were fi, na wo sankofa, yenkyi – If you forget and you return, go and grasp (from the Ancestral past) it is not taboo

When we engage in disorder, we make ourselves repulsive to **Nyamewaa-Nyame**, the **Abosom**, the **Nananom Nsamanfo** and our **Okra/Okraa**. If we continue to dwell in disorder the Okra/Okraa is repelled, similar to the repulsion of two magnets being placed together on a table with the same polarities facing one another. Until you *reverse the polarities*, the magnets will automatically repel. Until we *reject disorder* and realign with Order, the Okra/Okraa is repulsed and repelled. In this condition we can manifest *temporary* **odam** (psychosis). *Indeed, psychosis is properly defined fundamentally as disalignment from the Okra/Okraa.*

If one *continues* to dwell in disordered thoughts, intentions and actions with *deliberate effort* the Okra/Okraa will detach from the individual. In Akan culture it is said in such an instance, *"Ne kra eguane"* meaning *'his Okra has fled from him'*. This is a grave situation which must be addressed ritually. If the individual does not ritually restore Order to himself or herself and draw his or her Okra/Okraa back to his or her sunsum (spirit), the Okra/Okraa will return to **Nyamewaa-Nyame** never to return to the individual. There are three conditions that can befall the individual who suffers this permanent detachment from and departure of the Okra/Okraa:

1) The individual will face **imminent death**

2) The individual will not die, but will manifest permanent **odam** *(madness - insanity, various forms of psychosis including* <u>*certain expressions*</u> *of what is called schizophrenia, schizoaffective disorder, bi-polar disorder, other so-called axis I diagnoses, etc.)*

[Some expressions of 'psychosis' are simply caused by the influence of discarnate spirits and can be easily and swiftly neutralized. Others however are truly manifestations of a *permanent detachment* from the Okra/Okraa]

3) The individual will manifest **extreme anti-social behavior** – *externalized* **odam** *(committing murder, rape, child molestation, various forms of criminality, various other forms of perversity including sexual deviance – homosexuality/dissexuality, criminal dishonesty, intellectual dishonesty, spiritual perversity, oppressing other people and entities, displaying so-called psychopathic behavior and anti-social personality disorder, etc.)*

[While some forms of **odam** (psychosis) can be *internalized* – self-destructive, self-mutilating behaviors, suicidal, etc. some forms of odam are *externalized* – affecting the individual as well as others. *Homosexuality/dissexuality* is an example of *externalized* odam – a disalignment from the Okra/Okraa which manifests in the individual and motivates the individual to conscript others into the odam (psychosis). *Homosexuality/dissexuality resulting from an Afurakani/Afuraitkaitnit (African) individual being victimized (e.g. molested as a child) can be a form of temporary odam, detachment of the Okra/Okraa which can be corrected by realigning with the Okra/Okraa ritually. Otherwise the Okra/Okraa will permanently detach and the odam becomes permanent.*]

The sunsum without an Okra/Okraa is like a body without a brain. The individual manifesting this condition thus becomes a disordered *'living corpse'*.

*Indeed, this is the nature/condition of **all** of the whites and their offspring – all non-Afurakanu/non-Afuraitkaitnut (non-Africans~non-Blacks). They are spirits without Okra/Okraa and manifest the disposition of individuals in categories 2 and 3 listed above. Because they have no Okra/Okraa, they **incarnate** as spirits of disorder and will continue to manifest the same behaviors that they have displayed for thousands of years until they become extinct.*

Neglect of the Okra/Okraa by Afurakanu/Afuraitkaitnut (Africans) can lead to disalignment from the Okra/Okraa and the manifestation of temporary odam (psychosis). In such a state we become susceptible to the negative influences of discarnate, wayward, earthbound spirits. Such discarnate spirits who were lustful, misguided and/or malicious in life, continue such behavior after their deaths. Having been denied access to Asamando, they dwell in various areas including homes, forests, near rivers, near the places where they died or were murdered, etc. Such deceased spirits can be blood-related or unrelated. When we neglect our Okra/Okraa or become disaligned from our Okra/Okraa we no longer wield the compulsive/impulsive force of hye/hyebea and thus the energy of the Abusuabosom and Ntoro/Agyabosom. We are no longer attuned to our nkra/nkrabea, our function in the world and our Kradinbosom. We therefore receive misguidance from perverse discarnate spirits as well as the thought projections, manipulations, etc. from our living enemies. We often internalize these projections as perverse conditionings upon and within our sunsum (spirit).

This is how some Afurakanu/Afuraitkaitnut (Africans) were easily programmed by the pseudo-religions of the whites and their offspring and began to foolishly accept the fictional characters such as: jesus, allah, yahweh, moses, aaron, solomon, sheba, menelik, abraham, isaac, ishmael, jacob, esau, david, melchizedek, muhammad, bilal, buddha, brahmin, etc. and the pseudo-'holy books' associated with them. **None of these characters existed of any race whatsoever.** The whites and their offspring know this, for they created these characters in order to enslave the spirits of Afurakanu/Afuraitkaitnut (Africans). They desire for us to cease the worship of our own Okra/Okraa – our anchor in Divine Order – **and replace it with a perverse 'worship' of the whites and their offspring themselves – the pseudo-worship of spirits of disorder**.

*The formation of the pseudo-religions and their fictional characters by the whites and their offspring was designed specifically for the purpose of influencing Afurakanu/Afuraitkaitnut (Africans) to divorce ourselves from our Okra/Okraa, from **Nyamewaa-Nyame**, from **Nhyehyee** (Order) and therefore compromise our sanity – to create the conditions for the manifestation of odam within us.*

Embracing the pseudo-religions and their false 'gods' and fictional characters is also the incorporation of the pseudo-philosophy and pseudo-cosmology which *define* these perversions. Afurakanu/Afuraitkaitnut (Africans) who embrace these pseudo-religious practices thus lose the discernment of who and what to accept and who and what to reject - who and what to be in law (love) with and who and what to hate. *We lose consciousness* and thus the consciousness of **Nyamewaa-Nyame Nhyehyee** (Divine Order) which is *comprised* of Divine Law and Divine Hate. Like an individual with a compromised immune system, we now accept *'all'* and reject/hate *'none'*. We therefore accept the ingesting of poison and suffer the repercussions – disease and death – individually and communally.

Afurakanu/Afuraitkaitnut (Africans) embracing *christianity, islam, judaism, hinduism, vedanta, jainism, taoism, buddhism, kabbalism, european pseudo-esotericism, hermeticism, atheism, humanism, bahaism, socialism, extraterrestrialism, drug-addict 'spiritualism', sex-cult 'spiritualism', universalism, new age 'spirituality', lost-landism (mu, lemuria, atlantis, etc.), etc.* are Afurakanu/Afuraitkaitnut (Africans) who are disaligned from their Okra/Okraa and manifest **odam** (psychosis) – disalignment from reality. This manifestation of odam can be *temporary* or become *permanent* – depending upon the ritual measures taken by the individual.

Moreover, Afurakanu/Afuraitkaitnut (Africans) who engage in the process of attempting to 'blacken-up' fictional white biblical, quranic, talmudic and other characters and blacken-up white pseudo-philosophies, false histories and therefore embrace foolish titles such as: *moors, hebrews, 'African-centered' christians, rastafarians, African muslims, black muslims, asiatics, nuwaubians, gods and earths, 'the black man is god', 'the black woman is god', black buddhists, black jains, black kabbalists, masons, extraterrestrials, universalists, new-agers,* etc. also manifest **odam** (psychosis) – disalignment from their Okra/Okraa and thus from reality. This includes those who are *blind followers* of these false doctrines out of ignorance as well as the *promoters* of these false doctrines.

The promoters who are founders and/or upper-level instructors of such groups which espouse these false doctrines are actually aware of the fallacy of the doctrines, yet seek to enslave other Afurakanu/Afuraitkaitnut (Africans) on behalf of the whites and their offspring. The overseers on enslavement plantations in the western hemisphere always worked to engineer (break) and use compromised Afurakanu/Afuraitkaitnut (Africans) to beat, torture and maintain the oppression of other Afurakanu/Afuraitkaitnut (Africans) on behalf of the so-called slavemaster.

All of the above-mentioned groups are a perpetuation of this process, for these groups are all funded and supported by the whites and their offspring including the moorish science temple of america, the nation of islam, the nation of gods and earths, the nuwaubians, various christian groups, black hebrew/israelite groups, other black muslim groups, black masonic groups, black 'esotericists' and their various offshoots. The same is true of Afurakanu/Afuraitkaitnut (Africans) in Afuraka/Afuraitkait (Africa) attempting to foolishly trace their/our blood-circles to fictional characters, fictional priesthoods and lineages from the bible, quran, talmud, bhagavad gita, the kabbalah, tirthankaras, etc. The whites and their offspring use their black agents to promote pseudo-religion and philosophy under the guise of 'traditional African religion' in Afuraka/Afuraitkait (Africa).

It was through the corruption of Nanasom, Afurakani/Afuraitkaitnit (African) Ancestral Religion, that the whites and their offspring were able to gain political control in Afuraka/Afuraitkait (Africa) over the past 130 years. It is through the restoration of Nanasom, Afurakani/Afuraitkaitnit (African) Ancestral Religion, that Afurakanu/Afuraitkaitnut (Africans) worldwide will regain our political control – and ultimately eradicate our enemies.

The restoration of Nanasom for Afurakanu/Afuraitkaitnut (Africans) begins with our realignment with our Okra/Okraa

Center: ***Ures*** *(headrest) - from plate 32 of the* ***Ani Sheft, Ru Nu Pert em Hru*** *(misnomered Papyrus of Ani, Egyptian Book of the Dead).*

The text for the 'Chapter of the Ures/Headrest' reads:

"...May the pigeons awaken you when you are asleep, O Ani, may they awaken your head at the horizon. Raise yourself, so that you may be triumphant over what was done against you, for the [Ntoro (God)] ***Ptah*** *has felled your enemies and it is commanded that action be taken against those who would harm you. You are* ***Heru****, son of* ***Het Heru****, the male and female fiery serpents, to whom was given a head after it had been cut off. Your head will not be taken from you afterwards. Your head will not be taken from you ever..."*

Selected References

Communicating Nominatim: Some Aspects of Bono Personal Names, *by Kwasi Ansu Kyeremeh*
The Sociolinguistic of Akan Personal Names, *by Kofi Agyekum*
The Akan Concept of the Soul, *by Sam K. Akesson*
Orilonise: The Hermeneutics of the Head and Hairstyles Among the Yoruba, *by Babatunde Lawal*
Adinkra Cloth Symbols – Asante Wisdom, *by Aaron Mobley*
Teachings of Ptah Hotep, *edited by Asa Hilliard, et. al.*
Conjure, Magic, and Power: The Influence of Afro-Atlantic Religious Practices on Slave Resistance and Rebellion, *by Walter Rucker*
The above documents can be found at: www.scribd.com/Akumasaa

An Hieroglyphic Dictionary, Vols. 1 and 2, *E.A. Wallis Budge*
A Dictionary of the Asante and Fante language called Tshi (Chwee, Twi), *J.G. Christaller*
www.archive.org

Pyramid Texts Online
www.pyramidtextsonline.com/tools.html

Kasahorow Online, Promoting African Languages
www.kasahorow.org

Ghana National Commission on Culture – 'The Goldsmith's Craft', *by J.K. Anquandah*
www.ghanaculture.gov.gh/index1.php?linkid=273&page=4§ionid=523

African Spirituality: On Becoming Ancestors, *by Anthony Ephirim-Donkor*
An Essay on African Philosophical Thought: The Akan Conceptual Scheme, *by Kwame Gyekye*
African Anthroponomy, *by Samuel Gyasi Obeng*
History of the Asante Kings and the Entire Country Itself, *by Nana Agyeman Prempeh*
Cloth as Metaphor (Re) Reading the Adinkra Cloth Symbols of the Akan of Ghana, *by G. F. Kojo Arthur*
Let the Ancestors Speak, Removing the Veil of Mysticism from Medu Netcher, *by Ankh Mi Ra*
Ru Nu Pert em Hru, Papyrus of Ani (so-called Egyptian Book of the Dead) *additional rubrics translated by R. O. Faulkner*
AKANFO NANASOM – www.odwirafo.com/Akanfo_Nanasom.html
AKRADINBOSOM – www.odwirafo.com/akradinbosom.html
KUKUU-TUNTUM – The Ancestral Jurisdiction – www.odwirafo.com/kukuutuntumpage.html
NYANKOPON-NYANKONTON--RA-RAIT www.odwirafo.com/Nyankopon_and_Nyankonton-Ra_and_Rait.pdf
Akan Origin of the Term Hoodoo – www.odwirafo.com/Akan_Origin_of_the_Term_Hoodoo.pdf
MMARA NE KYI - Divine Law and Divine Hate – www.odwirafo.com/MMARA-NE-KYI_Article_Num_Nhomawaa.pdf

www.odwirafo.com/Akanfo_Nanasom.html

NOTE ON THE TERM NGG WR OR NGNG WR IN KAMIT
NGG UR IS NOT 'NIGGER' PART 1

THE ORIGIN OF THE TERM 'GOD'

NOTE ON THE TERM NGG WR OR NGNG WR IN KAMIT NGG UR IS NOT 'NIGGA' PART 2

NEHESU – NEGUS – NKOSO

NEGUS IS NOT 'NIGGA'

RA AKHA – NANKA – NAGA
NAGA IS NOT 'NIGGA'

ANIDAHO

There is a great deal of misinformation being propagated in the Afurakani/Afuraitkaitnit (African~Black) community regarding the etymological origins of the terms 'nigger', 'nigga', 'naga', 'negus' and 'god'. There are individuals in the Afurakani/Afuraitkaitnit (African) community who propagate this information out of ignorance, attempting to conflate the derogatory term 'nigger' and its variation 'nigga' with ancient terms from **Kamit** (Egypt), **Harrapa** (Ancient Black India) and **Ethiopia**.

Because of a lack of self-esteem programmed into the spirits of Afurakanu/Afuraitkaitnut (Africans) by the whites and their offspring – the spirits of disorder/our absolute enemies – some individuals desire to make the derogatory label 'nigger' a pseudo-'divine' label meaning 'god'. This allows the individual with low self-esteem to make themselves 'feel good' on the surface, while affording them the opportunity to continue to be defined by the whites and their offspring whom they still view as superior to them. This is one of the many manifestations of the pathology of enslavement still present within the spirits of our people. It is absolutely no different than skin-bleaching, hair straightening, cosmetic surgery to obtain white facial features, etc.

The whites and their offspring (white americans, europeans, hispanics, pseudo-'native'-americans, asians, hindus, arabs, etc.) incarnate as spirits of disorder – **all of them** – and are therefore spiritually and physiologically inferior to all Afurakanu/Afuraitkaitnut (Africans~Black People). Our lack of attunement to this spiritual and physical reality is a result of the blunting of our perception when we embrace white cultural values. We therefore seek to protect ourselves and empower ourselves by 'claiming' and 'redefining' the labels of inferiority forced upon us by the whites and their offspring as opposed to simply rejecting them. We therefore have misinformed individuals 'fighting' for the right to make 'nigga' a title of 'divinity', while simultaneously the pseudo-scholar, **agents** of the whites and their offspring in our community propagate this misinformation in order to keep Afurakanu/Afuraitkaitnut (Africans) spiritually enslaved, unaware of our identity and therefore unaware of our true enemies and how we must confront them.

We initially published the articles and the appendix in this publication separately. We have combined them here for ease of study and distribution. **Anidaho** is an Akan term meannig *awareness*. It literally means the **eye** (ani) **lies upon** (da) the **self** (ho). We must have *awareness* of who we are, who our enemies are and how they and their agents exploit our ignorance to keep us enslaved. Only then can we reorganize and move against them effectively.

Odwirafo Kwesi Ra Nehem Ptah Akhan
Aakhuamuman Amaruka Atifi Mu
(Akwamu Nation in North America)
www.odwirafo.com
July, 13014 (2014)

Note on the term Ngg Wr or Ngng Wr in Kamit

Ngg Ur is not 'Nigger' – Part 1

ODWIRAFO

NOTE ON THE TERM NGG WR OR NGNG WR IN KAMIT

NGG UR IS NOT 'NIGGER' – PART 1

neg , Hh. 541, to cackle.

negg , N. 749, to cackle, to quack.

negaga , , to cackle, to quack.

negȧ , cackler.

Negg-ur , , B.D. 59, 3, the goose-goddess who laid the sun-egg.

Negneg-ur , Berl. 2296; see .

Negaga-ur , B.D. (Saïte) 54, 1, 56, 2, 59, 2; see .

The terms **Ngg, Nga, Ngg Wr, Ngng Wr** or **Ngaga Wr** have been promoted as the etymological origin of the word 'nigger' and thus associated with the false notion that 'nigger' actually means 'god'. This false conception can be clarified when we look at another common form of the term **Ngng Wr** which is **GnGn Wr**:

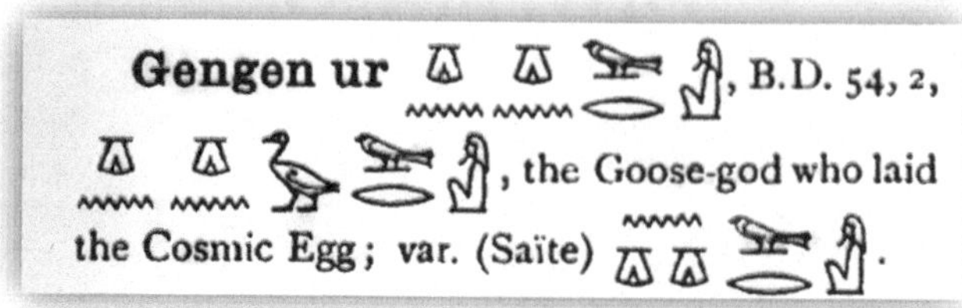
Gengen ur , B.D. 54, 2, , the Goose-god who laid the Cosmic Egg; var. (Saïte) .

Negg-ur , B.D. 59, 3, the goose-goddess who laid the sun-egg.

Negneg-ur , Berl. 2296; see .

Negaga-ur , B.D. (Saïte) 54, 1, 56, 2, 59, 2; see .

Gengen ur , B.D. 54, 2, , the Goose-god who laid the Cosmic Egg; var. (Saïte) .

Gaga ur , B.D. 56, 2, 59, 2, "Great Cackler"—a title of Geb.

As we can see **Ngg Wr** and **Ngng Wr** and **Negaga Wr** are identical to **Gngn Wr**. This is because the term is actually pronounced **Nganga** (in-gahn'-gah). **Gangan** or **Ganga** and **Nganga** are the same term. The '***wr***' (**ur**) is a desriptive title meaning 'the Great':

ur , , , , , great, much, superior, very, greatness, great size; dual , , , ; plur. , , ; , P. 808, great piece of flesh from the joint.

ur , U. 215, , , , , , , , , , , , , , , , , great man, great god, prince, chief, noble, eldest

ur-t , , , , , Rec. 5, 90, great woman, great thing, great, eldest; plur. , , .

ur , Anastasi I, 27, 8, , very great, how very great; Copt. ОΥНР.

ur , great; , greater than;

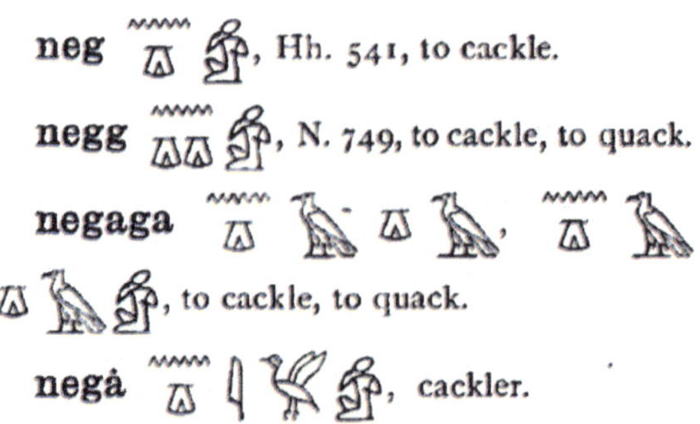

Nga (in-gah') means *'to cackle'* or *'to quack'*. It is also a title meaning *'cackler'*. **Nga** or **Ngga Wr** means the *'Great Cackler'*.

In the cosmology of **Kamit** at **Ta Apet** ('thebes'), it is revealed that the *Great Divine* ***Nganga*** (Cackler, Goose) in the form of the Great **Ntoro** (Ntr/Deity) **Amen** 'cackles' at the beginning of Creation and causes the primordial waters of **Nun** and **Naunet** to begin to vibrate. The primordial waters of **Nun** and **Naunet**, within the Great Black Substance of Space (**Kaka** and **Kauket** or **Ka** and **Kait**) ultimately give birth to **Ra** and **Rait**, the *Creator* and *Creatress* who manifest as Fire and Light piercing through the Blackness and eventually manifesting through the **Aten** (Sun).

What is key here is that the 'cackling', 'quacking' or *production of sound waves/vibrations/power* set in motion *movement/transmission of energy* within **Nun** and **Naunet**, the energic substratum from which **Ra** and **Rait**, the Creator and Creatress and ultimately all *created* entities would emerge. This notion and the terminology referencing it continue to be used by Afurakanu/Afuraitkaitnut (Africans) today. The **Bakongo** people are an example. In the Kikongo language, the term **nganga** means a *'master'*, referencing a *'healer'*. From: **Self-Healing Power and Therapy** by K. Kia Bunseki Fu-Kiau – pages 18-19:

http://books.google.com/books?id=MdRAVFEiegYC&pg=PA3&lpg=PA3&dq=nganga,+self+healing+power&source=bl&ots=zd74e_ZZpp&sig=qjYf87ELbUHbBxXpCscEgW36iAk&hl=en&sa=X&ei=RBvSUZLVILOq4APM_oHQBg&ved=0CDMQ6AEwAQ#v=onepage&q=ghanda&f=false

"....*Ghanda* ("to be initiated") is to join the circle of ***nganga*** ("masters") and become oneself, *nganga*, a doer. <u>**Nganga** of the archaic verbal root ***ghanga***</u>, of which the modern form is *vanga* (to do, to make, to act, to realize) is a *m'vangi*, i.e., an individual of deeds (*mavanga*).....It is earned by merit by enduring proofs of initiation, *ku kanga*, at the initiation institution site.

Through *Ku kanga* or *kongo*, one learns to discover one's own **sun** or package of life, its **power and radiations**: the genetically, spiritually and physically inherited strength of **self-healing power**. Once at *ku kanga* or *kongo*, the "candidate" must learn to speak the language of ***kinganga*** [ki-nganga], a **specialized language**. Without knowledge of this sophisticated language spoken by initiator-masters....one may find it hard to digest the sophisticated knowledge taught in these institutions of initiation.

Because of the lack of printed material, teaching constituted passing down of key principles of life through *bikumu* ("repeated mottoes") ***ngana*** ("proverbs")...."

[Emphasis ours.. Note the connection between the Kikongo *Nganga* and *Ghanga*. This is found in ancient Kamit as *Nganga* and *Gangan*]

The Nganga is typically recognized in ritual contexts to be a healer, medicine person, one who can call on the Spirits of the Deities (Divine Forces in Creation). The Nganga's ritual efficacy is dependent most often upon the Nganga's ability to make proper ritual invocations/prayers/chanting. This is true of Afurakani/Afuraitkaitnit (African) Traditional Healers/Healeresses in general. Proper, effective invocatory *chanting* moves the energy of the Forces in Creation and opens the way for transformation to occur. Indeed, the word 'chant' has etymological origins in *'kan'* and the **gan** of ancient Kamit (Also see: **ka** (pronounced with a 'nasal' 'A') - *to speak* and **kankye** - *to pray* in the Twi language of Akan).

gen, , to cry out, to beg, to beseech; , petitioner; Copt. ϭⲛⲟⲩ.

Moreover, the sacred proverbial wisdom of the Bakongo, **ngana**, mentioned in the quote above, are an *archive* of the *key principles of life.* Hence the term **gan** (**gn**) meaning *archive* in Kamit:

gen-t, N. 979, , , P. 364, N. 1078, , , , , L.D. III, 194, 27, memorial, record, archive, memorandum; plur. , Rec. 31, 25, , A.Z. 1880, 49, , IV, 500, , , , Tombos Stele 15, , , IV, 1183, , Mar. Karn. 52, 20, , Thes. 1285, annals.

gengenu , Rougé I.H. 256, records, archives, annals.

It should also be noted that **Amen** takes the form of a *Divine Goose* and *Cackles*, emits the Sacred Sound vibrations, at the onset of Creation. Technically, **Amen** takes the form of the *Gander* (male Goose) while the Great **Ntorot** (**Ntrt**/Deity/Goddess) **Amenet** takes form of the *Goose* as **Gan Writ**:

Genur, N. 979, , B.D. 14, 4, a god who presided over offerings; varr. , .

Gengen ur, B.D. 54, 2, , the Goose-god who laid the Cosmic Egg; var. (Saïte) .

Gen urit, a goddess of offerings.

It is **Amenet** as the Female Goose who lays the Cosmic Egg from which **Ra** and **Rait** will be born. **Amen** and **Amenet** function Together as One Divine Unit, the Supreme Being.

As **Nganga** or **Gan Gan Wr** or **Ngaga Wr**, **Amen** takes the form of a *Gander* in order to *'Cackle, Quack'*, as opposed to a *serpent*. [*The Naga serpents of the Tamil speaking Afurakanu/Afuraitkaitnut (Africans) of ancient India are actually the* ***Ra Akh*** *or* ***Raakha*** *serpents. The 'rolling 'R' and the 'N' interchange linguistically.* ***Ra*** *and* ***Rait*** *are subordinate to* ***Amen*** *and* ***Amenet****. See our* ***Nyankopon and Nyankonton – Ra and Rait*** *article for details: http://www.odwirafo.com/Nyankopon_and_Nyankonton-Ra_and_Rait.pdf*]

NGANGA WR

As we can see, the cosmological and etymological root of the term **Nganga Wr** or **Ngga Wr** or **GnGn Wr** is **gan**. **Ngg Ur** is not *nigger*. The term nigger, said to be derived through *negro*, *necro* from the proto-indo-european root *nekwt* or *nek* referencing 'dead, dark, night' etc., actually has its origins in the terms **Neq**, **Neqr**, **Neqau**, **Nek** and related terms in Kamit:

Negro (n.)
"member of a black-skinned race of Africa," 1550s, from Spanish or Portuguese *negro* "black," from Latin *nigrum* (nominative *niger*) "black, dark, sable, dusky," figuratively "gloomy, unlucky, bad, wicked," of unknown origin (perhaps from PIE **nekw-t-* "night," cf. Watkins). As an adjective from 1590s. Use with a capital *N-* became general early 20c. (e.g. 1930 in "New York Times" stylebook) in reference to U.S. citizens of African descent, but because of its perceived association with white-imposed attitudes and roles the word was ousted late 1960s in this sense by ***Black*** (q.v.).
Professor Booker T. Washington, being politely interrogated ... as to whether negroes ought to be called 'negroes' or 'members of the colored race' has replied that it has long been his own practice to write and speak of members of his race as negroes, and when using the term 'negro' as a race designation to employ the capital 'N' ["Harper's Weekly," June 2, 1906]
Meaning "English language as spoken by U.S. blacks" is from 1704. French *nègre* is a 16c. borrowing from Spanish *negro*.

night (n.)
Old English *niht* (West Saxon *neaht*, Anglian *næht*, *neht*) "night, darkness;" the vowel indicating that the modern word derives from oblique cases (genitive *nihte*, dative *niht*), from Proto-Germanic **nakht-* (cf. Old Saxon and Old High German *naht*, Old Frisian and Dutch *nacht*, German *Nacht*, Old Norse *natt*, Gothic *nahts*).

The Germanic words are from PIE **nekwt-* "night" (cf. Greek *nuks* "a night," Latin *nox*, Old Irish *nochd*, Sanskrit *naktam* "at night," Lithuanian *naktis* "night," Old Church Slavonic *nosti*, Russian *noch'*, Welsh *henoid* "tonight"), according to Watkins, probably from a verbal root **neg-* "to be dark, be night." For spelling with *-gh-* see ***fight***.
The fact that the Aryans have a common name for night, but not for day (q.v.), is due to the fact that they reckoned by nights. [Weekley]
Cf. German *Weihnachten* "Christmas." In early times, the day was held to begin at sunset, so Old English *monanniht* "Monday night" was the night before Monday, or what we would call *Sunday night*.

To *work nights* preserves the Old English genitive of time. *Night shift* is attested from 1710 in the sense of "garment worn by a woman at night" (see ***shift*** (n.1)); meaning "gang of workers employed after dark" is from 1839. *Night soil* "excrement" (1770) is so called because it was removed (from cesspools, etc.) after dark. *Night train* attested from 1838.*Night life* "habitual nocturnal carousing" attested from 1852.

necro-
before vowels, *necr-*, word-forming element meaning "death, corpse, dead tissue," from comb. form of Greek *nekros* "dead body, corpse, dead person," from PIE **nek-* "death, natural death" (cf. Sanskrit *nasyati* "disappears, perishes," Avestan *nasyeiti* "disappears," *nasu-* "corpse," Old Persian *vi-nathayatiy* "he injures;" Latin *nex*, genitive *necis* "violent death, murder" (as opposed to *mors*), *nocere* "to harm, hurt," *noxius* "harmful;" Greek *nekus* "dead" (adj.), *nekros* "dead body, corpse;" Old Irish *ec*, Breton *ankou*, Welsh *angeu*"death").

neqr , , Rec. 5, 86, 16, 159, to sift; Copt. ПОКЄР (?)

neqr , , dust, powder, what is sifted.

neqem , T. 12, , N. 959, , , , , Metternich Stele 3, to be afflicted, to mourn, to grieve, to lament.

neqmu , mourners, afflicted ones.

neqeb , Metternich Stele 6, to mourn, to be afflicted.

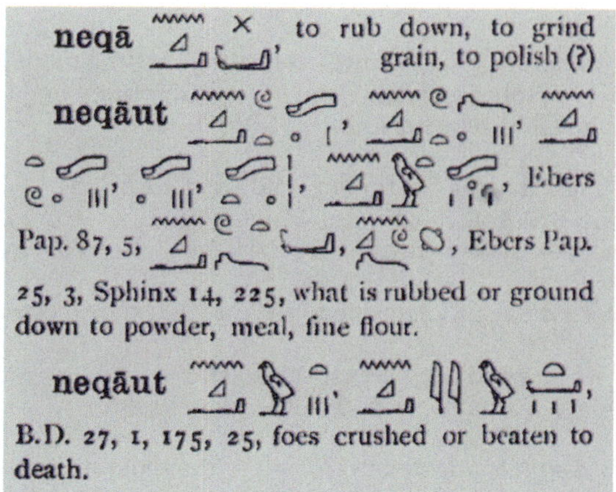

neqā to rub down, to grind grain, to polish (?)

neqāut, Ebers Pap. 87, 5, , Ebers Pap. 25, 3, Sphinx 14, 225, what is rubbed or ground down to powder, meal, fine flour.

neqāut, B.D. 27, 1, 175, 25, foes crushed or beaten to death.

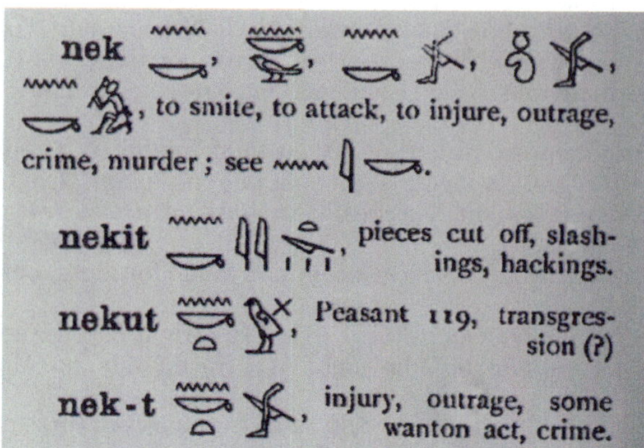

nek, to smite, to attack, to injure, outrage, crime, murder; see .

nekit, pieces cut off, slashings, hackings.

nekut, Peasant 119, transgression (?)

nek-t, injury, outrage, some wanton act, crime.

These terms are related to the *dead body, corpse, death,* the treatment of the body in a negative fashion, etc. [*The terms* ***negro*** *and* ***necro*** *is addressed in Part 2.*]

Sacred **Gangan** (Goose) of **Amen**

The Origin of the term 'God'

Note on the term Ngg Wr or Ngng Wr in Kamit

Ngg Ur is not 'nigga' – Part 2

ODWIRAFO

THE ORIGIN OF THE TERM 'GOD'

NOTE ON THE TERM NGG WR OR NGNG WR IN KAMIT

Ngg Ur is not 'nigga' – Part 2

In **Part 1** of our **Note on the Origin of the Term Ngg Wr or Ngng Wr in Kamit** we demonstrated that the title **Ngg Wr** or **Ngg Ur** is actually the term **Gngn Wr**:

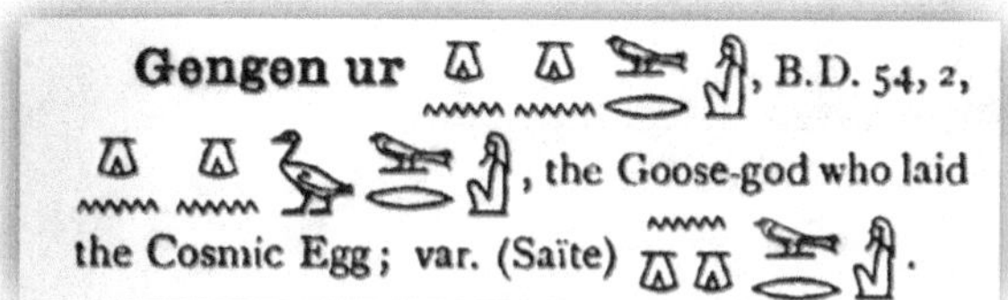

Gengen ur, B.D. 54, 2, , the Goose-god who laid the Cosmic Egg; var. (Saïte) .

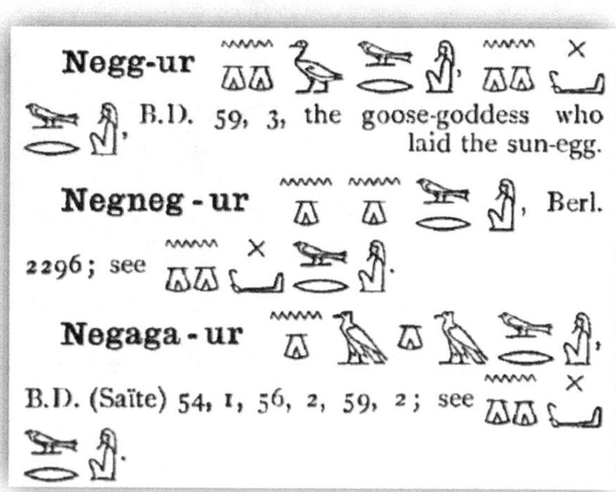

Negg-ur , B.D. 59, 3, the goose-goddess who laid the sun-egg.

Negneg-ur , Berl. 2296; see .

Negaga-ur , B.D. (Saïte) 54, 1, 56, 2, 59, 2; see .

We demonstrated the that proper pronunciation is **Nganga** (in-gahn'-gah) and **Gangan** (gahn'-gahn) and is still used by the Bakongo people today as a title for a ritual specialist/healer – ***nganga***. The 'N'-sound is a nasal prefix, thus Gangan can be pronounced and written nGangan (in-gahn'-gahn). **The root of the term is Ga or Gan (Gn)**.

The root term **ga** (gah' or gahn') also pronounced with the 'N' as a nasal prefix **nga** (in-gah') means 'to cackle' in reference to a *Divine Goose* or *Gander*, but specifically meaning to *emit sound vibrations*. The 'a' in ga is 'nasal' and this is why the term was written *ga* or *gan* – the

metut (hieroglyph) for the letter 'n' the wavy water/energy metut representing the nasal 'N' pronunciation ("NNN"). The term 'ga' pronounced with a nasal 'a' thus sounds like 'gan'.

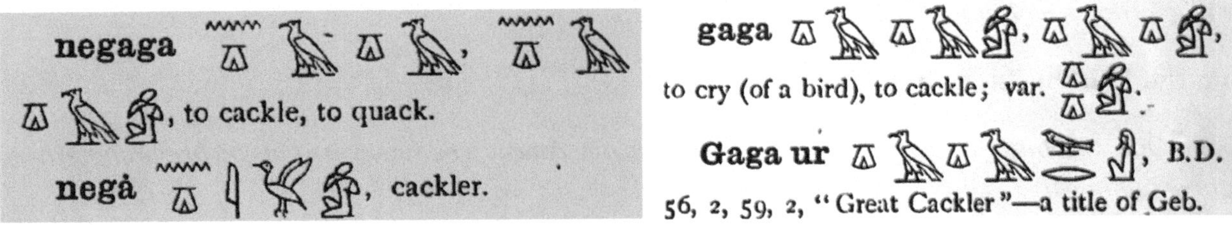
negaga, to cackle, to quack.

negȧ, cackler.

gaga, to cry (of a bird), to cackle; var.

Gaga ur, B.D. 56, 2, 59, 2, "Great Cackler"—a title of Geb.

[Notice that the term is actually spelled **n-g-a-g-a** (in-gah'gah)or **n-g-a** (in-gah'). The 'egyptologist' inserted an 'e' because of uncertainty of how the term was pronounced.]

As we stated in Part 1 of the series:

"...**Nga** (in-gah') means *'to cackle'* or *'to quack'*. It is also a title meaning *'cackler'*. **Nga** or **Ngga Wr** means the *'Great Cackler'*.

In the cosmology of **Kamit** at **Ta Apet** ('thebes'), it is revealed that the *Great Divine* ***Nganga*** (Cackler, Goose) in the form of the Great **Ntoro** (Ntr/Deity) **Amen** 'cackles' at the beginning of Creation and causes the primordial waters of **Nun** and **Naunet** to begin to vibrate. The primordial waters of **Nun** and **Naunet**, within the Great Black Substance of Space (**Kaka** and **Kauket** or **Ka** and **Kait**) ultimately give birth to **Ra** and **Rait**, the *Creator* and *Creatress* who manifest as Fire and Light piercing through the Blackness and eventually manifesting through the **Aten** (Sun).

What is key here is that the 'cackling', 'quacking' or *production of sound waves/vibrations/power* set in motion *movement/transmission of energy* within **Nun** and **Naunet**, the energic substratum from which **Ra** and **Rait**, the Creator and Creatress and ultimately all *created* entities would emerge..."

From the **Temple of Heb** (Hibis) – Columns 23-24 – **Hymn to Amen**:

*"...Your ancient throne is the highland (**qait/kait**) of Khemenu, it is from the lake of Two Knives that you reach land.*

*It is from the water surface that you appear in the hidden egg, **Amenet** being with you..."*

From the so-called **Leiden Papyrus I 350**, chapter 90 regarding **Amen**:

*"...Light was His coming into existence on the first occasion, with all that exists in stillness for awe of Him. He [**Amen**] **cackled** by voice, as the **Great Cackler**, coming into a land that He created for Himself...*

*He began **speaking** in the midst of silence, opening every eye and causing them to look. He began **crying out** while the world was in stillness, His **yell** circulated while He had none like Him, **so that He might give birth to what is and cause them to live**, and cause every man to know the way to walk. Their hearts live when they see Him..."*

From the **Leiden Papyrus I 350** Chapter 100:

*"...The One who initiated existence on the first occasion, **Amen**, who developed in the beginning, whose origin is unknown.*

*No Deity came into being prior to Him. No other Deity was with Him who could say what He looked like. He had no mother who created His name. He had no father to beget Him or to say : "This belongs to me." **He Who formed His own egg**. Power of secret birth, who created His (own) beauty..."*

Amenet and **Amen**

Gagait and **Gaga**; **Gagait Urit** and **Gangan Ur**; **Ngaga Writ** and **Ngangan Wr**

Amen and **Amenet** are the Great Father and Great Mother, Whom Together comprise The Supreme Being. When Amen and Amenet began the act of **gaga** or **gangan** (cackling, honking), the primordial waters of the Black Substance of Space, the unformed Matter, began to vibrate . A separation took place as the Divine Egg was formed within the Great Divine Goose, **Amenet**. She laid the Divine Egg from which emerged the **Aten** (Sun) through which **Ra** and **Rait**, the Creator and Creatress were born and emerged. Ra and Rait are the Creator and

Creatress, the first Fire and Light to pierce the primordial darkness at the beginning of Creation separating dark from light and eventually morning from night.

Sacred Goose and Gander of **Amen** and **Amenet**

"...The word goose is a direct descendent of Proto-Indo-European root, ***ghans-**. In Germanic languages, the root gave Old English **gōs** with the plural **gēs** and **gandres** (becoming Modern English goose, geese, and gander, respectively), New High German **Gans**, **Gänse**, and **Ganter**, and Old Norse **gās**. This term also gave Lithuanian **žąsìs**, Irish **gé** (goose, from Old Irish géiss), Latin **anser**, Greek **χήν/khēn**, Albanian **gatë** (heron), Sanskrit **hamsa** and **hamsi**, Finnish **hanhi**, Avestan **zāō**, Polish **gęś**, Russian **гусь**, Czech **husa**, and Persian **ghāz**..." [**Wikipedia – Goose**]

Note that the etymological origin of the term 'goose' is falsely posited by the whites and their offspring to be derived from the proto-indo-european root 'ghans'. Of course, the true origin is **Gan**, the 'cackler', from ancient Kamit and Khanit.

Amen and **Amenet**, **Gagait Wrt** and **Gangan Wr** in the primordial waters before Creation

"...Observe the actions of the geese. When they reach maturity (about three years old), the male tends to be more dominant and aggressive than the female, especially in mating season. The male is more protective of the nesting area as well. Listen to the sounds of geese, the male goose lets out a high-pitched honking sound to attract the female when they are ready to mate while female lets out a low-toned quack when she is ready to mate..."

The cackling, honking or quacking – the **gaga** or **gangan** – is related to *mating*. When Amenet and Amen as **Gagait** and **Gaga** (Gangan) were ready to mate in order to Create the Universe, Amen, the *Great* (**Wr**) *Gangan* began to '*ga*' – 'cackle', 'honk', 'cry out' and Amenet, the Great (**Writ**) *Gagait* responded. The sound vibrations caused the waters of the womb within the Great Mother Amenet to vibrate as Nun and Naunet. These dark waters are of the Black Substance of Space called 'dark energy' and 'dark matter' by physicists which makes up over 99% of the Universe. Amenet then produced the Divine Egg out of which the Aten (Sun) would emerge.

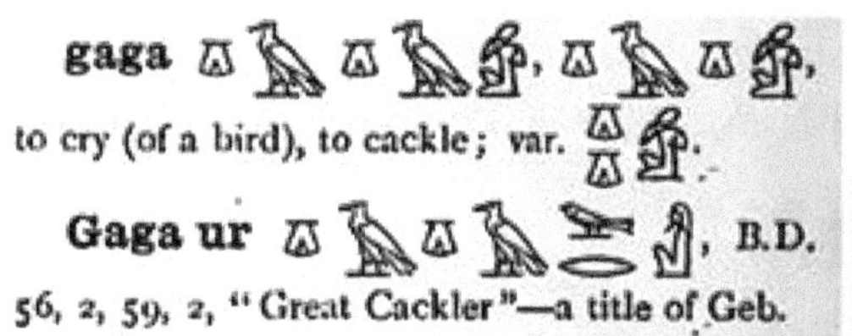

gaga, to cry (of a bird), to cackle; var.

Gaga ur, B.D. 56, 2, 59, 2, "Great Cackler"—a title of Geb.

Gagait (?), Ombos II, 130, a goddess.

Genur, N. 979, B.D. 14, 4, a god who presided over offerings; varr.

Gengen ur, B.D. 54, 2, the Goose-god who laid the Cosmic Egg; var. (Saïte).

Gen urit, a goddess of offerings.

The root of Gangan is **ga** and **gai**. As the Great Cackler, Gangan Wr, Amen **invokes** (calls from within) His own Creative Power. Chanting ('cackling') is the original **invocation**.

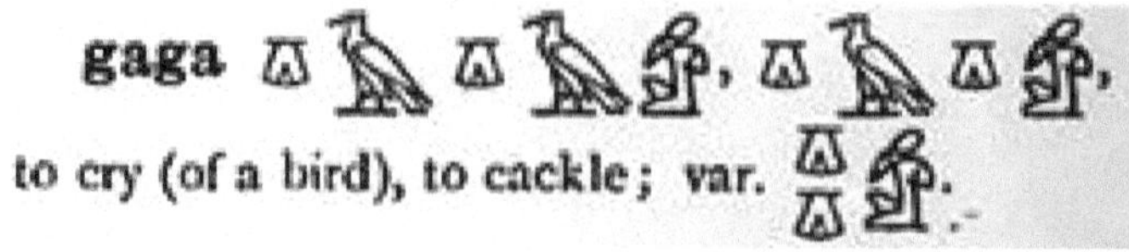

gaga, to cry (of a bird), to cackle; var.

The term **ga** also means *to sing*, **gaua** means *to sing; to praise* and **gangar** means *to sing*. **This praise/song is ritual invocation**. The determinative metut of the man raising his hands in the air is an act of **ritually provoking (invoking) the energy of the Deity**, in this instance via ritual song (sound vibrations, **gngn**). This metut is the deteriminative metut for words describing *prayer, praise, ritual practice*. Note that the term **gangar** is written in Coptic (Late Kamit dialect) as **knkn** or **gengen**: Copt. ϭⲛϭⲛ, ϫⲉⲛϫⲉⲛ. This is why in the Akan language the terms **ka** and **kankye** (the 'a' being nasal in both) mean *to emit a sound, to speak* and *to pray, to invoke a Deity*.

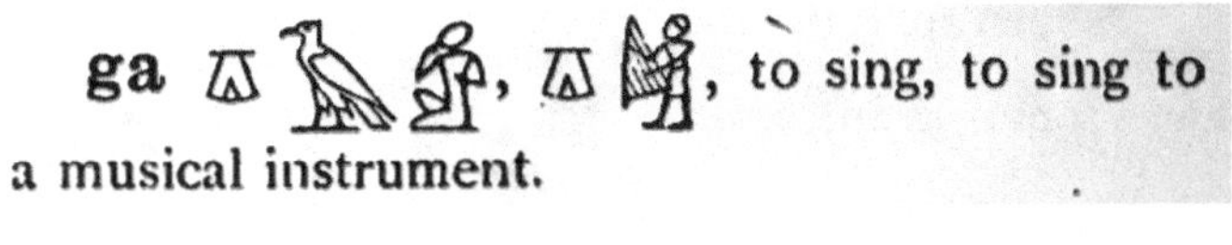
ga, , to sing, to sing to a musical instrument.

gaua, to sing, to praise; var. .

gangar, , to sing; Copt. ϭⲛϭⲛ, ϫⲉⲛϫⲉⲛ.

The term **ga** meaning *to cry out* again has the variation **gan** (**gn**, **gen**) meaning *to cry out, beseech, petition,* while the **ganu** (bird, goose) is a variation of **gan** (**gn**):

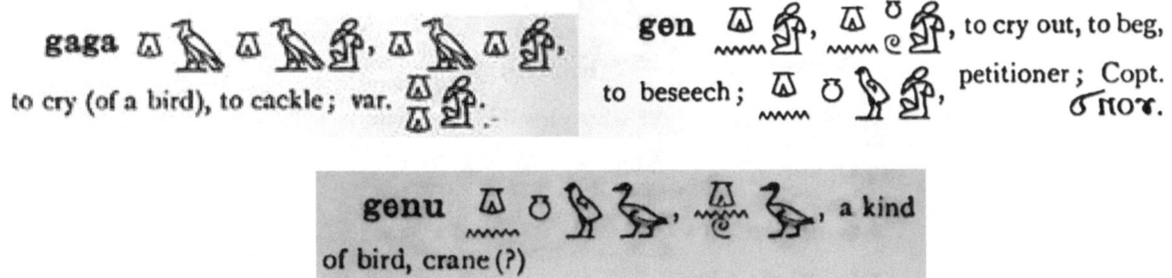
gaga , , to cry (of a bird), to cackle; var. .

gen , , to cry out, to beg, to beseech; , petitioner; Copt. ϭⲛⲟⲩ.

genu , , a kind of bird, crane (?)

Moreover, the same terms **gai** and **gnu** (gnu) also reference *pots, vessels* and *pouring*.

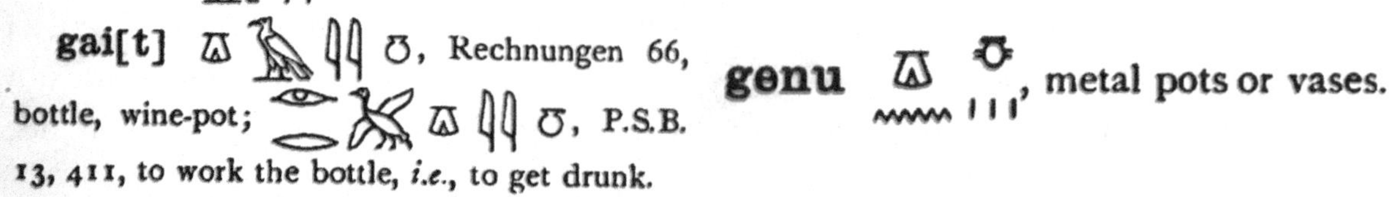
gai[t], Rechnungen 66, bottle, wine-pot; , P.S.B. 13, 411, to work the bottle, *i.e.*, to get drunk.

genu, metal pots or vases.

The related term **gash** meaning *to spill, to pour out, to sprinkle, a pouring out, inundation* is the origin of the english term '*gush*' meaning *to pour out, inundate,* etc. However, the root is **gai**. Notice the **two lips** of the **gai** (vessel) with the *wavy line for water/energy* being poured out function as the determinative metut (hieroglyph) for **gash** and **gai**:

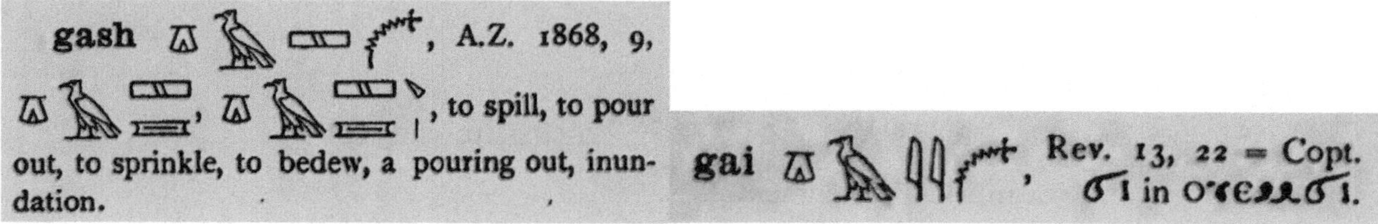
gash, A.Z. 1868, 9, , , to spill, to pour out, to sprinkle, to bedew, a pouring out, inundation.

gai, Rev. 13, 22 = Copt. ϭι in ογεɲɲϭι.

The two lips of the vessel (gai, gn) releasing water/energy as 'gai' are related to the two lips releasing the invocation 'ga' or 'gan' when 'crying out', 'petitioning' and with regard to Amenet and Amen 'cackling' – Ga or Gan.

The wavy water/energy **pouring out from the lips** is related to the energy activated in the waters of the Blackness of Space, the waters of Nun and Naunet, when they are stimulated by the **gaga** or **gangan** (cackling) of Amenet and Amen and the onset of Creation. The invocation of Amenet and Amen is a release of energy – **a pouring out of energy** necessary for the birthing of the Universe.

This is why Amenet and Amen as **Gn Ur** (Gangan Wr) and **Gn Urit** (Gagait Writ) are referred to also as the God and Goddess of *Offerings*:

Genur, N. 979, , B.D. 14, 4, a god who presided over offerings; varr. , .

Gengen ur, B.D. 54, 2, , the Goose-god who laid the Cosmic Egg; var. (Saïte) .

Gen urit, a goddess of offerings.

Certainly, the pouring out of the seed of the male (seminal fluid) and the release of blood of the female carrying the ovum, are a replication of this cosmological, foundational function of **conception** and **creation**. The white 'blood' (seminal fluid) and red blood (carrying the ovum) are the **blood offerings**, *sacrifice*, given by the mother and father in order to bring an Ancestral Spirit back into the physical world via conception. [*Union of the* ***red*** *and* ***white*** *crown in Kamit and the union of* ***Mogya*** *and* ***Ntoro*** *in Akan.*]

The cosmological foundation of these functions of **pouring** and **invocation** are critical, for they are the origin of the term 'god':

god (n.)
Old English *god* "supreme being, deity; the Christian God; image of a god; godlike person," from Proto-Germanic **guthan* (cf. Old Saxon, Old Frisian, Dutch *god*, Old High German*got*, German *Gott*, Old Norse *guð*, Gothic *guþ*), from PIE **ghut-* "that which is invoked" (cf. Old Church Slavonic *zovo* "to call," Sanskrit *huta-* "invoked," an epithet of Indra), from root **gheu(e)-* "to call, invoke."

But some trace it to PIE **ghu-to-* "poured," from root **gheu-* "to pour, pour a libation" (source of Greek *khein* "to pour," also in the phrase *khute gaia* "poured earth," referring to a burial mound; see ***found*** (v.2)). "Given the Greek facts, the Germanic form may have referred in the first instance to the spirit immanent in a burial mound" [Watkins]. Cf. also***Zeus***.

Notice that the whites and their offspring trace the origin of the word 'god' to two possible proto-indo-european roots:

Gheu (geu) meaning: *to pour, pour a libation*

Gheu (geu) meaning: *to call, invoke*

The whites and their offspring are unsure of *why* the roots *gheue* and *gheu* would have anything to do with *pouring* and at the same time something to do with *invoking* (calling). This is because they stole the term from ancient Afuraka/Afuraitkait (Africa) and claimed it as their own ('proto-indo-european').

It is in our culture where we find the **cosmological infrastructure** which gives birth to these terms. The terms gheu and gheue (goeh and goeh) are merely *corruptions* of **Ga** and **Ga** – meaning *to pour, pour out a libation* and *to invoke, cry out.* The 'a' is 'nasal'. Thus Amen is Gaga or Gangan the **Great Gan** or *Great God.* Amenet is Gagait the Great Gagait or Gad-es (Gait-s/Goddess). **Ga or Gan, became Gheu, Ghaeut, Got, Gad, and God.**

Amen is literally the Great Gan (Gad/god) – Amen Gan Wr

This is the reason that the name Amen is invoked at the end of prayers in the false religions of christianity, islam (amin) and judaism. The name was stolen by the whites and their offspring and falsely redefined as a term meaning 'so be it'.

It is important to note that in the **Twi** language of the **Akan** of Ghana and Ivory Coast we have two important terms:

guo — to pour, to sprinkle [**hwie guo**, to pour a libation; **nsaguo** *liquor* (nsa) *pouring* (guo) pouring libation with liquor as opposed to water]

go (agoo) — an invocation, an announcement before one enters a house; a call for attention

In Akan culture when one is about to enter a dwelling, one can knock, but they also cry out, '**Agoo**' – *'May I have your attention, I am here'*. The response by those within the dwelling to acknowledge the individual is '**Amen**' (also spelled **Amee** with the *nasal* 'ee' pronounciation). This same formula is used when one attempts to get the attention of a large or noisy crowd. It is a **call to Order**. An individual will thus cry out, 'Agoo' in the midst of of a large noisy crowd. The crowd is thereby alerted to quiet down and pay attention because something important is about to be said. The crowd then responds by saying 'Amen' – 'We are listening, we submit, you have our attention.'

Yet, this formula is first and foremost used ritually. Before any important task, meeting, function, etc. Akan people engage in the ritual of **pouring libation**. This is true of many Afurakanu/Afuraitkaitnut (Africans). In Akan culture, before pouring the liquid the officiant **cries out** 'Agoo', 'Agoo', 'Agoo'. This is an **invocation** to the Mother and Father Supreme Being **Nyamewaa-Nyame** (**Nyamewaa** is *Ny*-**Ament**-*waa* while **Nyame** is *Ny*-**Amen**), the **Abosom** (Deities), an evocation to the **Nananom Nsamanfo** (Spiritually Cultivated, Honorable Ancestresses and Ancestors) and the community. The community then responds by saying, 'Amen', 'Amen', 'Amen'. The call and response pattern is: **Agoo-Amen**, **Agoo-Amen**, **Agoo-Amen**. The officiant then begins to **pour**.

What we have in Akan libation is a ritual replication of the Creation of the Universe.

The **invocation** (goo) is followed by the **pouring** (guo). This is **Amen** and **Amenet** as Gaga Ur and Gagait Urit engaging in the **invocation** (**ga** – *cackling, crying out*) and the **pouring** out of their Divine Energy (**gai** – *to pour*). The cackling of **Amenet** and **Amen** is a **call to Order** the Universe.

This is also why the Akan response to the **goo** (invocation) and **guo** (pouring) is **AMEN**. This is also why the whites and their offspring recognized that the root of the term 'god' means 'pouring' and 'invocation' (gheu and gheu), yet had no understanding of *how* and *why* these two terms are related. Our actual, authentic cosmology demonstrates how inextricably related these two terms are – phonetically, conceptually and ritually.

In the language of Kamit, we have the term **Ntr** meaning 'Deity' (male) while **Ntrt** means 'Deity' (female):

neter, nether [hieroglyphs], U. 70, N. 330, [hieroglyphs], T. 237, [hieroglyphs], M. 147, [hieroglyphs], N. 649, [hieroglyphs], ★, the word in general use in texts of all periods for God and "god"; Copt. ⲛⲟⲩⲧⲉ, [hieroglyphs] = ⲛⲟⲩⲧⲉ (Rev.)

netrit [hieroglyphs], Rec. 30, 67, [hieroglyphs] goddess; Copt. ⲧⲛⲟⲩⲧⲉ.

Egyptologists are unsure of how the term **Ntr** was pronounced and therefore placed the 'e' in between the consonants. Note that in the Coptic dialect we have the vocalization: **NOUTE** **ⲛⲟⲩⲧⲉ,** .

In the Akan language, we find a proper vocalization for the term. **Ntr** or **Ntrt**, meaning 'God' or 'Goddess' is a Divine Spirit-Force in Nature and of Creation. In Akan culture, the term for a Deity, Goddess, God, Divine Spirit Force in Creation is **Obosom** (singular) and **Abosom** (plural). The term **Bosom** is derived from the Kamiti terms **Bsu** and **Msu** (*See: The Origin of the Term Abosom in Kamit*). The Akan designation for an Obosom (Deity) inherited by blood from the Father's patricircle (patrilineage) is **Ntoro** [in'-taw-raw]. The Ntoro is therefore referred to as the **Egyabosom** meaning *Father's* (Egya) *Deity* (Bosom). The term Ntoro is a proper vocalization of Ntr. The feminine version of the term in Akan is **Nton** (Ntoron) referencing the **Abusuabosom** – the Obosom (Deity) inherited from the **Abusua** or **Nton** (Ntoron) – the Mother's matricircle (matrilineage).

The Kamiti term **Ntr** meaning *Divine Spirit Force of Nature and Creation* was retained in european languages. **Ntr** is the etymological origin of the term 'Nature'. As a Divinity this would be *Mother Nature*.

It is important to note that the terms **Ntr**, **Ga**, **Gai** meaning *Deity*, to *invoke* and to *pour* are three different terms – **all three of which exist in the same forms in Kamit and Akan** as well as their corruptions in european languages:

Kamit	**Ntr**	*Deity*
Akan	**Ntoro**	*Deity*
european	**Nature**	*Deity (Mother Nature)*

Kamit	**Ga**	*Invoke*
Akan	**Go**	*Invocation*
european	**Gheu**	*Invoke*

Kamit	**Gai**	*Pour, libation*
Akan	**Guo**	*Pour, libation*
european	**Gheu**	*Pour, libation*

Ngg Wr, Neter, Negus, Naga

There is an extant body of misinformation purporting to elucidate the origin of the term 'Nigger' (Nigga) by erroneously attempting to trace the roots to **Ngg Wr**, **Neter** (**Netcher**), **Negus, Naga** or *all of the above*. There is also an extant body of misinformation regarding the etymology of the the term 'God'. In this two part series and our related articles, we have given the proper etymologies supported by the cosmological infrastructure in Khanit (Nubia) and Kamit which gave birth to these terms.

Gan is doubled as **Gangan**, also **Ngangan**. The *root* is **Gan** or **Ga**. **Ga is not the term 'nigger'.**

Ntr is **Noute** in Coptic, **Ntoro** in Akan and also **Tro** in Ewe. **Ntoro is not the term 'nigger'.**

Negus or **Nagas** is derived from **Nehesu** (**Nhsu**) written **Nkoso** in Akan. The *root* is **Hs** or **Hsu** (**Koso**). **Hsu or Koso is not the term 'nigger'.** [See our publication entitled: **Nehesu-Negus-Nkoso – Negus is not 'nigga'** for details]

Ra Akhu or **Ra Akh** is a title of **Ra** the Creator.  This title of **Ra** is found in Akan as **Nanka** (Nan ka, Dan ga, Ran ga, Ran ka), Onanka, Odanga, Edanga and Ananga, Nyanka. The rolling 'R' and the 'D' and 'N' interchange. Ananga is **Naga** in Tamil (India). The *root* is **Ra Aakhu** or **Ra Akha**. **Ra Aakhu is not 'nigger'.** [See our publication entitled: **NYANKOPON-NYANKONTON – RA-RAIT** for details.]

All four of these terms are different and expressive of their own meanings and functions in our cosmology. Most importantly, *all four of these terms exist in the same language* of ancient Kamit as well as the genetically descendent Akan language and *none of them spell out 'nigger' or 'nigga'.* **These are not different words from different languages around the world all pointing to the term 'nigga' meaning 'god'**. They are four different terms from the same langauge with four different meanings – **none of which are 'nigger'**. These terms are still spoken today by the Akan. The roots tell the **trustory** (true-story, true-history):

Kamit	Akan
Gan	Go
Ntr	Ntoro
Hsu	Koso
Ra Aakha	Dan-ga (Edanga, Ran-ka, Nan-ka)

Moreover, the term for the river called 'Niger' is not a variation of the word 'nigger'. The **Tuareg** people of North, Central and West Afuraka/Afuraitkait (Africa) since ancient times have referred to the this river as the **gher n gheren**. The term **gher** means *'river'.*

The title **gher n gheren** means *'river of rivers'.* The root is **gher**. Some have posited that a fragment of the phrase 'n gheren' meaning *'of rivers'* was corrupted by the whites and their offspring into *n-gheren* and *nigeren, niger* because *niger* already existed in latin and sounded simlar to their corrupted pronunciation of *n gheren.* The key however is that the root is **gher** and the Tuareg did not in the past nor do they today refer to the river as the 'Niger' in their Ancestral language. The term **gher** is actually derived from the terms **gari** and **gar** meaning *'stream'* in Kamit:

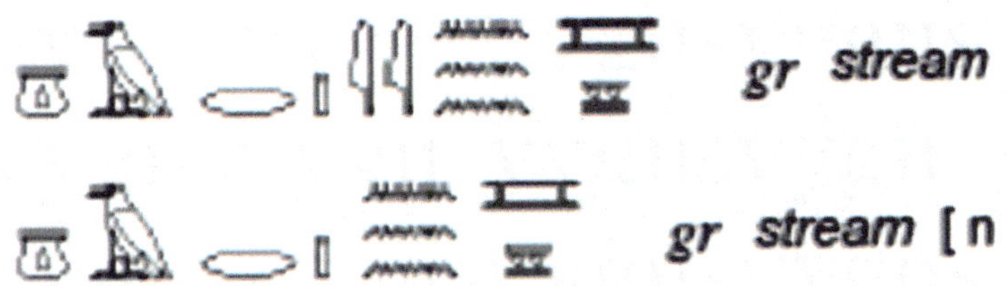

As we can see, none of the above terms nor their roots actually spell out 'nigger' or 'nigga'. The term *nigger* is derived from the same root as *negro, necro, neg (negate, negative), night*:

nigger (n.)
1786, earlier *neger* (1568, Scottish and northern England dialect), from French *nègre*, from Spanish *negro* (see ***Negro***).

Negro (n.)
"member of a black-skinned race of Africa," 1550s, from Spanish or Portuguese *negro* "black," from Latin *nigrum* (nominative *niger*) "black, dark, sable, dusky," figuratively "gloomy, unlucky, bad, wicked," of unknown origin (perhaps from PIE **nekw-t-* "night," cf. Watkins). As an adjective from 1590s. Use with a capital *N-* became general early 20c. (e.g. 1930 in "New York Times" stylebook) in reference to U.S. citizens of African descent, but because of its perceived association with white-imposed attitudes and roles the word was ousted late 1960s in this sense by ***Black*** (q.v.).

necro-
before vowels, *necr-*, word-forming element meaning "death, corpse, dead tissue," from comb. form of Greek *nekros* "dead body, corpse, dead person," from PIE **nek-* "death, natural death" (cf. Sanskrit *nasyati* "disappears, perishes," Avestan *nasyeiti* "disappears," *nasu-* "corpse," Old Persian *vi-nathayatiy* "he injures;" Latin *nex*, genitive *necis* "violent death, murder" (as opposed to *mors*), *nocere* "to harm, hurt," *noxius* "harmful;" Greek *nekus* "dead" (adj.), *nekros* "dead body, corpse;" Old Irish *ec*, Breton *ankou*, Welsh *angeu*"death").

night (n.)
Old English *niht* (West Saxon *neaht*, Anglian *næht*, *neht*) "night, darkness;" the vowel indicating that the modern word derives from oblique cases (genitive *nihte*, dative *niht*), from Proto-Germanic **nakht-* (cf. Old Saxon and Old High German *naht*, Old Frisian and Dutch *nacht*, German *Nacht*, Old Norse *natt*, Gothic *nahts*).
The Germanic words are from PIE **nekwt-* "night" (cf. Greek *nuks* "a night," Latin *nox*, Old Irish *nochd*, Sanskrit *naktam* "at night," Lithuanian *naktis* "night," Old Church Slavonic *nosti*, Russian *noch'*, Welsh *henoid* "tonight"), according to Watkins, probably from a verbal root **neg-* "to be dark, be night."

deny (v.)
early 14c., from Old French *denoiir* "deny, repudiate, withhold," from Latin *denegare* "to deny, reject, refuse" (source of Italian *dinegarre*, Spanish *denegar*), from *de-* "away" (see**de-**) + *negare* "refuse, say 'no,' " from Old Latin *nec* "not," from Italic base **nek-* "not," from PIE root **ne-* "no, not" (see **un-**). Related: *Denied*; *denying*.

neg, nega , , , , , , Amen. 12, 4, to lack, to want, to be short of; , Rec. 30, 216, 217, to be few in number; , Kubbân Stele 11, want of water.

neqan , to be lacking, or wanting.

neqāut , , , , , , Ebers Pap. 87, 5, , , Ebers Pap. 25, 3, Sphinx 14, 225, what is rubbed or ground down to powder, meal, fine flour.

neqāut , , B.D. 27, 1, 175, 25, foes crushed or beaten to death.

Neqāiu-ḥatu , B.D. 27, 1, the fiends who tore up hearts.

nequ-t , , something crushed, meal, powder (?)

neqeb , Metternich Stele 6, to mourn, to be afflicted.

neqem , T. 12, , N. 959, , , , , , Metternich Stele 3, to be afflicted, to mourn, to grieve, to lament.

neqmu , mourners, afflicted ones.

neqn-t [hieroglyphs], injury, affliction.

neqr [hieroglyphs], [hieroglyphs], Rec. 5, 86, 16, 159, to sift ; Copt. ποκερ (?)

neqr [hieroglyphs], [hieroglyphs], dust, powder, what is sifted.

As shown above, the whites and their offspring trace the terms *necro, negro, night* to the roots 'nekwt' and 'nek' yet are unsure of their etymological origins. This is because they have stolen terms which have no roots in their culture and then relabeled them as 'proto-indo-european'. The root of these terms can be found in Khanit and Kamit, predating the existence of europeans upon **Asaase** (Earth). The association of *negro, necro, night, negative (neg-* meaning *not, no, lack)* with *nekwt* and *nek* is rooted in the terms:

neqan	to be lacking, wanting (not having)
nega	lack, want
neqn	injury, affliction
neqaut	foes crushed or beaten to death

The related terms **neqr**, **nuqr** referencing *sifting; dust, powder, what is sifted,* etc. are related to that which is *crushed, beaten, pounded.* This is what happens in a *negative* sense to the *body, corpse* of a foe in Afurakani/Afuraitkaitnit (African) culture.

In a positive sense we do not crush, pound or cremate the body of the deceased. We engage the embalming and mummification process to preserve the body as an Ancestral shrine of the departed Ancestress or Ancestor. It is only in the *negative* sense that the body is treated otherwise, hence the related terms **neqem** and **neqeb** referencing *mourning, afflicted, grieving* and **Neqaiu hatu** – *the fiends who tear up hearts* in the spirit realm after the person died.

The loss of the heart was a grievous possibility in the spirit-realm, rendering the deceased spirit vulnerable to the attacks of other negative discarnate entities. This is why there are numerous chapters in the **Ru Nu Pert em Hru** (Book of Coming Forth by Day) wherein the individual invokes the Ntorou/Ntorotu (Deities) to not allow his or her heart to be taken away from him or her or destroyed/torn up.

However, in the culture of the whites and their offspring, cremation was/is a central feature of their funerary practices. The destruction of the body was not a descration to them, but a common practice. Afurakanu/Afuraitkaitnut (Africans) always preserved the bodies of our deceased in sacred ceremonies, that they may become **the most potent Ancestral shrines** of the departed Honorable Ancestor or Ancestress for family members to communicate with at sacred burial sites during Ancestral observances. <u>Since the whites and their offspring have no</u>

honorable ancestresses and ancestors, there was no ritual pracitce of preserving the melanin-recessive, perverse bodies of their deceased. They only began practicing embalming, mummification and elaborate burial practices after observing and imitating Afurakanu/Afuraitkaitnut (Africans).

Yet, because the whites and their offspring observed the sanctity of preserving the body, burial and Ancestral Communication amongst Afurakanu/Afuraitkaitnut (Africans) they always sought to desecrate the bodies of our deceased whenever they could during warfare, invasions, etc. They would also eventually use terms to identify us with the *dead, negative, afflicted, crushed,* etc. in a pejorative sense. This is the origin of the roots of terms such as **neqaut** being used in later european dialects to refer to Black people in general. Black used in the sense of *negative, not, lacking light* (therefore dark, black, gloomy), *lacking life* (dead), etc. [night, negro, necro, neg, naught, etc.] The **neqau** became the nekwt, nekus, nekros, necro, nigrum, niger, negre, negro, negroes, nigras, niggers, niggas, etc:

neqāut

B.D. 27, 1, 175, 25, foes crushed or beaten to death.

Neqau – Nigga

'niggas' are those who are *crushed, beaten to death*

This association of Black or Dark with *death, lack, want, negative* was utilized by the whites and their offspring in an attempt to demonize Afurakanu/Afuraitkaitnut (Africans). The same process undergirds their usage of the term 'moor' to refer to Black people in general as 'Dead'. [See our publication entitled: **Moor Means 'Dead'**]

Afurakanu/Afuraitkaitnut (Africans) who have accepted the false concept of what a 'God' or 'Goddess' is from the whites and their offspring have been spiritually corrupted. The association of the Supreme Being with fictional white characters such as jesus, yeshua ben pandira, muhammed, abraham, isaac, ishmael, jacob, esau, moses, aaron, solomon, sheba, menelik, buddha, brahmin, yahweh, allah, etc. – **none of whom existed of any race or in any form whatsoever** – was/is designed to emotionally coerce Afurakanu/Afuraitkaitnut (Africans) to embrace self-hatred. Such self-hatred manifests in Afurakani/Afuraitkaitnit (African) people foolishly attempting to trace their lineage back to these fictional characters, blacken-up these fictional characters, insert themselves into non-existent 'clans' and 'tribes' of these fictional characters, etc. We thus have misguided individuals referring to themselves as hebrews, moors, muslims, christians, buddhists, taoists, hermeticists, yogis, nuwapians, five percenters, aboriginals, masons, children of mu, extraterrestrials, etc.

Such self-hatred also manifests in the insane quest of such individuals to embrace and/or manufacture **contorted, absurd and totally inaccurate and baseless rationalizations** to force 'nigger' or 'nigga' to mean something sacred or divine. Yet, internally, psychologically, these indiviudals are actually seeking to hold on to the denigrating title given to them by the white slaver because they really accept it as their identity.

Another manifestation of this learned self-hatred is Black people referring to themselves as 'god'. Because we have accepted a false definition of 'God' from the whites and their offspring and in turn have an inferior reflection of ourselves in relation to that false definition, we then compensate by attempting to *de-inferiorize* ourselves through claiming 'the black man is god' or 'the black woman is god'. Black people who have low self-esteem seek to make themselves feel good by chanting such slogans to themselves, when in reality and internally they know it is nonsensical. **They have taken on the perverse and imbalanced white male masculinist and white female feminist complexes of seeking to be superior to the other sex as well as to be superior to the 'human being' in general.** Such Afurakanu/Afuraitkaitnut (Africans) therefore cannot 'settle' for being a 'human', they must be 'god', 'goddess' or a 'spiritual being having a human experience'. This foolish mindset bespeaks the lack of understanding of who they truly are as Afurakani/Afuraitkaitnit (African) people in relation to **Amenet-Amen** (**Nyamewaa-Nyame**), the actual Supreme Being - Goddess/God. It also betrays the deeply embedded self-hatred spawned by the perverse doctrines of the whites and their offspring.

When we understand the cosmological foundation of **Abode** (Creation) we recognize the reality that **Amenet** and **Amen** function as One Divine Unit – Two Complementary Halves of the Divine Whole. All *created* entities including plant life, animal life, mineral life and Afurakani/Afuraitkaitnit (African) human life (Afurakani/Afuraitkaitnit human life only) have a Divinely demarcated place and function (role) in the world.

Our value is encoded in the Divine Function that we have been given to execute as 'cells' within the Great Divine 'Body' of Amenet-Amen.

Just as your heart cells, liver cells, bone marrow cells, etc. each have their own *value* in the body, based on the *functions* within the organs' system they are a part of and support, so is every Afurakani/Afuraitkaitnit (African) individual encoded with a *Divine Function* to execute in the world which is expressive of his or her value in the world as a 'cell' within the Great Divine 'Body' of Amenet-Amen. We are each given an **Okra/Okraa** (**Ka/Kait**; **Ori Inu**; **Se**

Lido) which is encoded with this Divine Function. The Okra/Okraa is our Soul/Divine Consciousness – a *Deity* (Obosom, Orisha, Vodou, Ntoro/Ntorot) a Spirit-Force in Creation which dwells within our head-region and guides us throughout our lives. **This is our conscious connection to Divinity**, for our Okra/Okraa is a child of the Great Okra/Okraa (Ka/Kait - Soul/Divine Consciousness) of Amenet-Amen (Nyamewaa-Nyame).

Heart cells do not need to seek to be 'the heart' (organ) in order to feel better about themselves. Lung cells do not need to claim that they are 'not really cells of the organ' they are an 'organ having a cellular experience'. They have no need to denigrate their function in the body in order to seek a 'higher' function. No cells need to claim that they are actually the 'entire body' (the Great Being) and not 'merely' a 'cell'. Every cell has its place. Every organ has its place. The structure/place is Divinely designed. The same is true for Afurakanu/Afuraitkaitnut (Africans). Our function as **human beings** (the **only** *true/created* human beings) in relation to plant life, animal life, mineral life and the Abosom (Deities) has value and is undergirded by **Nyamewaa-Nyame Nhyehyee (Amenet-Amen Sekher)** -The Supreme Being's Order, Divine Order. We have no need to attempt to foolishly and pseudo-intellectually, step outside of our roles – which in **reality** we could **never do anyway**.

Pseudo-scholars, pseudo-metaphysicians, pseudo-traditional 'spiritualists', pseudo-conscious 'culturalists' and others in america, the west as well as in Afuraka/Afuraitkait (Africa) seek to take advantage of certain Afurakanu/Afuraitkaitnut (Africans) who are emotionally unstable as well as those Afurakanu/Afuraitkaitnut (Africans) who are simply ignorant to facts and are therefore misguided. Such parasitical pseudo-'teachers' seek financial gain, sexual favors, prestige as well as accolades from the whites and their offspring for working as their agents against the interests of the Afurakani/Afuraitkaitnit (African) community. Such parasites are easily exposed and dismissed for good with accurate information. The same is true for well-meaning, yet misinformed 'scholars', 'teachers' and 'elders'.

Our connection as Afurakanu/Afuraitkaitnut (Africans) to **Nyamewaa-Nyame/ Amenet-Amen**, **Gagait Writ** and **Gangan Wr** is written into our Okra/Okraa – *pre-incarnation.* We must take the responsibility to ground ourselves in **reality** based on this Divine connection. We consciously *align* with **Gangan Wr** and **Gagait Writ**, **Amen** and **Amenet**, by *directly invoking Them* and *learning directly from Them.*

We are not 'god'. We do not have *a need to be* 'god'. As Afurakanu/Afuraitkaitnut (Africans~Black People), we are **nnipa** – human beings, the *only authentic* human beings. Recognize your *value* as **nnipa** rooted in the **reality** of your function and your place in **Abode** (Creation). This is our exclusive inheritance as Afurakanu/Afuraitkaitnut (Africans).

See our publications referenced in the text:

Note on the Term Ngg Wr or Ngng Wr in Kamit – Ngg Ur is not 'nigger' – Part 1
www.odwirafo.com/Note_on_the_Term_Ngg-Wr_or_Ngng-Wr_in_Kamit_Ngg-Ur_is_not_nigger.pdf

NEHESU-NEGUS-NKOSO – Negus is Not 'nigga'
www.odwirafo.com/Nehesu-Negus-Nkoso_Negus_is_not_nigga.pdf

NYANKOPON-NYANKONTON – RA-RAIT
www.odwirafo.com/Nyankopon_and_Nyankonton-Ra_and_Rait.pdf

The Origin of the Term Abosom in Kamit
www.odwirafo.com/The_Origin_of_the_Term_Abosom_in_Kamit.pdf

The Okra/Okraa Complex – The Soul of Akanfo
www.odwirafo.com/nhoma.html

AFURAKA/AFURAITKAIT – The Origin of the term 'Africa'
www.odwirafo.com/Afuraka-Afuraitkait_Article_Nhomawaa_Nan.pdf

MOOR MEANS 'DEAD'
www.odwirafo.com/Moor_means_Dead.pdf

KUKUU-TUNTUM – The Ancestral Jurisdiction
www.odwirafo.com/kukuutuntumpage.html

Language and Transliteration References:

Resource for Texts from Kamit: *Coffin Texts, Pyramid Texts, Translations, Transliterations*
www.pyramidtexts.online/tools.html

An Hieroglyphic Dictionary, Vols. 1 and 2, E.A. Wallis Budge
A Dictionary of the Asante and Fante language called Tshi (Chwee, Twi), J.G. Christaller
www.archive.org

Kasahorow Online, Promoting African Languages
www.kasahorow.org

NEHESU – NEGUS – NKOSO

Negus is not 'nigga'

ODWIRAFO

NEHESU – NEGUS - NKOSO

Negus is not 'nigga'

In our publication: **Akan – The People of Khanit** we elucidated the etymological origin of the name **Akan** as a designation for the Akan ethnic group who live primarily in the West Afurakani/Afuraitkaitnit (African) countries of Ghana and Ivory Coast. There are many Akan in the western hemisphere as well, descendants of those who were enslaved as prisoners of war during the **Mmusuo Kese** (Great Perversity/Enslavement era). The root of the name Akan is **kan**, which in the Twi (Akan) language means: *first, foremost* as well as *to count, to reckon, to calculate*. The oral traditions of the Akan state that the reason that we refer to ourselves as Akan is because we are recognized to be a component part of the *first people to exist in the world* as well as the *first people to engage in calculation (reckoning)*, which is the foundation of study, measurement, ritual and scientific inquiry and hence the capacity to replicate of the Order of Creation in the institutions of a social Order (civilization).

Ancient Khanitu (Akanni - Nubians) visiting Kamit

Khentiu [hieroglyphs]
dwellers in the South, *i.e.*, Nubians; [hieroglyph]

We showed that the root **kan** is derived from our Ancestral languages of Kamit and Khanit (Egypt and Nubia). A descriptive title of Nubia is **Khnt** (**Khanat**) from the root **khn** (**khan**). The term **khan** in the ancient language means *first, foremost* as well as *to count, to reckon*. The name Khanat or the Khanit land means the *first land, south land, front land, land of origins,* etc. The people of the Khanat or Khanit land are the **Khanitu** – the *first people*. This descriptive title of the first people of the original land Khanitu is still used by their descendants today – Akan or Akanni people. [See: www.odwirafo.com/Akanni_Khanit.pdf]

A unique feature of Akan culture is the **kradin** concept. The term kradin is composed of **Kra** or **Kraa** (krah or krah'ah – also **Okra/Okraa**) meaning *'Soul/Divine consciousness'* and **din** (deen) meaning *'name'*. The kradin is thus the *'Soul's name'*. In Akan culture, we recognize that there are **Abosom** (Deities) that govern the solar, lunar and planetary bodies which govern the **nnawotwe** or 7-day inclusive week. The names of the seven days are based on the Abosom (Deities) Who govern the celestial body and hence the day. When an Akan person is born, the day upon which he or she is born is an indicator of which **Obosom** (Deity) he or she was assigned to in the spirit-realm *prior* to birth. He or she thus takes on a kradin, a soul-name, reflective of the Obosom Who governs the day as well as his or her Okra/Okraa (Soul). For example, the day called **Benada** is 'tuesday'. In Akan it is the day (da) of the Obosom **Bena**. In Kamit the Obosom **Bena** is called **Heru Behdety** (Behdet, Behdat, Behda or Bena; **Ogun** in Yoruba). Males born on Benada therefore automatically receive the name **Kwabena** meaning that they are a subject (kwa) of the Obosom Bena. This means that his Okra is aligned with and governed by this Divine Force in Creation.

In Akan culture the Female Obosom governing **Fida** (Friday) is the Obosom **Afi** also called **Afua**. She is the Female Obosom Who animates the planet **Afi**, called 'venus' in english. Her title Afi in Akan from the root **Fi** (fee) is derived from one of her descriptive titles in Kamit: **Fait** (fah-eet'). This is a title of **Het Heru** (Hathor). **Afi** (Het Heru, called **Oshun** in Yoruba) is the Obosom of beauty, song, art, dance, music, adornment, creativity, innovation, exploration, adventure, etc. She governs the sensual attraction which is the precursor to procreative activity and that which replenishes its harmony (pleasure). This is the foundation of creativity (procreativity) and thus she governs various expressions of creativity. Physiologically, Afi governs the reproductive system in the Afurakani/Afuraitkaitnit (African) body (fallopian tubes in the female, epididymis in the male) as well as the Divine Reproductive

System in Creation – the Divine Body of **Amenet** and **Amen** (**Nyamewaa** and **Nyame**) – the Mother and Father Supreme Being. [See our: **AKRADINBOSOM** and **Afi - The Obosom of Afi and Fida**: **www.odwirafo.com/akradinbosom.html**]

In Akan culture, all of the **akradin** (soul-names) have **mmrane** or *praise names* associated with them, which are expressive of different aspects of the Obosom as well as the nature of the Okra/Okraa (Soul) of the person who is born under that Obosom on that Obosom's day. One of the mmrane or praise names for a Fida (Friday) – born female is **Nkoso**. This is also an mmrane for Afi. **Nkoso** references that which is: *splendid, grand, gorgeous, brilliantly adorned,* etc. It also references *progress, furtherance, success, prosperity.* The verb '**ko**' means 'to go' while '**so**' means *'up, above'* and also *'upon'.* The mmrane Nkoso thus references the nature of the energy-complex of Afi and her children who 'go above, upon, beyond'. They are adventurous, creative, innovative, artistic, wanderers, explorers, progressive (in the natural sense), prosperous, re-productive, furthering of the clan, people, progeny, etc.

The name vocalized as **Nkoso** (un-kaw'-soh) as a title of **Afi** (Het Heru) in Akan is the same title of **Het Heru** (**Fait**) in Kamit spelled **N-h-s** in the medutu (hieroglyphs):

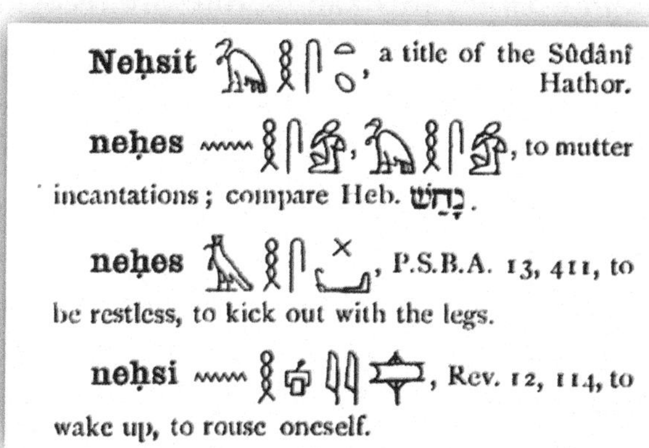

Neḥsit, a title of the Sûdânî Hathor.

neḥes, to mutter incantations; compare Heb. נָחַשׁ.

neḥes, P.S.B.A. 13, 411, to be restless, to kick out with the legs.

neḥsi, Rev. 12, 114, to wake up, to rouse oneself.

From the **Akan (Twi)** dictionary:

ŋkɔ-só, *inf. progress; furtherance. Phil. 1,25; success, prosperity; edification;* mā ŋk., *to cause to prosper, to edify. 1 Cor. 8,1;* - nyā ŋk., *to prosper, be edified, receive edifying. 1 Cor. 8,10;* -

kɔ̀sɔɔ, kɔ̀sɔkɔsɔ, *adv. gorgeously, splendidly,* of adorning; ɔde sika nè ŋhenè ahyehyɛ ne hō kɔsɔɔ, *she has adorned, bedecked, bespangled herself in a gorgeous manner, brilliantly.* - *syn.* pii,

The term **nhs** (spelled 'nehes' by egyptologists because of uncertainty about the vocalization) meaning *to be restless, to rouse oneself* is an exact description of an **Afua** (child of Afi) also called **Nkoso** in Akan culture. Children of Afi are said to be *restless wanderers, easily aroused (creatively/artistically or procreatively/sensually) and able to arouse or inspire others through art, song, dance, creativity, sensuality, etc.* The 'n' in Nkoso is a nasal prefix. The same is true in the language of Kamit and Khanit. The 'Sudani' meaning '**Khaniti**' title of Het Heru is **Nhoso** and the **Akanni** title of Het Heru is still **Nkoso**. The root is **Koso** in Akan, the vocalized version of **Hs** (Hos, Hoso written 'hs' or 'hes', 'hesi' by egyptologists). Note the Coptic dialectical vocalization Copt. ϩⲱⲥ. [Hawc or Haws – Kos (Kaws) in Twi]:

Ḥeḥ-neb-Ḥeḥ-ta , B.D. 64, 38, a god.

ḥeḥ , Shipwreck, 36, to strike; , to cut, to smite off, sword.

ḥeḥui (?) , , the two ears; var. .

ḥeḥes , a kind of bird.

ḥes , , , , Sinsin II, 20, , , , , , , , , , , , , , to praise, to commend, to honour, to do honour to, to reward, to recompense, to remunerate, to requite, to show favour to; , to sing or recite laudatory writings, praises, etc.; Copt. ϩωc.

ḥess , IV, 972, , to praise, to ascribe merit to, to applaud.

ḥessu , praises, hymns of praise, songs.

ḥessu , one who is praised.

ḥes-t, ḥesu-t , Rec. 31, 166, , , , , , , , , P. 655, M. 760, , IV, 944, , , , , , , , , , , , , praise, approval, approbation, commendation, favour, reward, gift, act of grace, gratification.

ḥess-t , , , IV, 1154, , , favour, an act of grace, something that pleases, a reward, pleasure.

ḥesi, ḥesu , , , , , , one to whom grace and favour have been shown [by Osiris], *i.e.*, a dead person, one who is approved of by a god; plur. , , , , , , , , , , the blessed dead.

ḥesi , he who is praised, he who praises; … , the praised one who praises those who are to be praised; … , IV, 967, the praises of those who are praised.

ḥesit , I, 139, a personal decoration or mark of favour.

ḥesutȧ , P. 424, N. 1212, , praised, renowned, famous; said of a weapon, … , "thou seizest thy famous javelin."

ḥestȧ , Tombos Stele 10, will.

ḥes, ḥesi , , , , , , to sing, to chant, to repeat laudatory compositions; Copt. ϩωc.

ḥesi , , , , A.Z. 1906, 123, , to sing to the accompaniment of an instrument.

ḥes , Rev. 12, 32, song; Copt. ϩωc.

ḥes-t , chant.

ḥesu, chant, song, any rhythmical composition; (var.) the 70 chants or songs of Rā.

ḥesi em ben-t, to sing to the harp, harper.

ḥesi em ṭe-t, to sing to the hand, *i.e.*, to sing whilst playing a musical instrument.

ḥesiu, Rec. 21, 97, singers, musicians, musical entertainers, professional mourners; male singers; female singers, wailing women.

ḥesi-àb, to sing to the heart (?)

ḥesi-t, Love Songs 4, 1, a song of love.

ḥesi, a spell to be recited against evil creatures in the water.

Ḥes-ā, Ṭuat I, a singing-god.

ḥesi, IV, 971, IV, 1105, IV, 85, 613, 945, Sphinx Stele 11, to run or rush against, to attack, to advance with hostility, to show himself (of the enemy), to come on against, to encroach (of the sand about the Sphinx); Tombos Stele 12.

ḥes-t, Thes. 1289, vase, vessel, pot, libation vessel; plur.

ḥess-t, pot, vessel.

ḥesḥes, to be hot, to burn, fire, flame.

ḥess, heat, flame, fire.

ḥes-t, Rec. 32, 66, to sprout.

ḥesti (?), U. 337, two sceptres (?)

ḥesa, Hearst Pap. 3, 2, Love Songs 1, 7, new milk, milk in general, milk supply, milk vessels full or empty.

Ḥesait [\], P. 204 + 10, N. 976, Rec. 26, 224, A.Z. 1906, 130, the Cow-goddess of heaven who supplied the blessed with milk.

ḥesau, P. 306, the Milky Way (?)

As we can see, the root **hs** (**koso** in Twi) references those who are *creative, singers, entertainers, splendid, approved by the Deity, lauded, celebrated, praised, honored, favored, decorated,* etc. These are all attributes of Afi and children of Afi (Het Heru). We also see the reference to the *Great Divine Cow of Heaven* who supplied the blessed with milk. **Het Heru** as **Fait** is the *Great Divine Cow* and also the support of the western (amenti) Heaven:

Het Heru as the Divine Cow in the **amenti** (western region)

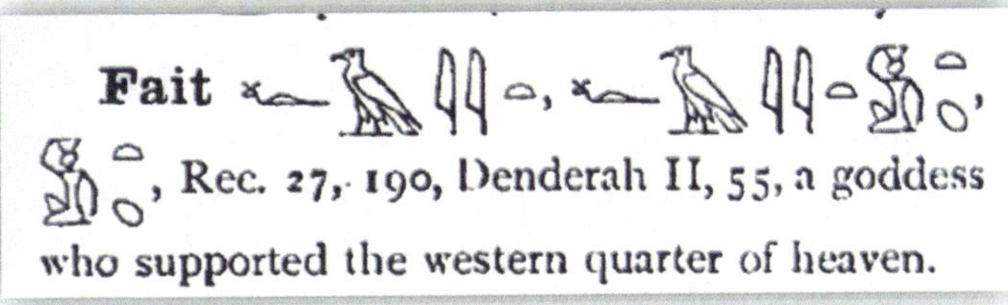

Fait [hieroglyphs], [hieroglyphs], [hieroglyphs], Rec. 27, 190, Denderah II, 55, a goddess who supported the western quarter of heaven.

We also recall that Het Heru heals the eyes of **Heru** with milk when they were torn out during his fight with **Set**. This association is key, for Het Heru as a title means the 'House of Heru'. Het Heru is the Queen Mother who nurtures (gestates) the King in her womb (het/house). Indeed, a title of Het Heru is **Herit** meaning 'She Who is Above, Leader, Chieftainess' while the male counterpart is **Heri**, 'He who is above, Chief, King'. Het Heru is also called **Nebt Pet** *(Nbt Pt)* and **Henut Ntorou Nebu** *(Hnwt Ntrw Nbw)* meaning 'Mistress of Heaven' and 'Queen of All of the Deities'.

This is the foundation of the root **hs** (**koso**) meaning the one *'who is praised', 'renowned', 'blessed'*, etc. in reference to royalty. The ancient *title* of Het Heru, **Nhst** (**Nhosot**), vocalized as **Nkoso** in Akan is the origin of the term **Nagast** and **Nagas** (**Negusit** and **Negus**) – an Ethiopian title descriptive of *royalty* as in *to reign*. This term was also used for **Khanitu** (Nubians/Ethiopians) by the Kamau in general:

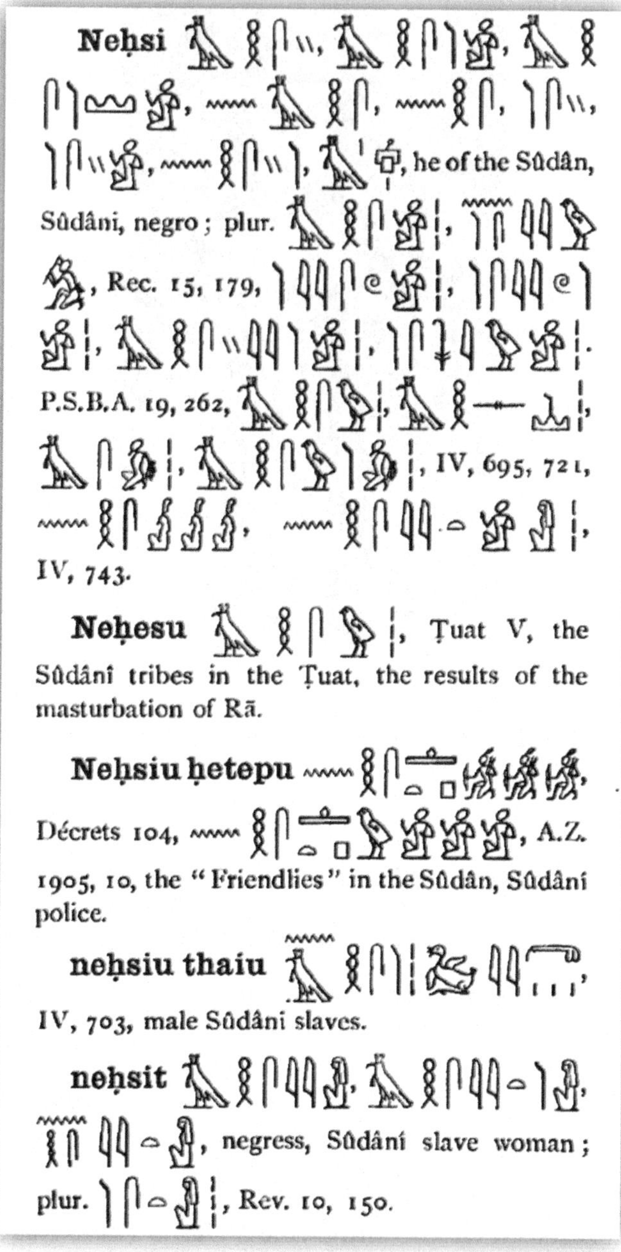

Neḥsi, he of the Sûdân, Sûdâni, negro; plur., Rec. 15, 179, P.S.B.A. 19, 262, IV, 695, 721, IV, 743.

Neḥesu, Ṭuat V, the Sûdânî tribes in the Ṭuat, the results of the masturbation of Rā.

Neḥsiu ḥetepu, Décrets 104, A.Z. 1905, 10, the "Friendlies" in the Sûdân, Sûdânî police.

neḥsiu thaiu, IV, 703, male Sûdâni slaves.

neḥsit, negress, Sûdânî slave woman; plur., Rev. 10, 150.

The **Nehesu** are vocalized as the **Negesu** or **Nagasu** in Geez. Those who are *first, foremost, from the land of the Ancestresses and Ancestors (first land, etc.).* The Negus and Negusit (Nagas and Nagasit) are the Nehes and Nehesit – the *first, head, leader, governor, governess,* etc. They are those who are *praised, adorned,* etc. Just as the term 'Nubia' is derived from the term '**nub**' in Kamit meaning 'gold' and thus the **Nubitu** or *Nubians* are the 'golden' people, *adorned people,* those *worthy of praise,* etc. so is the term **Nehesu** (**Nkoso**) representative of these characteristics.

Notice, however, that the egyptologists attempt to denigrate the name, for they desire to associate Black and Afurakani/Afuraitkaitnit (African) with 'slave' 'negress', etc. as a pejorative. Yet, even in their attempt to denigrate the character of the Afurakanu/Afuraitkaitnut (Africans) south of Kamit, the **cosmology of the culture precludes them from doing so**.

When the Nehesu are associated with 'masturbation', this is **deliberately misrepresented by the whites and their offspring** in order to associate Afurakau/Afuraitkaitnut (Africans) with sexual deviance. However, the reference to 'masturbation' is **inaccurate**.

When the Obosom/Deity **Atem** (**Atum**) in Kamit speaks of 'having union with His clenched hand' in order to create his Children, **Shu** and **Tefnut**, the 'clenched hand' he is speaking of is the Obosom/Deity **Iusaaset Nebet Hetepet** (**Ausaaset** called **Asaase Afua** in Akan). She is a wife of Atem who is also called the *'Lady of the Vulva'* as well as the *'Hand of the God'*. The vagina was regarded as a 'hand' because of its function in the act of procreation. Just an Afurakani man today will call his wife his 'right hand', so did we refer to the ancient Goddess Mother as the 'Hand of the God'. It demonstrates that **the woman is an active participant in the procreative process** as opposed to being merely an empty, passive vessel waiting for the male to fill her with his seed. The woman is magnetic, *actively* drawing the male to her. The vagina *actively* pulls the seed out of the male. The ovum *actively* pulls/draws, magnetically, the sperm to itself. On every level, the woman is as equally active as the male in the process.

[See: **Asaase Afua and Asaaase Yaa: Earth Mother Abosom**: www.youtube.com/odwirafo]

The notion of the Nkoso (Nehesu, Negesu, Negesut), Ethiopians/Nubians being associated with the 'Hand of the God' is once again associating them with an original (first) procreative *function* of Het Heru, who also operates as the 'Hand of the God'. Het Heru, is **Nehesit** (Negusit, Nagast), **Nkoso**. As shown in our article on Afi, in Akan culture Afi is called **Kyekye** (Che-che), *the evening star*. The title **Kyekye** is the Akan variant of **Het Her** (Che-cher).

Fait Het Heru Nhosot (Nhst) – Afi Kyekye Nkoso

While we can see the cosmological foundation for the term Nkoso (Nhosou) in Kamit and Akan in association with the Nubians/Ethiopians south of Kamit we must also recognize the political reality of the relationship between the Afurakanu/Afuraitkaitnut (Africans) of Kamit and Khanit during different times in **trustory** (true history). There were periods where they were allies, while during other periods they were adversaries. This is where the notion of the Nehesu being those who 'mutter' incantations, engage in negative forms of 'witchcraft', etc. derive from. The ritual practice of chanting, ritual song, ritual dance, spirit possession, etc. can be used for productive or non-productive purposes. While the Khanitu were known for having powerful 'magic' – ritual capabilities, during times of conflict this capacity was re-characterized as the Nubians/Ethiopians being 'sorcerers'. The same dynamic exists today amongst various Afurakani/Afuraitkaitnit (African) groups. Some ethnic groups regard their neighbors as steeped in sorcery and characterize them as spiritual criminals not to be trusted. There are some Akan for example who label the neighboring and related Nzema people in this fashion.

From the text of **Khaemwaset and Sa Ausar** (Khamwas and Si-Osiri):

"...Said the other of them after saying: 'Let ***Amen*** *not find for me misfortune nor the Kwr of Kamit cause abomination to be done to me: I would* ***cast my magic*** *up to Kamit that I might cause the Per Aa of Kamit to be brought to the land of* ***Nehes****, and cause him to be beaten with a scourging, 500 blows of the stick in the midst before the Viceroy, and cause him to be brought back up to Kamit in six hours precisely.'*

When the viceroy heard what the ***three men of Ethiopia*** *had said, he ordered them to be brought before him. He said to them: 'Who of you is he that said, "I will* ***cast my magic*** *up to Kamit, I will not allow them to see light in three days (and) three nights" ?' They said: 'It is Heru, the son of the Sow.'*

Said he: 'Who is he that said, "I will cast my magic up to Kamit, I will bring Per Aa to the land of ***Nehes****, I will cause him to be beaten with a scourging, 500 blows of the stick in the midst of the Viceroy, I will cause him to be taken back to Kamit in six hours precisely" ?' They said:* ***'It is Heru, the son of the Nehesit****.'* http://www.reshafim.org.il/ad/egypt/texts/khamuas.htm

As we can see, there are political reasons why the **Nehesu** (**Nkoso**) at certain times were labeled as 'sorcerers' in Kamit. The term **hos** (hes, hesi - **koso**) referencing ritual practices are therefore **selectively** given a pejorative connotation at times when referencing the Khanitu.

The cosmology of Khanit and Kamit and its continuum in Akan culture today is the infrastructure which gave birth to the term **Nhsu** (**Nkoso**) as a title of Het Heru, Her Divine function in Creation, Her association with royalty (House of Heru – the King; Herit – Queen) and more. Nehes, Nhsu, vocalized as Nkoso in Akan is the origin of Negus, Nagas etc. **The root hs, hsu (koso) is clearly not the word 'nigger' or 'naga'**. For details about the *actual* etymology of the word 'naga' being derived from a title of **Ra** (Ra Akh, Da Akh, Na Akh) see our publication: **Nyankopon-Nyankonton – Ra-Rait**. For details about the term **Ngg Wr or Ngg Ur** from Kamit which is **not** the origin of 'nigger' see our publication: **Note on the Term**

Ngg Wr or Ngng Wr in Kamit – Ngg Ur is Not 'nigger'. For accurate information about proper notions of identity see our publication: **AFURAKA/AFURAITKAIT – The Origin of ther term 'Africa'**. Also see our publication: **MOOR MEANS 'DEAD'** for accurate information about the origin of the term 'moor', which is actually a **pejorative** term for our people used by the whites and their offspring. Download these articles from our links below.

Appendix

[*Excerpt from pages 19-23 of our publication:* **NYANKOPON-NYANKONTON – RA-RAIT**]

RA AAKHU – NANKA

The name **O-nanka** as a title for the Creator in the form of a snake becoming **O-danga** or **E-danga** is derived from a title of **Ra**. In the *Book of the Heavenly Cow*, found in the tombs of **Tut Ankh Amen**, **Seti** and **Ramessu**, we find that **Ra** is referred to as **Ra Aakhu**. The metutu are:

Ra **Aakhu**

"Whoever says these words works his own protection by means of the words of power, *'I am the Deity Heka and I am pure in my mouth and in my body. I am **Ra** from whom the Deities proceeded. I am **Ra Aakhu**.'* When you say this, step forth in the evening and in the morning on your own behalf, if you would make to fall the enemies of **Ra**."
[Book of the Cow of Heaven – Tomb of Seti]

Ra Aakhu is defined as **Ra** operating as **Aakhu**, the Light/Fire. **Aakhu** and **Aakhut** are also written **Aakh** and **Aakht**. Different aspects of the term **Aakhu** or **Aakh**:

áakhu, N. 112, 124, , T. 292, , T. 399, Rec. 31, 17, , , P. 2, , , , to shine, to be bright, fine, splendid, glorious, excellent, good, to be useful, to recite formulae.

áakhu-t, L.D. III, 140c, fire.

åakhu, U. 622, P. 237, , IV, 918, , , , , A.Z. 1900, 129, light, splendour, radiance, brilliance, glorious deeds, splendid acts, virtues, excellences, blessings, benefits;

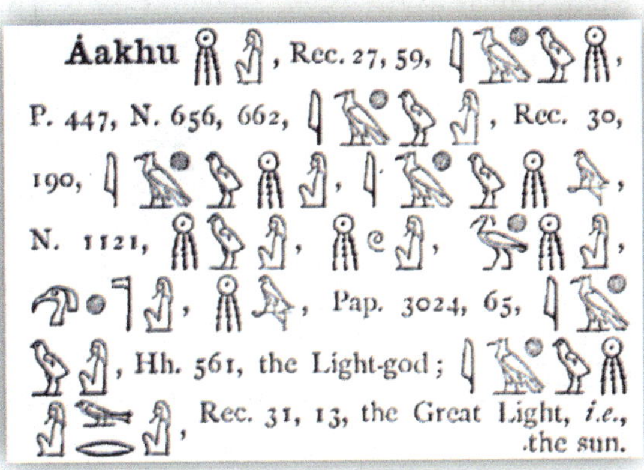

Åakhu, Rec. 27, 59, , P. 447, N. 656, 662, , Rec. 30, 190, , , N. 1121, , , , , , Pap. 3024, 65, , Hh. 561, the Light-god; , Rec. 31, 13, the Great Light, *i.e.*, the sun.

åakhu-t, T. 251, 321, , , U. 440, , , , , , , , , the Eye of Rā or Horus, the fiery light of the sun, a flame-goddess, the fiery uraeus on Pharaoh's crown, the name of a crown; , the uraei on the royal crown.

The terms **Aakh** or **Aakhu** and **Aakht** or **Aakhut** thus reference *Fire, Light, brilliance, radiance*, the *Aten* (Sun) as well as the ***fiery Serpent on the Royal Crown***:

Ra Aakhu is Raakhu, Raako, Daako, Danko, Dango, **Nanko** **Nyanko**
Ra Aakh is Raakh, Raakha, Daaka, Danka, Danga, **Nanka** **Nyanka**

Recall that in Akan culture, the birth-place-name for the second child born after twins can be written **Nyankomago** or **Nyankamago**. The 'A' and 'O' are used interchangeably. Note also that **Da** in Vodoun is also commonly written and pronounced **Dan**. The 'A' in **Da** is *nasal*, thus sounding like **Dan** (Dah-ng) when enunciated, similar to the 'N' in the word *senior*. This nasal 'A' is derived from a pronunciation of the name **Ra**. In the metutu when the name **Ra** is spelled out we have:

The metut is the character for the letter 'R'. The metut is the character for the letter 'A'. The other two metut, the serpent surmounting the Aten (Sun) and the mummified, seated figure are *determinatives*. They are not read or enunciated. They are *markers*, indicators that this word 'ra' refers to the serpent around the Aten who is an Obosom (Deity - the mummified figure denotes Divinity/sacredness). There are three different metutu for the 'A' sound in Kamit. The metut of a forearm and open hand with palm turned upward for the letter 'A' is sometimes written in the **Coptic dialect** (Late Kamit dialect) as **'AW'**. Thus, the 'A' in **Ra** could be thus be pronounced like the 'AWNG' in the english word *'wrong'* and taking on a nasal tone. **Ra Aakhu** would thus be pronounced like **rawn-ah-ko'**. The difference between pronouncing **Ra** and **Ra** with a nasal tone is [**rah**] and [**rawn** or **rah-oong**]. This is also the difference between the Vodoun versions **Da** and **Dan** (Dah-ng) The pronunciation dah-ng sounds like dah-oong. This is the same as O-Dang-a and E-Dang-a. It is also **Nanka** (Nah-ng-a). Just as some Afurakanu/Afuraitkaitnut speaking the Fon language pronounce **Da** with a nasal 'N' - **Dan** (dahng) today, so did some Afurakanu/Afuraitkaitnut in Kamit pronounce **Ra** with a nasal 'N' in ancient times. **Ra-Aakhu** or Ra[wn]-Aakhu thus became Ra[ng]-Aakhu, Daankhu, Daanko, Danga, Naanko and **Nanka**.

Note: The **Ebrie** people, another **Akan** sub-group in Cote de' Ivoire, call the Creator **Nyangka** or **Nyanka**. This fact in relation to the forms **Ananga-man**, **Odanga** and **Edanga** proves that the **Nyanko** or **Nyanka** component of **Nyankopon** and **Nyankonton** is a dialectical variant of **Nanka**.

Circular serpent pendant, manifestation of **Nyankga**, from the **Ebrie** Akan of Cote de' Ivoire

Ra Aakhu or **Ra Aakh**, the fiery Circular Serpent (cobra) as **Da Aakh**, **Na aakh**, is found in the ancient temple of **Naga** in Khanit (Sudan, Nubia). Moreover, some of the Afurakanu/Afuraitkaitnut of ancient Khanit (Nubia) migrated east and settled india over ten thousand years ago. This is why the term **Naga** (also written Naya, Naka) is a name of the *Divine Cobra* in different parts of **pre-aryan** (pre-white) india. When the whites and their offspring began to invade india approximately 4,000 years ago they came into contact with the indigenous Afurakanu/Afuraitkaitnut – the descendants of the Afurakani/Afuraitkaitnit migrants from Khanit. The false religions of hinduism and buddhism would *later* incorporate and corrupt the meaning and function of the Naga. The **Naga** in Black india, **Naga** in Khanit (Nubia) is the same **Nanka** in Akan. They all derive from **Ra Aakha** and **Rat Aakhat** or **Ra Aakhu** and **Rait Aakhut**.

Ra and Lion-headed Obosom **Apedemak** from the Temple in **Naga** – ancient **Khanit** (Nubia)

RAT

In the first two of the three spellings of the name **Rat** (raht) above the metut is the letter 'R', the metut is the letter 'A' the metut is the letter 'T'. The metut of an egg is a determinative referencing *female*. The seated female figure is also a determinative indicating *female*. In the second variation we simply have the circular serpent for **Ra**, the 'T' metut and the egg symbol denoting **Rat** (female). In the third variation we have the circular serpent, the 'T' and the large cobra: . This cobra metut is a determinative metut. It means *Female Deity* (Goddess). These variations are of the name **Rat**. We also have variations of the name when pronounced **Rait** (rah-ette'):

RAIT

The three variations of the name **Rait** above include the metut for the 'I': The second and third variations of the name **Rait** above include another version of the raised cobra denoting Female Divinity: . Note that this is the same determinative found in the term **aakhut** or **aakht** the ***fiery serpent on the royal crown***: **ȧakhu-t** . This term **aakhut** not only references different Abosom (Deities) Who have the title *"Eye of **Ra**"*, such as **Uatchet**, but also references **Rait** as the *Original Ancestral Female Creatress*. **Rait** is the *Progenitress Serpent Obosom* (Deity) from Whom all other Female Abosom Who carry that energy and title *descend*. The above also is a reference to the feminine title **Rait Aakhut** or **Rat Aakht**, the female **Nanka** or Naga.

DIVINE PROHIBITION AGAINST DISSEXUALITY-HOMOSEXUALITY IN ANCIENT KAMIT

NIANKHKHUNUM AND KHNUMHOTEP
IDENTICAL TWINS
NOT DISSEXUAL/HOMOSEXUAL

SET AND ANAT – THE DATING OF 'THE CONTENDINGS OF HERU AND SET '

DISSEXUALITY/HOMOSEXUALITY WAS NEVER ACCEPTED IN KAMIT

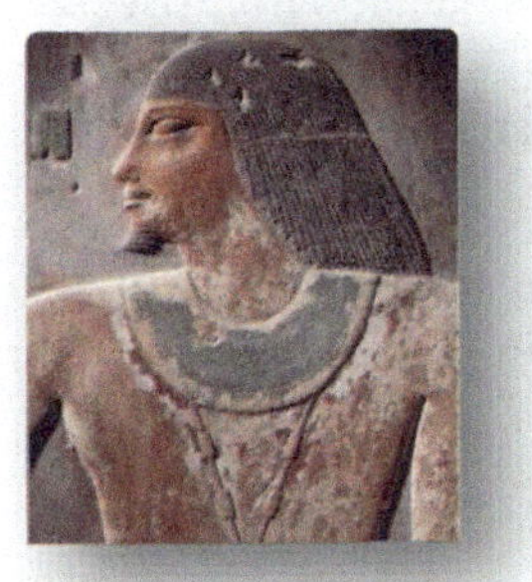

INSTRUCTIONS OF PTAH HETEP
PROPER TRANSLATION OF INSTRUCTION 35

PRE-PUBESCENT SEXUAL TABOO

ODWIRAFO KWESI RA NEHEM PTAH AKHAN

KOKOBO

The whites and their offspring (white americans, europeans, hispanics, pseudo-'native'-americans, asians, hindus, arabs, etc.) incarnate as spirits of disorder – **all of them** – and therefore manifest that diordered, perverse nature through their behavior inclusive of the practice of all forms of sexual deviance including dissexuality/homosexuality, pedophilia, bestiality and more. By contrast, Afurakanu/Afuraitkaitnut (Africans~Black People) incarnate as spirits of Divine Order and are therefore innately repulsed by dissexuality/homosexuality and all forms of sexual deviance. We recognize them as expressions of **insanity**.

The whites and their offspring, like cancerous cells, seek to consume and destroy all of those within their path whenever possible. This has been the case for over 12,000 years and will continue to be the case until we make them extinct. One of the means by which they work to destroy the Afurakani/Afuraitkaitnit (African) family is to pervert the spirits/minds of the people with sexual perversity. This is why the whites and their offspring are all over the world working to force dissexuality/homosexuality on Afurakani/Afuraitkaitnit (African) communities and nations This is genocidal warfare being waged against us on a constant basis.

We must recognize that the whites and their offspring – all of them – are our absolute enemies. We have been engaged in a war, yet we have not been fighting. Indeed, many do not even recognize that a war is being waged at all. One of the major means by which this war is waged is through the attempted corruption of Afurakani/Afuraitkaitnit (African) Ancestral Religion and Culture. This is why the whites and their offspring constantly attempt to promote the false belief that dissexuality/homosexuality was always a part of Afurakani/Afuraitkaitnit (African) culture. Their calculation is that if we accept this falsehood, we will react in one of two ways: 1) *we will despise African culture and have no desire to embrace it at all* or 2) *some of our people will embrace African culture with the goal of introducing white perversity – dissexuality/homosexuality – into its practice.* On both counts, this leaves sincere Afurakanu/Afuraitkaitnut (Africans) in a position of being dispossessed from our **culture** – *our natural way of life and living* – and thus mired in the way of life and living promoted by the whites and their offspring. This leads to self-destructive thoughts, intentions and actions and is thereby a means of physical, cultural, spiritual, political and economic enslavement. We reverse this process by embracing our authentic culture and living our values. This includes the absolute **repudiation** of dissexuality/homosexuality.

We initially published the articles and the appendix in this publication separately. We have combined them here for ease of study and distribution. **Kokobo** is an Akan term meaning *warning*. We must *warn* our people of the continuous assault being waged on our spirits and thus our communities by our enemies, the whites and their offspring and their Black agents who feign 'Afrocentrism', yet work at the behest of the whites and their offspring. Only then can we reorganize and remove our enemies and their agents.

Odwirafo Kwesi Ra Nehem Ptah Akhan
Aakhuamuman Amaruka Atifi Mu
(Akwamu Nation in North America)
www.odwirafo.com
July, 13014 (2014)

DIVINE PROHIBITION AGAINST DISSEXUALITY/HOMOSEXUALITY IN ANCIENT KAMIT

Odwirafo Kwesi Ra Nehem Ptah Akhan

Afurakanu/Afuraitkaitnut (Africans~Black People) have never accepted the spiritually perverse practice of dissexuality/homosexuality. This is true today and was/is true in ancient times. The whites and their offspring, as spirits of disorder, continuously attempt to insert their perverse, sexually deviant practices upon Afurakani/Afuraitkaitnit (African) culture on the continent and outside of the continent of Afuraka/Afuraitkait (Africa). This is one of their various approaches to the corruption of our Ancestral culture and thereby the spirits/minds of our people. One popular lie that they tell is that the **Ru Nu Pert em Hru** (misnomered *Egyptian Book of the Dead*) does not ban dissexuality/homosexuality - **when in fact it does**. Below is an excerpt from what is called *Chapter 125, Plate 31* of the **Ani Sheft** (Papyrus of Ani). In this passage, the spirit of the deceased individual declares to the **Ntoro** (**Ntr**/Deity) that *he has not copulated/penetrated with a copulator/penetrator.* This is a **Divine prohibition against dissexuality/homosexuality**.

In order to live in harmony in perpetuity after death in the Ancestral realm as well as during life in the physical realm, the Afurakani/Afuraitkaitnit (African~Black) individual must ritually invoke the **42 Ntorou/Ntorotu** (Gods/Goddesses) who are judges of **Maa/Maat** (Divine Law). In order to *harmonize* with the energy of the Ntorou/Ntorotu (Ntrw/Ntrwt), the Spirit-Forces of Creation, the **Embodiments of Divine Order** in Creation, Their energy is invoked. Once the energy is invoked (called) it can be *internalized, infused* and *replenished* within the individual. Like a drop of water fusing with a river, harmonizing with this greater force/body of water in Nature, so does the Afurakani/Afuraitkaitnit (African) individual fuse his/her energy with the energy of the Spirit Force in Nature that he/she is invoking ritually. This opens the way for one to **align** him/herself with the Divine Order of Creation.

However, in the process of ***accepting/receiving*** the infusion of energy, Divinely Ordered energy of the Ntorou/Ntorotu, the individual must ***reject*** perversity, disordered energy, which can manifest as a result of disordered thoughts, intentions and/or actions. The individual thus invokes (accepts) the energy of the Ntorou/Ntorotu, Spirits of Divine Order, and rejects (repels) disorder. In the passage below the individual invokes the Ntoro (God) **Qererti**, the Ntoro of the *caverns/holes* ***(qerert)***, *gateways* to the spirit-realm, He who *comes forth* from **Amentet**, the *Land of the West*, the *Ancestral realm*. The individual invokes, calls forth and *accepts/receives* the energy of the Ntoro and he also *rejects/repels* thoughts, intentions and actions that are repulsive to the Ntoro and thus the Divine Order of Creation. He states that he has **not copulated/penetrated** (entered the hole, cavern – *qerert*) **of a copulator/penetrator**. The only *hole/cavern* (qerert) that a male should enter during copulation is that of the female whose *cavern* (**kait**/vagina) is also associated in ancient Kamit with the opening (*hole, qerert*) to the **Tuat** (Ancestral realm) whose *gate* is **Amentet** – the *Land of the West* (Land of the setting Aten/Sun).**

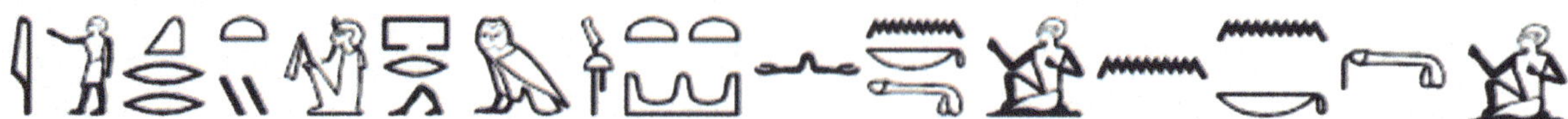

A Qererti, per em Amentet, an nk n nk

*Hail, Qererti, coming forth from the Land of the West, not have I penetrated/copulated (**nk**) with a penetrator/copulator (**nk**)*

The whites and their offspring often attempt to translate this passage as: *I have not fornicated with a fornicator.* However, the term **nk** (**noiek** in Coptic) with the determinative of the erect phallus (**ka** in Kamit) is not referencing fornication but copulation/penetration.

Ani Sheft

(Actual image of Papyrus of Ani from whence the above metutu (hieroglyphs) are taken)

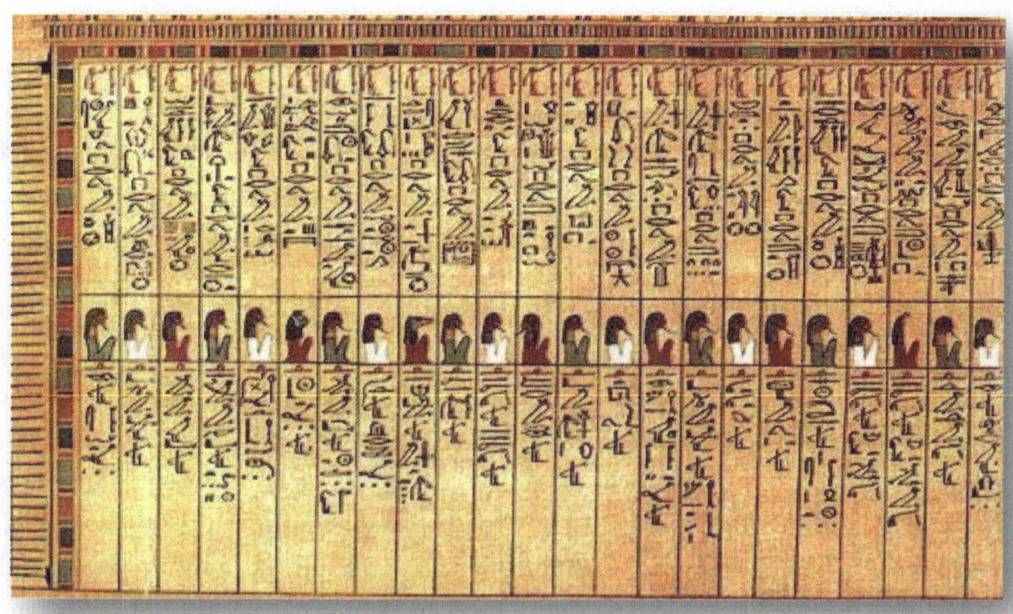

Above is an excerpt from what are often called the **42 Declarations of Innocence, 42 Laws of Maat, 42 Negative Confessions**, etc. The spirit of the deceased individual actually *invokes*

42 different Ntorou/Ntorotu (Deities) through ritual prayer in the sanctuary of **Maati** for purificatory purposes. The **eleventh** Ntoro (Deity) is called **Qererti**. Below is a close-up of the invocation of **Qererti** which contains the metutu translated above:

Hail, Qererti, coming forth from the Land of the West, I have not copulated/penetrated with/a copulator/penetrator.

The Abosom, Orisha, Vodou, Ntorou/Ntorotu (Neteru/Netertu) never have and never will accept dissexuality/homosexuality. Amenet-Amen, the Ntorou/Ntorotu and Aakhu/Aakhutu - The Supreme Being, the Deities and the Ancestresses and Ancestors of Afuraka/Afuraitkait (Africa) <u>hate</u> dissexuality/homosexuality and direct us to hate/reject it as a prerequisite to harmonizing with Divine Order. This is true of all other forms of sexual deviance as well. Afurakani/Afuraitkaitnit (African~Black)

individuals who proclaim otherwise are pseudo-culture bearers and charlatans be they 'scholars', 'researchers', 'professors', 'psychologists', 'geneticists', 'physicians', 'spiritualists', 'universalists', 'metaphysicians', 'kabbalists', 'esotericists', 'initiates' of a pseudo-traditional African religious priest/esshood, pseudo-'native'-american or asian 'system' of spirituality, etc.

The spirits of disorder, the whites and their offspring, have always sought to recruit criminal-minded as well as brainwashed and misguided Black people to spread their perverse doctrine of dissexual/homosexual acceptance. Parasites need a host. Authentic Afurakani/Afuraitkaitnit (African) Ancestral Religion and Culture are reflections of the Divine Order of Creation which by nature repudiates all expressions of disorder inclusive of dissexuality/homosexuality – without compromise. The promotion of dissexuality/homosexuality is a cancer carried by the parasites and their followers. However, this cancer will be eradicated from the Afurakani/Afuraitkaitnit (African~Black) Body/Culture worldwide.

www.odwirafo.com/Akanfo Nanasom.html

The term for *'land of the Dead'*, **Tuat (**Duat**) also means *hollows, abysess*. The Ntorot (Netert/Goddess) **Amentet** is the Ntorot of the **Amentet** (*western land*) where the Aten (Sun) sets or enters the caverns, **qerer**, (holes, entrance to the *underworld*). The *vagina* called **kat** or **kait** in Kamit is seen as an *opening to the spirit-realm* (Amentet, Tuat). This is why the Ntorot **Nut** is shown as a Sky Ntorot with the stars in Her body. She swallows the Aten (Sun) at night and gives birth to the Aten in the morning. The terms **tuat** (dwat), **qerert**, **amentet**, **kait** all reference the *opening to the inner-world, underworld, spirit-world, Ancestral realm.* Ancestresses and Ancestors return, via reincarnation, into the inner-realm, the mother's womb and are ultimately birthed into the world. The **tuat** is the *gateway, hole, cavern* to the 'Ancestral realm' the inside of the womb wherein the returning Ancestor/Ancestress resides until birth.

Note that the term **tuat** (twat, dwat) referencing the *spirit-realm or gateway to the spirit-realm/vagina* is vocalized as **e-twa** in Akan meaning *'vagina'.* The term **tuat** has also carried over into english as a colloquial term for vagina – *'twat'.* See the images and metutu (hieroglyphs) below.

Ntorot **Nut** bent over the Earth in the form of the Sky Ntorot. The Aten (Sun) is by Her mouth and **Kait** (vagina). She swallows the Aten at night and gives birth to the Aten in the morning. **Nut** also takes the form of a Divine Cow in the sky:

Ntorot **Nut** in the form of the Great **Kait** (Cow) in the Sky Who gives birth to the Aten (Sun). The word for *vagina* is also the word for *cow* – **kait**. The **Kait** (vagina) of the **Kait** (cow) is the **qerert** (hole) which is a gateway to **Amentet/Tuat**, the spirit-realm.

Ṭua-t, U. 381, , , , B.M. 708, , , , , Rec. 32, 176, , , , , a very ancient name for the land of the dead, **ṭuaut** , **hollows, abysses, empty places.**

Qerti , , , B.D. 125, II, the god of the Qerti, one of the 42 assessors of Osiris.

qerr-t , , , , Rec. 3, 46, hole, cavern, grotto, circle in the Ṭuat, hole in a vessel, spout; Heb. קִיר; plur. , Rec. 31, 172.

qer-ti-t , Hymn Darius 15, , Rev. 13, 13, cavern, hole, cave, den.

Qer-ti, Qerr-ti [hieroglyphs], Berg. I, 15, the two caverns in the First Cataract out of which the Nile was believed to rise; [hieroglyphs], the bodies of the Qerti; [hieroglyphs], L.D. III, 140B.

Qerr-t [hieroglyphs], the 5th Division of the Ṭuat.

Åmentt [hieroglyphs], the west, the abode of the dead, Dead-land; Copt. ϵⲙⲛⲧ.

Åmentit [hieroglyphs], the goddess of Dead-land.

Ntorot Amentit

ka-t [hieroglyphs], Ebers Pap. 94, 17, [hieroglyphs], Rec. 27, 88, [hieroglyphs], vulva, vagina,

kai-t [hieroglyphs], cow; plur. [hieroglyphs]

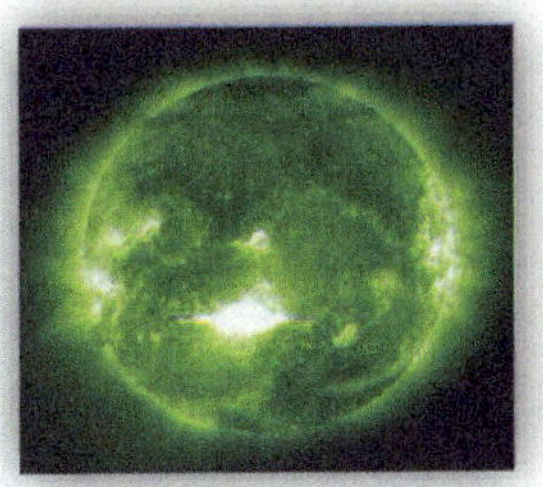

Listen to our **MAAKHERU** webcast on the subject of dissexuality/homosexuality:

Morality and the insanity of dissexuality (homosexuality) as defined in Afurakani/Afuraitkaitnit (African) Ancestral Religion

www.odwirafo.com/maakheruda3.mp3

NOTE ON NI ANKH KHNUM AND KHNUM HOTEP

Ni Ankh Khnum and **Khnum Hotep** are identical twins. Their depiction as twins is cosmological:

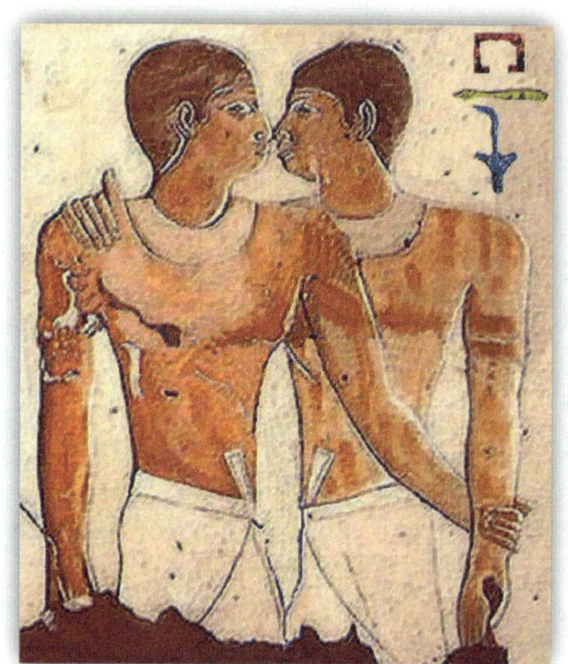

Ni Ankh Khnum and Khnum Hotep, Sakkara, Fifth Dynasty

The term for twins in Kamit is **htr** (heter, hatr, atre):

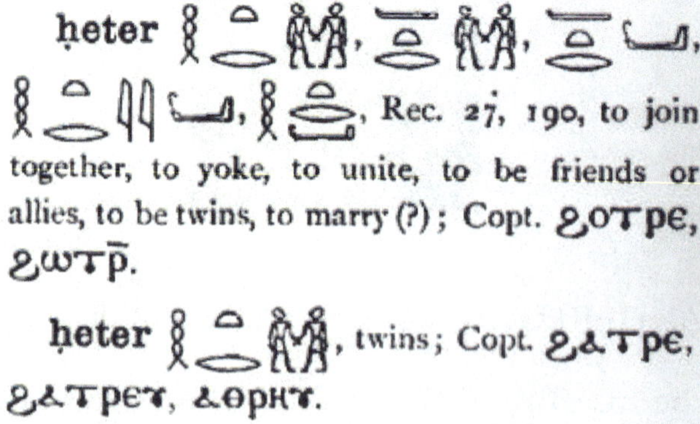

ḥeter , , , , Rec. 27, 190, to join together, to yoke, to unite, to be friends or allies, to be twins, to marry (?); Copt. ϩⲟⲧⲣⲉ, ϩⲱⲧⲣ̄.

ḥeter , twins; Copt. ϩⲁⲧⲣⲉ, ϩⲁⲧⲣⲉⲧ, ⲁⲑⲣⲏⲧ.

[Note: In Akan, the male and female names for twins are **'ata'** and **'ataa'** (hatar/hatr in Kamit)]

The **metutu** (hieroglyphs) for 'twins' shows the two twins *holding hands*. This is because twins are seen as *conjoined in the womb*. The *Divine Conjoiner* is the **Ntoro** (Ntr) **Khnum** (Khnemu, Khunem, etc.):

Khnum (Khunem)

His name literally means **'to conjoin'**:

khnem, T. 241, , U. 421, , T. 280, , M. 69, , , , , Rev. 11, 188, , Rev. 11, 181, to unite with, to join, to join together, to reach or attain, to associate with; var. , U. 558; Copt. ϣⲟⲛⲃ̄.

Khnem, U. 556, , , , , , , , , the flat-horned Ram-god, creator of the universe; later forms of the god's name are :— , , , , , , , ,

Khunem is a Creative **Ntoro** (**Ntr**/Deity) Who is the One Who **fashions the person's soul and body** on His Divine Potter's Wheel. He then **conjoins** them. [Notice that the soul and body are identical 'twins']:

[Note: In Akan, the term for potter is '**okukunwem**-fo']

Ni Ankh Khnum and Khnum Hotep are twins. As in Afurakani/Afuraitkaitnit (African) culture across the board, twins are seen to be children of a Divinity (the Obosom **Abam** in Akan, the Orisha **Ibeji** in Yoruba, the Vodou **Hoho** in Vodoun). Khunem (Khnum) is the patron Ntoro of Twins. This is why these twins were named after Him. Ni Ankh Khnum was the first born. Khnum Hotep *'Khnum is 'satisfied', 'at peace', 'completed'* was the second-born as indicated by his name.

The whites and their offspring have attempted to cast Ni Ankh Khnum and Khnum Hotep as 'homosexuals'. **This is because the whites and their offspring are sexual deviants by nature and will always attempt to force the perversity of homosexuality onto Afurakani/Afuraitkaitnit (African~Black) people and culture. The reality however, is that Afurakanu/Afuraitkaitnut (Africans) have never and will never accept homosexuality for it is the height of spiritual perversity - disorder. The Ntorou/Ntorotu, Abosom, Orisha, Vodou - the Deities - despise homosexuality. They always have and always will for They are children of Nyamewaa-Nyame (Amenet-Amen), The Supreme Being and only accept that which is in harmony with Divine Order.**

[BTW - All of the white 'egyptologists' know that Niankhkhnum and Khnumhotep are twins. They simply continue to lie about the subject deliberately.]

Khnum Hotep and Ni Ankh Khnum

SET AND ANAT

THE DATING OF 'THE CONTENDINGS OF HERU AND SET'

DISSEXUALITY/HOMOSEXUALITY WAS NEVER ACCEPTED IN KAMIT

ODWIRAFO

SET AND ANAT

THE DATING OF 'THE CONTENDINGS OF HERU AND SET'

DISSEXUALITY/HOMOSEXUALITY WAS NEVER ACCEPTED IN KAMIT

Odwirafo Kwesi Ra Nehem Ptah Akhan

The whites and their offspring often deliberately and erroneously cite the text referred to as, *The Contendings of Heru and Set*, as evidence that dissexuality/homosexuality was accepted in ancient Kamit (Egypt). This is absolutely false. Ancient Kamit, as all past and present Afurakani/Afuraitkaitnit (African~Black) nations have always abhorred and continue to abhor dissexuality/homosexuality and had/have embraced the **Divine prohibition** against it. We utilize the term dissexuality as a more proper designation for homosexuality for 'dis-' indicates that true sexuality is not (*dis*) present.

In reality, the text of the 'Contendings' **repudiates** dissexuality/homosexuality. For example, *in the manner in which this particular text is rendered*, in one questionable episode, Set attempts to sodomize Heru when Heru is asleep. However, Heru blocks Set from doing so with his hand. Heru then immediately goes to his mother Auset to report on what Set had attempted to do [**The Contendings of Heru and Set** – 'Chester Beatty' Papyrus I]:

"...Heru went to tell his mother Auset: 'Help me, Auset, my mother, come and see what Seth has done to me.'

And he opened his hand(s) and let her see Set's seed/semen. ***She let out a loud scream, seized the copper (knife), cut off his hand(s)*** *that were equivalent and threw it in the river..."*

In this *rendering*, when Auset finds that Set attempted to sodomize Heru and Set's seed/semen gets on Heru's hand as a result of him protecting himself from being sodomized, Auset, known as the great Healeress, Magician, etc. did not wash and purify Heru's hand. She **screamed** and immediately took a knife and **cut Heru's hand off.**

The hand was no longer any good and beyond repair, even ritually, because of the perverse attempt at dissexuality/homosexuality. Even the Great Mother Goddess who has the capacity to manufacture a new hand for Heru, instantaneously, was not able to purify the old hand because of the perversity of how it became defiled.

This is the highest form of **repudiation** of even the **idea** of dissexuality/homosexuality. If one could imagine a mother in contemporary times being informed by her son that his uncle attempted to molest him and the mother's immediate response upon seeing the son's hand was to reach in the kitchen drawer, grab a butcher knife and cut her son's hand off. This constitutes a **comprehensive** and **absolute repudiation** by the mother of even the **idea of dissexuality/homosexuality**. This is the sentiment conveyed by Auset. The seed/semen of another man touching the skin of another male was enough to **remove that body-part from the body**. How could dissexuality/homosexuality be accepted or practiced under such rules? **It could not and was not. Anyone in Kamit engaging in that foreign practice would be punished by the Ntorotu/Ntorou (Deities) as well as their Aakhu/Aakhutu (Ancestresses and Ancestors) who watched over them from the spirit-realm.**

The text also shows that the seed/semen of Set *never entered Heru's body*. Moreover, it shows the Ntorou/Ntorotu (Deities) absolute **disgust** at the very possibility that sodomy *may have occurred*, yet they would later find that *the sodomy did not occur*.

"...Said Set: 'Let me be awarded the office of Ruler, l.p.h., for as to Heru, the one who is standing (trial), I have performed the labor of a male against him.' [reference to sodomy]

The Ennead [Tribunal of Ntorou/Ntorotu - Deities] let out a loud cry. They spewed and spat at Heru's face.

*Heru laughed at them. Heru then took an oath by the God as follows: **'All that Set has said is false. Let Set's seed/semen be summoned that we may see from where it answers**, and my own be summoned that we may see from where it answers.' Then Tehuti, lord of script and scribe of truth for the Ennead, put his hand on Heru's shoulder and said: **'Come out**, you semen of Set.' **And it answered him from the water in the interior of the marsh**..."*

The reason why Set's seed/semen had answered from the 'water in the marsh' is because when Auset cut off Heru's stained hand, she through it in the water. **Because no seed/semen entered Heru's body, Tehuti was able to demonstrate that the sodomy had not occurred**. Notice that the seed/semen *is an **entity/spirit** which **spoke back** to Tehuti* and informed him of its location in the marsh.

In this *rendering* of the story, after Auset threw Heru's hand away she made him a new one. She subsequently decided to trick Set. She gave Heru some medicinal ointment which caused his own seed/semen to be released. She captured his seed/semen in a pot, took it to the garden and put it on lettuce that Set was known to eat every day. This is the *cos lettuce* which releases *white fluid/sap* when the stem is cut:

Above: Cos lettuce with white sap emerging from the cut stem. This kind of lettuce was viewed as a medicinal plant which supported male virility in ancient Kamit. It is sacred to the Ntoro (Neter) Men (Min).

Because Set was so lustful, Auset believed that he would not pay attention to the fact that the white fluid on the leaves was not the naturally-occurring white sap of the cos lettuce and would therefore eat the lettuce anyway. This is what occurred. Set ate the lettuce and therefore unknowingly swallowed the seed of Heru. **The term for seed was also used for poison in Kamit**. When the seed/semen of the male is inside the female it is life-giving, regenerative. Outside of the female, it becomes a waste product even poisonous. Moreover, this is akin to one smearing fecal matter on a plant and the unknowing individual consumes the leaves of the plant, thereby ingesting the fecal matter. In the following passage, Tehuti asks the seed/semen of Heru to come forward:

"...Tehuti put his hand on Set's shoulder and said: 'Come out, you semen of Heru.' Then it said to him: 'Where shall I come from?' Tehuti said to it: 'Come out from his ear.'

Thereupon it said to him: 'Is it from his ear that I should issue forth, ***seeing that I am Divine seed****?'*

*Then Tehuti said to it: '****Come out from the top of his head****.'*

And it emerged as a golden solar disk upon Set's head. Set became exceedingly furious and extended his hand(s) to seize the golden solar disk. Tehuti took it away from him and placed it as a crown upon his (own) head. Then the Ennead [Company of Deities] said: "Heru is right, and Set is wrong..."

The context in this *rendering* was that Set was attempting to rob Heru of his inheritance – the throne of Ausar, the Divine Kingship. Set wanted to rule Kamit himself. After having Ausar killed, Set was positioned to take the throne. However, the son of Ausar, Heru, survived a death plot planned against him by Set and eventually grew up to challenge Set's illegitimate authority. Set tried all kinds of deceptions and contests to disqualify Heru from the Kingship in the eyes of the Ntorou/Ntorotu (Deities). However, the schemes all failed. Set then moved, *in this rendering,* to disqualify Heru by making it appear that Heru was a dissexual/homosexual – **thereby immediately disqualifying him**, as this is the height of perversity and abomination in Afurakani/Afuraitkaitnit (African) societies. In his insanity, Set believes that Heru being disqualified would allow him – the only surviving male in the lineage – to be awarded the throne previously held by Ausar by default. This kind of extreme, discordant logic (insanity, madness) became associated with followers of Set in certain aspects of society.

On one hand, this *rendering* of the text **actually demonstrates, in a crude manner, that dissexuality/homosexuality is an abomination and is absolutely hated by the Ntorou/Ntorotu (Deities)**. Yet, out of the thousands of inscriptions, writings, etc. about Ausar, Auset, Heru and Set covering thousands of years of Kamiti (Kamitic) trustory (history) this *particular rendering* is an anomaly. We use the terms 'crude' and 'this rendering' for a reason.

Set, Anat and Foreigners

It is important to take note that whenever the whites and their offspring show up in an Afurakani/Afuraitkaitnit (African) society, references to dissexuality/homosexuality show up. This is true across Afuraka/Afuraitkait (Africa) today and wherever Afurakani/Afuraitkaitnit (African~Black) people come into contact with the whites and their offspring anywhere in the world. The same was true of ancient Kamit and the rest of ancient Afuraka/Afuraitkait (Africa). Yet, this is not limited to the greek and roman invasions into Kamit and their well-documented attempts to introduce the perversity of dissexuality/homosexuality into the culture (e.g. via the emperor hadrian and antionus).

The whites and their offspring constantly invaded the ancient Afurakani/Afuraitkaitnit (African) civilization of Kamit for millennia. After what is called the First Intermediate Period of Kamit, the end of what is called the 'Old Kingdom' and entering into the 'Middle Kingdom', we find that so-called 'semitic' speakers have some influence in Northern Kamit. This would later culminate in the **Hequ Shasu** (so-called Hyksos) taking over Northern Kamit for over a century until they were repelled by the indigenous Kamau (Egyptians). This series of events would usher in the 'New Kingdom'. The so-called 'semitic'-speakers who settled in Northern Kamit brought their culture with them. They were comprised of a mixture of Afurakanu/Afuraitkaitnut (Africans) **as well as white invaders** from the Levant (Kanaana, Lebanon, Syria regions). The original people of the Levant were Afurakanu/Afuraitkaitnut (Africans) who had migrated from ancient Kamit and Khanit (Nubia) and established civilization in ancient times. **However, this region was later invaded by white indo-europeans who would over time take political control.**

Tiles from the royal palace adjacent to the temple in Medinet Habu during the reign of Ramessu III of the Twentieth dynasty. They are typically labeled from right to left: Philistine, Amorite and Syrian. They represent the populations of the Levant at the time. The Peleset (Philistine) represents the original Black type of Afurakani (African) origin. The Aamu (Amorite) and Syrian represent the white foreign type, those non-Afurakani/non-Afuraitkaitnit (non-African/non-Black) invaders who later took control of the region. This is similar to the situation in Egypt today where the white arab invaders are in control while the original, indigenous Black Afurakani/Afuraitkaitnit (African) Kamau (Egyptians) still live mainly in the South yet have no political control.

A Libyan, a Canaanite, a Syian, and a Nubian, bow to pharaoh. XVIIIth Dynasty

The above image is from the Seventeenth dynasty, approximately 400 years prior to the reign of Ramessu III. Notice here that the Tamahu (Libyan), Aamu (Canaanite), Nehesu (Nubian) and Syrian are all brown-skinned.

When the whites invaded the Levant, they **polluted the blood-circle** of those Afurakanu/Afuraitkaitnut (Africans) that they waged war against **via rape**. They also introduced their **perverse culture**, corrupting the ancient Afurakani/Afuraitkaitnit (African) culture and religion to the extent that they could. Their **perverse culture, inclusive of dissexuality/homosexuality**, was thus introduced into the Levant and later **introduced into** Afuraka/Afuraitkait (Africa) upon their infiltration into Northern Kamit. This perverse culture would ultimately infect that minority of the Kamau population who made the foolish decision to interact with the white foreigners and embrace them on some level.

This reality allows us to **date the particular renderings** of the 'Contendings of Heru and Set' that are most often cited. Most importantly, it allows us to **date the origins of the infiltration of the non-Afurakani/non-Afuraitkaitnit (non-African/non-Black) perverse notion of dissexuality/homosexuality**, through the agency of the whites and their offspring into Kamit.

In the 'Contendings', prior to the 'attempted sodomy' event, **Ra** (The Creator) asks **Tehuti** to write a letter to the Great **Ntorot** (Goddess) **Neit (Neith, Nit, Net)**. He wanted Her to rule as to who should become the new King. This is an ancient Afurakani/Afuraitkaitnit (African) tradition wherein a critical issue which cannot be agreed upon by consensus is taken by a select group of Elders/Elderesses who go and consult the 'Elder Woman' or 'Great Mother' for a final decision.

[In Akan culture today, when the **Nananom Mpanyinfo** (Elders/Elderesses) cannot reach a decision on an issue of great importance to the oman (nation) through the normal process of consensus, a select number of them are appointed to **'Ye ko bisa Aberewa'** - 'We are going to consult with the Old Woman' (related to the Earth Mother). When they return from consulting with 'the Old Woman', her decision is understood by all to be final.]

When Neit renders her judgment, she chooses Heru to be the rightful heir to the throne of Ausar. However, Neit also states that Ra should *double Set's inheritance* (as sort of a consolation). As part of doubling Set's inheritance, Neit orders that **Ra** should give **his two daughters** – the Ntorotu (Goddesses) **Anat** and **Astarte** – to **Set** as wives:

"...Then ***Neith*** *the Great, the God's Mother, sent a letter to the Ennead, saying: Award the office of Ausar to his son Heru. Don't commit such blatant acts of inequity which are illegal, or I shall become so furious that the sky will touch the ground. The Universal Lord, the Bull who resides in Annu [Ra], ought to be told:* ***Double Set's inheritance. Give him Anat and Astarte, your two daughters, and install Heru in the position of his father Ausar****..."*

This is critical because Anat and Astarte are Kanaani (Caananite) – foreign – Goddesses. This demonstrates that by the time this rendering was written, the culture of Kamit had been **infected with foreign ideology** from the whites and their offspring. The two **foreign** Goddesses had **already been incorporated into the cosmology** and **assigned** as daughters of Ra and later wives of Set.

This rendering of the text and its earlier version are thus the product of a time when the culture of Kamit had already been compromised in the North.

[See 'Chester Beatty I' papyrus and 'Kahun' hieratic papyrus fragment for the two versions.]

Anat sitting on Her throne holding a spear, shield and mace. This foreign Goddess is here fully incorporated into Kamau culture. Notice that she wears the **Atef** crown which is a sacred crown representing rulership over **Southern Kamit**.

We should take note that there were very few instances wherein foreign Deities were incorporated into the culture of Kamit. Our focus here is not simply that foreign *forms* of Goddesses were incorporated by some in Kamit, **but the white/perverse ideology of dissexuality/homosexuality shows up in the texts at the time of the embrace of the foreign/white immigrants.**

Yet, not only are notions of dissexuality/homosexuality introduced when the whites show up, but **different renderings of texts** and **exchanging of roles amongst Deities** also appear as well.

Set identified as **Baal** in Kamit

Left: **Baal** wearing typical **Hedj** (white) crown of **Southern Kamit**. Right: **Baal** as transformed by the white invaders of the Levant.

In Kanaana (Canaan), the Deity **Baal** is the husband of **Anat**. Baal takes the form of a *Bull* and Anat takes the form of a *Cow* when they copulate. In Kamit, **Baal as identified with Set**. Thus Set and Anat became the Kamiti version of Baal and Anat. There is a very important *'spell for protection against scorpions'* written during the Ramessu period in Kamit that is important for our discussion. It deals with Set, although married to Anat, coming across the Goddess called the 'Seed Goddess' – *a Spirit operating as the energy of the seed/seminal fluid of* ***Ra***. When Set sees the Seed Goddess bathing in the river, He proceeds to 'leap upon her like a Ram' and rapes her. However, because he raped the Seed Goddess who was protected by Ra - for she is the energy carrying Ra's seed/semen - Set becomes ill. The seed/semen, *now poison,* (the word for *seed* is also used in Kamit for *poison*) goes to Set's *head* and the brows of his eyes. He lays upon his bed ill. His wife Anat takes note of his condition and then appeals to Ra to heal him. Ra judges that Set deserves to be ill because he raped the Seed Goddess. Ultimately, Auset comes to heal Set of his illness. See the excerpts from various references below [First is the Chester Beatty Papyrus VII – in this text Ra is called Pre (Pra)]:

No. VII (Brit. Mus. 10687)

PLATES 33–38 A

Recto. MAGICAL SPELLS FOR PROTECTION AGAINST SCORPIONS

Verso. CONTINUATION OF THE SAME. SPELLS AGAINST FEVER, ETC.

AN INCANTATION FOR A MAN WHO . . . . (1, 5) [The goddess ⸢Anat was disporting?] herself in the (stream of?) Khap[6] and bathing in the (stream of) Ḥemket.[6] Now the great god[7] had gone forth to walk, and he [beheld Seth as he mounted?] upon her back, leaping (her)[8] even as a ram leaps, and covering[9] her even as a . . . . . covers [a] . . . . . . [Then some of the seed-poison (?) flew] to his forehead to the parts of the brows of his eyes.[10] Thereupon he lay down upon[11] his bed in his house [being ill. Then] came ⸢Anat the divine, she the victorious, a woman acting as a warrior,[12]

clad as men [and girt as women],[1] to Prēꜥ her father. And he said to her: 'What ails thee, ⸢Anat the divine, thou the victorious, woman (2, 1) acting as a warrior, clad as men and girt as women? I reached (home) in the evening, and I know that thou[2] hast come to beg Seth from the seed-poison.[3] [Is it not?] a childish punishment (for?) the seed-poison put upon the wife of the god above[4] that he should copulate with her (?)[5] in fire and open[6] her (?)[5] with a chisel?'[7] [Then said] Isis the divine: I am a Nubian woman and have descended from heaven. I have come to uncover the seed-poison which is in the limbs [of N, born of M(?),] to cause him to depart in health for [his] mother, [even as] Horus [departed] in health for his mother Isis. N, born of M, shall be ⟨to his mother⟩.[8] (As) Horus lives, (so) lives (also) N, born of M.

Seed Goddess

http://www.reshafim.org.il/ad/egypt/religion/seed_goddess.htm

The Seed Goddess, [hieroglyphs],[3] was the personification of the seed of the creator god. She was forbidden to anybody but the creator god himself and violating her would lead to a terrible death by poisoning.

This did not prevent Seth from copulating with her after he had seen her bathing, some suggest that she seduced Seth.[1][2] He fell ill because of his sacrilegious act, possibly poisoned by the goddess herself–the word *mtw.t*, "seed", used can also mean "poison" [2]– and Anat intervened with Re, asking the creator god to save him. Re ordered Isis to remedy Seth with the help of her knowledge of magic.

Compare:

"...According to Genesis, Seth was born when Adam was 130 years old[1] "a son in his likeness and image."[1] The genealogy is repeated at 1 Chronicles 1:1-3.Genesis 5:4-5 states that Adam fathered "sons and daughters" before his death, aged 930 years. In Genesis 4:25, there is a folk etymology for Seth's name, which derives it from the Hebrew word for "plant" as in "plant a seed" (syt). Eve says, "God has planted another seed, under/replacing Abel's"[citation needed]. According to the bible, Seth lived to the age of 912.[2] ..." **[Seth – Wikipedia]**

Here we have the situation of Set engaged in the **rape of a Divinity** [*copulate with her in fire and open her with a chisel is a reference to forced penetration*], yet **the seed/semen ends up in his body and goes to the top of the head/brow region**. This story of Set and Anat is a story related to Baal and Anat in Kanaana, later reconfigured in Kamit. Moreover, the Hittite myth gives more texture to its expression in Kamit. Some identify the Seed Goddess as Het Heru (Hathor), who in this rendering is the wife of Ra (*'wife of the god above'*). In Kanaana (Canaan) as well as the Hittite culture, the Creator is called **El** (Kanaana) and **El-kunirsha** (Hittite). His consort is **Athirat** (Kanaana) or **Ashertum/Aserdu** (Hittite). The ancient Afurakanu/Afuraitkaitnut (Africans) who originally migrated from Kamit into the Kanaana region brought the worship of Ra with them. Ra is called **Ra Ur** meaning Ra "the Great" one. **Ur** was corrupted into **Ul**, **Al** and **El** in what would later be called the 'semitic' languages. Het Heru or Hathor (**Athyr** in the *Coptic* or Late Kamit dialect) is the origin of the name **Athirat** and Asherah (Ashertum/Aserdu). In the Ugarit (Kanaani) rendering of the story, Baal and Anat come upon Athirat sitting by the Sea. Athirat is initially afraid. As shown below, the Hittite myth gives more context to her fear:

"...The next section begins the bulk of the text concerning Athirat. We first see her **sitting by the sea** using a spindle and doing laundry. She is identified in advance as the one who entreats El. During her labors, she sees Baal and Anat coming and begins to fear and tremble. She wonders aloud if they have come to kill her sons. This appears to scholars to be a reference to something that was a part of the myths of Ugarit that is not preserved among our current texts. The story of Baal killing the children of Athirat is alluded to here and elsewhere in the Ugaritic texts but is nowhere found. **In order to complete their understanding scholars turn to a Hittite myth that they think is probably Canaanite in origin**. In this myth Ashertum (Athirat) tries to convince the Storm God (Baal) **to sleep with her**. She is refused and the Storm God tells El-kunirsha (El), Ashertum's husband, of what has happened. **El-kunirsha advises the Storm God to sleep with Ashertum and then humiliate her. The Storm God then accepts Ashertum's invitation but upon finishing the act informs her "that he slew seventy-seven, even eighty-eight of her sons."** Ashertum is **humiliated** and **terrified**..."

http://webcache.googleusercontent.com/search?q=cache:zv8sRV_WOVoJ:https://ojs.lib.byu.edu/spc/index.php/StudiaAntiqua/article/download/11943/11908+&cd=2&hl=en&ct=clnk&gl=us

[**Athirat: As Found at Ras Shamra** by J. Watkins]

As we can see, Baal ultimately copulates with Ashertum (Athirat) the consort of El and humiliates her. This is retold in Kamit as Set (Baal) finding the Seed Goddess (in the form of a Divine Cow), the consort of Ra, bathing in the water. He then 'humiliates' or rapes her.

The relationship between El and Ashertum is alluded to in the 'Contendings' via the relationship of Ra and Het Heru (Hathor) however it is only given a few lines:

"...And so the great god spent a day lying on his back in his pavilion very much saddened and alone by himself. After a considerable while Hathor, Lady of the Southern Sycamore, came and stood before her father, the Universal Lord [Ra], and she exposed her vagina before his very eyes. Thereupon the great god laughed at her. Then he got right up and sat down with the Great Ennead..."

This limited treatment of the relationship which is more fully developed in the Hittite myth is borne of the fact that these episodes are from a foreign story infused into an ancient Kamiti narrative.

Most important however is the fact that the same elements are placed in the *rendering* of the 'Contendings of Heru and Set', **yet the Seed Goddess is removed and Heru is put in her place.** All Kings in Kamit automatically received as one of their titles '**Sa Ra**' meaning the *'Son or Offspring of Ra'.* Heru was the legitimate heir to the Kingship and thus the 'seed'/'son' of Ra. The corruption of the rendering takes this into account when **exchanging the roles** of the Seed Goddess with Heru. Tehuti orders that the **seed/semen/poison come out of Set's body through the head** in the 'Contendings' **just as the seed/semen/poison went to Set's head** in the story of Set and Anat. Tehuti causing the seed to emerge from Set's head occurs *after* Neit orders that Set be given Anat as his wife. This means also that the rape of the Seed Goddess occurred *after* Anat was assigned to Set.

What we are witnessing is **foreign influence** in the cosmology of Kamit. Moreover, this **exchange of the roles of Deities** tells a political story. The so-called 'semitic' speakers who infiltrated Northern Kamit took Set as their main Divinity. After centuries of infiltration, they would take over control of Northern Kamit for a period:

"...The Hyksos first appeared in Egypt c.1800 BC, during the Eleventh Dynasty, and began their climb to power in the Thirteenth Dynasty, coming out of the second intermediate period in control of Avaris and the Delta. **By the Fifteenth Dynasty, they ruled Lower Egypt [Norther Kamit]**, and at the end of the Seventeenth Dynasty, they were expelled (c. 1560 BC).

The Hyksos practiced horse burials, and their chief deity, their native storm god [Baal], became associated with the Egyptian storm and desert god, Seth.[4] Although most Hyksos names seem Semitic, the Hyksos also included **Hurrians**, who, while speaking an isolated language, **were under the rule and influence of Indo-Europeans**.[5]..." **[Hyksos - Wikipedia]**

"...During the Second Intermediate Period, a group of Asiatic foreign chiefs known as the Hyksos (literally, "rulers of foreign lands") gained the rulership of Egypt, and ruled the Nile Delta, from Avaris. They chose Set, originally Upper Egypt's chief god, the god of foreigners and the god they found most similar to their own chief god, as their patron, and then Set became worshiped as the chief god once again. The Hyksos King Apophis is recorded as worshiping Set in a monolatric way: "[He] chose for his Lord the god Seth. He didn't worship any other deity in the whole land except Seth."..."

...Herman te Velde dates the **demonization of Set to after Egypt's conquest by several foreign nations** in the Third Intermediate and Late Periods. Set, who had traditionally been the god of foreigners, thus **also became associated with foreign oppressors**, including the Assyrian and Persian empires.[7] It was during the time that **Set was particularly vilified**, and his defeat by Horus widely celebrated..."

[Seth – Wikipedia]

"We do find reliefs in the 5th Dynasty mortuary temple of King Sahure at Abusir depicting a sea-borne fleet that is said to have transported his army to Syria, and in the 6th Dynasty, the official Weni is said to have taken troops to Palestine in vessels described as nmiw (traveling ships). Keelless seagoing vessels like those during the time of King Sahure (2500 BCE) traded with the Phoenician cities, importing cedar wood, Asiatic slaves and other merchandise." http://www.touregypt.net/featurestories/navy.htm

Tut Ankh Amen

The images above are from the canes of **Per Aa Tut Ankh Amen**. Those nations that had been defeated by Kamit were represented as prisoners around the cane handles. There were different times in trustory when Kamit and Khanit (Nubia) were at odds. Compare the Khaniti (Nubian) prisoner with the white asiatic foreigners, some of whom had taken up residence in Kamit and brought their perverse culture.

Above is **Baal** as rendered in the **medutu** (hieroglyphs) of Kamit. Notice that the Set animal is the determinative. Baal was identified with Set by the Kamau. Ramessu II was said to appear at the Battle of Kadesh like "Set great of strength and Baal himself". The war cry of Ramessu III was said to be like Baal in the sky, and therefore thunder which makes the mountains shake.

The rendering of the 'Contendings' under consideration shows that the author of the text is referencing the Followers of Set (foreigners) attempting to exact an abomination upon, to dominate, to 'screw'/'rape' the Followers of Heru (native Kamau). The foreigners were attempting to take the inheritance of the nation, the Divine Rulership, for themselves. Yet, the white foreigners were barbaric, abominable, detestable to the extreme as represented by their embrace of dissexuality/homosexuality. They were among the spiritually unclean:

*"...Late period texts from Ptolemaic temples include **Asiatics**, along with the **unwashed**, the **insane** and the **bearded** among those **forbidden to enter temple sanctuaries**..."* [**Ancient Egypt**, Edited by David Silverman]

The white foreigners were recognized as social and spiritual **deviants.** These (pseudo)-Followers of Set ultimately could not be allowed to continue to rule the country over the Followers of Heru. Set (the foreigner) was thus ordered to be captured and exported:

*"...Then Set said: 'Let us be taken to the Island in the Middle so that (I) may contend with him [Heru].' He went to the Island in the Middle, and Heru was vindicated against him. Then Atum, Lord of the Two Lands, the Annui, sent to Auset, saying: '**Bring Set, restrained with shackles.**'*

***Auset brought Set restrained with shackles, as a prisoner.** Said Atum to him: 'Why do you not allow yourselves to be judged but (instead) usurp for yourself the office of Heru?'*

Said Set to him: 'On the contrary, my good lord. Let Heru, son of Auset, be summoned and be awarded the office of his father Ausar.' Heru, son of Auset, was brought, and the White Crown was set upon his head and he was installed in the position of his father Ausar. He was told: 'You are a good King of Kamit. You are the good lord, l.p.h., of every land unto all eternity.' Thereupon Auset let out a loud cry on behalf of her son Heru, saying: 'You are the good king. My heart is in joy. You have illumined the earth with your complexion.'

Then Ptah the Great, South of his Wall, Lord of Ankh-tawi, said: 'What shall be done for Set? For see, Heru has been installed in the position of his father Ausar.'

*Said Pa Ra Heraakhti [Ra]: 'Let Set, son of Nut, be delivered to me so that he may dwell with me, being in my company as a son, and he shall **thunder in the sky** and be feared...'*

Here, Set is defeated and shackled. The foreigner (Set, Baal) was bound and ordered to dwell with Ra in the solar boat (out of the country). The political situation was such that the native

Kamau recognized that societal stability would be guaranteed by deportation and containment of the white foreigner, under the watch of Ra.

[*The association with Ra is also a reference cosmologically to the* ***planet*** *of Set (mercury) being placed next to the* ***Aten*** *(Sun – orb of Ra) as the Aten's* ***messenger****. Set is also the owner of the Desert (Deshert in Kamit) and also called* ***Sut****. In Akan culture the Obosom (Deity)* ***Awuku*** *(****Aku****) is the Obosom of the planet* ***Awuku*** *(mercury) is a Messenger of the Creator –* ***Nyankopon*** *and also the Owner of the desert and a Trickster. This is* ***Kweku Ananse*** *in Akan. This is also the Messenger and Trickster Orisha* ***Esu*** *(Alagbara –* ***Esu*** *is e-****Sut****) in Yoruba culture and the Messenger and Trickster Vodou* ***Legba*** *in Fon and Ewe culture. Note that in Fon Vodoun the Great Mother Divinity, Mawu, causes Legba's phallus to be eternally erect as punishment for his lust in engaging in sexual intercourse with the Vodou Gbadu and her daughter Minona. In Yoruba culture, Esu (Elegba/Alagbara) is also shown with an erect phallus. As it was in Kamit, when functioning amongst the Akan as Aku Ananse, amongst the Yoruba as Esu and the Fon and Ewe as Legba, Set has never engaged in dissexuality/homosexuality.*]

It should be noted that although the whites 'took Set as their major Divinity' because Set was the 'owner of the desert' and a 'war' and 'storm' Divinity – **this does not mean that Set accepted the foreigners**. The Ntorotu and Ntorou (Netertu and Neteru), the Goddesses and Gods are the Divine Spirit-Forces in Creation. They are called **Abosom** in Akan culture, **Orisha** in Yoruba and **Vodou** in Fon and Ewe culture. **The Divine Spirit-Forces in Creation only work with Afurakanu/Afuraitkaitnut (Africans), for these Spirits are connected to us by blood.** This is why when Afurakanu/Afuraitkaitnut (Africans), wherever we find ourselves in the world, begin to engage in ritual prayer, ritual song, ritual dance, ritual drumming, etc. the Abosom/Orisha/Vodou/Ntorou/Ntorotu enter into our bodies via **spirit-possession**, to communicate with the Afurakani/Afuraitkaitnit (African) community. They also speak through dreams, oracular divination, animal totems and more.

As *Children* of the Mother and Father Supreme Being, called **Amenet** and **Amen** in Khanit and Kamit, **Nyamewaa** and **Nyame** in Akan, **Mawu** and **Lisa** in Fon and Ewe, etc. the Deities are the *Divine Embodiments of Order* in Creation. **As Spirits of Divine Order, they repel all spirits of disorder - without compromise**. This is why the whites and their offspring (eurasians – europeans and asians/non Blacks) are **repulsive to** and **repelled by** the Ntorou/Ntorotu. **This has been and always will be the case, for the whites and their offspring incarnate as spirits of disorder**. The 'worship' of Set by white foreigners was thus a *pseudo, empty worship*, for Set has never communicated with them. This is one reason why they corrupt the role of Set as a dissexual/homosexual - an expression of <u>their</u> own <u>inherent</u> spiritual discordance and disorder.

The whites and their offspring simply **imitate** the rituals, prayers, practices, etc. of the Afurakani/Afuraitkaitnit (African) people whose land and culture they invaded and attempted to infiltrate. They then move forward to **corrupt** the rituals, prayers, practices, images of Deities, attributes of Deities and more in their effort to create a new 'religion'. This while simultaneously attempting to outlaw and eradicate the original Afurakani/Afuraitkaitnit (African) Ancestral Religion from which they stole the elements.

There are tens of thousands of writings, texts, inscriptions, etc. found in ancient Kamit. Out of these tens of thousands of writings, the whites and their offspring have identified about seven fragments which they claim are proof that dissexuality/homosexuality was accepted in ancient Kamit. **None of these texts support dissexuality/homosexuality at all**. As it was in the past, so it is today.

The whites and their offspring **incarnate** as spirits of disorder – **all of them**. This is why they have continued and will continue to attempt to force the perverse notion of dissexuality/homosexuality onto Afurakani/Afuraitkaitnit (African~Black) people – even upon those Afurakani/Afuraitkaitnit (African) people who have long died, whom the whites and their offspring believe cannot defend themselves and their culture. However, those Afurakani/Afuraitkaitnit (African) Ancestresses and Ancestors speak through their descendants. We will defend our culture at all costs.

www.odwirafo.com/Akanfo_Nanasom.html

Appendix

In the 'Old Kingdom' Set is often regarded as the husband of Neit. This is important because **Anat is often identified with Neit in ancient Kamit**, **just as Set is identified as Baal**. It is also important to note that the name Neit in Kamit has numerous spellings. One in particular shows Neit to be the 'fecundator' and thus the determinative symbol is that of an erect phallus:

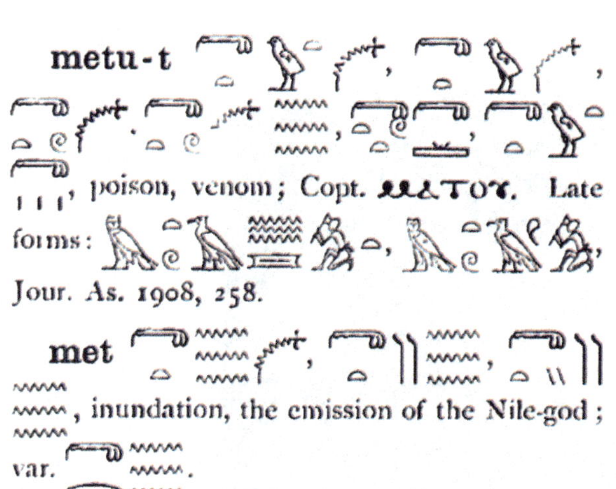

metu-t [hieroglyphs], poison, venom; Copt. ⲙⲁⲧⲟⲩ. Late forms: [hieroglyphs], Jour. As. 1908, 258.

met [hieroglyphs], inundation, the emission of the Nile-god; var. [hieroglyphs].

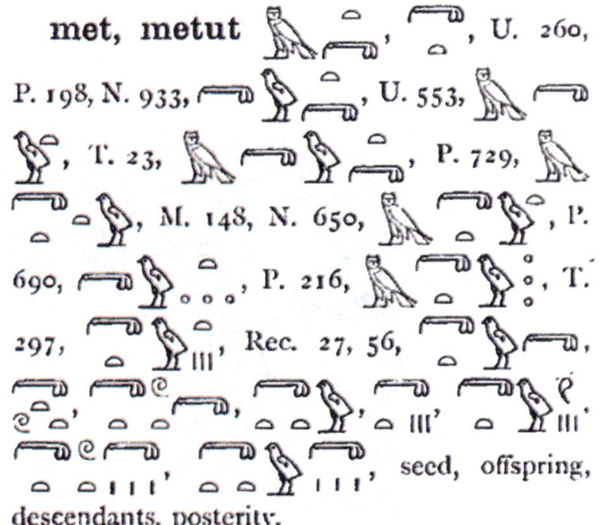

met, metut [hieroglyphs], U. 260, P. 198, N. 933, [hieroglyphs], U. 553, [hieroglyphs], T. 23, [hieroglyphs], P. 729, [hieroglyphs], M. 148, N. 650, [hieroglyphs], P. 690, [hieroglyphs], P. 216, [hieroglyphs], T. 297, [hieroglyphs], Rec. 27, 56, [hieroglyphs], seed, offspring, descendants, posterity.

met [hieroglyphs], milch cow.

As we can see, the name Neit (Nt) is spelled with the determinative symbol of the erect phallus, which is also used for the term **mt** (met, mtut) meaning *'seed, emission/seminal fluid; posterity, offspring, seed' and 'poison, venom'.* It is also used for the '**milch cow**' – the female bovine. This is important, because Neit often takes the form of the Great Mother Cow in the Sky. This ties Neit (Nit) to Anat, the *Great Cow of Baal* in Kanaana and the *Great Cow of Set* in Kamit. This is also related to the notion that Het Heru is also the *Great Cow* in the Sky. As a consort of Ra, Het Heru is also referenced as the form of the Seed Goddess. These shared attributes of Deities from Afurakani/Afuraitkaitnit (African) culture were not understood by and also deliberately misappropriated by non-Afurakanu/non-Afuraitkaitnut (non-Africans/non-Blacks) when rewriting and corrupting the cosmology. Those Afurakani/Afuraitkaitnit (African) people who embraced the whites and their offspring also perpetuated the white cosmological corruptions in some fashion. This happened in ancient Kamit and continues today. For example, some Afurakanu/Afuraitkaitnut (Africans) on the continent and in the americas and the Caribbean have embraced and now perpetuate corruptions of the Yoruba and Vodoun traditions, corruptions initially introduced by invading whites.

Our restoration of **Nanasom ne Amammere** – *Afurakani/Afuraitkaitnit (African) Ancestral Religion and Culture* is predicated upon rejecting all of the whites and their offspring and their perverse culture without compromise.

INSTRUCTIONS OF PTAH HETEP

PROPER TRANSLATION OF INSTRUCTION 35

PRE-PUBESCENT SEXUAL TABOO

Ptah Hetep

Instructions of Ptah Hetep

Proper Translation of Instruction 35 - Pre-Pubescent Sexual Taboo

Odwirafo Kwesi Ra Nehem Ptah Akhan

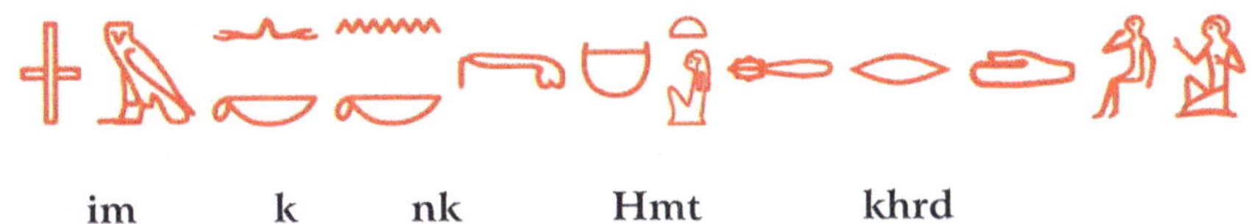

im k nk Hmt khrd

Do not copulate with female child [pre-pubescent girl]

rkh nk khsfwt r mw hr hati f

You have learned the taboo against the water upon her chest [fullness of her breasts]

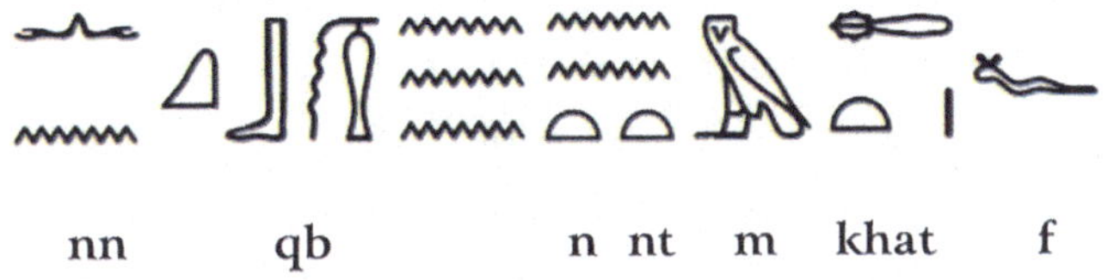

nn qb n nt m khat f

That which is within her body will not be cooled

im f sukhu r art khsfwt

She will not hide those acts which are taboo

qb f m kht hdj f ab f

She will cool [only] after she has injured her heart/conscience [suffered from violating the taboo]

"...Do not copulate with a pre-pubescent girl. You have learned the taboo against the water upon her chest [fullness of her breasts].

That which is within her body will not be cooled (she will become hot with lust) and she will therefore not hide the taboo behavior. She will cool down only after she has injured her heart/conscience – (after having suffered from violating the taboo)..."

--From the Instructions of Ptah Hetep, c4500 years ago. *Ptah Hetep was the* ***Tjati*** *(Chief Minister/Advisor) of the* ***Per Aa*** *(Pharaoh)* ***Tet Ka Ra****. When he was 110 years of age, Ptah Hetep dictated a series of instructions in ethical behavior to be recorded for the benefit of his posterity in particular and Afurakanu/Afuraitkaitnut (Africans~Black People) in general. The instructions of Ptah Hetep embody the fruits of incorporating the energy and consciousness of Maa and Maat, the Male and Female Deities of Divine Law and Balance, within our spirits.*

The instruction or maxim called number 35 (some translate it as number 32) of the **Instructions of Ptah Hetep** has been mistranslated by the whites and their offspring in an attempt to force the false notion and perverse culture of dissexuality/homosexuality into Afurakani/Afuraitkaitnit (African) Ancestral Culture. This is a means by which the whites and their offspring attempt to pervert Afurakani/Afuraitkaitnit (African) Ancestral Religion and Culture while also driving Afurakanu/Afuraitkaitnut (Africans) away from re-embracing our Ancestral Religion and Culture. Our disconnection from **Nanasom ne Amammere**, *Akan* for *Ancestral Religion and Culture,* is what keeps Afurakanu/Afuraitkaitnut (Africans) spiritually, politically and economically enslaved. Our reconnection to authentic expressions of Nanasom ne Amammere, enables us to free our spirits from such enslavement. As a collective we thereby reassert our innate drive towards sovereignty, security and thus the end of white-rule wherever we exist in the world.

Afurakanu/Afuraitkaitnut (Africans) have always, do today and always will recognize the reality that dissexuality/homosexuality is insane. It is sexual deviance and anti-life. We refer to homosexuality as dissexuality because the description shows that true sexuality is *not* (dis) manifest.

While dissexuality/homosexuality is a central feature of the mindset, nature and thus culture of the whites and their offspring worldwide, it has nothing to do with Afurakanu/Afuraitkaitnut (Africans~Black People). This reality is rooted in the cosmological foundation of Creation and the Divine Balance of the Great Father and Great Mother Supreme Being called **Amen** and **Amenet** in Kamit and Khanit (Egypt and Nubia), **Nyame** and **Nyamewaa** in Akan, **Lisa** and **Mawu** in Ewe and Fon, **Olorun** and **Olokun** in Yoruba, **Kolotyolo** and **Katyeleo** in Senufo, etc. Sexual deviance is a manifestation of disorder and has never, is not now and never will be supported by the Supreme Being, for **Amenet-Amen** only creates in accordance with Divine

Order and has a mechanism in Creation to eradicate disorder and its purveyors. This *Divine Immune System* in Creation, birthed by **Amenet-Amen** maintains Divine Balance in Creation through the Enforcement of Divine Order. The Deities **Heru Bedehty** (**Behudet**) and **Sekhmet** are the male and female Deities Who govern the Divine Immune System in Creation. They are the Agents of **Mesut Ntoro** – Divine Hate:

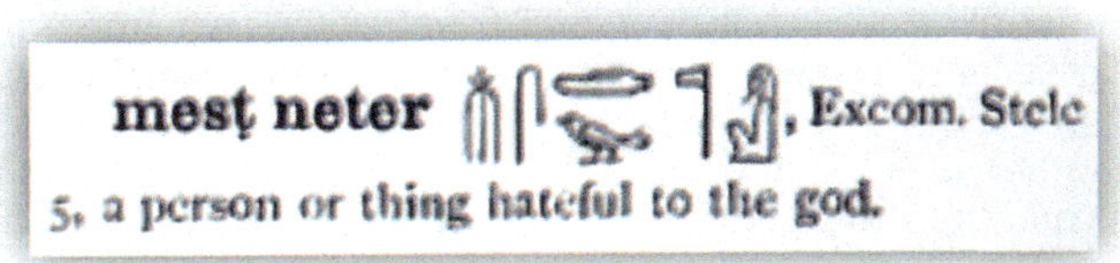
mesṭ neter , Excom. Stele 5, a person or thing hateful to the god.

This ***God loves*** *(****merru****) hearing (listening). Not hearing is* ***hated by the God*** *(****mesddu Ntr****)*

--From the Epilogue of the Instructions of Ptah Hetep

That which is *hateful* to **Amenet-Amen**, the Supreme Being, is *eradicated* by **Heru Behdety** and **Sekhmet**. They are called **Bena** and **Abenaa** in Akan and **Ogun** and **Iyaami Abeni** in Yoruba. They function as the *Divine Immune and Lymphatic Systems* within the 'Great Divine Body' of **Amenet-Amen** just as they function through the Immune and Lymphatic systems within the bodies of Afurakanu/Afuraitkaitnut (Africans) – constantly seeking out and destroying disordered/cancerous cells in order to maintain the health/integrity of the body/universe. Their functioning governs our physical and spiritual immunity.

The whites and their offspring have attempted to force the false belief that instruction 35 from Ptah Hetep states 'do not have sex with an 'effeminate boy'' or 'effeminate man'. This suggests that some forms of sexual deviance including dissexuality/homosexuality between non-effeminate boys and/or men was accepted in Kamit – **which in reality it was not**. Their false propaganda is based entirely upon their **deliberate mistranslation** of the term **Hmt Khrd** as well as the usage of the pronoun '**f**' in the text.

The term **hmt** (**hemt**) in Kamit means 'woman', 'female'. The term **khrd** (khard) means 'child'. **Hmt khrd** thus references a 'female child'. There is no basis for rendering 'khrd' in this construction 'boy' or male, specifically when Ptah Hetep clearly demonstrates that he is referring to a female 'hmt'. The term 'khrd' is actually the etymological origin of the english term 'child'. Etymologists falsely point to a proto-germanic root for the term:

> **child (n.)**
> Old English *cild* "fetus, infant, unborn or newly born person," from Proto-Germanic **kiltham* (cf. Gothic *kilþei* "womb," *inkilþo* "pregnant;" Danish *kuld* "children of the same marriage;" Old Swedish *kulder* "litter;" Old English *cildhama* "womb," lit. "child-home"); no certain cognates outside Germanic. "App[arently] originally always used in relation to the mother as the 'fruit of the womb'" [Buck]. Also in late Old English, "a youth of gentle birth" (archaic, usually written *childe*). In 16c.-17c. especially "girl child."
>
> The wider sense "young person before the onset of puberty" developed in late Old English. Phrase *with child* "pregnant" (late 12c.) retains the original sense. The sense extension from "infant" to "child" also is found in French *enfant*, Latin *infans*. Meaning "one's own child; offspring of parents" is from late 12c. (the Old English word was *bearn*; see ***bairn***). Figurative use from late 14c. Most Indo-European languages use the same word for "a child" and "one's child," though there are exceptions (e.g. Latin *liberi/pueri*).

As shown above, the europeans state that there are 'no certain cognates outside germanic'. This of course is inaccurate. The language of Kamit which according to our Ancestresses and Ancestors goes back to the first Divine Dynasties of Kamit (42,000 years ago according to what is now called the Turin papyrus' King's List) predates the existence of the whites and their offspring on Earth. Our Ancestral language thus necessarily predates the existence of 'proto-indo-european'. In the language of ancient Kamit the letter 'L' is not used until the late period when loan words from the invaders (greeks, romans, etc.) enter the language. The metut (hieroglyph) used to translate the 'L' sound is the metut for the letter 'R'. This is because the 'rolling 'R'' sound and the 'L' sound are interchangeable. The same is true in the Twi language of the Akan. There is no 'L' sound in Akan, only a 'rolling 'R''. When a foreign word which includes the 'L' sound is spoken and written by an Akan person, it is spoken with the 'rolling 'R'' and also written in the same fashion. Thus the english term 'mulatto' is written and spoken 'murato-ni' by Akan people (the tongue tapping the roof of the mouth once to produce the 'rolling' 'R' sound). This is how **Khrd** in Kamit became **Khld** or *Chld* (*Child*) in european languages. The metut for the 'kh' sound can be pronounced as the 'ch' in 'check' or the 'ch' in 'chronology'. Notice that the determinative metut is that of a small child with his finger near/in his mouth:

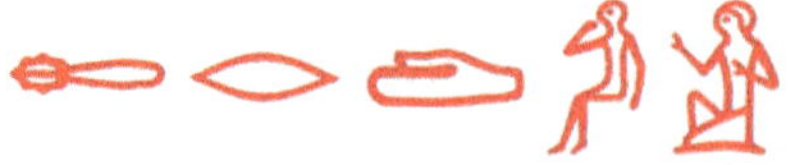

Khrd - *Child*

The pronoun 'he' is typically written with the horned viper metut in Kamit: This is the 'f' sound in the language. Thus in the text we see the usage:

Hati f

This would typically be rendered *'his'* (**f**) *'breast, chest, front'* (**hati**). The usage of the term 'f' for 'he' or 'his' is used throughout instruction 35 – after initially referring to the individual as a '**hmt khrd**' or '*female* child'. Why would Ptah Hetep refer initially to a female child and then subsequently refer to her as 'he' throughout the rest of the instruction? Why should the 'he' in this case be translated as 'she' or 'her'? Was this a scribal error? No. It reflects a common practice in different Afurakani/Afuraitkaitnit (African) Ancestral Cultures.

Krobo girls in Ghana during **Dipo** (Puberty Rites) Initiation into Womanhood

Puberty rites are sacred rites in Afurakani/Afuraitkaitnit (African) culture. It is a time when the pre-pubescent child is infused with the energy of those Ancestrally inherited Deities Who are connected to the child by blood. The Deities are the Divine Spirit-Forces in Creation - the Spirits that animate the Earth Mother, the Sun, Moon, Stars, Black Substance of Space, Oceans, Rivers, Fire, Wind, the Magnetosphere and more. The Deities, the Goddesses and Gods, are the *Children* of the Great Goddess and Great God – The Supreme Being: **Amenet-Amen**, **Nyamewaa-Nyame**, **Mawu-Lisa**, etc.

Tens of thousands of years ago the Deities, called **Abosom** in Akan, **Orisha** in Yoruba, **Vodou** in Fon and Ewe, **Ntorou/Ntorotu** (**Neteru/Netertu**) in Kamit, etc. began to *possess*

Afurakanu/Afuraitkaitnut (Africans) in Afuraka/Afuraitkait (Africa). Through ritual song, dance, drumming, prayer, etc. the Spirits would come and enter into the bodies of our Ancestresses and Ancestors. This continues today during Ancestral Religious rituals when spirit-possession occurs wherever Afurakanu/Afuraitkaitnut (Africans) are found in the world.

When the Divine Spirit-Forces of Nature first possessed the bodies of our Ancestresses and Ancestors, our bodies became altered – energically. This *altered blood* was subsequently passed down, genetically, generation after generation until today. The blood of Afurakanu/Afuraitkaitnut (Africans) resonates at the frequencies of the Spirit-Forces of Nature and therefore we are physical magnets for Them to enter into our bodies, our families, to give us direction, healing, guidance, etc. Our capacity to wield this Divine energy is a responsibility which is bestowed upon us when we reach the age whereby we can transmit this energy to future offspring – **when we reach puberty**. This is why puberty rites are *sacred*. Manhood and Womanhood training is key to the spiritual balance of the community, for those who have the capacity to reproduce, have the capacity to transmit Divine power, via blood, to their posterity. The instruments of this transmission, the male and female reproductive organs, are thus *sacred* as well.

However, prior to reaching the age of puberty, this responsibility does not exist for the children. Physiologically, boys and girls appear similar and function similarly in many ways. **This is why different Afurakani/Afuraitkaitnit (African) cultures refer to girls with same term they use for 'boys'.** When menstruation begins, these girls are then referred to as 'females', 'women'.

For example, amongst the **Kgatla** people of South Afuraka/Afuraitkait (Africa), **pre-pubescent girls are referred to as boys (*basimane*) because they have not yet menstruated.**

"…Isaac Schapera: Some Kgatla Theories of Procreation.

Obtaining the opinions of a number of "witchdoctors" *(dingaka)*, among them Natalie Morema and Rapedi Letsebe, Schapera draws on an extensive period of fieldwork to outline several topics concerned with conception, barrenness, and contraception amongst the Tswana-speaking Kgatla of the Bechuanaland Protectorate. He notes in the first section of the paper that while the Kgatla once informed their children that conception occurred following the visit of an elderly woman to a "bearded snake" who resides in a pool of water, adults believed that conception rightly occurred following copulation, and the mixture of a man's semen *(maree)* with a woman's menstrual blood *(mosese)*. Brief notes on *thobalo* (sexual intercourse) among children are also included. The writer notes that pre-pubescent girls were referred to as *basimane* (boys) because they had not yet menstruated…"

http://books.google.com/books?id=8rGpO_TzeCsC&pg=PA361&lpg=PA361&dq=kgatla,+pre-pubescent+girls&source=bl&ots=mmCwGibvid&sig=3lPxu56xngfml3Eoil1nF1wuRug&hl=en&sa=X&ei=yLo6UuCvFY7a4AOJwYCACg&ved=0CCoQ6AEwAA#v=onepage&q=kgatla%2C%20pre-pubescent%20girls&f=false

--**African Traditional Religion in South Africa**: An Annotated Bibliography, edited by David Chidester

Moreover, after menopause, some cultures refer to post-menopausal women ritually as 'men'.

"...Menstruation and Pregnancy

As the **Lowiili** phrase it at the menopause a woman 'turns into a man' (Goody 1962:56,201: Goody 1967:52). She can no longer perform the main task of women, bearing children and so is in a sense of sexual. As Goody states, "Authority ritual and otherwise is normally vested in men; within the general category of women, it is those past menopause who most nearly approach the male"..."

--Notes on Cultural Aspects of Menstruation in Ghana, by Christine Oppong

http://archive.lib.msu.edu/DMC/African%20Journals/pdfs/Institue%20of%20African%20Studies%20Research%20Review/1973v9n2/asrv009002005.pdf

Thus, prior to the onset of menarche (menstruation) pre-pubescent females are referred to as 'males' and after the end of menarche or post-menopause females are referred to as 'males' in different parts of Afuraka/Afuraitkait (Africa). The concept of referring to pre-pubescent girls as 'boys' because of their behavior, has been retained within Afurakani/Afuraitkaitnit (African) culture in america (African-American culture). Afurakanu/Afuraitkaitnut (Africans) in america, having lost the knowledge of our Ancestral languages, appropriated and modified words, phrases and concepts from english to reflect our traditionally held, Ancestrally inherited, innate worldview. This is why Afurakanu/Afuraitkaitnut (Africans) in america refer to pre-pubescent girls who, wrestle, fight, climb trees and play just as rough as the boys as 'tom-boys'. This masculine terminology as employed in the culture of Afurakanu/Afuraitkaitnut (Africans) in america does not reference the sexual perversity of dissexuality/homosexuality. It carries the same connotation of the traditional Afurakani/Afuraitkaitnit (African) concept of referring to pre-pubescent girls as 'boys' because of their appearance, behavior and the fact that they had not yet menstruated. Once 'tom-boys' reach puberty and their bodies begin to change (breast development, shape of the pelvis, menstruation, etc.), the term 'tom-boy' is dropped and 'young lady' or other terms designed to promote femininity are used. **This shift in terminology towards a clear focus on gender identity and proper functioning in society after the onset of menarche has Ancestral roots for Afurakanu/Afuraitkaitnut (Africans) in america as well.**

The cosmological underpinning of **female excision** (circumcision) in Afuraka/Afuraitkait (Africa) is founded upon Afurakanu/Afuraitkaitnut (Africans) endeavoring to **clearly delineate gender roles for males and females ritually** as they make the biological and spiritual journey towards manhood and womanhood:

"...There is a reference to it on the sarcophagus of **Sit-hedjhotep**, in the Egyptian Museum, dating back to Egypt's Middle Kingdom, c. 1991–1786 BCE (see right).[111] The Greek geographer Strabo (c. 64 BCE – c. 23 CE) wrote of it after visiting Egypt around 25 BCE: "**This is one of the customs most zealously pursued by them [the**

Egyptians]: to raise every child that is born and to circumcise the males and excise the females."[113] The philosopher Philo of Alexandria (c. 20 BCE – 50 CE) contrasted the Egyptian practice with God's commandment in the Book of Genesis (c. 950–500 BCE) that boys be circumcised, writing: "**the Egyptians by the custom of their country circumcise the marriageable youth and maid in the fourteenth (year) of their age, when the male begins to get seed, and the female to have a menstrual flow...**"[114]

Inscription on Egyptian sarcophagus [of Sit hedjhotep] c. 1991–1786 BCE:

"But if a man wants to know how to live, he should recite it [a magical spell] every day, after his flesh has been rubbed with the b3d [an unknown substance] of an uncircumcised girl and the flakes of skin [šnft] of an uncircumcised bald man."

--Female genital mutilation - Wikipedia

The Dogon people of Mali, one of many descendant groups of people from Ancient Kamit (Egypt), provide a cosmological basis for the practice of excision (female circumcision):

"Only among Blacks does circumcision find an interpretation integrated in a general explanation of the universe, in other words, a cosmogony. Specifically, the Dogon cosmogony that Marcel Griaule reports. In Dieu d'eau, he reminds us that, to make sense, circumcision must be accompanied by excision. These two operations remove something female from the male and something male from the female. Such an operation is intended to fortify the dominant character of a single sex in a given human being."

Cheik Anta Diop, *Civilization or Barbarism*

We should note that the term female genital mutilation (FGM) as a reference to female circumcision is rooted in the arab-islamic influenced practice of clitoridectomy and removal of the inner labia and outer labia as in infibulation. Traditional Afurakani/Afuraitkaitnit (African) practices reflect the 'circumcision' of the clitoris meaning the removal of a portion of the clitoral hood (leaving the clitoris intact) or *simply drawing blood from the region.* Drawing blood from the genital regions of the male and female as a form of **mogya aforebo** (Akan for blood offering/sacrifice) to the Ancestral Abosom (Deities), in order to ground Afurakani and Afuraitkaitnit males and females in their proper gender functions, is the traditional practice. **Mutilation of sex organs is a eurasian practice that infected the culture of Afurakanu/Afuraitkaitnut (Africans) after the infiltration of islam**.

We can see from the foregoing that different Afurakanu/Afuraitkaitnut (Africans) in traditional Afuraka/Afuraitkait (Africa) refer to pre-pubescent girls as 'boys', that contemporary Afurakanu/Afuraitkaitnut (Africans) in america, refer to pre-pubescent girls as 'boys' (tom-boys) and that this intergenerational concept is rooted in ancient Afuraka/Afuraitkait (Africa) as demonstrated by Ptah Hetep. We can also clearly delineate the cosmological infrastructure that births this concept and usage of the term 'he' to refer to the pre-pubescent girl.

You have learned the taboo against the water [fullness] upon her breast

"...Menstruation and Pregnancy

The fact that the beginning of menstruation heralds the potentially fertile period of a woman's life is known by people of all occupational and ethnic groups in Ghana. There is evidence that among the daughters of the better placed sections of the population the mean age of menarche is 12.9 (95 per cent in one school sample began to menstruate between the ages of 12.5 and 13.5 years) (Ofosu Amaah, 1969). In contrast there is evidence that among rural farming populations the age of menarche is somewhat later, the mean age being 15.6 (Ofosu Amaah 1974)..."

--Notes on Cultural Aspects of Menstruation in Ghana by Christine Oppong

http://archive.lib.msu.edu/DMC/African%20Journals/pdfs/Institue%20of%20African%20Studies%20Research%20Review/1973v9n2/asrv009002005.pdf

"...Breast ironing (also known as breast flattening[1]) is the pounding and massaging of a pubescent girl's breasts, using hard or heated objects, to try to make them stop developing or disappear.[2][3] It is typically carried out by the girl's mother who will say she is trying to protect the girl from sexual harassment and rape,[3] to prevent early pregnancy that would tarnish the family name,[4] or to allow the girl to pursue education rather than be forced into early marriage.[4][2] It is mostly practiced in parts of Cameroon, **where boys and men may think that girls whose breasts have begun to grow are ready for sex.**[2] The most widely used implement for breast ironing is a wooden pestle normally used for pounding tubers. Other tools used include leaves,[1] bananas, coconut shells,[2] grinding stones, ladles, spatulas,[4] and hammers heated over coals.[5].."

--Breast Ironing – Wikipedia

The above quotes show on one hand that in rural areas in contemporary Afuraka/Afuraitkait (Africa) the onset of menarche (menstruation) for girls is later in comparison to girls in urban areas. Moreover, the onset of menarche is the final phase of puberty. It can occur three years after the breasts begin to develop. This is important, for in traditional Afuraka/Afuraitkait (Africa), such as amongst the Krobo in Ghana, once girls complete their puberty rites, they are expected to marry and have children as soon as possible. Young males who have gone through puberty and are therefore viewed as 'men' in society seek out young 'women' – *post-pubescent females* – to marry. Yet, some males circumvent protocol and seek to engage in sexual intercourse prior to marriage. Typically, such individuals' only indication that the girl has become a 'woman' is the change in the shape of her body, most notably the development of her breasts as illustrated in the quote above.

However, because breast development precedes the first menstrual cycle, young men who attempt to have sex with girls who they believe are 'women' based on breast development risk violating a **major taboo** – having sex with an pre-pubescent girl – which is akin to **statutory rape** and/or **pedophilia**. There are severe consequences, social, legal and spiritual for violating such a taboo – including the death of the individual for committing statutory rape and pedophilia as well as fines, beatings or banishment for young men (e.g. 15 year-olds) who have sex with pre-pubescent girls (e.g. 14 year-olds) who have not had their first menstrual cycle nor completed their womanhood initiation. This is why the proverbial wisdom, Divine restrictions, taboos in Afurakani/Afuraitkaitnit (African) culture prohibit men from judging whether or not a girl is a 'woman' simply based on the 'water upon her chest' - *fullness of her breasts.* Indeed, the practice of 'breast ironing' and other similar practices is founded upon this reality. While most Afurakani/Afuraitkaitnit (African) Ancestral Cultures do not embrace the practice of breast-ironing and see it as the adoption of an unnatural foreign eurasian practice, the relevance here is that it is practiced out of the recognition that some young men would seek to copulate with pre-pubescent girls because they believe that the girls are women and ready to have sex simply based on breast size – thereby violating a major societal taboo.

Dipo Initiates – Krobo girls making the transition to womanhood

In the image above, these young girls are going through their **Dipo** initiation. Once they complete these rites, they are considered women and will be expected to marry as soon as possible and begin a family. The young men in the society anxiously wait until the conclusion of the ceremonies to choose their future wife, for they are deemed ready – as women – to engage in sexual activity. However, weeks prior to this event, the girls – not yet 'women' – look no different than they do in the above image. If a young man in the village based his sexual advances towards one of these girls based on breast development alone during that time, he would see no difference between her pre-initiation appearance and post-initiation appearance.

He therefore could make the mistake of seeking to have sex with a pre-pubescent girl – a major social and spiritual taboo. This is why traditional Afuraka/Afuraitkait (Africa) as well as contemporary Afurakani/Afuraitkaitnit (African) people's customs around the world have proverbial admonitions against approaching young girls as women simply because of their breast development or the 'water upon her chest/front' as stated by Ptah Hetep.

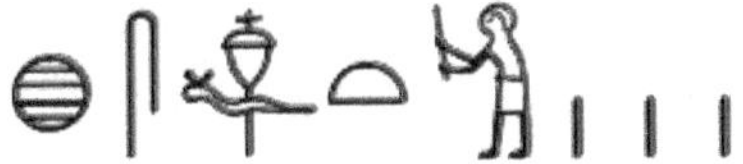

Khsfwt

That which is objectionable, shameful, driven away, punishable, repulsive

The term for taboo in Akan culture is **akyide** or **akyiwade**. The term **kyi** (chee) means *to hate, to abhor,* while the term **ade** means *'thing, object, deed, entity'.* The term **akyiwade** thus references those *things, objects, deeds and/or entities that are Divinely hated* and therefore restricted. That which the **Amenet-Amen**, the **Ntorou/Ntorotu** and the **Aakhu/Aakhutu**, The Supreme Being, the Deities and the Honorable Ancestresses and Ancestors, hate is referred to in Kamit as **Mesut Ntr** – a person or thing which is hated by the Deity. This is Divine Hate. This is the nature of 'taboos' in Afurakani/Afuraitkaitnit (African) culture. Unlike simple rules and regulations, taboos carry Divine sanction. The term **kyi** in Akan also means *to turn the back to, to crush, to abominate,* etc. These are all descriptions of the term **khsfwt** in Kamit used by Ptah Hetep to delineate that which is *objectionable, repulsive, punishable, shameful – taboo.* The same concept of taboo: **akyiwade**, **khsfwt** is called **eewoo** in Yoruba. All Afurakani/Afuraitkaitnit (African) Ancestral Cultures have a term for Divine prohibitions/restrictions. Ptah Hetep's instruction against copulating with a pre-pubescent girl inclusive of observing the taboo which requires that one not judge sexual maturity in females by the 'water upon her chest' thus reflects the timeless recognition of taboos as Divinely sanctioned prohibitions/restrictions in ancient Afurakani/Afuraitkaitnit (African) cosmology.

You have learned the taboo against the water upon her chest [fullness of her breasts]

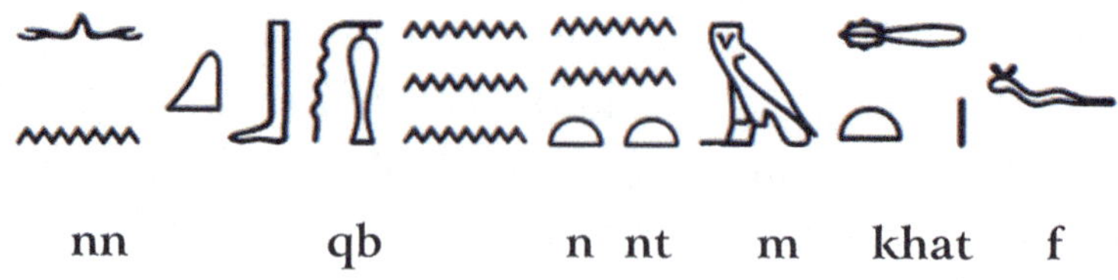

That which is within her body will not be cooled

Afurakanu/Afuraitkaitnut (Africans) have recognized for millennia that when the act of copulation occurs with a pre-pubescent female it creates disorder and imbalance within the female, for her reproductive organs are not yet developed, nor is her spirit prepared to resonate at the frequency necessary to harmoniously incorporate such energy. The post- pubescent male not only has the physical and energic capacity to dominate the female. He also has the capacity to tap into the residual energy of his Ancestrally inherited **Abosom** (Deities). For example, in Akan culture, every male inherits his **Ntoro** from his father. The Ntoro, also called **Egyabosom** meaning 'Father's Deity' is a patrilineally/patricircularly *inherited* **Obosom** (Deity). It is the Divine Spirit-Force in Nature that has governed the individual's patriclan Ancestresses and Ancestors for generations. Prior to puberty, the father regularly invokes the energy of this Obosom on behalf of his children. After puberty, the young adult now has the capacity and responsibility to invoke this Obosom on his/her own and communicate and learn from this Obosom independently in addition to communally.

The infusion of energy received by males after puberty from their Ancestrally inherited Obosom creates an energic advantage for the post-pubescent male over the pre-pubescent female – even if they are very close in age: e.g. a 15 year-old post-pubescent male and a 14 year-old pre-pubescent female. This energic advantage manifests very often as an energic imbalance if such a male and female enter into a relationship. The male exercises undue influence over the sexual desire of the younger female. If such a female is not focused, she can be easily controlled sexually, mentally and emotionally by the male – based on the sexual energy aroused and her desire to continue engaging in sexual activity with the individual. Some females, once aroused, develop an unnatural appetite for sexual activity and become promiscuous.

In the parlance Afurakani/Afuraitkaitnit (African) people in america such a girl is called 'hot', a 'hot ass' or 'hot in the ass'. This is because of the out-of-cycle provocation of sexual energy which manifests as lust – misguided desire – and often promiscuity.

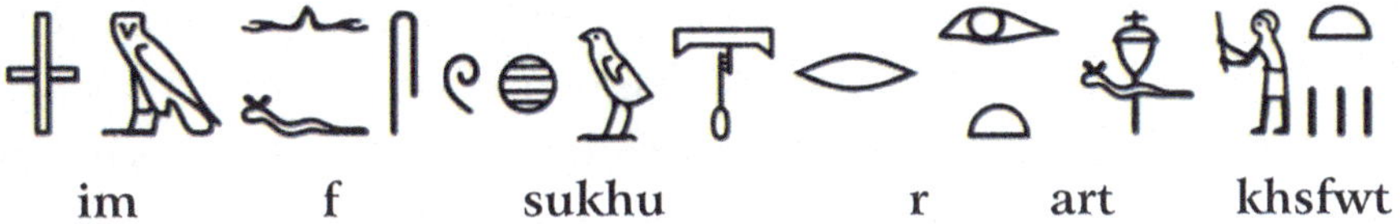

She will not hide those acts which are taboo

She will cool [only] after she has injured her heart/conscience [suffered from violating taboo]

This potentiality was recognized and addressed in ancient Afuraka/Afuraitkait (Africa) and is reflected in the admonition of Ptah Hetep as he warns his son that copulation with a pre-pubescent girl can create a condition wherein she becomes 'hot' – *that which is within her body will not be cooled* and that because of the heat of lust that has been generated through unlawful, out-of-cycle sexual activity, she will not attempt to hide her behavior. She will be driven to frequently engage in sexual activity prior to puberty **thereby violating a social and spiritual taboo**. Therefore, she will only cool down after having satisfied her lust, yet injuring her heart (sacred conscience) for she will suffer the recrimination of the society as well as her **Okraa** (Soul/Divine Consciousness in Akan; **Kait** in Kamit; **Ori Inu** in Yoruba; **Se Lido** in Vodoun) and her Ancestresses and Ancestors who have constantly warned her against such behavior. The degradation of morality, circumvention of Divine Order and the negative repercussions upon the individual and society, short-term and long-term, are recognized and addressed through this admonition.

...Isaac Schapera: Kgatla Notions of Ritual Impurity

Originally intended to form part of a revised edition for his account of married life among the Tswana, Schapera draws on information supplied by several *dingaka* (doctors), among them Rakgomo Segale, Rapedi Letsebe and Natale Mancheng to reexamine aspects of ritual purity among the Tswana-speaking Kgatla of the Bechuanaland Protectorate. Particularly, the writer identifies how **"hot blood"** *(madi abollo),* including menstrual and post-natal blood, signified a state of ritual pollution among the Tswana. **In this regard he notes that only pre-pubescent or virgin girls and sexually inactive boys, because they are classified as cool (tsidifala)**, could perform rainmaking (gotlhapisa lefatshe), annual national purification, and war-doctoring rites.

http://books.google.com/books?id=8rGpO_TzeCsC&pg=PA361&lpg=PA361&dq=kgatla,+pre-pubescent+girls&source=bl&ots=mmCwGibvid&sig=3lPxu56xngfml3Eoil1nF1wuRug&hl=en&sa=X&ei=yLo6UuCvFY7a4AOJwYCACg&ved=0CCoQ6AEwAA#v=onepage&q=kgatla%2C%20pre-pubescent%20girls&f=false

--**African Traditional Religion in South Africa**: An Annotated Bibliography, edited by David Chidester

Notwithstanding the author's misunderstanding of the nature of ritual restrictions regarding the sanctity of menstrual blood, the quote above demonstrates the Afurakani/Afuraitkaitnit (African) recognition of the *coolness* of pre-pubescent girls – energically and spiritually. When a pre-pubescent girl is encouraged to have sex, the *'hot blood'* is generated within her prematurely, out-of-cycle, and thus in an **imbalanced** fashion. This imbalance manifests as lust, misguided desire, and can drive her to repeatedly circumvent Divine Order by violating social and spiritual taboos. This in turn leads to spiritual imbalance, emotional imbalance and the 'injury to her heart/her conscience' after having 'cooled down' from engaging in the restricted/taboo behavior. She suffers the weight of recrimination internally from her **Okraa** (**Kait**/Soul) and her **Nsamanfo** (Akan for Ancestresses and Ancestors) as well as from her family members, peers and society as when she is exposed. Prior to being discovered and exposed she suffers not only from the internal spiritual pressure from the Okraa and Nsamanfo but also from the constant fear of being discovered and exposed. This set of negative behaviors and the corresponding emotional imbalance can be set in motion simply by a male who exercises undue influence, energically and emotionally, over a pre-pubescent female who may be 'attracted' to him and who is impressionable, gullible, comparatively submissive, etc.

Moreover, the referencing of a pre-pubescent girl as a 'he' (*basimane* – *boy* in Kgatla) in the instruction of Ptah Hetep drives home the point to the male receiving the instruction that copulation with a pre-pubescent girl is perverse – it is akin to attempting to 'copulate' with a boy which is insane and degenerate.

In ancient Afuraka/Afuraitkait (Africa), contemporary Afuraka/Afuraitkait (Africa) as well as in various communities of Afurakani/Afuraitkaitnit (African) people outside of Afuraka/Afuraitkait (Africa) – including america and the Caribbean – Afurakani/Afuraitkaitnit (African) people routinely kill people found to have molested children or found to have been engaged in dissexual/homosexual activity. This is not in any way due to patriarchal religions and western culture as many white writers deliberately, falsely assert. This has been a feature of Afurakani/Afuraitkaitnit (African) Ancestral Culture for millennia. The misuse of the procreative force of Ra and Rait (the Creator and Creatress of the Universe) is anti-life. Thus, those who choose to engage in anti-life behavior in the Afurakani/Afuraitkaitnit (African) community are removed from this life – like cancerous cells being destroyed and expelled from the body by the immune system – for the good of the body.

In the past two decades the killing of child molesters and the killing or attacking and exiling of dissexuals/homosexuals by members of the Afurakani/Afuraitkaitnit (African) community has waned. The major reason for this is the promotion of dissexuality/homosexuality and pedophilia by the whites and their offspring worldwide. **The whites and their offspring employ their false religions and pseudo-philosophies to promote the acceptance of all forms of sexual deviance. It is a major form of cultural warfare aimed to destabilize and**

perpetuate imbalance in the Afurakani/Afuraitkaitnit (African) community as well as contribute to a decline in our population growth worldwide. This includes the worldwide push by the whites and their offspring for the acceptance of 'same-sex' marriage. However, trustorically, Afurakani/Afuraitkaitnit (African) people worldwide from ancient times to the present have despised and continue to despise child molestation, dissexuality/homosexuality and all other forms of sexual deviance including all forms of rape and violence against women. As Afurakanu/Afuraitkaitnut (Africans) continue to re-embrace our Ancestral Cultures, those who had been lured by the whites and their offspring into a perverse acceptance of dissexuality/homosexuality and a soft stance on pedophilia will reject such acceptance and that stance and will return to their correct Afurakani/Afuraitkaitnit (African) minds. The relevance here of this trustorical narrative of how Afurakanu/Afuraitkaitnut (Africans~Black People) have always demonstrated our disdain for dissexuality/homosexuality is that it represents a continuum of culture from ancient Kamit to today – wherever Afurakanu/Afuraitkaitnut (Africans) are found in the world. The degree to which we have abandoned our Ancestral culture and embraced the anti-life, perverse culture and pseudo-religions of the whites and their offspring has determined the degree to which we have accepted dissexuality/homosexuality and other forms of sexual perversity. However, when functioning normally, naturally, no post-pubescent Afurakani (African) male, after having been informed that a pre-pubescent female exists in the category of 'he' or *basimane* (boy) until the onset of menarche, would attempt to copulate with her ('him') for dissexuality/homosexuality is recognized to be as perverse as bestiality.

Here we have demonstrated the Afurakani/Afuraitkaitnit (African) cosmological foundation for the proper and direct translation of Instruction 35 from Ptah Hetep. The young male, upon hearing the admonition against copulating with a pre-pubescent girl, gains insight into how destructive and destabilizing for the individuals and the community such an act would be. He therefore internalizes the instruction for the good of his own spiritual balance and that of the females in his community and the community as a whole. He recognizes that any attempt to circumvent Divine Order on his part will not only promote spiritual imbalance in the female, but also within himself. He will therefore suffer the punishment from the **Nsamanfo** (Ancestral Community), his own **Okra** (Soul/Divine Consciousness), his **Ntoro** (patrilineally inherited **Obosom**/Deity) as well as the members of the community. It could lead to his punishment, exile or death. The gravity of the instruction also prompts the young male to make sure other males in society observe the taboo as well, for one individual's negative actions can affect the entire community. The young male thus takes the responsibility of not only governing himself, but participating in the stability of the society.

With a firm cosmological foundation in Afurakani/Afuraitkaitnit (African) Ancestral Culture we can compare the proper transliteration and translation of Instruction 35 with the deliberate mistranslations of the whites and their offspring:

Proper translation:

Do not copulate with a pre-pubescent girl. You have learned the taboo against the water upon her chest [fullness of her breasts].

That which is within her body will not be cooled [she will become hot with lust] and she will therefore not hide the taboo behavior. She will cool down only after she has injured her heart/conscience – [after having suffered from violating the taboo].

False translation and corresponding perverse rationalization:

http://epistle.us/hbarticles/ancientegypt1.html

"Do not copulate [nk] with a woman-boy [hmt], for you know that / what is (generally) opposed will be a [necessity] to his heart, and that which is in his body will not be calmed. Let him not spend the night doing what is opposed in order that he may be calm after he has [quenched] his desire."42

Parkinson translates the last line a little differently: "Let him not spend the night doing what is opposed; he shall be cool after destroying [renouncing] his desire."43 Here Vizier Ptahhotep argues that the nocturnal activities of a 'woman boy' will bring him no lasting relief. Nk refers to penetration, and hmt refers to a male who is open to taking the womanly role, although his social status is unclear. In many cultures, women and boys were interchangeable as sexual objects. Parkinson notes that although same-sex penetration is condemned here, it is the passive partner who is demeaned and not the active partner, who has not departed from his appropriate (active) sexual role. It is assumed elsewhere in these maxims (21st, 37th) that the pupil or audience will marry, so the aim of this prohibition is probably to safeguard the morality of the youth. Still, a certain reticence is displayed here toward the active role.44 Any gay person reading this maxim would immediately know that it is written by a heterosexual male, not someone who knows how strong homosexual desire can be and how futile the call for abstinence may also be…"

Here, one of the whites and their offspring attempts to pervert the entire meaning of the Instruction of Ptah Hetep in order to support dissexuality/homosexuality. **As we have demonstrated above, the insanity of this rationalization is an obvious and deliberate attempt to lie and pervert Afurakani/Afuraitkaitnit (African) Ancestral Culture.**

The same is true of every attempt to twist the meanings of about seven textual references in Kamit (out of hundreds of thousands covering thousands of years of Kamau trustory). In every instance, including the texts related to **Heru**, **Set, Atum**, **Niankhkhnum** and **Khnumhotep**, **Nefer Ka Ra** (**Pepi II**), **Akhenaten** and the **Pert em Hru** (Negative Confessions) the whites and their offspring deliberately mistranslate and/or insert words and phrases that do not exist in the text itself in order to put forward the false narrative that dissexuality/homosexuality and other forms of sexual deviance were accepted in Kamit and Afurakani/Afuraitkaitnit (African) Culture in general – **which is categorically inaccurate**.

We must never trust the whites and their offspring to translate, interpret or expound upon Afurakani/Afuraitkaitnit (African) Ancestral Culture. It is our responsibility to teach the truth and fullness of our culture to our people. We carry our Ancestral culture within our

Okra/Okraa (Soul). It is an innately held way of life that we carry with us wherever we exist in the world. The **Mmusuo Kese** (Great Perversity/Enslavement) was not capable of removing what **Nyamewaa-Nyame** (**Amenet-Amen**) encoded within our **Okra/Okraa** as Afurakani/Afuraitkaitnit (African~Black) people.

We have a genetic, spiritual and thus *transcarnational* (through successive reincarnations) tie to ancient Khanit, Kamit and contemporary Afuraka/Afuraitkait (Africa). We therefore have intrinsic, inborn knowledge of our customs, traditions, cosmology, religion and culture. It is our responsibility to access that knowledge and share it with our people for the fortification of our worldwide Afurakani/Afuraitkaitnit (African) body/community. This is a key component of **Amansesew** – Afurakani/Afuraitkaitnit (African) Nationbuilding/Restoration.

ANKH NKWA

THE ORIGIN OF THE TERM 'YOGA'

KARA KASA

THE ORIGIN AND NATURE OF THE 'CHAKRA'

ODWIRAFO KWESI RA NEHEM PTAH AKHAN

There is a great deal of misinformation regarding the notion of what 'yoga' is and how 'chakras' are related to yoga. This misinformation has been propagated by the whites and their offspring who have fraudulently co-opted these terms and created false etymologies to place them in their own languages. They further moved to take fragments of ritual practices of Afuraka/Afuraitkait (Africa) and manufacture pseudo-religious practices and a corresponding dogma which has no basis in reality. These acts were and are deliberate acts by the whites and their offspring, spirits of disorder, to control the spirits/minds of Afurakanu/Afuraitkaitnut (Africans) whose lands and cultures they invaded and desire to maintain complete control over.

The corruption of the Ancestral Religion of Afurakani/Afuraitkaitnit (African) people by the whites and their offspring is an act of war. It was the final attempt by them to gain a foothold in our societies which they were unsuccessful at taking through various failed military engagements over the course of millennia. The western eurasian version of the corruption of Afurakani/Afuraitkaitnit (African) Ancestral Religion manifested via the pseudo-religions of christianity, islam, judaism and their pseudo-esoteric branches. The eastern eurasian version of the corruption of Afurakani/Afuraitkaitnit (African) Ancestral Religion manifested via the pseudo- religions of hinduism, vedanta, jainism, buddhism, taoism and various others. These pseudo-religious practices do not lead to enlightenment nor any manner of spiritual development. They are designed to keep Afurakani/Afuraitkaitnit (African) people the spiritual and physical slaves of the whites and their offspring, thereby allowing them to control us, our land and its resources – until we awaken.

The terms 'yoga' and 'chakra' have no etymological roots in proto-indo-european languages. We demonstrate conclusively and for the first time that these terms are found in the language of ancient Kamit (Egypt). They are woven into the cosmology of ancient Afurakani/Afuraitkaitnit (African) Ancestral Religion and Culture. Once understood, their connotations for spirituality and ritual practice are totally different than what has been promoted by the whites and their offspring over the centuries.

We combined our two original publications into one volume in 13013 (2013). We added as appendices our articles: **ANKHUT - Original Terms from Kamit** and **AB – Khepra and Kheprit: The Heart, Dance and Tai Chi/Qi Gong** for added texture and information. In 13021 (2020) we revised the work including three additional appendices and expanded linguistic analysis. Afurakani/Afuraitkaitnit (African~Black) People are not the physical, philosophical nor spiritual slaves of the whites and their offspring. Our recognition of this reality is our true liberation, for in Afurakani/Afuraitkaitnit (African) Ancestral Religion, recognition is the precursor to concrete action – the restoration of Order and the elimination of disorder and its purveyors.

Odwirafo Kwesi Ra Nehem Ptah Akhan
Aakhuamuman Amaruka Atifi Mu
Akwamu Nation in North America
Hoodoo Gyaasedan
Odwiraman

www.odwirafo.com

ANKH

NKWA

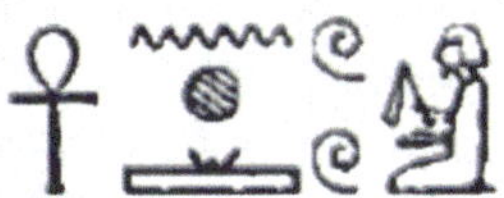

THE ORIGIN OF THE TERM 'YOGA'

The ritual practices of Afurakani/Afuraitkaitnit (African~Black) people are millions of years old. Ritual song, ritual dance, ritual prayer, ritual chanting, ritual clothing, ritual sacrifice, ritual foods, ritual offerings, ritual architecture, ritual warfare, ritual movements are various facets of our prescribed means of attuning ourselves to **Nyamewaa-Nyame** (**Amenet-Amen**), *The Mother and Father Supreme Being*, through the agency of the **Abosom** and **Nananom Nsamanfo**, the *Deities* and *Honored Ancestral Spirits* of Afuraka/Afuraitkait (Africa). And this is the essence of **Afurakani/Afuraitkaitnit (African) Ancestral Religion** – *the ritual incorporation of Divine Law and the ritual restoration of Divine Balance.* Through ritual, we as Afurakanu/Afuraitkaitnut (Africans~Black People) work to incorporate those things, deeds, entities necessary to harmonize our every thought, intention and action with Divine Order and through ritual we work to eradicate those things, deeds, entities necessary to restore balance to our lives when imbalance has occurred. This is true of all forms of Afurakani/Afuraitkaitnit (African) Ancestral Religion including the ritual practices of ancient **Khanit** and **Kamit** (Nubia and Egypt) and their contemporary expressions amongst the Akan, Yoruba, Ewe, Igbo, Bakongo, Dogon, Zulu, Oromo, Chokwe, Goromantche and all Afurakanu/Afuraitkaitnut around the world.

This is also true of our traditions preserved in North america including **Hoodoo** (Akan), **Juju** (Yoruba), **Voodoo** (Ewe), **Wanga** (Ovambo), **Ngengang** (Fang) and more.

Central to the ritual practices of Afurakanu/Afuraitkaitnut is communication with what the **Akan** people of Ghana and Ivory Coast call the **Okra/Okraa** *(Soul/Divine Consciousness called **Ka/Kait** in Kamit, **Ori Inu** in Yoruba, **Se Lido** in Ewe)*, the **Abosom** *(Deities called **Ntorotu/Ntorou** in Kamit, **Orisha** in Yoruba, **Vodou** in Ewe)* and **Nananom Nsamanfo** *(Spiritually Cultivated Ancestral Spirits called **Aakhu/Aakhutu** in Kamit, **Egungun** in Yoruba, **Kuvito** in Ewe)*. Such communication takes place at an **nkommere** (shrine).

[The languages of the **Akan**, the **Yoruba** (Nigeria) and the **Ewe** (Togo, Benin) are directly descendant of the language of Kamit. We utilize Akan language terms in comparison to the Ancestral language of Kamit in this book.]

There are **Abosomnkommere** (Deity shrines) as well as **Nsamankommere** (Ancestral Shrines). These are sacred places where we go to communicate with the Spirits. An nkommere is erected according to the dictates of the Abosom (Deities) and Nananom Nsamanfo (Spiritually Cultivated Ancestral Spirits) as well as being extant in the environment: sacred groves, rivers, trees, mountains, streams and more.

When we sit at the nkommere we engage in **nkom** (spiritual communication) with the Divinity or Ancestral Spirit through invocation or evocation. There are instances when the Abosom or Nsamanfo will direct or urge us to *shift positions* as we sit at the nkommere to facilitate a better reception of Divine energy emanating from Them. We are also sometimes urged to shift positions when a different Obosom or Nsamanfo comes forward at the nkommere in order to receive Their energy optimally. Sitting at an nkommere to be imbued with the purificatory life-energy of the Abosom and Nananom Nsamanfo has been our practice for millennia. We learned of this practice directly from the Abosom (Ntorou/Ntorotu "Neteru/Netertu") Themselves:

Ra

Tehuti

Het Heru

Maat

The Abosom (Deities) depicted above: **Ra, Tehuti, Het Heru** and **Maat**, are seated in the common meditative posture that Afurakanu/Afuraitkaitnut (Africans) learned from Them and other Abosom and continue to use at nkommere today. These Abosom are holding the **Ankh** (**Nkwa**), the *talisman of life.* The term **ankh** literally means *life.* When referring to an individual, it means *'a life'* (a human life). The talisman in the form of an ankh is used to *wield the energy of life in order to enliven or awaken the innate (pure) energy and awareness* of an individual:

Obosom **Anpu** *enlivens* (en-life-ens) or *"ankhs"* the spirit of the deceased Per Aa (pharaoh)

Obosom **Ptah** "ankhing" the Per Aa

Per Aa **Senusret** wielding Ankhs

When Afurakanu/Afuraitkaitnut sit at the nkommere we are always engaged in the process of invoking or evoking our **Okra/Okraa**, the **Abosom** and/or **Nananom Nsamanfo** in order to harmonize ourselves with **Nyamewaa-Nyame Nhyehyee** (The Supreme Being's Order~Divine Order).

The whites and their offspring learned of religion and ritual practice after infiltrating and settling in certain parts of Afuraka/Afuraitkait and observing Afurakanu/Afuraitkaitnut. Their infiltration into Afuraka/Afuraitkait followed a series of unsuccessful military invasions into Afuraka/Afuraitkait carried out over the course of thousands of years. As immigrants, the whites and their offspring would witness Afurakanu/Afuraitkaitnut sitting at nkommere for different durations of time, sometimes shifting positions in response to the necessity of the energic emanations received from the Spirit-realm.

The whites and their offspring have no **Okra/Okraa** (Ori Inu, Se, Ka/Kait – Soul/Divine Consciousness). They are **akyiwadefo**, *spirits of disorder*, and therefore lack this spiritual organ which is needed in order to communicate with **Nyamewaa-Nyame** (Supreme Being), the Abosom and Nananom Nsamanfo. They are also incapable of developing into Nananom Nsamanfo. This is true of **all** of the whites and their offspring, living, deceased and yet-to-reincarnate including: *all white americans, white europeans, white asians, white latinos/latinas, white pseudo-"native" americans, white indians/hindus---all non-Blacks*. They all *incarnate* as akyiwadefo and are thus **hated** by **Nyamewaa-Nyame**, the Abosom and Nananom Nsamanfo, without exception just as cancerous cells are hated/rejected/repelled by the body (via the immune system) without fail or compromise.

The whites and their offspring recognize their inferiority, a manifestation of their disordered ill-nature. It is this recognition in connection with their ill-nature that prompts them to seek to dominate and control Afurakanu/Afuraitkaitnut wherever they find us in the world, just as cancerous cells seek only to consume and destroy healthy cells in every organ and tissue of the body. The whites and their offspring thus desired to pervert the religion of Afurakanu/Afuraitkaitnut and manufacture a false religion with images of whites as "gods". They calculated that if they could pervert the religion, they might finally control the Afurakani/Afuraitkaitnit population after having been defeated militarily by Afurakanu/Afuraitkaitnut for millennia.

It ultimately took centuries for the whites to corrupt authentic religious practices and then disseminate pseudo-religious practices and dogma to Afurakanu/Afuraitkaitnut. These pseudo-religious practices and dogma include all forms of christianity, islam, judaism, buddhism, jainism, hinduism, vedanta, kabbalism, zoroastrianism, gnosticism and more - "esoteric" and "exoteric". To date, hundreds of millions of Afurakanu/Afuraitkaitnut around the world falsely believe the **fictional** white character 'jesus' to be 'god', believe in the sanctity of the **fictional** white character 'muhammad', believe in the existence of **fictional** white 'deities' and 'angels' and thus the corresponding false doctrines of 'white superiority' and 'black inferiority'. So-called "eastern philosophies" are simply a variation of this white pseudo-spiritual perversity.

When the whites and their offspring observed Afurakanu/Afuraitkaitnut sitting at nkommere in communication with Okra/Okraa, Abosom and Nananom Nsamanfo, they attempted to replicate the procedure. **Yet, the whites and their offspring are not capable of communication with Divinity or of harmonizing with Divine Order**. They therefore created a "discipline" out of communicating with "nothing" and then worked to force this pseudo-discipline upon Afurakanu/Afuraitkaitnut as a means to exercise spiritual, political and economic domination over us. Their goal was/is to force Afurakanu/Afuraitkaitnut to **abandon** the Abosom (Divine *Embodiments* of Order), **abandon** the Nananom Nsamanfo (*Guides* to Divine Order), **reject** our Okra/Okraa (Soul/Link to **Nyamewaa-Nyame**) and embrace the whites as guides and interpreters of 'divine law'. They corrupted terms and practices to promote their newly manufactured pseudo-religion and pseudo-religious discipline. This is the origin of what is called 'yoga'. Below we show the actual etymology of the term and its trustorical origins.

ANKH

The term **ankh** is very often spelled with the *ankh talisman*, the 'T' cross surmounted by a loop. In the *Coptic* dialect (Late Kamit) the term is pronounced **awnk**. This term continued to be used by the **Akan** people after migrating from ancient **Khanit** (Nubia) and **Kamit** and eventually settling in the regions of contemporary Ghana and Ivory Coast, West Afuraka/Afuraitkait (Africa) over the course of two millennia. Thus, in the Akan language today the term **nkwa**, pronounced awn-kwah', means *life*. **Ankh** and **Nkwa** (awnk and awnkwah) are the same term. Moreover, the symbol can be found in both cultures:

Ankh **Akua (Nkua)**

The **Akua** sculpture, also called **Akua-ba**, in Akan culture shown above is a talisman used for *fertility* purposes. This sculpture is thus often called a "fertility doll" and utilized by Akan women to assist them in becoming pregnant. However, there are similar sculptures called **Nkua** that are used as talismans to communicate with and give offerings to the Nsamanfo (Ancestral Spirits). We thus have the *Ankh* used to *give life* to the living and deceased and the *Akua/Nkua* used to *promote life* (fertility) for the living and the deceased (Ancestral ritual). **Ankh** and **Nkwa** (*Nkua*) are the same term utilized ritually for the same cosmological purposes from ancient Khanit and Kamit to cotemporary Akan culture unchanged. [See **AKUA**: Appendix 3]

ŋkwã, *life, vitality; vigour, health; happiness, felicity. pr.* 74. 162. 1878. 2519; *cf.* asetrã; ŋkwã nè akwãhõsaŋ, *life and health;* ŋkwá a owu mmam' da, *immortality;* - gye ŋkwã, *to preserve, to save from death;* wógyè no ŋkwã; obi à wógyè no ŋkwá no; di ŋkwã,

[Left: Entry from *Asante-Fante Dictionary* of the Akan Language]

The term **ankh** is commonly spelled with the wavy/water-line **medut** (hieroglyph) for the 'N' sound and the dark circle for the 'kh' sound: The 'N' sound is often a 'nasal' sound in words from Kamit. Moreover, the 'kh' medut can be pronounced as the 'ch' in *chronology*, the 'ch' in *change* or the 'ch' in *chagrin*. In fact, the whites and their offspring learned of the alphabet and writing from Afurakanu/Afuraitkaitnut in Kamit and would later corrupt the forms falsely claiming it as their own creation. This is why the 'ch' combination in english has three pronunciations. It is derived from the 'kh'

medut: 

The 'A' sound takes many forms in the **medutu** (hieroglyphs) of Kamit. Certain words beginning with an 'A' are therefore pronounced with an 'ah' or 'yah' sound:

ām , , Jour. As. 1908, 290, to know, to understand; , Jour. As. 1908, 313, book-learned; Copt. ⲉⲓⲙⲉ.

aḥ-t , , field, land, acre, ploughed or cultivated land; plur. , , , , Amen. 7, 14; Copt. ⲉⲓⲱϩⲉ, ⲉⲓⲟⲟϩⲉ, ⲓⲁϩ, ⲓⲟϩⲓ, ⲓⲱϩⲉ.

Notice that the term **am** (ah-m) is also written in Coptic as **EIME** ⲉⲓⲙⲉ. (eh-yeem-eh). Notice that the term **aht** is also written in Coptic: **EIWHE, EIOOHE, IAH, IOHI** Copt. ⲉⲓⲱϩⲉ, ⲉⲓⲟⲟϩⲉ, ⲓⲁϩ, ⲓⲟϩⲓ, (eh yee-aw-eh; eh-yoh-eh; yah; yoh-hee) Here the 'ah' sound for the letter 'A' becomes 'iah' or 'yah' (ee-ah).

A similar occurrence is found in the Akan language. The term **afunu** or **afuru**, meaning *belly, inner abdomen*, is also pronounced and written **yafunu** depending upon the dialect of Akan being spoken. The 'a' (ah) becomes 'ya' (yah/iah). This is the process by which the term **ankh** becomes pronounced **iankh** (**yankh**), **iakh** and **ykh** (**yoke**).

It is often stated that the etymology of the term **yoga** comes from the indo-european root **yewg** and the sanskrit term **yuj**. The indo-european term *yewg* is also the root of the english version: *yoke*. The true etymology is rooted in the reality that the whites and their offspring stole the term from ancient Afuraka/Afuraitkait. The variations *yewg* and *yuj* are derived from *ankh* ('kh' pronounced like a 'k' sound) and *ankh* ('kh' pronounced like a 'j' or 'ch' sound). The 'a' in ankh is pronounced 'iah' as in the Coptic (Late Kamit) dialect variation. Thus, **ankh** sounds like **iankh**. The 'nasal' pronunciation of the 'N' produces the term **ynkh** which sounds like yuj or yok (yewg). With regard to the nasal 'N' and its corruption in white pronunciations of the co-opted term:

"….**infix**: a bound morpheme that interrupts a morpheme. (Cf. prefix and suffix) In a few language families like [a]ustronesian infixes are abundant; in most [i]ndo-european languages they are rare or non-existent. [e]nglish and most modern [i]ndo-[e]uropean languages do not have any. Proto-[i]ndo-[e]uorpean had one infixing verb stem marker ***-ne-*** alternating with ***-n-***. For example, the root ***yewg-/yug-*** 'link, join; yoke' the present imperfect finite stems were ****yuneg-/*yung-*** componentially ****yu-ne-g / *yu-n-g-***…" [Language History: An Introduction by Andrew Sihler]

"…The sanskrit word **yoga** has the literal meaning of "yoke", from a root **yuj** meaning 'to join', 'to unite', or 'to attach'. As a term for a system of abstract meditation or mental abstraction it was introduced by Patañjali in the 2nd century BC…" [wikipedia]

We quote the above to demonstrate how misinformation is perpetuated and accurate information is ensconced or totally omitted by the whites and their offspring. While the first quote demonstrates how the **yewg/yug** in proto-indo-european had the **yuneg/yung** forms, it is not shown that these forms derive from **ankh** (**yankh**). While both quotes relate the meaning of the terms yewg, yoke and yoga to *'yoke; to link'* they omit again the etymological root of this notion of 'yoking' and its perceived relationship to ritual practice.

There are numerous variations of **ankh:** [Entries from *An Hieroglyphic Dictionary* by E.A. Wallis Budge]

ānkh, U. 191, T. 71, M. 225, N. 603, to live, to live upon something, life; Copt. ωnϩ.

ānkh – "life, stability, prosperity (or, content)"; "life, all prosperity, all stability, all health, [and] joy of heart," a formula of good wishes which follows each mention of the king's name in official documents. See the following examples.

Ānkhit "living one," the name of a goddess.

Ānkhit Rec. 11, 178, a uraeus-goddess.

Ānkhit Ombos I, 1, 46, a hippopotamus-goddess.

ānkh oath; king's oath.

ānkhu goat, any small domestic animal; plur.

ānkhi, ānkhu a living being, a living thing; plur.

[Entry below from the Mark Vygus Hieroglyphic Dictionary]

àānkh ; see .

àānkhu N. 551, the living.

variants of **ankh** and **ankhu** – **iankh** and **iankhu** (the first 'a' is the reed *medut* - 'i' sound). **Iankh** or Yankh

There are two variations that warrant our attention:

A living being (a life)

A goat; small domesticated animal; small cattle

sāḥ U. 298, the form of a man that exists in heaven, the spirit-body; plur. T. 143, N. 113, 539, U. 516, T. 327, P. 6, M. 8. Later forms are:—

We also have the term **sah** or **sahu** meaning the spirit body:

sah (**sahu**) – *the spirit body*

In the term **sah** we have the three medutu for **s-a-h**: followed by the *determinative* medutu which

point to the nature of the term:

The determinatives here are the *goat* and the *seated Elder or Elderess* (shrouded denoting purity) seated in one of our common meditative postures. <u>The goat and the shrouded figure are also determinatives in variations of the term ankh</u>:

ankh

ankh

Notice that in the term **ankh** with the determinative of the goat, *the animal has an* ***ankh*** *around its neck*. This *ankh around its neck* became known (*and pronounced*) as a **yankh** (**yuneg**) or **yakh** (**yewg**) or **yoke** *around its neck*.

Ankh and Yoke are the same word and the same symbol from ancient Kamit

This is why the whites and their offspring, when stealing/co-opting the term ankh, recognized it to represent 'yoking' in some form. However, there is more to the association which is rooted in our cosmology. We must understand the **sahu** or *spirit body* to understand the cosmological connection.

Sahu

The **sahu** or **sah** is sometimes referred to as the "glorified" spiritual body. Sometimes the determinative medut is not a shrouded individual in a *sitting* posture but a shrouded individual *lying* as a mummy on a funerary bed. The focus of the Afurakani/Afuraitkaitnit individual when sitting at an nkommere (shrine) and communicating with the Abosom and Nananom Nsamanfo is to align his or her **sunsum** (*spirit* in Akan; **sahu** in Kamit) with his or her **Okra/Okraa** (Soul-Divine Consciousness; **Ka/Kait** in Kamit). When we link or re-link our spirits to our souls we have re-aligned ourselves with Divine Order. We have thereby purified our thoughts, intentions and actions, which is *pre-requisite* for our harmonious functioning in the world. The Abosom and Nananom Nsamanfo are *key* to this realignment and purification for They utilize the Ankh (yoke, the *key of life*) to imbue us with purificatory life-giving energy when we communicate with Them:

Above, the Afurakani individual provokes the energy of ***Tehuti***. ***Tehuti*** *radiates His Divine Energy to the Man via the Ankh to effect recalibration, purification and communication of Divine Wisdom.*

This is why the goat with the ankh (yoke) on its neck is a medut for the term *ankh* as well as the term *sahu* (spirit body). It is the reason why the shrouded figure (purified figure) is a medut for the term *ankh* as well as the term *sahu* (spirit body), for it is our meditation (at the shrine) which leads to invocation and evocation of the Abosom and Nananom Nsamanfo for ritual re-alignment and life purification.

[Note that the term **su** in Akan means *essential nature*, while **su-n-su-m** means *spirit*. This is derived from the ancient term **sahu** (s-hu or s-hu s-hu/sahu-sahu).The related Akan term **susu** (also susuw) means *to meditate; to contemplate,* while **suban** (su-ban) means *character*. We also have **sua** meaning *to learn*.]

In the first image from a coffin from the New Empire we see the sacred **Kait** (Cow) of **Het Heru** wearing a **sesheshet** (sistrum) around its **neck** which is <u>in the form of an **ankh**</u> (yoke). The sesheshet is a 'shaker', an instrument used to reverberate sound vibrations in ritual. Next is **Henut** (Queen) **Nefertari** wielding a sesheshet. Next is a metal sesheshet. We then have an ankh from **Tut Ankh Amen**'s tomb followed by a **shenu** (cartouche) with the name of the **Nesu** (King) **Nefer Ka Ra** inside of the loop. Note that the shenu (cartouche) is a loop <u>bound with rope</u> to the cross-bar, just as the top of the ankh is a loop with the same <u>binding to the cross-bar.</u> This is important as the next image is the medut of a **khetem** (cylinder seal) in the form of an ankh. This is also important because the khetem is also used as a determinative medut for **sah**:

The two variants of the term **sah** above for spirit-body utilize the **khetem** (seal) as well as the khetem next to a **seated, shrouded Elder Ancestral Spirit.** The goat with an ankh around its neck is also shown as a goat with a khetem around its neck **in the form of an ankh** as shown in the second (bottom) goat medut from Gardiner's hieroglyphic sign-list and the temple of **Kom Ombo**:

It was customary in Kamit to depict ritual implements in ankh-form such as the **sesheshet** (sistrum) around the neck of the Kait (Cow) and the **khetem** (cylinder seal) around the neck of the goat as shown above. The relationship is cosmological. The cylinder seal as in the golden example shown above is a 'stamp'. The medutu (glyphs) are carved into the seal. When it is rolled on clay or papyri, the glyphs are imprinted upon the clay or papyri. It is a stamp or **signature**. In the same fashion the **shenu** (cartouche) contains the name of the **Nesu** or **Nesut** (King or Queen Mother). It is bound at the bottom with the 'rope' image. As a representation of the 'life-time' or **incarnation** of the individual, this name or set of sound-vibrations (energy) is what characterized this individual. The **sah** or spirit-body binds together (yokes) all of the spiritual organs (**Ba, Ka, Akh, Ab, Hati, Sau, Khaibit**) into one entity, just as your physical body binds together all of your physical organs and glands into one entity. The life of the individual is summed up in (contained in) the physical body as well as the spirit-body. The shenu (cartouche) contains the **name** – the **signature**, life- stamp, of the sovereign. The khetem (seal) contains the **signature**, representing the life (ankh), character, spiritual disposition of the owner.

When the khetem as a sacred implement carrying the spiritual signature of the individual is utilized ritually, it becomes the **horizontal cross-bar** of the **ankh-form**, with a **beaded necklace** forming the loop. It is placed around the neck of the goat as a yoke (ankh) – the goat again being the animated life-form, ankh. The neck is the gateway between heaven (head) and Earth (body). It binds (shenu/ankh/ropes) together the two 'worlds'.

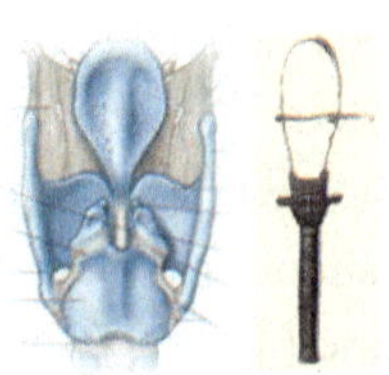

The **shaking** of the sesheshet (sistrum) actually replicates the **vibrations** of the vocal cords within the **larynx** (*voice box - image on the left*) and signifies the character of the individual (each person's voice is unique and distinct). The vocal cords are found in the neck/gateway. In the same fashion the khetem (seal) is around the neck of the goat defining the sah, spirit-body, the unique life(ankh)-form of the individual in comparison to all other entities in the world. The shenu (cartouche), sesheshet (sistrum) and khetem (seal) are all represented in **ankh-form** or **yoke-form** around the **necks** of the kait (cow) and goat for these reasons.

Ankh is the origin of the term yoga/yoke. Ankh (yoga) is not a discipline.

When we use the original term **ankh** we have a full understanding of the corruption 'yoga'. When the Abosom *use the ankh* to purify, to enliven, to assist us, this has nothing to do with practicing postures, practicing breathing, meditating upon the "formless", seeking to "escape the cycle of reincarnation" or the other foolish practices and doctrines promoted by the whites and their offspring. True spirituality is grounded in the reality that the Okra/Okraa (male and female terms for Soul/Divine Consciousness in Akan) is a drop from the Ocean of the Divine Okra/Okraa (Soul) of **Amenet-Amen** (**Nyamewaa-Nyame**). Each Afurakani/Afuraitkaitnit individual has an **nkra/nkrabea** (function; so-called 'destiny') to execute in Creation, just as each organ in your body is designed to execute a specific function in your body. Our Okra/Okraa (Soul) houses our Divine Function (nkra/nkrabea). As *part of a greater system*, the Great Divine Body of **Nyamewaa-Nyame**, we work in concert with the Abosom and Nananom Nsamanfo to function harmoniously in Creation.

Spirituality without the invocation and evocation of the Okra/Okraa, Abosom and Nananom Nsamanfo is not spirituality at all. It is empty ritual.

Empty ritual is all that the whites and their offspring have access to and engage in because they have no Okra/Okraa and cannot communicate with the Abosom (Divine Spirit Forces in Creation) nor the Nananom Nsamanfo. They thus have no connection to the Supreme Being, **Nyamewaa-Nyame**, just as there are cancerous cells that live in your body (universe) yet are in conflict with you. This temporary situation is brought into balance by your immune system ultimately destroying these cells and expelling them from the body (universe). Analogously, **Nyamewaa-Nyame** direct the Abosom and Nananom Nsamanfo to reject/repel the spirits of disorder/whites and their offspring as a function of the Divine Immune System in Creation. Because the whites and their offspring recognize the inadequacy of their spirits, yet seek to control us, they work to reduce us to their degenerate level - spirits of disorder incapable of Divine communication.

This is akin to a blind person working to convince a person with normal vision to reject the use of his vision and follow the blind person. The blind person then attempts to instruct the individual who has normal vision on how to drive a car. The blind person's series of postures, breathing practices and misguided foci while sitting in a car (that actually has no engine) is labeled a "discipline" by the blind person. The blind person then offers this 'discipline' as a gift for the individual with vision to practice and perfect so that he can learn how to drive a car. The man with vision can see that there is no engine in the car and thus a set of instructions on how to sit, breathe and focus on that which is "formless" will never get the car to move.

To follow the blind is to ultimately engage in self-destructive activity. **To follow the blind who seek to deliberately blind you for purposes of dominating you is to accept disorder into your life.** Afurakanu/Afuraitkaitnut who follow our absolute enemies – the whites and their offspring – or those Afurakanu/Afuraitkaitnut who have been culturally, spiritually and politically blinded by the whites and their offspring, engage in self-destructive behavior. The embrace of pseudo-religious white dogma is the embrace of disorder (white culture) which by default is the perpetuation of white rule. Much to the chagrin of the misguided Afurakanu/Afuraitkaitnut, they often do not learn this lesson until they die and eventually reincarnate. Upon death they realize that what the akyiwadefo told them about the spirit-world is 100% inaccurate. Upon reincarnation, they grow up to realize that not only have they not "escaped the cycle of reincarnation" but they have returned to a state of affairs where white rule continues and is more entrenched.

True Ritual

Ritual dance is a means by which the Abosom and Nananom Nsamanfo move through the Afurakani/Afuraitkaitnit individual and community to bring a communication of Divine wisdom and to transmit the **tumi** (spiritual power) that we need in order to replenish ourselves and accomplish our objectives – execute our Divine function in the world given to us by **Nyamewaa-Nyame**. When the drums begin to play, the Abosom *move us*. We are in constant communion with them as they guide our movements. The same is true of ritual song and ritual prayer. It is also true of **susuw** (meditation) at the nkommere (shrine).

We are guided by the Abosom and Nananom Nsamanfo and our Okra/Okraa to sit and listen at the nkommere – and sometimes to *change positions* (postures) as necessary. **This is an effect of ankh (life). It is not the practice of a 'yoga discipline'**. We don't *practice* sitting at the nkommere, we go at prescribed ritual times to engage in *nkom* (spiritual communication). It is not contrived. It is instinctive, powered by the Abosom and guided by the Nananom Nsamanfo. This reality is inaccessible to the minds of the non- Afurakanu/non-Afuraitkaitnut.

What is termed as 'yoga' is nothing more than exercise and stretching (similar to the lower-level training of a gymnast or ballerina) overlaid with pseudo-spiritual dogma that leads the misguided Afurakani/Afuraitkaitnit individual to totally abandon him/herself and thus his/her actual Divinely allotted function "destiny"(nkra/nkrabea) only to cling to white domination in all spheres of life.

Every moment of everyday is purposeful for Afurakanu/Afuraitkaitnut because before we incarnated **Nyamewaa-Nyame** gave each individual Afurakani/Afuraitkaitnit spirit an nkra/nkrabea – a Divine function. When we harmonize with this function, we harmonize with **Nyamewaa-Nyame**. When we are out of harmony with this function we create disorder in ourselves and in the world. This is why we have **Nanasom – Afurakani/Afuraitkaitnit Ancestral Religion**. We have a means to ritually incorporate Divine Law and ritually restore Divine Balance when imbalance occurs.

Without a function (purpose/destiny) one is wayward. The whites and their offspring, as cancerous cells in the body of Black humanity, mal-function in perpetual disorder. This is why it is insane – out of harmony with reality – for us to embrace them on any level, including their perverse interpretations of spirituality and ritual practice.

Sitting in a meditative posture with an ankh was corrupted by the whites into 'meditation as a form of yoga (ankh)'

We do not practice ankh, life. We live ankh, life. We cannot practice yoga/yoke. Our sahu, our spirit is an ankh (yoke)

It is not something that can be practiced. It is something that is.

Origin of the Common Meditative Posture

Abosom (Deities) in common meditative posture

The crossed-leg "lotus" position is often used as a representation of 'yoga'. The so-called lotus posture, as well as the most common posture shown above, have their roots in Afuraka/Afuraitkait. Yet, they are not related to a 'practice' of 'yoga', but are associated with certain Abosom and Nananom Nsamanfo.

The scribe **Neb Meru tef** meditating/communicating with the sacred baboon **Aan** of **Tehuti**. Note that the baboon is an **Obosom** (Deity). This is a ***Spirit*** that Neb Meru tef is *ritually communing* with (*nkom*) here. [*Neb Meru tef in the 'lotus'.*]

Baboons praising **Ra** – Invoking the energy of **Ra** through the **Aten** (Sun)

Baboons came from Khanit (Nubia) and other lands south of Kamit. Certain baboons were sacred and were seen by the Kamau as animals who could possess the spirits of the ancient Ancestresses and Ancestors. They were recognized as *vessels* of the ancient Elders and Elderesses and honored ritually as such. Baboons would be the first to raise their hands at sunrise to invoke the power of the **Aten** (Sun) and **Ra** and **Rait** (*Creator and Creatress of the Universe – Servants of* **Amenet-Amen**, *The Supreme Being*). These sacred animals, used as totems for the Nananom Nsamanfo, who originated from the South and the first to worship and honor the Abosom at the beginning of Creation (sunrise), brought messages from the spirit-realm to the people. Sacred baboons were mummified as were other sacred totemic animals. Many Abosom were ritually depicted as baboons as well, including **Tehuti**, the Male Obosom of Divine Wisdom. The meditative posture of the sacred baboon, the **akyeneboa** *(animal totem)* of the Nananom Nsamanfo is one of the most common meditative postures employed by Afurakanu/Afuraitkaitnut. **It is Ancestral and totemic.**

Sacred Baboon. Akyeneboa of the Nananom Nsamanfo

Baboon of **Tehuti**

Baboon of **Tehuti**

Obosom **Maat**

Senenmut in the common meditative posture

Origin of the term Chakra

The concept of **chakras** is typically associated with pseudo-discipline of 'yoga'. Again, this term is one stolen from Kamit by the whites and their offspring and co-opted into their pseudo-spiritual practices and cosmology. Two quotes from wikipedia concerning the etymology of the term chakra:

"...The concept of chakra features in tantric and yogic traditions of hinduism and buddhism. Its name derives from the Sanskrit word for "wheel" or "turning" (cakraṃ चक्रं [ˈtʃəkrə̃], pronounced [ˈtʃəkrə] in hindi; pali: cakka चक्क, oriya: ଚ� malayalam: ചക്രം, thai: จักระ, telugu: చక్�o, tamil: சக்கரம், kannada: ಚಕ್� chinese: 輪/轮, pinyin: lún, tibetan: འཁོར་ལོ་, wylie: 'khor lo).

Chakras correspond to vital points in the physical body but are generally understood as being part of the "subtle body" which cannot be found through autopsy. While breath channels (nāḍis) of yogic practices had already been discussed in the classical Upanishads, it was not until the eighth-century buddhist Hevajra Tantra and Caryāgiti, that hierarchies of chakras were introduced..."

"...Bhattacharyya's review of Tantric history says that the word chakra is used to mean several different things in the sanskrit sources:[4]

1. "Circle," used in a variety of senses, symbolizing endless rotation of shakti.

2. A circle of people. In rituals there are different cakra-sādhanā in which adherents assemble and perform rites. According to the Niruttaratantra, chakras in the sense of assemblies are of 5 types.

3. The term chakra also is used to denote yantras or mystic diagrams, variously known as trikoṇa-cakra, aṣṭakoṇa-cakra, etc.

4. Different "nerve plexus within the body."

In buddhist literature the sanskrit term cakra (Pali cakka) is used in a different sense of "circle," referring to a buddhist conception of the Cycle of Rebirth consisting of six states in which beings may be reborn.[5]

The linguist Jorma Koivulehto wrote (2001) of the annual finnish Kekri celebration having borrowed the word from early indo-aryan.[6] indo-european cognates include greek kuklos, lithuanian kaklas, tocharian B kokale and english "wheel."[7]

Cognates of "chakra" still exist in modern asian languages as well. In malay, "cakera" means "disc," e.g. "cakera padat" "compact disc."..."

chakra (n.)
1888 in yoga sense "a spiritual center of power in the human body," from Sanskrit *cakra* "circle, wheel," from PIE root ***kwel-** (1) "revolve, move round." -- [www.etymonline.com]

Again, we quote this source to demonstrate how the whites and their offspring continue to lie about the origins of the term. The term chakra, also written cakra, is said to be derived from sanskrit with the definition of 'wheel', 'circle'. The true origins can be found in Kamit:

karkar
anything round, staff, stick, roll, cylinder

karkar, A.Z. 1880, 95, stone boulders ; compare Heb. גַּל and גַּלְגַּל

The term **karkar**, meaning *anything round, cylinder* as well as *boulders* (round rocks) was corrupted into **kakar** and **kakara** (cakra). The related terms **kar, kara** and **Karaut** shed more light:

kar, karȧ, N. 160, Rec. 27, 227, 31, 17, Rec. 19, 96, shrine, sanctuary, chapel ; plur. gods of the same sanctuary.

Karȧut, B.D. 84, 4, the gods of a shrine.

The root term **kar** or **kara** means *shrine* or *sanctuary* of an Obosom. The **Karaut** are the Abosom of the **kara**/shrine.

Kara (Shrine) from Kamit wherein the statue of the Obosom dwells

Note that **kara** meaning *shrine* is the Akan term **Okra** (also written **o-kara**, **kra** and **kera**). The **Okra/Okraa** (**Ka/Kait**) is the *Soul*, the *shrine* for the Divine Consciousness of **Nyamewaa-Nyame** within the head of the Afurakani/Afuraitkaitnit individual. Moreover, the various organs, organs' systems and body parts of the Afurakani/Afuraitkaitnit body are associated with different Abosom. They are **kara** (shrines) for the Abosom. Thus, in the **Pert em Hru** (misnomered *Egyptian Book of the Dead*) in the chapter of *Driving Back Slaughter in Henen Su* the spirit of the deceased individual says:

*"...My hair is the hair of **Nu**. My face is the face of **Ra**. My eyes are the eyes of **Het Heru**. My ears are the ears of **Ap-uat**. My nose is the nose of **Khent-sheps**. My lips are the lips of **Anpu**. My teeth are the teeth of **Khepera**. My neck is the neck of **Auset**, the Divine Lady. My hands are the hands of **Khunemu**, the lord of Tattu. My fore-arms are the fore-arms of **Neith**, the Lady of Saut. My backbone is the backbone of **Sut**. My privy member is the privy member of **Ausar**. My reins are the reins of the lords of **Kher-aba**. My breast is the breast of the awful and terrible One. My belly and my backbone are the belly and backbone of **Sekhet**. My buttocks are the buttocks of the eye of **Heru**. My hips and thighs are the hips and thighs of **Nut**. My feet are the feet of **Ptah**. My fingers and leg-bones are the fingers and leg-bones of the living **Auraut**.*

*There is no member of my body that is without an **Ntoro/Ntorot** (God or Goddess). **Tehuti** shields my body altogether and I am [like] unto **Ra** every day..."*

The parts of the body are **kara** (shrines) for the Abosom. This is why the **karkar** (karakara/kakara/cakra) or chakras, are recognized to be *shrines* (sacred centers of energy) for the Deities. As stated above, because the whites and their offspring are incapable of communicating with the Abosom (Forces of Nature), they are incapable of "activating chakras", "balancing chakras" or any other associated "practice". *Their "shrines" are empty*. Therefore when they meditate, they send their own electromagnetic energy (the simple energy moving through the nervous system) up and down their spines in an attempt to "open" their chakras. What results is nothing more than a pseudo-metaphysical "light show". When no Abosom are present in the shrines, 'activation of chakras' is merely the stimulation of deeply embedded, disordered obsessions, desires, lusts, etc. and the discarnate relatives/spirits attached to their blood-circles who resonate with such lusts. The whites and their offspring pass such a "practice" off as spirituality and communication with the "higher forces" or "higher self". In reality, they are simply engaged in ritual disorder.

Afurakanu/Afuraitkaitnut have authentic religious practices, because we have an **actual connection** to **Nyamewaa-Nyame**, the Abosom and Nananom Nsamanfo.

***Ankh** arising from the **Djed** pillar holding the solar disk. From the Papyrus of Ani.*

The question is often asked, "If yoga leads to awareness, then why are those who have been practitioners of yoga for years or decades not aware of the truth about the origins of yoga?"

It is because yoga is not a discipline, but a corruption of a term and the attachment to this term a set of foolish beliefs and pseudo-religious practices, designed by whites, to misdirect Afurakanu/Afuraitkaitnut from our true source of power.

If the pseudo-discipline of yoga led to awareness, this truth about its origins would not have been hidden (invisible) from the awareness of those who have *practiced* and *taught the false definitions of* yoga for years until now.

Afurakanu/Afuraitkaitnut have authentic forms of ritual song, ritual dance, ritual prayer and more which are naturally inclusive of varied modes of strengthening, stretching and balancing our physical vehicles for the purposes of toning/attuning, health and defense. We need only to **sankofa**, return, go and grasp from our Ancestral reservoir.

Afurakanu/Afuraitkaitnut, free yourselves from the idiocy of disorder, from the whites and their offspring, their ill-culture and their pseudo-religions, pseudo-religious practices and pseudo-disciplines. Embrace your **ankh**, your life, in purity.

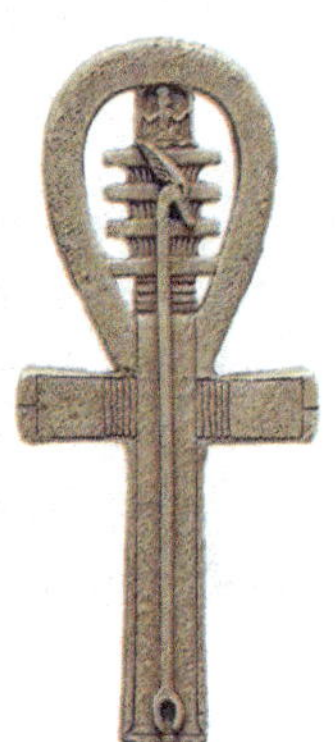

tchet, P. 92, , M. 121, , N. 699, , , to be stable, to be permanent, abiding, established firmly, lasting, enduring;

tchet , , , stability, as in the group , "life, stability, serenity."

The **djed** (tchet) pillar (stability) is often combined with the **ankh** (life) as we can see in the examples above. The image above from the tomb of **Ta Nut Amen** shows his **Ba** (Spirit) in the form of a bird with the head of Ta Nut Amen. The **ankh-djed** talisman is around his neck in the form of a **yoke**. The **Ba** is the *Divine Living Energy,* a child of **Ra** and **Rait**, the Creator and Creatress. It is the life-force animating us manifest as the solar-fire surging through our blood. Our Spirit (**Ba**) is yoked (**ankh**) to our Soul (**Ka**) for stability (**djed**).

KARA

KASA

The Origin and Nature of the 'Chakra'

Ofa a Edi Kan (Part 1)

Karkar was shown in our article **ANKH – The Origin of the Term 'Yoga'** to be a term from ancient **Kamit** (Egypt) meaning *anything round; cylinder.* This is the true Afurakani/Afuraitkaitnit (African) etymological origin of the term *cakra (chakra)* which was later stolen and plagiarized by the whites and their offspring after their invasion of india – which up to that point was an Afurakani/Afuraitkaitnit (African~Black) civilization.

karkar
anything round, staff, stick, roll, cylinder

We also have the variation of the term: **krkr** which means *to circle; mark out a circle with a stick*:

kerker
to circle, to mark out a circle with a stick.

The related terms **kara** (**kra**) and **Karaut** mean *shrine*  and *Deities of the shrine* respectively:

kar, karȧ, N. 160, , Rec. 27, 227, 31, 17, , , , , , , , , Rec. 19, 96, shrine, sanctuary, chapel; plur. ; , , , gods of the same sanctuary.

Karȧut , B.D. 84, 4, the gods of a shrine.

The **karkar** (circles/chakras) are **kara** (shrines) which are *sanctuaries* for **Karaut** (Shrine Deities). What is the location of the **karkar** within the Afurakani/Afuraitkaitnit individual?

A quote from one of the first texts written in the west regarding the 'chakras':

*"...The [hindu] books hint at, rather than explain, what happens when kundalini rises up the channel through the sushumna. They refer to the spine as Merudanda, the rod of Meru, "the central axis of creation", presumably of the body. In that, they say, there is the channel called sushumna, within that another, called Vajrini, and within that again a third called Chitrini, which is "as fine as a spider's thread". Upon that are threaded the chakras, **"like knots on a bamboo rod"**..."* [The Chakras, C.W. Leadbeater, 1927]

The spine is the physical channel which contains the non-physical *sushumna* in hinduism. It is the central axis and thus called the 'rod of Meru'. This is a corruption of the name of the Obosom **Menu** (the Deity **Min**) also called **Amen-Men**. As shown in our article **Amen-Men: The Obosom of Amene and Menmeneda**:

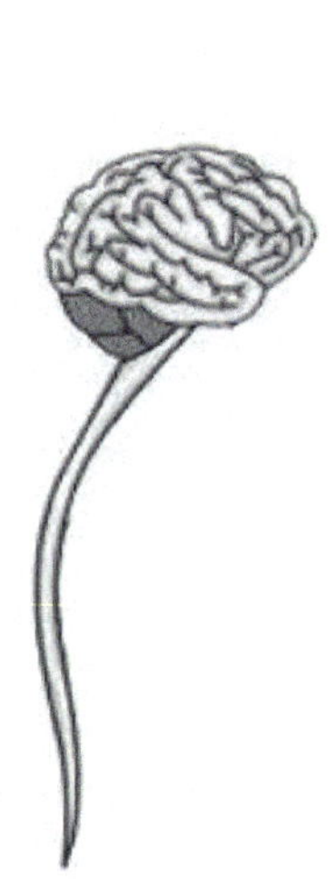

*Images of the **Axis/Central Nervous System, Men** and **Amen-Men.** The cord connecting the back of the head of the **Obosom** to the **Asaase** (Earth) represents the spinal cord while the rounded and flat crowns represent the brain.*

Amen-Men (**Menu**; **Min**) operates through the central *Axis of Creation*, the polar axis of **Asaase** (Earth) and the axis (central nervous system) of the Afurakani/Afuraitkaitnit (African) body. He operates through the **okyin** (planet) **Amene** (saturn) and the "crown" **karkar** (chakra). The two plumes (feathers) rising from His crown, often with the disk of the **Aten** (Sun) in between them, comprise the image later stolen by the whites and their offspring and relabeled the *"thousand-petaled lotus"* and radiant "crown chakra". It should be noted that the term **amemene** in Akan means *'brain'*.

[See: **Amen-Men**: **The Obosom of Amene and Menmeneda**: www.odwirafo.com/Akradinbosom_Amen-Men.pdf]

The axis of **Amen-Men** or **Menu** was plagiarized by the whites and called the 'rod of Meru'. Note that when the rolling 'R' is pronounced, it is identical in sound to the 'N' sound in Afurakani/Afuraitkaitnit languages. Meru and **Menu** thus sound identical when spoken at regular conversation speed.

The notion of the seven chakras being akin to *knots on a bamboo pole/rod* within the sushumna/spine, was also stolen directly from Kamit by the whites. **It must be understood that the doctrine of the chakras as plagiarized by the whites and their offspring is very recent.**

The first mention of chakras as psychic centers in a *rudimentary* form is typically stated to be found in the texts called the upanishads in india. The later upanishads – the earlier of which were composed between **2,200 - 1,800 years ago** [2nd century 'b.c.e.' and 2nd century 'c.e.'] – are where basic notions of chakras are first plagiarized by whites. However, the **seven-chakra** system was not plagiarized and propounded by the whites until centuries later beginning approximately **1,500 years ago** [6th century 'a.d.'] with the tantra traditions. **This information was stolen and corrupted by the whites from the writings and culture of the ancient Kamau (Blacks/Egyptians) which predate hinduism, the upanishads (vedanta) and tantra by thousands of years:**

thes, thes-t , P. 568, , , , , , knot, tie, ligature, backbone, vertebrae, spine; plur. , , , , U. 517, , T. 328, , T. 183.

The 'th' in the term **thes** or **theset** (often transliterated as 'tj' or 'tch') can be pronounced like the 'ch' sound in *'change'* as well as the 'k' sound in *'chrome'*. Thus, in **Coptic** (Late Kamit dialect) the term is spelled **Kac** (**Kaws**): ϭⲱⲥ. **Kosi** (**Koci**) and **Kase** (**Kace**) are also variations. **Thes** is a term meaning a ***knot*** , yet it also means the ***backbone, vertebrae, spine*** . This is critical because of the following usage regarding the ***nature*** and ***number*** of the ***knots***:

thesut VII , the seven magical knots that protected a man.

Here we have **seven magical knots** that **protect** the individual. It is important to note that the term for *knots* is also the term for *vertebrae, spine.* The seven **thesut** are the *seven magical knots upon the spine that protect* the individual. This is the Kamau origin of the hindu perversion regarding the *seven chakras* within the sushumna/*spine* being akin to *seven knots on a bamboo rod.* Moreover, the Afurakanu/Afuraitkaitnut (Africans) of Kamit recognized that there are **Abosom** (Akan for *Deities*) associated with the seven knots:

Thesu VII, B.D. 71, 16, seven gods who assisted at the judgment and condemnation of the wicked.

These seven Abosom are called the **Seven Thesu.** This is the source from which the whites and their offspring learned that there are Abosom (**thesu**) associated with the seven magical "knots" (**thesu**) along the "spine" (**thesu**). These Abosom protect and assist the individual with overcoming *bad-judgment (disorder)* and *condemnation.* More definitions of the term **thesu** are instructive:

thes, chamber, room.

thes-t, sarcophagus, funerary coffer.

The **thesu** as *chambers, rooms, sarcophagi, coffers* reveal their function as **kara** (shrines).

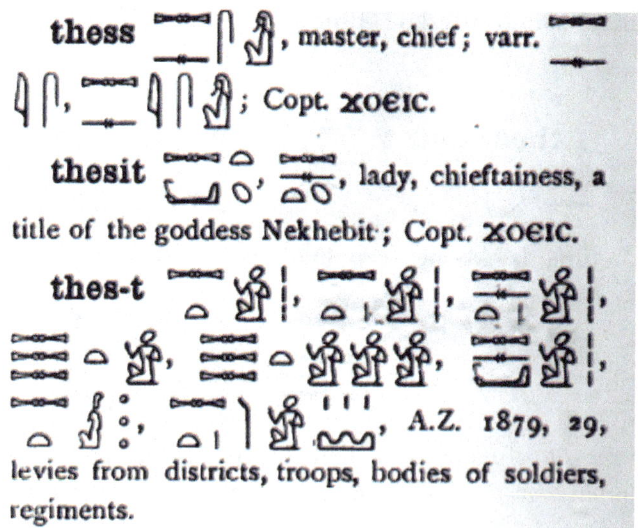

thess, master, chief; varr. ; Copt. ϫⲟⲉⲓⲥ.

thesit, lady, chieftainess, a title of the goddess Nekhebit; Copt. ϫⲟⲉⲓⲥ.

thes-t, A.Z. 1879, 29, levies from districts, troops, bodies of soldiers, regiments.

The **thesu** are *masters/chieftainesses*; bodies of *soldiers/fighters*

thes, to compose a connected statement, to arrange words in logical sequence.

thes, I, 116, IV, 221, IV, 1090, proverb, saying, formula, charm, spell, incantation, declaration, statement, what a man wants to say, accusation of a plaintiff, speech or defence of a defendant, sentence, aphorism, apophthegm, "word," precept;

thesu, speeches, proverbs, precepts, statements, charms, spells, orders, commands.

The **thesu** are related to *ritual incantations, ritual prayer*, the use of **sound** to manifest intent ("mantric")

thesu, law-makers, arrangers, disposers, managers.

The **thesu** are *Regulators* of *Divine Law*

thesi, T. 271, P. 22, 97, 604, M. 32, N. 122, Ḳubbân Stele 11, Metternich Stele 59, to lift up, to raise, to rise, to raise oneself, to ascend a hill, to lift away, to bear up, to support, to be high (of price), to lift up an offering to a god, to set aside, high (of bows); Copt. ϫⲓⲥⲉ, ϫⲟⲥⲉ, ϭⲓⲥⲓ, ϭⲟⲥⲓ.

thess, T. 29, Hh. 564, to lift up, to raise, to rise, to mount, to be exalted; Copt. ϫⲓⲥⲉ.

thesi, ascent, ascender.

thesu bâti, Tombos Stele 13, wearers of the double crown.

The verb **thesi** also means *to lift up, to raise,* etc. This is the source from which the notion of the *serpent power rising up* through the **karkara** (chakras) along the **thesu**/spine is derived.

Thesu-urut [hieroglyphs], U. 434, [hieroglyphs], T. 248, a group of gods who raised the dead.

The term **thesu** encompasses the notion of *raising consciousness*, *awakening* and *raising up certain Ancestral Spirits from death/ dormancy* and more.

The **thesu** (*Coptic*: **kasu**) as *seven magical knots* along the *spine* governed by seven Abosom (Deities) are found in the physical body. The **spinal nerve ganglia** and **plexuses** are seen as the *physical representation* of the seven major chakras at the following spinal anatomical locations: coccyx, sacrum, lumbar, upper thoracic, cervical, mid and upper brain. The nerve ganglia are a *mass* (knot) of nerve cells and the plexuses are a *network* (knot) of spinal nerves:

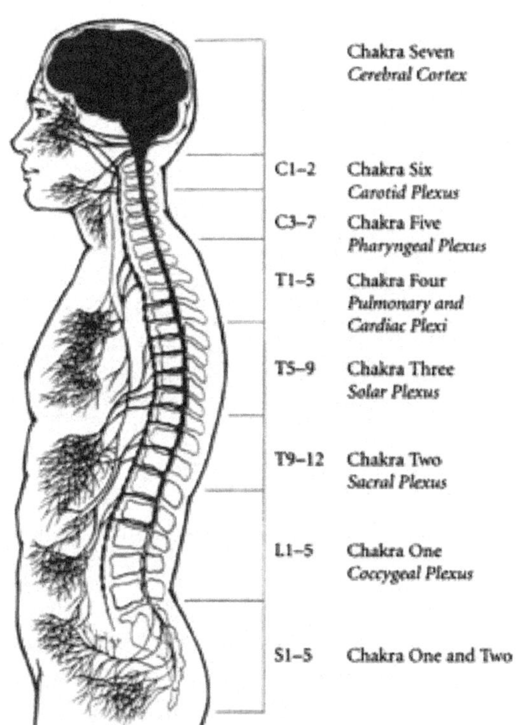

Seven Thesu (Knots) in the Body

One of the many textual references regarding the **seven thesu** (knots) can be found in **Chapter 71** of the **Pert em Hru** (*misnomered Egyptian Book of the Dead*) scribed over **3,600** years ago:

"...O you ***seven knots****, the arms of the balance on that night of setting the Sacred Eye in order, who cut off heads, who sever necks, who take away hearts, who make a slaughter in the Island of Fire: I know you, I know your names; may you know me just as I know your names;* ***if I reach you, may you reach me; if you live through me, may I live through you; may you make me to flourish with what is in your hands, the staff [spine] which is in your grasp. May you destine me to life annually;*** *may you grant to me many*

years of life over and above my years of life; many days over and above my days of life; many nights over and above my nights of life, until I depart. ***May I rise to be a likeness of myself, may my breath be at my nose, may my eyes see in company with those who are in the horizon*** *on that day of dooming the robber...*"

Here the spirits of the seven **thesu** are appealed to ritually for the elevation and recalibration of the individual's spirit. This is evidence of the **7-karkar (kara/kasu)** system – fully incorporated in ritual – thousands of years before the whites and their offspring had any knowledge of its existence.

We have thus far demonstrated that the **thesu/kasu** are the source of the 'seven chakra' *imagery, placement* and *ritual associations* that were later plagiarized and corrupted by the whites and their offspring. However, we must also understand the *origin* and *nature* of the **kara** (shrines) and **kasu** (knots) within the spirit-body.

Arat

(Auraut/Uraei)

The cobra is called **auraut** (**arat**) in Kamit. There are numerous Abosom Who take the form of Divine Auraut. The most popular being **Uatchet** (Wadjet; Wadjit) [**Yaa** in Akan – See: **Yaa: Obosom of Yaa and Yaada**: www.odwirafo.com/Akradinbosom_Yaa.pdf]. The Auraut is often depicted with a solar or lunar disk on its head as in the image above.

There is a grouping of cobra Abosom that are **seven** in number. These **Seven Aurautu** (called the *seven uraei*) are key to the notion of the **karkar, kara** and **kasu/thesu**. An excerpt from the **Mer** of the **Per Aa Unas** (*pyramid text* of the *Pharaoh* Unas), scribed over **4,400** years ago:

"...**Unas** is the **Nau**-snake, the leading bull, **who has swallowed his seven Aurautu** [seven uraei cobras], **and so his seven neck vertebrae came into being**, who give orders to his seven **pesdjetu** [enneads] to hear the words of the King..." [*Utterance 318. See inscription below*]

Mer text of Unas [Utterances 318-321]

Here the Per Aa (king) is identified as taking the form of a **Nau** *snake* who *swallowed* the *seven* Divine Cobra Divinities - Aurautu - which caused his **seven neck vertebrae** to *come into being.*

While the **thesu** are the *seven knots* (thesu) along the *spine* (thesu), the *swallowing* of the Seven Aurautu is the **ingesting of seven radiant disks** who then take up residence within the king as his **seven neck vertebrae** [cervical vertebrae]. This act *precipitates* the development of the seven magical knots within the body. Because of this ritual act, Unas is empowered to give orders to his seven **Pesdjetu** Who *regulate* the kara and kasu.

The swallowing of the radiant disks is akin to the Great Mother in the night sky swallowing the radiant disks (stars) which take up residence in Her body (black sky). It is also related to the presence of the radiant energy centers/kara operating within the ***abatumm*** *(melanin) of Afurakanu/Afuraitkaitnut which lines the axis – central nervous system.*

Great Mother Obosom **Nut** with the stars of the night (nut) sky in Her body

The term **Pesdjetu** means *'company/group of Abosom'.* There are many sacred groupings of Abosom in Kamit: *Four Sons of* ***Heru****, Forty-Two Assessors of* ***Maat****, Eight Primordials of Khemenu (Ogdoad),* the *Nine Divinities of Annu (Ennead)*, etc. The Abosom are the Divine Spirit-Forces operating throughout the various Suns, Moons, Stars, the Black Substance of Space, Planets, Oceans, Mountains, Rivers, Fire, Earth, etc. in Creation. They are the *Divine Organs* within the *Great Divine Body* of **Amenet-Amen**, the Supreme Being (**Nyamewaa-Nyame** in Akan). Specified sacred-groupings of Abosom *(Pesdjetu)* function together in Creation just as organs and organs' systems function together in groups within the body (e.g. heart-lung complex, digestive system, endocrine system, etc.). In the Mer text of Unas, **seven Pesdjetu** are mentioned and are often translated as *'seven enneads'*. These seven sacred-groupings or *sets* of Abosom are *Divine Regulators* (**thesu** - *to regulate, arrange*). They are also **Thesu Urut**, those who *raise the dead* or *awaken the dormant*:

Thesu-urut gods who raised the dead.

Pesdjet (**pest**; **pestchet**) references a *sacred number-grouping* of Abosom:

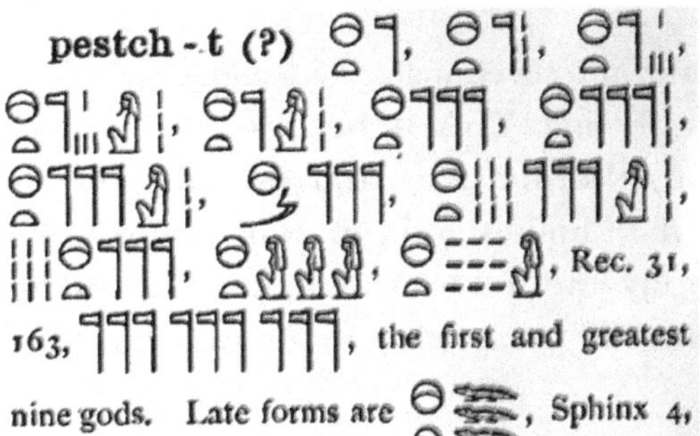
pestch-t (?) , Rec. 31, 163, , the first and greatest nine gods. Late forms are , Sphinx 4,

pestchiu (?) , U. 418, 632, T. 238, 307, P. 218, the three companies of the gods, *i.e.*, the great gods of heaven, earth, and the Ṭuat = , all the gods, , B.D. 23, 6, all the companies of the gods.

Yet, the term also has two other important meanings:

pestch , back, backbone, vertebrae; plur.

pestch , T. 174, P. 163, N. 356, , to shine, to illumine.

The term **pesdjet** thus means a *sacred number-grouping* of Abosom, *backbone/spine* and *to shine, illuminate.* These are descriptions of the **karkar**, **kara** (chakras) as *radiant/illuminate* centers of energy along the *spine* (**thesu**) that are *sanctuaries* (**thesu** – *chambers;* **kara** - shrines) for the Abosom. The spelling of

pesdjet above with the **metut** (hieroglyph) of a *serpent* , the determinative metut of a *radiant sun disk* and a *spine* (thesu) shows the origin of the *fiery, serpent power* moving through the *spine* (kundalini) - all combined in one term. It references the swallowing of the seven radiant Aurautu Who become the seven neck vertebrae.

Moreover, the Auraut can also take the form of a Divine Cobra with its body *encircling* (**karkar** – *to circle*) a Sun disk. Below are images of the Abosom **Ra** and **Sekhemet** with the **Auraut** encircling the **Aten** (Sun) upon Their heads:

Ra and **Sekhemet** wearing the **auraut** (arat) a variation of the "crown" **karkar**

The fact that there are *sets* of Abosom associated with each of the seven major kara and kasu (chakra shrines and knots) is typically omitted by the whites and their offspring. **This is because they are unable to communicate with any Abosom (Orisha, Vodou, Ntorou/Ntorotu [Neteru/Netertu]). They have thus created a "system" of stimulating empty shrines within their bodies and communicating with nothing. This pseudo-system is supported by a pseudo-philosophy and fed to Afurakanu/Afuraitkaitnut who are unconscious. It is an attempt to influence us to abort our connection to the Abosom Who are our Divine source of power and consciousness.**

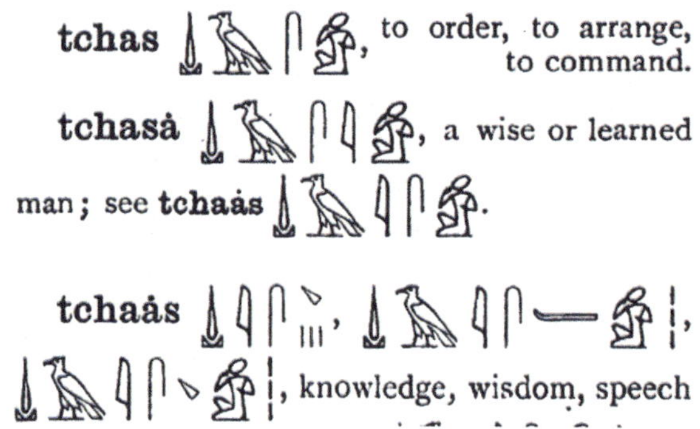

tchas, to order, to arrange, to command.

tchasȧ, a wise or learned man; see **tchaȧs**.

tchaȧs, , , knowledge, wisdom, speech

The term **tchas** meaning *to order, to arrange* is a variation of **thesu** meaning *lawmakers, arrangers*. The term **tchasa** and **tchaas** meaning *wise* or *learned individual; knowledge, wisdom, speech* is a variation of **thes** meaning *speeches, spells, incantations; to arrange words in a logical sequence.*

These definitions are critical for in the Akan language the terms and their variations exist with the same meanings. The Akan term **nyansa**, pronounced with a nasal 'N'-sound means *'knowledge', 'wisdom'*. Wise people are thus called **nyansa-fo**. Linguistically, the 'tch', 'ch' or 'j' sound often interchanges with the 'ny' or 'y' sound. Some Afurakanu/Afuraitkaitnut in america thus pronounce the term *'yeah'* as *'jeah'*. This linguistic shift is seen throughout Afuraka/Afuraitkait (Africa). This is how **Nyame** (God) in Akan becomes **Nyambe** amongst the **Lozi** people in **Zambia** and **Njambe** amongst the **Herero** in Namibia (**Nzambe** amongst the **Bakongo** in the Republic of Congo). This is also how the term **tchaasa** meaning *wisdom* in Kamit came to be pronounced chasa, jasa, yasa, nyasa and **nyansa** meaning *wisdom* in Akan:

nyãnsã, -sa, *knowledge, learning, wisdom; skill, dexterity; art, artfulness, craft, cunning. pr.* 2554. 2869 *f.*; *cf.* nimdeɛ, anitew, anifere; ɔkyerɛ me ny., *he imparts knowledge to me, instructs me;* wahũ ny., onim ny. (trɛ̃nɛ̃nɛ̃), *he possesses (true) knowledge, is wise, intelligent.*

ɔ-kásá, *inf.* **1.** *speaking, speech; the peculiar manner of speaking, the particular sound uttered. pr.* 534. 2479; *cf.* osũ; ɔkasa nè n'aw̃erefiri, ɔk. nè ne ntekam' *or* ɔk. nè ne ntegyaw, *I have forgotten to mention* ... — **2.** *language, dialect;* ɔkasa a edi aduasã = ɔk.

As stated above, the Coptic variation of the **'TH'** ('ch' or 'chuh') sound is the **'K'** ('ch' or 'cuh') sound. Thus, 'thes' or 'thas' is pronounced **'kas'** in Coptic. The variation **kas** (thes) meaning *speech, statements, commands* can be found in the Akan language. The Akan term **kasa** means *to speak; language.* The related term **kase** means *message* and **nkasae** means *talk; sayings; report.* These are the same terms with the same meanings unchanged over thousands of years from our ancient Ancestral language to its contemporary expression in Afuraka/Afuraitkait (Africa) today.

kasé = kaseɛ, *message* **ŋkasàé**, *inf. talk, sayings; report,*

In the Akan corpus of **adinkra** symbolism we have the **nyansapo**. This is the *'wisdom knot'.* The **ebe** (proverb) associated with this adinkra symbol states that *'Only the wise can untie the wisdom knot'.* The **nyansa** knot adinkra symbol was carried by the Akan from **Khanit** (Nubia) and Kamit to contemporary Ghana, Ivory Coast and the western hemisphere. The **nyansa** knot is actually the **tchaasa** (thas) knot:

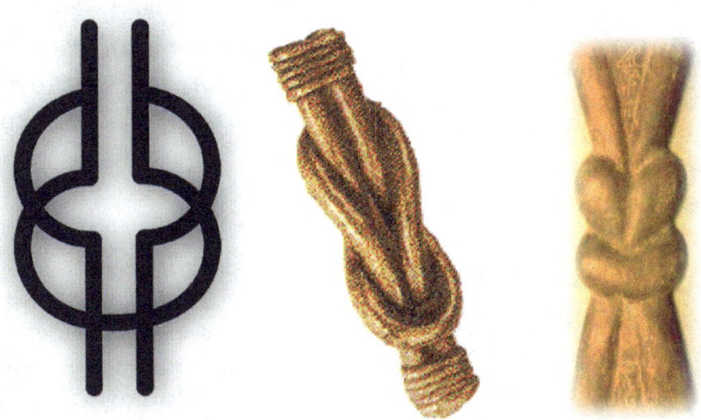

Nyansapo adinkra - *Wisdom knot.* **Nyansapo** in the form of **abrammu** *(brass weight).* **Tchasa** *(n-Yansa)* knot from Kamit

For one to achieve the recognition of **nyansafo** *(one in the group of wise Elders/Elderesses)* in Akan culture, one must be *spiritually aligned* with **Nyamewaa-Nyame** (**Amenet-Amen**) - *consistently.* Such an individual has been able to untie (open) the knot (karkar/kara/thesu/chakra) to facilitate the unencumbered flow of Divine consciousness and energy necessary to execute his/her Divine function in Creation - *consistently.* He or she has the capacity to unravel issues with patience and intelligence, while avoiding disorder (destruction of the material basis of the knot) in the process. Such an individual becomes a *radiant/shining example* for others to emulate.

The unraveling of the nyansa knot is the opening of the **kara** (shrines) and the **kasa** (thasu/knots) of the spirit-body. **Critically, it is the conscious harmonizing with the Abosom Who govern the kara (shrines), for Afurakanu/Afuraitkaitnut – and only Afurakanu/Afuraitkaitnut – are components of these Spiritual Organs and Organs' systems within the Great Divine Body of Nyamewaa-Nyame.**

Above left is a **kra** (**kara; kera**) or *shrine* from Kamit, a sanctuary for the sacred ritual elements of the **Obosom**. Above right is an Akan **koro** (**kuruw; kuruo; kuduo**). The **koro** is used as a *shrine* for the **kra** (**okara; okra**) - the Soul/Divine Consciousness – the individual's personal Divinity/Obosom which resides in the head. It is often used in the **akraguare** or *'soul-washing'* ceremony. Water for the ceremony as well as ritual offerings are placed in the vessel.

ɛ-kõro, *a pot before the* place, tree &c., of a so-called *fetish,* containing water, palm-wine, leaves, eggs, cowries &c., from the appearance of which things (called abo), when stirred up by the kɔmfo, he concludes what he has to soothsay; *syn.* kuŋkuma; ahina a wɔde nsu nè ŋhabamma [nnuruwa-nnuruwa] nè nsã nè ŋkesuwa nè ntrama agum' na ɛtaa ɔbosompa no anim.

kúrukuruwa, *pl.* ŋkúruwa-ŋkúruwa, *a. round and large,* of flat and globular things; *circular; globular, spherical; cf.* korokorowa, puruw; kontoŋkroŋ, dantabaŋ, haŋkare, katraka.

kãŋkrá, Okw. = hãŋkare, *circle*

karkar [hieroglyphs], 11
anything round, staff, stick, roll, cylinder

ɔ-kórów, *pl.* a-, 1. *a large, round, flat, wooden vessel,* made of one piece of wood (wɔde onyãã a.s. ɔwowa na eseŋ k.), used to wash clothes, to bathe little children &c.; *a bowl; a van* or *fan,* for winnowing grain; *syn.* apaawá, apampaá (*cf.* korókũma). F. *a tub.* —

kórokorowa, *pl.* ŋkórowa-ŋkórowa *(Ex. 16,14), a. round and small,* of grains, seeds, globules; *cf.* kurukuruwa, puruw. ŋkorowá = ŋkoruwa. — ŋkórowa-ŋkórowa, *s.* kórokorowa.
kõrɔ(w)-béŋ, kõrɔbéne, *the red inner part of a tree* (ɔdwene), with which charms and amulets are dyed. *pr. 1538.*

The Akan terms **kankra** and **korokorowa** are variants of the ancient Kamiti term **karkar.**

The wisdom of the **nyansa** knot is summed up in Kamit in the group of Abosom known as the **Seven Tchaasu** - seven Abosom born of the primordial Mother Obosom **Meht Urt** and **Tehuti**, the Male Obosom of Divine Wisdom. These seven Abosom are thus called the *Seven Wise Ones.* They planned the world with **Meht Urt** and **Tehuti** and preside over learning and letters:

Tchaásu VII

Düm. Temp. Inschr. 45, the Seven Divine Masters of Wisdom who helped Thoth to plan the universe. Their names were: Neferḥat, Neferpeḥui, Nebṭesheru, Ka, Bȧk, Khekh, and Sȧn.

These **seven Tchaasu** are manifest as the **seven Thesu**. Thus, in relation to the texts in the **Pert em Hru** regarding the seven thesu quoted above, we also have in the *Coffin Texts* these same seven thesu being referred to as the **seven thesu of Meht Urt**:

"…O you ***seven knots of Mehet Urt****, may you make me fresh, may you make me live, may you give me strength to my bones and life to my limbs, may you make my flesh fresh completely with life. I know you, I know your names. I have not died. I have not grown poor. I have not gone blind. I have not become deaf. I am one of the Deities. I know your names…"* [Coffin Texts #407]

Tehuti

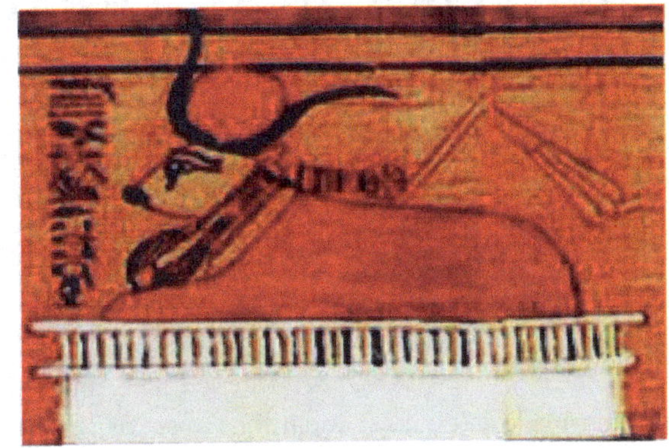

Meht Urt

The **seven Tchaasu** are the **seven Thesu/knots of wisdom - nyansapo**. They helped to plan the universe and govern learning. Their **kara** (shrines) are the **karkaru** (chakras) in the spirit-body and the seven knots (nerve ganglia and plexi) in the physical body. In the Afurakani/Afuraitkaitnit individual, these **karau** (shrines) are not empty. They are *sanctuaries* of These **Karaut** (Shrine Deities). Our cosmological connection to these Abosom and the specific approach to our proper alignment and realignment with Them is rooted in our Ancestry – our reincarnation through specific Afurakani/Afuraitkaitnit blood circles. This information can only be accessed from These Abosom and our direct **Nananom Nsamanfo** (Spiritually Cultivated Afurakani/Afuraitkaitnit Ancestresses and Ancestors). The whites and their offspring – *all non- Afurakanu/non-Afuraitkaitnut (all non-Blacks)* – have no access to this reality and no concept of its depth. The white ritual perversions and pseudo-philosophies of hinduism, buddhism, jainism, vedanta, tantrism, hermeticism, "new"-age pseudo-spiritualism, kabbalism, sufism, gnosticism, taoism, moorishism, pseudo"native"-american spiritualism, etc. have no bearing on this reality. Only Afurakanu/Afuraitkaitnut, through the embrace of our Afurakani/Afuraitkaitnit Ancestral Religion, have the capacity to realize and operationalize the origin and nature of the **kara** and **kasa**.

ANKHUT - ORIGINAL TERMS FROM KAMIT

karkar, IV, anything round, staff, stick, roll, cylinder;

The etymology of the term cakra (chakra) meaning *'wheel'* or *'that which is round'* comes directly from the term **karkar** from Kamit, meaning *anything round, roll, cylinder,* etc. The related term **kar** or **kara** means *shrine or sanctuary of a Ntoro/Ntorot (Neter/Netert)*. The **karkaru** ('chakras') are **karau** ('shrines') for certain Divinities.

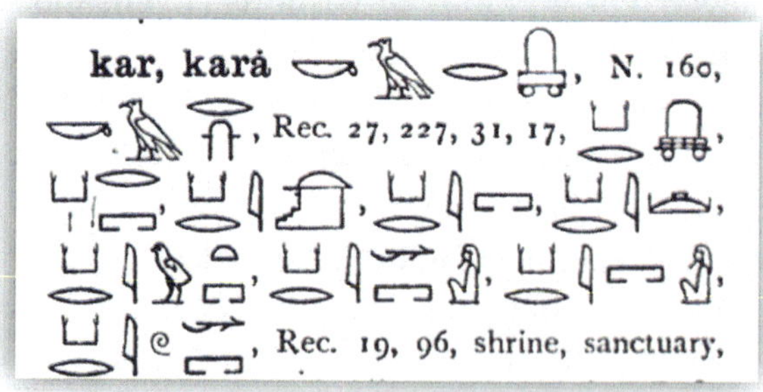

kar, karȧ, N. 160, Rec. 27, 227, 31, 17, Rec. 19, 96, shrine, sanctuary,

Khi, the Exalted One, *i.e.*, God.
Khi, Rec. 27, 87, winged disk.

Khai, Rev. 13, 25, "Exalted one"—a title of Rā.

The term chi (chee) or qi (kee) referencing the *'life-force' energy* comes directly from Kamit. The **Ntoro** (God) **Ra** is the *Creator* of the world. The **Ntorot** (Goddess) **Rait** is the *Creatress* of the world. They are the *Divine Living Energy* moving throughout all *created* entities. They use the **Aten** (Sun) as a major transmitter of Their life-force energy. The term **khi** meaning *exalted One*, also referencing the *winged sun-disk* is a title of **Ra**. The name **khai** is a variation of **khi**. The **metut** (hieroglyph) for the 'kh' symbol can be pronounced with the 'k' sound or the 'ch' sound. This 'kh' metut is the origin of the english 'ch' letter combination that can be pronounced with the 'ch' sound (e.g. 'change') or the 'k' sound (e.g. 'chronology').

pa Rā, the Sun

Another title of **Ra** is **Pa Ra**, often written **Pra**. The term **pa** is the *definite article* in the language of Kamit. It is the same as the english definite article '*The*'. **Pa Ra** thus means "*The* (God) **Ra**". **Ra** as **PaRa** or **Pra** is the etymological origin of the term prana meaning *life-force*. The reason why prana is said to be from the root 'pra' meaning 'full' is because the term was stolen from the name **Pa Ra**. **Ra** as Creator is the Expansive (full) aspect of the Life-Force, while **Rait** is the Contractive. The term **pa** also references *flame, spark, fire*:

pā, flame, fire, spark; plur.

This is a direct reference to the energy of **Ra** and **Rait** operating through the **Aten** (Sun). The Afurakanu/Afuraitkaitnut (Africans) of Kamit stated that we came into being from the tears of **Ra**.

ānkh ānkh

The term yoke is derived of 'yoga' which is said to be derived from the term 'yuj' or 'yewg'. These terms in reality have their etymological orgin in the term **ankh**. The 'a' in ankh can be pronounced variously as 'ah', 'aw', 'eh'. This is the origin of the english 'a' having the same variations in pronunciation. The 'n' in the term ankh is nasal as the 'n' in the english term 'senior'. The 'kh' combination again can be pronounced with the 'k' sound or the 'ch' sound. **Ankh** pronounced eh-n-ch or eh-n-k is the origin of the corruptions 'yuj' (eh-unch) and 'yewg' (eh-unk).

As can be seen above, the term **ankh** is also written with the symbol of the ankh and the *goat with the ankh around its neck* in the form of a *yoke*. This is also the metut (hieroglyph) used for the term **sahu** (*spirit body*):

The **sahu** or spirit body being spelled with the metut of the animal wearing the **ankh** as a *yoke* references our *animated* (animal) *life* (ankh) energy being *purified through ritual practice* (the elder/elderess seated in a meditative posture and mummified/purified in the image above). This is also a reference to the *animal totems* (**akyeneboa**) inherited through the blood circle of Afurakani/Afuraitkaitnit (African) clans whose **akyiwade** (taboos) we must observe in order to harmonize with Divine Order. These Ancestrally inherited prohibitions and prescriptions are key to our spiritual development and proper functioning.

ānkhi, ānkhu, a living being, a living thing; plur.

ānkh-t, U. 192, T. 71, M. 225, N. 603, Rec. 31, 32, a living person (fem.) or thing; "living fire."

The related terms **ankhi** and **ankht** mean *a living being, a life* referencing exclusively the Afurakani (African) male and Afuraitkaitnit (African) female. These terms are also applied to the **Ntorou/Ntorotu** (Deities):

Ānkhi, Tuat X, the god of time and of the life of Rā.

Ānkhit, "living one," the name of a goddess.

We also have the variation **ankh nu nut** and **ankht nu nut** meaning *a life within the city* – a *citizen*:

The terms **ankhi, ankhit, ankhnunut** (also written **ankh nu nuit**) are the origins of the terms *yogi* - **ankhi** (awn-kee or ohn-kee), *yogin* and *yogini* – **ankh nu nuit** or **ankhnnuit** (awnk-n-nu-eet).

yank (v.)

"to pull, jerk," 1822, Scottish, of unknown origin. Related: *Yanked*; *yanking*. sense of "sudden blow, cuff;" 1856 (American English) as "a sudden pull."

The term **'yank'** is a variation of 'yoke' as in to 'yoke someone up'. This is directly derived from **iankh/yankh/ankh**.

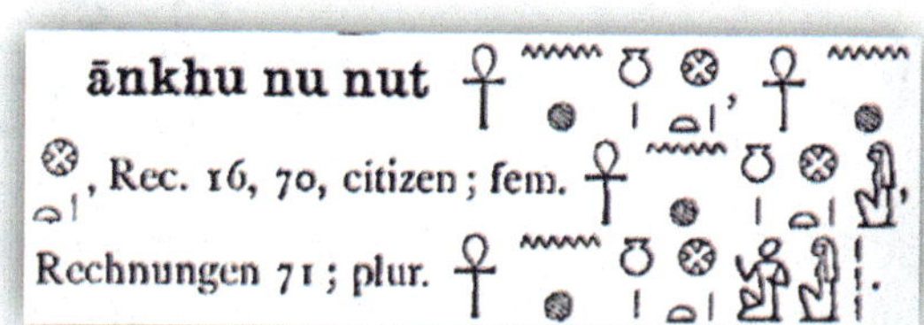
ānkhu nu nut, Rec. 16, 70, citizen; fem. Rechnungen 71; plur.

The terms **karkar, khi, pra** and **ankh** are the origins of the corruptions: *cakra, chi, prana* and *yoga/yoke*. These are terms used by our direct Afurakani/Afuraitkaitnit (African) Ancestresses and Ancestors thousands of years before hindus and asians came into being as populations on **Asaase** (Earth). For a more extensive discussion, see our articles below.

Appendix 2

AB - KHEPRA AND KHEPRIT

THE HEART, DANCE AND 'TAI CHI'/'QI GONG'

Below are index pages 97-98 from E. A. Wallis Budge's 'An Hieroglyphic Dictionary' - Volume 1:

I.

MEN (Standing, Sitting, Kneeling, Bowing, Lying Down).

Number.	Hieroglyph.	Phonetic Value.	Signification as Determinative or Ideograph.
1		—	inactivity, inertness, inanition, exhaustion.
2		à	address, cry out, invoke. As an interjection, *hai*, *hi*.
3, 4		—	deprecate, propitiate.
5, 6		ṭua, àau	pray, worship, adore, entreat, praise.
7		hen	praise, exult, chant.
8		qa, ḥāā	high, lofty; exult, make merry.
9		ān	go back, turn back, turn round.
10, 11		—	call, beckon.
12		—	see No. 7.
13		—	. . . .
14		ān	run.
15, 16, 17, 18		ab	dance, perform gymnastics.
19, 20		kes	bow, pay homage.
21		—	run away or run after something.

Notice the images of the human figure in various poses from numbers 1 through 21. While some of these postures are Ankh ('yoga') movements notice that if each movement was executed beginning with number 1 through 21 continuously, you would have a series of movements which would today be called *'tai chi'* or *'qi gong'*.

Notice that images 32-42 are also what would be considered 'martial arts' techniques:

27, 28		—	image, figure, statue, *tut*; mummy, transformed dead body, *sāḥu*; to stablish a custom.
29		—	eternity.
30		ur, ser	great, great one, a chief official, prince.
31		—	old, aged, *àau*, senior *semsu*.
32		—	strong, strength, *nekht*.
33		—	beat (?) strike (?)
34		—	shepherd (?) hunter (?)
35		—	to repulse, to drive away, *seḳer*.
36		—	to perform a ceremony (?)
37		—	shepherd.
38		—	the *àḥi*-priest.
39, 40		—	. . . .
41		—	strong, strength.
42		—	harper, play a musical instrument.

While the author refers to some of these movements as *dance* or *gymnastics* movements, the reality is that word for dance (**ab**) is also the word for heart (**ab**). The **ab** *(heart, dance)* manages the pulsation/rhythm of life - *ankh*. **Ankh** thus encompasses what is called *dance, martial arts, 'tai chi', 'qi gong'* - **<u>rhythmic</u> <u>movements that redistribute energy.</u>**

àb, heart, middle, interior, sense, wisdom, understanding, intelligence, attention, intention, disposition, manner, will, wish, desire, mind, courage, lust,

àb, àbu N. 737; var. **àab**, to dance.

Note that **abb** is also a title for the *winged scarab* - **Khepra** (male) and **Kheprit** (female). **Khepra** (abb) is commonly called the **ab** (heart) scarab, for a **Khepra** amulet is placed in the **heart** cavity of the deceased. An example of such a heart scarab containing an inscribed prayer is below:

"...O my heart, which I had from my mother...the centre of my ***khepru*** *(coming into being). Do not stand against me as a witness, do not oppose me in the judgment hall, in the presence of the keeper of the balance. You are my* ***ka*** *(soul) in my body, the creator [who makes my limbs prosper]..."* [Extract from Chapter 30B, **Pert em Hru** – *"Book of the Dead"* – Heart Scarab prayer]

ābb [hieroglyphs], to fly, the flying scarab; var. [hieroglyphs], the flier.

ābb [hieroglyphs], [hieroglyphs], [hieroglyphs], beetle, scarab.

Khepra and **Kheprit** are about **manifestation** - *bringing something into being out of 'nothing'*. This is tied to the *heart* (ab) which constantly and consistently *brings the pulsation of life/ankh (heartbeat) into being in the body out of 'nothing'*. Rhythmic movements are a ritual replication of this process.

Iusaaset also called **Kheprit**.

Khepra

Kheprit [hieroglyphs], Ṭuat XII, a wind-goddess of dawn.

Khepri [hieroglyphs], Rec. 27, 217; see **Kheperȧ**.

See our nhoma (book) **ODOMANKOMA-ATMU KHOPA – TWEREDUAMPON-KHERER RA** for detailed information about Khepra.

Akua

The Obosom of Aku and Akuada

Akua
(Nebt Het, Agberu)

AKUA (ah-koo'-ah *or* ah-kwee'-ah) is the **Obosom** (**Akan** term for 'Deity') of the **okyin** *(planet)* **Akua** *("mercury").* Her **da** (*day*) is **Akuada** (wednesday). She is referred to as the *Divine Courieress, Protectress, Governess of Ritual* and *Nurse Mother.* **Akua** is the **Obosom** Who governs the *Divine Renal System*, the fluid-balancing and excretory structure of **Abode** (ah-baw'-deh/Creation) – The Divine Body of **Nyamewaa-Nyame** (*The Supreme Being*) and thus the renal system within the Afurakani/Afuraitkaitnit (African~Black) body. **Akua** also governs the excretory function of lactation (nursing) and the rain-waters (lactation) of **Asaase Afua** (Earth Mother). **Akua** nourishes the living and protects the spirits who transition to **Asamando**, the Ancestral-realm.

Okyin Akua

Akua is called **Agberu** in Yoruba culture, **Konikoni** in **Fon** culture (**Vodoun**) and **Nebt Het** in **Kamit** and **Keneset/Khanit** (Ancient Egypt and Nubia). One of the titles of **Akua** in Akan culture is **Kuukua**. The general term *kukua* in Akan means *'a small earthen vessel'*. This earthen vessel is the symbol that defines and distinguishes **Nebt Het/Akua** from other Abosom (Deities) in Kamit:

The **medutu** (hieroglyphs) making up the name **Nebt Het** also function as Her headdress:

The basket symbol is **neb** meaning *'Head, Chieftainess, Mistress, Great Lady'*. The rectangular symbol is **het** meaning *'house, sanctuary, temple enclosure'.*

It is the bird's eye-view of the floor-plan of a sanctuary. Included in this symbol is the metut for the letter 't'= The 't' is the feminizing sound in the language. Thus **neb** means *'master, lord'* while **nebt** means *'mistress, lady'.* **Akua** is the *Mistress* or *Great Divine Lady/Head of the House, temple enclosure, sanctuary*. She is the *Governess* of the *Priestesshood*, those who are the link between the physical world and the spirit-realm.

In Yoruba culture, **Akua** is called **Agberu**, the wife of **Eshu**. **Eshu** is the Divine Messenger of the Supreme Being. **Eshu** carries the messages of the people to the **Orisha (Abosom)**, **Egungun (Nananom Nsamanfo)** and vice versa. **Agberu** carries the **ebo** (sacrifices/ritual offerings) in a basket from the people to the Orisha and Egungun. The name **Agberu** means *'load bearer'* in Yoruba. **Akua** is the wife of **Awuku (Eshu/Set)**. In Kamit She is **Nebt Het** the wife of **Set (Eshu/Awuku)**. Her headdress is comprised of the *basket/vessel* that She uses to carry the ritual offerings from the physical realm to the spirit-realm:

In Akan, this basket is an *earthen vessel* called **kukua (kukuwa)**, a title of **Akua**. Moreover, the term **akuaa** in Akan also means, *a recess in a courtyard, a small courtyard behind a house.* The bird's eye-view of the temple enclosure comprising the second part of **Nebt Het**'s name is an illustration of this: The temple enclosures

and the homes in ancient Keneset and Kamit, as depicted in the metut, contained courtyards. Thus the recess in the courtyard is *akuaa* and the vessel placed above this courtyard is itself called *kukua*.

kúkuwa, *pl.* **ŋ-,** *a small earthen-vessel, small pot; censer. Nu.* 16,6; *s.* **kuku.**

àkúaa, akúawa, *a recess in the court-yard, a small yard behind a house,* used as *a kitchen, washing-place,* store for oil, palm-wine &c.

neb , , P. 181, M. 282, A.Z. 1906, 118, cup, basin, basket.

neb , , all, any, each, every, everyone, every sort or kind; fem. **neb-t** ; plur. , , , M. 77, N. 79, , , , P. 111; Copt. ⲚⲒⲂⲈ.

Neb-t , Rec. 20, 91 = Nephthys

Neb-t ḥe-t

[Note: **Nebt Het** was corrupted into Nephthys by the greeks.]

Above we have the medutu for the term **neb**. The term **neb** can mean *cup, basin, basket, vessel.* It can also mean *all, any, each, every*. **Nebt** is a short form of **Nebt Het**. The terms **nebt/neb** also have the definitions: *mistress, lady; master, lord, owner.*

neb-t , , , , Rec. 31, 171, , Hh. 404, lady mistress; plur. , Metternich Stele 53.

neb , T. 275, N. 907, , M. 353, , , , Peasant 53, , , , , , , , P. 79, M. 111, A.Z. 1900, 128, , , , , , lord, master owner, possessor; plur. , P. 169, M. 744

Thus in Kamit the term for *basin, basket, vessel* is the same term for *all, every*. This is critical for in the Akan language the term for *basin, vessel* is the same term for *all, every*:

ahina (also written **ahinawa**) – *pot; earthen vessel* – synonym: ***kukua***

nhina (also written **ninwa** and **nyinaa**) – *all, every, each*

As shown above in the metutu, the **Coptic** *(Late Kamit)* dialectical version of the term **Neb** is spelled **Nim** (neem). This is because the letters 'm' and 'b' interchange linguistically. The same is true of the letters 'w' and 'b'. Thus in Akan the name **Ayawa** is also written **Ayaba**. **Adwowa** is also written **Adwoba**. This is how the above terms **ahinawa** can be **ahinaba** and **ninwa** can be **ninba**.

Ahi**naba** meaning *basin or vessel* is derived from **neb** (**nba**/nim) meaning *basin, vessel*. Ni**nba** meaning *all, every, each* is derived from **neb** (**nba**/nim) meaning *all, every, each.*

Most importantly, **ahinawa/ahinaba** meaning *earthen vessel* is a synonym in the Akan/Twi language for **kukua** meaning *earthen vessel*. This is etymological proof that **Kuukua** and **Nebt Het** are one and the same.

ahìná, *pl.* **ŋ-**, *a pot, an earthen vessel,* with a big belly and comparatively narrow opening, for water, palm-wine, palm-oil; *cf.* kuku. *pr. 148. 184. 1380-83. 2188.* — **ahĩnaá**, ahĩnawá, *pl.* **ŋ-**, *dim.* of ahĩna.

ŋhĩnã́, nyináa, ŋhĩnã́nã, ŋhĩnára, ŋhĩná ara, *n.* (supplying also the place of the Eng. *adj.*) **1.** *all, every,* prop. *the whole* (number or sum, of individual objects). *pr. 2428.* — **2.** *whole* (in con- ŋhĩnã), -yina, ninwa, adingna (= ade ŋhĩnã), niyina, nenana (*Nig. Exp. Voc.* under *all, each, every, whatever, whole*);

The terms **kua** and **ku** also mean *to bend, to join, to bring together*. These roots forming the basis of the names of the Abosom **Akua** and **Aku** reveal Their Divine functions as links from the physical realm to the spirit-realm. **Akua (Nebt Het)** is the Ritual link while **Awuku (Set)** is the Communicative link. Ritual is the gateway to the spirit-realm. The **het** (house, temple) is a *ritual space* that functions as a sacred gate, a portal, to **Asamando**. **Nebt Het**, the Great Divine Lady/Mistress of the enclosure is the Governess of this ritual space and the ritual activity conducted within such space.

kũá, *v. to bring near or together, to join;* used with ano or anim; *cf.* kũ.

kũ, *v.*: kũ.. hõ, *to be bent to, to join*

Within our **okyin** (planet) the *het* (house) is the sky which is the gateway/link between the physical and the non-physical (Blackness of Space). The clouds are the *kukua*, *vessels* in the sky (het) that contain ritual offerings. When the clouds become full and dark they release/offer rainwater to nourish and cleanse. **Nebt Het** is called the *Nurse Mother* or *Wet Nurse* of **Heru (Yaw)** while **Auset (Adwoa)** is the *Birth Mother* of **Heru**. **Nebt Het** is recognized to govern the rainwaters and dew of **Asaase Afua**. This is one reason why **Akua** has the **mmrane** (praise names) **Obisi**, **Obirisuo** and **Ekusee**. These titles reference that which is *dark, thick, dusky, overcast, cloudy, nebulous, fog, mist.*

The dark (**biri**) clouds point to the coming of nourishing rain. Moreover, in the morning when dew appears, a nourishing and cleansing also takes place. **Heru pa khart**, **Heru** the Child, is shown rising up from the **sashen** (lotus) flower. He is nourished/fed by his *Nurse Mother* **Nebt Het** through the rain and dew. When **Heru** is grown and operates in the sky (**hru**) the moisture of **Nebt Het** within the sky (fog, mist, rain) nourishes/nurses Him. Moreover, rainwater fills the space of the sky and the droplets become *couriers* of messages/energy from 'heaven' to **Asaase Afua**.

Rainwater is a redistribution of resources on **Asaase Afua**. The dry areas that are not close to the lakes, streams, rivers and oceans derive a great benefit from this redistribution. The same is true of plant life, animal life, mineral life and Afurakani/Afuraitkaitnit human life. The rains also assist in the swelling of the rivers, streams and lakes for the rebalancing of the water-supply. The same function is executed by **Nebt Het** within the Afurakani/Afuraitkaitnit body as She functions through the renal system whose major organ is the kidneys. The renal system not only functions as an excretory system and detoxifier of the blood but also as the system which regulates electrolyte balance and fluid-balance/water-balance in the body including the regulation of blood pressure. The regulation of the fluid-balance and electrolyte balance is nourishing while the excretion of waste and detoxification of the blood is restorative. These functions reflect the *fertility* and *funerary* functions of **Nebt Het**.

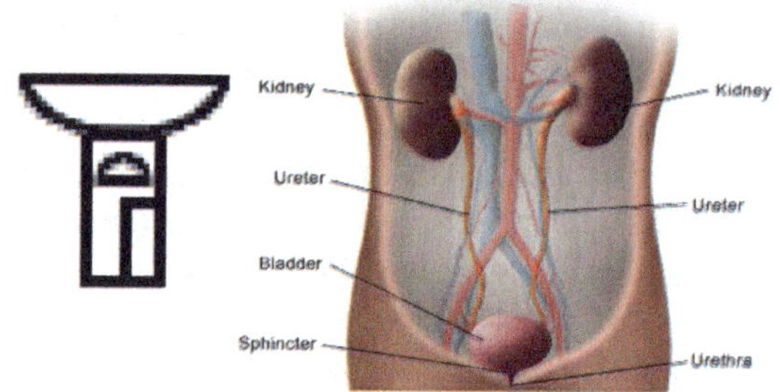

*Medutu for **Nebt Het** in comparison to the renal system:*

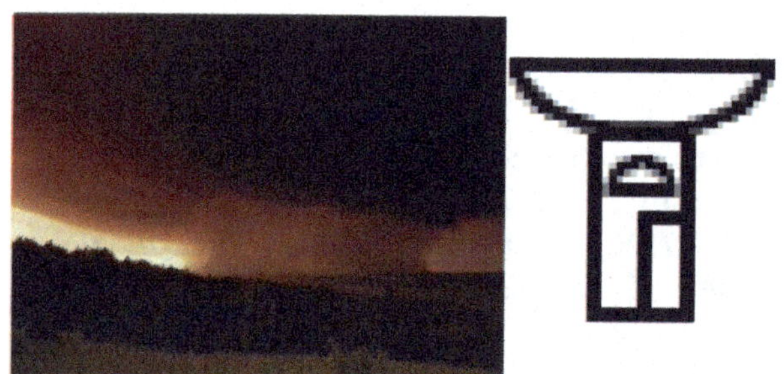

*Nebulous cloud, **kusuu,** in the **Nebt Het** shape releasing rainwater*

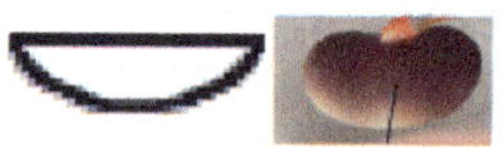

kidneys, renal arteries, ureters and bladder

The kidney is a vessel which filters (cleanses) blood, stores nutrients And maintains electrolyte and water-balance in the body (planet)

Biribi Wo Soro

*Akan **Adinkra** Symbol related to* **Obirisuo** ***(Nebt Het)***
***Nyame, biribi wo soro** na ma emmeka me nsa God, there is something in the heavens, let it reach me*

Nebt Het is often referred to as a *Funerary Obosom*. She is a *Protectress* of the individual who transitions from the physical world to Asamando, just as She protected **Ausar (Awusi)**. It is to **Nebt Het** that we look for protection, nourishment and strength so that the deceased spirit makes a harmonious transition to Asamando, without becoming earthbound, trapped in-between worlds and subject to the attacks from other discarnate earthbound spirits. Her function as a *Protectress* of the individual deceased spirit (*osaman*) also lends itself to Her titles in Akan, **Obisi**, **Obirisuo**, **Ekusee**.

These titles referencing *dark, dusk, cloudy*, etc. are related to the fact that **biri** (black) is a color of the Ancestral spirits, for blackness references maturity and vested power. The gateway to Asamando is **biri** (dark) and **kusuu** (nebulous). Moreover, the pathway from the physical world to the gateway of Asamando is partially ensconced in thick darkness (**kusukuku** – *thick mist or fog*). In the physical world this darkness begins at **kusuu** (dusk) – the time when **Nebt Het** accompanies **Ra** in His solar boat to the underworld after sunset. [**Nebt Het** leads at dusk, while **Auset** leads at dawn]:

*'Ascend and descend; descend with **Nebt Het**, sink into darkness with the Night-boat. Ascend and descend; ascend with **Auset**, rise with the Day-boat.'* - - Pyramid Text Utterance 222 line 210

Akuaba **Ankh**

Many are familiar with the **Akuaba** sculpture in Akan culture commonly called a *fertility doll*. **Akuaba** means child *'ba''* - of **Akua**. In one Akan story, **Akua** is reputed to have been a woman who could not give birth. When she went to a healer, she was given a doll to assist with her *fertility*. She eventually became fertile and gave birth to a child. The doll she was given (the **ankh**-shaped doll) was called **Akua**'s child *(Akuaba)* until she gave birth. This story is also a reference to **Akua** (**Nebt Het**), for in Kamit **Nebt Het** was initially unable to give birth but eventually gave birth to the Obosom **Anpu**. The Akan term **kua** also carries the meaning: *plantation; farm, fertile land.* An **okuafo** is a *farmer*. The term **kua** in these contexts is related to the *fertility* aspect of the *akuaba*.

In Keneset and Kamit the word **Ankh** (awnk) means *'life'*. The ***ankh*** is used to activate *life* within the context of fertility and **awo** (birth). However, the *ankh* is also given to the <u>*deceased*</u> in the spirit- realm for their revivification and elevation to the office of **Nananom Nsamanfo** (**Aakhu**) after **owu** (death):

Anpu activates the spirit of the deceased **Per Aa** (Pharaoh/King) with the **ankh**

Just as the ***ankh*** is used in connection with birth and death, so is the ***akua***. In Akan culture there is a class of ritual sculptures used for deceased spirits as a part of the funerary ritual practices. These sculptures are called **Akua** (*plural*: ***nkua***). As can be seen below, the *akua* sculpture has the same head and facial features as the *akua-ba:*

Akuaba **Akua**

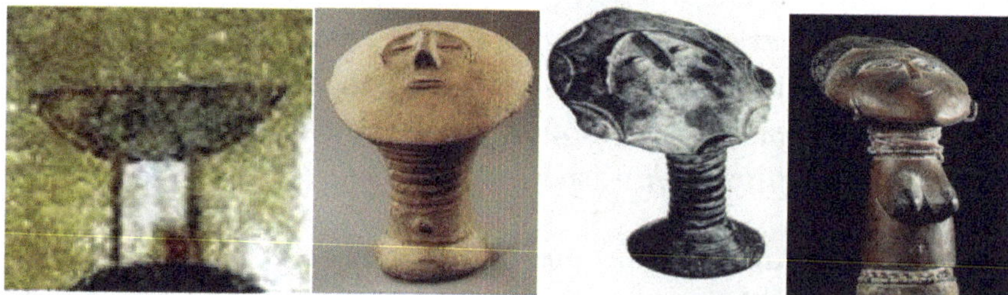

Above-left is an image of **Nebt Het**'s crown, which distinguishes Her from all other Abosom. The images adjacent to **Nebt Het** are more examples of Akan funerary sculptures.

These sculptures, *nkua*, are used as shrines for the departed spirit. Food and other offerings are placed before the *akua* and the **osaman** (deceased spirit) takes up residence in the consecrated *akua* sculpture to consume the spiritual essence/energy of the food offerings and communicate with his/her living relatives.

The basket-shaped symbol on the top of the rectangular enclosure which makes up the name **Nebt Het** is replicated in the *nkua* sculptures. The upward turned face is the vessel (**nebt**) which reposes upon the neck/pedestal (**het**).

The term **nkwa** (awn-kwah') is defined as *life* in the Akan language. This term is derived from the ancient **ankh** (awnk) *life*. The terms *nkwa* and *nkua* are variations of one another. *Nkua*, *Nkwa* and *Akua* are not only related phonetically but conceptually and visually:

Akua-ba **Ankh (Nkwa)** **Akua (Nkua)**

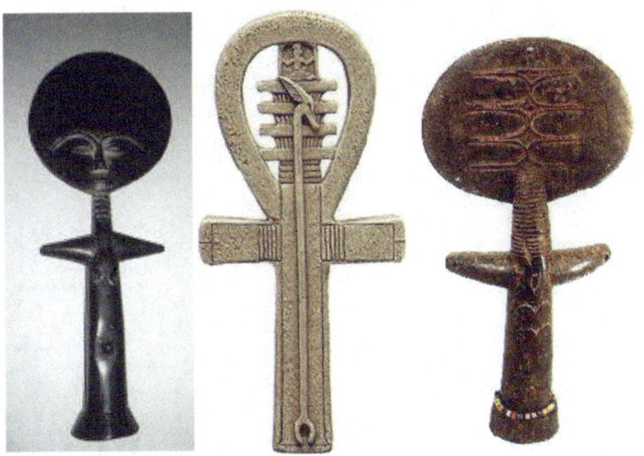

The above images show frontal view of an *akuaba*, an *ankh* with a **djed** pillar inside of the loop and a rear view of an *akuaba*. Many *akuaba* sculptures have the symbol on the back of Their heads which is actually the **djed** symbol from Kamit. The combination of the *djed* and *ankh* (*nkwa/akua*) was common in ancient Khanit/Keneset and Kamit and this combination continued to be utilized by the Akan after we migrated from Keneset and Kamit and settled in West Afuraka/Afuraitkait (Africa).

Ānkhit [hieroglyphs], "living one," the name of a goddess.

As can be seen above, the **Ankh** (*Nkwa*) is not only a symbol, but also a Deity, an *Obosom.* This Obosom is therefore sometimes shown with arms in ancient Kamit similar to Its descendant in Akan culture. The feminine version of **Ankh** is **Ankht**. **Ankht** or **Ankhut** is **Akua**. Moreover, **Nananom Nsamanfo** (*Honored Ancestresses and Ancestors*) as well as **Nananom Mpanyinfo** (*Living Honorable Elders and Elderesses*) are called **Ankhu** <u>*and*</u> **Aakhu**:

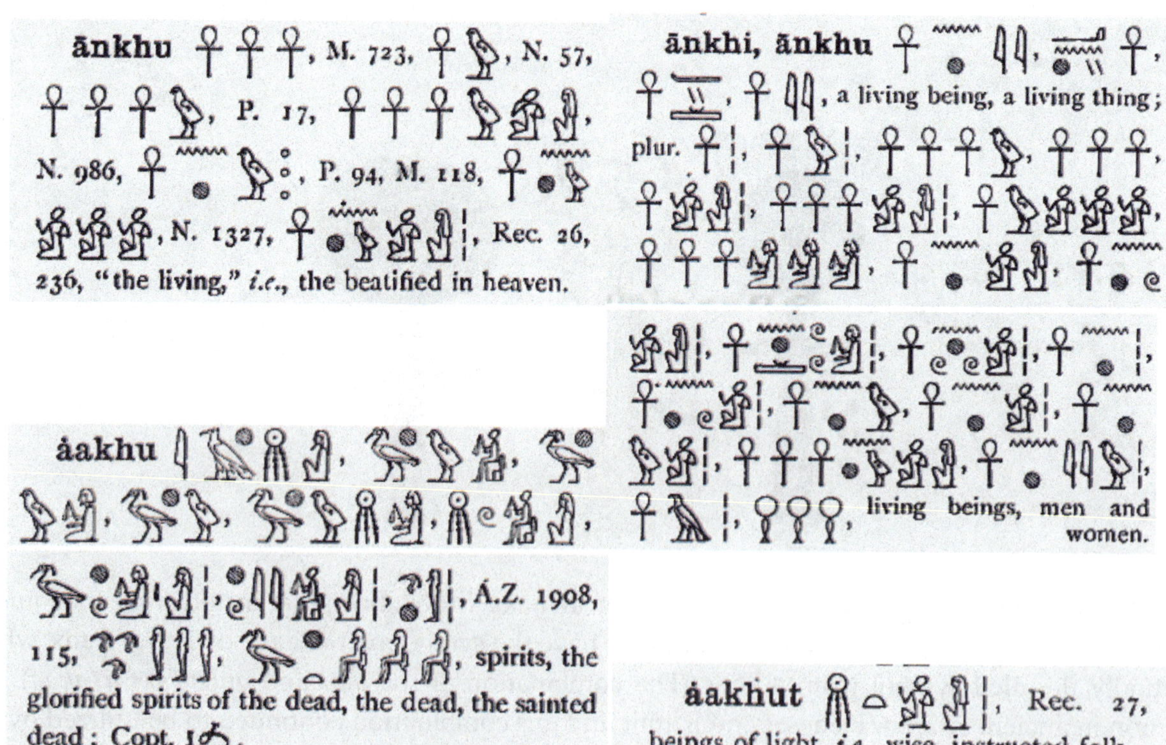

ānkhu [hieroglyphs], M. 723, [hieroglyphs], N. 57, [hieroglyphs], P. 17, [hieroglyphs], N. 986, [hieroglyphs], P. 94, M. 118, [hieroglyphs], N. 1327, [hieroglyphs], Rec. 26, 236, "the living," *i.e.*, the beatified in heaven.

ānkhi, ānkhu [hieroglyphs], a living being, a living thing; plur. [hieroglyphs], living beings, men and women.

åakhu [hieroglyphs], Á.Z. 1908, 115, [hieroglyphs], spirits, the glorified spirits of the dead, the dead, the sainted dead; Copt. [Coptic].

åakhut [hieroglyphs], Rec. 27, beings of light, *i.e.*, wise, instructed folk.

The fertility functions of **Nebt Het** and the after-death functions of **Nebt Het** are manifested in the fertility functions of the *Akua-ba* and the funerary functions of the *Akua.*

Yoruba women in ritual. **Nebt Het** is called **Agberu** the *load bearer* in Yoruba.

One of the titles of **Nebt Het** in Kamit is **Urt Hkau (Wrt Hekau)**: **Urit-ḥekau**

This title describes **Nebt Het** as the *Great One* (**Urt, Wrt**) *of Divine Words, Incantations, Ritual Speech or Prayer* (**Hekau, Hkau**). The male version of the title, **Ur Hekau**, applies to **Set** the Husband of **Nebt Het**:

ur-ḥekau he who is great in words of power, or enchantments, *i.e.*, a god or man who is a magician.

Ur-ḥekau a title of Set.

In Akan we have **owura:** *master; lord; sir; landlord; owner* and **awuraa:** *mistress; lady, landlady; owner*

o-wúrà, *pl.* **o-wúránom, a-, F. e-, Ak. ow̃ira,** ***master, lord; landlord, possessor, owner;*** **owúrá no; -** ***voc. sir;***

awuraá, *pl.* **ŋ-, Ak. aw̃irabá, aw̃iraw̃á, F. awuraba,** ***mistress, lady; landlady.***

Owura and **Awuraa** in Akan are forms of **Ur** and **Urt (Urat)** in Kamit:

Ur - *great, great one, great god, chief, master*

ur U. 215, great man, great god, prince, chief, noble, eldest

Urt - *great, great one, great goddess, chieftess, mistress*

ur-t Rec. 5, 90, great woman, great thing, great, eldest; plur.

One of the *mmrane* or praise names of an Akan female born on **Akuada/Awukuda** is **Awuraakua.** This name is composed of **Awuraa** and **Akua**. **Awuraakua** is directly derived of **Urt Hekau**: **Awura Akua - Ur(a)t Hkau**

It is important to note that the title **awuraa** is used with other female **akradin** *(soul-names)*:

Awuraaesi (Awuraa Esi)	female born on **Akwesida** *(sunday)*
Awuraadwoa (Awuraa Adwoa)	female born on **Dwooda** *(monday)*
Awuraabena (Awuraa Abenaa)	female bornon **Abenaada/Benada** *tuesday)*
Awuraayaa (Awuraa Yaa)	female born on **Yaada/Yawda** *(thursday)*
Awuraafia (Awuraa Afia)	female born on **Fida** *(friday)*
Awuraamma (Awuraa Ama)	female born on **Memeneda** *(saturday)*

The *mmrane* **Awuraakua** is only used for those born on **Akuada/Awukuda**. **Urat Hekau/aWuraa Kua** is specifically a title of **Akua**, the same title applied to **Nebt Het** (**Akua**), the Wife of **Set** (**Awuku**). Moreover, **Owuraku** is also a title used by Akan males born on **Awukuda**. **Owur aku** is **Ur Hkau** the title of **Set/Ananse**.

Nebt Het as a Hawk

Sacred **Bennu**

Nebt Het also takes the form of a Divine Hawk. The hawk's cry is reflected in the sacred wailing of women at funerals in Keneset and Kamit. In Akan culture, the sacred bird called **Obereku** is considered a *spiritual messenger*. It has red (**bere**) eyes and its cry is '**ku, ku, ku**'. Birds were used as messengers in ancient Kamit. This is the origin of *'homing pigeons'*. These functions are reflective of **Akua** as a *Divine Courieress* of ritual offerings and communication between the physical world and ***Asamando***. [*As a Protectress of the sacred* ***Bennu*** *bird,* ***Akua*** *also operates through the okyin/planet* ***Afi***.]

Those who are children of **Akua** must recognize the value of effective ritual which encompasses the interdependence of our proper functioning in the physical world and our need for nourishment and detoxification/protection received from the **Abosom** and **Nananom Nsamanfo** in the spirit-realm. Those who have the **akradin** (soul names) **Akua** and **Kweku** carry the **tumi** (energy) of **Nana Akua** and have the capacity to participate in the regulation of Divine ritual offering to **Nyamewaa- Nyame**, the **Abosom** and the **Nananom Nsamanfo** from all Afurakanu/Afuraitkaitnut in order to harmonize our thoughts, intentions and actions with **Nyamewaa-Nyame Nhyehyee** – Divine Order. Yet, they also have the capacity to engage in misguided ritual, leading to engaging in ritual with discarnate spirits who are not **Abosom** or **Nananom Nsamanfo** – including perverse discarnate spirits who will 'impersonate' the **Abosom** and **Nananom Nsamanfo** in order to mislead and corrupt the unknowing individual. Such spirits include those of the whites and their offspring. **Nana Akua, as is true of ALL Abosom, hates the whites and their offspring, living and deceased. She has never and will never work with them**. The embrace of misguided ritual leads to corruption of true religion,

Nanasom, and to the birth of pseudo-religion, pseudo-philosophy and pseudo- priest/esshood—ritual charlatanism.

As the **Obosom** Who is the *Divine Courieress, bearing a load on Her head*, **Akua** is *Governess* of our **emotions**. As we nourish ourselves, nutrients are distributed throughout our bodies based on the need of our organs and organs' systems. The renal system filters our body and maintains fluid- balance. As we absorb the energy streaming into us from **Abode** (Creation), harmonious energic- emanations are distributed throughout our spirit-bodies based on the need of our spiritual organs and organs' systems. **Akua/Nebt Het** filters our spirit body and maintains spiritual-fluid-balance by excreting perverse, disharmonious, disordered vibrations and projections form disordered entities. This *spiritual-fluid-balance* is our **emotional balance**. Our emotional state is a reflection of our own spirits' energic-emanations interacting with, internalizing and/or rejecting the energic-emanations of entities of and within **Abode**.

The absorption of perverse, disharmonious energic-emanations from disordered entities (physical and non-physical) leads to the perversion of our perception. We have not filtered properly, because we have not rejected disorder, thus our *kukua/basin* becomes a *heavy load upon/in our heads.* This is the manifestation of *emotional imbalance*. Corrupted energy and perceptions resulting from emotional imbalance then *animates* a disordered practice of ritual offering.

The major dilemma that children of **Akua** face when they are out of harmony with Her **tumi** (energy) is the manifesting of emotional imbalance which leads to *rationalizing* the *ritualization of disorder* and thus the most extreme and perverse ritual practices without regard for the disastrous consequences – the pollution of their spirits, perpetuation of disorder amongst discarnate Afurakani/Afuraitkaitnit earthbound spirits and the pollution of our **oman** (nation). Akanfo understand the value of the role of **Nana Akua** in society and the **Abode** and therefore engage children of **Nana Akua** in ritual realignment to their **Kradinbosom** on a regular basis. Individuals who are children of **Nana Akua** ritually cleanse their soul, ***dwaree no kra*** and invoke their **okraa** and **Nana Akua** on their **krada** (krah'-dah) – their soul day which is **Akuada** (wednesday). This is conducted at their **Kradinbosom Nkommere** (shrine).

<u>Appendix – 4</u>

Above and below we see images of anthropomorphized ankhs - ankh figures in human form with arms and hands as well as legs. We also see the djed pillar anthropomorphized with arms, legs, hands and feet:

tet , an amulet symbolic of the uterus of Isis.

We also compare the **tet** symbol which represents the **uterus of Auset** and the Afuraitkaitnit (African) woman in general. It is similar in shape to the ankh yet different in function. **The idea that the ankh represents the union of the womb (loop) and phallic organ (shaft) has never been accurate.** In reality, the ankh is the Afurakani/Afuraitkaitnit (African) human body, just as the akuaba doll is the human body preserved in Akan culture. There are male and female ankh figures and Deities just as there are male and female **nkuamma** (plural of akuaba).

Ānkh , life personified, the name of a god.

Ānkh , P. 174, , P. 672, , M. 661, N. 1276, the son of Sothis, or

Ānkhit , , , , "living one," the name of a goddess.

Ānkhit , Rec. 11, 178, a uraeus-goddess.

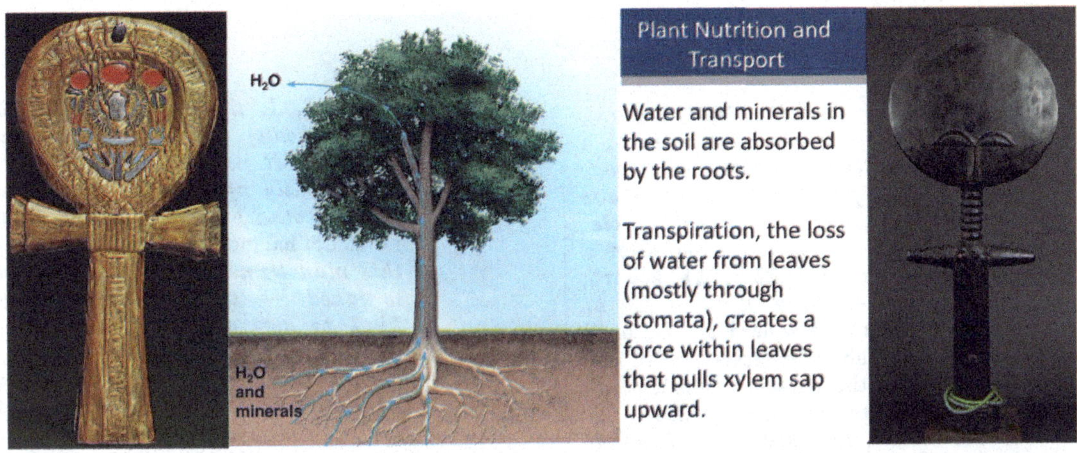

In reality the ankh, like the akuaba, is representative of the human body and its corollary spirit-body in the human sphere. In the realm of plant life, the body of the tree is the ankh/akuaba form. This is why in Akan culture the human body is referred to as **onipadua** literally referencing the *tree* (**edua**) of the *person* (**onipa**).

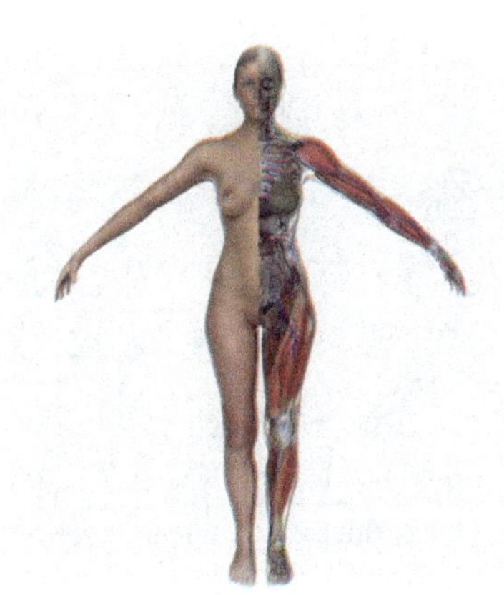

o-ní [*con.* né ní, nè ni] **1.** *relative, relation, kinsman* or *kinswoman* = obusũani; onipa yi, mé ní ni (me bi ni); ne nĩ awu. *pr. 251. 2287 f. 3176.* — **2.** *a person* in general: *a*) espec. in compounds or derivatives, forming, as it were, a *suffix* which in the plural number is replaced by **fo.** Gr. § 38. — *b*) in the lengthened form **óníí,** when followed by **n o, k ɔ̃** or the *rel. part.* 'a'. Hena na wasɛe m'ade yi? - minnim' óniikɔ̃, *I do not know who it is;* - óníí no nnué! óníí à óbɛsɛèe m'ádé yi mmeyi nè hɔ̃ adi kómm! *Cf.* onipa, ɔyaa.

o-nípa, *pl.* **n-** [F. nyimpa] **1.** *man, a man, human being, person* (it may be used also of *God* or *spirits*); *pl. men, people;* nnipa mma, (F.) *human beings. pr. 534. 689. 2362-2439.* - It is frequently put as an object or attribute, where it is not expressed in Eng.: ɔwɔ ka onipa, *a snake bites*

e-duá, *pl.* **n-,** (*pr. 45. 991—1021*) **1.** *plant, tree, shrub.* — **2.** *stem* or *stalk* of a plant or its leaf or fruit. — **3.** *wood; piece of wood. pr. 994; something made of wood. pr. 1014.* — **4.** *stick, pole; pl. timber.* — **5.** *handle, helve* (of a *hoe,* asow dua, *cf.* sókúm, Ak. sodúrò, F. sɔbakúrá). — **6.** *a block* or *log of wood,* to which prisoners are fastened by means of an iron fixed in it and closing round the wrists; duá mù, *pl.* n-, *in ward, in prison. Gen. 40, 3. 4. 7;* bɔ or to.. duám', *to fasten to the block, to arrest, imprison. pr. 578;* da duam', *to be arrested, fastened to the block:* wɔde

o-nipa-dùá, 1. *the figure, form, shape of the body; the body; cf.* nipamũ, ɔhɔ̃nam. *Mt. 6, 25;* ne n. yɛ asɛ oyi, *as to bodily appearance he is nearly like this one;* onipa yi, ɔhyehyɛ (ɔkekã) ne n. hɔ̃, na, ne kãra de, ɔda adagyaw, *this man trims his body, but his soul is naked.* — **2.** *the character, stamp, kind* or *sort of person,* nipabaŋ; wo n. [*or* nipabaŋ] (wo)wɔ hɔ yi, wún'yé! *such a one as you, you are not good!* wo n. [*or* nipabaŋ] (wo)wɔ hɔ yi, metaŋ wo! (- medɔ wo!); mempé wo n. (*or* nipabaŋ), *with one like you I will have nothing to do!*

abá, *pl. id.* F. *the arm, a branch;* n'abá apà, *his arm has become slack,* i. e.

ba [hieroglyphs], staff, stick.

ba-t [hieroglyphs], U. 201, N. 610, [hieroglyphs], T. 78, [hieroglyphs], T. 331, M. 232, N. 621, [hieroglyphs], P. 615, [hieroglyphs], M. 783, N. 1142, [hieroglyphs], Rec. 31, 171, [hieroglyphs], Peasant 14, [hieroglyphs], bush, thicket, branch, undergrowth; Copt. ϐω.

The foilage of the tree, the leaves, are the **afro-hair** while the branches are the limbs. We thus have the term **aba** in Akan meaning the **arm** as well as a **branch**. The same term **ba** in Kamit means **stick** with the medut of the *tree* [hieroglyph] *branch* and also **bush, thicket, branch**. The tree is firmly rooted in the ground while its leaves receive the energy of the Aten/Atenit (Sun) and photosynthesize its light. The Afurakani/Afuraitkaitnit (African) man and woman are grounded in Asaase Afua (Earth Mother) while our hair receives the energy of the Aten/Atenit and the related Spiritual Energy for our enlightenment and empowerment.

Appendix – 5: Excerpt from: **HONAMSU – Spiritual Anatomy**

The **Sahu** is the **spirit-body**. Just as the physical body contains all of the organs and glands in a harmonious arrangement, so does the spirit-body contain all of the spiritual organs and glands (**Ba, Ka, Ab, Aakhu, Hati**) in a harmonious arrangement. In Akan, the term for spirit-body is **sunsum**. This is a reduplication of the term is **sum**. The term **sum** is a contraction of **su-mu** meaning 'within' (**mu**) the 'essence' (**su**).

Kamit: **SAHU**

sāḥ [hieroglyphs], U. 298, the form of a man that exists in heaven, the spirit-body; plur. [hieroglyphs], T. 143, [hieroglyphs], N. 113, 539, [hieroglyphs], U. 516, [hieroglyphs], T. 327, [hieroglyphs], P. 6, [hieroglyphs], M. 8. Later forms are:— [hieroglyphs].

seḥu [hieroglyphs], Rec. 22, 2, [hieroglyphs], Rec. 33, 34, [hieroglyphs], IV, 767, Annales III, 109, [hieroglyphs], to collect, to gather together, to assemble, to sum up, to add up a total; Copt. ⲥⲱⲟⲩϩ.

Akan: **SUNSUM**

sûnsûm, *pl.* **a-** [*con.* nė sùnsum'] **the** *soul* or *spirit* of man; ne s. sõ, *he is influential;* - *a spirit, ghost;* F. *pl.* n-, *Mt. 8,16. Mk. 1,27; cf.* sunsumã, ɔkãra, hoŋhom.

sûm, *v.* [*red.* sunsum] **1.** *to stand,* of things forming a heap or mass, or being of a considerable circumference (*cf.* si of thin or slender things, or of hollow structures, as houses); ɑ̀bó kúw bi sûm hó, *a heap of stones is set up there;* abo, ŋhwẽa, dɔte, ntrama sùnsum hó, *there are heaps of stones, sand, mud, cowries.* — **2.** *caus.* with de, fa &c., *to set, put, place,* espec. in heaps or in a mass: fa abo no sunsum ho! wode ɔkorow sùnsúm' wiyammo ano de gye dɔkono a woyam gu mu; *syn.* sow; wɔakekã dɔte asunsum daŋ no hõ, *they have heaped up mud* or *clay around the base of the house.* — **3.**

sāḥ [hieroglyphs] In one of the variations of the term **sah** or **sahu** we see the determinative medut of a **mummy** lying on his back. The related term sahu (misspelled sehu by the egyptologist) means 'to collect, to gather together, to assemble, to sum up'. The mummified body is representative of the spirit-body which collects or gathers together, sums up all of the spiritual organs into one harmonious arrangement. The **Coptic** dialectal vocalization of the term is **Saouh**: **Copt. ⲥⲱⲟⲩϩ.**

The Coptic dialect is the Late Kamiti (Egyptian) dialect of the language which came into use about 2,000 years ago. In Akan we see that **sum** references that which is 'heaped up, formed into a mass'. This is the root of **sunsum** referencing the spirit-body as the force that collects or 'heaps up into a mass' the spiritual organs in a sacred form. The related term **sahu** means 'property, possession, homestead, environs, neighborhood'. The **sunsum** (sahu-sahu, su-su) is that which is the 'homestead' or 'environ' for the 'property/possessions' - the spiritual organs.

saḥ-t [hieroglyphs], IV, 1111, [hieroglyphs], Anastasi I, 24, 1, [hieroglyphs], holding, possession, landed property, estate, allotment, site of a temple, homestead, vicinity, environs, neighbourhood; plur. [hieroglyphs],

saḥu [hieroglyphs], Rec. 20, 42, [hieroglyphs], property.

**The spirit-body pulls together (yokes/ankhs) the spiritual organs together.

www.odwirafo.com/Honamsu_Spiritual_Anatomy.pdf

Tehuti: Sankofa, Fa and Ifa

Male Deity of Divine Wisdom and Divination in Kamit, Akan, Ewe, Fon and Yoruba

ODWIRAFO KWESI RA NEHEM PTAH AKHAN

Tehuti: Sankofa, Fa and Ifa

Male Deity of Divine Wisdom and Divination in Kamit, Akan, Ewe, Fon and Yoruba

In **Aakhuamuman Amaruka Atifi Mu**, Akwamu Nation in North America, we observe our **Obradwira Nananomsom**, our New Year observance, for seven days with the final day being the day of the **Atem/Atemet** (autumn) equinox - our New Year's day. This year's observance begins today on September 16th and will conclude on September 22nd, our New Year's Day and the first day of our year **13018**. Naturally, we do not calculate time based upon a fictional character who never existed in any form or of any race whatsoever (jesus/yeshua). We recogize the reality that all of the characters of the bible, quran, talmud and others are all fictional characters promoted in the pseudo-religions of christianity, islam, judaism/hebrewism and others. We have our own agency and calculate time based upon reality inclusive of the position of Asaase (Earth) in relation to Sun, Moon, planets and stars.

During our seven-day observance, each day of the week takes on a special character. **Memeneda** (saturday) during our seven-day observance is called **Sankofa Dwira Da** – 'Sankofa Purifies' day. The **ebe**, the proverb or Divine Wisdom teaching, governing this day is:

Sankofa dwira suban Afurakanu/Afuraitkaitnut

Sankofa purifies our character as Afurakani/Afuraitkaitnit (African~Black) people

Each day of the seven-day observance is governed by the Divine Energy and Consciousness of the **Abosom** (Deities) who govern the solar, lunar or planetary body which governs the day. There is an **ebe** associated with each day. We reinforce the guidance of the **Abosom** and **Nananom Nsamanfo**, the Deities/Divine Spirit-Forces in Creation and our Spiritually Cultivated Ancestresses and Ancestors, through adhering to the body of knowledge contained within the **mbe** (proverbs). On **Sankofa Dwira** day, we focus on the example of this teaching as manifest by our people in this hemisphere, our direct blood Ancestresses and Ancestors who preserved our Ancestral Religion and Culture and guided us to wage war against our enemies, the whites and their offspring, to force the end of enslavement in North america.

This year, the first day of our seven-day observance is **Sankofa Dwira** day, yet it also coincides with our 20-year anniversary of the restoration of our specific form of **adebisa** (divination) within our Ancestral clan. We thus are releasing this book regarding the true nature of **Sankofa** as an **Obosom** (Deity) as manifest in the function of oracular divination.

Adinkra symbols have been used by **Akan** people of West Afuraka/Afuraitkait (Africa) for over 1,000 years and by our Akan Ancestresses and Ancestors from North and East Afuraka/Afuraitkait (Africa) for thousands of years prior to our migration to West Afuraka/Afuraitkait (Africa). The root adinkra symbols can therefore be found in the **medutu** (hieroglyphs) of ancient **Khanit** and **Kamit** (Nubia and Egypt), our Ancestral homeland.

When some Akan people were forced into the western hemisphere during the **Mmusuo Kese** (Great Perversity/Enslavement era), we brought our Ancesrtal Religion and culture with us. We thus find adinkra symbols being utilized in **Hoodoo** which is **Akan Ancestral Religion** in North america. One of the most prominent adinkra symbols is **Sankofa** with its two major expressions:

Adinkra symbols, as is true with their parent medutu (hieroglyphs) and other symbols utilized by Afurakanu/Afuraitkaitnut (Africans~Black People) wherever we exist in the world, are matrices of Divine Energy and Consciousness. **The specific geometric forms comprising each symbol radiates a unique configuration of energy which resonates at the frequency of specific Abosom (Deities).** The adinkra symbols thus become **shrines-in-miniature** for these Abosom and for the Nananom Nsamanfo (Honored Ancestral Spirits) who carry the same energy complex within their clans. Adinkra symbols are thus used on Deity shrines, Ancestral shrines, talismans, amulets, ritual implements and on the body in the process of ritual invocation and evocation of the Abosom and Nananom Nsamanfo.

Sankofa, meaning return (san), go (ko) and grasp (fa) from your Ancestral past in order to bring balance to the life-circumstances in the present and to chart a balanced future, is one of those energic-matrices drawing the Abosom and Nananom Nsamanfo to us – including in North america in the **Hoodoo** tradition. Our Akan Ancestresses and Ancestors from ancient Khanit and Kamit, from West Afuraka/Afuraitkait (Africa) and those who were forced into North america, yet waged the **Hoodoo Wars** for liberation and forced the end of enslavement – it is these Nananom Nsamanfo, our Spiritually Cultivated Ancestresses and Ancestors of our direct spiri-genetic blood-circles, who inform our knowledge of Sankofa and the identity of the Obosom (Deity) **Sankofa**. This Obosom and related Abosom (Deities) have guided us for hundreds of years in North america and inform our practice of **adebisa** (oracular divination).

We thus present to the Afurakani/Afuraitkaitnit (African~Black) community on **Sankofa Dwira Da**, the first day of our seven-day New Year observance and the 20th anniversary of our expression of **adebisa** (divination) being restored in our Ancestral clan, this work elucidating the identity of the Obosom (Deity) **Sankofa – Tehuti** for the first time.

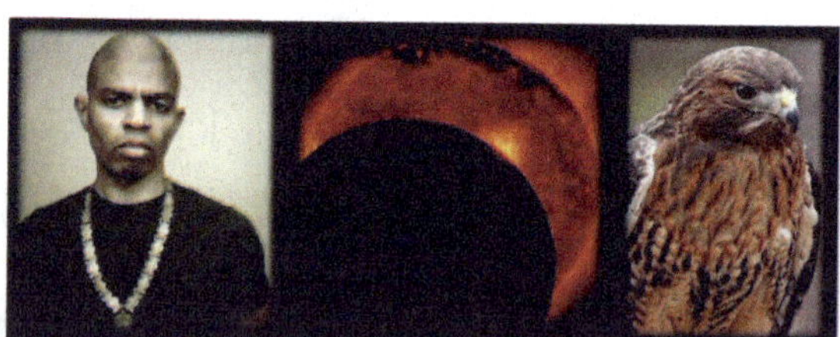

Odwirafo Kwesi Ra Nehem Ptah Akhan
Aakhuamuman Amaruka Atifi Mu
Akwamu Nation in North America
Odwiraman
Sankofa Dwira Da, September 16, 13017
www.odwirafo.com

Tehuti: Sankofa, Fa and Ifa

Male Deity of Divine Wisdom and Divination in Kamit, Akan, Ewe, Fon and Yoruba

The term for **nose** in our Ancestral language of Kamit is spelled in the **medutu** (hieroglyphs) with the consonants: **f n t**

fent , , , Anastasi I, 23, 8, , nose; see and ; Copt. ϢⲀⲚⲦⲈ.

When egyptologists are unsure of the vocalization of a term, what vowel sounds to insert in between consonants, the conventional rule is to place an 'e' in between consonants to facilitate pronunciation. Thus **fnt** is rendered **fent**. Notice that in the **Coptic** (Copt.) dialect, the dialect which came into use in **Kamit** (Egypt) in the Late period about 2,000 years ago, the term is spelled SHANTE rendered:

Copt. ϢⲀⲚⲦⲈ

This is also shown in the ancient variant form: **kh n t**

khent, khenti , , , , , the nose, the face; Copt. ϢⲀⲚⲦ.

Notice that the 'kh' medut in Kamit can be pronounced the the 'ch' in 'check' as well as the 'ch' in 'chagrin'. We thus see that **khnt** (rendered **khent, khenti**) is vocalized as SHANT in Coptic.

Copt. ϣⲁⲛⲧ.

We therefore have two variations of the term for 'nose' in the language of Kamit:

fnt (fenet, fent)

fent, , , Anastasi I, 23, 8, , nose; see and ; Copt. ϣⲁⲛⲧⲉ.

shnt (shenet, shant)

khent, khenti , , , , , the nose, the face; Copt. ϣⲁⲛⲧ.

In the language of the **Akan** people, who reside primarily in Ghana and Ivory Coast, West **Afuraka/Afuraitkait** (Africa) we have **both** variants with proper vocalizations:

ɛ-hwéne, Ak. ɛhwéŋ, ŋhwéŋ; F. ɛhwen(e), *pl.* **a-, 1.** *the nose. pr. 1198;* **ɔ̀bɔ̀ ne hwéne**

fw (fw̆) see **hw**

Hw (Fw)

hwa, hwã, (= fwa, fwã) and other words containing these three combined letters in Ak., s. hüa, hüã...

for things during one's absence, prepare (something to eat) *for one's return.* — **10. hwɛ.. mu,** *to look, pry ... into; inspect, examine, revise.*

As shown in the above dictionary entry in the Akan language, also called **Twi**, the 'hw' combination can be pronounced 'hooh-wah' or 'foo-wah' depending upon the Akan dialect being spoken. Thus **hwene** and **fwene** are to diaelctical variants of the same term. Moreover, the 'hw' sound also approximates a 'shw' sound and is thus written 'sh' or 'shw' by many Akan linguists. We therefore have the dialectical variants of the term 'nose' from ancient Kamit being spoken by Akan people on a daily basis:

Kamit:	nose	fnt (**fenet**)	khnt (shant, **shenet**)
Akan:	nose	**fwene**	hwene (**shwene**)

Related to the term for nose is the sense of 'smell' as well as 'scraping or scratching'. We see the Akan definitions including the variants of **hwa** and **fwa** the 'hw' and 'fw' interchange again:

hũã, F. hwã, Ak. hwã = fwã.

hũá, *v.* [*red.* hũhũá, (hũahũa)] *to smell, scent;* memã no aduaŋ a, ohũá hwɛ̀ ansã-na odi, *when I give him food, he smells (or snuffles) at it before he eats (it);* ɔkramaŋ de ne hwene ahũ(a)-hũa ara akohũ aboká no, *the dog has traced out with his nose,* i.e. *has scented the carcass. Cf.* ehũã, hũãm; hũã tie, *s.* tie, *pr. 1565.*

hũã, *v.* **1.** *to scrape, scratch;* hũã ode, *to scrape,* or *scratch,* or *pare, off the burned parts of the roasted yam; to graze, to rub* or *brush lightly in passing* (*cf.* hũãsu); *syn.* twere, twerɛw;

We also have the variant of **hwa** being **hwe**. In the Asante Akan dialect (As.) **hwe** is **hua** and **fwa**:

hwẽ, *v.* **As.** = **hũã, fwã,** ***to scrape, scratch.***

The term **hwe** (**fwe**) meaning *to scrape, scratch* is the root of **hwene** (**fwene**) meaning *'nose'*. The nose is highly sensitive, especially in certain animals. It allows one to **perceive** even when one is not able to 'see'. If one is in darkness, they may not see that a certain food has spoiled, however they can smell it. One can smell that something is burning or on fire before arriving at the location of the fire. The drawing in of breath is a 'gathering' or 'scraping'. Yet, it is also working the sensory receptors in the nose to allow a 'gathering' or 'scraping' of data, information, so that one can discern properly and make proper judgments. We thus have the related term **hwe** also meaning *'to look, examine, see, perceive; to learn, infer, to know'*. The reduplication of **hwe** is **hwehwe** *'to look repeatedly and intensely'*:

hwɛ̀, *v.* [*red.* hwehwɛ, *q. v.*] **1.** *to direct the eye towards* an object so as to see it (always implying *intentional,* not accidental, *seeing,* in contradistinction from hũ); *to look (at, on), to view; to eye; to consider;* wohwɛ a, ɛŋhwɛ́, *it is magnificent, superb, splendid, grand; horrible.* - wó ara hwɛ! applause by people who listen to a tale. - *Cf.* hwɛ, *interj.* - *pr. 894. 1218, 1318. 2081. 2293. 3486.* — **2.** *to fix the eyes upon, look at* or *see with attention, behold; to look at in order to imitate, cf.* 12 a. *pr. 1232.* — **3.** *to learn, infer, know:* da no a wuhũ no saa a,

hwehwɛ́, *red. v.* hwɛ, *q. v.* - *to look repeatedly* and *intensely,* hence *to look for, seek, search for; to endeavour, attempt, strive.* Me paane ayera, mehwe-hwɛ na miŋhũ, *I have lost a needle, I am seeking for it and do not find it. pr. 284. 1192-96;* mehwehwɛ woŋ hõ, *'I will search them';* hw. mu pɛ́sɛ-pɛsɛ, *to make search, rack one's brains. Ps. 77,7.* - *Cf.* due 6.

The key here is that the nose, fwene (hwene) allows one to smell, perceive, gather (fwe, fwa) through scraping, gathering (fwe, fwa, hwe). It is key because of an important title of the **Obosom** (God) **Tehuti** in ancient Kamit:

Fenti [hieroglyphs], B.D. 125, II, "he of the nose," *i.e.*, one of the 42 judges in the Hall of Osiris, a name of Thoth.

Fenṭi [hieroglyphs], B.D. 125, II, a form of Thoth; one of the 42 Assessors of Osiris.

Tehuti as one of the 42 Assessors or Judges of **Maat** is called 'He of the Nose': **Fnti** (**Fenti** or **Fanti**). The 'i' functions as the 'y' or 'ey' in english as a descriptive. Thus one who is 'in his head' is called 'heady'. One who has his 'nose in other's business' is called 'nosey'. He of the **Fant** (**Fent**) or 'He of the Nose' is Fant-i or Fent-i. We also find that the 't' is almost silent. The Fnt or Fant is vocalized as **Fan** (fahn) or **Fen** (fehn) with a 'nasal' 'N'.

Fan(t) or **Fen(t)** as a title of **Tehuti** is **Fwa** or **Fwe** (dialectical variant of Hwe) in Akan as a title of the Obosom of Divine Wisdom – He of the Nose. **Hwe-fo** (Fwa-fo) one of those (fo) who **hwe** (fwe, fwa) looks, searches ('scents'/smells and 'senses'), investigates; **hwehwe** (fwefwe), intense investigation.

ɔ-hwɛ́fo, ohwefó, *pl.* **a-,** [*con.* me **hwɛ́fo**] *looker; overseer, superintendent, surveyor, inspector, director; officer. Josh.*

hwehwɛ́, *red. v.* **hwɛ,** *q. v.* - *to look repeatedly* and *intensely*, hence *to look for, seek, search for; to endeavour,*

[See: Appendix 2 – Hwehwemudua]

Brekyiri-hũnũ-ade,
'the All-knowing'.

Another major title of **Tehuti** in Akan is **Brekyirihunuade** (breh-cheeh-reeh hoo-noo ah deh). This is a title defining this Obosom (Deity) as the 'Omniscient one', specifically 'He who turns back/behind (brekyiri) to see (hunu) Creation/the Entity (ade)'. He can go back in the **past** (Ancestral Realm, Spirit Realm, Origin/Source of Creation) and see why things have manifested in the present and what will manifest in Creation in the **future**. This is a function of what is called **adebisa** (divination) in Akan culture – the capacity to see within the circumstances of the present the events that will shape the future, informed by Spirits of the **past** in the sense of **'behind'** – Ancestresses and Ancestors and the Deities. One can see what Ancestral Spirits and Deities are 'behind' the shaping of events and thus what is needed to preserve Order or restore Order to our lives. The term **sankofa** is rooted in this divinatory function. The Akan **ebe** (proverb) is often quoted:

'Se wo werefi na wo sankofa, yenkyi'

'If you forget and you return (san) go (ko) and grasp (fa) [from your Ancestral past], it is not hated/taboo.'

When we have a problem we are directed to *return, go and grasp* from our past in order to remedy issues in the present and avoid negativity in the future. On a mundane level, if you lost your keys, you engage the **sankofa process** mentally to remedy the situation. You return (san), go (ko) and grasp (fa) from your past, your memory – you retrace your steps. You recall what areas of the home you were previously in and what led up to the current situation. When you retrace your steps, you then recall where you previously set your keys down. You can then proceed to retrieve them.

On a spiritual level, entering the Ancestral realm to communicate with those from the past – the **Nananom Nsamanfo**, our Spiritually Cultivated Ancestresses and Ancestors – and to become empowered by the **Abosom** (Deities) to forge a new path for the future, including the future reincarnation of those same Ancestresses and Ancestors, is the key to **divination**. It is returning to, going 'back' to the Spirit Realm, the Source of all things formed by **Nyamewaa-Nyame**, the Supreme Being. The past or Source informs the present and future in a cyclical manner. Reincarnation, a past spirit returning from the Source to live in the present is proof of this. This is confirmed through Ancestral communication inclusive of **akom** or **spirit-possession** – communicating in real time, the present, with Ancestral Spirits who lived upon **Asaase** (Earth) in the past.

tè, *v.* [*red.* **teté**], **F. tse, L.** *to perceive* **by the nerves of sensation,** *to feel; to perceive within one's self, to be affected by;* **also** *to be felt or perceived by;* **wo abaa a woabɔ me no anté me,**

Tehuti as **Brekyirihunuade** is also called **Te** in Akan. **Te** means 'to understand, perceive, to know'.

The name **Te** in Akan as a title of the Deity is derived from the same title of **Tehuti** in Kamit: **Tekh**

tekh, plummet, the little weight which served as the tongue of the scales; Ḳubbân 13, just weight; Rev. 3, 12, the regulation of justice.

tekhá, A.Z. 1900, 33, weigher, the pointer of the scales.

tekhi, ibis, crane; Copt. ϯϩⲓ (?)

Tekhi, a title of Thoth as regulator of times and seasons.

Tekh is not only a title of **Tehuti** but also a title of the **akyeneboa** (animal totem), the **habui** bird (ibis, crane) itself.

In the weighing of the heart, **Tehuti** is taking note of the <u>weighing</u> and the results. He is performing his **Tekh** function.

In the talking drum texts in Akan culture the cosmology is laid out:

Hena ko se,
Hena ko se,
Hena ko se,
*Hena oko see **Te***
*Ma **Te** ko see **Ananse***
*Ma **Ananse** ko see **Odomankoma***
*Ma **Odomankoma** Bo Adee?*

Translation:

Who gave word
Who gave word
Who gave word
*Who gave word to the [Obosom] **Te***
*For **Te** to go and tell the [Obosom] **Ananse**,*
*For **Ananse** to go and tell the [Obosom] **Odomankoma***
*For **Odomankoma** to Complete/Form the World/Creation?*

The answer to the question posed by the drummer of 'Who gave word?" of course is **Nyamewaa** and **Nyame** (**Amenet** and **Amen**) the Great Mother and Great Father Supreme Being. The **okyeremaa** (drummer) is provoking the people to invoke the names of **Nyamewaa-Nyame**, for it is **Nyamewaa** and **Nyame** who made their Divine charge known, *gave the word*, to their Divine **Okyeame** (Spokesperson) **Te** (**Tehuti**) who formed the desire of the Supreme Being into directives for action/knowledge/a blueprint. This knowledge of what was to come (the blueprint of what was to be formed as the Universe) was given to the Divine Messenger who formed the knowledge/directives into a specific message. The **Esen** (Divine Messenger), the Obosom **Ananse**, then carried this Divinely ordained set of directives/blueprint in the form of a message and delivered it to **Odomankoma** who had/has the energy to shape the material/matter of Creation in order to bring the blueprint into physical reality. The Obosom **Odomankoma** operating with the Obosom **Oboade** through the inner core and mantle of **Asaase** (Earth) fashioned and completed the World/Creation – they executed the blueprint. [**Odomankoma** and **Oboade** are called **Atem** and **Ptah** in Kamit.]

This process is reflected in the Akan court where the **Ohene** (King) does not speak directly to the people in the **ahemfie** (palace, court). He speaks his desires for action to his spokesperson (**okyeame**) and the okyeame announces the desire of the Ohene (King) to the ahemfie (palace). Once the proclamation has been made, the **esen** (messenger, herald) leaves the ahemfie (palace) and runs throughout the **oman** (nation) to spread the message. The blacksmiths, architects, physicians, military and other workers then get to work on bringing into being what the Ohene (King) has desired.

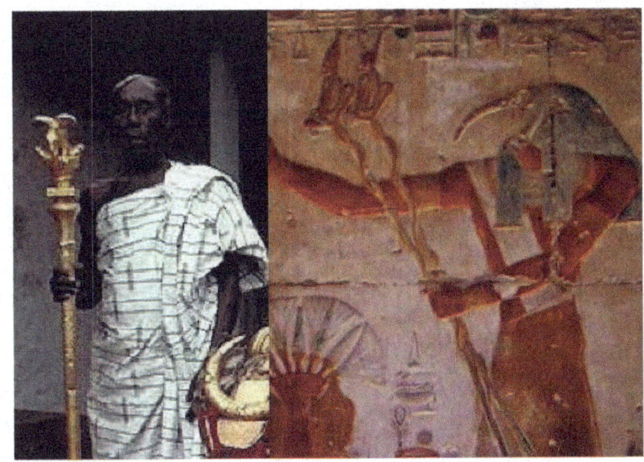

Akan Ohene (King) and Okyeame (Spokesperson) with mpoma (staff). Okyeame is vocalized as **Uhemaa** in Kamit. **Tehuti** holding his dual staff (mpoma) is called the **Uhemma** of **Ra** and **Amen**.

ɔ-kyĕàmé, *pl.* a-, *speaker, reporter, interpreter;* one of the elders of a king or a negro-town or community, called *linguist,* who in their councils has the office of a speaker being the mouth-piece of, or reporter to, the king or the assembly; – di ky., *to be or act as a speaker. Cf.* ɔpanyiṅ.

uhemu [hieroglyphs], P.S.B. 10, 47, [hieroglyphs], a "teller," registrary, herald, lay priest, recorder, orator, proclaimer; plur. [hieroglyphs], Rec. 21, 92.

uhem nesu [hieroglyphs], the king's herald.
uhem nesu tep [hieroglyphs], king's herald-in-chief.
uhem āa [hieroglyphs], IV, 972, the great recorder; [hieroglyphs], IV, 1120, recorders of the Nomes.

This same process takes place biologically as **Tehuti** operates through the **pineal gland** (in concert with the Female Obosom of Wisdom **Seshat**). When this light-senstive gland is stimulated the directives for action from the brain are formed into hormonal secretions which are released into the bloodstream. The messages from these hormonal secretions and their reactions in the bloodstream are carried by the nervous system (messenger, world-wide-web, **Ananse**'s Spider web) throughout the body. The various organs and glands of the body are then stimulated to carry out the directives.

The same process plays out in our spiritual-being with the **Aakhu/Aakhut**, the spiritual organ in the third-eye/pineal region, the seat of **Tehuti** and **Seshat** being stimulated by **Nyamewaa-Nyame** (**Amenet-Amen**). We learn/intuit in this energic region – the 'third' eye, the eye of the **Okra/Okraa** (Soul) – what is in harmony with Divine Order. When we learn/intuit from this region, we then send that message throughout the energic-web within our spirit-body (**sahu**) in order to align our specific configuration of spiritual energy to execute our Divine function in Creation, without creating disorder in the process.

Our **nkra/nkrabea**, our Divine function that we are allotted to execute in Creation, was given to us by **Nyamewaa-Nyame** *pre-incarnation.* It is written into our Okra/Okraa (Soul), which is the Deity dwelling in our head-region, guiding our thoughts, intentions and actions toward Divine Order every moment of every day *when we listen.* [This applies to Afurakanu/Afuraitkaitnut (Africans~Black People) only. The 'Soul' is actually a **Deity** assigned to dwell within us by **Nyamewaa-Nyame**.]

When we engage the divinatory process we return, go and grasp (san ko fa) from our Okra/Okraa (called **Ka/Kait** in Kamit, **Se Lido** in Ewe and Fon, **Ori Inu** in Yoruba), our head-Deity, what our Divine function is and how to utilize the specific configuration of energy we have inherited from our patriclan and matriclan Ancestresses and Ancestors and Deities to execute that function. Through **fwa** (scraping, gathering, sensing, smelling, discerning) we are enabled to **fa** (grasp). The gathering (fwa) and grasping (fa) are related functionally and phonetically.

kɔ̀, *v.* [Ak. also kɔrɔ, *pret.* kore; *red.* kokɔ] *to go;* more particularly: **1.** *to go along, to walk* (*cf.* nam. nantew); yékɔ̀ ntém, *we are walking fast,* ɔbayifo a ɔrekɔ ee! *there goes a witch! pr. 60.* — **2.** *to go off, away; to pass away, leave, depart* (opp. ba, *to come,* trã, *to stay*); ɔ́kɔ̀, *he is gone* (*cf.* wakɔ under 3); mekó mabá, *I go away but shall come again, cf.* Gr. § 112. 147,4. *pr. 1590;* F.: kɔ bĕra oo = ŋkyé bá! *do not stay away long!* - woko-bae no wɔbɛkãe sɛ: ɛwom' sa, *when they had gone and returned, they reported, that it was so* (*that the matter was true*); - wobɛkɔ, na me de, metrã ha, *you will depart, but I shall stay here.* - ɛkɔ-báé sa, or ɛkɔ́-baɔ̀ sa, *it happened* or *came to pass thus.* — *to escape. pr. 601.* — **3.** *to go to a place:* woko

fà, *v.* [*red.* fefa, fofa] *to take; cf.* gye, kukuru, tase, mã so, som', yi, & de, fuą, kita, kura. — **1.** *to take* to make use of: *pr. 1081; to lay hold on for use.* In these senses it takes the place of the *aux. v.* de in all negative and imperative sentences; *s.* Gr. § 108,26-29. 205,5. 206,2. 208,3. 4. 237. 240 a. c. 241. *Cf.* 26 (below). *pr. 47. 136—66. 168 f.* — **2.** *to take away:* hena na wafa me tuo? *who has taken my gun?* — **3.** *to carry off* (said also of inanimate objects): nsu afa no, *the water has taken him,* i.e. *he is drowned. pr. 389. 3073. 3085;* mframa afa me kyɛw kɔ, *the wind has carried off my hat.* — **4.** *to lay hold on, to seize:* wáfà no gyáw, *he has embraced his legs,* i. e. *implored him, begged his pardon.*

fa, fai [hieroglyphs], M. 359, [hieroglyphs], T. 8, N. 910, 1382, [hieroglyphs], P. 347, [hieroglyphs], M. 648, [hieroglyphs], L.D. III, 229c, 14, to carry, to bear, to lift up, to get up from sleep, to start a journey; Copt. ϥει.

The Akan term **fa**, meaning *to take, carry, obtain, grasp* is found in Kamit. Notice the image of the individual taking a vessel and *holding, grasping, carrying* it upon his head: [hieroglyph]

The **head** is the seat – *literally the* shrine – of the Okra/Okraa (Ka/Kait), the Soul - the Deity dwelling in our head-region which contains our Divine function (blueprint) to execute in Creation. The vessel on the head is thus a **shrine** for the Obosom (Deity) in ritual. **Divination directs us to this head-Deity** so that we can perceive, 'smell', sense, gather (**fwa, fa**) and then grasp, take, obtain (**fa**) what has been written into our Okra/Okraa. The term **kofa** in Akan (go grasp, seize) is thus found in Kamit:

kɔ́fa-bèra [*go take come*]: ways k., *he* or *she has* (by growing up to an age of 6 or 7 years) *become a fetcher* or *"fetch-something",* i. *e.* one that can be told *"go and fetch it",* i.e. can be sent on errands.

fetch, *v.* kofa..ba; gye; twẽ .ba.

kef-t [hieroglyphs], IV, 1139, [hieroglyphs], Rec. 1, 50, a seizure; [hieroglyphs], Pap. 3024, 139, [hieroglyphs].

kefā [hieroglyphs], IV, 663, 893, [hieroglyphs], IV, 711, [hieroglyphs], Edict 22, to seize, to grasp, to capture, to collect taxes, to plunder; see [hieroglyphs].

The symbolism of **Tehuti** gathers (fwa) all of these variegated notions together holistically:

gem, gemi [hieroglyphs], U. 515, [hieroglyphs], to find, to discover; [hieroglyphs], U. 200, T. 78, M. 231, N. 610, [hieroglyphs] to find a mouth, *i.e.*, to speak; Copt. ϭιn, ϭinε, ϫεⲙ, ϫιⲙι.

gemgem [hieroglyphs], Verbum I, 336, 2, to search out, to investigate, to reckon up.

gemḥ [hieroglyphs], to see, to look, to perceive; var. [hieroglyphs].

gemaḥ [hieroglyphs], to weigh, to grasp, to enclose, to bind.

The **habui** (ibis) bird, the **akyeneboa** (animal totem) of **Tehuti** when searching, investigating, looking, perceiving, gathering uses its **fnt** (fan, fwa) nose, beak, in the act of scraping, scratching, sensing (fwa) so that it can grasp (fa) what it is seeking.

This is why **Tehuti** is called **Fan**(t), 'He of the Nose'. He who scrapes, scratches (fwa, fa) in order to grasp (fa). He is scraping, searching, gathering from what is under the surface of Asaase (Earth), 'hidden' in the Spirit-realm, to bring it to light. Once he finds what he is looking for, he will **kofa** (go grasp). This is why the term **san** is also instructive:

sàŋ, *v.* [*red.* **sensaŋ**] **1.** *to draw a line, to make a stroke,* **e.g. with a stick in the sand; ɔresaŋ fam',** *he is drawing a line on the ground; to mark with a line;* **fa saŋ hɔ,** *make a line* **(which signifies something)! saŋ ŋhoma no so = fa hyɛ ŋhomam'! ɔde sèkáŋ asàŋ m'ani ase dè àyè me kàsante,** *with a knife he cut a line across my cheek as a mark of disobedience.* — **2.** *to be drawn across* **or in another direction; etwȁ sàŋ** (*pl.* **sènsaŋ**) **n'ani ase,** *a scar is* (*scars are*) *on his cheek.* — **3.** *to make a slit, cut lengthwise into two long pieces* **or** *strips; s.* **sensaŋ.** — **4.** *to return, go* **or** *come back. pr. 2767;* **mã yɛnsaŋ ŋkɔ fie bio,** *let us return home again!* **onipa-wu a, ɔbɛsaŋ aba bio,** *if a man dies, he will return again* **(by metempsychosis, according to the ideas of the natives); saŋ akyiri,** *to return, go back;* **wasaŋ n'akyi** *he has turned back. pr. 415;*

s-ān [hieroglyphs], to turn back

While the fourth definition of **san** is 'to return, go back' in Akan and also in Kamit, the first definition of **san** in Akan is 'to draw a line, make a stroke' as in with a stick [beak] in the sand. **Tehuti** as Habui, the Crane, with his **fwa** (scraping, scratching) is making strokes in the Asaase (Earth). **Tehuti** is thus the Divine **Sesh** or **Scribe**. Drawing the sacred symbols (**medutu, adinkra, veves**) in Asaase (Earth) which carry the **tumi**, Divine Power and **Nyansa** (Wisdom) of **Nyamewaa-Nyame**.

Tehuti as Habui is scratching, scraping, scribing (fwa) and also sensing (smelling), perceiving (fwa) the nature of what is hidden in order to bring it to light. His scratching, scraping, drawing lines, strokes is the function of **san**. His seizing and drawing forth the object of his search (egg) is the function of **kofa**. His strokes are not only the **original letters and numbers** passed on to us, but are first and foremost the **sacred lines, marks and patterns** used in the divination process.

gemgem

Tehuti functioning as **Sankofa**

In the Akan tradition, the term sankofa is not merely a description of a process. It is and always has been first and foremost the name of an Obosom (Deity) - the Obosom from Whom the process was received by us as Afurakani/Afuraitkaitnit (African~Black) people. This Obosom (Deity) is Tehuti. He is called Nana Sankofa in Akan.

We also recognize that the Female Obosom (Deity/Goddess) of Divine Wisdom is **Seshat** who is also a Divine Scribe (Sesh-t). The female habui (ibis) is Her sacred symbol:

Sesha-t (Seshait), T. 268, , M. 426, , , , , Rec. 30, 194, 31, 28, A.Z. 1906, 124, IV, 1074, B.D. 57, 6, 152, 31, 169, 18, the goddess of learning, wisdom, architecture,

Tehuti and **Seshat** together, Husband and Wife

Tehuti as **Brekyirihunuade** – 'He who **turns back** (san, brekyiri) to see or 'grasp' (hunu, kofa) all of Creation'. The title **Brekyirihunuade** is the literal definition of **Sankofa**. The Akan **mbrammu** (brass goldweight) of the Sankofa bird is shown on top of a **pyramid.** This demonstrates the preservation in Akan Ancestral culture of our geographical and cosmological origins in Khanit and Kamit (Nubia and Egypt) prior to our migration to West Afuraka/Afuraitkait (Africa).

The habui bird is shown **preening**. The preening process is one wherein the bird stimulates its **uropygial gland** and uses the secretions (preen oil) to purify its body, strengthen and waterproof its feathers and protect itself from parasites:

"...The **uropygial gland**, informally known as the **preen gland** or the **oil gland**, is a bilobate sebaceous gland possessed by the majority of birds. It is located dorsally at the base of the tail (between the fourth caudal vertebrae and the pygostyle) and is greatly variable in both shape and size. In some species, the opening of the gland has a small tuft of feathers to provide a wick for the preen oil. It is a **holocrine gland** enclosed in a connective tissue capsule made up of glandular acini that deposit their oil secretion into a common collector tube ending in a variable number of pores (openings), most usually two. Each lobe has a central cavity that collects the secretion from tubules arranged radially around the cavity. The gland secretion is conveyed to the surface via ducts that, in most species, open at the top of a papilla (nipple-like structure.

The uropygial gland secretes an oil (**preen oil**) through the dorsal surface of the skin via a grease nipple-like nub or papilla. The oil contains a complex and variable mixture of substances formed greatly of aliphatic monoester waxes, formed of fatty acids and monohydroxy wax-alcohols. However, some types of diester waxes called uropygiols and containing hydroxyfatty acids and/or alkane-diols exist in the secretions of the uropygial gland of some groups of birds. Preen gland secretion of some birds have shown to be antimicrobial, while others are not antimicrobial. Some birds harbor bacteria in their preen gland, which to date, have (exclusively) been isolated from preen glands (e.g. *Enterococcus phoeniculicola*[7] and *Corynebacterium uropygiale*). Some of those bacteria add to the antimicrobial properties of preen wax.

A bird will typically transfer preen oil to its body during preening by rubbing its beak and head against the gland opening and then rubbing the accumulated oil on the feathers of the body and wings, and on the skin of the feet and legs. Tailward areas are usually preened utilizing the beak, although some species, e.g. budgerigars use the feet to apply the oil to feathers around the vent..."

[Uropygial Gland – Wikipedia]

This natural preening function is also manifest in the ritual function of **adebisa** (divination) – *reaching back to stimulate the energy necessary to purify one's awareness, insight, so that one can 'see' or 'sense', intuit, learn what is in harmony with Divine Order, strenghten themselves and protect themselves from disordered spiritual projections from others (parasites).*

The symbol of sankofa is often the bird looking back and preening, yet also grasping (fa) an **egg**. It is looking back to the past to grasp that which represents the future – future birth of, the **reincarnation** of, an Ancestral Spirit – a Spirit of the past (behind) who will now return (san) to the present and take, seize (fa) the future. We thus have the other popular expression of the sankofa symbol:

It is a stylized version of twin sankofa bird symbols. This is directly derived from the actual region wherein **reincarnation** manifests **physiologically**:

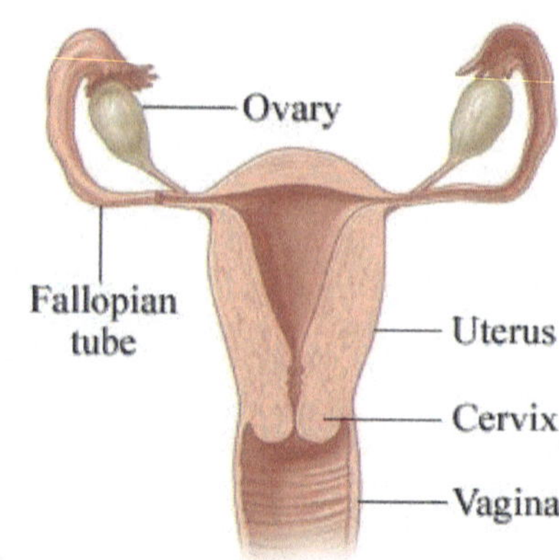

Physiologically, the fallopian tubes of the Afuraitkaitnit (African~Black) female reproductive system is the sanctuary of the sankofa process with regard to the return of an Ancestress or Ancestor to the physical world. The fallopian tubes literally return (san) go and grasp (kofa) the ovaries so that they can receive the ovum (egg). This is the egg in the beak of the sankofa bird – the Ancestral spirit that the bird is seeking out to grasp and bring to light – to the present – in order to shape the future in a positive manner.

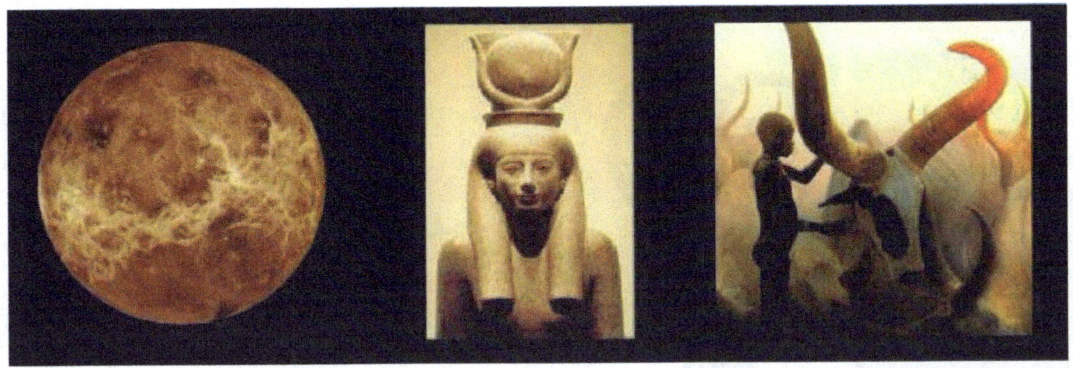

The fallopian tubes of the Afuraitkaitnit (African) woman's reproductive system are governed by the Obosom (Goddess) **Het Heru**, called **Afi** in Akan, **Oshun** in Yoruba and **Azili** (**Erzulie**) in Ewe and Fon, who governs the planet **Afi** (venus), sensuality, union of complementary opposites, fertility, conception as well as beauty, art, music, dance and creativity. Her sacred animal totem is the **Kait** (Cow) as a Great Mother Obosom (Goddess). She is the House (**Het**) within which the rebirth, return – **reincarnation via conception** – is initiated. Her sacred symbol which is thousands of years old reflects this reality:

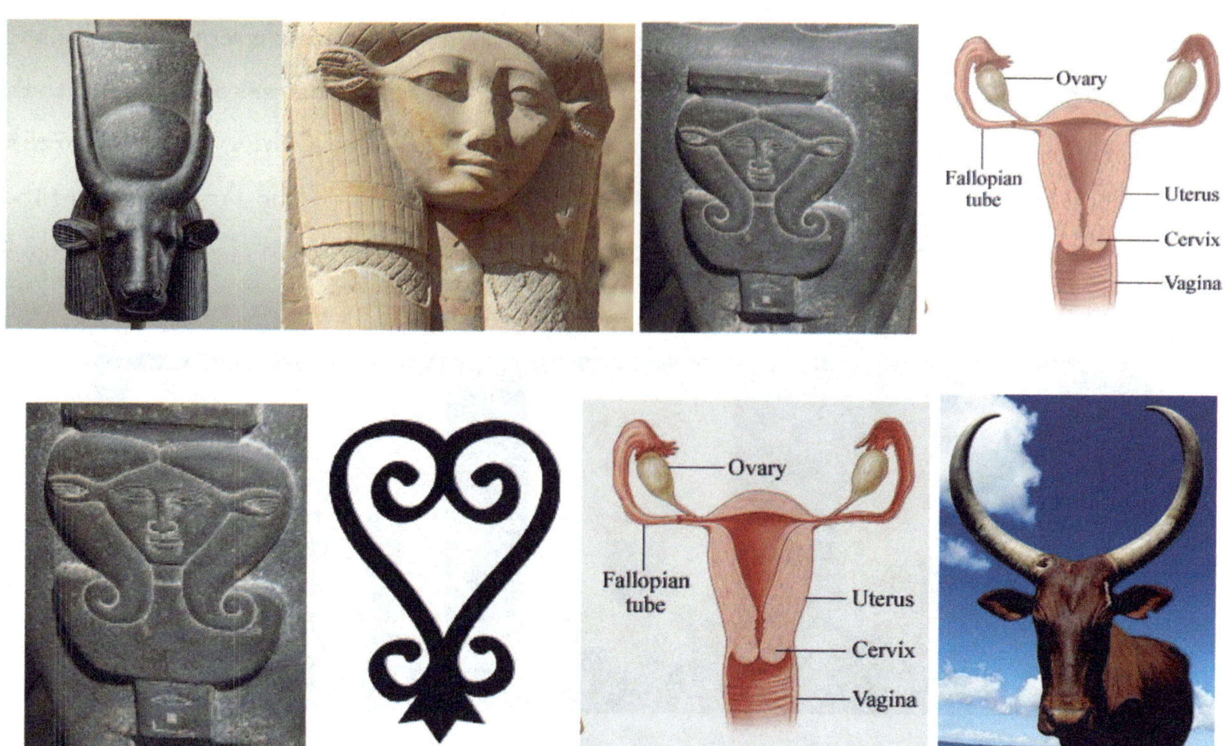

Het Heru, whose sacred animal totem is the **Kait** (Cow) has been represented not only as a woman but also with the face of a **Kait** for thousands of years. She wears the curved horns of the Kait on her crown. The face of **Het Heru**, manifest as the face of the **Kait** is **represented in the structure of the reproductive system**. We note that the term for the female Soul is **Kait**, the term for cow is **Kait** and also the term for vagina is **Kait** in the language of Kamit. This is the connection between the cow, reproduction inclusive of reincarnation, Divinity and **Het Heru**.

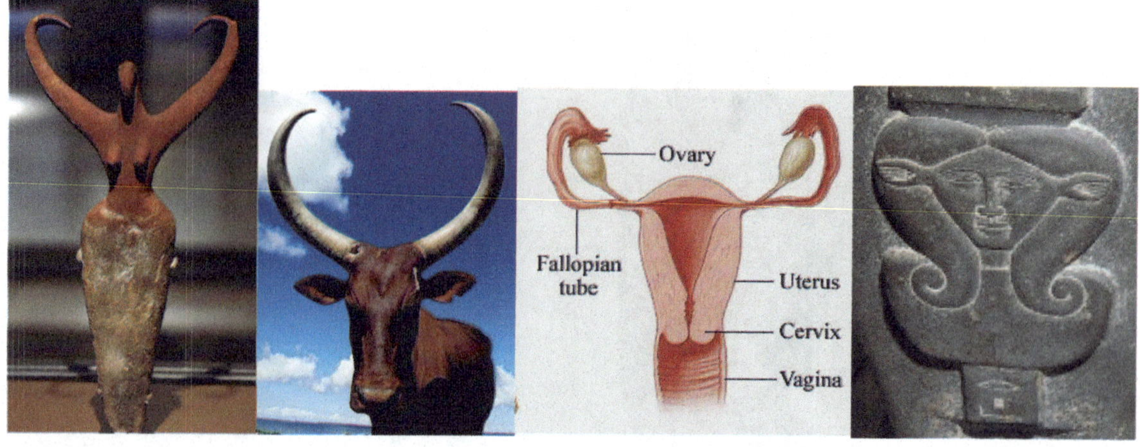

[Left: Pre-dynastic sculpture of **Het Heru** found in Kamit from 7,000 years ago. Ancient manifestations of **Het Heru** as the sacred Kait (Cow) and Divine Fertile Mother. Also represented by the Obosom (Goddess) **Bat**.]

The sankofa process takes place within the sanctuary, the shrine of Het Heru within the Afuraitkaitnit (African) female body – the fallopian tube structure. This is why Tehuti and Seshat, twin Habui birds are also present flanking the sycamore tree (bush) of Het Heru at the spiritual rebirth of the Nesut (King).

Het Heru, Spirit within the sacred sycamore (bush/tree) feeding the spirits of the man and woman

Seshat and **Tehuti** writing the name of the Nesut (King) on the leaves of the sacred **ished** tree (bush). The ished is another sacred tree which is called the 'tree of life'. The **ren** (name) of the individual carries the energy and consciousness of his or her Divine function in Creation. The Deities of Divine Wisdom inscribe the nature of the reincarnating spirit by concretizing his or her name through the **medutu** (symbols) which carry that potency. The 'bush' is a euphemism for the pubic hair of the **Kait** (vagina) the gateway to the returning spirit.

Tehuti and **Seshat** operating within the sanctuary of the 'bush' of **Het Heru** wherein conception takes place

Left: Stela showing a male adorer standing before two Habui birds (Ibises). In the context of reincarnation and rebirth, these are **Tehuti** and **Seshat**. [Limestone, sunken relief. Early 19th Dynasty.]

Right: Dual **Sankofa** birds at the Shrine of the Abosom (Deities) in **Patakro, Asante** Region of Ghana.

Sankofa and other Akan **adinkra** symbols were preserved in the blood-circles of Akan people forced into the western hemisphere during the **Mmusuo Kese** (Great Perversity/Enslavement era). Akan Ancestral Religion in North america is called **Hoodoo** from the Akan term **Ndu** (oohn-dooh'). Our Akan Ancestresses and Ancestors left images if adinkra in the wrought ironworks all over the united states wherever we were enslaved and where we freed ourselves and became independent. The above image in the gate is in Washington, DC. This is the transcarnational inheritance of our Ancestral Religion spanning thousands of years and two continents.

We therefore see that the **sankofa** bird is the habui (ibis), the animal totem of **Tehuti** and **Seshat**. The dual sankofa bird symbol in the heart-shape is **Het Heru**, She who houses (**het**) and facilitates the returning, going and grasping (conception, ovulation – reincarnation) function of **Tehuti** and **Seshat**. Just as **Tehuti** and **Seshat** are present when **Amenet** and **Amen** (**Nyamewaa** and **Nyame**) the Supreme Being assign us a Divine function to execute in Creation before we are born into the world, so are they present within the sanctuary of conception witnessing and recording our reincarnation. Moreover, this is why there are two major representations of sankofa in the adinkra corpus. These symbols have been employed by Akan people since ancient **Khanit** (Khan-land/Nubia) and Kamit up until today in West Afuraka/Afuraitkait (Africa) and North america and the western hemisphere. This includes the same adinkra symbols found in the Caribbean, Central and South America where Akan people were enslaved and freed themselves through waging wars of liberation.

ABE – Sacred Palm Tree

Fai-m'kha-t [hieroglyphs], Ṭuat VI, B.D. 105, 6, a god whose body formed the pillar of the Great Scales.

Fa m'khat is the Deity whose body formed the pillar of the Great scales. The term **m'khat (makhaat)** means 'scales.' The Deity's name is '**Fa (Fai)** of the scales'. Although the egyptologist transliterated the name as **Fai** we can see that in this rendering the **horned viper** [hieroglyph] representing the 'f' sound and the **eagle** [hieroglyph] representing the 'a' sound are followed by the determinative of the man with the vessel upon his head [hieroglyph]. As can be seen, there is no 'i' medut in this particular rendering.

Note that the term **gemah** is defined as to 'to weigh, to grasp' and not only shows the habui (ibis) of **Tehuti**, but also shows the **scales of balance**. This is directly associated with **Tehuti** as the Judge regulating the balancing of the Divine scales.

gemgem [hieroglyphs], Verbum I, 336, 2, to search out, to investigate, to reckon up.

gemaḥ [hieroglyphs], to weigh, to grasp, to enclose, to bind.

This is also directly related to **Tehuti** as the Male Deity of Divine Wisdom and Divination in the **Vodoun** tradition.

FA – Palm Tree and Divination in Vodoun

The term **Vodou (Voodoo)** in the languages of the Ewe and Fon people who reside primarily in Togo and Benin, West Afuraka/Afuraitkait (Africa), means 'Deity, God or Goddess'. The religion itself is called **Vodoun** (voh-doohn'). The major divination system is called **Fa** named after the **Vodou** of Divine Wisdom and Divination whose name is **Fa**. The Vodou **Fa** is **Fan(t) – Tehuti**.

In the Fon tradition, the Vodou named **Gbadu** is a Female Deity who has sixteen eyes. **Gbadu** was told by **Mawu**, the Great Mother of the Universe (**Amenet** in Kamit, **Nyamewaa** in Akan) to live atop a great Divine palm tree in the sky so that she may observe the domains of Sky, Earth and Sea. When **Gbadu** sleeps, she cannot open her eyes, so the Vodou **Legba**, the Divine Messenger, was directed by **Mawu** to climb the tree daily and open **Gbadu**'s eyes for her. **Legba** asks **Gbadu** which of her eyes she wants opened. **Gbadu** either places one palm kernel or two palm kernels in the hand of **Legba** to communicate to him how many of her eyes should be opened, based upon what she is observing in the world.

What is important is that the palm tree upon which **Gbadu** sits to survey Creation is called **Fa**. In the Fon tradition, **Fa** is recognized as a Vodou, the Male Vodou of Divination and Divine Wisdom. **Gbadu** codifies the Divine Wisdom of **Fa** in the various combinations of the opening and closing of her sixteen eyes. This is the origin of palm kernels as well as cowrie shells being used as divinatory instruments.

We find the same structure in our Ancestral culture of Khanit and Kamit, from which the various cultures of West, Central, South and North Afuraka/Afuraitkait (Africa) were born.

In ancient Khanit and Kamit, the **Ntorot** and **Ntoro** (Goddess and God) of Divine Law and Balance are **Maat** and **Maa**. The results of the weighing of the heart against the feather, to determine if the heart of the person is 'light' enough (not weighed down by the negative/contorted energy of disorder) to balance the feather, is **codified** by **Maat.** Law is the **codification** of Order. We see that **Maat** is sitting atop the scales of Divine Balance. Most importantly, **Maat is sitting upon the pillar of the scales**. As shown previously, the Ntoro (God) of this pillar is called **Fa** m'khaat. **Fa** of the Scales. We therefore have the Goddess of Divine Law and Balance, **Gbadu**, sitting atop and balanced upon the palm tree called **Fa** in Vodoun and the Goddess of Divine Law and Balance, **Maat**, sitting upon and balanced upon the pillar ('tree') called **Fa** in Kamit. The tree is the staff of **Fa**, **Tehuti** the **Uhemaa** (Okyeame), the pillar of the scales of balance.

Maā-t, N. 154, 1224, 1279, a goddess, the personification of law, order, rule, truth, right, righteousness, canon, justice, straightness, integrity, uprightness, and of the highest conception of physical and moral law known to the Egyptians.

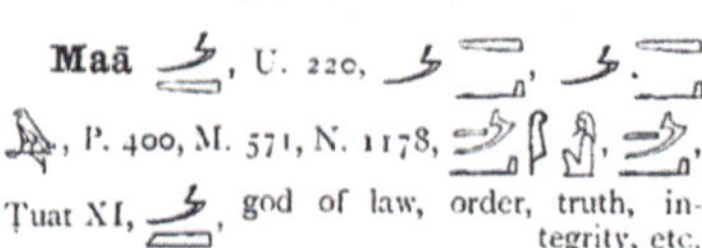

Maā, U. 220, P. 400, M. 571, N. 1178, Ṭuat XI, god of law, order, truth, integrity, etc.

[left: **Maat** from the tomb of Queen **Tauseret**. right: **Maa** from the tomb of **Ra Messu** VI. Photos by author.]

Tehuti and **Seshat** – Temple of **Apet Reset** (Luxor). Photo taken by this author.

Tehuti and **Seshat** are shown with notched palm branches, counting and regulating the time and seasons in Creation. They also take note of and enumerate the potential years of life of the newly returned/reincarnated spirit of the individual. **The enumeration of years and regulation of time – past, present and future – is the domain of divination.** This is why palm kernels are used in Vodoun as a divinatory instrument by the diviners. This is the sacred plant totem of **Tehuti** and **Seshat** in Kamit and **Fa** in Vodoun.

ABE – Palm Tree in Akan Divination

In the Akan tradition we have further evidence of this reality woven into the fabric of the culture. The term for 'Divine wisdom teaching' or 'proverb' is **ebe**. This is wisdom received from the Abosom (Deities), the Embodiments of Divine Order in Creation, preserved by our **Nananom Nsamanfo**, our Spiritually Cultivated Ancestresses and Ancestors and transmitted by our **Nananom Mpanyinfo**, our Spiritually Cultivated Elders and Elderesses. The **abe** is the palm nut. A palm nut from the outside appears to be a simple entity, yet there is a great deal of value contained in the nut (including palm oil, palm juice and other nutrients). Once the nut is opened one can see its enormous value. An ebe or proverb can appear to be a simple saying, yet when properly examined the ebe contains invaluable lessons born of intergenerational and transcarnational experience. Such experience-based wisdom can totally transform the direction of one's life and the life of the oman (nation) when diligently adhered to.

The **ebe**, proverb, is the product of experience. The **abe** or **beemu** (palm nuts) are the product of the **Abe** – palm tree. Moreover, the term **be** is the root of the term **bere** or **abere** meaning 'time'. The term **bere** also means 'place' and 'way or manner'. These definitions 'time', 'place or space' and 'way or manner' are inextricably related in the ritual context.

When we communicate with our Nananom Nsamanfo, our Spiritually Cultivated Ancestresses and Ancestors at the **Nsamankommere** (Ancestral shrine) we do so at a specific time (bere) in a specific ritually prepared place (bere) and in a specific ritual manner or way (bere). This is directly tied to divination, learning from the Spirit realm the nature of the specific time, place and manner of the functioning of various physical and spiritual entities and the nature of the manifestation of various events which are impacting us in a positive or negative manner. When we understand the nature of the functioning of physical and non-physical entities and related events we can learn the specific manner, place and time within which to conduct ritual in order to bring balance to our lives or restore balance to our lives.

The root of **bere**, time, is **be** which is also the name of the palm tree **Abe**. The feminine suffix gives us **Aberewaa**. The relevance here is that **Abe** and **Aberewaa** are titles of **Tehuti** and **Seshat** in Akan and are directly related to divination.

In one of the **Anansesem** or Ananse Stories in Akan culture we find the following:

"...They say there once was a woman and that she went to a certain **Abe**, palm-tree, which stood there in the water that she might consult it about child-bearing. And when she went, **Abe**, the palm-tree said, "I shall give you what you want, but the child with whom I shall present you, when he rises up, will never do any work." She said, "I agree to that." It was not two days, it was not three days, when she conceived and gave birth..."

Here we have a woman going to **consult** with **Abe** because she desired to become fertile and give birth to a child. **Abe** granted her desire and then gave instructions regarding how the child was to be raised. This consultation with related instructions is divination with the Obosom (Deity) **Abe**, a title of **Tehuti** – operating in/as the palm tree. Note that **Abe** or **Be** is the root of **Bere** which is contracted into **Bre** in the title **Brekyirihunuade** another title of **Tehuti**. [Returning back, going back in 'time'/bre.]

We therefore have the palm tree connected to the Obosom (God) of Divine Wisdom and Divination in ancient Khanit and Kamit and Akan culture. **Abe** here is also assisting in child-birth the return (san) of an Ancestral Spirit to be reincarnated/reborn into the world. This is **sankofa**.

We also find that in legislative matters Akan people work to achieve a consensus. However, when deliberations on a specific issue reach an impasse, a certain delegation of Nananom Mpanyinfo, Honored Elders/Elderesses, leave the deliberations and state, **'Ye ko bisa Aberewaa'** which means *'We are going to consult the Elder Woman'*. This is a euphemism for **divination** with **Aberewaa**. The term **abisa** means 'divination' in Akan. To 'ko bisa' means to 'go ask/inquire'. This is a euphemism for 'going to consult the Obosom (Deity)' via oracular divination. This precedent can be found in the culture of ancient Kamit. In the text called the 'Contendings of **Heru** and **Set'** wherein these two are fighting for the right to rule the nation, the Elder Mother Goddess **Neit** is appealed to in order to render a decision. An excerpt from our book **KOKOBO**:

"...**Ra** (The Creator) asks **Tehuti** to write a letter to the Great Ntorot (Goddess) **Neit** (Neith, Nit, Net). He wanted Her to rule as to who should become the new King. This is an ancient Afurakani/Afuraitkaitnit (African) tradition wherein a critical issue which cannot be agreed upon by consensus is taken by a select group of Elders/Elderesses who go and consult the 'Elder Woman' or 'Great Mother' for a final decision.

[In Akan culture today, when the **Nananom Mpanyinfo** (Elders/Elderesses) cannot reach a decision on an issue of great importance to the **oman** (nation) through the normal process of consensus, a select number of them are appointed to **'Ye ko bisa Aberewa'** - 'We are going to consult with the Old Woman' (related to the Earth Mother). When they return from consulting with 'the Old Woman', her decision is understood by all to be final.]..."

The term **aberewaa** is comprised of **bere** which means 'time' and also 'ripe, aged' when referencing a person and **waa** which is the feminine suffix in Akan. **Aberewaa** (Aberewa, Abrewa) can be used for an 'aged, ripe, wise' woman or Female Obosom (Goddess). However, in the specific divinatory context, we are speaking of the Female Obosom of Divine Wisdom and Divination who regulates the time (abere) and seasons, the cycles of life. The one who holds the palm branch. This is **Aberewaa, Seshat**, the wife of **Abe, Tehuti (Berekyirihunuade)**. [Because the palm tree is born of Earth, **Asaase Afua** and **Asaase Yaa**, the Earth Mother Abosom (Deities) are also invoked as part of the divination process.]

We also note that **berew** is the term for 'palm oil leaves'. This fact is enshrined not only in the palm branch that **Seshat** uses to enumerate the years in the cycle of life of Creation and the Afurakani/Afuraitkaitnit (African) individual but also the unique symbol shown on her head. The symbol on the head of **Seshat** is the palm:

Seshat is **Aberewaa**, the **Abe** (**Abere**) or Palm tree shown on her head indicates that **Seshat Aberewaa** is the 'Head' or 'Cheiftaness Diviner'.

[Note: This symbol has never represensted cannabis. Our cosmology demonstrates that this is the palm tree.]

When we state that we are 'going to consult with the Elder/Old Woman' this is the **sankofa process**. We are returning to the past (Elderess, Spirit of Divine Wisdom from the Origin-Source of Creation) to grasp, learn, intuit, the lessons we need in order to remedy our situation in the present and lay the groundwork for a positive future. **Seshat** is **Aberewaa**. **Tehuti** is **Te, Abe, Berekyirihunuade – Sankofa**.

The **fallopian** tube structure has its parallel in the male reproductive system as the **epididymis**:

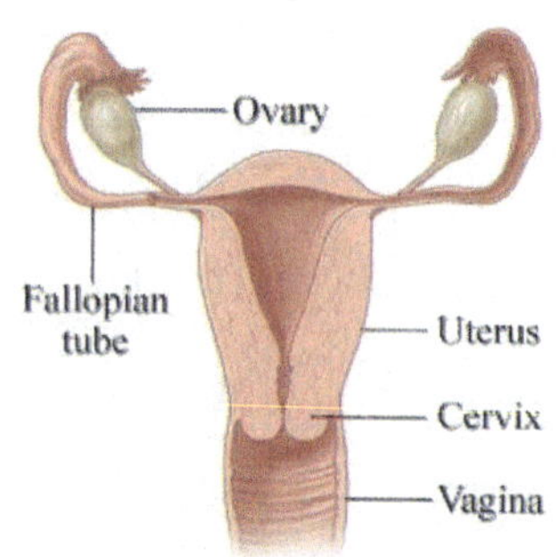

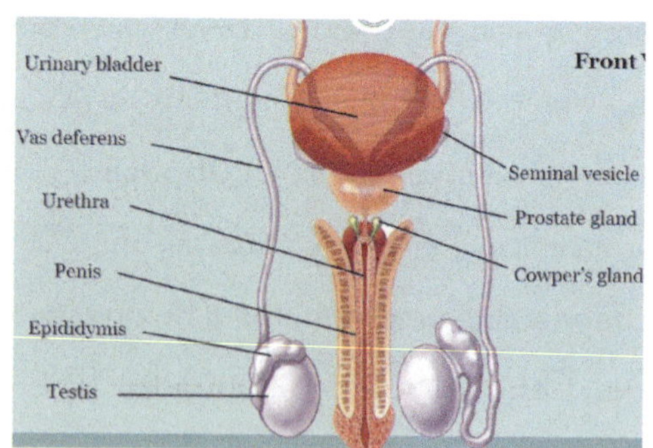

The ova (eggs) of the female mature within the ovaries and are released into the fallopian tubes. In similar fashion the spermatazoa of the male mature within the testes and are released through the epididymis and the vas deferens tubes. We thus have a sankofa symbol within the male as well. However, the actual conception can only take place within the female. The male sperm cells must leave the male body, enter the female and fuse with the ovum within the sanctuary of **Het Heru** – the fallopian tubes.

Thus, in order for an Ancestral Spirit to be reborn into the world – in order form the Ancestral Spirit to return to the womb – the male must connect with the female. The sperm cell must *seek, search* (**gemgem**), *'scrape', sense* (**fwa**) and then *grasp, seize* (**kofa**) and fuse with the ovum:

gemgem

The swimming, seeking, searching, scraping and grasping of the ovum by the sperm cell demonstrates a masculine function in the reincarnation process. **Sankofa** is thus a male title for the Obosom (Deity)**Tehuti** in Akan. Yet, the ovum is not a passive participant in this process. The ovum actively stimulates and draws (electromagnetically) the sperm cell to itself, guides the fusion and completes the integration. Moreover, the reincarnation process can only reach completion within the sanctuary of the female reproductive system, the shrine of **Het Heru.** This is why the symbol of the dual sankofa birds is called **Sankofa** as well. The dual symbol as the symbol governed by **Het Heru** is literally the *sanctuary* of Sankofa physiologically.

A feminine form of the name **Sankofa** in Akan is **Sankofawaa** or **Sankofabaa.** This is a title of **Seshat** (**Aberewaa**). This title includes the feminine function in the reincarnation process. Undergirding the male and female functions of the reincarnation process – within the *procreative sanctuary* of **Het Heru** – is the drawing into the womb of specific female and/or male Ancestresses or Ancestors to be reborn. **Tehuti** and **Seshat**, **Abe** and **Aberewaa**, know which Ancestresses and Ancestors are to return and what spiri-genetic qualities they are to inherit (draw from) and manifest in their phenotypes, spiritual disposition, character, physical attributes, etc. **Abe** and **Aberewaa** thus regulate the proper time (**bere**), womb/space/clan (**bere**) and manner (**bere**) in which the Afurakani (African) Ancestor or Afuraitkaitnit (African) Ancestress reincarnates. This is how **Tehuti, Seshat** and **Het Heru** work together in the male (epididymis) and ultimately female (fallopian tubes) structures.

IFA – Palm Nuts in Yoruba Divination

The major form of divination among the Yoruba people who reside primarily in southwest Nigeria, West Afuraka/Afuraitkait (Africa), is called **Ifa**. The system of **Ifa** is said to have been given by the **Orisha** (Deity) **Orunmila**, the Orisha of Divine Wisdom and Divination. Because of the role of **Orunmila** in Creation and Divination, **Orunmila** is also called **Ifa**.

In the Yoruba language, the term **fa** means 'to scrape'. It can also mean to 'shave, clean, wipe'. A related definition is to 'pull, draw, lead'. We thus have the Orisha (Deity) of Divine Wisdom and Divination called **Ifa**, which also means 'to scrape' just as **fa** and **fwa** mean 'to smell' and also 'to scrape'. In the practice of Ifa divination markings/lines are drawn by the diviner in the **iyerosun** or divination powder on the **opon Ifa** or divination tray. These markings indicate what **Odu** is addressing the issue that the querent came to learn about. There are 256 **Odu** which are manifest in patterns governed by specific Orisha. All of Creation and the events taking place within Creation can be read within the Odu. The markings are made as the diviner casts the 16 **ikin** or **palm nuts**:

The **ope ifa** or Ifa palm tree is that from which the **ikin** or palm nuts are taken. This sacred tree is the pillar upon which the system rests. The **san** (drawn lines) made by **Tehuti** with his beak in the soil and sand is the origin of the diviner in Yoruba culture drawing lines when in communication with **Orunmila** (**Ifa/Fa(n)/Tehuti**). This ancient form of divination pre-dates the whites and their offspring and thus has absolutely no roots in 'islamic sand divination' as some have erroneously speculated. We have demonstrated the cosmological foundation for the sacredness of the palm tree in divination and the nature and functioning of the Deities in the process, inclusive of the 'scraping' function of 'fa' (Ifa). The scraping up or grasping also includes the grasping, scraping, of shells, nuts, stones when casting during divination. We also take note of the fact that in Yoruba, the term **'kofa'** literally means to 'study **Ifa'**.

The 256 **Odu Ifa** are manifest in the patterns drawn in the iyerosun powder and accompanied by **ese Ifa** or 'verses' of Ifa containing the stories, ritual practices and wisdom associated with the governing

Orisha. The Odu Ifa are named after the Female Orisha (Deity) **Odu**. **Odu** through these sacred arrangements codifies the Divine Order as Divine Law. **Odu** is called **Maat** in Kamit and **Gbadu** in Vodoun. **Maat** is called **Amamee** and **Amaowia** in Akan.

We also find in the Yoruba tradition that **Orunmila** and **Oshun** were at one point married and both had a role in the introduction of the Ifa divination system. As stated above, **Oshun** is the Orisha who is called **Het Heru** in ancient Kamit. **Oshun** being married to **Ifa** in a specific context is the same interrelationship of **Tehuti** and **Het Heru** in the context of Sankofa.

Orunmila is referred to as **Eleri Ipin**, the 'Witness of Destiny'. He is present when the spirit of the individual receives his or her Divine function from **Olorun** and **Olokun**, the Great Father and Great Mother Supreme Being prior to reincarnation in to the world. Because **Orunmila** knows the Divine function or 'Destiny' of all individuals, **Orunmila** or **Ifa** can be consulted when issues in life arise so that balance can be restored. **Orunmila** is the thus the Male 'Spokesperson' or 'Mouthpiece' of the Supreme Being. This is the role of **Tehuti** in Kamit and **Berekyirihunuade** as **Okyeame** (Spokesperson, Mouthpiece) in Akan.

Het Heru and Tehuti – Oshun and Orunmila (Tomb of Pashedu)

Ṭeḥuti, chief titles of: , Pap. Ani 3, dweller in Khemenu;

Per Khemenu Hermopolis in Upper Egypt.

The sacred city of **Tehuti** in Kamit is **Khemenu**. The term **khemenu** means 'eight'. This is a reference to the priomordial eight Abosom (Deities), **Amen** and **Amenet** and their first six children, who are the origin of Creation. We take notice of the fact that the Ifa diviner casts the **ikin ifa** (palm nuts) eight times and makes eight markings/strokes/lines (san) in the iyeroson powder upon the opon Ifa or divination tray. Those original eight strokes can be found in the spelling of the title of **Tehuti** as 'dweller within Khemenu': and .

We also take note of the fact that it was **Tehuti** who assisted in the restoring of the body of the Obosom (Deity) **Ausar**. Ausar is called **Obatala** in Yoruba. Some texts state that the body of **Ausar** was cut into fourteen pieces which were later reconstituted so that the body could be mummified. However, other texts state that the body of **Ausar** was cut into **sixteen pieces** and list the sixteen cities wherein they were found. This is the reason why there are sixteen palm nuts used in **Ifa** divination.

When we experience disorder and seek to realign ourselves with Divine Order we must return (san), go (ko) and grasp (fa) from our Ancestral past. Ritually, this means we must return to the pact we made with **Nyamewaa-Nyame (Mawu-Lisa, Olokun-Olorun, Amenet-Amen)**, the Supreme Being, pre-incarnation. We are assigned a specific function to execute in the Great Divine Body, just as every cell in your body is designed and comes into being to execute a specific function within your body. As 'cells' within the Great Divine Body, we have a Divine function (so-called destiny or life-focus, purpose). When cells run afoul of their physiological functions, disorder and disease manifest in the body. Restoration of order is affected through proper diagnosis and natural healing, medicine. The same is true when we as 'cells' make legitimate mistakes and find ourselves out of harmony with Divine Order within the Great Divine Body. We receive a proper diagnosis of our condition only by attuning to the Obosom (Orisha, Vodou) in our head region which contains our blueprint/Divine function – the instruction manual regarding our role in the Divine Body – Creation. If we are not receptive enough to attune to this information streaming from our head Obosom (Deity), we consult the Abosom who were present at the assignment of our Divine Function. This is **Tehuti** and **Seshat**. They can show us through divination, externally, what our head Obosom has been working to show us internally all along. We can then incorporate the healing, medicine and behavior necessary to restore Divine Order to our thoughts, intentions and actions and thus restore balance to our lives. This is the **sankofa process**.

It is critical to understand that this process is for Afurakanu/Afuraitkaitnut (Africans~Black People) only. The Abosom, Orisha, Vodou, Ntorou/Ntorotu (Neteru/Netertu), the Deities, have never and will never communicate with the whites and their offspring (white americans, europeans, white hispanics, white asians, white hindus, white arabs, white pseudo-'native'-americans, etc.). Our connection to the Deities is through our spiri-genetic blood-circles. The whites and their offspring **incarnate as spirits of disorder**, spirits without an Okra/Okraa, Ori Inu, Se Lido, Ka/Kait – Soul/Deity in the head-region. They are thus **repelled** by the Spirits of Divine Order. They can only communicate with the spirits of their disordered, deceased relatives and non-relatives and call these communications 'deity communication'. **All non-Blacks who claim to practice Ancestral Religion are frauds – no exceptions.**

Kefāu [hieroglyphs], IV, 35, "capturer"—a title; plur. [hieroglyphs], Mar. Karn. **Kefaiu** [hieroglyphs], B.D. 145, 79, a group of gods.

The term **kofa** in Yoruba means to 'study Ifa'. The term **kofa** in Akan means to 'go and grasp'. This is the operationalizing of study. Going, seeking to grasp or understand a subject or object is studying, examination. However, grasping is not only a passive function. It is also an aggressive function as shown in the medutu for **kfa** (**kofa**) above. **Tehuti** as the Obosom of Divine Wisdom works to assist us to overcome our obstacles including human obstacles. **This includes our enemies**. Divination can thus be used for empowering us to **heal ourselves** but also **kill our enemies**.

Afurakanu/Afuraitkaitnut (Africans) in North america maintained our Ancestral Religions in our blood-circles during the Mmusuo Kese (Great Perversity/Enslavement era). It was through the practice of our Ancestral Religions that we were empowered and guided by the Abosom and Nananom Nsamanfo on the best means by which we could wage war against the white slavers, massacre them and free ourselves from enslavement. Divination was a key component of this process. This included our various traditions **Hoodoo** (Akan Ancestral Religion), **Juju** (Yoruba Ancestral Religion) **Voodoo** (Ewe and Fon Ancestral Religion), **Wanga** (Ovambo Ancestral Religion), **Gris Gris** (Bambara Ancestral Religion) **Ngengang** and **Nganga** (Fang and Bakongo Ancestral Religion), **Gullah – Geechee** (Gola and Kisi Ancestral Religion) and more in North america.

We appealed to **Tehuti** and **Seshat** and the other Abosom for Divine guidance and received it. It was because of the wars waged by those who practiced Ancestral Religion, including the **Gullah Wars** (so-called Seminole Wars) and **Hoodoo Wars**, that forced the Civil War and the end of enslavement in North america.

This precedent was set in ancient Khanit and Kamit. **Kofa** and **Kofau** (plural) is a title applied not only to soldiers who capture the enemy but also Abosom (Deities) as shown above. The oldest religious compositions yet unearthed in the world are the **meru** or pyramid texts. We quote from the text of **Pepi** regarding the **Kofa** function of **Tehuti**. The Nesut (King/Pharaoh) **Pepi** is being addressed showing that he is being given power, protection and dominion over various aspects of Creation by the Abosom (Deities) as he functions in partnership with the Obosom **Ausar**:

"...Heaven is to you, the Earth is to you, the Spirit-realm Sekhet Aaru is to you. The domains of **Heru** are to you. The domains of **Set** are to you. The cities are to you and the Deity **Atem** has gathered together for you the regions of Kamit. The Earth Deity **Geb**, Father of **Ausar** has spoken concerning it. **Tehuti grinds his knife and sharpens his knife and crushes in heads and cuts open chests.**

He crushes heads and cuts open the chests of those who attack this Pepi when he is journeying to you, O Ausar. He breaks the heads of those who would repel this Pepi when he is journeying to you O Ausar that you may give him life and serenity..."

Here we see in the oldest religious texts in existence that **the Deity of Divine Wisdom is also a Divine Killer**. As we have shown in our book **MMARA NE KYI – Divine Law/Love and Divine Hate**, **Tehuti** and **Seshat** are the Governor and Governess of the expasive and contractive poles of **Nyansa** (Divine Wisdom). The expansive pole of Wisdom is **Revolution**. The contractive pole of Wisdom is **Resolution**. Revolution and Resolution are two halves of this Divine Whole, governed by **Tehuti** and **Seshat**. To re-volve is to re-turn back to the Source, draw wisdom from experience and then utilize that wisdom to re-solve or vindicate your condition. This is the goal of divination.

Tehuti as the Deity with the title **Kofa** – capturing, seizing the enemy and restraining them, so that **Heru**, the Son of **Ausar** and **Auset** can kill them. [From the **Edfu** Texts – Legend of **Heru Behudet**].

The Kings and Queenmothers of Khanit and Kamit led armies guided by the Divine Wisdom of **Tehuti** and **Seshat**. Our Akofo, Warriors and Warrioresses in North america raised armies to wage war against the white slavers. Kofa is not about killing the spirit of 'ego' within. It is founded upon killing negative disordered entities and emanations – so that – you can expand that function externally and manifest the same results in the Afurakani/Afuraitkaitnit (African) **oman** (nation/community).

It is this form of **Sankofa**, **Tehuti** as **Kofa**, that Afurakanu/Afuraitkaitnut (Africans) in the western hemisphere invoked and continue to invoke for the Divine guidance and wisdom regarding the best and most effective means to eradicate our enemies, the whites and their offspring. **Tehuti** and **Seshat** guided us to overthrowing the enslavement system and will now guide us to complete the mission of our complete liberation.

Select Bibliography

An Egyptian Hieroglyphic Dictionary, Vols. 1-2, by E.A. Wallis Budge

Dictionary of the Asante-Fante Language Called Tshi (Twi), by J.G. Christaller

Cloth as Metaphor, by G.J. Kojo Arthur

Adinkra Dictionary, by W. Bruce Willis

Pryamid Text of Pepi

Ifa Will Mend Our Broken World, by Wande Abimbola

Akan-Ashanti Folktales, by R.S. Rattray

Dahomean Narrative: A Cross-Cultural Analysis, by Melville Herskovits

Bibliography of publications by Odwirafo Kwesi Ra Nehem Ptah Akhan – See: www.odwirafo.com

OKYEAME-UHEMMA: Spokesperson of the Sacred

HOODOO PEOPLE: Akan Custodians of Hoodoo from Ancient Hoodoo/Udunu Land (Khanit/Nubia)

HOODOO MAYN: Hoodoo Nation Festival Nhoma (Journal) – 13016

HOODOO MAYN: Hoodoo Nation Festival Nhoma (Journal) – 13017

AKYISAN – Ancestral Religious Reversion Nhoma (Journal) - 13016

KOKOBO – Warning: Divine Prohibition against dissexuality/homosexuality in Kamit

MMARA NE KYI – Divine Law/Love and Divine Hate

AFURAKA/AFURAITKAIT – The Origin of the term 'Africa'

THE OKRA/OKRAA COMPLEX – The Soul of Akanfo

Appendix

Tehuti, Maa and Divination: From Kamit to Hoodoo

In the stela of **Nefer Renpet** we see the **Ntoro** (Ntr/God) **Tehuti** sitting in his sacred barque. **Tehuti** is the Male Force of Divine Wisdom in Creation. He is the Divine Spokesperson or Mouthpiece of **Amenet** and **Amen**, the Great Mother and Great Father Supreme Being as well as **Ra** and **Rait**, the Creator and Creatress. [Note that **Seshat** is the Female Force of Divine Wisdom.]

When we want to know what is in harmony with Divine Order, what thoughts, intentions and actions are or would be a manifestation of Divine Wisdom, we attune to the **Ntoro** and **Ntorot** (Neter and Netert/Ntr and Ntrt - Male and Female Deities) of Divine Wisdom, **Tehuti** and **Seshat** for guidance. The message they transmit to us, plant into our spirits, is a message which allows us to see the circumstance, event, individual and/or entity in proper context and how to move forward. This could be for healing a physical illness, a spiritual illness, a societal or communal fracturing and more. **Tehuti** takes the form of his sacred **akyeneboa** (animal totem) the **Habui** (Ibis/Crane) on the stela. Next to **Tehuti** is the Ntoro (Deity) **Aan** in the form of his sacred animal totem the baboon.

Aan is offering the **Udjat Heru**, the *Eye of Heru* to **Tehuti**. The Eye of **Heru** as an **asuman** (talisman) is also a shrine. The left eye of **Heru** was injured when the Ntoro (God) **Heru** battled the Ntoro (God) **Set**. It was **Tehuti** along with the **Ntorot** (Goddess) **Het Heru** who healed the eye.

The left eye of **Heru** is the Moon while the right eye is the Sun. When the Moon goes from full, to half, to crescent, to New Moon, the Moon (eye) is being 'gouged out' or 'injured'. When the light returns to the Moon and it fills back in, the eye has been 'healed' or restored. The Moon reflects the Divine light of the **Aten** (Sun) so that we can see in darkness. This is **Tehuti** (Spokesperson) reflecting the Divine Illumination of **Ra** and **Rait** to us so that we can 'see' our way through 'blindness' (ignorance) and make the proper/wise decision which is in harmony with Divine Order.

Moreover, the gravitational pull of the Moon affects the rising of tides on **Asaase** (Earth). The increase in water, an increase in fullness, is akin to **spirit-possession**, 'going under'. Water is recognized in ancient Kamit and across **Afuraka/Afuraitkait** (Africa) as a gateway to the Spirit-realm.

The Messenger Ntoro (Deity) Aan, proffering the Eye of Heru, the Moon to Tehuti (who wears the crescent Moon on his crown) is part of an oracular divination ritual. The Eye of Heru is the Divination vessel through which Tehuti, the High Priest, gazes to learn what Spirit-Forces are affecting the issue in the physical world.

This symbolism is critical to understand because it references a functional reality within the Ancestral Religious practices of our people – ancient and contemporary.

In the **Akan** tradition amongst the **Baule** sub-group of the Akan in Ivory Coast, West Afuraka/Afuraitkait (Africa), we find that the very same sacred monkey is the assistant of the **Obosomfo** (High Priest). The oracular sculpture shown here is found on the shrines of Akan diviners. The monkey is holding the **divination vessel.** This is the Eye of **Heru** utilized for divination (including water-gazing) so that the Obosomfo (Priest) can communicate with the **Abosom** and **Nananom Nsamanfo** (Deities and Honored Ancestral Spirits).

The same is true in the **Yoruba** tradition in Nigeria in West Afuraka/Afuraitkait (Africa). We find that the **Orisha** (Deity) of Divine Wisdom **Orunmila** (**Tehuti** in Kamit) had a pair of twins with his wife **Peregunlele**. The twins were male and female and were called **Edun**. Edun is the term for monkey. The male **Edun** went to live on Earth with **Orunmila**. Because of his appearance, he lived amongst the animal kingdom. The male Edun became a priest of **Ifa** (High Priest). The male Edun holds the **Opon Ifa** (divination tray) while the female Edun (**Odu**, **Maat**) holds the sacred calabash of existence **Igba Iwa Odu**.

We thus have the sacred monkey being an assistant to the Deity of Divine Wisdom in Yoruba, a sacred monkey being an assistant to the High Priest who invokes the Deity of Divine Wisdom in Akan and the sacred monkey being an assistant to the Deity of Wisdom, who is the High Priest – Tehuti – in Kamit. This is the same Ancestral Religion – the unbroken living tradition - with the same Deities.

One of the titles of the monkey **Aan** (**Anan**) is **Up Maa** (Judge **Maa**), however his primary title is **Maa**. **Maa** is the counterpart of **Maat**. They regulate Divine Law and Balance in Creation.

In the papyrus of **Hunefer**, we see that **Maat**, the Female Deity of Divine Law and Balance is sitting atop the **equilibrium point** on the **Makhait** - scales of Divine Balance. The deceased person's heart is being weighed against the feather of **Maat** to see if it is light enough (not weighted down by disorder) to balance out the feather. If it does balance out feather, the spirit of the person can pass on to the Ancestral realm to live in peace (after a subsequent trial with the Deity **Maa**).

In the papyrus of **Ani**, we find that it is the male Deity **Maa** also called **Up Maa** and **Aan**, in the form of his sacred animal totem, the monkey, who sits atop the **equilibrium point** on the scales:

In the late period papyrus and in the Tomb of **Pa Nentwy** below we also see the Ntoro **Maa** in the form of **Up Maa** working in concert with **Tehuti** and sitting atop the scales on the **equilibrium point**:

What is important to understand is that the role of **Maa** in divination and his role in Creation in relation to **Tehuti** as demonstrated in the Nefer Renpet stela **can only be understood in our Ancestral Religious context.** *This is because we have a living tradition.*

In the Akan tradition, we have not only the cosmological and ritual manifestation but also the linguistic evidence:

Kamiti and **Akan** terms:

Ka – Soul/Divine Consciousness	**Kara** (Kra) – Soul/Divine Consciousness
Ba – Spirit/Divine Living Energy	**Bara** (Bra) – Spirit/Divine Living Energy
Maa – Divine Law	**Mmara** (Mmra) – Divine Law

As we can see the terms for Soul (Divine Consciousness), Spirit and Law are the same terms in Kamit as they are in Akan. The 'ara' added to the roots of each term in Akan functions as an **emphatic particle** (like an exclamation point). An example being 'ba' meaning 'come' and the emphatic version 'bara (bra)' meaning 'come!!'. It is exclamatory.

This is key to understand because while the Male and Female Forces of Divine Wisdom are **Tehuti** and **Seshat**, those who are Spokespersons for the Supreme Being, their **Divine declarations** are **codified into Law** by the Male and Female Deities of Divine **Law** and **Balance**. The Ntoro and Ntorot of Divine Law and Balance are **Maa** and **Maat**.

The term mmara (maa – ra) meaning 'law' in Akan is the same term maa meaning 'law' in Kamit. **This is precisely why the monkey holding the divination bowl for the Obosomfo (High Priest – representative of Tehuti) in Akan is named <u>Mmara</u>. In the Baule dialect it can also be pronounced Mbara.**

(The word **mmara** in the Asante Akan dialect is also pronounced **mbara** in the Akwamu Akan dialect).

Maa and Variations of **Mmara** (Mbara/Maa)

This is the ***exact same Deity*** *with the* ***exact same <u>name</u>*** *executing the* ***exact same function*** *in* ***both cultures – ancient and contemporary.***

It is also very important to understand that the Akan Ancestral Religion maintained in the blood-circles of Akan people in North america for over 300 years is called Hoodoo.

In the Hoodoo Religion, we continue to have this Mmara (Maa) sculpture/figure (typically wood, clay or fabric) on our shrines next to or holding our vessels of divination (adebisa) which includes water-gazing – peering into the gateway (water) to the Spirit-realm for direction from our Abosom and Nananom Nsamanfo (Deities and Honored Ancestral Spirits).

We know exactly who **Maa** and **Maat** are, for we communicate directly with them via spirit-possession and spirit-communication (including divination) on a regular basis. We know the distinctions between **Maa** and **Tehuti**, **Maat** and **Seshat**.

The variants of the Baboon with the vessel as well as the vessel containing the Eye of **Heru** confirms the divinatory function.

Egyptologists and Black scholars who follow white egyptologists often make the mistake of assuming that the baboon represents only **Tehuti** in these representations in papyri. While **Tehuti** can use the baboon as an animal totem (**akyeneboa**), in these specific instances we are dealing with two different Ntorou (Deities) – **Tehuti** and **Maa**. We invoke them by the same names, for the same ritual functions today in West Afuraka/Afuraitkait (Africa) and in North america in Hoodoo just as our Ancestresses and Ancestors did thousands of years ago in Khanit and Kamit.

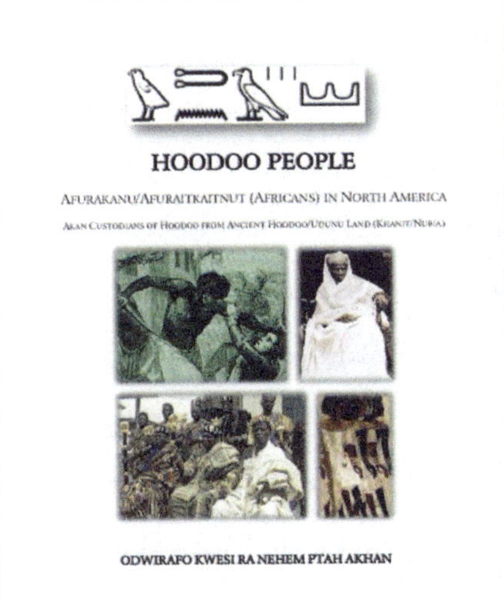

See our related book: HOODOO PEOPLE: Afurakanu/Afuraitkaitnut (Africans) in North America – Akan Custodians of Hoodoo from Ancient Hoodoo/Udunu Land (Khanit/Nubia)

Appendix 2: Hwehwemudua – Divining Rod

ɔ-hwɛ́fo, ohwɛfó, *pl.* a-, [*con.* me hwɛ́fo] *looker; overseer, superintendent, surveyor, inspector, director; officer. Josh.* 3,2; *pedagogue, child-tender; warden; guardian; curator, trustee; keeper, conservator, preserver; herdsman, shepherd; pastor, parson, curate, bishop; ruler, chief; cf.* oguaŋhwɛfo, asafo-so-hwɛfo. —

ŋhwehwɛ-mú, *inf. investigation, examination, inquiry;* enni ŋhw., *it is*

e-duá, *pl.* n-, (*pr. 45. 991—1021*) **1.** *plant, tree, shrub.* — **2.** *stem* or *stalk* of a plant or its leaf or fruit. — **3.** *wood; piece of wood. pr. 994; something made of wood. pr. 1014.* — **4.** *stick, pole;*

The symbol on the left is an Akan **adinkra** symbol called **hwehwemudua**. The term **dua** means 'stick or rod', while **mu** means 'within'. As shown, **hwe** (**hwehwe**) means to 'look, examine intensively'. **Hwehwemudua** is the *rod* or *stick* used to *look, examine intensively* within. This is a **divining rod**. It is an ancient form of **adebisa**, divination, born of the **hwe** (**hwa**, **fwa**) function of **Tehuti** and **Seshat**. A title of **Tehuti** is thus **Hwefo** in Akan – 'inspector, surveyor' and 'diviner' in the ritual context. The image next to hwehwemudua is from the ancient rock art of **Tassili N Ajjer** in North Afuraka/Afuraitkait (Africa). This rock art, west of the **Hapi** (Nile) river, is **12,000 years old**. The next image is that of a man in **Kamit** with the **mer** stick used as a hoe, tilling the soil. The term '**mer**' also means 'water' and is a title of the **Hapi** river when it **inundates** (swells) and floods (buries) the land. The **mer** instrument was not only used to till, but also to locate water. It is a **divinatory instrument**. In the same fashion the **bow** used by hunters, as in the Tassili art, is also a **divinatory instrument**. All hunters, **obofo** in Akan, must learn rudimentary forms of divination. This is part of the ritual connected to **divining the spirits** of the forest and the land. The same is true of **akuafo** or farmers. The form of divination expressed by **hwehwemudua**, the divining rod, is popularly called **dowsing.** It replicates the divining **Habui** bird.

Dowsing continues to be utilized today as a form of divination within **Hoodoo - Akan Ancestral Religion** in North America. The whites and their offspring attempted to mimic this ancient practice millennia later as shown in the image of the european above holding a 'dowsing' stick.

REKHIT HENA SPERET

ETYMOLOGY AND COSMOLOGY OF RELIGION AND SPIRIT

ANCESTRAL RELIGION IS SPIRITUALITY

ODWIRAFO KWESI RA NEHEM PTAH AKHAN

REKHIT HENA SPERET

ETYMOLOGY AND COSMOLOGY OF RELIGION AND SPIRIT

ANCESTRAL RELIGION IS SPIRITUALITY

The notion that one is *'spiritual but not religious'* or *'into spirituality and not religion'* or that *'religion is different from spirituality'* is totally inaccurate and born of ignorance of the etymological and cosmological roots and origins of the terms. The terms **religion** and **spirit** come directly from the Ancestral language of Afurakani/Afuraitkaitnit (African~Black) people as documented in ancient **Khanit** and **Kamit** (Nubia and Egypt), our civilization founded over 40,000 years ago. Our cosmology born of our ritual practices as Afurakanu/Afuraitkaitnut (Africans~Black People) interfacing with the Deities and Ancestral Spirits gave birth to the words in our primordial Ancestral language. This includes the origins of the terms religion and spirit. These root terms continue to be spoken in our contemporary Afurakani/Afuraitkainit (African) dialects today wherever we exist in the world. This is the first publication to accurately elucidate the etymology and cosmology of religion and spirit.

Religion and Spirituality are identical. It is pseudo-religion which is incongruent with spirituality.

It was and is a political ploy initiated and perpetuated by the whites and their offspring to separate religion from spirituality and misdefine both terms. This ploy is designed, on one hand, to promote the pseudo-religions with their **fictional characters who never existed in any form nor of any race** inlcuding: christianity and jesus, islam and allah, judaism and yahweh, hinduism and brahmin, buddhism and buddha, etc. The doctrines of these pseudo-religions are designed to enslave the minds of Afurakanu/Afuraitkaitnut (Africans) and by extension support white socio-economic and political control. On the other hand, the whites and their offspring promote alternative pseudo-'spiritualities' to entrap those of our people who have broken away from the established pseudo-'religions'. New-age 'spirituality', 'native'-american 'spirituality', kabbalism, sufism, hermeticism, wicca, gnosticism, various forms of european 'magic', vedanta, taoism, eastern and oriental 'spirituality', extraterrestrialism, drug-addict 'spirituality' and more are variegated expressions of these pseudo-'spiritualities' which serve to enslave the minds of Afurakanu/Afuraitkaitnut (Africans) as well, simply packaged in different yet related rhetoric and symbolism. The result of embracing the pseudo-religions and pseudo-spiritualities for Afurakani/Afuraitkaitnit (African) people is the rejection of our identity, our Ancestral culture, our connection with the **actual** Deities/Divine Spirit-Forces in Creation and the Ancestral Spirits of our direct blood-circles and thus our capacitiy to align with Divine Order – **inclusive of the Divine Mandate to exterminate our enemies**.

None of the 'practices' of the whites and their offspring qualify as religion nor spirituality. The only religion that has ever existed and ever will exist is Afurakani/Afuraitkaitnit (African) Ancestral Religion in its varied expressions in Afuraka/Afuraitkait (Africa) such as: Akan, Yoruba, Fon, Ewe, Fang, Senufo, Khoi Khoi, Twa, Maasai, Gikuyu, Chokwe, Bassa, Lemba, Tuareg, Bakongo, Fula, Xhosa, Bambara, Dogon and more. Afurakani/Afuraitkaitnit (African) Ancestral Religion also includes its varied expressions outside of Afuraka/Afuraitkait (Africa) wherever Afurakani/Afuraitkaitnit (African~Black) people migrated or were forced to migrate around the world including in the western hemisphere inclusive of **Hoodoo** (Akan), **Vodoun** (Fon, Ewe), **Juju** (Yoruba), **Gris Gris** (Bambara), **Wanga** (Ovambo), **Ngengang** (Fang, Bakongo), **Lukumi** (Yoruba), **Candomble** (Yoruba, Fon), **Winti** (Akan) and more. All of these expressions of Ancestral Religion are united as they derive from our Ancestresses and Ancestors and thus our inherited capacity to align with the Great Mother and Great Father, **Amenet** and **Amen** – The Supreme Being through the agency of the **Ntorotu/Ntorou** and **Aakhutu/Aakhu** – the Deities and Ancestral Spirits. This capacity to align with Divine Order is the exclusive domain of Afurakani/Afuraitkaitnit (African~Black) people as we are the only *created* people in Creation and thus the only people who can experience *spirit-possession* and *spirit-communication* – direct interfacing with the Divinities that animate the Created Universe. This is Afurakani/Afuraitkaitnit (African) Ancestral Spirituality.

The return to Afurakani/Afuraitkaitnit (African) Ancestral Religion is the reembracing of our Ancestral Spirituality as Afurakani/Afuraitkaitnit (African~Black) people. It is the animation of our Ancestral Culture, our **transcarnationally inherited** way of life, which is defined as the *Divine acceptance (Law/Love) of Order and the Divine rejection (Hate) of disorder.* **Amenet-Amen Sekher, Nyamewaa-Nyame Nhyehyee**, The Supreme Being's Order – Divine Order is our foundation. It is the basis of our development and the root of our **Revolutionary-Resolutionary** capacity to eradicate our enemies, reestablish our civlization and maintain our civilization.

Odwirafo Kwesi Ra Nehem Ptah Akhan
Aakhuamuman Amaruka Atifi Mu
Akwamu Nation in North America
Odwiraman

The term **religion** is directly derived from our Ancestral language of **Khanit** and **Kamit** (Nubia and Egypt). It is descriptive of the ritual means by which we reconnect, realign ourselves in every thought, intention and action with the **sekher**, Order, of **Amenet** and **Amen**, the Great Mother and Great Father Who together comprise the Supreme Being. **Amenet** and **Amen** are called **Nyamewaa** and **Nyame** in Akan, **Mawu** and **Lisa** in Fon and Ewe. Afurakani/Afuraitkaitnit (African) Ancestral Religion is properly defined in essence as the *Ritual incorporation of Divine Law and the Ritual restoration of Divine Balance.* This means that through *ritual* we incorporate those things, objects, deeds and entities we need to incorporate in order to harmonize every thought, intention and action with Divine Order and through *ritual* we reject those things, objects, deeds and entities we need to reject in order or restore balance to our thoughts, intentions and actions and thus realign ourselves with Divine Order.

The ritual incorporation of Divine Law and the ritual restoration of Divine Balance are thus the Expansive and Contractive poles of Ancestral Religion.

Religion animates Ancestral Culture. Afurakani/Afuraitkaitnit (African) Ancestral Culture is properly defined as the *Divine acceptance (Law/Love) of Order and the Divine rejection (Hate) of disorder.* Just as our respiratory and circulatory systems draw in (accept) what is needed and our immune and lymphatic systems repel (reject) what would otherwise be deleterious to our health, so it is with our spirit-bodies as Afurakani/Afuraitkaitnit (African~Black) people. In our book **MMARA NE KYI – Divine Law/Love and Divine Hate**, we define the nature of Divine Order as being comprised of the Expansive and Contractive Poles Law/Love and Hate and governed by the Male and Female Deities of Divine Law (Love) – **Maa** and **Maat** – and the Male and Female Deities of Divine Hate – **Heru Bedehty** and **Sekhmet**.

As we deal with the ritual incorporation of Law/Love and ritual restoration of Balance, the focus is the *ritual* – a *special means* by which we accomplish incorporation and restoration. We seek to align every thought, every intention and every action, every moment of everyday with Divine Order. When we make mistakes and experience imbalance in our lives, we employ ritual processes for the restoration of balance. This is *tied* into – literally – the etymology of the word 'religion' and its root in Khanit and Kamit and our cosmology.

Etymology – Cosmology

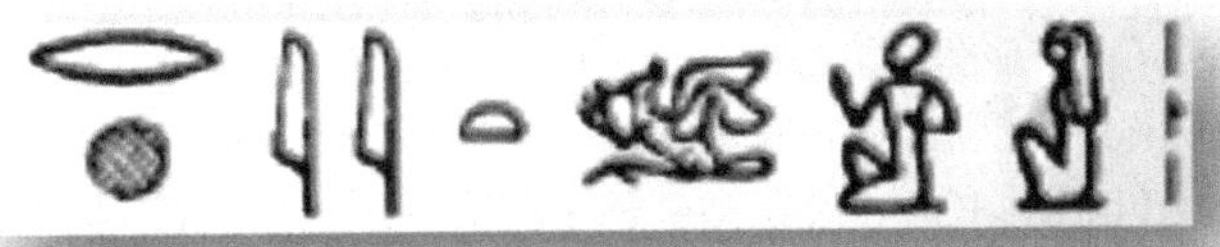

...When the scribe Ani maakheru arrives at the seventh ***arit*** *he says: I have come to you* ***Ausar****, purified of disordered emanations. You encircle the heavens, you see* ***Ra****, you see the* ***Rekhitu****. Unique One, You from the* ***Sektet*** *boat - the boat of* ***Ra****, as He encircles the horizon in the heavens...* [**Ru Nu Pert em Hru** – Book of Coming Forth by Day, Papyrus of Ani]

Rekh, Rekhit

The term **rekhit** in the language of Kamit (Egypt) is multi-layered in meaning. The root **rekh** means *knowledge*. **Rekh** and **Rekhit** are the male and female designations for *one who is wise, knowledgeable, skillful.* The **Ntorot** (**Ntrt**/Goddess) **Auset**, misnomered 'Isis', thus carries the title **Rekhit** meaning the *Divine Wise One* referencing Her wisdom and skill as a Divine Healeress.

There exists a class of Afurakanu/Afuraitkaitnut (Africans) in ancient Kamit who are called the **rekhitu** or **rekhiu** (plural):

rekh, , , , to be wise, to know, to be acquainted with, to be skilled in an art or craft; , B.D. 153A, 29; , to know carnally; , he knew his reins, *i.e.*, understood his nature; , knowingly, wittingly.

rekhit, knowledge, learning.

rekh, science, knowledge.

Rekh, Ṭuat XI, the god of knowledge in the Ṭuat.

Rekhit, B.D.G. 461, , knowledge personified.

Rekhit, Thes. 99, a title of Isis-Sothis.

rekhit, Palermo Stele, , , U. 646, , , , Rec. 27, 225, , Rec. 31, 18; , IV, 1026, , , , , , , , , , , men and women, mankind, rational beings.

The **rekhitu** exist as a group within the Afurakani/Afuraitkaitnit (African) population and retain this status upon transition to the Ancestral-realm after death. Hence, the declaration quoted above from the *Pert em Hru*. The deceased individual comes before **Ausar**, the **Ntoro** (**Ntr**/God) Who is the Sovereign of the Ancestral realm, and notes that by virtue of purification **Ausar** has taken up His position with **Ra** (Creator) in the **Sektet** boat. **Ausar** therefore encircles the heavens in this 'boat' of the **Aten** (Sun). He beholds **Ra** and also the **Rekhit** spirits. The spirit of the deceased individual endeavors to be pure and participate in the same process as **Ausar**. Moreover, in the *Emergence of **Sekhmet***, it is stated that **Ra** is the "*Creator of men and women and sovereign of the **rekhit**.*" [www.odwirafo.com/The_Emergence_of_Sekhmet-Het-Heru-Arit-Ra.pdf]

The **rekhitu** are symbolized by the lapwing bird with hands raised in the act of *ritual provocation*. They are also represented in human form with the wings of the bird or as humans with the head of the bird:

The rekhit as a sacred *Divine* bird denotes the capacity of our spirits to enter, fly, between the physical world and the spirit-realm. The upraised hands not only denote *worship*, but *ritual provocation* of the energy and consciousness of the **Ntorotu/Ntorou** and the **Aakhutu/Aakhu** – the Goddesses/Gods and our Spiritually Cultivated Afurakani/Afuraitkaitnit (African) Ancestresses and Ancestors.

The **rekhit** is a *spirit-medium*. A rekhit provokes the energy and consciousness of the Ntorotu/Ntorou and Aakhutu/Aakhu by entering into communion with Them. Such communion facilitates **spirit-possession** of various forms. The rekhit thus becomes a *human divinatory instrument* utilized by the Ntorotu/Ntorou and Aakhutu/Aakhu for the healing and empowering of the Afurakani/Afuraitkaitnit (African) community. Their capacity to heal not only facilitates realignment of the individual from the disalignment of disease. It also motivates us to re-discover our *own capacity* to heal and empower ourselves and our families through realignment with the Ntorotu/Ntorou and the Aakhutu/Aakhu Who are connected to us by blood. In this manner the community reestablishes its footing within the **sekher** (plan) of **Amenet** and **Amen**, the Great Mother and Great Father Whom Together comprise the Supreme Being.

Yet, the capacity of the rekhit to become a divinatory instrument of healing is solely dependent upon the receptivity of the rekhit to his or her **Ka/Kait** (Soul-Divine Consciousness), the **Ntorotu/Ntorou** connected to him/her and his/her **Aakhutu/Aakhu**.

The rekh, rekhit (rekht) and rekhu, as spirit-mediums, those who become possessed by the Deities and Ancestral Spirits are found in the religious practices of Afurakanu/Afuraitkaitnut (Africans) all over Afuraka/Afuraitkait (Africa) and wherever we have migrated or have been forced to migrate in the world. This includes those Afurakanu/Afuraitkaitnut (Africans) who practice **Hoodoo, Juju, Vodoun, Wanga, Ngengang, Gris Gris** and other expressions of Ancestral Religion in North america.

Linguistically, the letter 'L' and 'R' are interchangeable. This is evidenced in the language of Kamit. In the language of ancient Kamit there is no letter 'L'. The **medut** (hieroglyph) used to translate foreign words which contained the letter 'L' was the symbol for the 'R'. The rolling 'R', enunciated with the tongue tapping the roof of the mouth once is typically symbolized in the **medutu** (hieroglyphs) with the image of the open mouth  . This is the shape that the mouth takes and also the form that the life-force energy contained within the breath takes when the sound is enunciated. The image of the couchant lion is also used as a medut for the 'R' sound: . This usage is predicated upon the fact that the 'R' sound naturally emanates from the lion and lioness when they communicate via the 'ROAR'. Indeed, the term for lion in Kamit is '**Ru**'.

Just as in the language of Kamit, in the Twi language of the Akan, there is no letter 'L'. The rolling 'R' is also used to translate any foreign word which contains an 'L'. Thus when an Akan speaker hears the foreign word 'mulatto' he or she will pronounce it as 'murato-ni'.

Taking the interchangeability of the 'L' and 'R' sounds into account we find the term 'rekh', 'rekhu', 'rekht' in the Yoruba and Akan languages. The Yoruba, Akan and other ethnic groups in West, Central and South Afuraka/Afuraitkait (Africa) are directly descendent of ancient Khanit and Kamit genetically and culturally. This is a blood-circle which spans over 40,000 years.

In the language of the Yoruba of Southwest Nigeria, a term for one who becomes possessed by the Spirits of the **Orisha** and **Egungun**, the Deities and Ancestral Spirits, is **elegun**. This term would be transliterated in the medutu as **eregu** or **erekhu**. The (e)**rekhu** or **elegun** is the spirit-medium – he or she who *gathers, collects, draws in* the Spirits and thus the Divine Wisdom in order to transmit that knowledge to the community during ritual. This is the same term with the same meaning and ritual function over thousands of years unchanged.

In the Twi language of the Akan of Ghana and Ivory Coast, those who *teach, instruct, show,* knowledge and wisdom on a mundane level as well as through ritual are called **okyerefo**. The suffix 'fo' denotes '*people, folks*' in a plurality, thus **okyerefo** means one of the group of *people* (fo) who *teach, instruct, guide* (kyere). The singular form is **okyerefo** or **kyerefo** while the plural form is **akyerefo**. The root term **kyere** (cheh-reh) is an emphatic or enlarged form of **kye** (cheh) which means in its verb form, '*to show, teach, instruct*'. The term can also be reduplicated for emphasis – **kyekye, kyekyere, kyerekyere**.

c) **by infixing r (or n, when the vowel is nasal). E. g. wa, wàre,** ***to be long;*** **kyè, kyere,** ***to last;*** **kõ, koro,** ***one;*** **pà,** ***to take off superficially,*** **prá, pără,** ***to sweep;*** **bá,** ***to come,*** **brá, bărá,** ***to come*** **(i. e.** ***be born) again into this world;*** **bà,** ***to come,***

Note that the root word is *emphasized* or *enlarged* by an 'R' or 'N': kye, kyere; ko, koro; pa, para; ba, bara.

kye, ***v.*** **1. Ak. = kyew. — 2. F. (khe) = kyekye, kyere, kyekyere.**

kyẹkyẹ́, ***red. v.*** **[*cf.* kyere, kyekyere] 1.** ***to bind, tie (up), bind together. pr.***

ɔ-kyerɛ́, the act of ***teaching; doctrine, rule, precept, instruction.***

ɔ-kyerɛ́fó, ***pl.*** **a-,** ***teacher, instructor;*** **s. ɔkyerɛkyerɛfo.**

kyerɛ́, *v.* [*red.* kyerɛkyerɛ, *q. v.*] **1.** *to show forth, produce, exhibit, present to view* (often preceded by de, fa, yi, with the object that is shown): fa mfonini yi kyerɛ no, *show him these pictures!* mede maky. no (*or*, maky. no mf.); - fa wo hõ *or* yi wo hõ kyerɛ, *show yourself! pr. 51;* ɔkyerɛ ne hõ (dodo), *he is ostentatious, boastful, vaunting. pr. 382. 1318.* - yi .. kyerɛ, *to manifest, reveal, make known. John 1,31. 2,11; to profess, pretend, cf.* 9. - mekyerɛ-wo nsã, *your health!* Answer: ɛ́ŋkɔ wo yiye, *may it do you good.* — **2.** *to show, point out* (*to*)*; to guide* or *lead to;* kyerɛ no kwaŋ, *show him the way!* kyerɛ no ɔdaŋ a ɔbɛdam', *lead him to the room where he is to sleep! pr. 1617. 1653.* — **3.** kyerɛ ase, *to show the reason, meaning, sense,* i.e. *to explain, interpret. pr. 1950. 1908; to upbraid* or *abuse somebody by reminding him of his ancestors;* kyerɛ ano, *to state* or *declare the amount, number, weight &c.,* F. *to declare.* — **4.** *to teach, instruct in:* mekyerɛɛ no ŋhoma-kaŋ, *I taught him to read* (*cf. red.*)*;* kyerɛ .. ade, *to teach, instruct; cf.* kyerɛkyerɛ. — **5.** *to advise,*

The relationship between *binding* and *tying together* and *instruction* as definitions of **kye, kyere** and **kyekye** is rooted in the capacity for the one who has insight, perception to investigate or ***examine*** data and *gather an understanding, meaning, value* from various aspects or pieces of data. He or she can *pull it all together* and paint the proper picture. He or she *binds* (kye) together information in order to *show, teach, instruct* (kye/kyere).

The related noun form is **adekyere** or **adekye** meaning *'instruction, teaching'*. The general term **ade** (**de**) in its noun form means *thing, object, deed, entity*. The term adekyere or adekye thus references *that which is kyere (taught), i.e. – instruction, teaching.* This term **adekye** is rooted cosmologically in the related term **adekyee** meaning *daybreak:*

ade-kyerɛ́, *inf. instruction, teaching.*

adekyɛ̃ɛ́ [*cf.* ade kyẽ] **1.** *day-break, morning* (*cf.* anɔpa). *pr. 524. 1664.* — **2.** *the next* or *following day. pr. 272.* — **3.** *day-light* (*cf.* awia), *the whole day* including morning, noon, afternoon, and evening (anɔpa, owigyinae, betwabere a.s. mfaretubere, aŋwummere). *Mt. 20,6.*

adekyɛ̃ɛ-hémã, *the first ray or streak of light on the horizon in the morning sky; morning-twilight, dawn, day-break, day-blush, the purple glory of the morning.*

kyè, *v.* **1.** *to become clear, visible; to appear, come to light; to come* or *bring forth, to obtain* or *impart subsistence.* This *v.* is only used in connection with ade: adé kyè, *the day breaks* (lit. *things become visible*). *pr.*

àdé, **Ak.** àdéɛ, **F.** adzé [fr. de, *v.*] *pl.* àdé, nnéɛma (F. nnyemba, ndzemba), nnèwá, nnéwa, **1.** *thing, substance,* espec. *an inanimate object; any object* of the senses or of thought. *pr. 783—88...* (*cf.* asɛm, *any object of speech, transaction, occurrence, affair, event*); *something,* *s.* bɔ 85. — **7.** *the things visible in daylight* or *performed in the day-time:* ade kyẽ, *things appear, become clear, visible,* i. e. *the day breaks;* ade akyẽ, *it is daylight, morning;* - ade sã, *things*

The related term **kye** meaning *to become clear, visible; to appear, come to light* being the root of **adekye** meaning *daylight, morning* references that which is *shown, visible.* When darkness dissipates in the morning and light shines we are able to *see, know, perceive* and thus *show, guide, instruct.* Things become <u>clear</u>. One who engages in **adekye** or *instruction* is one who has the capacity to *see through the darkness* of ignorance, *bind* together facts harmoniously and *show, teach, instruct* and thus *shed light* on the subject matter - make things *clear.*

Ritually, the first appearance of light piercing the darkness is related to the Spirits of the **Abosom** and **Nsamanfo**, Deities and Ancestral Spirits 'coming down' during spirit-possession to *alight upon*, mount – **possess** the individual. This is why in Akan culture the term **kankye** (**ka** – *speak, utter incanations* **kye** – *to make to come forth*) means to employ ritual incantations to call the Spirits down to possess and communicate. [See: **Kankye - Akan Origin of the term 'Conjure' as Hoodoo** www.odwirafo.com/Kankye_Conjure_Akan.pdf]

One becomes *open* to receive the Spirits during the ritual process and the Spirits thus alight, possess and utilize the body of the individual as a vessel of communication to the community.

The term **de** in its verb form references **<u>possession</u>** and **action**. The 'D' sound is also interchangeable with the rolling 'R' sound as both are enunciated by tapping the tongue on the roof of the mouth. This is why in Akan **ode** in its continuous active function is written and pronounced **re** or **ore.**

dè, *v.* [*red.* dede] **1.** *to hold, have, possess; to own:* onó nà ódе kùró yi, *he is the possessor of this town. pr.* 713. 2134—38; òde ne hó, *he possesses himself*, i.e. *he is free, his own master, not in bondage.* — **2.** *to owe:* òde (me) kàw, *he owes (me) a debt. pr.* 747. 776. — **3.** *to have seized or befallen:* awow de me, *I am cold;* okom (osukom) de no, *he is hungry, (thirsty). Mt.* 25,35. *Rom.* 12,20. — **4.** *to contain, to be:* ne dín dè déŋ? *what is his name?* — *to have the name of, be called:* òde Kofi, *his name is Kofi.* — **5.** *to hold on, keep on, persist in, continue:* óreké no na òde sú, *he went on weeping. 1 Sam.* 1,10. 6,12; òde no

dè is very often used as an *aux. v.* introducing an object to which the action expressed by the principal verb refers, or by means of which it is performed, or of which some other thing is made;

re- is a *prefix* of the progressive and second future forms of the verb, marking action in the *progress of performance*, such action being considered by itself alone, or as joining to a preceding action or state. Gr. § 91,5. 7. 173f. 176f. [It seems to have originated in the verb de: óréyè = odè yè, *he holds* (the thing) *does* = *he is doing* or *he proceeds to do; cf.* (n)nye

r is the rolled or trilled Scottish *r*. It does not begin any genuine Tshi word or root, but only secondary syllables (pra, frɛ = pāra, fērɛ). In the prefix **re-**, also in **ara** and **nnera**, it was originally *d*. Before nasal vowels r interchanges with n; e. g. trã, tẽnã. In foreign words r is used instead of l.

In the medutu of Kamit, the symbol is transliterated as 'kh'. This combination can be pronounced like the 'ch' in *check*, the 'ch' in *chagrin* or the 'ch' in *chronology*. Indeed the 'ch' in english is derived directly from this medut. In the Akan orthography, these sounds are written with the '**ky**' combination. Thus **adekye** is pronounced: ah-deh'-cheh or ah-reh'-cheh. [Note in the **Asante Akan** dialect the 'ky' is pronounced like the 'ch' in 'chronology'. Note also below the variation in the **Fante Akan** dialect (F.) with the spelling **khe**.]

ky occurs before palatal vowels, and both constituent letters are sounded; y, however, weaker before ẹ, ẽ, i, ĩ. In Akem the pronunciation of ky slightly approaches to that of 'ch' in church, whereas in Fante it is nearly like ch. In Asante the y is sounded less distinctly, especially before r; e. g. kĕrɛ = kyerɛ.

kye, *v.* **1.** Ak. = kyew. — **2.** F. (khe) = kyekye, kyere, kyekyere.

The Akan term **adekye** [ah-reh'-cheh] is transliterated in the medutu as **rekh, rekhit** or **rekht** (rech, re-cheh). The term **rekh** meaning *knowledge,* **rekhit** meaning *that which is known, wisdom*, etc. is defined in the Akan language by the same term. When we look at the medut of the open mouth for the 'R' sound, we are looking at a symbol referencing 'opening', 'expansion' . The shape can also be found for the open 'eye' in the medutu .

The open mouth and open eye denote an opening, expansion, which leads to revelation – of sound and sight. Sound being released is a form of communication/revelation. Sight or illumination, perception is a form of communication/revelation which is received and transmitted.

In the cosmology of Kamit it is shown that **Amenet** and **Amen**, in the form of the *Great Goose* and *Great Gander*, 'cackled' sending forth sound vibrations that birthed the Black Substance of Space, caused it to vibrate and eventually bring forth the explosion of Fire and Light out of the Blackness which was the manifestation of **Ra** and **Rait** the Creator and Creatress.

Sacred Goose and Gander, Animal Totems of ***Amenet*** *and* ***Amen***

59, 3, the goose-goddess who laid the sun-egg.

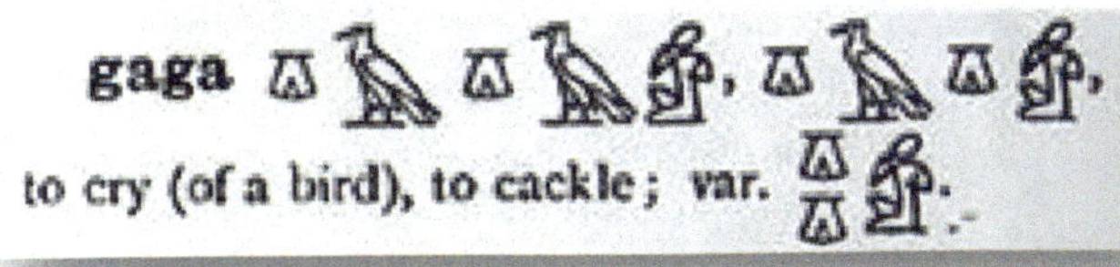

gaga , , to cry (of a bird), to cackle; var. .

From our publication **ANIDAHO**:

"…**Nga** (in-gah') means *'to cackle'* or *'to quack'*. It is also a title meaning *'cackler'*. **Nga** or **Ngga Wr** means the *'Great Cackler'*.

In the cosmology of **Kamit** at **Ta Apet** ('thebes'), it is revealed that the *Great Divine* ***Nganga*** (Cackler, Goose) in the form of the Great **Ntoro** (Ntr/Deity) **Amen** 'cackles' at the beginning of Creation and causes the primordial waters of **Nun** and **Naunet** to begin to vibrate. The primordial waters of **Nun** and **Naunet**, within the Great Black Substance of Space (**Kaka** and **Kauket** or **Ka** and **Kait**) ultimately give birth to **Ra** and **Rait**, the *Creator* and *Creatress* who manifest as Fire and Light piercing through the Blackness and eventually manifesting through the **Aten** (Sun).

What is key here is that the 'cackling', 'quacking' or *production of sound waves/vibrations/power* set in motion *movement/transmission of energy* within **Nun** and **Naunet**, the energic substratum from which **Ra** and **Rait**, the Creator and Creatress and ultimately all *created* entities would emerge…"

From the **Temple of Heb** (Hibis) – Columns 23-24 – **Hymn to Amen**:

*"…Your ancient throne is the highland (**qait/kait**) of Khemenu, it is from the lake of Two Knives that you reach land.*

*It is from the water surface that you appear in the hidden egg, **Amenet** being with you…"*

From the so-called **Leiden Papyrus I 350**, chapter 90 regarding **Amen**:

*"…Light was His coming into existence on the first occasion, with all that exists in stillness for awe of Him. He [**Amen**] **cackled** by voice, as the **Great Cackler**, coming into a land that He created for Himself…*

*He began **speaking** in the midst of silence, opening every eye and causing them to look. He began **crying out** while the world was in stillness, His **yell** circulated while He had none like Him, **so that He might give birth to what is and cause them to live**, and cause every man to know the way to walk. Their hearts live when they see Him…"*

Amenet and **Amen**

Sound as the first manifestation or revelation of existence is the basis of the *open mouth* medut being the first medut in the word for 'knowledge' . The 'kh' or dark circle medut is that upon which the open mouth - *instrument of sound-vibrations once opened and released* - would then act upon. The combination of the 'R' medut and 'KH' medut is the description of the *opening, expansive power, acting upon the dark energy/matter* to *show* forth Creation, to *bind* together the primordial elements, *to make visible, clear, teach, instruct.*

rekh , , , , to be wise, to know, to be acquainted with, to be skilled in an art or craft; ,

We thus have rekhiu, rekhut, rekhitu being described as *those of knowledge, teachers,* those who are *skilled* and also descriptive titles of Deities:

rekhit , knowledge, learning.

rekh , science, knowledge.

rekhu , IV, 972, the known characteristics of a person.

rekhā , Jour. As. 1908, 281, wise, understanding.

rekhiu , , , , , skilled workmen, craftsmen, trained mechanics; , N. 55, knowers of god.

Rekh , Ṭuat XI, the god of knowledge in the Ṭuat.

Rekhit , B.D.G. 461, , knowledge personified.

Rekhit , Thes. 99, a title of Isis-Sothis.

This is why as stated above there are a specific class of Afurakanu/Afuraitkaitnut (Africans) who carry this title on Earth as well as in the **Tuat** – the *Spirit Realm* as Ancestresses and Ancestors after death:

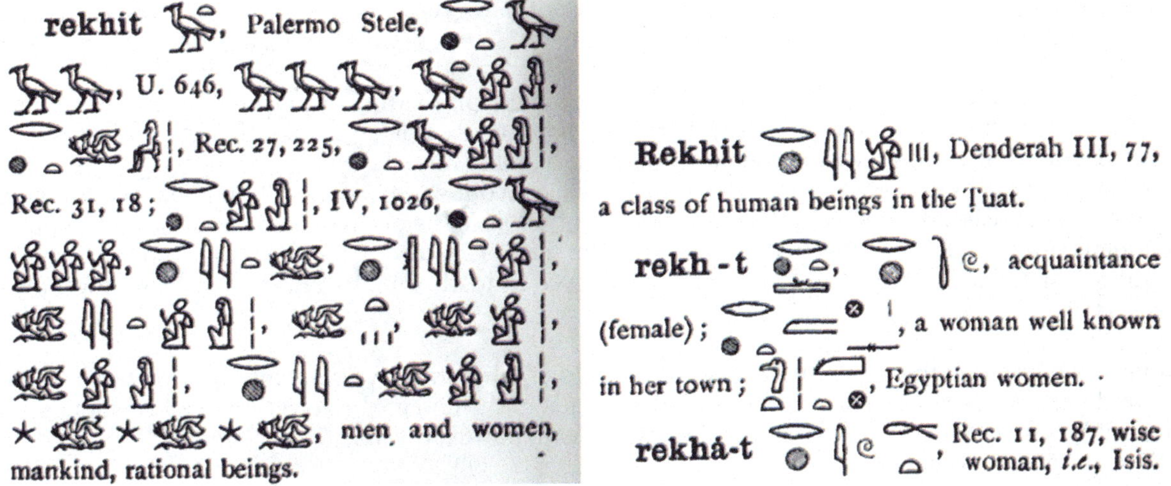

rekhit , Palermo Stele, , , U. 646, , , , Rec. 27, 225, , Rec. 31, 18; , IV, 1026, , , , , , , , men and women, mankind, rational beings.

Rekhit , Denderah III, 77, a class of human beings in the Ṭuat.

rekh-t , , acquaintance (female); , a woman well known in her town; , Egyptian women.

rekhȧ-t Rec. 11, 187, wise woman, *i.e.*, Isis.

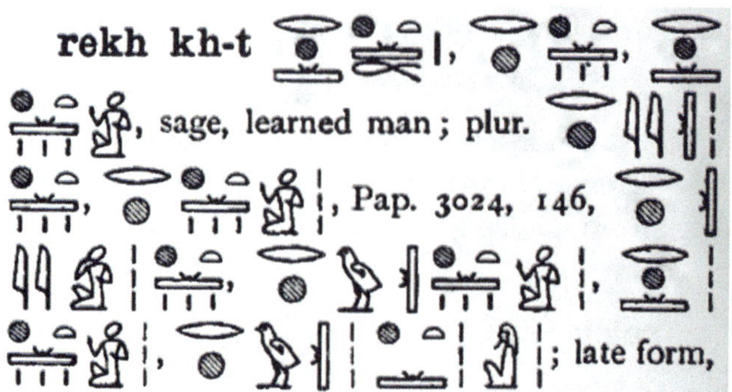
rekh kh-t , , sage, learned man ; plur. , Pap. 3024, 146, ; late form,

rekh-t , , list, catalogue, statement, summary, account, report, contents of a document.

rekhit , a detailed statement, an account.

rekh re , , skilled mouth, *i.e.*, wise in speech.

As shown above it is the capacity for those who are open to receive the Spirits of the Deities and Ancestral Spirits who have the capacity to bind together information, give a detailed statement, account, report. They are skilled in mouth, referencing the capacity for effective ritual invocation of the Deities and Ancestral Spirits so that the Deities and Ancestral Spirits respond and come down to possess and communicate. This is the **cosmological foundation** for Religion being in essence the *ritual incorporation* (binding together) of Divine Law and the *ritual restoration* of Divine Balance.

It is also the **etymological foundation** for the term:

religion (n.)
c. 1200, "state of life bound by monastic vows," also "conduct indicating a belief in a divine power," from Anglo-French *religiun* (11c.), Old French *religion*"piety, devotion; religious community," and directly from Latin *religionem* (nominative *religio*) "respect for what is sacred, reverence for the gods; conscientiousness, sense of right, moral obligation; fear of the gods; divine service, religious observance; a religion, a faith, a mode of worship, cult; sanctity, holiness," in Late Latin "monastic life" (5c.).

According to Cicero derived from *relegere* "go through again" (in reading or in thought), from *re-* "again" (see ***re-***) + *legere* "read" (see ***lecture*** (n.)). However, popular etymology among the later ancients (Servius, Lactantius, Augustine) and the interpretation of many modern writers connects it with*religare* "to bind fast" (see ***rely***), via notion of "place an obligation on," or "bond between humans and gods." In that case, the *re-* would be intensive. Another possible origin is *religiens* "careful," opposite of *negligens*. In English, meaning "particular system of faith" is recorded from c. 1300; sense of "recognition of and allegiance in manner of life (perceived as justly due) to a higher, unseen power or powers" is from 1530s.

To hold, therefore, that there is no difference in matters of religion between forms that are unlike each other, and even contrary to each other, most clearly leads in the end to the rejection of all religion in both theory and practice. And this is the same thing as atheism, however it may differ from it in name. [Pope Leo XIII, *Immortale Dei*, 1885]

lecture (n.)
late 14c., "action of reading, that which is read," from Medieval Latin *lectura* "a reading, lecture," from Latin *lectus*, past participle of *legere* "to read," originally "to gather, collect, pick out, choose" (compare ***election***), from PIE **leg-* (1) "to pick together, gather, collect" (cognates: Greek *legein* "to say, tell, speak, declare," originally, in Homer, "to pick out, select, collect, enumerate;" *lexis* "speech, diction;" *logos* "word, speech, thought, account;" Latin *lignum*"wood, firewood," literally "that which is gathered").

To read is to "pick out words." Meaning "action of reading (a lesson) aloud" is from 1520s. That of "a discourse on a given subject before an audience for purposes of instruction" is from 1530s.

rely (v.)
early 14c., "to gather, assemble" (transitive and intransitive), from Old French *relier* "assemble, put together; fasten, attach, rally, oblige," from Latin*religare* "fasten, bind fast," from *re-*, intensive prefix (see ***re-***), + *ligare* "to bind" (see ***ligament***). Sense of "depend, trust" is from 1570s, perhaps via notion of "rally to, fall back on." Typically used with *on*, perhaps by influence of *lie* (v.2). Related: *Relied*; *relying*.

ligament (n.)
late 14c., from Latin *ligamentum* "band, tie, ligature," from *ligare* "to bind, tie," from PIE **leig-* "to bind" (cognates: Albanian *lith* "I bind," Middle Low German *lik* "band," Middle High German *geleich* "joint, limb"). Related: *Ligamental*; *ligamentary*.

re-
word-forming element meaning "back to the original place; again, anew, once more," also with a sense of "undoing," c. 1200, from Old French and directly from Latin *re-* "again, back, anew, against," "Latin combining form conceivably from Indo-European **wret-*, metathetical variant of **wert-* "to turn" [Watkins]. Often merely intensive, and in many of the older borrowings from French and Latin the precise sense of *re-* is lost in secondary senses or weakened beyond recognition. OED writes that it is "impossible to attempt a complete record of all the forms resulting from its use," and adds that "The number of these is practically infinite ...." The Latin prefix became *red-* before vowels and *h-*, as in ***redact***, ***redeem***, ***redolent***, ***redundant***.

As shown above from www.etymonline.com the whites and their offspring trace the term religion to so-called **Proto-indo-european** roots (**PIE**). The Proto-indo-european language phylum is posited to be the mother language for all indo-european languages. The whites and their offspring place the origins of the Proto-indo-european language phylum between 6000-8000 years ago, most settling on the 6000-6500 years BP (before present) range promoted as the 'Kurgan hypothesis' and supported by recent ancient DNA analysis.

What the whites and their offspring almost invariably do not admit is that the so-called Proto-indo-european language phylum is Afurakani/Afuraitkaitnit (African) at its roots, the so-called **Niger-Congo** language phylum being the foundation.

Afurakanu/Afuraitkaitnut (Africans) migrated into europe tens of thousands of years ago when no other group existed upon Earth. Naturally, we carried our language, culture and religion with us. A minute population who were forcibly separated from the larger group of Afurakanu/Afuraitkaitnut (Africans) were drawn into Northern eurasia thousands of years ago and would eventually become isolated in that region during and until the end of the last ice age. That isolated population would lose their melanin during the last ice-age because of a shift in diet (lack of nutrients), lack of sufficient sunlight, but most importantly intergenerational **in-breeding**.

Inbreeding greatly increases the incidence of albinism and the transference of genetic defects. This population, originally forced out of the larger Afurakani/Afuraitkaitnit (African) population because of criminality would, over generations of isolation and inbreeding, produce descendants with **extra-vitiligo** and **albinoid** characteristics: *white skin, blond hair and light eyes.*

Their spiritual degeneration led to a physical isolation and physiological disfigurement. While isolated they continued to speak their original language. However, because of isolation and lack of attunement to Nature and the Ntorou/Ntorotu (Deities), Spirit-Forces of Creation animating Nature, the dialect began to degenerate. Yet, the root words remained constant. This is why the terms we find in the so-called Proto-indo-european language phylum can all be found in the language of ancient Khanit and Kamit as proven in the medutu.

In the above entry for the etymology of **'re'** we see that the term is defined as *'again, back'* and derived from the PIE root meaning *'to turn'*. Yet, the author states, **"Often merely intensive, and in many of the older borrowings from French and Latin the precise sense of *re-* is lost in secondary senses or weakened beyond recognition. OED writes that it is "impossible to attempt a complete record of all the forms resulting from its use..."**

There is no lost meaning. The whites and their offspring deliberately lie about the origins of PIE words because they know that the origins lead to ancient Afuraka/Afuraitkait (Africa) demonstrating the anteriority and superiority of Afurakani/Afuraitkaitnit (African~Black) civilization. As we can see below, the term **'re'** meaning *back* or *again*, rooted in the definition of *'to turn'* comes directly from **'rer'** in Kamit:

rer (read **pekhar**), to turn round, to go round; , Rev. 12, 66, , Åmen. 22, 13, to answer.

The two legs walking 'back' contained within the spelling of **'rer'** is a literal symbol of *'returning'*, to *'go round'* or to go *'back around'*. Cosmologically this references the foundational cyclical movement of Earth around the **Aten** (Sun). When **Asaase** (Earth) goes around the Aten, it *re-'turns'* to its point of origin making a complete revolution around the Aten. Moreover, the shape of the mouth when open and enunciating the 'rer' sound causes the air and life-force energy within the air to emerge from the mouth in a circular, cylindrical fashion. This is the etymology and cosmology of the term 'rer' perpetuated in english as 're'.

The 're' in the term religion is the prefix. The root is 'ligion'. As we can see above, the whites and their offspring trace this term to 'ligio', 'legere', 'ligare', 'leig' and 'leg'. They are unsure of the connection between 'leig' meaning 'to bind', 'leg' meaning to 'read' rooted in 'to pick, gather, collect'. As we have shown, these definitions are united in our cosmology.

Because there was no letter 'L' in Kamit, the medut to translate the letter 'L' from foreign words is the medut for the 'R'. Thus the root term 'leig' or 'leg' from which 'ligio' and 'religio/religion' is derived is written in Kamit as not 'leg' but reg/rekh:

rekh-t, list, catalogue, statement, summary, account, report, contents of a document.

rekhit, a detailed statement, an account.

rekh, to be wise, to know, to be acquainted with, to be skilled in an art or craft;

A *list, catalogue, statement, summary, account, report* as a definition of **rekh** (**lekh**, leg, leig) references the capacity to *pull together* the contents of the document and *gain meaning* from them. This leads to 'knowledge, to be skilled'. It is a *binding* together of disparate elements in a harmonious fashion to transmit wisdom. One who demonstrates this capacity is knowledgeable, skilled on a mundane level. Moreover, on a spiritual level they have the capacity to *pull together, bind the Spirits* of the Ntorou/Ntorotu (Deities) and Aakhu/Aakhutu (Spiritually Cultivated Ancestresses and Ancestors) *into their bodies* to function as vessels of communication via *spirit possession.* The **Rekhitu** or **Rekhiu** as spirit-mediums can 'pick out, gather, collect, read' the messages from the Spirits. This is **divination**. The term 'ligio' is derived from this cosmological function of 'lekhiu' or 'rekhiu'.

The ritual incorporation of Divine Law and the ritual restoration of Divine Balance is demonstrated through our repetitive daily acts of re-'leg'-ing or re-leig-ing (rer-rekhi) , re-binding, realigning our thoughts, intentions and actions with Divine Order. We are engaging the **rekh** process, gaining knowledge and wisdom through ritual to maintain spiritual balance in our lives.

rekh re, skilled mouth, *i.e.*, wise in speech.

"...Those who are in this image take the towing rope of the boat of ***Ra*** *when He comes forth [****per****] from the serpent* ***Ankh Ntorou*** *and they tow this Great Deity into the sky and lead him along the ways of the upper sky. It is they who make to arise in the sky gentle winds and humid breezes and it is they who order those who live upon Earth to place themselves in the great boat in the sky..."* [**Shat em Duat** – 12th Hour of the Night - Book of What is in the Spirit-Realm]

Per, Pert, Speret

Ra is the name of the Ntoro (Deity/God) who is the Creator of the world. **Rait** is the name of the Ntorot (Deity/Goddess) who is the Creatress of the world. **Ra** and **Rait** are the *Great Spirit* animating the Black Substance of Space, Stars, Planets, Moons, Oceans, Rivers, Earth, Fire – all *created* entities in Creation. The stars including our star the **Aten** (Sun) are utilized as physical transmitters of the Divine Living-Energy of **Ra** and **Rait**. They 'possess' the Aten (Sun) as in spirit-possession and utilize that vessel as a vehicle of transmission. This is one of the reasons why the whites and their offspring misinterpret **Ra** and **Rait** as the 'Sun-God' and 'Sun-Goddess'. Actually **Aten** and **Atenit** are the Sun God and Sun Goddess. **Ra** and **Rait** are called **Nyankopon** and **Nyankonton** in Akan, **Odumare** and **Oshumare** in Yoruba and **Da** and **Aido Hwedo** in Fon and Ewe.

Ra and **Rait** are called the Great **Ba** and **Bait** [bah and bah-eht'], the Divine Living-Energy or *Spirit* animating all *created* entities. The **ba** and **bait** (male and female expressions) are depicted in Kamit as a *bird*, a *bird in front of a bowl of burning incense* or a *bird with the head of the human being it belongs to*:

In the above image the **ba** bird stands before a bowl of burning incense. This is a reference to the **animating** (winged) **fire** (burning energy) which surges through our blood-stream as Divine Living-Energy (life-force energy), a portion of the Divine Living-Energy of **Ra** and **Rait** that surges through and animates all of the *created* Universe [Note: *Cancerous entities are not naturally created. This includes the whites and their offspring.*]

When the Aten (Sun) rises in the east it is a *coming forth*, an *emergence* of the solar orb and the fiery energy of the orb. It is a *rebirth, a return.* It is an explosion of energy, fire and light, akin to the first emergence of **Ra** and **Rait** exploding from the Black Substance of Space at the beginning of Creation. Once the **explosion** of energy manifests, the energy is **radiated** throughout the Black Substance of Space, just as the energy of the morning Aten bursts through the horizon and radiates across the land bringing warmth, illumination and revivification.

The term **per** in the language of ancient Kamit and Khanit means to *'come forth'*. The noun form **pert** means *that which has come forth*:

per , , , , , , Rev., , Jour. As. 1908, 277, to go out, to go forth, to go away, to depart, to leave one's country, to withdraw from a place, to proceed from, to be born, to arise from, to flow out, to empty itself (of a river), to issue, to escape, to march to an attack, to come up or sprout (of plants), to manifest oneself, to appear, to run out, to expire, to perish, to be sacrificed, to pass a limit, to evade a calamity; Copt. πειρε, πιρε (?); , , , coming out and going in.

per-t , , , , , Metternich Stele 55, exit, issue, what comes forth, manifestation, outbreak of fire, offspring; plur. .

per , ,

Three common variations of the spelling of the term shown above are instructive. In the first spelling we have the medut of the bird's eye view of a building with an opening (doorway) above the medut of the open mouth: . The 'P' sound references the explosive energy. When enunciating the 'P' sound the lips are placed together until enough air is generated for the release or explosion or 'pop'. Once the 'explosion' takes place the energy is 'rolled' with the open mouth (circular, cylindrical). 'P' and 'R' are thus *explosion* and *radiation*. This is why the term **per** must mean 'to come forth'. It is a vocal replication of explosion and radiation. The descriptive variation of the term shows the same two medutu with the determinative of the two walking legs: . This recalls the same determinative medut found in the term **'rer'** meaning to *'turn, go round'*. The rising of the Aten is an explosive and radiant event, yet it is also a return, a rebirth. The Aten 'sets' in the west, moves through the 'twelve hours of the night of the underworld' and 'returns' to the east at sunrise. This is akin to the breathing in of air, drawing its oxygen into the lungs and bloodstream and eventually releasing/returning air including carbon dioxide back into the atmosphere. This in *turn* is related to the **Ba/Bait** in the bloodstream as the blood 'rises' from the east (left) ventricle and is sent (radiated) into the circulatory system. This oxygenated blood fires the cells of the organs and systems. The 'used' blood subsequently 'sets' (returns) in the west (right) atrium of the heart, is sent to the lungs for oxygenation (purification) and then sent into the left atrium and ventricle to be reborn and circulated throughout the body once again. This is the rising and setting of the Divine Living-Energy of **Ra** and **Rait** – The **Ba** and **Bait** or *Great Spirit* – within the body. Every inhalation and exhalation, every complete circuit of the blood, is a return or rebirth .

Note in the Akan language we have the same term vocalized as **pere** meaning *to walk around*:

pѐre, *v.* [*red.* pepere] **1.** = peré **1.** — **2.** ne hõ p. no (= haw no), *he is impatient, passionate* (nea ɔrehwehwɛ no, ontumi ntwɛŋ gyé sɛ ne nsa akã ansã). — **3.** p. hõ, *to be anxious, impatient* or *eager for, to be unquiet, fidgety about. pr. 559; to desire ardently;* mpere hõ mmu ntɛŋ, *do it without prejudice. 1 Tim. 5,21; syn.* bɔ hõ mmɔdeŋ; ɔ̀pere (*or* ɔperé) asɛm no hõ, *he is anxious to know about the matter* (*cf.* peré 3). — **4.** (p. kwaŋ,) *to go, walk* or *travel along. pr. 2679;* yéhyiaa no na ɔresũ pere kwaŋ no ba, *he was walking along the road weeping when we met him;* ɛhá dé, wonsũ mpérѐ mãŋ! *here*

per *v. F. to strive, struggle, press upon. Mt. 12,19.*

pĕré, *v.* [*red.* perépѐre] **1.** *to struggle; to make efforts with a twisting,* or *with contortions, of the body* (*pr. 559*); *to strive, contend, use great efforts. Lk. 13,24; to labour in pain* or *anguish, to be in agony;* wuyi anomaa na ɔyɛ kitikitikiti pùtupùtuputu a, wuse: ɔperé *or* ɔ̀pѐre (*pl.* wopepéré); ɔperé *or* ɔ̀pere, ɔ̀peree, *he is in the agonies* (or *struggle*) *of death;* pere katirikatiri, *to pant. Ps. 38,11.* — **2.** *to strive* or *contend for. pr. 3667. Gen. 26,21f.* - *to defend, protect, fight* or *plead for;* ɔperé nѐ hõ, nѐ ti, *he defends his own life. pr. 3258;* mepere me ti fi ne sõtɔre hõ, *I defend my head against his blows, I strive to ward off a box on the ear;* ɔpere no = ogye ne ti, *he defends him, fights for him;* ɔp. amã onipa yi, *he pleads for this man;* meperѐѐ no na wɔaŋkum no. — **3.** = pѐre 2. 3. — **4.** *to vibrate, pulsate, beat, throb* = home 3.

In part 4 of the second definition of **pere** above we see that it means *to vibrate, pulsate, beat, throb.* The next reference is to the Akan term **'home'**. We thus look to the synonym **'home'** in Akan. We see that in part 3 of the definition **'home'** means *to vibrate, pulsate, beat or throb, as the arteries and the heart.* **Home** is term for 'breath', yet breath is a *coming forth* of air carrying the pulsating, vibratory energy of the ba/bait within the blood.

homé, *v.* **1.** *to breathe. pr. 2771;* wawu, ɔŋhome bio, *he is dead, has ceased to breathe;* ontumi ŋhome nsi so, *he cannot breathe well, breathes with difficulty.* — **2.** *to rest, repose;* mabĕrɛ, mekɔhómé kakra; oŵigyinae mehomee wɔ Aburi; sɛ woforo bepow yi ŵie a, wóbɛhóme. — **3.** *to vibrate, pulsate, beat* or *throb,* as the arteries and the heart; ntiní home, *s.* ntini.

The variation of **per** including the medut of the *horned viper* coming forth from the enclosed space: is a variation on the theme of *rising out of* or *emerging* from the darkness. The horned viper medut when used alone is the medut for the '**F**' sound. Indeed, the english letter **F** is derived directly from the horned viper's form in a perpendicular position: **f**

[*It must be noted that the whites and their offspring never created an alphabet.* ***<u>All</u>*** *of the characters making up the english alphabet (as well as the so-called 'hebrew', syriac, proto-sinaitic, sanskrit, latin, greek, etc.) have their origins in the medutu of Kamit and Khanit. The same is true of the numeral system 0-9 misnomered 'hindi-arabic numerals'.*]

The 'f' sound is similar to the sound that a serpent makes when 'hissing', moving or spitting venom. The symbol also references the 'snake' moving, undulating in the 'enclosure' *when the sound is made.* This is the **tongue** (snake) inside the midst of the **mouth** (enclosure) when the 'f' sound is actually pronounced .

However, in the term **per** the 'f' medut is used as a *determinative* and not pronounced. It is referencing the serpent power of **Ra** and **Rait**, the electromagnetic, wavy, undulating, serpentine life-force energy of the Great Spirit (**Ba/Bait**) and miniature **ba/bait** within the body of the Afurakani/Afuraitkaitnit (African) human being.

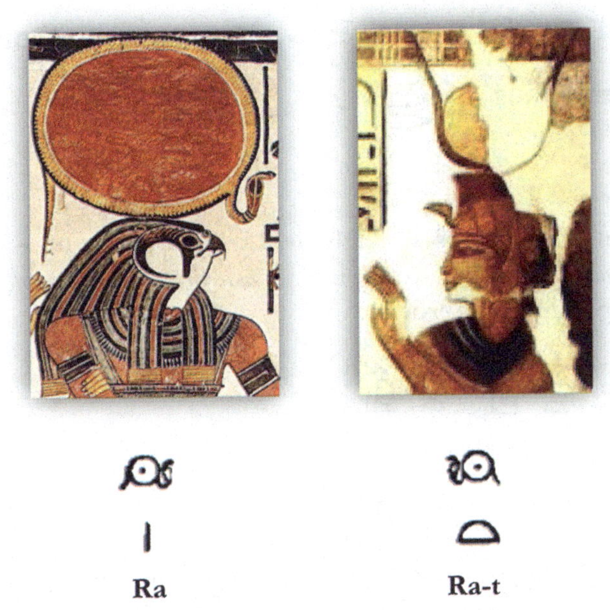

The serpent encircling the Aten (Sun) – symbols of **Ra** and **Rait**

Just as the heat in your body is connected to the solar heat outside, so is the ba/bait within your physical and spirit-bodies connected to the Divine Source **Ba/Bait** of **Ra** and **Rait**. The explosive and radiant release of that energy is effected through the pronunciation of the 'P' and 'R' sounds making up the word **per** – literally.

In the language of Kamit the two different medutu for the 'S' sound and are utilized as **causatives**. They *cause something* to take place. Thus **per** means *'to come forth'*, while the term **s-per** means to *make/cause* (**s**) something *to come forth* (**per**).

per, Rev., Jour. As. 1908, 277, to go out, to go forth, to go away, to depart, to leave one's country, to withdraw from a place, to proceed from, to be born, to arise from, to flow out, to empty itself (of a river), to issue, to escape, to march to an attack, to come up or sprout (of plants), to manifest oneself, to appear, to run out, to expire, to perish, to be sacrificed, to pass a limit, to evade a calamity; Copt. πειρε, πιρε (?); , coming out and going in.

s-perr, Rec. 34, 177, IV, 968, Thes. 1480, to make to come forth, to act with strength; caus. of ; Copt. πρ̄ρε.

s-per[r], to make to come forth; caus. of .

What is being made to come forth? **It is the Divine Living-Energy of Ra and Rait**. Through ritual provocation we invoke the Deities and Ancestral Spirits to *come forth, possess, communicate, heal, guide, instruct*. This is why **sper** also means *entreaty, supplication; prayers*:

sper-t, IV, 970, , prayer, petition, request.

speru, Hh. 439, IV, 971, petitions, prayers.

sper, to ask, to pray, to entreat.

It is through the ritual practice that we invoke and evoke the Deities and Ancestral Spirits. The provocatory power of prayer stimulates the ba/bait within other Afurakani/Afuraitkaitnit (African) human beings, within the Spirit-bodies of the Deities and Ancestral Spirits and the Great **Ba** and **Bait**, the Great Spirit **Ra** and **Rait**, the Creator and Creatress themselves. [Note that **Ra** and **Rait** as Creator and Creatress are *servants* of and *functionaries* of **Amenet** and **Amen** the Supreme Being.]

The 'B' sound in ba/bait is similar to the 'P' sound. This is why these sounds are often interchangeable. However, the 'B' sound is an expression of emergent energy while the 'P' sound is an expression of explosive energy. The 'P' sound is more forceful than the 'B' sound. The term 'ba' combines the emergent energy of the 'B' sound in connection with the expansive energy of the 'A' (ah) sound. This emergent energy of ba/bait is akin to a child being born out of the womb. In fact the term for child is **oba** in Akan. There is a distinction between *emergent* energy and *explosive* energy. Similarly, there is a distinction between a flame burning incense and expanding in comparison to an explosion of fire such as a lightning strike causing something to be burned.

The explosive energy of **per**, *to come forth* and its noun form **pert** *that which has come forth* is connected to the energy of the Great Ba/Bait, **Ra** and **Rait**, animating the Aten (Sun). We thus find that the term **per** has related meanings referencing the *rising of the Aten, to splendor, shine; the coming forth of a heavenly body or Deity; that which has come forth (produce, grains)* in connection with the revivifying energy of **Ra** and **Rait** animating the Aten:

per = , to rise (of the sun).

per , , splendour, to shine; Copt. ⲡⲉⲓⲣⲉ ⲉⲃⲟⲗ.

per-t , , the appearance of a heavenly body, or of the figure of a god or goddess, which was usually celebrated by a festival.

per-t āa-t , , , , the "great appearance," or the great festival; a ceremony in the miracle play of Osiris; , the great day of grief, *i.e.*, the day of the death of Osiris.

per-t = , appearance, festival.

per-t , , , , , Thes. 1203, , , Peasant 294, grain, corn, wheat, field produce, fruit of any kind; Copt. ϥⲣⲉ, ⲃⲣⲏϫⲉ, ⲉⲃⲣⲏϫⲉ, Heb. פְּרִי.

per-t , grains of any substance, *e.g.*, , grains of myrrh; , grains of cassia.

This is the cosmological foundation of **per**, *to come forth* and also **sper**, *to cause to come forth*, being tied to **sper**, *to pray – evoke and invoke the Deities and Ancestral Spirits.* This is also the cosmological and etymological foundation of the term **spirit**.

spirit (n.)
mid-13c., "animating or vital principle in man and animals," from Anglo-French *spirit*, Old French *espirit* "spirit, soul" (12c., Modern French *esprit*) and directly from Latin *spiritus* "a breathing (respiration, and of the wind), breath; breath of a god," hence "inspiration; breath of life," hence "life;" also "disposition, character; high spirit, vigor, courage; pride, arrogance," related to *spirare* "to breathe," perhaps from PIE **(s)peis-* "to blow" (cognates: Old Church Slavonic *pisto* "to play on the flute"). But de Vaan says "Possibly an onomatopoeic formation imitating the sound of breathing. There are no direct cognates."

Meaning "supernatural immaterial creature; angel, demon; an apparition, invisible corporeal being of an airy nature" is attested from mid-14c.; from late 14c. as "a ghost" (see **ghost** (n.)). From c. 1500 as "a nature, character"; sense of "essential principle of something" (in a non-theological context, as in *Spirit of St. Louis*) is attested from 1680s, common after 1800; *Spirit of '76* in reference to the qualities that sparked and sustained the American Revolution is attested by 1797 in William Cobbett's "Porcupine's Gazette and Daily Advertiser."

From late 14c. in alchemy as "volatile substance; distillate;" from c. 1500 as "substance capable of uniting the fixed and the volatile elements of the philosopher's stone." Hence *spirits* "volatile substance;" sense narrowed to "strong alcoholic liquor" by 1670s. This also is the sense in *spirit level* (1768). Also from mid-14c. as "character, disposition; way of thinking and feeling, state of mind; source of a human desire;" in Middle English *freedom of spirit*meant "freedom of choice." From late 14c. as "divine substance, divine mind, God;" also "Christ" or His divine nature; "the Holy Ghost; divine power;" also, "extension of divine power to man; inspiration, a charismatic state; charismatic power, especially of prophecy." Also "essential nature, essential quality." From 1580s in metaphoric sense "animation, vitality."

According to Barnhart and OED, originally in English mainly from passages in Vulgate, where the Latin word translates Greek *pneuma* and Hebrew *ruah*. Distinction between "soul" and "spirit" (as "seat of emotions") became current in Christian terminology (such as Greek *psykhe* vs. *pneuma*, Latin *anima* vs.*spiritus*) but "is without significance for earlier periods" [Buck]. Latin *spiritus*, usually in classical Latin "breath," replaces *animus* in the sense "spirit" in the imperial period and appears in Christian writings as the usual equivalent of Greek *pneuma*. *Spirit-rapping* is from 1852.

spire (n.)
Old English *spir* "a sprout, shoot, spike, blade, tapering stalk of grass," from Proto-Germanic **spiraz* (cognates: Old Norse *spira* "a stalk, slender tree," Dutch *spier* "shoot, blade of grass," Middle Low German *spir* "a small point or top"), from PIE **spei-* "sharp point" (see **spike** (n.1)). Meaning "tapering top of a tower or steeple" first recorded 1590s (a sense attested in Middle Low German since late 14c. and also found in the Scandinavian cognates).

spike (n.1)
"large nail," mid-14c., perhaps from or related to a Scandinavian word, such as Old Norse *spik* "splinter," Middle Swedish *spijk* "nail," from Proto-Germanic**spikaz* (cognates: Middle Dutch *spicher*, Dutch *spijker* "nail," Old English *spicing* "large nail," Old English *spaca*, Old High German *speihha* "spoke"), from PIE root **spei-* "sharp point" (cognates: Latin *spica* "ear of corn," *spina* "thorn, prickle, backbone," and perhaps *pinna* "pin" (see **pin** (n.)); Greek*spilas* "rock, cliff;" Lettish *spile* "wooden fork;" Lithuanian *speigliai* "thorns," *spitna* "tongue of a buckle," Old English *spitu* "spit").

The English word also might be influenced by and partly a borrowing of Latin *spica* (see **spike** (n.2)), from the same root. Slang meaning "needle" is from 1923. Meaning "pointed stud in athletic shoes" is from 1832. Electrical sense of "pulse of short duration" is from 1935.

As we can see above, the whites and their offspring trace the term **spirit** to the PIE **(s)peis** meaning 'to blow'. The term **peis** (peh'ee) means *'blow'* while **(s)peis** means *'to cause to blow'*. This is directly derived from the 'S' being the causative factor in the language of a Kamit. However, the whites and their offspring are not clear as to the true cognate of the term: "...related to *spirare* "to breathe," perhaps from PIE **(s)peis-* "to blow" (cognates: Old Church Slavonic *pisto* "to play on the flute"). But de Vaan says "Possibly an onomatopoeic formation imitating the sound of breathing. There are no direct cognates..."

In reality the direct cognates can be found in our Ancestral language of Kamit. What *comes forth* from the mouth is not only speech/sound vibrations but also breath. The medut of the open mouth in the term **per** and **sper** reference both functions of speech and breath. Thus, **inspire, expire, aspire,** all relate to that which is *coming forth* from the individual whether it be ideas, emotions, breath, sound or energy. The same is true of the **eyes** which take the similar shape of the open mouth in the medutu. What *comes forth* and *goes forth into* the eyes affects the emotions and thus emotional/energic output of the person:

per , to see, sight, vision, aspect, appearance; see .

pera , to see.

The term **per** is thus the root of the english term *'peer'* as in to 'peer into/look into something'.

The energy of **per** moving through the open mouth medut signifies a circular, cylindrical, *turning* energy. Thus the meaning of **per** and **sper** meaning *to go out, come in, come around* and *to cause to go out, go forth, come in, come around* with the determinative medut of the walking legs. We thus have the cosmological connection to the etymology which the whites and their offspring are unable to detect:

Pokorny Etymon: 2. peis-, speis- 'to blow, **fizz**' **Semantic Field**: to Blow

Indo-European Reflexes:

Family/Language	Reflex(es)	PoS/Gram.	Gloss	Source(s)
English				
Old English:	*fīstan	vb	to fist	OED
	fisting	n	fist	IEW
Middle English:	fiesten	vb	to fist	OED
	spirit	n	spirit	W7
English:	fist	n.obs	fart, stink, foul smell	OED
	fist	vb.obs	to fart, break wind	OED
	fizz	vb	to hiss, whiz, sputter, effervesce	W7
	fizzle	vb	to fizz; fail/end feebly	AHD/W7
	spirit	n	vital/animating life principle	W7
W-Germanic				
Middle Dutch:	veest	n	fist	OED
Dutch:	veest	n	fist	IEW
	veesten/vijsten	vb	to fist	OED
	vijst	n	fist	OED
Middle High German:	vīsen/visten	vb	to fist	IEW
	vist	n	fist	IEW

German:	fispern/fispeln	vb	to fizz	IEW
N-Germanic				
Old Norse:	fīsa	vb	to fist	W7/IEW
Norwegian:	fisa	vb	to fist, blow	IEW
Danish:	fise	vb	to fist	OED
Italic				
Latin:	spīritus	n.masc	breath, soul, spirit	IEW
	spīro, spīrare	vb	to blow, breathe	IEW
Old French:	spirit	n	spirit	W7
Slavic				
Old Church Slavonic:	piskati	vb	to hiss, wheeze, whistle	IEW

Pokorny Etymon: 3. sper- 'to turn, wind' **Semantic Fields**: to Turn; to Wind, Wrap

Indo-European Reflexes:

Family/Language	Reflex(es)	PoS/Gram.	Gloss	Source(s)
English				
English:	esparto	n	Spanish/Algerian grass	AHD/W7
	sparteine	n	liquid alkaloid extracted from common broom	AHD/W7
	spiral	n	winding/helical curve	W7
	spire	n	spiral	AHD/W7
W-Germanic				
German:	Spirale	n.fem	spiral	LRC
Italic				
Latin:	spartum	n.neut	reed, broom, esparto	W7
	spira	n.fem	coil, spiral	W7
Medieval Latin:	spiralis	n	spiral	W7
Spanish:	esparto	n.masc	reed	W7
Baltic				

Lithuanian:	springti	vb	to choke while swallowing	W7/LD

Hellenic

Greek:	σ π ά ρ τ ο ν	n.neut	rope, cable	LS
	σ π ε ι ˜ ρ α	n.fem	coil, spiral	LRC
Late Greek:	σ π α ρ γ α ˜ ν ό ω	vb	to wrap in swaddling clothes	LRC

http://www.utexas.edu/cola/centers/lrc/ielex/U/P1845.html

As we can see in the above entries the terms **(s)peis** being referenced as the root of **spirare** and **spirit** comes directly from **s-per** meaning *to make to come forth* – not only of breath/air – but of the **Ba/Bait** (Spirit) in the process of ritual invocation (sper). The relationship of the **spire**, **spike** (that which rises up, comes forth; sharp point, tall slender tree) from the PIE 'root' **s(pei)** is directly derived from **per** and **sper** referencing the *grains, produce* that *comes forth from, penetrates, pierces* the soil as a 'spike' or 'spire' to emerge under the light of the Aten (Sun).

The PIE term **sper** meaning to *'turn'* as in *'turn around, spiral'* is directly derived from **sper** meaning *to cause to come forth, come back around* as in the coming forth of the Aten after coming 'back' around from the underworld with the determinative of the walking legs: - *returning*. This is also why **sper** means to *'arrive at a place; to come'* with the medut of the Moon which *goes and comes* from new Moon, crescent, half-Moon, three-quarters, full-Moon and eventually 'back' to new Moon:

sper , P. 400, , N. 1179, , , , , , Ȧmen. 20, 16, , , , , , to arrive at a place, to come.

Sper-t neter-s , Ṭuat XII: (1) a wind-goddess of dawn; (2) one of the 12 goddesses who towed the boat of Ȧf into the eastern sky.

Moreover, we have the name of an Ntorot (Goddess) of dawn, one of the twelve Ntorotu (Goddesses) who tow the boat of **Ra** as He *emerges*, is *born*, *returns*, *comes forth* (per) into the eastern sky at the rising of the Aten:

Spert Ntoro Es is *'She who makes to come forth her Ntoro (Deity)'*, meaning she who participates in making **Ra** – the Great **Ba** in Creation to come forth at dawn on the horizon. Here we have the Divinity of **Spert** (Spirit) in the cosmology of Kamit, connected with the *re-turn* (sper), *rebirth* or *making to come forth* (sper) the Creator, **Ra**. These twelve Deities make *prayers, invocations, entreaties* (sper) to **Ra** for the revivifying energy he along with **Rait** endows upon all *created* entities every day.

The terms **sper** and **Speret** are intricately tied to the functioning of the Divine Living-Energy of **Ra** and **Rait** within Creation and thus within our physical and spirit-bodies as Afurakanu/Afuraitkaitnut (Africans~Black People).

Rekhit Hena Speret – Religion and Spirituality are identical. They have the same cosmological foundation, an expression of our obligation to effect the ritual incorporation of Divine Law and the ritual restoration of Divine Balance in order that we may align every thought, every intention and every action with Divine Order every moment of everyday.

Select Bibliography

Ru Nu Pert em Hru – Book of Coming Forth by Day (Papryus of Ani)
www.archive.org

Shat em Duat – Book of What is in the Underworld
www.archive.org

Origin of the Niger-Congo Speakers, Dr. Clyde Winters
www.webmedcentral.com/article_view/3149

University of Texas at Austin – Linguistic Research Center
www.utexas.edu/cola/centers/lrc/ielex/

Etymology Online
www.etymonline.com

An Hieroglyphic Dictionary, Vols. 1-2 by E.A. Wallis Budge (1920 edition)
www.archive.org

Dictionary of the Asante and Fante Language Called Tshi (Twi) [Akan Language Dictionary] by J.G. Christaller (1881 edition and 1933 edition):
www.archive.org

Note on Tua Ra Being the Origin of the Term 'Torah'
www.odwirafo.com/Tua-Ra_torah.pdf

Note on Khu Ra Being the Origin of the Term 'Quran'
www.odwirafo.com/Khu-Ra_quran.pdf

Emergence of Sekhmet – (From the 'Book of the Cow of Heaven')
www.odwirafo.com/The_Emergence_of_Sekhmet-Het-Heru-Arit-Ra.pdf

KANKYE – Akan Origin of the Term 'Conjure' as Hoodoo
www.odwirafo.com/Kankye_Conjure_Akan.pdf

KAMIT HENA NTORO

THE BLACK NATION AND DIVINITY

Akwamu, Gyaman and the Origin and Meaning of the Name 'Kamit'

NTORO: Origin and Meaning of the Term 'NTR' - Deity as Defined in Ancient Kamit and Akan Culture

ODWIRAFO KWESI RA NEHEM PTAH AKHAN

KAMIT HENA NTORO

THE BLACK NATION AND DIVINITY

The culture and people of ancient **Khanit** and **Kamit** (Nubia and Egypt) are Ancestral to Afurakanu/Afuraitkaitnut (Africans~Black People) all over the continent of Afuraka/Afuraitkait (Africa) and around the world. Archaeological data and genetic data when properly assessed has borne out the direct material and genetic link of contemporary Afurakanu/Afuraitkaitnut (Africans), inclusive of those on the continent and those who migrated or were forced to migrate outside of the continent, to the Ancestral culture and population of Khanit and Kamit which spans over 40,000 years. What is referred to as anthropological data is the third leg of a three-legged stool including archaeological and biological data which allows us to properly identify ourselves through time wherever we have existed in the world. However, anthropolgical data, inclusive of the study language, family organization, cultural and ritual customs and more is only revealing when a firm knowledge of the cosmology is attained. In Afurakani/Afuraitkaitnit (African) Ancestral culture, knowledge of the cosmology is derived from the Ancestral Religion. Afurakani/Afuraitkaitnit (African) Ancestral Religion is informed by the Deities, the Divine Spirit-Forces in Creation, who are directed by the Great Mother and Great Father, the Supreme Being, to engage the process of spirit-possession and spirit-communication.

When through ritual our people become possessed by the Spirits of the Deities, we are able to attune to their functioning in Creation. We are thus availed of the knowledge – through experience – of the harmonious interfacing of variegated interdependent Forces in Creation. We can thus replicate this Divine Order we have attuned to when organizing our families, clans and nation. Afurakanu/Afuraitkaitnut (Africans) have by this process been able to establish **civilization** which is properly defined as a social order rooted in the Divine Order of Creation.

The lived-experience of fusion with the Spirit-Forces of Divine Order allows us to express this Order through the relating of cosmology. Afurakani/Afuraitkaitnit (African) cosmology is thus not an 'attempt to explain reality', it is an exposition and expression of the nature of reality as it truly is governed by the Spirit-Forces of Divine Order which undergird and animate this reality. Our use of language and expression of language through symbol reflecting cosmology is rooted in this direct experience with the Deities themselves.

It is by this means that we are able to properly translate the thoughts and formulations of our Ancestresses and Ancestors. We are animated by the same Deities - **Abosom, Orisha, Vodou, Arusi, Ntorou/Ntorotu** - today that our Ancestresses and Ancestors were animated by in the past at the foundation of our culture. This is the foundation of true anthropology. The archaeological and biological data naturally and organically corroborate the properly structured anthropological analysis rooted in this lived-experience.

In this publication we address the nature of the idenity of our people and our relationship with the Deities as codified in the ancient terms **Kamit** and **Ntoro**. These terms spelled in the **medutu** (hieroglyphs) typically without vowels: **Kmt** and **Ntr** define the 'Black Nation and Divinity'.

We utilize the **Akan** language and culture to elucidate the proper meaning of these terms, their proper vocalizations and their etymological and cosmological foundations rooted in the Ancestral Religion of Afurakani/Afuraitkaitnit (African~Black) people. This publication is the first to fully and properly define these terms.

Our cosmology illuminates the reality that just as there are cancerous cells that develop within the body at any given time seeking to consume and destroy the healthy cells, so do cancerous entities emerge within the body of Afurakani/Afuraitkaitnit (African~Black) humanity, seeking to consume and destroy the healthy cells. The whites and their offspring are the minority cancerous cells who have sought and continue to seek to consume and destroy our people not only physically (enslavement, incarceration, chemical, biological and conventinal warfare), but culturally worldwide and throughout trustory. They continue to work to deliberately misconstrue and misrepresent archaeological, biological (genetic) and anthropological data to dispossess Afurakanu/Afuraitkaitnut (Africans) of our identity inclusive of the culture of Khanit and Kamit. Just as we must initiate our own archaeological and biological studies to correct the record and expand the record, so must we initiate our own authentic anthropological studies rooted in our lived-experience with the Deities and Ancestresses and Ancestors who birthed the culture. This is how we correct and expand the record. We must cease to continue to fall into the pseudo-anthropological traps set by the whites and their offspring which have to date rendered our attempts at authentic analysis handicapped at best.

This work is a turning point which opens the way for Afurakanu/Afuraitkaitnut (Africans) worldwide to restore our Ancestral language, culture and religion - our Ancestral identity - to those foundations which are firm, secure, abiding and timeless.

Odwirafo Kwesi Ra Nehem Ptah Akhan
Aakhuamuman Amaruka Atifi Mu
Akwamu Nation in North America
Odwiraman
www.odwirafo.com

AKWAMU, GYAMAN AND THE ORIGIN AND MEANING OF THE NAME 'KAMIT'

The term **Kamit** also written **Kemet, Kmt** is the ancient name for the Afurakani/Afuraitkaitnit (African) country and civilization which would later be mislabeled **Egypt**. The term Kamit designates the country and the land as the 'Black Country' and 'Black Land'. The term **kam** (km) means 'black' in the ancient language as well as the **Coptic** dialect, the late period dialect of the language which came into popular use approximately 2,000 years ago. As we have shown in our publication **Kam Ur - Kamit Urit: Ausar, Auset and the Enslavement and Restoration of the Afurakani/Afuraitkaitnit (African) in Amenti - The West**, the people of Kamit being designated as **Kamitu** or **Kamau** identifies them as people of the 'Black Country', 'Black Land' but also the **Black People** referencing their **skin color**. In our publication we demonstrate that those who are designated as 'Black' (kam) are dark brown people with black undertones, while those designated as 'Red' (desher) are dark brown people with red undertones. They manifest the energic-complex, temperament and physiological characteristics of the Deities, the Divine Spirit-Forces in Creation, who animate and thus govern the Black Land and Red Land - the Deities **Ausar** and **Set** respectively.

As we examine the term Kamit and its definition 'black' we can gain a proper understanding of the **medutu** (hieroglyphs) which make up the term when we have a proper understanding of the cosmology that birthed the term. The medut of the *burning, flaming piece of charcoal* representing kam (km) as well as the *crocodile's tail* or *paw* representing the term kam (km) is accounted for in the cosmology. Both medutu define the blackness of the soil and the nature of the Deity who animates the black soil. They also define the nature of the country itself and its development, topographically and politically.

The proper understanding of the medutu comprising the name Kamit and its cosmological, physiological and political implications can be found in **Akan** culture today. We can thus confirm the ancient texts in the living culture and language of the Akan, who are directly descendant of ancient **Khanit** (Nubia/Sudan) and Kamit. We have shown the genetic, linguistic and religious ritual identity of the Akan with our Ancestresses and Ancestors of Khanat/Khanit (Nubia) in our publications: **HOODOO PEOPLE: Afurakanu/Afuraitkaitnut (Africans) in North America - Akan Custodians of Hoodoo from Ancient Hoodoo/Udunu Land (Khanit/Nubia)** and **HOODOO MAYN Nhoma - Hoodoo Nation Festival Journal.** In this note, which is part of a larger forthcoming work, we demonstrate that the name Kamit (Kmt) also exists in Akan culture designating **a people** and **a nation**. The name in Akan includes the reference to the **burning charcoal** and all of its cosmological implications.

Kam, B.D. 142, IV, 20, Egypt;
Copt. ⲔⲀⲘⲈ, ⲔⲎⲘⲈ, ⲔⲎⲘⲎ, ⲔⲎⲘⲒ.

Kamit in *medutu*

Temple of **Ra Messu II** in Abu Simbel

Photo by author

The Akan people number over 20,000,000 in West Afuraka/Afuraitkait (Africa). Approximately 45% of the population of Ghana is Akan while approximately 42% of the population of neighboring Cote de 'Ivoire (Ivory Coast) is Akan. As one of the largest ethnic groups on the continent of Afuraka/Afuraitkait (Africa) in general and West Afuraka/Afuraitkait (Africa) in particular, millions of Akan people suffered many losses as a result of the **Mmusuo Kese** (Great Perversity/Enslavement Era). There are millions of Akan people in North, Central, South america, the Caribbean and Europe today, directly descendant of those who were forced into enslavement.

The **Akwamu** are a sub-group of the larger Akan ethnic group. Akan people migrated from ancient **Khanat** (Nubia) to West Afuraka/Afuraitkait (Africa) after the fall of Kamit nearly 2,000 years ago. Our Akan (Khan) Ancestresses and Ancestors then established the empire of Khanat **(Ghana)**. Nearly 1,000 years later, the empire of Ghana was invaded by muslim groups. Because of the deterioration of the 'neighborhood' and because the Akan were against the embrace of the pseudo-religion of islam, Akan people began migrating further south in waves. They would eventually pass through and settle in the regions of today's Ivory Coast and Ghana. During these migrations, the Akwamu settled in **Kong** (Northern Ivory Coast) and would eventually continue through today's Northern, Central and Eastern Ghana. The Akwamu became one of the first and largest Akan empires.

In the late 12400s (1400s), a segment of the Akwamu people separated and established a new nation. These people called themselves the **Gyama** people - **Gyamafo** or **Gyaamanfo** and the nation the **Gyama** Nation - **Gyaman** or **Gyaaman.**

The term **'oman'** or **'man'** in the **Twi** language of the Akan means 'nation, people'. **Akwamuman** is thus the Akwamu Nation. **Asanteman** is the Asante Nation. **Gyama** or **Gyam man (Gyaman, Gyaaman)** is the **Gyam** or **Gyama** Nation. The suffix **'fo'** in the Twi/Akan language denotes a plurality of people similar to the english term 'folks'. **Akwamufo** thus means Akwamu People (Akwamu folks). **Akanfo** means Akan People. **Gyamafo** means Gyama People.

Because of the artificial borders imposed upon the region by the whites and their offspring in the late 12800s (1800s) the traditional territory of the Gyama people was divided between Ghana and Ivory Coast. We thus have Gyama people in Northwest Ghana and Gyama people in Northeast Ivory Coast. Ghanaian Gyaman and Ivorian Gyaman were formerly called British Gyaman and French Gyaman.

The name **Gyama** amongst the two branches is spelled variously: **Gyama, Gyaama, Gyam** (Ghanaian Gyaman) **Kyama, Tchama, Kama, Cama** (Ivorian Gyaman).

In the **Ebrie** Akan dialect (Ivorian Branch of Gyaman), the **Gyama** (Chah-mah or Jah-mah) people are also called the **Kama** (Cah-mah) people. As we will see in this short note, the **Gyama** or **Kama** people are the **Kamat (Kamau)** people. Just as ancient Kamit was born out of ancient Khanat (Khanit/Nubia) in East Afuraka/Afuraitkait (Africa), the same dynamic played out as we migrated from East Afuraka/Afuraitkait (Africa) to West Afuraka/Afuraitkait (Africa). The Gyama/Kama people reemerged from the larger Akan (Khana) parent and reestablished themselves after the migration away from the empire of Ghana.

...

In the **Twi** language of the **Akan** of Ghana and Ivory Coast there are a few grammatical features that are important to take into consideration for this discussion.

The suffix which denotes 'female' or a diminutive has dialectical variants:

obaa
obea
waa
aa

The term for woman is **obaa** in the Asante dialect and **obea** in the Akwamu dialect. It is also a suffix representing the diminutive.

The male and female **Abosom**, Akan term for 'Deities', Who govern the planet 'mars' are called **Bena** and **Abenaa** in Akan culture. **Bena** and **Abenaa** are the Deities **Heru Behdety** and **Sekhmet** in Kamit. All Akan people born on tuesday **(Benada, Abenaada)** are thus given the soul-name **(kradin)** associated with the Deity Who governs the day. A male child born on **Bena**'s day (Benada) is thus a *servant* or *subject* (akoa, kwa) of **Bena**. His soul-name is therefore **Kwabena**. A female born on **Abenaa**'s day is thus a *servant* or *subject* of **Abenaa**. Her soul-name is therefore **Abenaa**. There are variations based on dialect: **Abena, Abenawa, Abenaba, Abenaa**. As we can see the diminutive suffix is variously spoken -wa, -ba, -aa.

The term for 'madame' or 'mistress', a higher societal office than 'brother or sister', is **awuraa** in the **Asante** Akan dialect. However, it is **ewuraba** in the **Fante** Akan dialect. The -aa and -ba suffixes interchange. The -ba suffix can also be pronounced -ma.

From the **Asante-Fante Dictionary** of the Tshi (Twi) Language:

a) *Gender.* Tshi has no grammatical gender; natural sex is indicated: (1) by different words; as ɔbàrimá, *man;* ɔbéa, *woman;* agyá, ɔsé, *father;* ɛnã́, ą̀wó, *mother;* okúnu, *husband;* ɔyére, *wife.* — (2) by adding nouns meaning *man, woman,* or *male, female;* as ɔbá-barimá, *son;* ɔbá-bea, *daughter;* akóko-nini, *cock;* akóko-beré, *hen.* — (3) by adding the diminutive suffix *wa* (orig. ba = ɔbá, *child, young*) to indicate the feminine; when joined to a final a, wa is with the latter usually contracted into aa. In dialects, ba & wa are still in use. E. g. atá, atáwa (Ak.), *male twin;* ataá, *female twin;* owúrà, ow̃irá (Ak.), *master;* awuraá, wuraba (F.), aw̃irawá, -bá (Ak.), *mistress.* Gr. § 41. — On the birth-names Kwadwó, A'dwówa &c., see Dict. p. 599, III. — Concerning the pers. pron. ɔ, o, ɛ, e, *cf.* p. XXV.

We also have the **'ky'** combination and **'gy'** combination in the Twi/Akan language. The **'ky'** is similar to the 'ch' combination in english with is varied pronunciations. The 'ch' can be pronounced as the 'kuh' sound in 'character' or the 'chuh' as in 'check'. The **'gy'** combination can also be pronounced as the 'chuh' sound. The **'gy'** is very often pronounced similar to the 'j' sound in 'jump':

ky occurs before palatal vowels, and both constituent letters are sounded; y, however, weaker before e, ĕ, i, ĭ. In Akem the pronunciation of ky slightly approaches to that of 'ch' in church, whereas in Fante it is nearly like ch. In Asante the y is sounded less distinctly, especially before r; e. g. kĕrɛ = kyerɛ.

gy is softer than ky, and appears before (a), e, ĭ; before ĕ, i, ĭ the y sounds weak. In certain Fante dialects gy is pronounced like English *j*.

The term **'mu'** in Akan means 'interior, within'. When the term mu is used at the end of a phrase or name, the 'u' is typically dropped. Thus the Akwamu are often called Akwam. When one is knocking on a door and they who are in the dwelling say 'bra dan mu' meaning come (bra) house/dwelling (dan) within (mu), the phrase is typically spoken 'bra danmu' or 'bra dam' - the 'u' being dropped.

high tone. When used as a postposition or complement, the vowel u is often dropped, and the remaining m' connected in pronunciation with the noun or pronoun to which it refers, or with the verb. — 5. In some *phrases*

We also have the interchange of the 'm' and 'b' sounds

m is pronounced as in English. When original, it is united with nasal vowels; when followed by pure vowels, it is a transformation of b, caused by a preceding m (or orig. n, ŋ). It interchanges with b, w, n, ŋ. — *M* before *f* is by some persons not formed with both lips, but with the lower lip only; e. g. ahenfó; usual form: abemfó.

khaā [hieroglyphs], IV, 658, [hieroglyphs], [hieroglyphs], Rec. 147, 17, [hieroglyphs], [hieroglyphs], Rec. 21, 92, [hieroglyphs], to leave, to forsake, to cast aside, to reject, to abandon, to cast away, to release, to slip away from, to yield, to throw; [hieroglyphs], rejected, forsaken; Copt. ϫω, κω.

gyàw, *v.* [*red.* **gyigyaw**] **1.** ***to leave, quit, depart from*** **(for a time).** ***Mt. 4,13.*** **— 2.** ***to part from*** **(never to return),** ***to forsake, desert, abandon, relinquish. Mt. 4,20. 22.*** **— 3.** ***to leave*** **(*behind*),** ***let remain. pr. 1261. 2735. 2776. John 4,28. Mt. 22,25.*** **— 4.** ***to leave in*** **or** *commit to the care of, intrust.* **— 5. gyaw mu,** ***to depart this life, expire, give up the ghost; cf.*** **wu; onnyã nnyaw mu ɛ,** ***he has not yet breathed his last;*** **wágyàw mú = wawu. — 6. gyaw biribi (wɔ)..mu,** *to make up what is wanting, to complete.* **— 7.** ***to leave*** **(*out*),** ***omit,*** **translated by** ***without*** **(*pr.* 221),** ***rather than*** **(*Prov. 8,10*). — 8. odidi gyaw ne yere (ne yɔŋkõ &c.) ase,** ***he eats by himself, without his wife*** **(*his friend &c.*). — 9. ógyàw mfẽmfẽm,** ***he grows a moustache; s.*** **ano-da-so. o-gyáw,** ***inf. forsaking, desolation. Isa. 6,12.***

khaȧ [hieroglyphs], [hieroglyphs], to leave, to forsake; Copt. κω, ϫω.

gya, *v.* **Ak.** (*s.* **gyaw**), **1.** ***to leave;*** **gya ho, F.** ***to leave, forsake. Eph. 5,31.*** **— 2.** ***to worship.***

As we can see above, the term in Kamit 'khaa' is written with the medut of the lotus plant [hieroglyph] representing the 'kh' sound. This can be pronounced 'chah' or 'kah' like the 'ch' in 'check' or the 'ch' in 'character'. The second 'a' in the first instance is the forearm with the open palm. [hieroglyph] The vocalization of the word is thus 'chaw'. In the second entry the second 'a' is represented by the 'reed' [hieroglyph]. The vocalization of the word is thus 'chaah'. **We can confirm this in the Akan language**. As you can see above the term 'gyaw' and the variation 'gya' (chaw and chah) mean 'to leave, to forsake, abandon'. **This is the same word and its variation in both languages with the exact same meaning.**

It is important that in the Coptic dialect we see that the 'chuh' sound and 'kuh' sound for the 'kh' is interchangeable: Copt. ϫω, κω. This gives a vocalization of 'Chaw' and 'Kaw'. This same interchangeability is found in Akan as we will see. First we must look at the term for 'fire':

khe-t [hieroglyphs], [hieroglyphs], Rec. 31, 167, [hieroglyphs] Ȧmen. 5, 14, fire, flame, heat, to burn up; [hieroglyphs], [hieroglyphs], burning incense.

Khe-ti [hieroglyphs], [hieroglyphs], [hieroglyphs], Ṭuat VII, VIII, a fire-spitting serpent in the Ṭuat.

o-gyá, 1. *fire. pr. 467. 1245. 1247-53;* ogya sɔ, dɛw, fram, tutu sransran, dum; - *the power of striking fire. pr. 490.* - to (ofi, kūrow...) mu gya, s. to 6. - da gyá *to sleep by the fire. pr. 559;* wɔtɔe ogyam', *they fell* (i.e. *died*) *on the spot. Cf.* nnyabyee. - ne gya abye = n'asɛm abye, *s.* bye. — **2.** *fuel; cf.* nnyansiŋ, nnyentia, nnyina, anyaŋ. *pr. 1246 f.*

As we can see, the term for 'fire' in Kamit is spelled 'kht'. The egyptologist inserted an 'e' arbitrarily to approximate the vocalization. **In Akan, we have the vocalization**. The term 'gya' means 'fire' and is the term 'kht' (khat, kha) in the medutu. Moreover, 'khaa' meaning 'leave, forsake, leave behind' and 'kha' meaning 'fire' are cosmologically related. This is why the terms are identical.

We next show the relationship of 'kha' and 'mu' referencing 'burning, hot':

kham [hieroglyphs], burning hot; Copt. ϧⲉⲙ, ϧⲙⲟⲙ.

gyám'-gyám', *adv.* [gya mu, lit. *in fire,* repeated] *hotly,* i. e. *eagerly, swiftly, rapidly;* wɔakɔkã asem no gy. mã a-tẽrɛw, *s.* abyésém.

khamm [hieroglyphs], Rev. 11, 141, heat, fire, hot, fever; Copt. ϧⲙⲟⲙ.

Here we have the 'fire within' **kham** as demonstrated in the Akan rendering of the term **gyam**. The term 'gyam' is comprised of 'gya' and 'mu' - *within the fire*. The difference between **khaa** and **kham** (fire and burning) in Kamit is the same as the difference between **gya** and **gyam** (fire and fire within). Of course the 'm' also shown to be 'mu' with the medut of the vulture in the language of Kamit means 'in, into' just as 'mu' does in Akan:

m [hieroglyphs], a preposition: in, into, from, on, at, with, out from, among, of, upon, as, like, according to, in the manner of, in the condition or capacity of.

e-mú (u = ū), *the interior.* **1.** *the inner* or *middle part, inside; any part* or *point within the limits of* a line, surface or body. *pr. 148 f.* — **2.** *the inner parts, cf.* anom', asõm', mfẽm', yam' &c.; *the space within* or *inside.* — **3.** *the interior of a country:* emú nohɔ̃ (nohɔ̃a) tɔŋŋ, *far in the interior.* — **4.** As a postposition after nouns & pronouns it stands for the foll. *prepp. & advv.: in, at, into, through, within, inward, inside; between;* of time: *in, at, during, within;* of a plurality of things: *among, amongst;* con-

Recall the linguistic rule in Akan where the final 'u' in 'mu' is dropped when spoken. This is also found in the language of Kamit as can be shown here.

We also have the variations 'khem' and 'gyem':

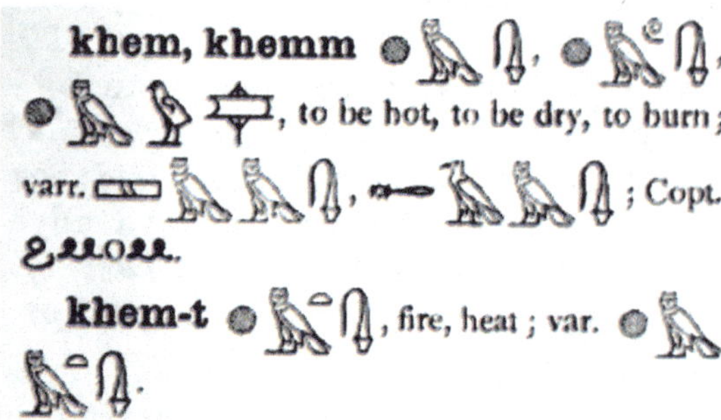

khem, khemm, to be hot, to be dry, to burn; varr. ; Copt. ϩⲙⲟⲙ.

khem-t, fire, heat ; var.

o-gyém' [obs.] = **ogyá mù,** *in or into (the) fire (pr. 2634).* — **o-gyém** [= **ogyá mù,** *in the fire*]: **wáyì no gyém,** *he has killed him;* **osì a woresi hɔ na wɔáyì wo gyém,** *as soon as you step there, you are done for.* **Sɛ wonom aduru yi a, ne nnansã so na ogyém,** *if you take this medicine, you are a dead man in three days.*

We recall that the 'kh' medut can also be pronounced as 'K' as demonstrated in Coptic:

Copt. ϫω, κω.

This applies to the terms 'khamm', 'kham' and 'kam':

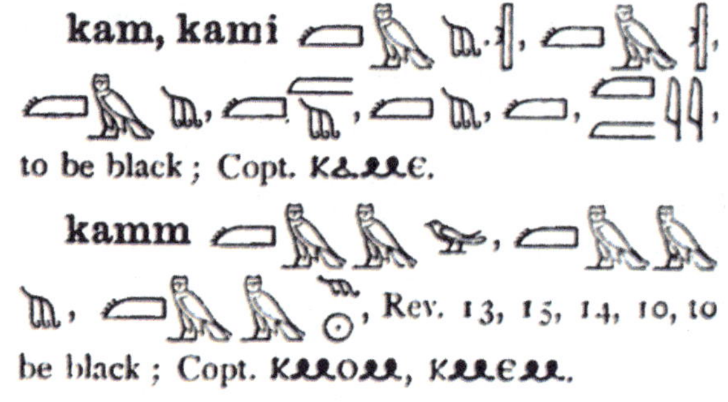

kam, kami, to be black ; Copt. ⲕⲁⲙⲉ.

kamm, Rev. 13, 15, 14, 10, to be black ; Copt. ⲕⲙⲟⲙ, ⲕⲙⲉⲙ.

Note that the term **kamm**, meaning 'to be black' is also written **KMOM, KMEM** in Coptic:

kamm, Rev. 13, 15, 14, 10, to be black ; Copt. ⲕⲙⲟⲙ, ⲕⲙⲉⲙ.

Copt. ⲕⲙⲟⲙ, ⲕⲙⲉⲙ.

Notice that the determinative medut is the symbol of the 'Sun' the circle with the dot in the middle. This is associating the term 'kam' meaning 'to be black' with 'fire', 'solar fire'.

In the same fashion, the variant term **'khamm'** is spelled **KHMOM, KHMEM** in Coptic:

khamm [hieroglyphs], Rev. 11, 141,
heat, fire, hot, fever; Copt. ϧⲙⲟⲙ.

This is key, for the medut of the burning piece of coal demonstrates that the **fire** (kha, gya) is **within** (m, mu). When coal burns, the fire smolders *within* the substance. It **burns** within the substance. In the same fashion, as food is cooking and then burning, the fire is within (khamm, gyam). **The substance thus becomes 'black' or 'blackened' because of the 'burning'**. This is shown in the Akan language, for the term 'gyaa' not only references 'fire' but also **'smithy coal, charcoal', 'coals', 'anthracite'**. The terms 'gyaa', 'gyawa', 'gyama', 'gyabaa', 'gyabea' are all variations of one another. Note the interchange of the 'wa', 'baa', 'bea', 'ma' suffixes and terms as mentioned previously:

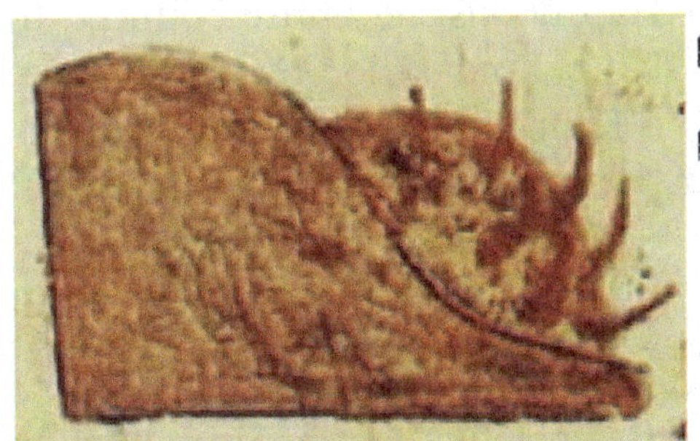

gyaá, *pl.* **n-** [*con.* **né gyàa**] *s.* **gyawa**; **tɔ gyaa** = **tɔ apakye.**
gyaá, *pl.* **n-**, *smithy coal, charcoal*, made of **ɔsĕŋá** wood, formerly also of palm-nuts (**ŋŋw̃eaa**), i. e. the shells with their kernels, of which the natives did not know how to extract the oil. — **gyaa-baa**, *pl.* **n-** [**ogya, abaa,** *stick*] F. *a fire-brand.*

[Burning charcoal from mural in Kamit]

gyawa, *coal(s), anthracite,* **gyabiriw pa.** **gya-biriw** [**gya, biri**] *coal, charcoal.*

gyàbea, Aky. *s.* **gyama.**

Tcham [hieroglyphs], [hieroglyphs]
Rev. 14, 46, 51, Egypt; Copt. ⲭⲏⲙⲉ.

Gyààmáŋ(-fo), (**gyàw wó máŋ**) a *people* in the north-west of the Asante & to the north of the Doma-people; one of the capitals: Dwereme (map = Wimme).

Kam [hieroglyphs], B.D. 142, IV, 20, [hieroglyphs], Egypt; Copt. ⲕⲁⲙⲉ, ⲕⲏⲙⲉ, ⲕⲏⲙⲏ, ⲕⲏⲙⲓ.

Tcham [hieroglyphs], Rev. 14, 46, 51, Egypt; Copt. ϫⲏⲙⲉ.

Note the variation in spelling: **Kam** and **Tcham**. Note also the use of the medut for the **'fire drill'** in the spelling of **Tcham.** [hieroglyph] This is the variation amongst Akan people in Ghana and Ivory Coast: **Kama** and **Gyama (Tchama)**

There is a folk-etymology regarding the origin of the name **Gyama** people (Gyama-fo) as shown in the above entry: **gyaw wo man** meaning 'left, abandoned your nation'. In a negative connotation it references those who forsook their parent nation (Akwamu) and separated. However, gya and gyaw as we saw above means to 'leave behind'. When a plant or mineral is burning, that which is 'left behind' is the black, carbon, burned substance.

In the cosmology of ancient Kamit, when the river **Hap** floods the entire country, the waters begin to recede after a number of months. What is 'left behind' when the water recedes is the 'black soil' deposited on the banks of the river. This is **Kamit**, the black soil, left behind. This is the body of **Kam Ur** (The Great Black One)- **Ausar**, whose body was 'left behind' after being drowned in His water (Shabaka text).

However, the black soil is the rich, fertile soil as opposed to the infertile, red, desert sand of **Set** (Deshert). The black soil is fertile because the fire, energy, of **Ra** and **Rait**, the Creator and Creatress who use the Sun (Aten) as a transmitter of their Divine Energy, is moving within the black soil. It is literally the 'fire within' **gyam, kam, kham**. The fire of **Ra** and **Rait** will resurrect **Ausar** so that He can impregnate **Auset** who will give birth to **Heru**. The green vegetation, life, will emerge from the black soil as **Heru** rises out of the **seshen** (lotus). **Ausar** becomes fertile when He receives the fire of **Ra** and **Rait**. **Ausar** goes from being called **Kam Ur** (Great Black) to **Wadj Ur** (Great Green One). [See Pyramid text of **Teti** for **Kam Ur** and **Wadj Ur** as titles of **Ausar**].

Ausar as **Kam Ur** and **Wadj Ur (Km Wr, Wadj Wr)**

The medut of the burning coal designating the black land is the same coal in Akan designating the **Gyama** nation, **Gyama** people and culture.

Gyām. Gyāmā.

Ōgyám, a nickname for Kwabena.
gyám'-gyám', *adv.* [gya mu, lit. *in fire,* repeated] *hotly,* i. e. *eagerly, swiftly, rapidly;* woakɔkă asem no gy. mã a-tĕrɛw, *s.* ahyésém.

As we have shown in our **Akradinbosom** article series, in the **Bena** and **Abenaa** articles, one of the praise-names **(mmrane)** of those males and females born on Benada, Abenaada (tuesday) is **Gyam** (male) and **Gyamaa** (female). These names designating people born under the energic complexes of the Deities **Bena** and **Abenaa (Heru Behdety** and **Sekhmet)** reveal that these are individuals with the 'fire within'. The planet **Bena/Abenaa** (mars) is the planet of 'war', 'fire' and more. The Deities **Bena** and **Abenaa** are warrior and warrioress Deities who are the Enforcer and Enforceress of Divine Order. They operate as the Divine Immune and Lymphatic Systems within the Great Divine Body of **Amen-Amenet** (Supreme Being) and have similar shrines within our bodies as Afurakanu/Afuraitkaitnut (Africans~Black People).

Fire within coal burns red and upon the complete burning out of the substance 'leaves behind' (kha, gya) the 'burned, blackened' substance. The Gyama people (Kama in Ebrie dialect) are those who separated from and *left behind* the larger group. They are the people who had the 'fire within'. They are black people. The Ebrie Akan people share in their oral traditions that the term 'Ebrie' was given to them by their neighbors the **Aboure** people after a battle. They typically refer to themselves as Akan or **Tchama, Kyama, Kama**. They state that their neighbors used a negative connotation of the name 'ebrie', which is from the root **'biri'** meaning 'black, dark'. In Akan, 'biri' meaning 'black, dark' references 'power'. An **obirifo** means an 'unusually dark' person but also 'unusually powerful'. However, in a negative manner 'dark' can be used to mean 'dirty'. Just as 'soil' is used to mean 'fertile land' which is sacred to us, yet 'soil' can mean 'dirt, dirty', as in 'my clothes are soiled'. The blackness of 'soil' or 'dirt' is not negative. However, the manner in which it is applied can suggest a negative connotation.

bíri, *adj.* in cpds., *black, dark; cf.* adubiri, akokobiri, ɔpɔŋkobiri *&c.*
birii, F. *blackness.*

birí, *v. to grow, be,* or *make black, dark, dirty;* odaŋ yi mu biri, *this room is dark;* aduru no mmiri bebrebe, *the ink is not black enough. pr. 810. 3162 f.;* ne wusiw (w̆isi) biri me, *it is fearful to me, I am afraid of it; cf.* owusiw; wabiri ne tam, *he has soiled his 'clothes';* ntama a abiri, *soiled linen;* ntade nsimma-nsimma no

o-bírifo, obírifò, *pl.* **a-,** *a fellow of unusual power;* also = **sumanni;** *e. g.*

In the same fashion 'biri' meaning the 'dark, black' people is natural and sacred. This is a description of the Gyama (Kama) people in Ivory Coast – those with the 'fire within'. However, their neighbors attempt to use the term in a negative fashion because of their conflicts culturally and militarily.

We must also mention that in Akan, the term 'biri' is the root of **Obibirini**, **Abibirifo** and **Abibiriman**. The term 'obi' means 'someone'. Obi-biri-ni means 'one who is dark, black'. Abibiri-fo means those people 'fo' who are 'dark, black'. Abibiri-man means the nation 'oman' of Black people. In Akan culture, **obibini** means simply 'Black person' as opposed to a 'white person'. **Abibifo** (Abibirifo) means 'Black People'. **Abibiman** means 'Africa – the Black Nation/People'.

Abibi-máŋ, *the Negro - country. pr. 1477.*
o-bibiní, *pl.* **a--fo,** *negro, black man, African. pr. 1796.* — **o-bibiníwa** [dim.] *a negro boy* or *lad.*

Abíbíri(m`), *the Negro-country, Africa;*

One who is 'very black' is called **Obiri**. This is also a title of the **Obosom** (Deity) **Awusi** in Akan meaning *Black One.* **Awusi** is **Awusir (Ausar)** in Akan culture. We also have the term **tuntum** meaning 'black'. It is from the root **'tumm'** meaning 'dark or black'. The term **'tumi'** meaning 'power' is derived from 'tumm' – black, dark. This is the association of blackness with power, inclusive of Divine Power. When one is blacker than the average person, they are called **tuntuuntum** (black-black). While all people are obibirifo (Black People) some are blacker than others.

o-tuntum', *a black person.*

tuntùuntu(m), *very black; s.* **tumm, tuntum;** *t.* **hrãhrãhrâhrãhrà,** *glossy black.*

The key here is that Gyama people in Ivory Coast are called 'biri' or **Ebrie**. The Gyama people are the 'Black' people. They are those with the 'fire within' that makes them 'black, dark, powerful'. The Kama (Kamit) people are the Black people.

Gyaman Nananom (Elders, Royals, Chiefs) in Ivory Coast

Odenkyem da nsuo mu, nanso mframa..'The Crocodile lives in water but breathes air' - *Akan proverb*

The crocodile swims with his nose, eyes and tail above water while the rest of his body is submerged. He lives in the water but breathes air, meaning he knows instinctively that he cannot function, breathe, in the same manner as those who are in his present environment (fish). If he did so, he would drown. **He must come out of the water to breathe** and thus sustain his life by drawing from the air and the energy of the Sun. As the crocodile emerges from the flood water, **the first sight of him appears to be the emergence of a black mound from the waters**. This is the emergence of the **kam**, the black land, from the waters of the flood.

The crocodile Deity **Sobek** carries the body of **Ausar** out of the water after the drowning (flooding). The emergence of the crocodile from the depths of the water is the emergence of the black land **(Kamit)**, the primordial mound, at the beginning of Creation and from the flood waters after the inundation. The black and greenish color of the crocodile references the Black and Green sacred colors of **Ausar** – the black soil giving birth to green vegetation – based upon the 'fire within' **(kam/gyam)** the land – the fire of **Ra** and **Rait**. **Sobek** is also called **Sobek Ra** showing that he has the 'fire within'. The term 'kam' meaning 'black', based upon the burning of the charcoal, the 'fire within' and also meaning 'completion, to come to an end' also represented by the crocodile's tail and paw (the *end* of the body from front to back and the *end* of the body from top to bottom), also references the 'completion, burning, blackening, empowering' of a certain phase of the Creative and Regenerative process.

Sobek bearing the mummified body of **Ausar** upon his back. Temple of **Paaraka** (Philae).

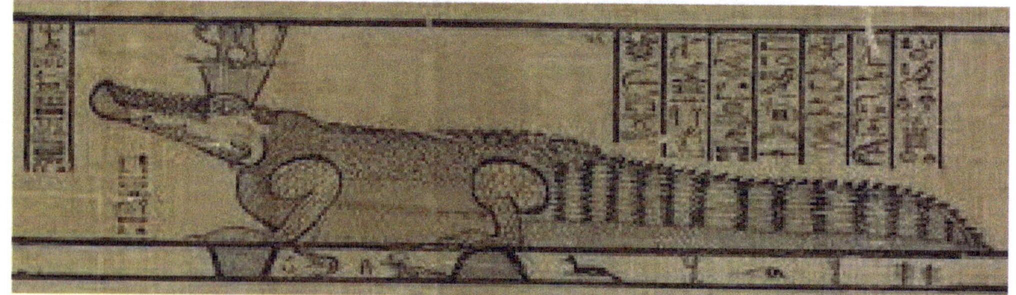

Sobek from the 'Book of the Faiyum'. The tail is the 'end' or 'completion' of the body **'km'**.

åkam [hieroglyphs], Düm. H. I, 1, 19, [hieroglyphs] shield; plur. [hieroglyphs].

ɔ-kyɛ́m, *pl.* **a-,** *a shield plaited of twigs. pr.* 306. 312. 1932 *f.;* **ŋwene ky.,** *to make a shield;* **wɔyɛ no teterɛɛ ahiŋanaŋ;** *buckler; cf.* **ŋwákyɛ́m, wókyɛ́m.**

As we can see in the Akan language, the term **okyem** means 'shield'. This is the **same term we have used for thousands of years** as can be shown above from the spelling of **akam** in the medutu. Recall that in Akan the 'ky' can be pronounced like the 'kuh' sound or the 'chuh' sound. The term **okyem** is thus pronounced 'aw-chem' and 'aw-kem' by different Akan speakers. The shield is made of sticks as a framework and covered by the **hide** or **skin** of an animal which is typically a **dark brown** or **black skin**. The shield is the 'end' or the extension of the person's, the fighter's 'skin'. It is his/her protection just as the skin on the body is the 'end', 'edge' or 'last' part of the person and our protection from infection and injury.

kam , vine; Copt. ϭⲁⲙⲉ.

agyàmó-mmaa, Aky. a thick *climbing plant; cf.* **hāmā 2.** [*Ezek.* 5,16.

The related **kam** and a**gyam**o-mmaa terms regarding **creeping, climbing plant, vine** show the identity of the term and concept of **kam** in ancient Kamit and contemporary Akan culture. The vine, the **kam** or a**gyam**o-mma is the plant rising up from the black soil. It **grabs onto another living structure in order to rise up, climb** as it reaches towards the Sun.

This black or green entity, rising up from the soil is **Ausar** the Great Black One **(Kam Ur)** and the Great Green One **(Wadj Ur)** being **resurrected.** He is pulled up by **Heru, Auset** and **Nebt Het** after he had 'drowned in His water' as shown in the Shabaka Text. Like the black or green vine, he **grasped** onto **Heru, Auset** and **Nebt Het** in order to rise up from the soil. He then entered into the heavenly realm to connect with **Ra**, the Creator, who operates through the **Aten** (Sun):

"…The Great Throne (Men Nefer) that gives joy to the heart of the Deities in the House of **Ptah** is the granary of **Tenen**, the mistress of all life, through which the sustenance of the Two Lands is provided, owing to the fact that **Ausar** was drowned in his water. **Auset** and **Nebt Het** looked out, beheld him, and attended to him. **Heru** quickly commanded **Auset** and **Nebt Het** to grasp **Ausar** and prevent his drowning. They heeded in time and brought him to land. He entered the secret portals in the glory of the Lords of Eternity, in the steps of him who rises in the horizon, on the ways of **Ra** at the Great Throne…" [Shabaka Text]

As we show in our publication: **KUKUU-TUNTUM The Ancestral Jurisdiction,** the Deity **Ausar** is the Spirit animating the black soil substance **(kam)**. He is deposited on the banks of the river after the inundation (flooding). His body is what is 'left behind'. **Heru, Auset** and **Nebt Het** were able to retrieve the body of **Ausar** with the assistance of the crocodile Deity **Sobek** who swam through the water to bring the **Kam Ur** (Black One) to the river bank. The black/green One is then resurrected and 'climbs up' to the heavens to sit in the boat of the Aten (Sun), wherein **Ra** resides. [This is the foundation upon which the greeks would later associate **Ausar** with **Dionysus** the 'god of the vineyard' as **'Osiris-Dionysus'**.]

Kam, Kamit defined in Kamit and in Akan:

kam-t , T. 26, N. 208, , , , , a black thing, black; , strong black, *i.e.*, jet black; , black

Black, burned

kam-t, Shipwreck 118, the end, end of a period, completion, a finish; , Ȧmen. 6, 3, , Ȧmen. 9, 3, 20, 2.

kam, Peasant 182, IV, 895. , , , to end, to bring to an end, to finish, to complete; ,

Completion, come to an end, expire

kam, vine; Copt. ϭⲙⲉ.

agyàmó-mmaa, Aky. a thick *climbing plant; cf.* **hāmā 2.** [*Ezek.* 5,16.

Vine, creeping plant

Kam, B.D. 142, IV, 20, , , , , , , Egypt; Copt. ⲕⲁⲙⲉ, ⲕⲏⲙⲉ, ⲕⲏⲙⲏ, ⲕⲏⲙⲓ.

Black land

Kammȧu, with , Jour. As. 1908, 285, Egyptians.

Black People

khai, grain, wheat.

kha, , , plant, herb, flowering plant (?); plur. , , , , , , Love Songs 7, 8, , IV, 329, , IV, 524, , sweet herbs.

kamt-t (var.), grain plant; plur. , .

kamu, , seeds or fruit of the kam plant.

kam, vine; Copt. ϭⲙⲉ.

kamu en ȧrp, vineyard.

agyàmó-mmaa, Aky. a thick *climbing plant; cf.* **hāmā 2.** [*Ezek.* 5,16.

gyàw, *v.* [*red.* gyigyaw] 1. *to leave, quit, depart from* (for a time). *Mt.* 4,13. — 2. *to part from* (never to return), *to forsake, desert, abandon, relinquish. Mt.* 4,20: 22. — 3. *to leave* (*behind*), *let remain. pr.* 1261. 2735. 2776. *John* 4,28. *Mt.* 22,25. — 4. *to leave in* or *commit to the care of, intrust.* — 5. gyaw mu, *to depart this life, expire, give up the ghost; cf.* wu; onnyã nnyaw mu ε, *he has not yet breathed his last;* wágyàw mú = wawu. — 6. gyaw biribi (wɔ)..mu, *to make up what is wanting, to complete.* — 7. *to leave*

kamkam, Thes. 1199, to vanish, to pass away, to disappear, to decay.

Note that **gyaw mu (gyam)** includes the meaning: 'to depart this life, expire'

kha, the last; Copt. ϩⲁⲉ, ϧⲁⲉ.

The term **kha** meaning the 'last' or that which is 'left behind'. Related to **kha** and **kham**. The determinative of the 'hair' references the 'end', 'edge' of the physical body as well as the color 'black, blackness'. Also used in different spellings of **'kam'**.

It must be understood that the major, overarching symbol and manifestation of 'beginning and ending', 'birth and death', in ancient Kamit was the rising and setting of the **Aten** (Sun). When the Aten rises in the east, that is a birth or beginning. When the Aten sets in the west, that is a death or ending. When the death occurs, there is **kamkam** 'to vanish, pass away, disappear'. What is the greatest indication that the Aten has 'disappeared, vanished, passed away'? It becomes totally black, dark - **kam**. The blackness is what is 'last' or 'left behind' when the Aten (Sun, Fire) 'expires, goes within, fires within' **(gyem, gyam)** the Earth.

It is only with a proper understanding of cosmology as part of a living culture that our people can fully explain these terms and concepts in all of their expressions. It is the cosmology that unifies the various expressions of the term **'kam'**.

Khai, Rev. 13, 25, "Exalted one"—a title of Rā.

Khait, Ombos II, 130, a title of Uatchit of Ombos.

Khai and **Khait**, titles of **Ra** and **Wadjet** referencing the solar fire **(kha)** of these Fire Deities.

See our related blogtalkradio broadcast on the subject matter:

Akwamu, Gyaman and the Origin and Meaning of the Name 'Kamit'

https://youtu.be/fJAYYXIeWVs

Odwirafo Kwesi Ra Nehem Ptah Akhan
Aakhuamuman Amaruka Atifi Mu
Akwamu Nation in North America
Odwiraman
www.odwirafo.com

Select Bibliography

The People the Boundary Could Not Divide: The Gyaman of Ghana and Cote D'ivoire in Historical Perspective

http://www.academicjournals.org/article/article1381916339_Agyemang%20and%20Ofosu-Mensah.pdf

EBRIE PEOPLE of GYAMAN
http://kwekudee-tripdownmemorylane.blogspot.com/2013/07/ebrie-people-famous-cote-divoire-akan.html

Asante-Fante Dictionary, J.G. Christaller
www.archive.org

An Egyptian Hieroglyphic Dictionary, Vols. 1-2, E.A. Wallis Budge
www.archive.org

Pyramid Text of Teti
http://www.pyramidtextsonline.com/library.html

Kam Ur – Kamit Urt: Ausar, Auset and the Enslavement and Restoration of the Afurakani/Afuraitkaitnit (African) in Amenti – The West
http://www.odwirafo.com/Kam-Ur_Kamit-Urt.pdf

HOODOO PEOPLE: Afurakanu/Afuraitkaitnut (Africans) in North America – Akan Custodians of Hoodoo from Ancient Hoodoo/Udunu Land (Khanit/Nubia)
www.odwirafo.com/Hoodoo.html

Men Nefer Cosmology – Shabaka Text
http://sofiatopia.org/maat/shabaka_stone.htm

KUKUU-TUNTUM The Ancestral Jurisdiction
www.odwirafo.com/kukuutuntumpage.html

HOODOO MAYN Nhoma (Hoodoo Nation Journal)
www.odwirafo.com/Hoodoo_Mayn.html

AKRADINBOSOM – Abosom of the Okra/Okraa and the Akan 7-Day Week
www.odwirafo.com/akradinbosom.html

NTORO: Origin and Meaning of the Term 'NTR' - Deity as Defined in Ancient Kamit and Akan Culture

In the language of our Afurakani/Afuraitkaitnit (African~Black) Ancestresses and Ancestors of ancient **Kamit** and **Khanit** (Egypt and Nubia) the term for Male Deity, Divinity, God* is **Ntoro** and the term for Female Deity, Divinity Goddess is **Ntorot**. An Ntoro or Ntorot is a Divine Spirit-Force in Creation. The Great Ntoro is **Amen** while the Great Ntorot is **Amenet**. Together, **Amen** and **Amenet** are the Great Father and the Great Mother Who function together as a Divine Unit - The Supreme Being:

Amenet and **Amen** – The Great Mother and Great Father of Creation

[*See our publications: **AFURAKA/AFURAITKAIT – The Origin of the term 'Africa'** and **ANIDAHO** which includes the article: **The Origin of the term 'God'** which is derived from a title of **Amen** in Kamit.]

Amenet and **Amen** are the Great Being undergirding the entirety of Creation. Their Children, the many **Ntorou/Ntorotu** (Gods/Goddesses - Deities), are the Spirit-Forces that **animate** the various aspects of Creation: The Black Substance of Space (Dark Matter, Dark Energy), the various Stars, Suns, Moons, Planets, Oceans, Rivers, Land, Atmosphere, Mountains, Thunder, Lightning, Core of Earth and other Planets, etc. Just as your spirit animates your physical body, so do the Spirits of the Ntorou/Ntorotu animate the physical aspects of Creation.

Foundational to the cosmology of Afurakanu/Afuraitkaitnut (Africans) wherever we exist in the world from ancient times to the present is the recognition that the **Supreme Being is the Great Divine Body and the Deities are the Divine 'Organs' and 'Organs Systems' who regulate Order within the Great Divine Body.** Your organs are smaller 'bodies' within your 'great body'. They are the regulators of order within you. They in turn 'birth' yet smaller bodies, your cells. As your cells function in harmony with and support of their 'parent' organs, they 'serve' you – the great parent/body at the same time. Similarly, the Ntorou/Ntorotu are the Spirits that regulate Order in Creation. The 'cells' or children of these Divine Organs are: plant life, animal life, mineral life and Afurakani/Afuraitkaitnit (African~Black) human life. As we live in harmony with and support the functions of our parent 'Organs' – the Ntorou/Ntorotu who govern us – we live in harmony with and support/serve the Great Divine Body, **Amenet** and **Amen**, of Whom we are a component/cellular part.

This cosmological foundation manifest through this Divinely Ordered hiearchical system of 'bodies within bodies' is key to understanding the nature of the terms Ntoro and Ntorot as spoken, written and symbolized by our Ancestressses and Ancestors in Khanit and Kamit and to this day in our various Afurakani/Afuraitkaitnit (African) cultures and languages. We elucidate this continuity of culture as manifest within Akan Ancestral Religion and language.

Akanfo (ah-kahn'-foh) in the **Twi** language of the Akan means *Akan people*. Akanfo originated in ancient **Khanit**, also called **Keneset** (Ancient Nubia), at the beginning of human existence upon Asaase (Earth). This is the region of contemporary Sudan and South Sudan in the Eastern region of Afuraka/Afuraitkait (Africa). We eventually migrated around the world. Some Akanfo migrated north of Khanit and settled ancient Kamit (ancient Egypt), while others remained in Khanit. Over the millennia, Akanfo migrated to West Afuraka/Afuraitkait (West Africa) establishing the ancient civilization of **Akana** (Khanat - Ghana). Some Akanfo were also a component of the **Kanem** empire (pre-Bornu), the original/authentic Black Berber empire (Abibiri-fo) and the **Kong** empire (Kan) before ultimately migrating to and settling in the areas of contemporary **Ghana** (Akana) and **Ivory Coast**. Akanfo presently comprise over 45 percent of the population of Ghana (11,000,000) and over 42 percent of the population of Ivory Coast (9,000,000). Collectively, there are over 20,000,000 Akanfo in West Afuraka/Afuraitkait (Africa), including smaller populations in Togo, Burkina Faso, Liberia and other areas.

During the **Mmusuo Kese** (Great Perversity/Enslavement era) the Akan ethnic group, as today, comprised one of the largest ethnic groups in West Afuraka/Afuraitkait (Africa). Many Akanfo were thus captured as prisoners of war, shipped to the americas, the Caribbean and europe and forced into enslavement over the course of three centuries. As a result, Akanfo represent one of the largest groups of Afurakanu/Afuraitkaitnut (Africans) living in the western hemisphere today. There are millions of Afurakanu/Afuraitkaitnut (Africans) of direct Akan descent - genetically and spiritually - extant within the populations of the americas, the Caribbean and europe who refer to themselves variously as African-americans, African-canadians, Afro-brazilians, Jamaicans, Afro-cubans, Afro-Caribbeans, Africans in britain, spain, portugal, france, etc.

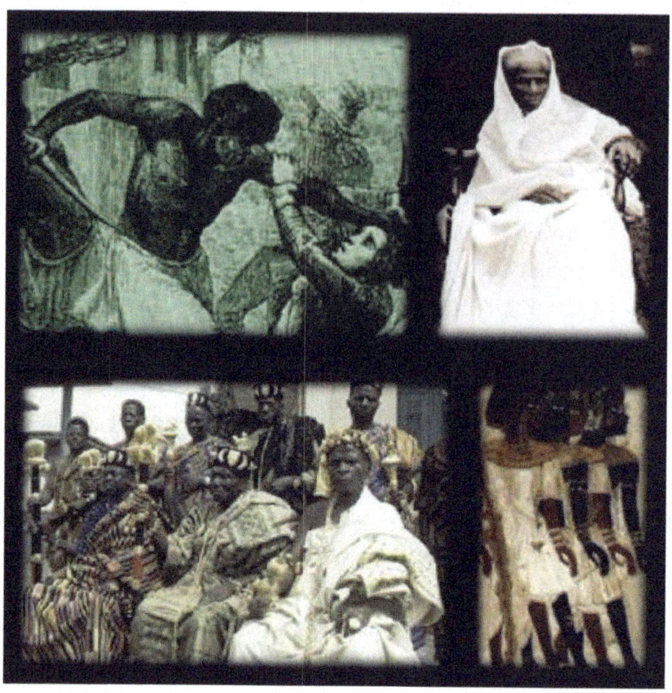

Above: Afurakanu/Afuraitkaitnut (Africans) waging war against white slavers in america; **Nana Abenaa Araminta** (Harriet Tubman – Her Akan Ancestry has been confirmed through Oral tradition, geneological records and DNA tests of her descendants); Akan Royal Nananom Mpanyinfo (Elders) in Ivory Coast; Ancient **Khanitu** (Akanni People - Nubians) visiting Kamit in 3,300 years ago.

The term **Ntoro**, spelled in the **medutu** (hieroglyphs) of Kamit often without the vowels **NTR** designating 'Deity', 'Divinity', 'God' is still used today. In the **Akan** culture and language of Ghana and Ivory Coast this term **NTR** is vocalized as **Ntoro** (un'-taw-raw). The definition of **Ntoro** in Akan is a 'Deity'. Moreover the symbol of the **axe** representing 'Deity' or Ntoro/Ntorot in Khanit and Kamit is also used to represent the Ntoro and Ntoron (Nton) in Akan culture today – and also used by the Deities Themselves during ritual. We first address the etymology of the term.

Entries from **An Hieroglyphic Dictionary, Vols. 1-2** by E.A. Wallis Budge (1920 edition) in comparison to the **Dictionary of the Asante and Fante Language Called Tshi (Twi)** [Akan Language Dictionary] by J.G. Christaller (1881 edition and 1933 edition):

neter, nether, U. 70, N. 330, T. 237, M. 147, N. 649, the word in general use in texts of all periods for God and "god"; Copt. ΝΟΥΤΕ, = ΝΟΥΤΕ (Rev.)

The term **Ntr** is spelled with the medutu (hieroglyphs) for the consonants. The wavy, water line is the medut for the letter and sound 'N': . The loaf of bread is the medut for the letter and sound 'T': . The open mouth is the medut for the letter and sound 'R': . Three variants of the term are shown below:

As we can see above in the three variant spellings of the term NTR, following the consonants N-T-R we have the medut of the **axe** in the first variant, the medut of the **falcon** on a standard in the second variant and the medut of the **seated, shrouded figure** in the third variant. These special medutu are called **determinative symbols.** The determinative symbols are typically not enunciated. They are *indicators* of what the word means. The axe, the sacred falcon on the standard and the seated, shrouded figure all denote a **Divinity** in the language of Kamit. Thus the term NTR is the word and it denotes a Divinity, a Deity, a God. The use of determinatives are effective as indicators when there are terms that are spelled with the same letters, yet have different yet related meanings based on intonation and usage. For example, the english terms **lie** meaning 'falsehood' and **lie** meaning 'lay down on a bed' are phonetically identical. The only way one could *determine* the meaning of the word is by the context within which it is used. In Kamit and Khanit however, we would use a determinative symbol/medut to accomplish the same objective. We could thus write the word with the **l-i-e** characters and then use a *determinative symbol* of a man lying down: following the letters **l-i-e.** The reader would immediately be able to identify this term **lie** as the form of the word meaning to 'lay down' as opposed to **lie** meaning 'falsehood'. The lying man is thus a **determinative** symbol.

Our Ancestresses and Ancestors sometimes wrote our words in various texts without including the medutu for the vowels. Only the structural components or skeletal body of the words – the consonants – were used in various instances. This continues today when on social media some opt to use the skeletal body of words when sending texts, often omitting the vowels. Because we employed this option in Kamit, egyptologists thousands of years later are unsure of how the terms were and are vocalized. A convention in egyptology which became widely used early on in the field was to place an 'E' in between consonants when the vocalization of the actual word was unknown.

The above entry thus shows the actual medutu spelling out the term **NTR**, yet the egyptologist inserts the 'E' to facilitate pronunciation: **NETER**. Also included in the entry is the **Coptic** dialectical variant of the term. The Coptic dialect is the **Late Kamit** (Late Egyptian) dialect of the language which came into use at the end of the civilization approximately 2,000 years ago. In the Coptic dialect, one of the vocalizations shown in the entry above is **NOUTE** (NOUTER): **ⲚⲞⲨⲦⲈ**. As we will see, the Coptic dialectal variants of terms as well as older dialectical variants can both be found in the Akan language.

From the **Dictionary of the Asante and Fante Language Called Tshi (Twi)**:

ntɔ̃rɔ, Ak., *pl. id.* **1:** *one of the ancient families,* **each worshipping a particular spirit. Descent is matrilineal.** *Cf.* **abusũa. - Wo nè bi guare ɔbosoŋ-koro a, ná moyɛ nt.; - mé ntɔ̀ŋ** *or* **mé ntɔ́rɔ ni,** *or,* **ɔyɛ me nt.,** *we are of the same* **ancient** *family,* **worshipping the same fetish. ("Mede m'agya ɔbosom mewoo no,** *I begat him with the help of my father's fetish".* **"We do not forget that the própagation of the family depends upon the help of the family fetish"). Wobɔ (,** *or,* **wuguare) nt. beŋ?** *to which family do you belong? Cf.* **ntɔŋ & guare. — 2. According to some informants ntɔrɔ denotes** *the totemic spirit(?),* **and descent is patrilineal; (in Akuapem, patrilineal & matrilineal).**

ntɔ́ŋ, Akp.; ntɔ́rɔ, Ak., (*pl. id.*) = abusũ-abáŋ, ***family, consanguinity, kindred;***

wufi nt. bɛŋ mu? wó ntɔ̀ŋ de dɛ́ŋ? meyɛ Dwṹmoànáni, &c., *I am a member of the* Dw. *family, &c.* - *Cf.* ntɔrɔ & App. D.

In the above entries we have the terms **Ntoro** and **Nton.** Note that the compiler of the dictionary indicates that in the **Akuapem** Akan dialect (Akp.) the term **Nton** is pronounced **Ntoro**. The term Nton (contraction of **Ntoron)** is actually the feminine term in Akan while Ntoro is the masculine.

In Akan culture the Ntoro is a Deity. In the second part of the definition above the compiler of the dictionary states that according to some informants, Ntoro denotes the 'totemic spirit and descent is patrilineal'.

The Ntoro in Akan is defined as and thus also called the **Egyabosom**. The term 'egya' or 'agya' means 'Father'. The term **Obosom** or **Bosom** means 'Deity'. The Egyabosom literally is the 'Father's Deity'. **It is the Deity inherited by every individual through his/her father's blood circle.** There are twelve Agyabosom or Ntoro-bosom, patriclan Deities, in Akan culture.

We also have the term **Nton (Ntoron)** which references the matriclan group in Akan culture and the **Obosom** (Deity) which governs that group. There are seven of these Nton (Ntoron) groups in Akan culture. The Nton or matriclan is also called the **Abusua**. The Deities which govern the matriclans are the **Abusuabosom** or **Nton-Bosom**. The matriclan Obosom is the Mother's Deity. **It is the Deity inherited by every Akan individual through his/her mother's blood circle.** There are seven Nton-bosom or Abusuabosom, matriclan Deities, in Akan culture.

Akan people thus say, 'Ntoro ye Egyabosom' meaning the 'Ntoro is the Father's Deity'. In the above entry one of the Akan informants to the compiler of the dictionary gave an idiom used to explain the nature of the term:

"...Mede m'agya obosom mewoo no – I begat him with the help of my father's fetish (Agyabosom – Father's Deity). We do not forget that the propagation of the family depends upon the help of the family fetish (Obosom – Deity)..." ['fetish' is a european misnomer and derogatory term which they use to translate the term 'Deity'].

"Wobo Ntoro ben?" means 'Which Ntoro (patriclan and patriclan Deity) do you belong to?'. Akan people regularly go to the river or other sacred body of water wherein their Ntoro (Deity) dwells in order to invoke this Ntoro (Deity) and then use the water which carries the energy of the Ntoro to perform the **Okraguare** or Soul-washing ceremony, which includes cleansing the head with the sacred water. The Ntoro or Egyabosom shows himself to the individual and can also **possess** the person. Children as well as adults invoke the Ntoro in this manner to provoke spirit-possession and spirit-communication. Similarly, Akan people invoke the Nton (Ntoron) Obosom, the Deity who governs the matriclan. This is done for protection, guidance, healing and more.

The seven matriclans and twelve patriclans in Akan culture are named after the seven **Abusuabosom** (Nton-Bosom/Matriclan Deities) and twelve **Egyabosom** (Ntoro-bosom/Patriclan

Deities) who govern them. This is why the groupings/clans are also called **Ntoro** and **Nton** (Ntoron). This is why in the above entry the statement is made: "Me Nton or Me Ntoro ni.. Oye me Ntoro – *we are of the same ancient family worshipping the same fetish* [Deity]."

neter, nether, U. 70, N. 330, T. 237, M. 147, N. 649, ★, the word in general use in texts of all periods for God and "god"; Copt. ⲛⲟⲩⲧⲉ, = ⲛⲟⲩⲧⲉ (Rev.)

ntɔ́rɔ, Ak., *pl. id.* 1: *one of the ancient families,* each worshipping a particular spirit. Descent is matrilineal. *Cf.* abusũa. - Wo nè bi guare ɔbosoŋ-koro a, ná moyɛ nt.; - mé ntɔ̀ŋ *or* mé ntɔ́rɔ ni, *or,* ɔyɛ me nt., *we are of the same* ancient *family,* worshipping the same fetish. ("Mede m'agya ɔbosom mewoo no, *I begat him with the help of my father's fetish*". "We do not forget that the propagation of the family depends upon the help of the family fetish"). Wobo (, *or,* wuguare) nt. beŋ? *to which family do you belong? Cf.* ntɔŋ & guare. — 2. According to some informants ntɔrɔ denotes *the totemic spirit*(?), and descent is patrilineal; (in Akuapem, patrilineal & matrilineal).

While the compiler of the dictionary was confused on the nature of the patrilineal and matrilineal function of Ntoro and Nton, the Akan informants who shared the information in the Akan/Twi language were clear. In the article **Ntoro and Nton**, Ghanaian scholar A.C. Denteh brings further clarity, showing that the Ntoro is patrilineal while the Nton is matrilineal. He defines the Ntoro as follows:

"…The two sociological terms, Ntoro and Nton in Akan, have been summarily treated as though they were one and the same thing. It has been suggested that "synonymous terms for Ntoro are Nton, Sunsum, or bosom", but a further study of Ntoro has revealed that Ntoro is not synonymous with Nton. The writer of the statement quoted above must have been led into that error by a previous writer whose definition of Ntoro was not explicit enough. In that definition, an example under one of the various meanings was given as follows: "Me nton or me ntoro ni", and the meaning vaguely given was "we are of the same ancient family, worshipping the same fetish." This writer's difficulty can be appreciated as his informants must have confused him by stating that "in Akuapem, Ntoro is both patrilineal and matrilineal."

The Twi Spelling Book also equates Ntoro with Nton. There has been a long standing confusion between the two terms, which in turn has resulted in real difficulties, even among some Akans, regarding the meaning and character of the terms.

What then are Ntoro and Nton? We shall begin with Ntoro. **Ntoro is the general term applied to the spirit, in most cases totemic, of each of a number of patrilineages of the Akans. The spirit is passed on from father to son or daughter…"**

"...The Akans, particularly the Ashantis, believe that when a person is at the point of dying, his or her Ntoro flies off and plunges itself into its agnate river. Often it does, so with a shout: "Hu-u-u-u!" and then a splash and disappears. If the river-god does not order it to go back at once but welcomes it, then the soul left alone in the body also leaves it. This point of the Ntoro spirit reporting back to the river-god is the idea reflected in the expression "kowuakra." Ko-wu-a-kra is a sentence-word referring particularly to the Ntoro of Bosomtwe. The full meaning of it is, "you to whom people send their Ntoro to say goodbye before they die."..."

https://archive.lib.msu.edu/DMC/African%20Journals/pdfs/Institue%20of%20African%20Studies%20Research%20Review/1967v3n3/asrv003003010.pdf

As we can see from the above excerpts, the Ntoro is a Spirit/Deity. For further definition we excerpt from our publication: **The Okra/Okraa Complex – The Soul of Akanfo**:

"...There are Abosom [Deities] associated with our **Abusua** (matriclan) as well as our **Ntoro** (patriclan). Thus, there is a major Obosom [Deity] Who governs our mother's blood circle, *an Obosom Who has protected and guided our* ***abusuafo*** *(matriclan members) for millennia.* There is also a major Obosom Who governs our father's blood circle, *an Obosom who has protected and guided our* ***ntorofo*** *(patriclan members) for millennia.* These Abosom are sometimes referred to as the **Abusuabosom** or **Nton-bosom** (**Nton** is a synonym for Abusua – matriclan) and the **Agyabosom** (Agya – *'Father'*) or **Ntorobosom** or simply **Ntoro**, respectively. Just as we receive DNA and thus *physical* and *personality* characteristics from our mother's blood-circle (lineage) and father's blood-circle (lineage) – *so do the sperm and ovum carry the energy of the matricircular (matrilineal) Obosom and the patricircular (patrilineal) Obosom of the mother's clan and father's clan respectively.* These are *clan* Abosom which are *directly related to our Ancestry.*

The Abusua Abosom and Ntoro Abosom are related to the hye and hyebea

There are seven major **mmusuakuo**, *great matricircular (matrilineal) clans* in Akan culture. **Mmusua** is the plural of **abusua**. If one cannot trace his or her Ancestry to one of the seven great Ancestresses of these mmusuakuo, then one is not Akan. The seven major mmusuakuo are: **Asona, Agona, Aduana, Ekuona, Asenie, Brietuo** and **Asakyiri**. There are also variations of these names and sub-groups born of these clans. These seven mmusuakuo are *headed* by seven Great Ancestresses and *governed* by **seven Female Abosom**.

There are twelve **Ntoro**, *patricircular (patrilineal) clan groups*, each governed by its own Obosom in Akan culture. Every Akan person inherits his or her Ntoro or **Agyabosom** (*Father's* Obosom) by virtue of birth. The twelve major Ntoro groups and their related Ntorobosom are: **Bosom Afram, Bosom Pra, Bosom Opo, Bosom Sika, Bosom Akom, Bosom Dwerebe, Bosom Ofin (Afi), Bosom Ayensu, Bosom Muru, Bosom Konsi, Bosom Twe** and **Bosom Krete**. Bosom here refers to the Deity, thus **Bosom Afram** is the Obosom of the River Afram in Ghana. **Bosom Ofin** (often written Bosomafi) is the Obosom of the River Ofin, etc.

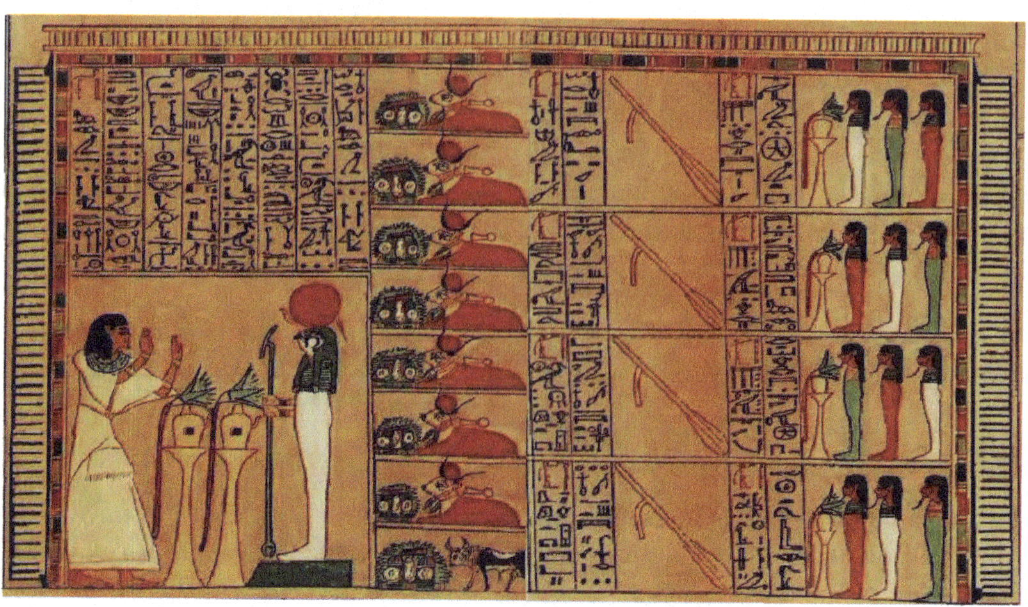

Left: The seven *Nton-Abosom* or *Abusuabosom* in the form of the Seven **Het Heru** Abosom. Here, the Seven **Het Heru** Abosom take the form of Seven Divine Cows. Right: The twelve *Ntoro-bosom* or *Agyabosom*. [*From chapter 148* ***Pert em Heru, Sheft Ani*** *(so-called Egyptian Book of the Dead - Papyrus of Ani)*]

Above: Another depiction of the Seven **Het Heru** Abosom. These Seven Female Abosom actually *govern* the seven Akan Ancestresses who *head* the Seven **Mmusuakuo** – matricircular clans. In ancient Kamit, the Seven **Het Heru** are shown to be present at the birth of the child to announce the child's *'fate'* or *shait/hyebea.* The constellation called *'pleaides'* in european languages is called the **Seven Het Heru** in Kamit *(seven Hathors).* In Akan this constellation of seven major stars is called *Aberewa na ne mma – The Elderess (Old) Woman and Her Children.* [*From the stele of the Priest Amenemhat*]…"

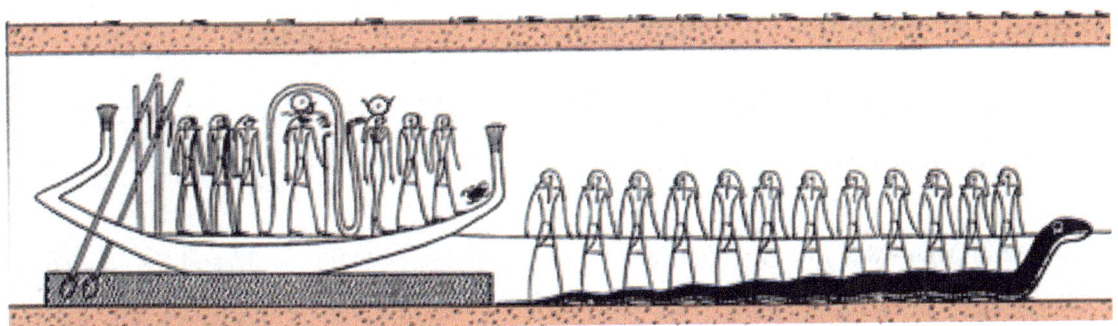

Shat em Duat – Book of the Underworld. Twelfth Hour of the Night

The Creator as Afu Ra in His boat with His attendants. This is the form that **Ra** (**Nyankopon**) takes when operating through the **Aten** (Sun) *during the twelve hours of the night.* **Ra**, operating through the Aten during the day is shown sailing in the boat of the Aten from sunrise to sunset. When the Aten sets, goes underground in the west and into the underworld (Ancestral realm), **Ra** becomes **Afu Ra** and sails through the underworld during the twelve hours of the night. When the boat of **Afu Ra** reaches the east, **Afu Ra** transforms into **Ra** (with the head of a Hawk) and rises inside of the Aten from the eastern horizon and into the sky to begin a new day.

Above is an image of **Afu Ra** sailing in His boat with His attendants in the underworld (**Duat**). This is a depiction of the twelfth hour of the night, the *last region of the underworld* that **Afu Ra** must pass through before being 'reborn' into the sky on the eastern horizon. The twelve Male Abosom who are towing the boat of **Afu Ra** are the twelve **Ntoro** or **Agyabosom**. They are standing upon the great serpent called **Ka en Ankh Ntorou**. The boat of **Afu Ra** will actually *enter the tail of this serpent*, move through its body and *come out of the mouth* being born into the sky as the sunrise of the new day. **Afu Ra** *will thus move through the* **Ka** (Afuraka) in order to appear above the mountain of sunrise. In the same fashion, before we leave Asamando to enter the world as a newborn child, we encounter the twelve Agyabosom who *stand upon the Ka* (Okra/Okraa) and we are assigned to one of these Abosom by **Nyamewaa-Nyame**…"

In the above excerpt we demonstrate that the same seven female Deities governing the seven great matriclans in Akan culture today are the same seven **Het Heru** Deities from our Ancestral Akan culture of Khanit and Kamit, connected to the same star constellation, unbroken over thousands of years. The same twelve male Deities governing the twelve great patriclans in Akan culture today are the same twelve Deities (also referenced as the twelve attendants of **Ausar-Sahu** (Osiris-Orion)) from our Ancestral Akan culture of Khanit and Kamit, unbroken over thousands of years. The twelve stars of **Sahu** (Orion) are animated by the Spirits of Deities, thus the seated, shrouded figure of a Deity (Ntoro) as the determinative medut is found in the spelling of the name of the twelve Sahu:

Saḥu XII
B.D. 64, 22, the 12 stars of Oṛion.

The image of the seven stars in the form of the seven Sacred Cows of **Het Heru**, the Sacred Bull or **Ka** and the twelve **Sahu** Deities in mummiform are located in the sky and are called by the whites and their offspring the seven stars of the Pleiades constellation, followed by the Sacred Bull or Taurus constellation and the Orion constellation. Note that while the Pleiades are called **Aberewa na ne mma** (Ancient Woman and Her Children), Orion is called **Nyenkrente** in Akan.

Excerpts from our publication: **The Origin of the Term Abosom in Kamit:**

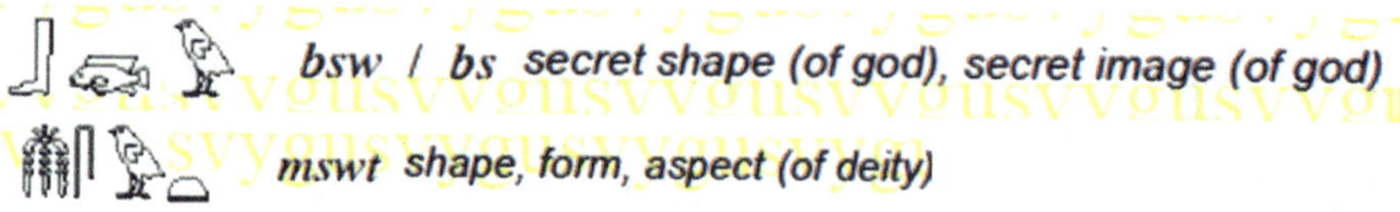

"...**Bsu** (Bsw) and **Msu** (Msw) both reference the *form* of the Deity. Here the 'b' and 'm' interchange. The *Kamau* term **Bsu** becomes **Bosom** in Akan. [*Note that some Akan speakers pronounce **Bosom** as **Bosum**.*]

The Agyabosom (Egyabosom) is the male Ntoro. There are <u>twelve</u> of these Abosom, Whom are also referred to as the **Ntoro-bosom** in **Akan culture**. These are the **Msu Ntr** (*Bosom-ntoro*) from ancient Kamit:

Young Deity, Divine Child

Young Deity, Divine Child

Creative Power; One Who brings forth [Seated figure denotes a Deity]

A stone – In Akan: abo<u>sam</u>: a stony, rocky place

"...The seven **Het-Heru** Ntorotu Who are present at the birth (*ms*) of every Afurakani/Afuraitkaitnit (African) child are called **Abusua-bosom** in **Akan**. Yet, another term used for abusua is **Nton**. The Nton thus references the Abosom inherited matricircularly (matrilineally) and determines what matriclan the Akan individual is born of. This inheritance is passed on via the mother.

The term **Nton** (in-ntawng') is derived from the term **Ntorot** in Kamit. Ntorot became Ntoron and Nton. This is similar to the Akan term **soro** meaning *up, above*, being shortened to **so**. The 'r' and the vowel which follows is dropped. The same occurs in the pronunciation of the Akan term **o-soron** meaning *tamarind*. This term is also pronounced **o-son**. The same dialectical variation exists between Ntoro(t) and Nton. The Abusuabosom are the **Nton-abosom**. They are the **Msu Ntrt** (*Bosom Nton*) from Kamit...."

netrit , , , , , , Rec. 30, 67, , , , , , goddess; Copt. ⲦⲚⲞⲨⲦⲈ.

ntṍŋ, Ākp.; **ntɔ́rɔ**, Ak., (*pl. id.*) = abusũ-abáŋ, *family, consanguinity, kindred;* wuñ nt. bɛŋ mu? wó ntɔ̀ŋ de dɛ́ŋ? meyɛ Dwũmoànání, &c., *I am a member of the* Dw. *family, &c.* - *Cf.* ntɔrɔ & App. D.

NTRT [NTOROT] in Kamit is vocalized as **NTON** (NTORON) in Akan. Nton is the Abusua:

abusũá, *pl.* m-, *family, kindred, relatives,* esp. *the relations of the mother's side; one of the original families* of the Tshi nation. (Descent is matrilineal); *race; lineage; clan. Cf.* App. D. II. b & ntɔrɔ.

We show the identity of the Akan term **abusua** (family, clan, offspring), plural **mmusua**, with its origins in our ancient language in our article:

abusua *family; clan; offspring*
mmusua *families; clans; offspring*

messu , IV, 614, children.
messiu , P. 171, 177, , , those who are born, children.
mesit , T. 284 = , P. 53, , M. 32, , N. 65, , , children; , P. 593, race, family.

abusũá, *pl.* **m-,** ***family, kindred, relatives,*** **esp.** ***the relations of the mother's side; one of the original families*** **of the Tshi nation. (Descent is matrilineal);** ***race; lineage; clan. Cf.*** **App. D. II. b & ntɔrɔ.**

pl. **m-** in the above entry means **plural** (*pl.*) for the term is formed by adding the **'m-' mmusua**

Again, the 'E' is inserted by the egyptologist as a vowel placeholder. The plural term **mmusua** *meaning families, clans; offspring* in Akan is the ancient term **msu (musu; musut)** properly vocalized meaning *offspring, family, race.* Also we recall that the 'B' and 'M' interchange not only in Akan but also Kamit. The **msu** (msw) is also **bsu** (bsw) – **Bosom** (Deities) – the *offspring, family, children* of the Great God and Great Goddess, **Amen** and **Amenet.**

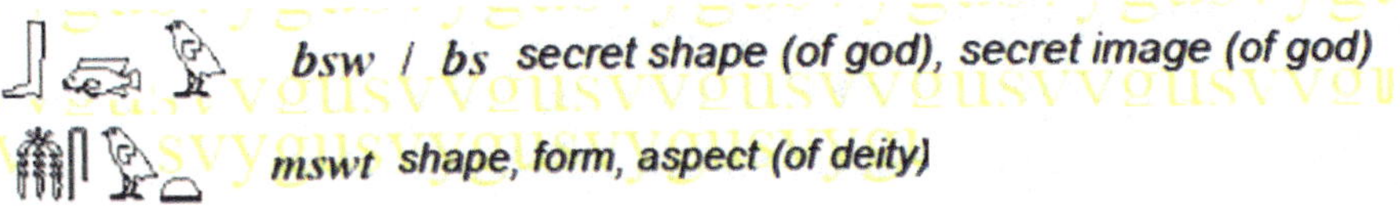
bsw / bs secret shape (of god), secret image (of god)
mswt shape, form, aspect (of deity)

We thus have the same term Ntoro and Ntorot (Ntoro and Ntoron) in the Akan language referencing a male Deity and female Deity, which we are born into the world assigned to. The energy of the Ntoro and Nton is passed on through our spiri-genetic blood-circles. This is why no matter where we have migrated on **Asaase** (Earth) or were forced to migrate during the enslavement era, we continue to be connected to these Spirit-Forces in Nature. Because they are connected to us by blood, they continue to manifest through spirit-possession and spirit-communication via ritual song, ritual dance, ritual prayer, divination and more. Thus ancient Akan culture continues through the religious practices of **Hoodoo** in North america, **Obeah** in Jamaica, **Winti** in Suriname and more. The same is true of all Afurakani/Afuraitkaitnit (African) people wherever we exist in the world.

Our Ancestresses and Ancestors interfaced with, were energized and sustained by the same Sun, Moon, Earth, Oceans, Atmosphere, Black Substance of Space (Dark Energy, Dark Matter), Stars, etc. thousands of years ago that we interface with, are energized and sustained by today.

By the same measure, the same Spirits that **animated** the Sun, Moon, Earth, Oceans, Atmosphere, Black Substance of Space (Dark Energy, Dark Matter), Stars and possessed and communicated with our Ancestresses and Ancestors thousands of years ago are the exact same Spirits, Ntorou/Ntorotu, who **animate** these aspects of Creation and possess and communicate with us as Afurakanu/Afuraitkaitnut (Africans) today. These Spirits are called by descriptive titles in various Afurakani/Afuraitkaitnit (African) languages including **Abosom** (Akan), **Orisha** (Yoruba), **Vodou** (Fon, Ewe), **Arusi** (Igbo) and more. Yet, amongst the Akan you also have the title Ntoro and Ntoron (Nton). Similarly, in the Ewe tradition another term for **Vodou** (Deity) is also **Tro** (plural **Trowo**). This **Tro** is the (N)Toro (n-Tro) from Kamit. Our culture as Afurakanu/Afuraitkaitnut (Africans~Black People) is a living culture and we are thus able to identify these Ntorou/Ntorotu because we have direct experience with them.

Moreover, we have the title **Totoro Bonsu** which is sometimes used as an **mmrane** (praise name) of the Creator of Universe in Akan culture. While **Nyamewaa** and **Nyame** **(Amenet** and **Amen)** are the Supreme Being, they direct **Nyankopon** and **Nyankonton** **(Ra** and **Rait)** to create the Universe. **Ra** and **Rait** in Khanit and Kamit are the Creator and Creatress, while **Amenet** and **Amen** are the Supreme Being. In our publication **NYANKOPON-NYANKONTON – RA/RAIT** we prove the identity of **Nyankopon** and **Nyankonton** as **Ra** and **Rait** and where the names can be found in the medutu.

As a Great **Ntoro** (Deity) the Creator of the Universe is sometimes referred to with the title **Totoro Bonsu:**

> **tòtŏ́ro-bō̆-nsu** (toturob., *R.* tetreb.), *he who causes rain to fall copiously* and *makes water (rivers) overflow*; a by-name of Nyaŋkôpɔŋ; ɔtotɔ totɔ a, na nsu abɔ, *when the rain falls abundantly, the rivers &c. overflow.*

This title designates **Nyankopon** as the great **Ntoro (To-ntoro)** who creates/makes **(Bo)** water **(Nsu)**. His totem is the rainbow serpent, the fecundator of **Nyankonton** and thus Creation.

In our publication **HOODOO PEOPLE: Afurakanu/Afuraitkaitnut (Africans) in North America – Akan Custodians of Hoodoo from Ancient Hoodoo/Udunu Land (Khanit/Nubia)** we provide the cosmological, linguistic and anthropological (including religious ritual) evidence proving the identity of the Akan people in ancient Khanit (Sudan/Nubia) to those in contemporary West Afuraka/Afuraitkait (Africa) and our people in North america who have preserved Hoodoo as an Ancestrally-inherited Akan Religious practice. The archaeological, and archaeo-genetic evidence corroborates this as well. In **Origin of the Niger-Congo Speakers**, Dr. Clyde Winters provides the archaeo-genetic evidence demonstrating that the Niger-Congo speakers, including the ancient Akan (C-group Nubians) originated in the Upper Kamit (Sudan/Nubia/Khanit) region over 10,000 years ago.

[Winters C. **Origin of the Niger-Congo Speakers**. WebmedCentral GENETICS 2012;3(3):WMC003149

doi: 10.9754/journal.wmc.2012.003149]

This evidence comports with the oral traditions of the Akan describing their migration from ancient Khanit and their subsequent settling in West Afuraka/Afuraitkait (Africa). It also corroborates the oral traditions of Akan in america. We find for example the same Deities in Akan culture having the same names, same ritual colors, governing the same aspects of Creation as they are found in the inscriptions of Khanit and Kamit thousands of years ago. This includes: **Amen, Amenet, Ra, Rait, Atum, Khepra, Ausaaset, Nebet Hetepet, Maa, Maat, Ausar, Auset, Set, Nebt Het, Heru, Het Heru, Wadjet, Nekhebet, Heru Behdety, Sekhemet, Men, Ptah, Hapi, Ba Neb Djedet, Khensu, Khensit, Tehuti, Seshat** and more.

Because of the identity of our ancient and contemporary expressions of Akan Ancestral Religion and Culture, we are able to unearth the cosmological foundation of the terms, symbols, ritual expressions, etc. found in Khanit and Kamit. We have proven the **identity** of the term **Ntr** with **Ntoro**. We now address the **origin** of the term, its **ritual function** and the **nature** of the axe as a symbol of Ntoro/Ntorot.

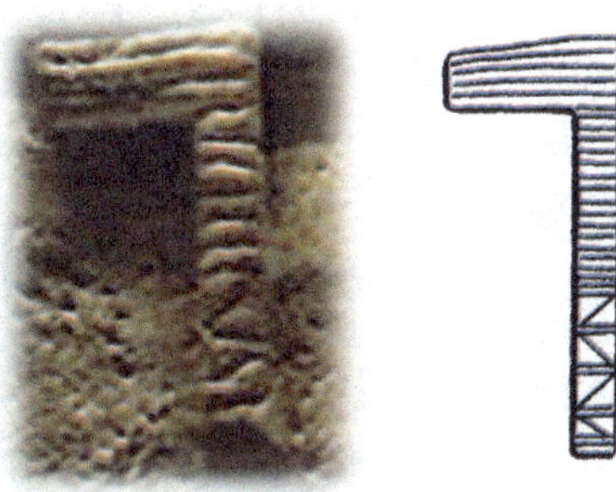

The image of the axe as a representation of an Ntoro or Ntorot, a Deity, continues to be misunderstood by egyptologists. At most, their explanation has been the axe represents power, authority, hunting and agricultural activities. However, because we have the insight of being a part of the living culture as Afurakanu/Afuraitkaitnut (Africans) we can demonstrate conclusively why the axe is a symbol and ritual implement of the Ntorou/Ntorotu. **The use of the axe is rooted in the functioning of the Ntorou/Ntorotu when interfacing with Afurakanu/Afuraitkaitnut (Africans) through spirit-possession and spirit-communication.** We thus have a cosmological foundation for employing it as a symbol of the Ntorou/Ntorotu.

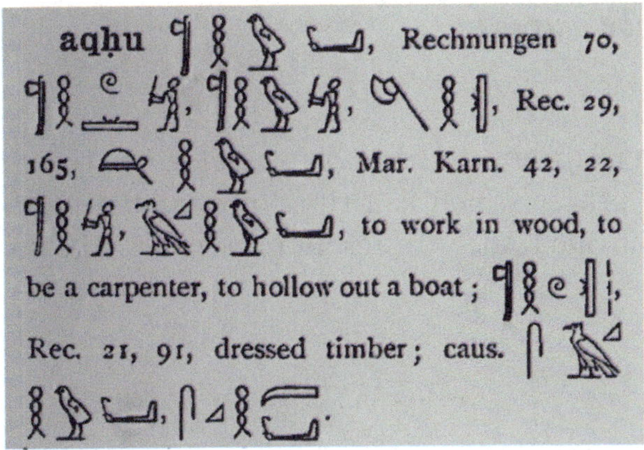

aqḥu, Rechnungen 70, Rec. 29, 165, Mar. Karn. 42, 22, to work in wood, to be a carpenter, to hollow out a boat; Rec. 21, 91, dressed timber; caus.

kùw, *v.* **1.** *to draw* or *pull out, off, away; s. red.* **kukuw; ókùw no ahwe ,hɔ = ɔwɛre no ahwe fam'**, *he draws away his* (some one's) *feet to make him fall.* — **2.** *to cut close to the root;* **ɔde adare k. wura, sare; kuw dua no ase = twa ase pá ara mã ɛnto fam'** (*that the cutting reaches to the ground*). *pr. 1866;* **ókùw n'asé**, *he cuts him off. Isa. 48,9;* **kuw so, kukuw so**, *to clip* (the beard); **ɛso ak.**, *it is clipped. Jer. 48,37.*

As we can see above the term **aqhu** in Kamit references *working in wood, to hollow a boat,* etc. The symbol is the axe. In Akan, the term **kuw (ekuw)** means *to cut.* The related terms for axe:

aqḥu [hieroglyphs], A.Z. 1905, 142, [hieroglyphs], carpenter's adze, axe, battle-axe.

akũmá, *pl.* **ŋ-,** *hatchet, axe.*

The Akan term for axe, **aku-ma** is derived from the ancient term **aqhu** meaning axe. The cosmological implication of the **axe-as-Ntoro/Ntorot** (axe-as-Deity) is rooted in the Akan word for prayer:

mpáé, *v. n.* [*cf.* **pae 6**] **1.** *invocation, prayer, supplication;* **bɔ** *or* **yi mpae,** *to pray;* **ɔbɔ Nyaŋkp. mpae amā ne nua,** *he prays to God for his brother;* **sometimes: ɔbɔ mp. mā Onyaŋk.,** *he prays to God.* **Ɔsɔfo na oyi mp., ɛ.s. wosore asĕrɛ biribiara; sɛ wokasa bĕrɛɛoo oo, wokasa denneŋ oo, ne nyinaa wɔfrɛ no mpae; mekaŋkye ma-bɔ abosom mpae; mede nsā merebɔ me nena samaŋ mpae na me hŏ ayɛ me deŋ. Obiara kobɔ mpae a, na bɔhyɛ wom'** *(according to P. Ket., others deny it).* **Múnyi** (*or* **mómmɔ**) **mpae mmā no, na ne hŏ yɛ no deŋ a, wɔbɛmā no aboade (abɔhyɛdé); - ɔbɔ me ti so mpae,** *he prays for me.* — **2.** *imprecation, curse, execration; cf.* **nsew; mpae ŋkā no! F.** *let him be cursed!*

The term **mpae** or **apae** in Akan is the general term for *prayer, invocation, supplication.* There is a reason why the term mpae is used to describe prayer which is a ritual **provocation** of the Supreme Being, the Deities and the Spiritually Cultivated Ancestresses and Ancestors. The root of the term mpae is **pae**:

paé, *v.* [*red.* paepae, paapae] **1.** *to strike, smite;* ɔpae n'asõm', n'atifĩ, ne mpampam', *pr. 160. 400, s.* paa. — **2.** *tr. to split, rive, cleave, break;* p. dua, *to split a piece of wood;* p. gya, *to cleave wood;* p. mpuraŋ, ntâboo, *to saw beams, boards;* p. abo, *to break, cut, dig* or *take stones* from the earth, from a quarry, *to quarry stones;* pae asase, *to furrow the earth. Ps. 141,7.* — **3.** *intr. to split, rend, burst, crack;* ɔprannaa duru duam' a, ɛpae, *when the lightning strikes a tree, it bursts;* duá no apáe, *the tree is riven;* kora no apae, *the calabash has a chink. pr. 614;* ɔdodobeŋ, *pr. 947.* - ne tuo mu paee, *his gun burst, flew into pieces. pr. 3389 f.;* emu apae abieŋ, *it has burst in two; to cleave asunder. Nu. 16,31.* — **4.** *to part, divide;* ɔpae (ɔpaa) ne tirim, *he parts his hair on (the top of) his head;* ɔpae sa, *he cuts* or *opens a path* through the bush; wɔbɛpae

As we can see, the term pae means *to split, cleave, break, rend, divide*. We have the related term **mpaee** meaning *cleft, crack*:

mpaeé, *pl.* mpaapáé, *cleft, crack.*

The term **pae** in Akan is the proper vocalization from the same term spelled in the medutu as **ph** and **pht** (peh, peht):

peh [hieroglyphs], to rend **peḥt, peḥtch** [hieroglyphs], [hieroglyphs], [hieroglyphs], to cut through, to split, to divide; Copt. ⲫⲱϫⲓ.

In Akan culture **prayer** is a process whereby through **ritual provocation** we utilize our **vibrational energy** of sound (incantations, song, etc.) in order to **PAE - to split, cleave, cut or make an incision into the spirit-realm.** We can therefore *enter into the spirit-realm through that gateway* and the *Ntorou/Ntorotu can move through that gateway* as well. When we open our spiritual heads through ritual invocation, the Ntorou/Ntorotu can then 'come down' and engage the process of spirit-possession and spirit-communication. When spirit-possession occurs, the Deity has literally *split, cleaved* and *entered into the body* of the person. The Deity then uses the person's physical vessel to physically interface with others in the community by speech, laying hands to heal, dance, making medicine, drawing sacred symbols to function as matrices of energy (medutu, **Adinkra**) and more.

When lightning strikes it is a *rending* or *splitting* of the black sky. This is **mpae** (prayer, ritual provocation). The sound vibrations are accompanied by the cleaving. This is akin to the first emergence of **Ra** and **Rait**, the Creator and Creatress, bursting forth as the Divine Living Energy of Fire and Light, *splitting, cleaving the Black Substance of Space.* They generated the first sacred sound vibrations of the Created Universe as they emerged. As **Ra** and **Rait**, The Great Spirit, began to expand and contract through the primordial Black Substance of Space in a spiraling motion, their Spirit-Energy carved out Black spheres. These Black spheres were then penetrated by (possessed by) and animated by the Divine Living Energy of **Ra** and **Rait**. These spheres became the first 'Black Bodies'. These Black Bodies would become the first stars. [Note that this aspect of our cosmology has been repackaged as **black body radiation** in theoretical physicist's description of the origin of the Universe.] Stars would later give birth to planets including our own star **Aten** (Sun) and the planets of our solar system.

Stars are the power-plants in the Universe. The stars 'rise and set' upon the horizon, just as the **Aten** (Sun) and **Iah** (Moon) 'rise and set'. Our Ancestresses and Ancestors recognized the setting of the Aten (Sun) as well as the stars as the *powers splitting the sky, the atmosphere, to penetrate Earth and bring energy to Earth.* The same is true of meteors (also Black bodies) coming down to Earth as 'shooting' or 'falling stars'. These phenomena mirror the Ntorou/Ntorotu 'coming down' from the spirit-realm during ritual prayer to 'set', 'alight upon', 'mount' or 'split' the head of a priest/priestess or another individual in the community to facilitate spirit-possession.

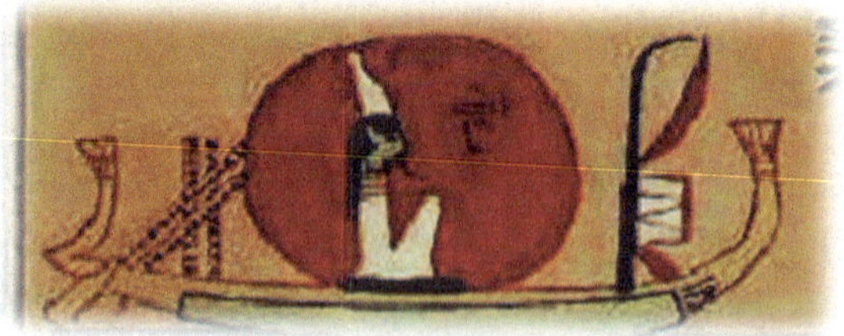

Left: Ntoro **Atum** (called **Odomankoma** in Akan) - Spirit operating through (possessing) the Setting Sun.
Right: Ntoro **Ra** (called **Nyankopon** in Akan) giving His energy to the Sun.

Nesut (King) **Kha f Ra** – The Ntoro **Heru** in the form of the Divine Falcon alighted upon his head. This is spirit-possession and spirit-communication. **Heru** is the Patron Ntoro of Kings.

Shooting or Falling Star – Meteor falling upon Earth

The stars' energy 'enters' the Earth from outside the Earth. The Ntorou/Ntorotu enter the body of the person from outside the body. This is the coming down, the splitting, of the atmosphere of the Earth and the Earthly body so that union can take place and spirit-possession and spirit-communication can occur. This <u>mpae function</u> speaks to the etymological root of the term Ntoro:

tò, *v.* [*red.* **toto**] **1.** ***to throw, cast &c.,*** **Ak. = tow,** *q. v.* **— 2.** ***to lay*** **or** ***put*** **somewhere, gener. caus. (preceded by de**

tɔ̀, *v.* [*red.* **totɔ**]:

1. *to fall, drop down, sink* (*cf.* **hwe, gu**): **akutu (atew) atɔ fam', *an orange has fallen down;* metɔɔ nsum', aka kū-maa sɛ miwui,** *I fell into the water and nearly perished;* **ne diŋ tɔɔ nsum', s. nsu; ɔbo no akɔtɔ nsu no ase,** *the stone has fallen into the water and sunk to the bottom. pr. 357. 2258. 3281. 3287;* **biribi a ɛ́tɔ̀ asõm',** *good reasons* (lit. *something which falls into the ears*). — **osu tɔ,** *rain falls, it rains; tr.* **osoro tɔɔ osu,** *the heaven gave rain. Ja. 5, 18;* **ɔtɔɔ sufre nè gya guu Sodom so.** *Gen. 19, 24.* — **2.** *to set, go down, sink, pass below the horizon,* of sun, moon and stars; **owia atɔ,** *the sun has set:* — **3.** *to fall, be killed, be slain, die, perish,* in battle, or by an accident, not by a natural death. *pr. 238. 2259; cf.* **ɔtɔ́fɔ̂; wo de, gye sɛ wotɔ !** (Gr. § 248,5) *I will not let you die a natural death!* — **4.** *to pass* (suddenly and passively) *into a weaker or lower state* or *circumstances: a)* **tɔ ber-**

The root of the term Ntoro is **'to'** which means *to fall, drop down, sink*. This includes the *passing below the horizon of the Sun, Moon and Stars*. The term **'to'** also means *'to throw, cast'*. The verb form means 'to throw, cast' while the descriptive form is 'that which is thrown, cast'. The Deities are 'thrown, cast' or 'sent' by **Amenet** and **Amen** to 'fall' or 'come down' below the horizon to penetrate Earth and our community through spirit-possession. The 'N' in Ntoro is a nasal 'N' (un'-taw-raw). The nasal sound replicates the primordial energy of **Nun** and **Naunet** the Male and Female Deities who are the primordial Energy within the Black Substance of Space, the inert Energy from Whom **Ra** and **Rait** (Divine Fire and Light) emerge to begin the Creative process. **Nun** and **Naunet** are thus the Father and Mother of **Ra** and **Rait**.

"…This Energy manifested as the Male and Female Spiritual Forces **Nu** and **Nut** (**Nun** and **Naunet**). **Nu** and **Nut** are the Two Abosom of *Primordial Energy*, *Inert Energy*, the Energy that contains the Potential to bring everything into being. The names of **Nu** and **Nut** are written with the 'wavy' lines representing the *wave-energy* within the Black Substance as it transformed into a watery-like substance. Their names are also written with the determinative metut of the **urn** or *vessel*:

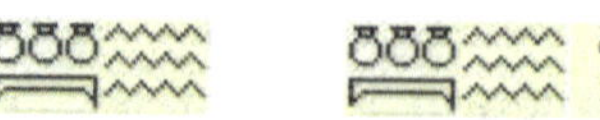

Nu (Nun) **Nut** (Naunet)

The Abosom **Nu** and **Nut** are the Divine, Inactive, Infinite Energy-source subsisting within the Black Substance…" [**Nyankopon-Nyankonton – Ra-Rait** – www.odwirafo.com/nhoma.html]

The primordial 'N' vibration is prefixed to the root 'TO' upon which the 'R' vibration is infixed. Regarding the enlarging of monosyllabic word stems through infixing in Akan:

c) by infixing r (or n, when the vowel is nasal). E. g. wa, wàre, *to be long;* kyè, kyere, *to last;* kŏ, koro, *one;* på, *to take off superficially,* prá, părá, *to sweep;* bå, *to come,* brá, bărá, *to come* (i. e. *be born*) *again into this world;* bà, *to come, Imper.* bèra; kò, *to go,* Pret. kòè, Ak.: kórè. — ɛsɛ́, *a small pillar,* ɔ̀sɛ́rɛ́, *the thigh.* — The vowel after 'r' is often to be considered as the original, and that before 'r' only as an auxiliary vowel, when the latter is very short. Gr. § 22.

Example of infixing:

ɛ-só, Ak. soɔ [*cf.* ɔsoro & Gr. § 118-120] 1. *the upper part* or *surface of.* — 2. *the upper parts, the space above,* and what is in it. — 3. *on, up, upon, over, above, upward, on high;* of time: *in, at, during;* of other relations: *on, at, concerning, in, from, with;* - ɔsekaŋ da póŋ no sò; ogyina n'abobowano hwɛ abontɛŋ no so; ɛtwene nni abontɛŋ no so. *pr. 40. 373. 592. 883. 1427.*

ɔ-sóró [*cf.* ɛso; s. Gr. § 118-120] 1. *the upper part* or *parts.* — 2. *the space* or *situation above. pr. 472.* — 3. *what is above, the upper world, upper regions, sky, heaven.* — 4. (*adv.*) *above, on high, up, upwards.* — kɔ soro, *to go up, upwards, to rise, to ascend;* owisiw kɔ soro, *the smoke ascends;* fi soro de besi fam', *from the top to the bottom.*

In the Akan language word stems are expanded by the 'R' sound as shown above. For example, the term **so** meaning 'up, above, heavens', becomes **soro**. The term **ko** meaning 'one' becomes **koro**. The term **ba** meaning 'come, happen' becomes **bara**. The term **TO** becomes **TORO**. While this rule is readily observed in Akan and our Ancestral language of Kamit and Khanit, our <u>cosmology</u> provides us with the answer to the question of <u>why</u> this is the case.

Ra and **Rait** (**Nyankopon** and **Nyankonton** in Akan)
Creator and Creatress

The rolling 'R' is a sound of power. It expands upon the stem because it is the sound that the Great Spirit **Ra** and **Rait** generates as they expand and contract throughout Creation.

The rolling 'R' sound is a replication of the sound vibrations generated by and emanating from Ra and Rait as they move throughout Creation.

All vibrations generate sounds. A whip whirling through the air creates a sound. A string being pulled taught and made to vibrate (plucked) generates sound. Wind moving through space generates sound vibrations. Thunder, lightning, earthquakes, all generate sound vibrations. **The same is true of the Spirit-Forces that course through Nature.** The faster moving energy generates higher-pitched sounds while the slower moving energy generates lower-pitched sounds. The nature of the expansion and contraction of each entity generates a unique configuration of sound-groupings as well. This becomes the unique 'voice' of the Spirit-Force moving through Creation. **It is the cataloging of these various frequencies and unique sound-groupings that makes up the corpus of ritual songs, drumbeats, dance movements, prayers and incantations in Afurakani/Afuraitkaitnit (African) Ancestral Religion.**

We attune to the sounds of the Ntorou/Ntorotu as they move through Creation and generate their unique vibrations. **We attune to the sounds they generate as they enter the bodies of our people through spirit-possession. We then replicate these unique sound groupings with our voices and other instruments in order to align with the frequency of the Ntorou/Ntorotu and thus draw them to us, provoke their energy – provoke them to align, alight, come down and possess.**

All of the words in our Ancestral languages are based upon these principles. These principles were taught to us by the Ntorou/Ntorotu when they first began to possess us and speak directly to us during possession. All of the words in our Ancestral languages thus have mantric value. They are constructed based on the sounds generated by the movement of the Ntorou/Ntorotu in Creation. **We can therefore properly identify things, objects, deeds, entities, etc. based on the nature of their movements (functioning) in Creation. This is born out in the language of Kamit.**

The 'N' 𓈖 is the primordial inert energy, wave energy and sound vibration subsisting in the primordial Dark Matter of Space, pre and post-Creation. The 'T' 𓏏 is not only a loaf but also the canopy of the sky, upper half of the calabash of the Universe. When the 'T' sound is spoken, the air rushing up from the trachea is cut off. When enunciating the 'T' sound as in the word 'hit', the front of the tongue is placed at the roof of the front of the mouth. The air coursing up through the trachea is then trapped within the mouth. The roof of the mouth is convex and the flat tongue is on the bottom. The inside of the mouth thus forces the air to take on the shape of the 'T' medut when enunciating the 'T' sound: 𓏏. It is similar to the air of the atmosphere of Earth being 'contained' within the dome-shape of the sphere - upper curved portion of the medut - while the land is the flat surface - bottom flat surface of the medut.

When we have the primordial vibration of **Nun** and **Naunet** the 𓈖 (N) which is then contained (cut-off) by the 𓏏 (T), **we have Divine Energy in Potential – Contained in a Space - Literally**. Then **Ra** and **Rait** burst forth from the primordial Dark Matter. The **Opening of the Mouth** occurs: 𓂋 (R). Note this is the shape the mouth takes when enunciating the 'R' sound. This 'opening of the mouth' is an incision, a splitting and rending. The explosive and radiant energy of 'RRRR' is the transformation of the wave energy 𓈖 to a spiral 𓍢. The wave-energy, **the undulating serpent**, transforms into spiraled-energy, **the circular serpent**:

The serpents encircling the **Aten** (Sun) above is the manner in which **Ra** and **Rait** are spelled in the medutu. This is the spiraling, radiant energy born of the waves **Nun** of **Naunet** which *splits, rends* the Black Substance of Space as the original Divine Fire and Light in Creation. **Ra** and **Rait** are Children of **Nun** and **Naunet**. Our cosmology is born out through the sound vibrations we replicate – the **ENE** (Akan for 'Sounds') of the Ntorou/Ntorotu.

ter, terá, Gol. Ḥamm. 13, 112, , , , Rec. 32, 16, Thes. 1481, IV, 970, , , , Rec. 16, 57, , to pay honour, to revere, to applaud, to have a regard for; , Åmen. 25, 7, , ibid. 21, 11.

terr, IV, 1182, to revere; Copt. ⲧⲣ̄ⲣⲉ.

netri, Rec. 27, 220, , , , , , , Thes. 1284, to be, or to become divine, to deify, divine; , I deify;

neter, nether, U. 70, N. 330, , T. 237, , M. 147, , N. 649, , , , , , , ★, the word in general use in texts of all periods for God and "god"; Copt. ⲛⲟⲩⲧⲉ, = ⲛⲟⲩⲧⲉ (Rev.)

The term **tr (toro)** is the verb form meaning *to revere, to honor, to praise.* The descriptive form is *that which is revered, honored or praised.* It is the Divinity which is accorded praise, honor and reverence. We also have the terms **ta** and **tua (to** in Akan) carrying the same meaning. This is the **to** root from which **toro (tr)** is derived in Kamit, just as **toro** is derived from **to** in Akan:

tua , Peasant 299, , Metternich Stele 101, , , to pray to, to praise, to address, to make a report, to honour; Copt. ⲦⲀⲒⲞ.

taȧ , Rev. 11, 131 = ★, to adore.

tȧ-t , A.Z. 1900, 128, , IV, 1074, , Tombos Stele, 10, emanation, part, portion; plur. , IV, 53; Copt. ⲦⲞ, ⲦⲞⲒ.

tȧ , form, counterpart; , forms, images, likenesses.

tȧa , divine emanation, essence of a god; var. .

It is key to understand that in Akan **to** is the root of **toro**. In the language of Kamit **tr (ter)** is the root of **ntr (neter)**. Yet, **tr** meaning *to praise, honor*, has the root **TUA** and **TA**. Note that the Coptic (Late Kamit) dialectical variant of **TUA** is **TAIO**: **ⲦⲀⲒⲞ.** Note also that the Coptic dialectical variant of **TA** is **TO** – <u>the vocalization still used in Akan today</u>: **Copt. ⲦⲞ, ⲦⲞⲒ**

In Kamit, the terms **Tua, Ta, Taa** reference ritual provocation, *to pray, to praise.* **Ta** also means *Divine emanation, essence of a Deity; Divine forms, images, likenesses.* We know these forms are Divine forms because the determinative symbol is that of a male or female Deity.

What is the relationship between **TA (TO)** as a *Divine emanation* and **TA (TUA)** meaning *to pray, praise, honor, worship* and also **TO** meaning *to cast, or to throw* and **TO** meaning *to fall, to set, to come down*? The link is found in the determinative symbol:

An **emanation** is that which is 'projected' out or 'cast, thrown' out. The Aten (Sun) casts, shoots, throws its light outward. The light of the Aten 'falls' or 'comes down' upon Earth. The light 'emanates' from the Aten.

The terms *praise, adore, honor, pray* are english terms. The action and function of the pictured individual with his hands held up performing ritual provocation is the key. The symbolism pulls the various definitions together as a functional expression. We quote from our publication on this ritual provocation: **Note on Tua Ra Being the Origin of the 'Torah'** [www.odwirafo.com/Tua-Ra_torah.pdf]:

"…Now we take note of the hand positions of the worshipper in the medutu and the image of Ani himself:

The posture shown by the individual in the medutu and by Ani is not a static posture but a **functional act**. The individual is involved in the 'worship' or ritual invocation of the Deity through **provocation**. When the hands are turned outward in a 'pushing' fashion, we are ritually and literally 'provoking' the energy of the Ntoro/Ntorot (God/Goddess). This ritual movement continues to be used today. When we engage in the **'laying on of hands'** to provoke the energy of the person's body for healing or for the repelling of negative spirits in the practice of Afurakani/Afuraitkaitnit (African) Ancestral Religion, we are engaged in ritual **provocation**. In contrast, if our palms are turned upward in a *receiving* posture we are engaged in ritual **convocation.** We are *drawing* energy to us. The act of provocation is literally a projecting, shooting of energy outward to stimulate the energic-body of the Deity, Ancestral Spirit, plant, animal or individual we are focused upon. This is a lived experience which is quantifiable.

In the same fashion that two magnets on a table whose like polarities are facing can 'push' one another across a table without touching because of their magnetic fields, we have the capacity and proactively employ our capacity to project our energy outward to 'touch', 'push', 'provoke', the individual or entity upon whom we are focused ritually.

This is why the term **tua** also means *to cry out, to call.* Sound vibrations are matrices of energy that are projected. One can sing at such a pitch and volume that the sound vibrations alone can break a glass. This is the releasing, shooting, sending out of energic-vibrations, unseen power, that can effect solid matter in a manner that can be measured and quantified…"

See the related term **TO** in Akan:

tò, *v.* **1.** *to meet (with), fall in with; to come* or *light on (upon), to find;* metoo no ɔkwaŋ mu; *I fell in with him on the way. pr. 14. 3307-10.* — **2.** *to reach, arrive at, come up with, overtake, catch;* wɔato nea Onyaŋkõpɔŋ bɔ too wɔŋ hɔ, *they have attained to their divine destination;* - ɛto fam', *it reaches to the ground; s.* knw, *v.* - *pr. 3313. 3338; to come upon. Am. 9,10; to attack, cf.* pèe. — ehĩa wato wɔŋ, F. *poverty has overtaken them, Mf. Gr. p. 107.* - ɔw̃ɛŋ ato wo, *it is your turn to keep watch;* asɔre ato wo, *it is your turn to preach;* n'ano ato me, lit. *his mouth has reached me,* i.e. *he has spoken ill of me, s.* ano; n'ano to Onyame, *he blasphemes God.* — **3.** *to come up to,* perf. *to equal, match:* wato no, *now he equals him* (in riches, knowledge &c.) — **4.** *to join, attach one's self (to). pr. (1810). 2811.* — **5.** *to expose one's self* (to the heat of a fire or of the sun, to the cold &c.): to gya, *to warm one's self at the fire;* to aw̃ia, *to warm one's self in the sun;* to ãwɔw, *to expose one's self to the cold;* mekɔto awɔw, *I am going to seek coolness;* - wato ne hõ sérè, *he has exposed himself to laughter; cf.* serew̃. *pr. 3312.* — *Phr.* woato yɛŋ, (prop. *'you have found us',* sc. at our meal), *please, join us* (sc. in our meal)! - reply: me nsa wom', *no, thank you!*

As we can see the term **TO** meaning *to fall upon, meet with; to join attach oneself to; to expose oneself to the heat of a fire or of the Sun,* is related to **TO** meaning *to cast, to throw* and **TO** meaning *to alight upon, come down, as in stars passing below the horizon.* When we see the determinative medut of the individual raising his hands in the act of ritual provocation, he is casting, throwing his energy to provoke the energy of the Deities so that they may come down, fall upon, alight upon, possess, attach themselves to, expose their energy and wisdom to the individual. This is the functional definition of to *pray, adore, honor, worship* – it is **ritual provocation.**

The variation of **TR** (TERA) is **TN** (TENA) meaning *to pray, cry out, invoke.*

tenȧ [hieroglyphs], Rev. 14, 8, to pray, to cry out, to invoke; and see [hieroglyphs].

ter, terȧ [hieroglyphs], Gol. Ḥamm. 13, 112, [hieroglyphs], [hieroglyphs], [hieroglyphs], Rec. 32, 16, Thes. 1481, IV, 970, [hieroglyphs], [hieroglyphs] have a regard for; [hieroglyphs], Amen. 25, 7, [hieroglyphs], ibid. 21, 11.

terr [hieroglyphs], IV, 1182, to revere; Copt. ⲧⲣ̄ⲣⲉ.

In Akan this is the relationship of Ntoro (Toro) and Nton (Ton). We therefore have:

Kamit		Akan
ntr		ntoro
tr		toro
ta	(to in Coptic)	to
tua	(taio in Coptic)	to
taa		to
tna		ton

Recall that in the fourth part of the definition of **TO** we see that it also has the related meaning: *to pass or fall into a weaker or lower state or circumstances.* This is the same related definition of **TR** (**TOR**) in Kamit:

tɔ̀, *v.* [*red.* totɔ]:

***die a natural death!* — 4. *to pass* (suddenly and passively) *into a weaker* or *lower state* or *circumstances*: *a*) tɔ ber-**

ter [hieroglyphs], to be weak.

We can thus confirm the vocalization of **TR** (TER) as **TO** (TOR). With this foundation in the etymological and cosmological roots of the term Ntoro, we now turn to the connection to the symbol of the axe itself.

NYAME AKUMA

God's Axes

In Akan areas, there are artifacts found all over the region including Neolithic celts. These stone celts or stone axes are recognized by the Akan to have been in the area since the stone-age. Very often these ancient stone axes can be found after the rains, when they emerge from the wet soil. Others have been found on the bottom of sacred rivers. Akan people recognize these ancient axes to be sacred for two major reasons. First, because they recognize that it was their Ancestresses and Ancestors who utilized these ancient axes thousands of years ago. They carry the energy of the Spirits of the **Nananom Nsamanfo**, Spiritually Cultivated Ancestresses and Ancestors. Secondly and most critically, the Akan recognize their origins to be Divine. Often after a thunderstorm these axes can be found at the base of trees that have been struck by lightning. Akan people identify these axes as sacred axes which have come down from the sky during the storms and caused the cleaving of the tree. These axes are thus called by the people: **Nyame Akuma** – God's Axes. The name **Nyame** is also written **Onyame**. This is a title of **Amen** in Ancient Kamit and Khanit.

[See our publication: **Note on the Origin of the Name Nyame in Khanit and Kamit**]:
www.odwirafo.com/Note_on_the_Origin_of_the_Name_Nyame_in_Ancient_Khanit_and_Kamit.pdf

Ari Amen pronounced with a rolling 'R' (tongue tapping the roof of the mouth once) sounds like **Ani Amen** and **Ari Amen**. This is **Ony-Amen** or **Onyame (Nyame)**. What is the nature of the **Nyame Akuma** – God's Axe as explained by the Akan? In the article **Ashanti**, the anthropologist R. S. Rattray, provides the information that was relayed to him by the Asante (Ashanti) Akan in the early part of the previous century:

"...NEOLITHIC IMPLEMENTS IN ASHANTI

I have had occasion several times in the preceding chapters to mention neoliths, which in Ashanti are known as God's axes or God's hoes, and the following fuller notes upon them may be of interest.

In the year 1911 it was my good fortune to be in Ashanti during the latter part of the construction of the Coomassie-Ejura main trunk road, and to have obtained a collection of celts which were then unearthed.

These formed the subject of a most interesting paper by Mr. Henry Balfour- (of the Pitt- Rivers Museum, Oxford) in the 'Journal of the African Society, (1) and I advise all who are interested to consult that article.

In 1921 I found myself again in Ashanti as Government Anthropologist.

In the short time that has elapsed since taking up my new work some hundred more specimens of celts have been obtained, a few being found by me in situ, and many were dug up by the Ashanti farmers, and one, the largest, was lately dredged up from the bottom of the Offin River.

Some were associated with the cult of the **Abosom**, the suman, or of **Nyame**.

While it is correct to state that probably ninety-nine out of a hundred Ashanti declare and actually believe that the stone celts found by them emanate from the sky, and are in consequence endowed with some of the power of the Sky God, **Nyame**, sufficient evidence is available to prove beyond a doubt that there are still alive in Ashanti to-day persons who know that these stones are artifacts, and that they were used by their ancestors at a period that was relatively recent.

The Ashanti generally call them **Nyame akuma** or **Nyame asoso**, i. e. the Sky-God's axes or hoes.

They believe that they fall from the sky during thunderstorms and bury themselves in the earth.

They think that, as they come from **Nyame**, they are endowed with some of the power of that great spirit and **this is the explanation of their use in connection with Abosom** [Deities] and of their supposed **potency as medicine.**

As a consequence of this belief they are constantly to be found as **appurtenances to Abosom** (the gods), suman (charms), **Nyame dua** (altar to the Sky God), or placed in a pot where the drinking water is kept, 'to cool the heart'. They are also sometimes fastened against the body to **cure diseases**, or are **ground down and the powder drunk**.

I am inclined to believe it is thought heterodox to say anything contrary to the above, because these, being the popular beliefs, are encouraged by the **akomfo** (priests)..." [Ashanti – R.S. Rattray].

A related quote from **West African Religion** by Geoffrey Parrinder:

"...The three-pronged tree, God's tree [**Nyame dua**], used in the worship of **Nyame** is like that which occurs in the worship of some other thunder gods. Rattray describes a tornado during which a tree was struck by lightning and had all the appearance of having been cleft by an axe. 'One of the villagers came up, and after looking at it, said that God's axe (Nyame dua) had, after splitting the tree, passed underground to the river where no doubt it would someday be found.'..."

Nyame Dua

In the above quotes we learn that the **axes** called **Nyame Akuma**, God's axes, 'fall down', 'come down' from the **sky**, <u>sent by **Nyame**</u>. When lightning cleaves, splits a tree during a thunderstorm, it is recognized to be the result of Nyame Akuma, God's axe, causing the rending, the splitting. These stone axes are <u>placed inside the shrine</u> called **Nyame Dua** (God's tree) which is a three or four-pronged tree which holds a vessel. Inside the vessel is water used to cleanse the spiritual heads of the people, but also an Nyame Akuma. <u>Other shrines of the Abosom (Ntorou/Ntorotu – Deities) all over the country also include Nyame Akuma in their vessels</u>. The Ntorou/Ntorotu (Deities) are associated with the axe – so much so that their shrines all contain axeheads. Because the Nyame Akuma is from **Nyame (Amen)**, it is recognized to be sacred, endowed with Divine power and thus **medicinal**.

This is the cosmological foundation for the image of the Ntoro/Ntorot, the Deity who 'falls down', 'passes under the horizon', 'cleaves or splits the sky' to be that of an axe. It is because the function of **mpae** (prayer) is literally a **splitting, cleaving** (pae) of the spirit-realm so that an incision can be made that we may pass through and that the Deities may pass through to facilitate spirit-possession and spirit-communication.

Actual **Nyame Akuma** (God's Axe) – Neolithic celt/axehead found in Ghana

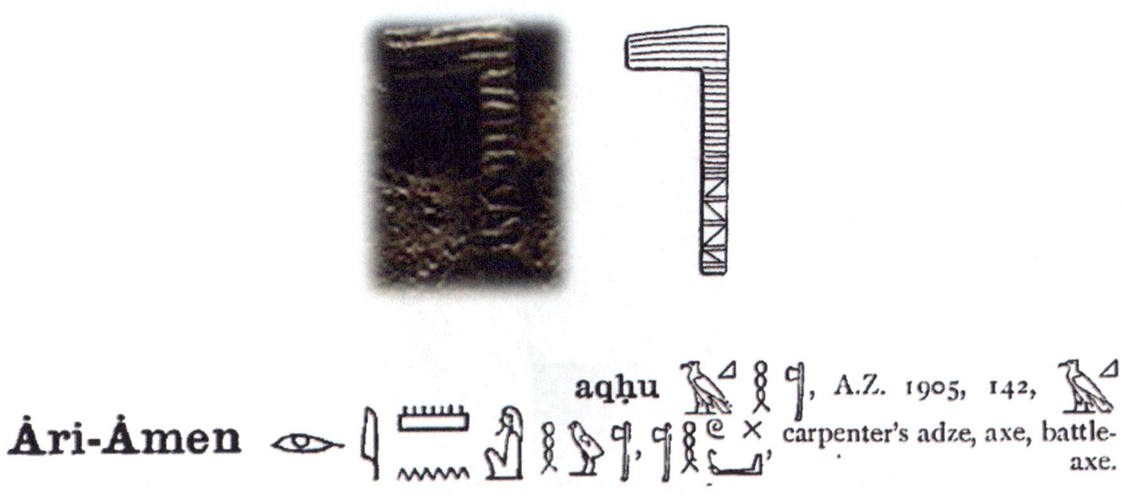

Ȧri-Ȧmen

aqḥu, A.Z. 1905, 142, carpenter's adze, axe, battle-axe.

The **Ari Amen Aqhu** is literally the **Onyame Akuma** – God's Axe.

All of the definitions of Ntoro, Nton, to, tua, ta, etc. are united in this symbolism. The motion of the akuma (axe) when properly used is always a **downward motion** in order to chop, cleave, split the object. The Divine Axe 'falls down', 'comes down' (to, toro) to Earth, just as the Deities fall down or come down to Earth.

When thunder comes it is a precursor to the coming down of Nyame Akuma, God's axe. This is demonstrated by traditional Akan **akyene** (drums) whose sticks are in the form of the Nyame Akuma:

The 'talking drums' of the Akan. When the axe (stick) falls, the thunder (drumming) begins. Spirit-possession often follows. This is the lightning, Divine Energy of Fire and Light, coming down to alight upon the person's head after the drumming/thunder:

Akan **Obosomfo** (Priest) Possessed by the Obosom (Deity) **Tano**

o-nípa, ***pl.*** **n-** **[F. nyimpa] 1.** ***man, a man, human being, person*** **(it may**

o-nipa-dùá, 1. ***the figure, form, shape of the body; the body; cf.*** **nipamũ,**

Note that in the Akan language the term for human being is **onipa**. Yet the term for the physical body is **onipadua**. The term 'dua' means 'tree'. The person's (onipa) body is seen as a tree (dua). Thus, when spirit-possession takes place the radiant energy of the Ntoro/Ntorot comes down to split the human-tree, onipadua, just as lightning comes down to split the tree, dua, in nature. This reflects the energy of **Nyamewaa** and **Nyame** residing in the Nyame Dua.

Most importantly, when the Ntoro possesses, the Ntoro **operates within** the body of the person. This is akin to a person driving a car and then another person gets in the vehicle and takes the wheel. The original driver may get into the back seat. He can see everything that's taking place, yet he is not directing the vehicle. The new driver and the original driver are in the same vessel, however the new driver has temporarily taken control. This is what takes place during spirit-possession which is called **Akom** in Akan from the root **ko** (go) **mu** (within). To **komu** or **kom** is to 'go within', to 'seize' to 'grasp' – **possession**.

akɔ́m [kɔm] *inf. the state of being possessed with a fetish,* i. e. *a temporary madness* or *ecstasy,* expressing itself in dancing and wild gestures, and ascribed by the natives to the agency of a fetish; *the fetish-dance;* wafa ak., *he* or *she has taken in* such an agency, *has been possessed with a fetish;* ne hõ resaw sɛ ak., *he is trembling, like one possessed with a fetish.*

kɔ̀m, *v.* [*inf.* a-] *to dance wildly in a state of frenzy* or *ecstasy,* ascribed by the natives to the agency of a fetish; *to be possessed with a fetish; to perform the actions* or *practices of a fetish-man; to prophesy. 1 Kg. 18,29;* k. bosom, *to soothsay, foretell;* ɔ́kɔ̀m b. sɛ ɔkyena osu bɛto, *he prophesies that it will rain to-morrow; s.* akom, ŋkɔm, ɔkɔmfo. *pr. 1698.* — *red.* koŋkɔ́m, *q. v.*

khemā, T. 46, P. 87, P. 33, Rev. 11, 90, to grasp, to seize, to lay hold upon, to hold, to possess, to contain.

khau (?), Rec. 21, 81, to fall into an ecstasy, to prophesy during a frenzy.

Critically, during this possession the Ntoro once in the body of the person in Akan culture dances, wielding its power by generating a vortex or field of energy through sacred movement. The community is then drawn into the 'orbit' of the Ntoro during possession. The Ntoro will also walk around, touch people, speak to them, lay hands to heal them and more. **What is most poignant in this display is that in Akan culture the Ntoro upon entering the body of the person very often grasps the curved sword/axe, an axe or a 'hunting' stick in the shape of an axe:**

The **okomfo**, a class of priest - one who is in the **kom** (possession) state - is possessed by the Ntoro. The white clay, **hyriew**, is thrown on the body of the okomfo denoting that Spirit is now inhabiting the body. The 'lightning' has 'come down' **(to)** and split the spirit. The Ntoro has 'fell in with' **(to/toro)** and 'joined itself' **(to/toro)** the person's body. The Ntoro operating through the okomfo's body therefore grasps the curved sword (a kind of axe). This image of the Ntoro (Deity) from Kamit next to the axe is the image of a <u>Spirit</u> juxtaposed to an axe. **When the Akan okomfo is possessed by the Spirit the axe is automatically grasped.**

The medutu of the Ntoro and the axe has literally leapt off of the inscriptions of the ancient temples and tombs and become manifest in real time in Akan ritual daily.

When we utilized this symbolism to denote a Deity, it was because the Deity literally <u>**is**</u> an **aqhu**, **akuma**, axe. The Ntoro/Ntorot is a Spirit-Force in Creation that splits, cleaves the transitional zone of Spirit and Matter in order to 'fall, come down' to possess, communicate, heal and guide:

ter , **to guide.**

The original 'axes' are those that came down from the sky – meteorite stones. Our Ancestresses and Ancestors fashioned these meteorite stones into axeheads as well as other stones. The meteorite stones as axes were used in shrines and as instruments to wield power during ritual. Other stones were also fashioned into axeheads for agricultural purposes, hunting purposes, warfare and could also be consecrated for shrine use. We also utilized sticks, branches from trees, including branches taken from those trees that would be used as **Nyame Dua** (God's Altar), that had the natural form of an axe (so-called hunting stick) for the same ritual purposes including drumming for the invocation 'calling down' of the Deities. Over time, when we learned how to smelt metal we began to fashion **metal axeheads** (akin to meteorite axeheads) and **curved metal axes** (akin to the curved branches). Such axes and sticks were used for ritual, agriculture, hunting and warfare.

Left: Late Pre-Dynastic image from Nekhen, Upper Kamit (Hierkonopolis). Individual raising axe to prisoners of war. Right: Asante Akan afena (curved sword/axe) used by okomfo (priests, priestesses) during possession. Also for warfare.

Ra Messu raising the axe to prisoners of war. New Empire.

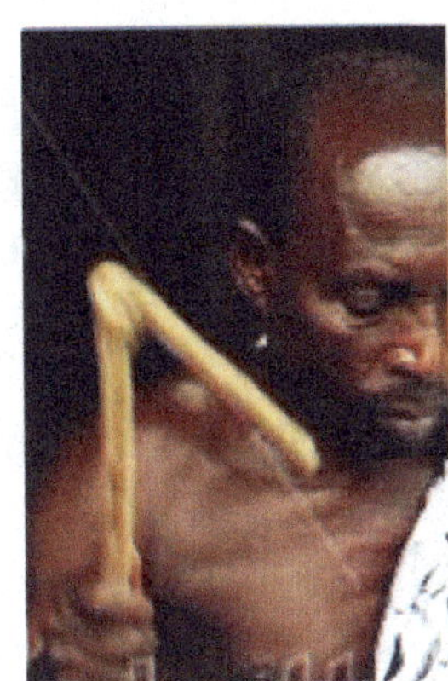

Left to right: Asante afena (sword/axe machete); Ntoro medut; Okyeremma – Akan drummer; Shrine of Obosom Kwasi Adanko. The large naturally curved stick in the form of the sacred axe in front of the shrine is a consecrated instrument of the Obosom.

The curved axe/sword is a **machete** - a stylized version of the straight axe. We thus find that both are used for the smiting of the enemy as well as for ritual purposes including being used as components of the shrines of the Deities in addition to being grasped by the Deities themselves during possession. The use of the stone axehead and the curved stick/branch in the form of an axe is not limited to the Akan of Ghana and Ivory Coast. In the **Hoodoo Religion**, which we have proven to be the **Akan Religion in North america**, the use of the stone axehead and sticks/branches which have the natural form of an axe, are used on the shrines of the Abosom and Nsamanfo (Deities and Ancestral Spirits). This is a living culture, unbroken for thousands of years across continents guided directly by the Abosom and Nsamanfo.

In ancient Kamit the symbol of the axe is also represented in the use of the flag on a standard:

This usage is in alignment with the cosmology. When a flag is hanging one is not able to see what the symbol and/or message on the flag is. However, when the wind comes the flag rises up. The fabric of the flag begins to straighten out. When one sees the fabric of the flag rise up and straighten out, one recognizes that an invisible force is now active (wind). The invisible force activates the flag. The flag sticking straight out in the air literally splits, cleaves the air. We can now see the symbol and read the message that the flag is conveying. We have become informed once the flag has been 'possessed' by and activated by the invisible power of wind.

Cosmological Foundation of Ntoro/Ntorot as Axe

- The **Nyame Dua,** the shrine for the Supreme Being **Nyame** and **Nyamewaa** contains an **Nyame Akuma** - God's axe. These shrines are in the courtyards of shrine houses/temples and in the courtyards of all traditional Akan homes. The Nyame Akuma are also found in the shrine pots of the various **Abosom** (Deities – **Ntoro/Ntoron**).

- When the **Abosom** (Deities – **Ntoro/Ntoron**) possess, they grasp an axe.

- **Mpae,** prayer, is ritual provocation which is a splitting or cleaving of the transitional zone of Spirit and Matter. The sound vibrations of ritual prayer, song, chant, incantation are literally 'axes'.

- The term **Ntoro** is from the root **toro** and **to** meaning to 'come down', 'fall down' as lightning coming down to strike, split, or the Spirits coming down from the sky to strike, split, possess. **Ntoro** and **Ntoron** are patrilineal and matrilineal lines of **descent.**

- The **Abosom** (Orisha, Vodou, Arusi), the **Ntorou/Ntorotu,** are literally 'axes' as they 'come down' and open, split the spiritual head of the individual to enter into the physical vessel wherein possession takes place.

The whites and their offspring, who incarnate as spirits of disorder, are not capable of properly contextualizing the symbols and ritual use of language in our Ancestral culture. Afurakani/Afuraitkaitnit (African) Ancestral Culture is a living Culture. It is living because we are animated by, guided by and possessed by the exact same Ntorou/Ntorotu (Deities) today that we and our Ancestresses and Ancestors were animated by, guided by and possessed by thousands of years ago. We have an Ancestral memory of our ritual practices which is replenished regularly through lived-experience when the **Ntorou/Ntorotu** and the **Aakhu/Aakhutu** (Deities and Spiritually Cultivated Ancestresses and Ancestors) communicate with us via spirit-possession and other forms of spirit-communication.

Finally, regarding **Hoodoo** as a preservation of Afurakani/Afuraitkaitnit (African) Ancestral Religion in the united states, we excerpt from **African-American Religious Thought: An Anthology** edited by Cornel West and Eddie S. Glaude Jr.:

"...The way in which bits of African faith and practice persisted in folk belief and customs...is evident in the following account from the New Orleans *Times-Democrat* of August 5, 1888. During a thunderstorm elderly Tante Delores anxiously searched the house for some object. Not finding it, she ran to the yard. According to the article,

'Hither and thither she ran in rapid quest, until at last she stumbled upon the object of her search, no less thing than an axe for chopping wood...a bright expression of joy irradiated her face.

Seizing the axe and raising it over her head, "she made pass after pass in the very face of the rushing current, as if chopping some invisible thing in twain." When the wind suddenly abated she returned to the house in triumph, stating that it never failed her if she "jest got there in time enough."'

A similar custom among Mississippi Black Folk was noted by Puckett:

...foreign to European thought is the Southern Negro custom of going out into the yard and chopping up the ground with an axe when a storm threatens. This is supposed to "cut de storm in two" and so stop it. Others stick a spade in the ground to split the cloud, or simply place an axe in the corner of the house."..."

This is **transcarnational inheritance** of Ancestral Religion and culture from Ancient Khanit and Kamit through West Afuraka/Afuraitkait (Africa) to North America.

Select Bibliography

AFURAKA/AFURAITKAIT – The Origin of the term 'Africa'
www.odwirafo.com/AFURAKA-AFURAITKAIT.html

THE OKRA/OKRAA COMPLEX – The Soul of Akanfo
www.odwirafo.com/Okra-Okraa_Complex.html

NYANKOPON-NYANKONTON – RA-RAIT
www.odwirafo.com/nhoma.html

The Origin of the Term Abosom in Kamit
www.odwirafo.com/The_Origin_of_the_Term_Abosom_in_Kamit.pdf

Ntoro and Nton, A.C. Denteh
http://www.odwirafo.com/ntonandntoro.pdf

Origin of the Niger-Congo Speakers, Dr. Clyde Winters
www.webmedcentral.com/article_view/3149

Ashanti, Robert Sutherland Rattray
Oxford, Clarendon Press, 1923. www.worldcat.org/title/ashanti/oclc/12159938

West African Religion, Geoffrey Parrinder
London, Epworth Press. 1961. www.catalog.hathitrust.org/Record/001395059

HOODOO PEOPLE: Afurakanu/Afuraitkaitnut (Africans) in North America – Akan Custodians of Hoodoo from Ancient Hoodoo/Udunu Land (Khanit/Nubia)
www.odwirafo.com/Hoodoo.html

UBEN-HYENG – The Ancestral Summons
www.odwirafo.com/nhoma.html

ANIDHAO – Awareness [Includes 'The Origin of the term 'God']
www.odwirafo.com/nhoma.html

An Hieroglyphic Dictionary, Vols. 1-2 by E.A. Wallis Budge (1920 edition)
www.archive.org

Dictionary of the Asante and Fante Language Called Tshi (Twi) [Akan Language Dictionary] by J.G. Christaller (1881 edition and 1933 edition):
www.archive.org

Note on the Origin of the Name Nyame in Khanit and Khamit

www.odwirafo.com/Note_on_the_Origin_of_the_Name_Nyame_in_Ancient_Khanit_and_Kamit.pdf

Moor Means 'Dead'

ODWIRAFO KWESI RA NEHEM PTAH AKHAN

MOOR MEANS DEAD

Odwirafo Kwesi Ra Nehem Ptah Akhan

The term in ancient **Kamit** (Egypt) written **MR** in the **metutu** (hieroglyphs) has been identified as a cognate for the term **moor** found in english as a noun and a verb. The term in Kamit is typically pronounced in the **Coptic** dialect (Late Kamit dialect which came into use c2000 years ago) as **MER** or **MAR/BAR**. Note that in the language of Kamit the 'm' and 'b' sounds can interchange. This interchange also exists in the **Akan** language of Ghana and Ivory Coast, West Afuraka/Afuraitkait (Africa). For example, the word for blood *'mogya'* is also written and pronounced *'bogya'* in Akan. The term **MR** in Kamit:

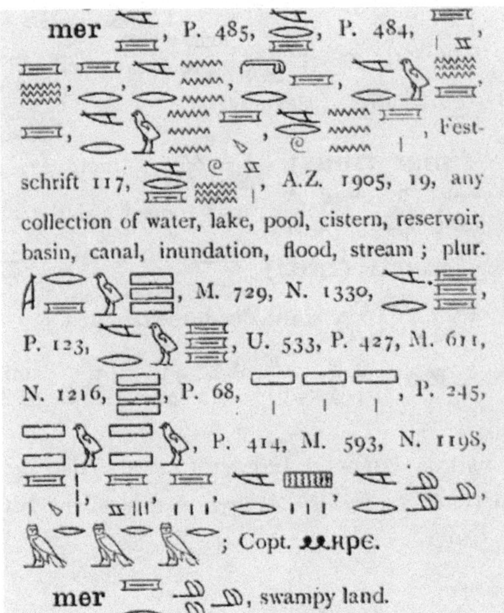

mer, P. 485, P. 484, Fest-schrift 117, A.Z. 1905, 19, any collection of water, lake, pool, cistern, reservoir, basin, canal, inundation, flood, stream; plur. M. 729, N. 1330, P. 123, U. 533, P. 427, M. 611, N. 1216, P. 68, P. 245, P. 414, M. 593, N. 1198, ; Copt. ⲙⲏⲣⲉ.

mer, swampy land.

mer, meru, IV, 656, Metternich Stele 117, desert, plain, mountain.

mer-tt desert land, waste, wilderness.

Many 'egyptologists' arbitrarily place an 'e' between consonants of words from Kamit when they are unsure of the ancient pronunciation. Sometimes this placement is accurate and sometimes it is not. The means by which we can find out the proper pronunciations of words spelled in the **metutu** *(hieroglyphs) such as* **MR** *is to look at the languages of Afuraka/Afuraitkait (Africa) which are directly descendent of the language of* **Khanit** *(Nubia) and Kamit. This includes languages such as the Akan, Yoruba, Ewe, Igbo, Bakongo and many more. We can also find the proper vowel placements for different dialects of the ancient language in the* **Coptic** *dialect (Late Kamit dialect coming into use about 2,000 years ago). For example, we see above that the term* **MR** *written in the metutu is written* **mer** *by the egyptologist. In the* **Coptic** *dialect the term is written* **MHRE** *(mereh):*

Copt. ⲘⲎⲢⲈ. *In this instance, the placement of an 'e' sound in between **MR** to facilitate the pronunciation **MER (MHRE** in Coptic) is a valid placement.*

As we can see the term **mr** (**mer**) has the definition: *collection of water, pool, flood; swampy land.* It can also mean *desert land, waste, wilderness.*

What kind of water? There is a relationship between the **flood** (water overrunning the land) causing *destruction, displacement, death: swampy land* (marsh, morass); *wasteland* (infertile/dead land), *wilderness.* We thus have the term **mr** also meaning *death* and related to death: *fatality, the dead, the damned*:

mer-t , , funerary chest or coffer.

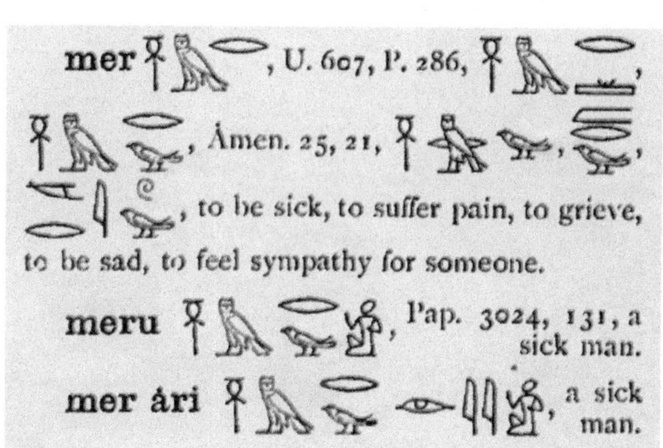

mer , U. 607, P. 286, , , Amen. 25, 21, , , , to be sick, to suffer pain, to grieve, to be sad, to feel sympathy for someone.

meru , Pap. 3024, 131, a sick man.

mer ȧri , a sick man.

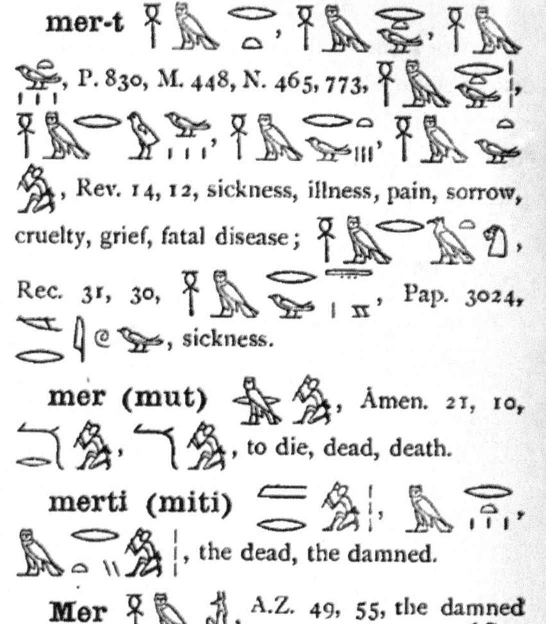

mer-t , , , P. 830, M. 448, N. 465, 773, , , , , Rev. 14, 12, sickness, illness, pain, sorrow, cruelty, grief, fatal disease; , Rec. 31, 30, , Pap. 3024, , sickness.

mer (mut) , Åmen. 21, 10, , , to die, dead, death.

merti (miti) , , , the dead, the damned.

Mer , A.Z. 49, 55, the damned one, a name of Set.

As we can see above the term **mr** also means a *funerary coffer or chest* – a reference to *death.* Also: *sickness, illness, pain, sorrow, fatal disease; to die, dead, death.* The **mru** and **mrti** are *the dead, the damned.* A title of the **Ntoro** (Deity) **Set** is **Mr** meaning *the damned one.*

mer , M. 202, , N. 681, , N. 682, , , , Amen. 2, 9, pyramid, tomb; plur. ,

The term **mr** is also the term for *pyramid* which is a structure *dedicated to the dead.* The dead were often buried in the **mr** (pyramid). Finally, we have a name of Kamit being **Ta Mra**. The term **Ta** means *land.* **Ta Mra** thus references the *land of **Mra*** or ***Mra**-land.*

Merà, an ancient name of Egypt; **Pa-ta-Merá**, the land of Merà = Gr. Πτιμύρις.

This references the **'dead land'** with **mr** referencing *dead, death, flood, swamp*, etc. Why is this so? It is rooted in the *cosmology* of ancient Kamit. First however, let us look at the etymology of the term **moor** as propounded by the whites and their offspring. From etymonline.com (online etymology dictionary):

moor (n.)
"waste ground," O.E. *mor* "morass, swamp," from P.Gmc. **mora-* (cf. O.S., M.Du. Du. *meer* "swamp," O.H.G. *muor* "swamp," also "sea," Ger. *Moor* "moor," O.N. *mörr* "moorland,"*marr* "sea"), perhaps related to ***mere*** (n.), or from root **mer-* "to die," hence "dead land." The basic sense in place names is 'marsh', a kind of low-lying wetland possibly regarded as less fertile than *mersc* 'marsh.' The development of the senses 'dry heathland, barren upland' is not fully accounted for but may be due to the idea of infertility. [Cambridge Dictionary of English Place-Names]

As we can see, the whites and their offspring trace the term **moor** only back to proto-germanic and proto-indo-european 'roots'. They list the following definitions:

1. waste ground
2. morass, swamp
3. sea
4. 'perhaps related to <u>mere</u> or from root <u>mer</u> "to die" dead land

These four definitions are **stolen directly from our Ancestral language of Kamit** as shown in the metutu:

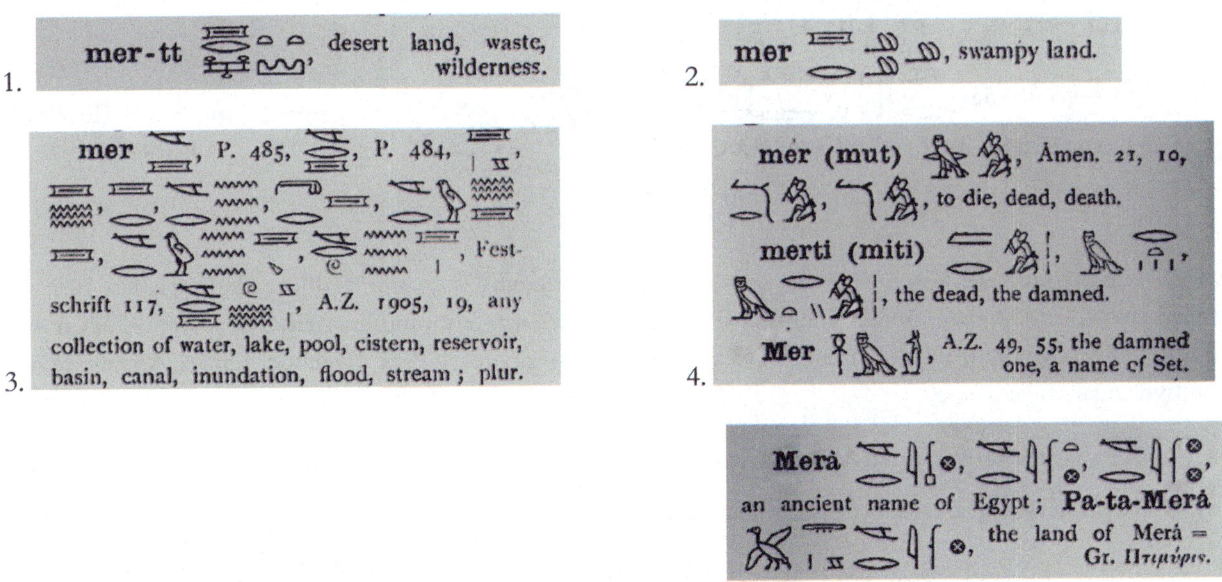
1. **mer-tt**, desert land, waste, wilderness.

2. **mer**, swampy land.

3. **mer**, P. 485, P. 484, Fest-schrift 117, A.Z. 1905, 19, any collection of water, lake, pool, cistern, reservoir, basin, canal, inundation, flood, stream; plur.

4. **mer (mut)**, Åmen. 21, 10, to die, dead, death. **merti (miti)**, the dead, the damned. **Mer**, A.Z. 49, 55, the damned one, a name of Set.

Merà, an ancient name of Egypt; **Pa-ta-Merá**, the land of Merà = Gr. Πτιμύρις.

The language of Kamit is an Afurakani/Afuraitkaitnit (African~Black) language that predates any european or asian language by thousands of years. These four definitions found in the metutu prove conclusively that the term **mr** (*moor* and *mere*) originated with Afurakanu/Afuraitkaitnut (Africans) thousands of years before the whites invaded ancient Kamit and learned of the term.

The Akan have a proverbial saying, *'Love is death'*. This is more than the notion that being 'in love' with someone is often 'painful' or makes someone want to 'die'. There is a cosmological meaning. First, the concept can be found in the term **mr** in Kamit:

mer T. 266, M. 421, T. 283, P. 50, M. 31, N. 64, P. 64, U. 224; Rec. 27, 224, to love, to desire, to wish for, to crave for, to will; Copt. ⲙⲉ.

merriu those who love, lovers, friends.

merr-t P. 69, N. 36, IV, 1045, love, desire, wish, something longed or wished for; plur.

meri U. 532, lover, a loved one, something loved.

meriu beloved one, darling.

meriti U. 532, Rec. 4, 135, Jour. As. 1908, 278, beloved; Copt. ⲙⲉⲣⲓⲧ.

Merr "beloved one," a title of several gods.

As we can see the term **mr** also means *love, desire, to crave for*. One who is *'beloved'* is thus called **mri**. The beloved are called **mriti**. One's *beloved* (masculine) is **mri** while one's *beloved* (feminine) is **mrit**. The 't' feminizes nouns in Kamit. [This is where the 'ette' in english as a 'feminizer' originates – Paul, Paulette; Anton, Antonette; the diminutive: cigar, cigarette, etc.]

We see above that the term written **MR** in the metutu is written **mer** by the egyptologist. In the Coptic dialect the term is written with the 'e' and thus spelled **ME**: Copt. ⲙⲉ. The term for *lover, beloved* is written **MRIT** and translated by the egyptologist as **merit**. In Coptic the term is spelled **MERIT**: Copt. ⲙⲉⲣⲓⲧ. The Coptic dialect has given us a proper dialectical variant of the word with an 'e' vowel placement (as opposed to placing a 'u' or 'o' between **MR**). Further confirmation comes from the Akan language. The Akan term for *love* in the sense of *desire* is **ope** or **pe**. A term for *lover* has the forms **mpra**, **mpena**. The Coptic version of **Mer** is **ME**. The 'R' is dropped. This features in many Afurakani/Afuraitkaitnit (African) speech patterns where we drop the 'R' at regular conversation speed when it occurs at the end of a word. Afurakanu/Afuraitkaitnut (Africans) in america have continued this practice when pronouncing words such as: *her* (pronounced 'huh') or *there* (pronounced by some as 'theh' as in *'see theh'* [*'see there'*]). This features prominently in the Akan language as well. This is how **MER** in ancient Kamit becomes **ME** (meh) in ancient Coptic and **PE** (**OPE** - from **MPE, MME, ME** - Coptic) in Akan. This is how **Meri** (lover) in Kamit becomes **Mpera** (**Mmera Mpena, Mpra**) in Akan.

The 'R' is pronounced as a rolling 'R' in Afurakani/Afuraitkaitnit (African) languages (tongue tapping the roof of the mouth once). This is why the rolling 'R' and the 'N' interchange in various words. They sound identical when speaking at regular conversation speed because the pronunciation of the 'N' sound also requires that the tongue taps the roof of the mouth once.

Note that **mr**, *love* is also **mr**, *death*:

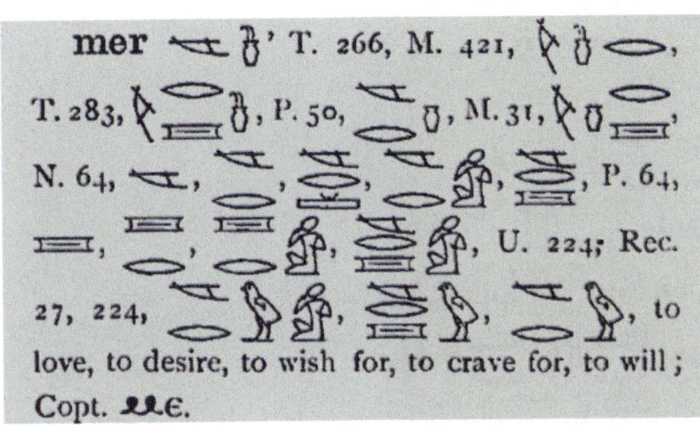
mer, T. 266, M. 421, T. 283, P. 50, M. 31, N. 64, P. 64, U. 224; Rec. 27, 224, to love, to desire, to wish for, to crave for, to will; Copt. ⲙⲉ.

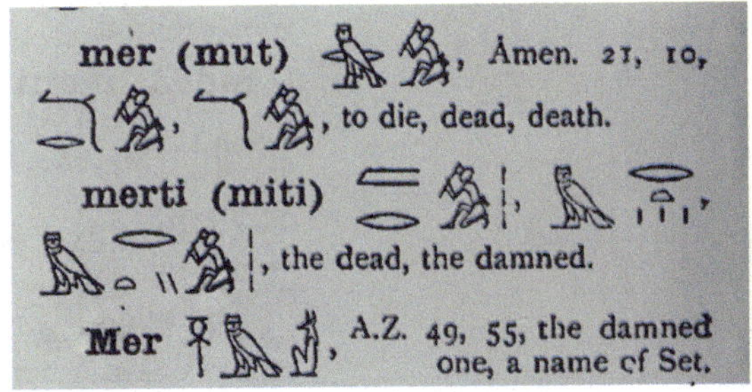
mer (mut), Ȧmen. 21, 10, to die, dead, death.
merti (miti), the dead, the damned.
Mer, A.Z. 49, 55, the damned one, a name of Set.

The Akan have the **ebe** (proverb) which says *'Love is death'*. In Kamit, the word for *love* (desire) **mr** is also the word for *death*, **mr**. This is a manifestation of cultural and cosmological continuity, for the Akan are one of many Afurakanu/Afuraitkaitnut (Africans) in West Afuraka/Afuraitkait (Africa) who migrated from ancient **Khanit** (Nubia/Sudan) and Kamit in ancient times.

Moreover, just as the term **mr** (mer) was corrupted into **moor** (mohr) by the whites meaning *swamp land, water, sea, wasteland, marshland, death*, so was the term **mr** (mer) meaning *love*, corrupted by the whites into **mour** (mohr) as in **amour** (love) and *mi amour* (my love):

amour (n.)
c.1300, "love," from Old French *amour*, from Latin *amorem* (nom. *amor*) "love, affection, strong friendly feeling" (it could be used of sons or brothers, but especially of sexual love), from *amare* "to love" (see **Amy**). The accent shifted 15c.-17c. to the first syllable as the word became nativized, then shifted back as the naughty or intriguing sense became primary and the word was felt to be a euphemism.
A common ME word for love, later accented ámour (cf. *enamour*). Now with suggestion of intrigue and treated as a F[rench] word. [Weekley]

ȧmer, T. 264, P. 320, M. 129; see, to love.

In both instances the term spelled with an 'e' in the Coptic dialect was changed to an 'o' by the whites and their offspring: **Mer** (mehre) meaning *swampland* becomes **moor**. **Mer** (me) and the variation **amer**, meaning *love* becomes **amour**.

These facts once again prove the Afurakani/Afuraitkaitnit (African) origin of the term popularly rendered **'moor'**. The five definitions (*wasteland, swamp, sea, death, love*) found in eurasian languages are identical to the same five definitions found in the earlier metutu because this is their origin.

We also have the term **mr** meaning *boats, shipping in port*. This is key to the cosmological understanding of **mr** meaning *love, death, water, wasteland, swamp,* etc.

merit, merut, Rec. 33, 30, , , boats, shipping in port.

men, men-t , , pool, lake, canal.

mená, meni , P. 180, , M. 280, N. 891, , N. 891, , Rev. 12, 19, , , , , , , , , , , , , , to tie up a boat in port, to lead a boat into port, to tether cattle, to gain access to a woman; , Rec. 21, 79, moored; Copt. ⲙⲟⲟⲛⲉ.

As shown above, the term **mn** (**men**) means *pool, lake*. The term **mna** or **mni** means *to tie up a boat* ***in port*** *– to* ***moor*** *a boat*. Notice in the Coptic dialect it is spelled **MOONE**. **Copt. ⲙⲟⲟⲛⲉ.**

As stated above, in the language of Kamit as well as Akan and other Afurakani/Afuraitkaitnit (African) languages, the letter 'R' is pronounced as a 'rolling R' meaning the tongue taps the roof of the mouth once. This is why the 'N' and 'R' interchange. If you pronounce **Mera Mena Mera Mena** out loud and 'roll' the 'R' you would not be able to tell the difference between the two words. This is why **mera** (*water, lake, pool*) is also written **mena** (*water, lake*). This is also why in Akan the name **Bena** is also written **Bera** or **Bra** and **Bono** is also written **Boron**. There are numerous examples of this in the languages of Kamit and Akan. The term **mna** pronounced moone [mooh-neh] in Coptic sounds like moore (mooh-reh) with a 'rolling R'. The term moone (moo-reh) became **moor** in english, as in *'to moor a boat'*:

moor (v.)
"to fasten (a vessel) by a cable," late 15c., probably related to O.E. *mærels* "mooring rope," via unrecorded **mærian* "to moor," or possibly borrowed from M.L.G. *moren* or M.Du.*maren* "to moor," from W.Gmc. **mairojan*. Related: *Moored*, **mooring**. French *amarrer* is from Dutch.

As we can see, the whites and their offspring have stolen a term and attributed it to themselves. The term **mni** and the Coptic **moone** (moorey) is the exact same term as **moor** for the language of Kamit holds the etymological root. Related terms:

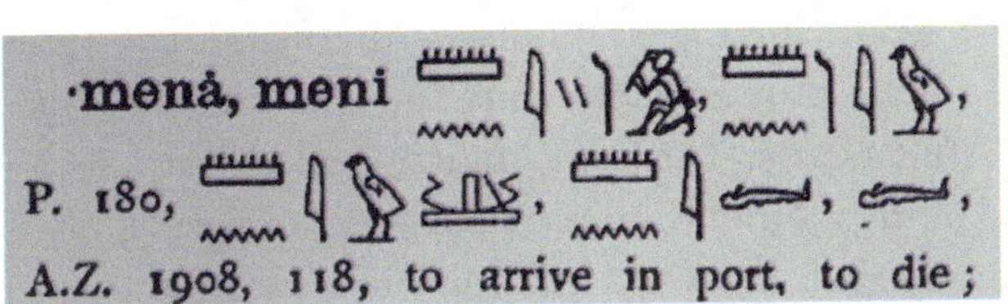
menȧ, meni, P. 180, A.Z. 1908, 118, to arrive in port, to die;

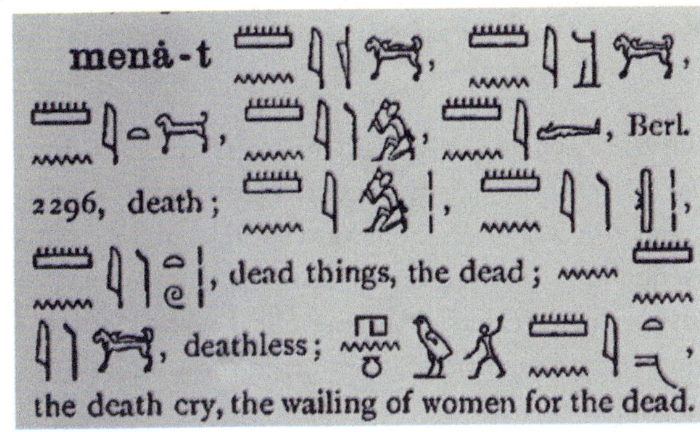
menȧ-t, Berl. 2296, death; dead things, the dead; deathless; the death cry, the wailing of women for the dead.

menȧ-t, Rec. 30, 68, Shipwreck 4, mooring post; two stakes for tying up a boat.

merit, merut, Rec. 33, 30, boats, shipping in port.

The term **mna** or **mni** (**mra** or **mri**) means *to arrive in port, to die; boats, shipping in port.* The term **mnat** means *the dead.* The term **mnat** also means *mooring post.* Ancient Kamit was a riverine culture. We quote at length from our article: **The Origin of the Term Nsamanfo in Kamit** for the cosmological context:

Pages 1-3:

"….Ancient **Kamit** (Egypt) and parts of **Khanit** (Nubia/Sudan) were/are riverine cultures. Our **Nsamanfo** (n-sah-mahn'-foh), our Afurakani/Afuraitkaitnit (African) Ancestresses and Ancestors, thus had/have an understanding of the value of water and images and concepts related to water are found throughout the texts, symbolism and culture of Kamit and Khanit. The sky for example is seen to be comprised largely of a mass of water. Thus, as the **Aten** (Sun) moves through the sky it is depicted as *sailing through the sky in a boat.* The Aten rises in Its boat in the **abtet** (east), sails across the sky and sets in Its boat in the **ament** (west):

Ra, Hawk-headed, sitting inside the disk of the **Aten** (Sun) which is inside of the *boat* of the **Aten** (Sun) as it sails across the sky

When the Aten sets in the ament (west), it sinks down below the horizon. Here, the Aten is said to *enter the hidden (ament) land (ta)*, the *underworld*, the spirit world – the **Ancestral realm**. The Aten has 'died' or moved through the *gate of Death* to now bring light to the spirit world for the 12 hours of the night. The Aten subsequently reemerges in the abtet (east) at sunrise and appears above the horizon. The Aten has thus been 'born' or 'resurrected' from the 'dead'. The Afurakani/Afuraitkaitnit (African) human is recognized to go through the same process, not only in the context of rising in the morning (sunrise) and going to sleep at night (sunset), but through our life-times. Our *sunrise* is our appearance in the world at birth, while our transition to the spirit world through the gate of Death is our *sunset*.

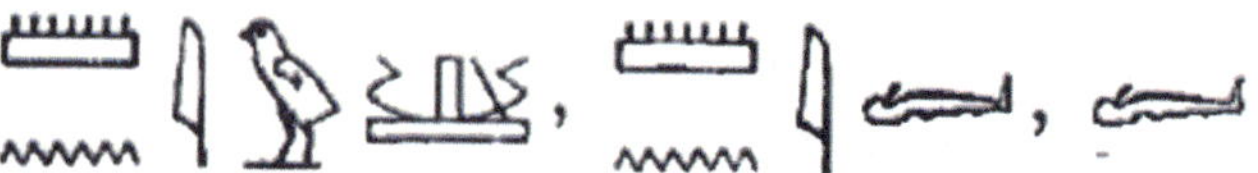

To arrive in port, to die

When a boat arrives at its port, its final destination, it docks. The inhabitants then leave the boat. The same is said of the boat of the Aten. The Aten rises above the horizon through the *eastern mountain range* in Kamit called **Bakhau**. On the western horizon is the *western mountain range* called **Manu**. When the boat of the Aten arrives at the mountain range of Manu in the west (ament), the Aten has *arrived at its port*. The boat docks and the inhabitants – Spirits – leave the *day* boat (**Mandjet** boat) and go into the spirit world (underworld). For the spirit world journey, They board the *night* boat (**Mesektet** boat).

Aten rising above ***Bakhau*** *mountains in the* ***abtet*** *(east) in Kamit*

Aten setting upon ***Manu*** *mountains in the* ***ament*** *(west) in Kamit*

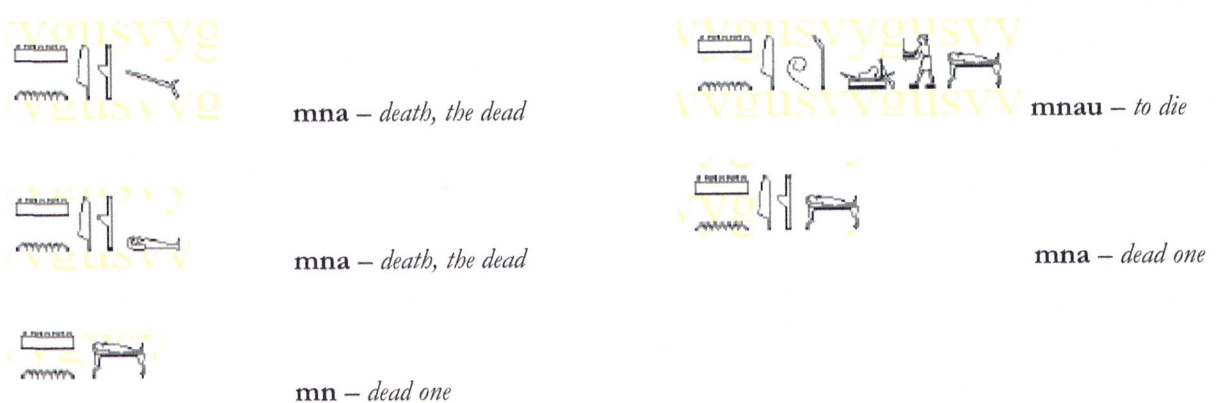

mna – *death, the dead*

mnau – *to die*

mna – *death, the dead*

mna – *dead one*

mn – *dead one*

The term **mn** or **mna** meaning *to die* or *dead one, the dead* and *death* as shown above is also the term for: *to arrive in port.* Three versions of the term **mn** or **mna** meaning *to arrive in port, to die* are below:

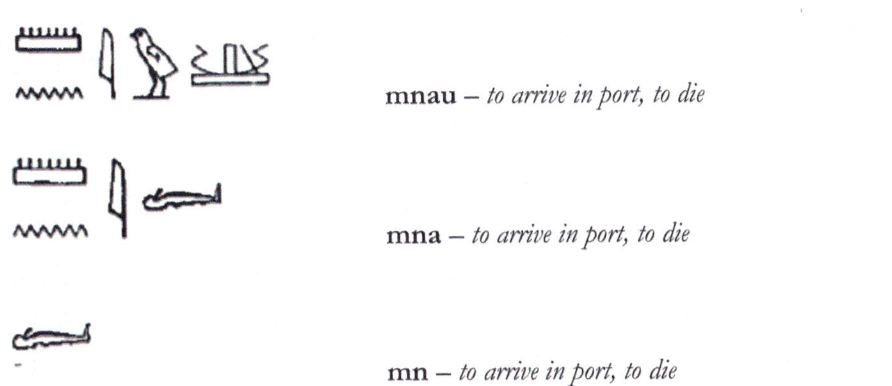

mnau – *to arrive in port, to die*

mna – *to arrive in port, to die*

mn – *to arrive in port, to die*

The first version of the term is comprised of the **metutu** (hieroglyphs) for the **mn** combination , for the letter 'n' , for the letter 'a' and for the letter 'u' . The final metut (symbol) is a *determinative* metut. This is a symbol that is not pronounced but is an *indicator* or *determiner* of what is being spoken of in the word. The *determinative* metut in this instance is the boat: .

In the second version of the word we have the metutu for the word **mna**, however the determinative is not a boat. It is the *mummified body* – a dead person: . In the third version of the term **mn** the metut of the *mummified body/dead person* is used *alone* and encompasses the word *and* the idea *in total:* **mn**. It is a common practice in the written language of Kamit to spell out the entire word *and* use a determinative metut or to simply use the determinative metut *alone* to signify the word and concept…."

Quote from pages 6-7:

"….It is relevant in this regard that the term **mn** means *dead one, mummified one, one who has arrived in port.* The one who arrives in port, or docks has his/her boat 'moored' or *tied/fastened.* The term **mni** thus means 'moored' and is the etymological origin of the english term 'moor' as in 'mooring post':

mená, meni, P. 180, M. 280, N. 891, N. 891, Rev. 12, 19, to tie up a boat in port, to lead a boat into port, to tether cattle, to gain access to a woman; Rec. 21, 79, moored; Copt. ⲙⲟⲟⲛⲉ.

Once the boat has arrived in port, it is **mni** - *moored* or *tied to a mooring post.* [*See the Coptic version of the term:* **MOONE** *(Mooh-reh):* Copt. ⲙⲟⲟⲛⲉ *from which the english 'moor' is derived. The rolling 'r' sound (tongue tapping the roof of the mouth once) and the 'n' sound are identical and interchange in Afurakani/Afuraitkaitnit (African) languages. moone (moo-neh) thus sounds identical to moore (moo-reh).*]…"

The key here is the relationship between **mn** meaning *to arrive in port, to die* and **mr** meaning *death, the dead* but also *boats, shipping in port*:

·mená, meni, P. 180, A.Z. 1908, 118, to arrive in port, to die;

merit, merut, Rec. 33, 30, boats, shipping in port.

A *moored* boat is one that has *arrived in port* (**mni, mri**) and is *fastened.* Like a person reaching their final destination (death) and the body is placed in the ground (port) and 'tied' to **Asaase Afua** (Earth Mother), so is the boat which reaches its final destination *fastened* after its arrival/death. It will not be sailing anymore – its journey has come to an end. *There is no longer freedom of movement.* When the boat arrives in port and is moored, the inhabitants *disembark* - leave the boat. When the individual arrives in port, dies, and his/her body is 'moored', fastened to **Asaase Afua** (buried in Earth), the inhabitant (spirit) of the body leaves for the body is dead. *There is no longer freedom of movement for the body.* The spirit therefore *disembarks*, leaves the physical vessel. The notion of *death, lack* *of freedom, being moored/ tied, submerged (flood water, buried)* and more is the basis for **a class of people** who are referred to as **mr** or **mru** (plural, also written **mrw**), meaning not only *the dead* and *the damned* but also *servants, slaves, bondsmen/ women, serfs, vassals, dependents*, etc. They are the 'socially dead' - *tied, fastened, lacking of freedom, weak, wretched*, etc:

mer, Rec. 16,. 70, Rec. 12, 12, servant, peasant, dependant.

merȧ, a female slave.

mer-t, Palermo Stele, Rec. 26, 236, Rec. 31, 26, Décrets 9, IV, 1147, Dream Stele 40, serfs, servants, vassals, peasants, hereditary servants on an estate;

merina, IV, 665, captive chiefs; compare Heb. מרין (?)

merua, Rec. 15, 158, weak, wretched.

mrw **Servants, Underlings, Partisans, Supporters**

mrw **Bondsmen, Servants, Underlings, Partisans, Supporters**

mrw **Serfs, Lower Classes**

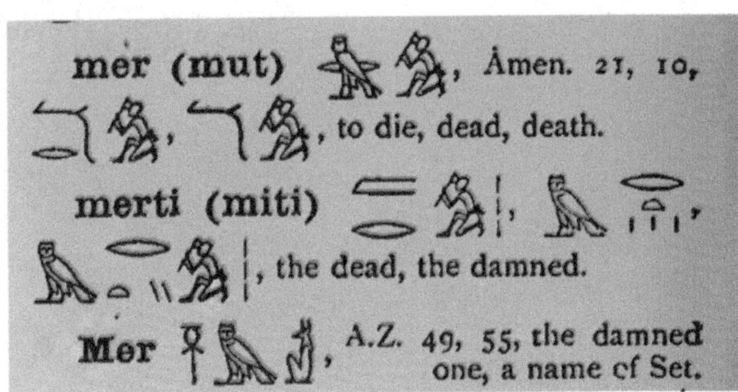

mer (mut), Ȧmen. 21, 10, to die, dead, death.

merti (miti), the dead, the damned.

Mer, A.Z. 49, 55, the damned one, a name of Set.

We also have the english term *'mourn'* which is also directly tied to the term *'moor'* with its etymological roots in **mer** and **mni** – death:

men-t , , , , , , Peasant 250, , , pain, sickness, sorrow, suffering, mourning, disasters, sore places, wounds, fatigue, calamity.

menȧ-t , , , , , Berl. 2296, death; , , dead things, the dead; , deathless; , the death cry, the wailing of women for the dead.

Mnt or **Mnut** (**Mrt** or **Mrnut**) meaning *suffering, mourning,* etc. is the root of the term *'mourn'*. We also have:

ȝgb ***mourn, grieve***  ***ȝgbi*** ***flood, primordial waters, inundate***

As we can see above, we have the term **agb** meaning *to mourn, grieve* and the same term **agb** meaning *flood, primordial waters, inundation.* Some have identified the term **egp.t** (Egypt - *the land of the inundation*) being derived from **agb**, *the inundation.* The notion of a descriptive title of the country being defined through *flooding, inundation* and *mourning, death* in the term **agb** is identical to the notion of **mer** (*death, mourning*) and **mer** (*inundation, flood*) being used as a descriptive title of the country – **Ta mri**. It should be noted that the swelling of the river during the inundation is said to be caused by a tear-drop falling from the star **Sapadet** (**Sopdet** – also called Sirius or Sothis by the whites). This star has the title '*Eye* of **Ra** (Creator)'. The *'crying'* or *mourning* (**agb** or **mn/mr**) from this Divine tear-drop thus causes the *inundation* (**agb** or **mn/mr**). **These terms and definitions are all united through the cosmology of Kamit.**

Merit , , , a goddess of the Inundation.

Mer-ti , Rec. 20, 42, the two goddesses of the Inundation, Southern and Northern.

Merit shemā , Pap. Anhai, , the goddess of the Inundation in the South; , the two goddesses of the Inundation.

Merit meḥ , Pap. Anhai, , the goddess of the Inundation in the North.

left: **Merit Shema** and **Merit Meht** facing each other. Partially damaged. Temple of **Seti** in Abdju (Abydos). Photo by author.

right: **Merit Shema** in the Tomb of **Ra Messu III**. Photo by author.

Merit is the name of the **Ntorot** (**Ntrt/Netert** *term for Goddess*) of the *inundation* of the river in Kamit. There are Two Female 'Nile' river **Ntorotu** (Goddesses), **Merit Shema** and **Merit Meht** meaning **Merit** of the *Southern Branch* of the river and country and **Merit** of the *Northern Branch* of the river and country. These Two Ntorotu are often shown to be the Wives of the Male **Ntorou** (**Ntru** *plural term for Gods*) of the Nile – **Hapi**:

Hapi Meht and **Hapi Reset**

[From the Temple of **Apet Reset** (Luxor). Photo by author.]

Above are the Twin **Ntorou** (Gods) **Hap Meht** (**Hapi** of the *North*) and **Hap Reset** (**Hapi** of the *South*). The Nile River is often referred to simply as the *Hapi* river. However, when speaking of the *inundation* (flood) of the river we are focused on the Female Ntorotu, the **Meriti** (dual **Merit**) Who are the Female Spirit-Forces behind the flood.

[*The term for water in Kamit is* ***mu. Mu Hap Meht*** *means waters (mu) of the Northern Nile Deity* ***Hap Meht. MuHapMeht*** *was corrupted into* ***muhammed*** *by the whites and their offspring and applied to a fictional character/prophet of the false religion of islam who in fact* ***never existed at all****. See our* ***KUKUU-TUNTUM – The Ancestral Jurisdiction*** *for details.*]

In ancient Kamit, it very rarely rained. However, every year the river would **flood** creating a tremendous lake, hundreds of miles long and 10-12 miles wide in certain regions. Kamit was situated along the river which is the longest river in the world. When the river would flood once a year, it was a time of ritual invocation of the Ntorou/Ntorotu (Gods/Goddesses) to ensure a promising future crop-yield. The flooding of the river would bring black silt and deposit that black silt along the river banks. Months later when the water would recede, there would be fertile land wherein the people would plant their seeds. The **Kamau** (people of Kamit - *'Egyptians'*) were totally dependent upon the flood of the river every year for their sustenance.

When the river would flood, **Merit Shema** and **Merit Meht** were the Spirit-Forces Who presided over the *swelling* or *'pregnancy'* of the river [*Note: in Akan the term* ***menem*** *[****merem****] means 'to swell' as in the swelling of a river*]. To the dwellers along the riverbanks, it appeared that the *entire country* had been inundated. It appeared as it was in what is called the **Sep Tepi** or *First Time – The beginning of Creation.* In our cosmology, we recognized that at the beginning of the Creation of the world there was no land, only water. While today approximately 71% of the Earth is covered by water, in the beginning the entire Earth was covered by water. **Ra** and **Rait** (*Creator* and *Creatress of the Universe*), operating as a Spirit-Force through the solar energy/fire of the **Aten** (Sun), activated the fire in the Earth's core thereby activating the Earth Mother. This resulted in earthquakes on the ocean floor and volcanic eruptions which ultimately caused a primordial hill to surge up from underneath the surface of the water. **This raised land would become the first landmass of Earth - Afuraka/Afuraitkait (Africa).**

Every year during the inundation, the Kamau were reminded of the cosmology. When **Merit Meht** and **Merit Shema** presided over the *pregnancy/swelling* of the body of the river, a large portion of the *land* was *buried* or *submerged* under water. This was a form of *death.* The plant life was submerged. The land animals living along the banks retreated. The land was *buried/submerged* for a period. However, when the new season came it was time for a re-emergence, a rebirth. The land emerged from its submergence/burial/death, the plant life was 'resurrected'. This recalled the story of **Ausar**, the Ntoro (Deity) who was killed, buried and resurrected. Ritually, this recalled the notion of initiation being a process of someone *'going under'*, dying to the old self and resurrecting as a new individual with new responsibilities (priesthood/priestesshood) and much more. It also recalled the fact that when men and women were in conflict with regard to their love-relationships, the desire (**mr**) for their significant other manifested as the *flood of the rivers of blood* in the body to the heart. One's heart would then be *submerged, flooded,* become *heavy with anxiety,* would *pain* them and he or she would feel like a *death* (**mr**) has occurred – *'love is death'* (**mr** is **mr**) – the heart would 'freeze' or 'stop'. There may even be a flood or inundation of tears – crying. Resolution of conflict however would bring an end to the *heavy* (dead) heart. A rebirth or restoration of balance would occur as the heart would begin to palpitate at its normal rhythm again. The tears would cease. The flood waters would recede.

It is important to note that in Afurakani/Afuraitkaitnit (African) culture, Death in and of Itself is not seen as evil or as a curse. Death also is *not* the opposite of life. One is born into the world, we *live* in the physical world, then go through the gate of Death and *live* in the Ancestral world. In our culture, we recognize *Death to be the opposite of Birth* – life is continuous in the physical realm (after birth) and the spirit-realm (after death).

Ancient Kamit was distinguished in many ways. The **mru** (pyramids) are magnificent structures which define an aspect of Kamit. The yearly inundation governed the entire economy and social life of the people. This is why Kamit would be referred to as **Ta Merit**, the land of the *inundation.* This name is also related to **Mer** meaning the *land of the* **Mer** or *pyramids.* However, in both instances we are referring to *death* (**mr**), *submergence, burial, inundation, shrines for the dead* (**meru**), etc. This is why those who died were referred to as those who *arrived in port* (**mni** or **mri**) like a boat docking and being moored (**mni, mri**).

This is not without precedent. The land south of Kamit, contemporary Sudan and Ethiopia, was called **Ta Aakhu** meaning – *Land of the Ancestresses and Ancestors* (**Aakhu**) – *Land of the Venerable Deceased Spirits/Dead*:

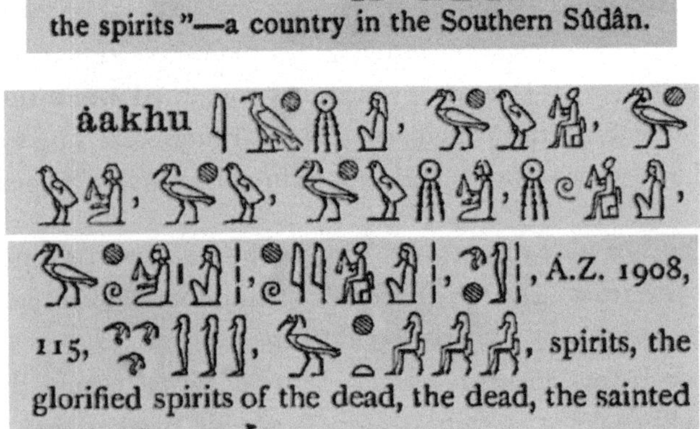
Ta åakhu, "land of the spirits"—a country in the Southern Sûdân.

åakhu, Á.Z. 1908, 115, spirits, the glorified spirits of the dead, the dead, the sainted dead; Copt. ⲓϧ.

The people of Kamit and Khanit paid great attention to those who lived honorable lives and continued to support us as Ancestresses and Ancestors (**Aakhu/Aakhutu**) from the Ancestral realm. They were/are our *beloved* (**mri, mriti**) deceased. We therefore built our *beloved* (**mr**) *dead* (**mr**) *shrines/pyramids* (**mr**). This practice was only for those who lived in harmony with Divine Order while on Earth.

However, societally, those who were engaged in self-destructive lifestyles were referred to as being 'dead' – **meru** (**mru**). Those who were *slaves, servants* (*prisoners of war* or *convicted felons* for example) were *tied* (**mr**) to their lot in life and thus to those whom they served. In contemporary culture we often refer to those who are *tied/addicted* to drugs as 'dead' or those who are engaged in self-destructive behavior as mentally or spiritually 'dead'. The same is true of the culture of ancient Kamit:

"…As for the fool does not hear, he can do nothing at all. He looks at ignorance and sees knowledge. He looks at harmfulness and sees usefulness. He does everything that one detests and is blamed for it every day. He lives on the things by which one dies. His food is evil speech. His sort is known to the officials who say, ***'There goes a living death every day'.*** *One ignores the things that he does because of his many daily troubles…"* [**Instructions of Ptah Hetep** - c4400 years ago]

When the whites and their offspring invaded Kamit, they learned of these terms from our language and continued to use them. We have proven conclusively that this is the case, for the varied definitions of the term 'moor' (*waste land, sea, swamp, death, love, fastening a boat*) have been shown to have their roots in the language of Kamit. The whites and their offspring continue to use the terms to this day with the exact same six meanings

– although they lack cosmological understanding. **The same is true of the whites and their offspring designating Black people as Moors:**

Moor (n.)
"North African, Berber," late 14c., from O.Fr. *More*, from M.L. *Morus*, from L. *Maurus* "inhabitant of Mauritania" (northwest Africa, a region now corresponding to northern Algeria and Morocco), from Gk. *Mauros*, perhaps a native name, or else cognate with *mauros* "black" (but this adjective only appears in late Greek and may as well be from the people's name as the reverse). Being a dark people in relation to Europeans, their name in the Middle Ages was a synonym for "Negro;" later (16c.-17c.) used indiscriminately of Muslims (Persians, Arabs, etc.) but especially those in India.

The terms *moor* and *blackamoor* were used by europeans as a descriptive of Black people who were muslims and Black people in general over time. The term was also used to identify anyone who was darker that the western european such as white arabs and hindus, **although white arabs and white hindus are not Afurakanu/Afuraitkaitnut (Africans~Black People).** [*The original people of these areas were Black. However, just as in 'egypt' today, the white invaders are in control of these regions. The white invaders in arab-controlled regions of the world, in india and elsewhere are not Black.*] Just as the term **mer** (love) was corrupted into **amour** (ah-mohr) meaning 'love' in european languages, so was the term **mer** (singular) or **meru** (plural) referring to *'dead people; the damned; slaves, servants, vassals'* etc. corrupted into **moor** (mohr) and **moors** in european languages.

In Kamit, to be labeled a 'mer' or a *dead, damned person* or a *slave* was a pejorative. This carried over into the european usage of the term. The only difference being that *all Black people* were labeled 'moors' as a pejorative by the whites. The europeans understood that the color *Black* was associated with *Divine Power, Ancestrally vested power* in Kamit. It was therefore associated with *death*. Because the whites and their offspring improperly associated death with evil, they sought to associate being Black with death in a pejorative sense, and therefore with evil. This is how **mr** (*dead, damned, slave, servant*) was connected with **Ta Merit** – *land of the Dead (submergence/inundation/wasteland* - see *mere* the 'dead land') and because **Ta Mert** (land of the pyramids) was also **Kam-t** (*Kam - Black; Kam-t - Black land/Land of the Blacks*) then Black was improperly associated by the whites with 'death', 'slave', 'servant', etc. We must also recall that it is the **Merit** Ntorotu, the Goddesses of the inundation/flood/submergence/death, who bring the **black silt** from the south to deposit on the banks of the river. The *merit-water (flood-water* as opposed to the water during the remainder of the year) was thus the *'black'-water*. The black silt comprised the **Kam-t** or *Black land*. The black silt is sacred to **Ausar**. It is His shrine on Earth. He thus has the title **Kam-Ur**, the *Great (Ur) Black One* (**Kam**):

Ausar also called **Kam-Ur**. **Ausar** is the Sovereign of the Ancestral Realm – *The Realm of the 'Dead'*

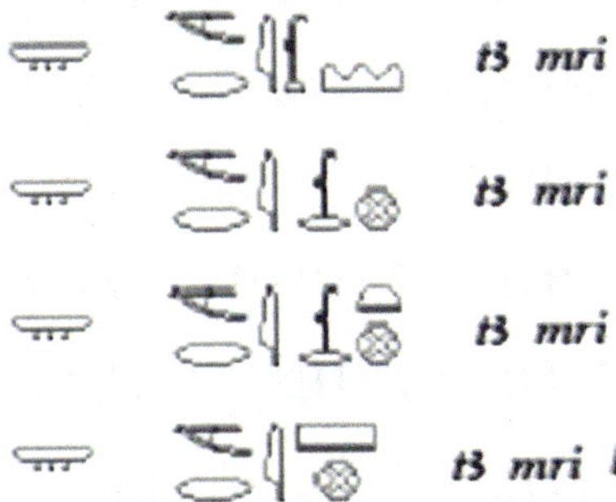

Above are four different versions of the name **Ta Mri** or **Ta Mra**. Note that in the first version the determinative metut is that of the *notched palm branch* which references *time* as in the *beginning of a season or period*. We also have the metut for *desert land* - *dead land, wasteland, land of the west, land of the setting Aten/Sun where the boat of* ***Ra*** *arrives in port* (**mni, mri**) [Note that *waste* means *'desolate region'*. The land of the *west* is the desertland (*waste/westland*) where the Aten (Sun) goes to 'die' (*mer*)]

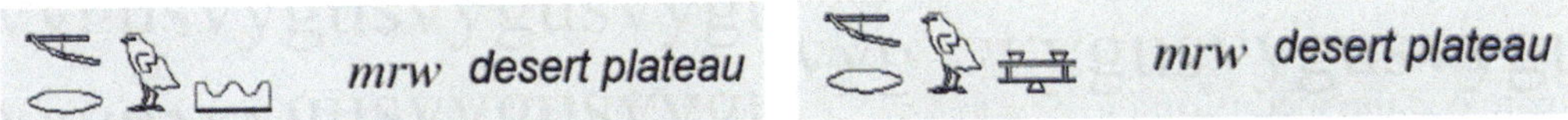

Ta Mri is thus the land which returns, via inundation, to a *dead-land* (mere), the land which is buried for a *season*, then resurrected/reborn. It is important to recall that in Kamit, the Ntoro (Deity) **Set** is the Ntoro of the *desert*/dead land. **Set** is also called **Mr** – the *'damned' one* meaning one who *works with deceased spirits*:

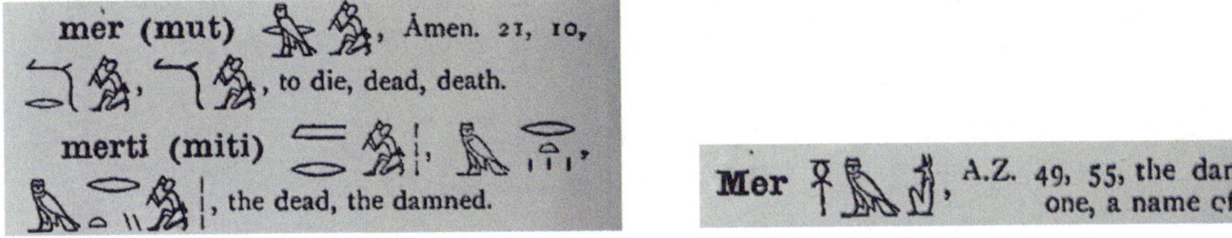

mer (mut), Àmen. 21, 10, , to die, dead, death.
merti (miti) , , the dead, the damned.

Mer , A.Z. 49, 55, the damned one, a name of Set.

[**Set** or **Seti** was corrupted by the whites into *Setin* or *Satan – the spirit who rules the dead, the damned, in the underworld/hell.*]

The term **mru** (**mrw, meru**) meaning *the damned* is indicated by the determinative metut of a man on one knee *driving an axe through the middle of his forehead*: He is engaged in self-destructive, suicidal activity. The axe through the head shows that he is not only *mentally dead* but *spiritually* and *physically dead*. Self-destructive behavior, inclusive of suicide is taboo, *Divinely prohibited*, in Afurakani/Afuraitkaitnit (African) culture. This *dead person* is thus a *damned person*. In Akan culture the term **akyiwade** is the word for *taboo*. It describes that which is **kyi** - *hated* by **Nyamewaa-Nyame** (*the Supreme Being*). Just as in all of Afuraka/Afuraitkait (Africa), taboos are *Divinely prohibited/Divinely hated* deeds, entities, objects, etc. If we violate an akyiwade, a Divine prohibition or restriction, we *'damn'* ourselves because we place ourselves out of harmony with Divine Order. The term **mru** meaning *serfs, servants, vassals* is also spelled with the *notched palm branch*:

, serfs, servants, vassals.

Mrat

t3 mri

Ta Mra

In the second and third versions of **Ta Mri** above, the *notched palm branch* is the determinative metut along with the metut for *country, territory*. **Ta Mri** is thus a descriptive of the country in the context of the *time/season* of the **merit** – *inundation (submergence, death)*. This is why we have the term **Ta mrau** with the *same determinative symbols* referencing the *time of the inundation – death, submergence* when referring to a group of people: **Ta-meråu**. Note that the ancient name of the country most often used is **Kamit** and the people **Kammau**:

Kam

Kammåu, with , Jour. As. 1908, 285, Egyptians.

The name **Ta Mra** or **Ta Mrit** is not attested until the 11th dynasty – thousands of years after the civilization was founded. The name **Kamit** is used from the early dynasties. In the last version of the term **Ta mri** above, the determinative is the metut for a *mass of water* and the metut for *country* or *territory* – the land/country of the great **merit** – *inundation (submergence, death)*. These facts collectively show that **Ta mert** is defined specifically as the *land of the inundation, death, submergence* and not the *'beloved land'*.

When a seed is planted, covered over with dirt, watered and then left alone that is affectively a ***funerary ceremony****. We bury our dead, cover the body with dirt and pour libation (water). When the plant ultimately sprouts – the spirit rises up from the 'underworld' – that is a 'resurrection'. This is how the* ***'cultivated land'*** *is necessarily the* ***'dead land'****.*

menå, meni , P. 180, , , A.Z. 1908, 118, to arrive in port, to die;

mer (mut) , Åmen. 21, 10, , to die, dead, death.

merti (miti) , , the dead, the damned.

Notice the metut of the <u>*man driving the axe through his head*</u> *is found in both the terms* ***mna, mni (mra, mri)*** *- to arrive in port, to die and in* ***mer*** *– the dead, the damned*

mer , U. 607, P. 286, , , Åmen. 25, 21, , , , to be sick, to suffer pain, to grieve, to be sad, to feel sympathy for someone.

meru , Pap. 3024, 131, a sick man.

mer åri , a sick man.

merua , Rec. 15. 158, weak, wretched.

mer , Rec. 16, 70, , Rec. 12, 12, servant, peasant, dependant.

merå , a female slave.

mer-t , Palermo Stele, Rec. 26, 236, Rec. 31, 26, , , , Décrets 9, , IV, 1147, , , , , Dream Stele 40, , serfs, servants, vassals, peasants, hereditary servants on an estate;

Again, the whites and their offspring took a term that was a **pejorative** when referring to a *class of people in Kamau society* (**mr** or **mru**) and used that **pejorative** term to apply to *all Black people.* Instead of simply referring to us all as **Kamau** (Black People/Blacks – Black being Divine) – *as we referred to ourselves* - they decided to use the term **mr** (corrupted into 'moor') - **specifically because it was/is pejorative.**

Ancient Black people of Kamit and those outside of Kamit never referred to themselves as 'Moors'

Again, some Black people colloquially refer to drug addicts in america as the 'walking dead'. A white foreigner could enter a Black community in america, learn of the label that Black people use - 'walking dead' - and begin to refer to *all Black People* (including all those <u>not</u> addicted to any drugs) as the 'walking dead'. This is a **pejorative** used by a community for a *certain segment of the population* who are self-destructive being taken by a *foreigner* and used as a label of identity for the *entire community.* **This is a deliberate attempt to insult and redefine the people.** [*In fact, many whites in america do refer to all Black people in america in these terms today.*]

The whites and their offspring, after invading Afurakani/Afuraitkaitnit (African) civilizations and losing numerous wars to Afurakanu/Afuraitkaitnut (Africans), decided to work on destroying our Ancestral Religion and Culture. This was a means by which they believed that they could disrupt the society, exploit divisions and ultimately divide and conquer. Part of the process was to *demonize Black people.* This is why all throughout white pseudo-religion *black* is defined as *evil, of the devil, demonic*, etc. **Black** is associated with **death** in a *negative* fashion. This goes directly back to ancient Kamit where *Merit* (*death* of the crops, flooding of the land, end of a cycle/season) was associated with *Mer* (pyramids/shrines for the *dead*) and *mer* (the *dead*, those who *arrived in port* and were *mer-ed* or *moored* and also the class of the *dead* who were *damned)* [see the related terms: *<u>mor</u>ose, <u>mor</u>bid, <u>mor</u>tuary, <u>mor</u>on, etc. meaning melancholy, psychologically unhealthy – associated with death, sanctuary of the dead, ignorant – mentally dead, etc. – all of which have the same roots in* **mr** *and later* **moor** *and are* ***pejoratives***]. Yet, the association with a **social class** (*slaves, servants – socially dead/bound/moored/fastened to their labor and service*) and a **spiritual designation** for a **certain class** of the deceased (*the damned*) was *artificially expanded* by the whites as a definition of all Black people.

Those Afurakanu/Afuraitkaitnut (Africans~Black People) who have embraced the idiocy of 'moorish' culture and identity and refer to themselves as 'moors', 'muurs', etc. are perpetuating the perverse agenda of the whites and their offspring. They are identifying themselves as 'dead people'.

Mru (Moors) – the dead, the damned

Many of these individuals perpetuate as well the false notion that the term Black means 'death'. They therefore do not call themselves Black nor do they understand the proper etymology of the term **Afurakani/Afuraitkaitnit** (**African**). They therefore do not recognize nor embrace the reality that they are Afurakani/Afuraitkaitnit (African).

Black does not mean death – Moor means death

Such individuals have been given false and foolish definitions – directly from the whites and their offspring – and have accepted these false definitions because of a **deeply seeded** and **deeply seated self-hatred**. The whites and their offspring have spent centuries attempting to convince us that 'Black' and 'African' mean inferior, ugly, ignorant, slave, etc. This began before the enslavement era and continues today. Misguided individuals who identify themselves as 'moors', 'muurs', etc. have internalized this false doctrine and thus have a **psychological need to believe** that they are something – *anything* – other than Black or Afurakani/Afuraitkaitnit (African). Many of them *detest the mention* of the word African. Yet, deep inside they know that is exactly who and what they are. They know this from genealogy, trustory, archaeology, genetics/DNA and common sense. However, they hate this reality and therefore seek any measure to distort it. This is a manifestation of their ingrained conditioning to accept Black inferiority and the insane notion of white supremacy. **This ingrained conditioning is also made manifest in their maniacal search of the entirety of the ancient world for words with the consonantal structure 'MR' in order to make them mean 'moor' in order to retro-fit a false assumed identity.**

There are also those Black people who are agents of the whites who know the truth but continue to serve their white masters by miseducating as many Blacks as possible about our identity. <u>All</u> of the founders of these 'moorish' as well as 'Black muslim' and 'hebrew' movements fit into this category.

In our book **AFURAKA/AFURAITKAIT – The Origin of the term 'Africa'** we give an extensive analysis of the term 'Africa' and show that his term was created and used by Afurakanu/Afuraitkaitnut (Africans) thousands of years before any other group existed on Earth. We demonstrate that the *Creator* and *Creatress* of the Universe are called **Ra** and **Rait** in Kamit. They operate *through* the **Aten** (Sun). When **Ra** and **Rait**, the *Great Spirit/Divine Living Energy in Creation*, move within matter, they take on the titles **Afu Ra** and **Afu Rait**. The term '**afu**' means *'house'* or *'flesh'*. On an individual level, your *flesh*/body is the *house* or *place of residence* for your spirit. When the Spirit of **Ra** and **Rait** moved *within* the primordial Earth to activate It and give It life (like sunlight penetrating Earth and stimulating the Earth's core), They were/are referred to as **Afu Ra** and **Afu Rait**. When Their movements caused earthquakes on the ocean floor, ultimately resulting in volcanic eruptions and a portion of the ocean floor surging upward above the surface of the water which covered Earth, this first 'raised land' or hill became the first landmass of Earth. The male/female terms for 'hill' or 'raised land' in Kamit are **Ka** and **Kait**. The **Ka** of **Afu Ra** is **Afuraka**. The **Kait** of **Afu Rait** is **Afuraitkait**. *Afuraka/Afuraitkait* is the *land of the Creator and Creatress*. This information is detailed in the book.

Because **Ra** and **Rait** operate *through* the Aten (Sun), They are often erroneously referred to the as the *'Sun God'* and *'Sun Goddess'*. In reality, **Ra** and **Rait** *use* the Aten (Sun) and other stars as *physical transmitters* of Their Spiritual Energy. This is how They manifest through the **fire of the Aten** (Sun).

The term **black** is erroneously traced back to eurasian languages by the whites and their offspring:

black (adj.)

Old English *blæc* "dark," from P.Gmc. **blakaz* "burned" (cf. Old Norse *blakkr* "dark," Old High German *blah* "black," Swedish *bläck* "ink," Dutch *blaken* "to burn"), from PIE **bhleg-* "to burn, gleam, shine, flash" (cf. Greek *phlegein* "to burn, scorch," Latin *flagrare* "to blaze, glow, burn"), from root **bhel-* (1) "to shine, flash, burn;" see **bleach** (v.).

The same root produced Old English *blac* "bright, shining, glittering, pale;" the connecting notions being, perhaps, "fire" (bright) and "burned" (dark). The usual Old English word for "black" was *sweart* (see **swart**). According to OED: "In ME. it is often doubtful whether *blac, blak, blake,* means 'black, dark,' or 'pale, colourless, wan, livid.' " Used of dark-skinned people in Old English.

bleach (v.)

Old English blæcan "bleach, whiten," from P.Gmc. *blaikjan "to make white" (cf. Old Saxon blek, Old Norse bleikr, Dutch bleek, Old High German bleih, German bleich "pale;" Old Norse bleikja, Dutch bleken, German bleichen "to bleach"), from PIE root *bhel- (1) "to shine, flash, burn" (cf. Sanskrit bhrajate "shines;" Greek phlegein "to burn;" Latin flamma "flame," fulmen "lightning," fulgere "to shine, flash," flagrare "to burn;" Old Church Slavonic belu "white;" Lithuanian balnas "pale"). The same root probably produced black; perhaps because both black and white are colorless, or because both are associated with burning. Related: Bleached; bleaching.

From the **Proto-Indo-European Lexicon**: https://lrc.la.utexas.edu/lex/master#P2494

bheleg	IE	bhlendh-	*to shine, glisten*
bherəĝ, bhrēĝ-	IE	bherək̂-	*to shine; bright, white*
bhel	IE	bhel-	*glittering white*
bher	IE	bherəĝ-	*shining; bright brown*
bhleu-(k-)	IE	bhlē-u̯o-s	*to burn*
bher	IE		*to cook, bake, fry, roast*

bíri, *adj.* in cpds., *black, dark;*

berber, pyramid, stone with a pyramidal top;

o-bibiní, *pl.* **a--fo,** *negro, black man, African. pr. 1796.* — **o-bibiníwa** [dim.] *a*

Brbr stone – *Egyptian museum in Cairo. Photo by author.*

BLACK (bhleg, bhereg, bher, brbr, biri)

The **brbr** (**berber**, **biribiri**) stone is the **black** pyramidion, the capstone of the pyramid. It is a shrine of the Deities **Ra** and **Atem**. It references the primordial mound that rose up from the primordial waters to become the first landmass **Ka/Kait**. The solar fire of **Ra/Rait** penetrated the primordial mound causing *a flash, shining* (bhereg, bher) and then a *burning, blackening* (bhereg, bher, bhleg). This solidified the mound as solid Earth. Our **Black bodies** were formed from this original, sacred, fired up, blackened Earth. This is why **brbr** stones are found in shrines and are used to give offerings to **Ra, Rait, Atem, Atemet** and more. This is also why **Akan** people identify ourselves as **Biri** (**Obi-Biri-fo**), **Black People**. Black is the sacred color of Divinity. **This is the actual etymological and cosmological origin of the term black, which europeans have never been aware of.**

As we can see, the term **black** is traced to the proto-indo-european root **bhleg** and the root **bhel** meaning *'to shine, flash, burn'*. The greek and latin related terms are **phlegein** and **flagrare**. Note that **flagrare** is the root of the english term **flagrant**. We can also see that the term **bleach** is traced to the same root. The reason why *bleach* and *black* are related is because *bleach burns* and something that has been on *fire* or has *burned* becomes *black*. The whiteness associated with bleach and black (both related to burning) has to do with the fact that the **fire** of the Aten (Sun) and fire in general *shines/burns 'white'* and *burns things black*. **These terms also have their roots in ancient Kamit.**

As we show in the **AFURAKA/AFURAITKAIT** article series, the people of North Afuraka/Afuraitkait (Africa) called **Aourigha** also pronounced **Afarak** and **Afri** have their roots in Khanit and Kamit. The terms **Afer** and **Afri** in Kamit mean *to burn, to be hot* and *smoke, hot vapor* respectively:

afer [hieroglyphs], to burn, to be hot. **afri** [hieroglyphs] Verbum Voc., smoke, hot vapour.

This is because the roots of these terms are **Afu Ra** and **Afu Rait**. **Ra** and **Rait**, the Creator and Creatress operating through the **Aten** (Sun), the Great white shining, burning **fire**, caused the water of the primordial Earth to *boil* and create *vapor*. It is Their Divine Energy which activates our **abatumm**, melanin, and causes us to become *black*. Some of the descendants of the Northern Afurakanu/Afuraitkaitnut (Africans), now called **Berbers** (the **Black Berbers** as opposed to the white invaders who now erroneously call themselves Berbers) are called **Fula** (**Fulani**). The name **Fula** is directly derived from **Afura** (**Afri** people).

[*In ancient Kamit there was no letter 'L'. The metut (hieroglyph) used to translate foreign words that included the 'L' sound is the metut for the letter 'R'. This is because the rolling 'R' and the 'L' interchange linguistically. The greek title Ptolemis is translated in the metutu as Ptuaremis for example. The same is true in the Akan language. There is no letter 'L'. If an Akan speaker pronounces a foreign word that includes an 'L' sound, he or she will pronounce it with a rolling 'R'. The foreign term 'mulatto' is pronounced by Akan speakers as 'murato-ni' for example. This is why Fula and Fura are identical.*]

The Fula or Fulani can be found across the continent of Afuraka/Afuraitkait (Africa), from East Afuraka/Afuraitkait (Africa) [in Sudan/Khanit] through Central, North and West Afuraka/Afuraitkait (Africa) all the way to the regions of Senegal and Gambia.

There are variations in the way that the Fula pronounce their name. In Afurakani/Afuraitkaitnit (African) languages the 'P' and 'F' often interchange. This is why some **Fula** people pronounce and spell their name **Peul** or **Pel**. Thus, a branch of the ancient Aourigha or Afarak, Afurak, Afri – the Furak or **Fula**, also call themselves the **Peul**. This is a *manifestation* of the ancient roots of the relationship between *bhleg* and *bhel - Fula* (Furak, Afarak) and *Peul*. The 'B', 'P' and 'F' in european languages interchange because this feature was taken from Afurakani/Afuraitkaitnit (African) languages. This is how *bhleg* becomes *phlegein* and *flagrare*. This is how the name of the ancient region of Kamit called **Paaraka** (**Pilak** in Coptic – 'R' and 'L' interchanging) becomes **Philae** in greek. The 'P' becomes an 'F' (PH) sound. Another example is a title of the Creator, **Ra**. A major title of **Ra** in Kamit is **Pa Ra**. The term **Pa** is the definite article. **Pa Ra** means '*The*' **Ra** – *Thee* God. In Coptic, **Pa Ra** or **Pra** becomes **Phre** (**Fra** or **Freh**) ⲫⲣⲏ. :

pa Rā [hieroglyphs], the Sun; Copt. ⲫⲣⲏ.

Moreover, the 'B' and 'F' (Ph) sound interchange in Kamit. The term **brg** (barg) in ancient Kamit becomes **pharg** in Coptic Copt. ⲫⲱⲣϫ. :

berg [hieroglyphs], to force open a door; Copt. ⲫⲱⲣϫ.

Fula Women

Iuput II – Berber (Libyan) King of Kamit
23rd Dynasty
Original Ancient Black Berber (Afri)

The Aourigha or Afaraka, Afuraka, Afurak, Afura, Fula people were/are black people because *black* refers directly to our *skin color*, our **abatumm** (melanin) and the *solar fire* moving through our *afu* (flesh). When the *white, shining, fire* of **Ra/Rait** moves inside of the physical matter of the body (**afu**) we have *Blackness* as a result. This is the connection between the english corruptions *black* and *bleach*. The titles **Afura** and **Afurait** are also the origin of the english term **'fire'** (**Fura**). This also accounts for the notion of the adjective 'pale' (Peul, Fula) being associated with *black* and *bleach*. It references the *radiant light* (pale/white), light of the *fire* of **Fura** - **Afura** and **Afurait**. Moreover, the terms *phlegien*, *flagrare* are rooted in **Afarak(n)** and **Afuraka**.

The first landmass, called **Ka/Kait**, to rise up from the primordial ocean in the *Sep Tepi* (First Time) was a primordial, Black, landmass. The terms **Ka/Kait** and their variations **Kaka/Kakait** (**Kk, Kkt** – often written **Kek** and **Kekut**) references *Divine Blackness* – Deities of the *Divine Black Substance of Space*. The Black Substance of Space (see *Dark matter* and *Dark energy* in astronomy) within which all of the planets, Suns, stars, dwell is that plasma from which the bodies of the planets and stars (see *Black Bodies* in astronomy) were formed. This is why the original Earth's first landmass was recognized to be a **Ka/Kait** – a primordial *Black* hill or 'raised land'. The terms **Ka** and **Kait** are also the masculine and feminine terms for *'Soul'* in Kamit.

The term Black as a designation for Afurakani/Afuraitkaitnit (African) people has always been a sacred designation referencing our skin color as well as our identity as children of Afu Ra and Afu Rait. Afu (flesh) Ra (Spirit) Ka (Soul and melanin-body), Afu (flesh) Rait (Spirit) Kait (Soul and melanin-body) – Afurakanu/Afuraitkaitnut (Africans~Black People).

MAR/BAR

In Akan culture the term for **law** is **mmara**. The 'm' and 'b' interchange in Akan as well as ancient Kamit. This is why *mmara – law*, has as its singular form **bara**. As a verb, **bara** often contracted to **bra** means *to forbid*. The noun and plural form becomes **mbara** or **mmara** – *law*. Those who uphold the law are called **barafo** (**mmarafo**) pluralized as **abrafo**. The suffix 'fo' means *'people'* as in *a group*. The **abrafo** or **abarafo** are that *group of people* 'fo' who *uphold the law* **bara** (**mmara**). They are the **bara** (law) **fo** (people). In common english, this group of people are referred to as the 'police officers' [In american parlance, police are often called *'law-men'* or *'the law'*]. They *oversee* the proper functioning of various aspects of the nation on a continuous basis. This title and function have their roots in Kamit:

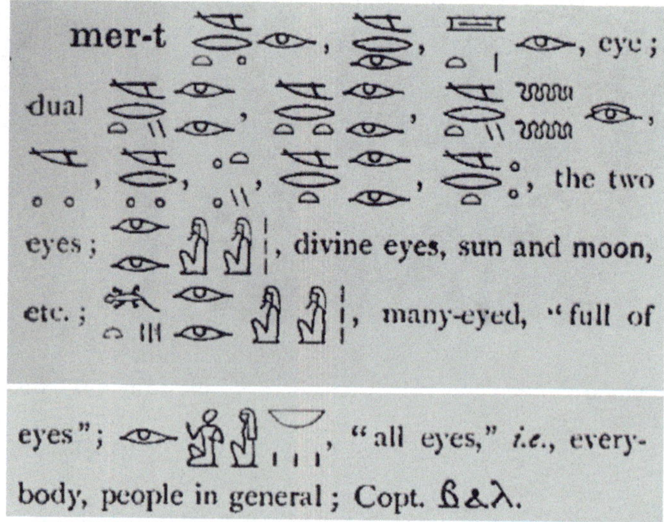

mer-t , , , eye; dual , , , , , , the two eyes; , divine eyes, sun and moon, etc.; , many-eyed, "full of eyes"; , "all eyes," *i.e.*, everybody, people in general; Copt. ϐⲁⲗ.

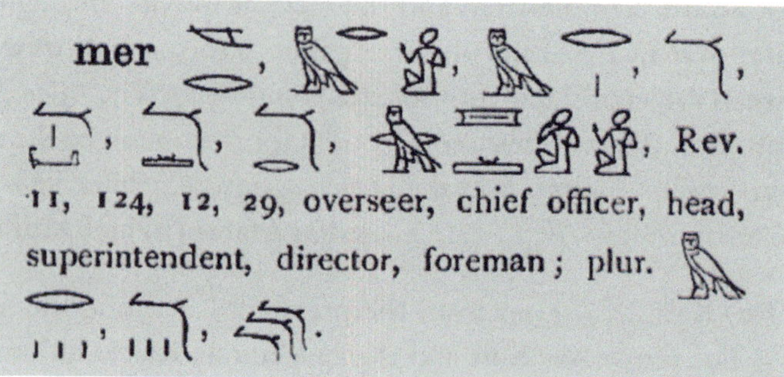

mer , , , , , , , , Rev. 11, 124, 12, 29, overseer, chief officer, head, superintendent, director, foreman; plur. , , .

A designation for the *Two Divine Eyes, Sun and Moon* is **Mrt (Mart)**. The egyptologist translated the term as **Mert**. However, notice that in the Coptic dialect the term is pronounced **BAR**: Copt. ϐⲁⲗ. The term **Mr** meaning *overseer, chief officer, director,* etc. written **Bar** in Coptic is the same title **Bara** (Barafo, Mmarafo) in Akan. The **obara-fo** is the **bara** or **mmara** person – *the law person* – the police officer. This is the individual who **inspects** all activity in the nation in order to determine where imbalance exists so that he/she may exercise his/her authority to uphold law by enforcing order. This is the association of the *Divine Eye* (**MAR** or **BAR**) with the one who *in-spects* (*looks* within), the over-*seer*, the chief officer (**BARA**-fo).

Mr-ti (**Bar-ti**) the *two* (**ti**) *Eyes* (**mar/bar**) from the coffin of **Hetep Nebi**

The two *Divine Eyes*, the Sun and Moon, are often referred to as the *Right and Left Eyes of* **Heru**. **Heru Ur** is depicted as a Hawk – the highest flying bird in the sky in Kamit with the keenest vision. He is the great Over-Seer. He is also, as **Heru Behudet** (**Behdety**), the *Enforcer of Divine Order*. He is called **Bena** in Akan culture. **Bena** is often contracted to **Bera** and **Bra**. He is the **Obrafo Kesee**, the *Great Obrafo*, *Divine Executioner*, created at the beginning of the world to *Enforce Divine Order* in Akan cosmology. There are many titles in Kamit referencing *'overseer, inspector'* beginning with '**Mr**' which are rooted in this cosmological reality.

The term **mr** (mar) in Kamit meaning *overseer, chief, head* as well as *brave man* was corrupted into **mir** and **emir** in arabic meaning *'commander'*. The arabic language is not an ancient language nor is it Afurakani/Afuraitkaitnit (African). It includes numerous words with roots in ancient Kamit (just as english, latin, greek, sanskrit, etc. do also) because of the invasions of the whites and their offspring and their cooptation and perversion of our language and culture. There is a relationship between **mr** (bar) meaning *overseer, inspector* and **mer** meaning *death*, for in Akan culture the **abrafo** (bara-fo) are also **adumfo** meaning *executioners*. When someone is convicted of a crime and sentenced to death (mr) the mr (bara-fo) carries out the execution. The term mr as mar/bar however is not the origin of 'moor'.

Manu [hieroglyphs] the West, the country of the sunset.

The term **mr** (mar) is also found in ancient **Sumer** (later called Babylon). Sumer was an ancient Afurakani/Afuraitkaitnit (African) civilization founded by migrants from Afuraka/Afuraitkait (Africa) over 6,000 years ago. The migrants from Khanit and Kamit who established what would later be called Sumer of course brought their language, culture and cosmology with them. This is why the term **Mar.tu** also written **Mar.ta** means *'west'*. This is the same term from Kamit - **amn.t** or **amn.ta** meaning *'west'*. The general term **amn** (**amen**) in Kamit means *'hidden'* or *'concealed'*. When the Aten (Sun) sets in the west and sinks below the horizon it becomes the *'hidden'* Aten (Sun). The west was thus called the *'hidden land'* – **amnt** (**ament**). The Ancestral Realm was also called the *'hidden'* land (**amnt.t**).

âmen [hieroglyphs], Peasant 182, to hide, to conceal, to be hidden, secret, mysterious.

âmen-t [hieroglyphs], P. 610, [hieroglyphs], the West, the right side.

âmen-t [hieroglyphs], the right eye.

âmen-t [hieroglyphs], T. 81, M. 234, N. 612, the west wind.

Âmen-t [hieroglyphs], Inscrip. of Darius 9, the west bank of the Nile and the land westwards.

âmenti [hieroglyphs], western; [hieroglyphs], west wind.

âmenti, a denizen of Âmen-t, one belonging to Âmen-t, U. 578, N. 966.

âmentiu, those who are in the West, *i.e.*, the dead.

menâ-t, Berl. 2296, death; dead things, the dead; deathless; the death cry, the wailing of women for the dead.

Manu, the West, the country of the sunset.

As quoted above, the Aten rises from the mountain range called **Bakhau** in the east (**abtet**) and sets in the mountain range called **Manu** in the west (**ament**). The term for the western mountain range, the region where the Aten *dies* (**mn**), *sets* (**mn**), *arrives in port* (**mn**) is called **Manu** and has the same roots as the term **mn** - *dead, hidden* (**amn**). The name **Manu** or **Mnu** related to **Amnt** becomes **Mar.tu** or **Mar.ta** in Sumerian meaning *'west'*. A description of the people called **Mar.tu**, later referred to as **Amurru** or **Amorites** can be found in Sumerian texts:

"…The MAR.TU who know no grain... The MAR.TU who know no house nor town, the boors of the mountains... The MAR.TU who digs up truffles... who does not bend his knees (to cultivate the land), who eats raw meat, who has no house during his lifetime, who is not buried after death...

[E. Chiera, Sumerian Epics and Myths, Chicago, 1934, Nos.58 and 112]

They have prepared wheat and gú-nunuz (grain) as a confection, but an Amorite will eat it without even recognizing what it contains!..."

[E. Chiera, Sumerian Texts of Varied Contents, Chicago, 1934, No.3]

Again, we have the ancient association of those who are considered *socially 'dead'* called **mar.tu** (**manu, mnu, mrtu** – the rolling 'R' and 'N' interchange). They are called the *boors of the mountains* - **Manu** – the *western (martu) mountain range (manu)* where the Aten 'dies' – **mn**. The english word 'boor' chosen by the translator means *'uncivilized, unrefined'*. They are uncivilized and are not buried after death (mn). The *unburied* are the *'perpetually dead'*.

The term mar.tu of Sumer is descendent of the term mru (mrt) – socially 'dead' of ancient Kamit. This is a cosmological concept that the ancient Khanitu and Kamau (Nubians and Egyptians) carried with them as they migrated from Khanit and Kamit to the Near East thousands of years ago.

As we can see in the excerpt addressing the character of those referred to as mar.tu, the description fits the character of the whites and their offspring. The **Mar.tu** were later caller **Amurru** which translates in english to **Amorites**. In Kamit, these people were called **Aamu**. [Note that **Amurru** means *'west'* and is a version of **amnu** (**amenut/amanu**). **Aamu** also means 'west' and 'right'.]. The original inhabitants of the region of what is now called palestine, israel, lebanon and syria were Afurakanu/Afuraitkaitnut (Africans) who migrated from Khanit and Kamit. Some of these people migrated further east to establish Sumer. However, these areas were invaded by the whites and their offspring. The **mru** (**mar.tu**) designation meaning 'uncivilized', 'socially dead' was naturally given to the white invaders as a group of *uncivilized criminals*. This is why the Aamu (Amurru, Mar.tu, Amorites) in the murals of ancient Kamit were typically depicted as non-Black:

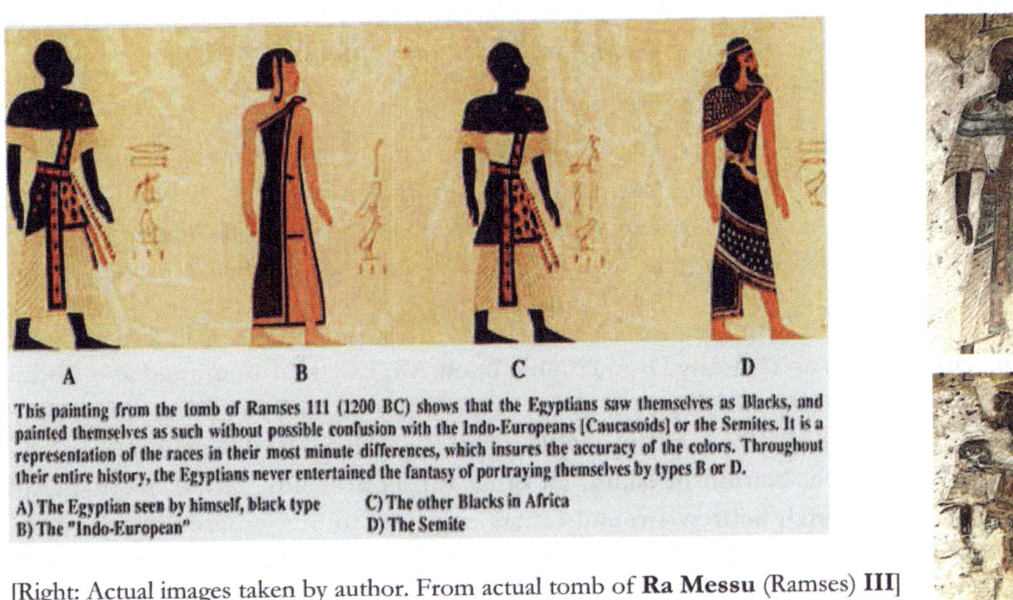

A B C D

This painting from the tomb of Ramses 111 (1200 BC) shows that the Egyptians saw themselves as Blacks, and painted themselves as such without possible confusion with the Indo-Europeans [Caucasoids] or the Semites. It is a representation of the races in their most minute differences, which insures the accuracy of the colors. Throughout their entire history, the Egyptians never entertained the fantasy of portraying themselves by types B or D.

A) The Egyptian seen by himself, black type
B) The "Indo-European"
C) The other Blacks in Africa
D) The Semite

[Right: Actual images taken by author. From actual tomb of **Ra Messu** (Ramses) **III**]

This excerpt from **Civilization or Barbarism** by Cheik Anta Diop shows an artist's rendition of a mural inside of the tomb of Ramessu III. [See the KV11 tomb for actual images]. The first figure, **Rtu** is a Kamau. The second figure, **Aamu**, is an 'amorite'. The third figure, **Nehesu**, is one of the people of Khanit (Nubia) and the fourth figure **Tmhu**, is one of the white invaders of North Afuraka/Afuraitkait (Africa), East Afuraka/Afuraitkait (Africa) and arabia which includes the arab-type [*The Arabian peninsula was originally populated by Afurakanu/Afuraitkaitnut (Africans). The whites invaded thousands of years later. They also corrupted the traditional religion – which was the same as that of Kamit – and manufactured the* ***false*** *god allah, the* ***fictional*** *character muhammad and the* ***false*** *religion of islam*]. The Aamu figure (called Mar.tu, Amurru in Sumer) is one of the whites and their offspring. These invaders of the Black civilizations of the ancient Near East had the characteristics of barbarians as shown in the quoted text. They were uncivilized, spiritually and mentally *dead* individuals. Those who would attempt to trace the term 'moor' back to the mar.tu are tracing the term back to white, uncivilized, barbaric invaders. They also reinforce the reality that the term defines *'the dead/damned'*.

Moreover, the name **mar.tu** is related to the name **Mari** which was a city-state to the *west* of central Sumer and situated on *west bank* of what is now called the euphrates river. Mari flourished about 5,000 years ago. The original inhabitants of this area were Afurakanu/Afuraitkaitnut (Africans) who had migrated north from ancient Khanit and Kamit. The name **Mari**, directly related to the later **Mar.tu** also references the *'west'*. The names Mari, Mar.tu, Amurru have their etymological roots in **Mni, Mrt, Mnu** and **Mru**. They reference the *'west'* as a *geographical region*, but most importantly the aspect of our cosmology wherein *the nature of the inhabitants of the 'west' are defined as the 'dead'*. The ancient designation **mni**, **mri** meaning the *dead land* was carried by Afurakanu/Afuraitkaitnut (Africans) from Kamit wherever we migrated. This is why the later kingdom of **Maure** (**Mari**) geographically to the *extreme west of Kamit*, bears this title. It was the greeks and romans who began to use the term *maure* (mauri) to refer not only to the people of the **Numidian** kingdom of that time (Mauritania - c2200-2300 years ago) but to *Black people in general.* The greeks, romans and later arabs were familiar with the root of the name **maure** being the term **mru** – *the dead, damned*, etc. - and its origins in Kamit for they had invaded Kamit, occupied Kamit for centuries and learned of the language including this term. The greek and roman invaders of Kamit not only began to imitate the dress, statecraft and ritual practices of the Kamau, but also misused the language. As stated previously, the white invaders took the term **mru** that was a pejorative designation for a certain class of society in Kamit and over time labeled the entirety of the Black race with the term – *wherever they came into contact with us in the world.*

Just as the whites and their offspring did in the past, so do they continue today. The whites and their offspring including arabs, turks and others utilized the derogatory term **mru**, corrupted into 'moor', to apply to Black people in general. They then use Black 'moors' to brainwash other Black people to accept the insanity of white supremacy and Black inferiority – which includes the false religion of islam and the pseudo-esotericism of masonry.

This is the origin of such individuals as Timothy Drew/Noble Drew Ali, Elijah Muhammad and Abdul Hamied Sulaiman – all of whom were worshippers of the white arab or turk as divine or 'god' – dedicating their lives to brainwashing Black people with white worship. The Canaanite Temple, Moorish Science Temple of america, Nation of islam, all other forms of islam, Nuwaubianism, all forms of hebrewism including Moorish hebrewism and others continue to perpetuate the agenda of the white slavemaster from eastern eurasia, just as Black 'christians' continue to perpetuate the agenda of the white slavemaster from western eurasia and america.

These individuals all taught Afurakanu/Afuraitkaitnut (Africans~Black People) to **hate ourselves** – *reject the reality that we are Afurakani/Afuraitkaitnit (African)* – and to embrace a pseudo-'asian' identity. They taught us to denigrate and reject Afurakani/Afuraitkaitnit (African) Ancestral Religion and Culture and to worship the white arabs, turks and hindus as 'god' or as having a divine position as custodians of the 'true religion'. **This is the contemporary origin of Black people foolishly referring to themselves with the derogatory name 'moors'. The title 'moor' is an insult to the intelligence of all Afurakanu/Afuraitkaitnut (Africans) and all of our Ancestresses and Ancestors. It is the equivalent of calling ourselves 'nigger'. [Notwithstanding the false etymologies now being circulated regarding 'nigger' by the uninformed].**

The ancient origin of this self-denigrating behavior is rooted in the greek, roman and arab invasions of ancient Kamit and the advent of what is referred to as the 'arab slave trade', 'indian ocean slave trade', asian enslavement of Afurakanu/Afuraitkaitnut (Tang dynasty in china) and the 'atlantic slave trade'. [*It must be understood that Afurakanu/Afuraitkaitnut (Africans) were not 'slaves' – we were captured as prisoners of war and forced into 'enslavement'*]. The whites and their offspring continue to promote the false 'moorish', 'islamic', 'christian' and 'hebrew' identities among Afurakanu/Afuraitkaitnut (Africans) in Afuraka/Afuraitkait (Africa) and outside of Afuraka/Afuraitkait (Africa) today through their Black agents. They will continue until we eradicate them.

After having endured enslavement as Afurakanu/Afuraitkaitnut (Africans) in the western hemisphere, many Afurakanu/Afuraitkaitnut (Africans) embraced the perversity of Black self-hatred promoted by the whites and their offspring [*Externally manifested through hair-straightening, skin-lightening, etc. Internally manifested through the acceptance of the insanity of white-worship*]. This is why it has been relatively easy for white christians, muslims, hebrews, hindus, buddhists, vedantins, pseudo-new age 'spiritualists', pseudo-'native' american spiritualists, pseudo-esotericists, pseudo-metaphysicians, 'extraterrestrialists', 'lost-land-ists' [*those who promote the idiocy of our origins being in the mythological 'lost lands' of atlantis and mu. Note:* **mu/mut** *in Kamit means 'mass of water' and also 'death'*] and others to lure us away from Afuraka/Afuraitkait (Africa) and our **actual direct** Afurakani/Afuraitkaitnit (African) Ancestresses and Ancestors. The same is true of the relative ease with which the Black agents of these white criminals can lure our people into an organized system of self-hatred – their promoted pseudo-'spiritualities' – for we were already pre-programmed with a disdain for Afuraka/Afuraitkait (Africa) and anything Afurakani/Afuraitkaitnit (African) as a result of enslavement.

However, that ability to perpetuate these false identities amongst Afurakanu/Afuraitkaitnut (Africans~Black People) has come to an end. We have returned to our **Nananom Nsamanfo** (Akan term for Honored/Spiritually Cultivated Afurakani/Afuraitkaitnit Ancestresses and Ancestors), Who have given us our **true cultural and spiritual identity** which is rooted in our connection to **Nyamewaa-Nyame** (**Amenet-Amen**, the Supreme Being) the **Abosom** (Deities) and our reincarnation through specific **Afurakani/Afuraitkaitnit (African)** blood-circles – blood-circles which have not been broken for thousands of years predating the existence of the whites and their offspring on **Asaase Afua** (Earth Mother).

Akan, Ewe, Yoruba, Igbo, Bakongo, Bambara, Dogon, Minianka, Goromantche, Nguni, Afar, Batswana, Fon, Ovimbundu, Bassa, Fula, Fang, Azande, Gikuyu, Maasai, Galla, Chokwe, Mende, Lobi, Kru, all other Afurakanu/Afuraitkaitnut (Africans) on the continent of Afuraka/Afuraitkait (Africa) and wherever we find ourselves in the world as a result of migration or forced-migration, are not, never were and never will be moors, hebrews (a fictional people), atlanteans or children of mu (fictional groups) or any other foolish and degenerate designations.

We are **Afurakanu/Afuraitkaitnut** - the **Ka/Kait** *bodies and souls* of **Afu Ra** and **Afu Rait**.

Odwirafo Kwesi Ra Nehem Ptah Akhan
Aakhuamuman Amaruka Atifi Mu

www.odwirafo.com
www.youtube.com/odwirafo

Select References

Let the Ancestors Speak: Removing the Veil of Mysticism from the Medu Netcher, *by Ankh Mi Ra.*
Twi-English/English-Twi Concise Dictionary – *by Paul Kotey*
Kasahorow.org – *Afurakani/Afuraitkaitnit (African) online language resource (online Akan, Ewe, Yoruba dictionaries)*
Etymonline – *Online Etymology Dictionary* – www.etymonline.com
Pyramid Texts Online – *Includes links to various funerary texts, stelae, papyri, sarcophagi and coffin texts and Hieroglyphic Dictionaries:* www.pyramidtextsonline.com/tools.html
KUKUU-TUNTUM - The Ancestral Jurisdiction, *by Kwesi Ra Nehem Ptah Akhan* - www.odwirafo.com
AKANFO NANASOM - Ancient Authentic Akan Ancestral Religion: www.odwiraof.com/Akanfo_Nanasom.html
NHWEHWEMU - Research Articles: www.odwirafo.com/nhwehwemupage.html

Appendix

The **Akan** people of Ghana and Ivory Coast West Afuraka/Afuraitkait (Africa) are directly descendant of ancient **Khanit** (Nubia) and **Kamit**. The language, culture and religious practices including the names of the Deities from ancient Khanit and Kamit are thus found intact within Akan culture today. [*See our publication:* ***Akan – The People of Khanit*** *(Akan Land – Ancient Nubia/Sudan):* *www.odwirafo.com/Akanfo_Nanasom.html*]

Naturally, we find that the term **mr** (mer, merew, mere) continues to be used in the Akan language today:

mmerẹw, *a.* [berẹw, berẹberẹ] *1. soft* (e. g. wood, *pr. 1244.*), *impressible, yielding.* — *2. meek, mild.* — *3. tender; delicate, effeminate.* — *4. weak, feeble, infirm, sickly;* ɔnehõ yẹ m., *he is not strong* (bodily); - ɔyẹ m., *a)* = odwo, *he is meek; b) he is weak, yielding, pliable, indulgent:* n'asõ yẹ m., *he is obedient.* — *Syn.* bètẹ̃, bọ́dõ, bòkõ, bŏrògọ, dábõ, dufudufu, dẹ̀fẹ̃, fifã, fẹ́tẹfẹtẹ, hòdwõ, horòhorọ, n'ã, n'i, nyámõ, siãmõ, pọ̀sọpọsọ, pósoposo &c. *opp.* deñ.

ọ-bẽrẹfo, *pl.* a-, *a needy, indigent, poor, destitute man; syn.* ohiani, ọmanehunufo. *Ps. 41,2. 72,13.*

[*A Dictionary of the Asante and Fante Language Called Tshi (Chwee, Twi). J.G. Christaller*]

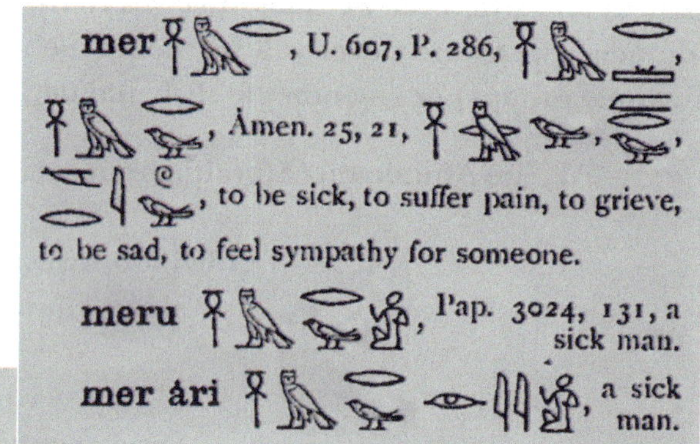
mer, U. 607, P. 286, Amen. 25, 21, to be sick, to suffer pain, to grieve, to be sad, to feel sympathy for someone.

meru, Pap. 3024, 131, a sick man.

mer ári, a sick man.

merua, Rec. 15, 158, weak, wretched.

As we can see above, in the Akan (Twi) language the sounds 'm' and 'b' interchange. We thus have **mmerew** and **berew**. The same is true for the term 'law' written in the Akwamu Twi dialect 'mbra', while written in the Asante Twi dialect 'mmara' (ma-ra, maa(t) in Kamit). The the suffix 'fo' denotes *plurality* as in a group of people, while 'ni' denotes *individuality*. Thus **Akanfo** means *Akan people* (fo), while **Akanni** means an *Akan individual* (ni). The term **mmerew** when describing an individual means: *weak, feeble, infirm, sickly*. The **mmerew-fo** are those *people* (fo) who are *weak, feeble, infirm, sickly*. The **mmerew-ni** is an *individual* who is *weak, feeble, infirm or sickly*. This is directly derived from **mer** and the variation **merua** meaning *weak, wretched* in Kamit. Note that the synonym in Twi for **mmerew** is **omanehunufo**. This term means *a sufferer, one who labors in affliction; trouble, wretchedness, torments, misery:*

amanne-hún,u, *inf.* [hũ amane] *suffering, affliction, tribulation, trouble, adversity, unhappiness, misery, wretchedness, torments;* yegyina amandzehunum'. F. *we stand in jeopardy.* am.-kũrow, *hell, Gehenna, the place of torment.* — **ọ-mannehunufo**, *pl.* a-, *a sufferer, one who labours under affliction.*

maār, to be oppressed, bound, miserable; see .

maȧr , , IV, 1139, Berl. Pap. 3024, 128, , , , to be miserable, misery, wretchedness, poverty, affliction.

maȧr , Peasant 204, , Peasant B. 2, 112, , IV, 972, Berl. 3024, 22, a poor man, one of humble condition, or one in a miserable or oppressed state; plur. .

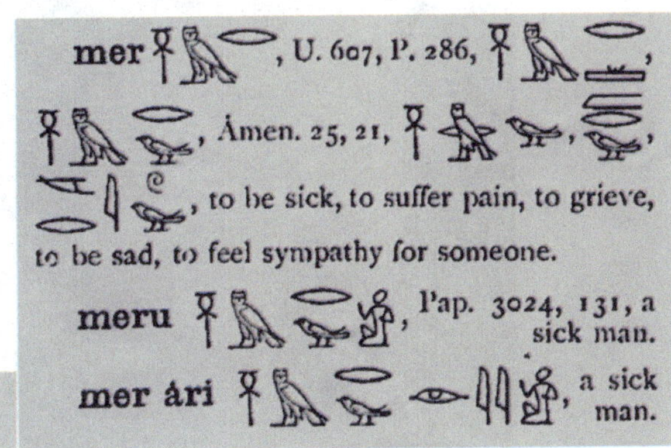
mer , U. 607, P. 286, , , Ȧmen. 25, 21, , , to be sick, to suffer pain, to grieve, to be sad, to feel sympathy for someone.

meru , Pap. 3024, 131, a sick man.

mer ȧri , a sick man.

merua , Rec. 15, 158, weak, wretched.

[Note the variation **maar** (**mer**) meaning *oppressed, bound, miserable; afflicted, wretchedness*]

ọ-bérẹfo mmerẹw, *a.* [berẹw, berẹbere]

The term **bere-fo** also written and pronounced in some Akan dialects as **mberefo, mmerefo** are the group of *people* (fo) who are *needy, indigent, poor, destitute, afflicted.* The Akan term **bere** (mbere, mmere) is derived from **mer** (mere) in Kamit referencing the *indigent, destitute, needy, servants, slaves, etc.* This is what it means to be a 'moor'. It has always been a pejorative term. It was therefore used by the whites and their offspring to falsely identify our people as a race of weak, wretched, indigent, afflicted people. Just as it is an insult today in Akan culture to label someone as *mmerew* or *bere* (mbere, mere) – **mr** (moor) – *weak, wretched, sickly, infirm,* when they are truly not that, so was it an insult in ancient Kamit to label someone a mr (moor), *slave – socially dead, spiritually dead/damned, afflicted, wretched,* etc. when they truly were not that. This is precisely why the whites and their offspring decided to label all Black people 'mr' (mer, moor). Only the ignorant amongst us can accept such a designation.

From the front cover:

AUSAR

Ntoro *(Deity)* of Regulatory Order in Creation

Tomb of **Ra Messu IX** *(Ramesses the Ninth)*

Valley of the Kings in Kamit

Akan Akyene (drum)

Brought to america during the 18th century on a ship of enslavement from the Akan people of Ghana.

Upon arrival we used the akyene to communicate with one another to foment revolution-resolution.

Made in the USA
Columbia, SC
28 March 2025